Continued on next page

Contents at a Glance

Continued from previous page

Mac OS X® Panther™

Brian Tiemann

SAMS
Teach
Yourself

Sams Publishing, 800 East 96th Street, Indianapolis, Indiana 46240 USA

Mac OS X Panther in a Snap

International Standard Book Number: 0-672-32612-4

Library of Congress Catalog Card Number: 2003108462

Printed in the United States of America

First Printing: January 2004

07   06   05   04   4   3   2

Acquisitions Editor
Betsy Brown

Development Editor
Alice Martina Smith

Managing Editor
Charlotte Clapp

Senior Project Editor
Matthew Purcell

Copy Editor
Seth Kerney

Indexer
Mandie Frank

Proofreader
Eileen Dennie

Technical Editor
John Traenkenschuh

Publishing Coordinator
Vanessa Evans

Designer
Gary Adair

Page Layout
Bronkella Publishing

Graphics
Tammy Graham

Trademarks

Warning and Disclaimer

Bulk Sales

Sams Publishing offers excellent discounts on this book when ordered in quantity for bulk purchases or special sales. For more information, please contact

U.S. Corporate and Government Sales

1-800-382-3419

corpsales@pearsontechgroup.com

For sales outside of the U.S., please contact

International Sales

1-317-428-3341

international@pearsontechgroup.com

About the Author

Brian Tiemann is a freelance technology columnist and software engineer who has written extensively in online magazines about the Macintosh, Apple software, and the philosophy of user-friendly design that has always been synonymous with them. A creative professional in the graphic arts and Web design world as well as in networking and software quality, he uses Mac OS X because of its Unix-based stability underlying the powerful built-in creative tools that let him bring his graphics, music, movies, and photography to life.

Having been a Mac user for nearly 20 years, Brian has observed Apple's growth from a maker of simple personal computers to the powerhouse of film production, digital music, online lifestyle, and publishing that it is today. A graduate of Caltech and the coauthor of *FreeBSD Unleashed* and *Sams Teach Yourself FreeBSD in 24 Hours*, Brian enjoys animation, motorcycles, technological gadgets, the outdoors, and writing about them all. He lives in Silicon Valley with Capri the collie, who posed for pictures used throughout this book.

Dedication

To my parents, Keith and Ann; my brother, Michael; and his wife, Julie.

Acknowledgments

Bringing out a thickly illustrated book on a brand-new Apple operating system is no easy feat, especially when you only get a couple of months' time from the first public betas until the final release. This book would never have seen the light of day without the efforts of the team of editors at Sams Publishing: Alice Martina Smith for heroically squeezing down the text until it all somehow fit between the covers; Matt Purcell for gamely putting up with all my constant additions and afterthoughts; John Traenkenschuh for making me feel as though I know what I'm talking about—even when setting me straight on how public-key cryptography works; Seth Kerney for making everything nice and consistent; Betsy Brown for taking over this careening ship mid-course and bringing it in to port; and Kathryn Purdum for giving me this great opportunity in the first place. These and the rest of the Sams staff have my deepest thanks.

I would also like to thank all those who have served to hone my passions both for writing and for the Mac: James Lileks for bolstering my ego with his very presence; Steven Den Beste for toughening me up; Mike Hendrix for keeping that torch lit and that flag flying; and Paul, Mike, Damien, Kevin, Aziz, and J for always keeping me on my toes. Lance, Kris, Chris, David, John, Van, Trent, Marcus, and all the rest: Thank you for understanding during these past three months, and for making sure that I didn't completely lose touch with reality while sequestered with the iMac. You do remember me, don't you?

We Want to Hear from You!

As the reader of this book, *you* are our most important critic and commentator. We value your opinion and want to know what we're doing right, what we could do better, what areas you'd like to see us publish in, and any other words of wisdom you're willing to pass our way.

You can email or write me directly to let me know what you did or didn't like about this book—as well as what we can do to make our books stronger.

Please note that I cannot help you with technical problems related to the topic of this book, and that due to the high volume of mail I receive, I might not be able to reply to every message.

When you write, please be sure to include this book's title and author as well as your name and phone or email address. I will carefully review your comments and share them with the author and editors who worked on the book.

Email: **consumer@samspublishing.com**

Mail: Mark Taber
         Associate Publisher
         Sams Publishing
         800 East 96th Street
         Indianapolis, IN 46240 USA

Reader Services

For more information about this book or others from Sams Publishing, visit our Web site at **www.samspublishing.com**. Type the ISBN (excluding hyphens) or the title of the book in the **Search** box to find the book you're looking for.

PART I

Understanding Mac OS X

IN THIS PART

1

✔ Start Here

Ever since the very first days of the Macintosh, Apple Computer, Inc., has prided itself on building computers that were "different." Back in the early years, Macs were marketed on the principle of being graphical, easy-to-use alternatives to the arcane, command-line–driven DOS computers that were most common then. Later, Apple's "Think Different" campaign presented the Mac as a stylish and elegant niche machine for the artists, writers, and free thinkers of the world. Today, the computing world is unarguably dominated by Windows PCs, but the Macintosh holds an indomitable (if small) percent of the market—an unbending cadre of loyalists, their numbers bolstered by newcomers attracted by the stability and modern design of Mac OS X.

The Macintosh's operating system, known as the "Mac OS" since version 8.0 (Mac OS 8) in 1996, has often seemed to be quirky, oddly designed, even clumsy—particularly to those people who were used to other kinds of computers.

When Windows 95 was released, however, it incorporated many graphical features that seemed to mimic features of the Macintosh, and Windows users found themselves using their computers in ways that Mac users had been accustomed to doing for years. Still, Microsoft implemented the features of Windows in such a way as to be *just* different enough from the Mac that Windows users came to think of Windows' way as the more common and natural, despite the fact that the Mac was specifically designed, through thousands of hours' worth of human interface study, to be the most intuitive system for controlling a personal computer that could possibly be created. (At least, that was Apple's theory.)

 NOTE

The first Macintosh hit the shelves in 1984; at that time, before Windows had become widely used on PCs, the Mac—"the computer for the rest of us"—was often derided as a "toy" because its operating system was graphical—using icons and menus and multiple windows for different applications, when many computer users preferred to think of computers as being something that only a privileged few ought to be able to understand, something that should be controlled only with austere keyboard commands.

The original Macintosh.

Meanwhile, open-source Unix operating systems such as Linux and FreeBSD had come onto the scene, bringing their own ideas about how computers should work, as well as their much-vaunted advantages of stability, security, and networking versatility. Windows grew to incorporate many Unix concepts as the Internet age dawned. By the time the translucent iMac was released in 1998, the Mac OS had fallen behind the technological curve, despite its fans' insistence that it was still the most pure and elegant operating system on Earth.

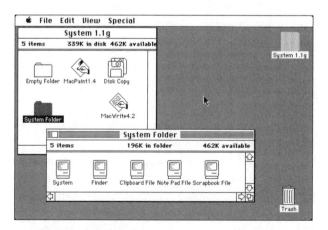

The Macintosh System 1.1, the operating system of the original Macintosh, is the distant ancestor of Mac OS X.

When Apple co-founder Steve Jobs returned to Apple after being exiled from the company for over 10 years, he brought with him an infusion of ideas from the company he had been running in the meantime, NeXT, which made a line of computers based on the BSD flavor of Unix. Apple put all its efforts behind turning NeXT's system into a new generation of system software, which was released to the public in 2001 under the name Mac OS X, with the "X" pronounced "Ten." This new operating system replaced the aging Mac OS 9's core technology with the BSD Unix undercarriage derived from NeXT, and laid on top of it a redesign of the familiar Macintosh operating system that boasted many new features and deep alterations to the venerable user interface. The goal was to create a hybrid operating system that would be as intuitive and elegant as the old Mac OS, but immediately familiar to users of Windows or people brand-new to computers altogether. Now, the world's most easy-to-use computer was also a true Unix workstation, and compatible in most important ways with a Windows-dominated computing world.

With Mac OS X, Apple gave Macintosh users a platform they could again be proud of using, one that gave them bragging rights over the competition.

The components of the 2003 17-inch iMac are all contained inside the hemispherical base.

Whether designed to be superbly intuitive or not, Mac OS X is not guaranteed to be easy for a new user to figure out. Depending on whether you are used to Windows, familiar with Mac OS 9, or new to computers altogether, Mac OS X offers a specific set of unfamiliar metaphors and technical challenges to overcome. Nonetheless, Mac OS X enables the user to accomplish very nearly everything that a user of any other operating system can do, if in a slightly different way. This book explains how to do those tasks, step by step, introducing the concepts fundamental to Mac OS X along the way. Whether you are a Windows user, a longtime Mac user, a Unix geek, or a first-time computer user, the procedures in this book should leave you with an understanding of why Mac OS X is designed the way it is, which in turn should enable you to accomplish things far beyond the scope of this book.

 **Start Here**

Coming from Windows

If your exposure to computers has only been through the various flavors of Microsoft Windows, Mac OS X is likely to seem strange and non-intuitive at first, even backwards. However, with an introduction to a few basic concepts, you should be able to find your way around the system with ease.

The first major difference between Windows and the Mac OS is that on the Mac, applications are *modal*. This means that whatever application you are currently using is in the foreground, and it effectively takes over the entire area of your screen. The menu bar across the top of the screen changes to reflect the controls provided by that application. For instance, if you are using TextEdit, the menus shown at the top of the screen are TextEdit's menus. By contrast, Windows is designed so that each application fits within a single window, which can be any size up to the full size of the screen. Each application window in Windows contains its own set of control menus, and nothing outside the application window applies to any given application.

Mac OS X has no "Start" button. How do you launch applications, then? Applications are started by double-clicking them where they reside on the hard disk, typically in the systemwide **Applications** folder. Because it can be time consuming to open the **Applications** folder each time you want to access an application, Mac OS X provides the Dock as a shortcut. The Dock is a broad horizontal strip across the bottom of the screen that stores the icons representing commonly used applications, documents, and other items; it allows you to control these objects with a single click. You will learn more about the Dock later in this chapter.

Finally, if you're a Windows user sitting down at a Mac for the first time, you might notice that there is only one mouse button. You might be used to two or three buttons, a scroll wheel, and other such features. However, all Macs ship with a single-button mouse. You might find this to be absurdly limiting; you might be so used to using the mouse's scroll wheel that you can't imagine computing without it. Don't worry—the good news is that Mac OS X supports scroll wheels, multiple buttons, and all the rest of the advanced mouse features. However, the Mac OS has always been designed with the new computer user in mind: a single mouse button is much easier to understand than multiple buttons. Everyone has been confused by which mouse button to use at some point in their life. Apple's solution is to stick with the one-button mouse,

KEY TERM

Modal—A style of computer interface in which all your keyboard or mouse input is interpreted by a single application. In Mac OS X, you can run dozens of applications at once, but the menus at the top of the screen belong to whichever application is currently active in the foreground.

NOTE

Because applications in Mac OS X take over the entire screen context, there is no such thing as "full-screen mode," as Windows users are accustomed to having. All applications are effectively full-screen, even if the window you're working with is very small. This is why there is no "maximize" button in Mac OS X, but rather a Zoom button. You will learn more about the Zoom button later in this chapter.

and to design Mac OS X and all Mac applications to use no more than one mouse button. If you have a second or third mouse button, it's a bonus; but it's never, ever *required* to properly use the computer.

Coming from Mac OS 9

Many die-hard Macintosh users see Mac OS 9 as the ultimate expression of the purity of vision that was the original Macintosh; they claim that Mac OS X is a travesty, a sellout, a mongrel that never should have been. Although there is something to be said for some of the classic Macintosh's admirable design goals, it has to be acknowledged that times have changed. It's not the same computing world that it was in 1984. Most people know basic computing concepts nowadays, such as files and folders and dragging-and-dropping. Moreover, it's a Windows world now; and although no dyed-in-the-wool Mac user will admit to Windows having any technical advantages over the Mac, there is one Windows advantage that cannot be denied: ubiquity. That being the case, the Macintosh must evolve or die.

Fortunately, the compromises that Mac OS X has had to make are of minimal impact, and the advantages it provides are very tangible. For instance, Mac OS X no longer uses the venerable Type and Creator codes to identify (respectively) what kind of file a document is, and what application created it. Instead, Mac OS X uses filename extensions to determine the file type (the extension can be hidden, simply by renaming the file, or by using a check box in most **Save** panels). Mac OS X also provides a global "opener application" framework that allows you to specify the application in which a file will open. This might seem less symmetrical and elegant than the old way, but in practice it's a lot more flexible.

NOTE

If you have a JPEG image file with the .jpg extension hidden, you never have to see the extension (nor does any other Mac user with whom you share the file); but if you send the file to a Windows or Unix machine, the extension is visible and tells that operating system what kind of file it is.

More visible and less technical differences are, of course, present between Mac OS 9 and Mac OS X. The Dock is the biggest one. In Mac OS 9, you had to launch applications from their locations on the disk or create aliases to them to place on your Desktop. That approach is no longer necessary now that you can simply place applications into the Dock. For the same reason, there is now much less need to keep important documents and folders on the Desktop; they can be kept filed away in your **Home** folder, while simultaneously appearing in the Dock for one-touch access. The Desktop can be kept much tidier this way.

The Control Strip is gone. Quick one-touch actions that once resided in the expandable tab at the bottom of the screen are now incorporated

NOTE

The idea that the entire disk is no longer your playground for placing files wherever you please can take some getting used to; but in the long run, especially if you share your computer with other users, you'll find that a Mac OS X system is typically far better organized and easier to navigate than any well-used Mac OS 9 system.

KEY TERMS

Boot—The process of starting up your computer. The term comes from the early tongue-in-cheek concept of the computer "pulling itself up by its own bootstraps."

Login or *Log in*—Mac OS X is a multiuser operating system. This means that each person (or *user*) can start a session with the computer with personalized settings and security privileges. Starting one of these sessions is known as *logging in*, and the window from which you begin a session (by picking a username from a list and typing in a password) is the Login window.

into the system menus that occupy the right half of the menu bar. Other functions from the Control Strip now appear in the **Apple** menu, which is now a global control menu with fixed content, rather than the free-form list of user-defined shortcuts that the Apple menu was in the old days. (Those shortcuts now go into—you guessed it—the Dock.)

The old Control Panels are now consolidated into the **System Preferences** application. Users of Mac OS 9 and earlier will probably not miss the ever-lengthening list of Control Panels that caused interminable conflicts, lockups, and other incompatibilities; also gone are the Extensions, which were incremental additions to the operating system, such as device drivers (and not to be confused with filename extensions). Mac OS X still has Extensions, but they're much more tightly controlled and much less user-accessible in the new, security-conscious Unix architecture of the system.

Finally, because of the multiuser nature of Mac OS X, your starting point in the system is no longer the Desktop, but the **Home** folder inside **Users** on the startup disk. Rather than placing all your files in folders on the Desktop or in the top level of the disk, the new way to keep things organized is to start at your **Home** folder and use the labeled subfolders inside it: **Pictures**, **Music**, **Documents**, and so on.

The Nickel Tour of Mac OS X

Switch on your Mac. The first thing you will notice—apart from the musical chime that tells you the system is starting up—is that unlike Windows, Mac OS X is graphical from the very first moment the computer begins to *boot*. A gray screen with the Apple logo signifies the first phase of booting, in which Mac OS X examines the computer and its devices, makes sure that they're all in working order, and prepares to start. After this phase is complete, the Mac OS X logo screen appears with a progress bar, along with informative statements about which parts of the operating system are being started. Finally, depending on whether you have enabled automatic *login* or not, you will either be presented with the Login window or be taken directly to the Desktop of your account.

The Desktop

As has become traditional in the computer world, your entire screen area is known as the Desktop. This virtual work area contains files (usually referred to as *documents*) and folders, which can be scattered anywhere on the screen, as is true with a real-life desktop. However, Mac OS X's Desktop has numerous features that aren't likely to be found on any office desk.

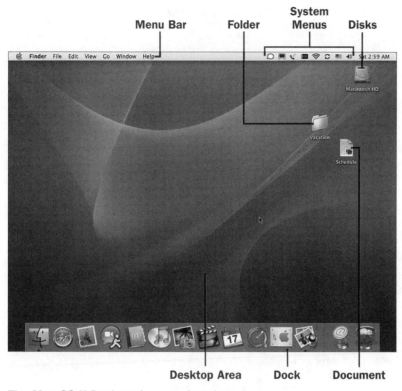

The Mac OS X Desktop is your virtual work area.

NOTE

If this is the first time you have started your Mac, after it finishes booting you are guided through a one-time initial personalization process. Enter your name, address, and other personal information into the system for use in many of Mac OS X's convenience features. If you're worried about your personal data being collected by Apple or third-party companies, don't; Apple has one of the best track records in the industry for treating its customers' private information with confidentiality.

In Mac OS X, the Desktop contains nothing but the files and folders you choose to put there. There are no fixed items, as with **My Computer** in Windows or the hard disks in Mac OS 9. The whole Desktop area is yours to scatter with documents and folders; however, considering the ways Mac OS X provides for you to organize your stuff, you shouldn't have to keep documents on the Desktop except for those files you're currently working on.

The Menu Bar

The permanent bar across the top of the screen is the menu bar; it contains all the menus for whatever application is currently active, as well as the **Apple** menu at the far left.

The **Apple** menu contains global options and controls for the entire system; these options are always the same no matter what application is in the foreground. Its contents include general information about your Mac, shortcuts to the controls for the Dock and the **System Preferences**, and controls for shutting down or sleeping the computer.

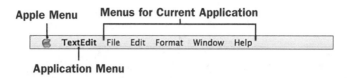

Apple Menu   Menus for Current Application

Application Menu

The menu bar changes based on the application that's currently open.

Next to the **Apple** menu is a menu in bold, labeled with the name of the current application. This menu always contains certain controls for the application, such as the application's preferences, the "About" information, and the **Quit** function.

The System Menus

The right side of the menu bar is taken up with the system menus. These are a series of specialized informational icons, each conveying some useful piece of data about the system, and each containing a menu with further information or options.

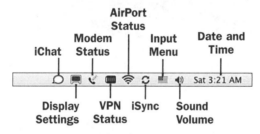

The system menus are iconized to give you visual cues about what functions each controls.

Shown here are only a few of the possible system menus that can be displayed by the various parts of Mac OS X. Each can be turned on or off at its appropriate place in the **System Preferences**.

The Dock

At the bottom of the screen is the Dock, a unique feature of Mac OS X. The Dock is a flexible combination of taskbar and document holder. You can place anything you like into the Dock by dragging it into place; applications go on the left side of the vertical dividing line, and documents and folders go on the right side. The Dock is anchored on the left by the icon for the **Finder**, which is the means by which you navigate the Mac OS X system; the right-most icon is the **Trash** can.

Running Applications   **Web Shortcut**   **Minimized Window**

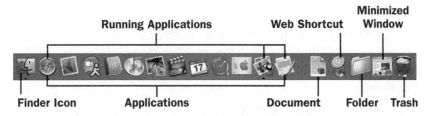

Finder Icon   **Applications**   **Document**   **Folder**   **Trash**

The Dock contains whatever you want it to; applications go on the left and files and folders go on the right.

When an application is running, a black triangle appears underneath it. You can launch an application from the Dock by clicking its icon once; after the application is running, clicking its icon switches you from whatever else is in the foreground to that application.

On the right side of the Dock are the documents and other items you place there. If you click a document in the Dock, the document's designated opener application launches and opens that document. Click and hold on a folder in the Dock to see a list of the folder's contents from which you can open individual documents.

You can remove any document or any non-running application from the Dock by simply clicking its icon, holding, and dragging it off the Dock. The item disappears in a poof of smoke when it is successfully removed from the Dock; however, this does not mean the item is deleted from the system. It's just no longer shown in the Dock. Think of the Dock as your quick-access system to whatever resources you use frequently.

The smiley-faced **Finder** icon at the far left of the Dock is what you click to open a new **Finder** window, with which you can navigate your Mac's disks and the surrounding network.

On the far right, the **Trash** can icon is where you put items you want to delete. Drag documents, folders, and other items into the Trash to throw them away; you can retrieve these items by clicking the Trash and dragging them out of the window that appears. You can retrieve thrown-away items until you empty the Trash (using the **Finder** menu at the top of the Desktop). After you empty the Trash (which you should do periodically to regain disk space), the items in the Trash are gone for good.

The **Trash** icon is also used for ejecting removable disks, burning writable CDs or DVDs, and disconnecting from remote servers. When you drag one of these items to the Trash, the **Trash** icon changes to an **Eject** symbol or a **Burn** symbol as appropriate to the kind of item you are dropping onto it.

 NOTE

Hold the **Control** key and click the vertical divider line in the Dock; from the menu that pops up, select **Dock Preferences**. With the dialog box that opens, you can play with some of the Dock's coolest features—size, position on the screen, automatic hiding, and magnification.

 TIP

Items from different disks can be in your Trash. Until you empty the Trash, thrown-away items still take up space on whatever disks they're stored on. If you need to free up space on a hard disk, it isn't enough to merely throw unneeded items into the Trash—you must also empty the Trash before the space is recovered.

The Finder

The **Finder** is the built-in application that allows you to navigate through the disks in your Mac. If you click the **Finder** icon at the left end of the Dock, you will get a window that shows you the items in your **Home** folder.

Clicking the folder icons in the **Finder** allows you to move from one part of the system to another, or from one disk to another, and to view and manipulate your documents. More on navigating the disk later in this chapter.

The Finder window shown here exhibits a crucial part of Mac OS X: the window control buttons. These three buttons, colored like a traffic light (red, yellow, and green), appear on every window of every Mac OS X application:

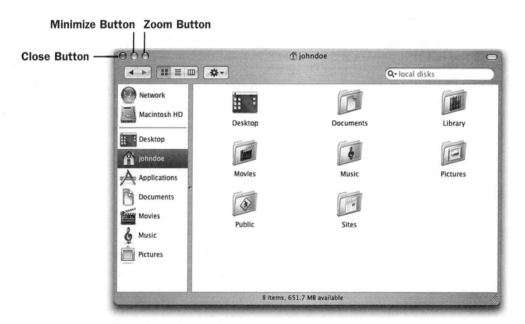

A Finder window.

- Clicking the red **Close** button closes any window. If the window contains a document that has been changed (such as a text file in TextEdit), and therefore cannot be closed without either saving the changes or discarding them, a dot appears in the middle of the close button to show that if you click it, you will be prompted for what to do.

- Clicking the yellow **Minimize** button sends the window to the Dock, getting it off your screen so that you can retrieve it later.

- Clicking the green **Zoom** button, in any window, causes the window to automatically size itself to the most efficient size possible—the smallest it can be while showing all the contents of the window, if possible.

Your Disks

Disks, including the built-in hard disk inside your Mac, appear in the upper-right corner of the Desktop. When you *mount* any new disk on the system (a CD-ROM or an external hard disk, for instance), the new disk's icon appears on the Desktop as well. Double-click any disk to open a **Finder** window showing the disk's contents.

When you insert a disk, such as a CD-ROM, it appears on the Desktop. To *eject* the disk, you drag it to the **Trash**, which appears at the right end of the Dock. While you're dragging a removable disk, the **Trash** can icon turns into an **Eject** icon to show that the disk will be ejected when you release the disk icon on top of it.

Your Home Folder

When you open a **Finder** window, it opens by default to your **Home** folder. This folder has the same name as your account's "short name," and it resides in the **Users** folder at the top level of your startup hard disk.

Your **Home** folder is where you spend the majority of your time when organizing and navigating your documents and folders. Inside your **Home** folder are several more folders, each with their own special purpose. Many of these folders are used by applications to store documents of the appropriate types for your quick access.

- **Desktop.** This special folder is an alias to your actual Desktop space; any documents or folders that appear on the Desktop are actually stored in this folder.

- **Documents**. Any saved files from applications, such as word processing or text documents, project files, spreadsheets, and HTML or PDF files, can be stored in this folder. Many applications default to this folder for saving documents.

- **Library**. The special **Library** folder contains items you install, such as fonts, screensavers, System Preference panes, and plug-ins for applications; it also stores automatically generated items such as application preferences (in the **Preferences** subfolder), Web bookmarks, and logs.

→ **146** Add a New User

Start Here

There's nothing stopping you from putting, for instance, a Word document in your Movies folder or an MP3 file in the Pictures folder. The folders are intended to help you keep your different kinds of data organized, but they don't force you to do so.

KEY TERMS

Application—Also known as a *program*, an application is any piece of software you run within Mac OS X. Adobe Photoshop, Microsoft Word, any game, and the Finder are all applications.

Utility—An application designed for a small, specific purpose. Often, when you close a utility's single window, the entire application quits.

- **Movies**. Keep your video files in this folder.

- **Music**. Store digital audio files here, such as MP3 and AAC files. iTunes keeps your music files organized within this folder.

- **Pictures**. Image files are typically stored in this folder; iPhoto keeps its photo collections here.

- **Public**. Place files in this folder that you want to share with other users over a network.

- **Sites**. Files placed in this folder are accessible to remote users accessing your computer through Personal Web Sharing.

Applications

The **Applications** folder sits at the top level of your startup disk and contains all the applications you have installed. *Applications* in Mac OS X are nearly always single objects, like folders or documents, and can be moved to any place in the system without any ill effects; however, it is usually best to keep all your applications in their designated folder. You can quickly access your applications from the icon directly below your **Home** folder in any Finder window.

*The **Applications** and **Utilities** folders contain all the programs available to you on your Mac.*

Within the **Applications** folder is a folder called **Utilities**. Tools essential for the management of Mac OS X are kept in this location. Over the course of this book, you will become familiar with many of the *utilities* in this folder.

The Library

There is a **Library** folder at the top level of the disk, as well as one inside your **Home** folder. You have two **Library** folders because of the hierarchical, multiuser nature of Mac OS X. The global and user-level **Library** folders contain much the same sort of items, but the difference is that items installed in the global **Library** apply to all users, whereas the ones in your **Home** folder apply only to you. For instance, you can install a new font in the global **Library** folder, and all users in the system can access it; but if you place the font in your own personal **Library** folder, only you will be able to use it.

System Preferences

The central control system for Mac OS X is an application called **System Preferences**. The quickest way to access **System Preferences** is to select it from the **Apple** menu, which is available no matter what application you are currently running.

*The **System Preferences** window is the control center for managing how your Mac looks and acts.*

> **NOTE**
>
> Generally speaking, you will not need to manually work with the files in either **Library** folder. These folders are mostly maintained by the applications you run.

TIP

Feel free to explore the many preference panes and see what kinds of options are available to you; this book explores nearly all of them in the course of explaining the myriad specific tasks that Mac OS X enables you to do.

The "preference panes" that make up **System Preferences** are grouped into conceptual arrangements. Some preferences apply only to you and the customizations you want to apply to your own login sessions; other preferences apply to the entire system. Some preferences control how certain hardware components will behave, such as the sound system and the display hardware; others manage networking and Internet access.

The Mac's Keyboard

Understanding how the Mac keyboard is laid out, and what its special keys do, is a crucial part of understanding how the Mac works. If you're new to the Mac, the special keys at the bottom of the keyboard might seem weird or esoteric; however, there is a method to their apparent madness.

Modifier Keys

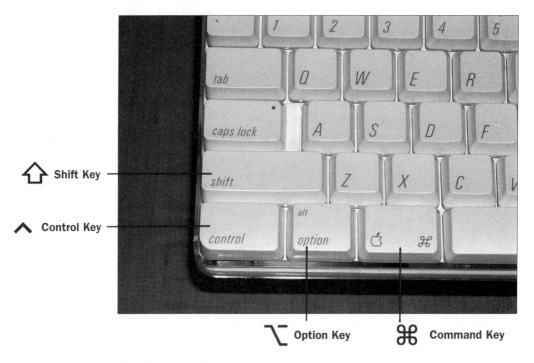

The Mac's modifier keys.

First of all, the Mac has three special modifier keys, found at the bottom of the keyboard. These keys are **Control**, **Option**, and ⌘ (also known as the **Command** or the **Apple** key and represented as ⌘). These keys, like the **Ctrl** and **Alt** keys on Windows keyboards, are used in combination with other keys on the keyboard to accomplish certain common functions in the operating system as well as in most applications. However, unlike the modifier keys in Windows, the Mac's modifier keys each have their own specific meanings, which are usually carefully observed by application developers. The keys are also each expressed by their own special symbols, as shown in the following chart.

Key	Symbol	Purpose
Command	⌘	In combination with alphanumeric keys, ⌘ (also often called "propeller," "Apple," or "splat") creates shortcuts to actions that are available from the menus in an application.
Option	⌥	The "magic" key. The **Option** key combines with letter keys to allow you to enter special accented or alternate letters or symbols. When combined with mouse actions or graphical buttons, **Option** changes the meanings of common functions to a less-used "alternate" version.
Control	∧	This key simulates the second (right) mouse button of a two-button mouse. Normally, if you click and hold the mouse on an item for a second or two, you will get a contextual menu with shortcuts and other options; however, if you hold down **Control** while clicking, the contextual menu pops up immediately. If you're used to right-clicking things in Windows, **Control**-clicking does much the same thing. Also, **Control** is used for compatibility with Unix applications designed with the PC **Ctrl** key in mind.
Shift	⇧	**Shift** is usually used for capitalizing letters or creating common special characters; however, it is also often used similarly to **Option** to trigger an "alternate" version of some function.

Key Combinations

The Mac has function keys—**F1** through **F15**—along the top of the keyboard; however, unlike the function keys in Windows, the Mac function keys are hardly ever used for any strictly predefined purpose. In

Windows, for example, you can press **Alt+F4** to close a window; this does not work on the Mac. Functions such as closing windows have different, carefully chosen key combinations, designed to be easily remembered and consistent across nearly all applications. Most of these key combinations involve the ⌘ key, although the **Option** or **Shift** key can be combined with other keys to create a secondary, related command.

TIP

Mac OS X and its applications have many more key combinations; you can find them all by looking in the menus, which show the key combinations along with the commands to which they correspond.

Common Key Combination	Meaning
⌘N	New (window, document, and so on)
⌘W	Close window
⌘Q	Quit application
⌘S	Save document
Shift+⌘+S	Save document as
⌘P	Print
⌘;	Preferences
⌘H	Hide application
⌘C	Copy
⌘X	Cut
⌘V	Paste
⌘.	Stop

Return and Enter

It must be noted that, on the Mac, the **Enter** key and the **Return** key have different meanings. **Return** is a text-editing key, using the original "carriage return" meaning from the days of typewriters. When you press **Return**, the cursor moves down a line and to the left end of whatever window you're typing in.

The **Enter** key (which in Windows has the same meaning as the Mac's **Return** key) is a little more specialized. When you press **Enter** (usually found on the numeric keypad), Mac OS X interprets the keystroke to mean "Perform the default action in the current window." A window typically has a single flashing blue button, which represents the default action for that window; pressing **Enter** simulates clicking that button. In other words, if you're typing in a text box, pressing **Return** will start a new paragraph; pressing **Enter** will cause the program to accept the changes and close the window, as though you had clicked the **OK** button.

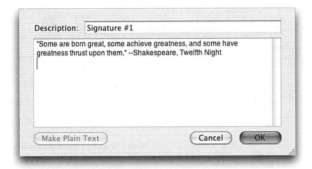

*In this application window, press **Return** to start a new line of text; press **Enter** to accept the changes and close the window (as if you'd clicked the **OK** button).*

Concluding the Tour

Now that you have seen the highlights of Mac OS X and have a basic understanding of what features do what, a few final notes are in order.

Put the Computer to Sleep

To put your Mac into a state of suspended animation, select the **Sleep** option from the **Apple** menu. The computer will appear to shut down, the fans and hard drive will spin down, and the display will go dark; but the power indicator light, which varies from model to model but which is usually purple, will pulse gently. This means that you can immediately wake the computer from sleep at any time by pressing a key or moving the mouse. The computer will immediately become usable again, without having to go through the entire boot cycle.

Because a Mac uses almost no power during sleep, it is the preferred means for turning the computer off for the night; Sleep mode is especially well suited to laptops, which automatically go to sleep when you close the lid. However, a sleeping Mac must still be connected to power; you can't unplug a sleeping iMac or remove an iBook's battery, or the computer will shut off entirely.

Log Out

To end your login session, select **Log Out** from the **Apple** menu. This will automatically quit all your running applications and return you to the **Login** window. If you use a Mac that is shared among several users, you will want to *log out* each time you're done using the computer.

NOTE

If your computer does not shut down cleanly—for instance, if the power cord is pulled, there is a power outage, or a sleeping laptop runs out of battery power—it will take longer to boot the next time you switch it on. Mac OS X has to repair the fragmentation on the disk that is caused when the machine shuts down unexpectedly, and these repairs can take a minute or more.

See Also

→ **165** Secure Your Files with FileVault

🔍 **KEY TERMS**

Log out—To end a login session. When you log out, you are returned to the **Login** window.

Restart—To shut down the entire system and immediately restart it, as though you had turned off the power and switched it back on again. This process is also known as a *reboot* or a *warm boot* (a cold boot is when you start the computer after it's been shut off completely), and is typically necessary only if something goes badly wrong with the operating system—an unlikely occurrence in Mac OS X.

Volume—Any disk (or portion of a disk that has been partitioned) is a separate resource that can appear on the Desktop or in the Finder.

Filesystem—Generally a Unix term; a filesystem refers to the software architecture that allows the operating system to read from and write to a volume. It also can mean simply a volume; for instance, your startup disk is both a volume and a filesystem.

Logging out protects your documents and settings from being altered or even seen by any other users (to see your documents, another person must have your login password). It's always a good idea to log out if there's any chance of someone else using the computer or of the computer being lost. If someone steals your laptop, logging out protects your sensitive documents from a thief's prying eyes.

Shut Down

If you want to completely shut down your Mac, choose **Shut Down** from the **Apple** menu. As with the **Log Out** option, the Mac automatically quits any open applications and ends your session; however, it will then proceed to clean up the system and then methodically power down. There is no need to press any switches; the computer will shut itself off completely. This is the safest method for deactivating your computer when you're done using it; it's safe to unplug the Mac or open it up to change the internal hardware after it has shut down. However, because shutting down and then *restarting* (a "warm boot") takes much longer than simply waking from sleep (which is almost instantaneous), it is usually not desirable to shut down completely unless you have a good reason to do so.

Navigating Mac OS X

Particularly if you're already familiar with another operating system (Windows or Mac OS 9), navigating through the structure of a Mac OS X system can be a challenging and unusual task. Mac OS X isn't any more complex than these other operating systems, but it's *different* enough from them that if you don't know what to look for, you could find yourself at a loss for what to do next.

Following this chapter, this book is filled with step-by-step demonstrations of useful tasks you can accomplish with Mac OS X. However, before we can proceed to those tasks, it is necessary to provide some detailed background on the **Finder**—the application that allows you to move through the system and find the resources you're looking for.

Structure of a Disk

Without disks, Mac OS X is nothing. The system must boot from a "startup disk," which is a disk with a full installation of Mac OS X on it. A startup disk (or startup *volume*) can be a hard disk, a CD-ROM or DVD, an external drive connected with FireWire or USB cables, or even a remote disk accessible over the network—anything with a readable *filesystem*.

The entire operating system (which consumes about two gigabytes of disk space) must be available on a mounted disk for the Mac to function.

Beyond just the operating system, however, is the part of the disk that you will be using. As you saw earlier in this chapter, your **Home** folder also resides on the startup disk of the operating system, in the **Users** folder. As you use the system, the applications you run will create files, all of which will be stored within the **Home** folder; this goes for documents you create, files you download from the Internet, and preference files and other supporting data for your applications. To use all these files, you must be able to find them; that's where the Finder comes in.

Know the Finder

Click the **Finder** icon at the left end of the Dock. A window opens up that should look like the one shown here.

NOTE

Every item in the system can be located by describing its *path* (the names of the folders you have to open to get to that item). You will seldom see a path written out in text; but if you do, it is described as a series of folder names separated by slashes or colons. For instance, the **Home** folder for a user called **johndoe** is inside the **Users** folder of the startup disk (**Macintosh HD**); its path is **/Volumes/ Macintosh HD/Users/johndoe**. Older applications might show the path as **Macintosh HD:Users:johndoe**.

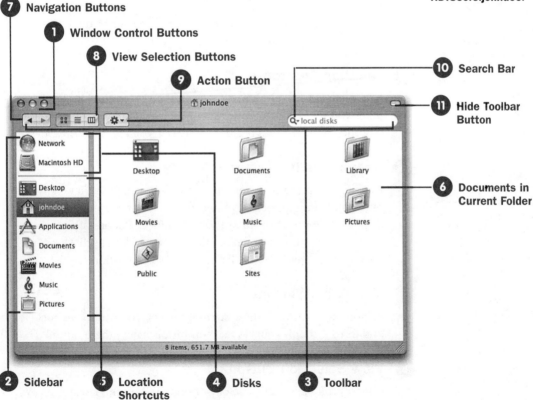

A Finder window.

❶ Window Control Buttons

Use these buttons to close, minimize, or zoom the window.

❷ Sidebar

The entire Dock-like section on the left side of the Finder window is the sidebar. It provides starting points for you to use in navigating the disk.

❸ Toolbar

The buttons across the top of the window are all part of the toolbar, which provides controls that apply to all Finder windows. You can customize which buttons appear in the toolbar using the **Customize Toolbar** command in the **View** menu.

❹ Disks

This area shows all the disks and other data sources available in your system. Click any disk to show its contents.

❺ Location Shortcuts

Each item here is a link to a folder in the system; clicking an icon takes you to that folder's contents. You can add folders to this pane by dragging them into position, much as you can with the Dock.

❻ Documents in Current Folder

Depending on the view you have selected (using the **View** selection buttons), icons representing the contents of the current folder are displayed arbitrarily or in organized listings. Double-click any folder to open it in the same **Finder** window; double-click any document to open it in its default opener application.

❼ Navigation Buttons

As you move through the system of folders, you can move back and forth through your navigation history using these buttons.

❽ View Selection Buttons

Choose Icon view, List view, or Column view. Each view has its own advantages and specialized options. You will see each of these views in detail later in this chapter.

9 Action Button

Use this button to perform specific actions on any documents or folders you have selected. Available actions include opening documents or folders, setting color labels, getting detailed file info, or moving items to the Trash.

10 Search Bar

Type in this field to perform an instant search on whatever text you type. Pull down the menu to select the disks or resources you want to search in.

11 Hide Toolbar Button

This button allows you to hide or show the toolbar (the row of control buttons) and the sidebar.

The Finder is a flexible piece of software that can be tailored to however you are most comfortable using it. Let's take a look at what some of its controls do. First we have the three different view modes, which you can switch between at any time.

Icon View

The first view option is Icon view. Each document and folder in the window appears as a pictograph or icon, with a label underneath it or to the right. Depending on your settings for the folder, the icons can be arranged in a strict grid pattern or scattered arbitrarily around the window. You can click and drag icons from one part of the window to another; some application developers create artistic presentation folders this way, as you will see in Chapter 2, "Working with Applications."

Icon view is the most configurable of the views. To configure the view, choose **Edit**, **View Options**; a panel opens in which you can select your viewing preferences, such as the background color or picture, or the icon arrangement.

To open a folder shown in Icon view, double-click it; the new folder opens in the same Finder window, its contents replacing those of the folder you were in previously. Alternatively, you can have the new folder open in a new Finder window, by holding down the ⌘ key while you double-click. If you hold down the **Option** key while double-clicking a folder icon, the new folder will open in a new window *and* the old window will close.

 TIP

You can assign a different view mode to every folder in the system. One folder can be in Icon view (with large icons); another might be in List view (with small icons); and a third can be in Column view. Each folder stores the view settings that were in effect when you closed the window in which you were viewing that folder; if you then open that folder directly, it opens with the same view settings it had when you last closed it.

Icon View Button

*A Finder window in Icon view, and its **View Options** panel.*

Hold down the ⌘ and **Option** keys, then click and drag to pan around a window in Icon view.

Hold down the ⌘ key and click the title of the Finder window to see a pop-up menu showing all the folders in the path to your current location. This action lets you easily jump to any point along the folder path.

Icon view is aesthetically pleasing and very useful for displaying folders with a few special items in it; but for easier sorting or quicker navigation, the other two views are often preferable.

List View

List view provides the most information about the items in a folder. Documents and folders are listed alphabetically (if you're accustomed to Windows, you might be surprised at first to see that folders are alphabetized right along with documents, instead of being shown first in the listing as in Windows). However, several additional columns show extra information about each item. You can click the column headings to sort the items based on whichever column you choose. These columns include the time of last modification, size, kind, version, and label color; in the **View Options** panel, you can enable or disable these columns according to your taste.

List View Button

*A Finder window in List view, and its **View Options** panel.*

Navigating in List view is more flexible than in Icon view. To the left of each folder is a small triangular arrow pointing right; if you click the arrow, it turns downward, and the folder's contents are displayed, indented under the folder. This arrangement allows you to open branches of the hierarchy of folders underneath the current folder. However, to see folders higher up in the hierarchy, you must use another method to move back along the path, such as clicking the **Back** button at the top of the window or holding down ⌘ while clicking the window title.

List view is tailored for showing the maximum amount of item information possible, at the expense of prettiness and navigability. For the ultimate in easy navigation, you need Column view.

Column View

Although Icon view and List view have been in the Mac OS for many years, Column view is a new addition to Mac OS X—but not a new idea. It first appeared in the NeXT operating system, which also pioneered features such as the Dock, which eventually made their way—in heavily altered form—into Mac OS X.

 TIP

If you've got an Icon view window that has icons scattered haphazardly all over the place, select **View**, **Clean Up**. The icons all snap to an organized grid layout.

🔅 TIPS

You can select a set of items in the same spatial area by clicking and dragging to create a selection box around the items. You can click to select one item, scroll to another item further down the list, and press **Shift** while clicking to select the entire intervening range of items.

Hold down ⌘ while clicking individual items in succession; each additional item you click is added to the selection. ⌘+click individual selected items to deselect them while leaving the rest selected.

⌘**A** is nearly always a key combination for **Select All Items**.

The idea of Column view is pretty simple: your window contains a series of columns, each of which represents a folder. The columns can be scrolled left and right, and picking a folder from any column causes that folder's contents to be shown in a new column to the right. This way, the entire path through a folder hierarchy can be represented in a single left-to-right view, and you can scroll horizontally to any point along the path.

Column View Button

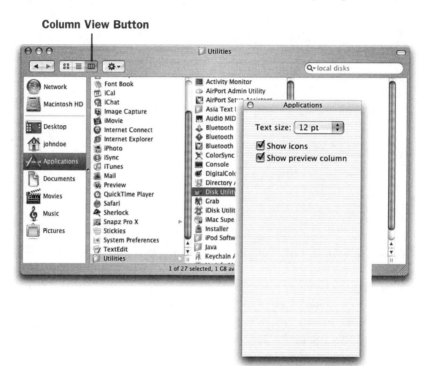

*A Finder window in Column view, and its **View Options** panel.*

If you select a file in a folder, the column to the right displays that file's preview and vital information. However, you don't get to see much else in the way of item information in Column view. All that's visible are the icons and item names, which are always sorted alphabetically. Column view is designed with easy navigation as its primary goal, and the trade-off in this case is information visibility. If you need to move quickly up and down through the folders on a disk, but you don't especially need to see the detailed information on all the items along the way, Column view is the most efficient way to do it.

The Action Button

In a Finder window, there are several things you can do to a document or folder directly without need for any extra applications; these include labeling items, creating new folders, getting detailed information on items, duplicating items, and moving items to the Trash. These operations are all grouped into the **Action** button.

The Action button and its contextual menu.

If you click the **Action** button without having selected any items, you will see only two options listed in its contextual menu: **New Folder** and **Get Info**. However, if you select one or more items first, the menu is filled with options.

Use the Second Mouse Button

Contrary to popular belief, the Mac does not limit you to a single-button mouse, even if that's all Apple sells; you are perfectly free to plug in a two-button or three-button mouse, or one with a scroll wheel, and Mac OS X will support the extra features without any need for extra drivers. The operating system is designed to require no more than a single mouse button; but if you have more mouse buttons, they can provide you with shortcuts to commonly used functions.

For instance, in the Finder, right-clicking a document or folder opens a contextual menu that matches the one you get from selecting the item and then clicking the **Action** button. (You can also get the same menu by holding down **Control** while clicking on the item.) The right-click contextual menu lets you perform an action on the item with two clicks in the same general vicinity, rather than three or four clicks and drags that require you to move the mouse all around the window. The **Action** button provides all the functionality available in the system, so a single-button mouse can

TIP

Most of the actions that can be launched from the Action button are described in ⑪ **Find an Item**, ⑫ **Create a New Folder**, and ⑯ **Set a Color Label.**

accomplish everything the system offers; but a multibutton mouse saves
you time and effort.

The contextual menu resulting from right-clicking an item.

Hide the Toolbar and Sidebar

The elongated white button in the upper-right corner of the Finder window is an interface element that appears in the Finder and a handful of
other applications; its purpose is to let you shrink the window to its bare
minimum components, hiding the toolbar and data sources from view
so that all you see is the window and its contents.

 TIP

Double-click the vertical
divider between the sidebar
(on the left) and the navigation pane (on the right)
in the Finder window to
hide the sidebar. You can
also drag the divider back
and forth to adjust the size
of the panes.

*A Finder window with the toolbar (at the top of the window) and the
sidebar hidden.*

If you hide the toolbar, be aware that you won't be able to change view modes or navigate back and forth using the mouse; you can use keyboard shortcuts for navigating (⌘[and ⌘]), and you can change the view mode using the **View** menu. But actions from the **Action** button's contextual menu must be selected from the **File** menu or by right-clicking the item you want to work with. A window with the toolbar hidden can be more streamlined and take up less space, but it's missing many amenities you might decide are too useful not to have available.

The Get Info Panel

Each document or folder has a wealth of information associated with it. On the Mac, documents can have custom icons, version numbers, opener applications, access permissions, comments, and other bits and pieces of data that are normally useful only to applications. The **Get Info** panel lets you examine that information for each item in the system.

NOTE

In Icon view with the toolbar hidden, if you double-click a folder, the new folder opens by default in a new window; if the toolbar is shown, double-clicking a folder opens the new folder in the same window. It's assumed that if you have the toolbar hidden, you expect to have your navigation path available in the form of the windows you have opened to get to your current position.

*The **Get Info** panel for a document.*

The **Get Info** panel consists of several subpanels, each of which can be expanded or collapsed by clicking the triangle arrow in the left corner of each one. You can use the **Get Info** panel to change many of a file's attributes: You can show or hide the filename extension (or remove it entirely), you can change the opener application, you can set a comment, and you can modify the access permissions. Some of these processes are covered in **7** **Assign an Opener Application to a File**, **13** **Rename a Folder or Document**, and **15** **Change an Icon or Label**. For now, remember that the **Get Info** panel can always be accessed for any item by selecting **Get Info** from the **Action** button menu or by pressing ⌘**I**.

Customizing the Finder

The control buttons you see in the toolbar at the top of the Finder aren't all you get; there's actually more to the toolbar than you have yet seen.

 NOTE

⌘+click the **Hide Toolbar** button (at the top-right corner of the Finder window) to cycle through the various types of icons and labels you can use—small or large icons, with or without labels. Adding the **Option** key (⌘+Option+click) opens the **Customize Toolbar** sheet.

One of the unique features of Mac OS X is that many applications have toolbars that can be customized however you like; the Finder is one of these applications. Select **Customize Toolbar** from the **View** menu to see a sheet full of controls you can place in the Finder's toolbar.

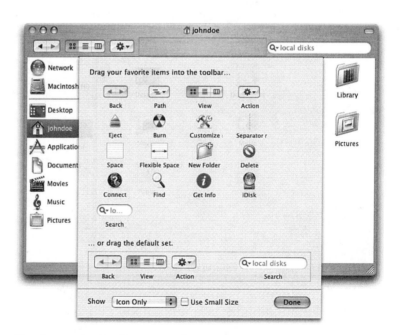

*The **Customize Toolbar** sheet for the Finder.*

To add any of the listed controls to the toolbar, simply drag them into place where you want them to appear. To remove a control from the toolbar, drag it off the window; it will disappear in a puff of smoke. If you put too many items on the toolbar for them all to be visible simultaneously, the ones that can't be shown are accessible by clicking an arrow at the right end of the toolbar.

Feel free to experiment with these controls; you can arrange them any way you like, and you can always go back to the way it was before by dragging the "default set" of controls into the toolbar; this resets the controls to their factory settings.

You can also use the controls at the bottom of the sheet to specify whether the toolbar controls are shown as icons or as text labels or as both. You can reduce the size of the buttons by enabling the **Use Small Size** check box.

You can control another set of global Finder options in the **Finder Preferences** window. Open this window by selecting **Preferences** from the **Finder** menu.

Options you can configure in these panels include (as you have seen earlier) which types of storage devices you want to display on the Desktop as well as the following behaviors:

1 New Finder Windows Open Menu

You can select whether opening a new Finder window starts you in your **Home** folder (the default behavior) or with the entire Computer view, which lets you see all the available disks and resources attached to your Mac. Because the Finder already shows you all the disks in the sidebar, it's probably best to leave this option set to **Home**.

2 Always Open Folders in a New Window Check Box

You can select to have each folder open in a new window. Enabling this option is equivalent to holding down the ⌘ key while you double-click a folder icon.

3 Open New Windows in Column View Check Box

You can choose to have all new folder windows open in Column view.

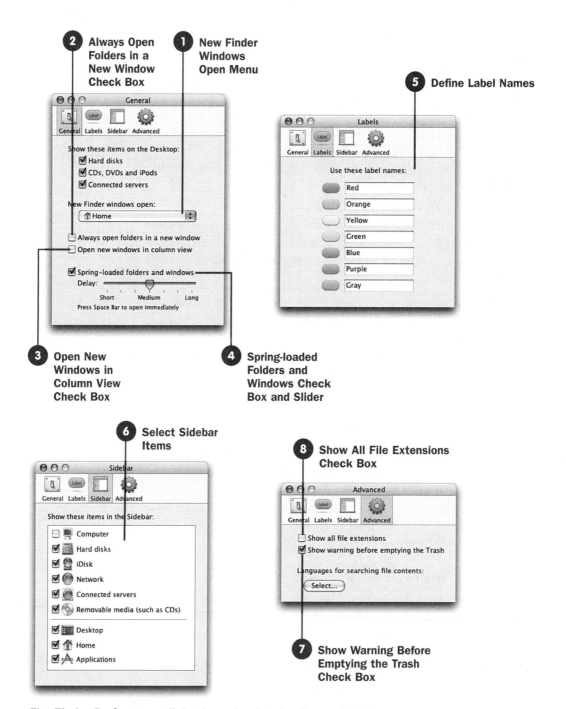

② Always Open Folders in a New Window Check Box

① New Finder Windows Open Menu

⑤ Define Label Names

③ Open New Windows in Column View Check Box

④ Spring-loaded Folders and Windows Check Box and Slider

⑥ Select Sidebar Items

⑧ Show All File Extensions Check Box

⑦ Show Warning Before Emptying the Trash Check Box

The **Finder Preferences** dialog box, showing the **General**, **Labels**, **Sidebar**, and **Advanced** panes.

4 Spring-loaded Folders and Windows Check Box and Slider

Spring-loaded folders is a convenience feature that allows you to navigate through the folders in your disk while dragging a file at the same time. While holding down the mouse button and dragging a file icon, hover the mouse over a folder in the Finder; regardless of what view you're using, after a short delay the folder blinks and then pops open. You can then drop the file into that folder (and it will close), or you can drive still deeper into other folders using the same method. The slider in the **Finder Preferences** dialog box lets you control the length of the delay before the folder pops open.

5 Define Label Names

In the **Labels** pane, you can customize the names for each of the seven different colored labels available. For instance, if you like to use red labels for items that are urgent, you can change its name from **Red** to **Urgent**. The new label name will appear in all textual representations of the label in the Finder, such as in the **Label** column in List view.

6 Select Sidebar Items

The **Sidebar** pane lets you select which kinds of media (disks, servers, and other data sources) as well as which folders or documents will appear in the Finder's sidebar. Use the check boxes to enable or disable the indicated items. The options you select here do not affect items you drag into the sidebar manually.

7 Show Warning Before Emptying the Trash Check Box

In the **Advanced** pane, you can turn off the warning that appears when you empty the Trash, permanently deleting whatever items are in it.

NOTE

See **16** Set a Color Label for more on setting colored labels on files.

NOTE

Because the hiding of a file's extension can be toggled on and off simply by renaming the file and adding or removing an extension as appropriate, this option is probably not likely to be useful unless you're a hard-core purist.

⑧ Show All File Extensions Check Box

If you want, you can choose to show filename extensions under all circumstances, even if the extension is hidden. This can be useful if you do a lot of cross-platform work and don't want to be confused about whether a file has a hidden extension that will appear when transferred to a Windows or Unix system, or whether it has no extension at all.

Finally, you can select as many languages as you like from the list accessible from the **Select** button at the bottom of the **Advanced** panel; the more languages you select, the more relevant results you will get when you perform a search on the contents of files. However, the more languages you select, the larger the indexes will be, the longer searches will take, and the more disk space the system will take up. It's probably best not to select any additional languages unless you have a lot of documents in those languages that you want to be able to search.

2

Working with Applications

IN THIS CHAPTER:

Without *applications*, all you can do with Mac OS X is move files around and change their names, or customize your work environment. Applications are what make a computer into a tool for accomplishing useful tasks, which is what this book is all about.

Mac OS X comes with many applications bundled by Apple as part of the operating system. Indeed, it is entirely possible to live the Digital Hub life (as promoted by Apple's marketing team) using only the applications that come with your Mac; after all, Apple produces more cutting-edge software for more diverse purposes than just about any other technology company in the world. Software such as iTunes, iMovie, and Safari that come with your Mac have one thing in common with high-end third-party applications such as Adobe Photoshop and QuarkXPress: They're all *applications*, which is to say they're self-contained programs you run to accomplish some task and quit when you're done using them.

This chapter addresses the skills necessary to manage your applications, install and delete them, and make them interact with your files so that they do what you need them to do.

1 Install an Application from Disc or Download

See Also

→ **3** Add an Application to the Dock

→ **9** Uninstall an Application

Installing an application under Mac OS X is considerably different from the way it's traditionally done under Windows. Because Mac OS X has no Registry, and because Mac OS X applications are single monolithic "bundles"—which can be moved around from place to place or from disk to disk as though each application is a single file (rather than being folders full of DLLs and config files, as it's usually done in Windows)— oftentimes installing an application involves nothing more complicated than dragging an icon from one disk window to another.

Some applications under Mac OS X do use installer programs, as is typical of Windows; this is usually the case with large and complex software, such as Adobe Photoshop or Microsoft Office. When an application uses an installer program, it's usually because the installer has to add resources to the system, such as Library frameworks or kernel extensions, or because it has to apply certain low-level system settings. The more complex the software, the more likely you will need to run an installer.

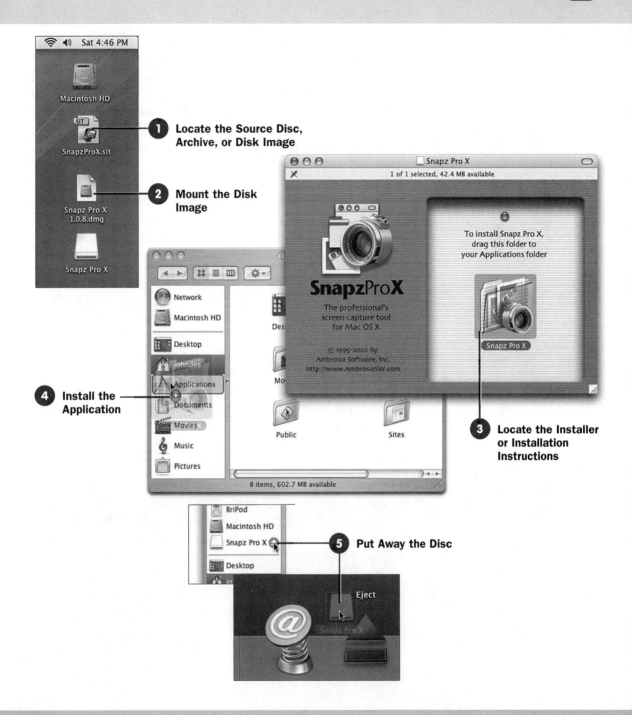

1 Locate the Source Disc, Archive, or Disk Image

2 Mount the Disk Image

3 Locate the Installer or Installation Instructions

4 Install the Application

5 Put Away the Disc

KEY TERMS

Disk image—A specialized kind of archive file, a disk image is a file that when opened acts like a regular disk that you mount on the system. Disk image files end in **.dmg** or **.img**; if you double-click on one, the Disk Utility application opens up and expands the disk image into a virtual disk mounted in the Finder. You can then browse it or manipulate its contents just as you would any real disk.

Archive—A collection of documents, folders, or applications that are packed into a single file, which is usually compressed so that it can be easily downloaded. On the Mac, archives can be Windows-style ZIP files (with **.zip** extensions), **.sit** (StuffIt) files, **.tar.gz** files (for Unix utilities), or disk images.

TIP

Check the **Preferences** of your Web browser to see where it is configured to save downloaded files. Safari, the built-in Mac OS X browser, is normally set up to save downloads to the Desktop, but if you can't find files you've downloaded, the browser might be set to save them somewhere else.

Applications typically are installed from either a disc (CD-ROM or DVD) or a *disk image*. In either case, the process for installing the application is generally the same: You must **mount** the source disk, then open it up to see what the installation procedure is. We will look at both an application that requires an installer program (iTunes), and one that must simply be dragged from its disk image to your **Applications** folder (Snapz Pro X, a screen-capture program that was used to capture all the screenshots in this book).

① Locate the Source Disc, Archive, or Disk Image

An application downloaded from the Internet is usually in the form of an *archive* file. This file can be either a compressed folder (usually with a **.zip** or **.sit** extension) or a disk image.

Downloaded files usually appear directly on the Desktop. If you don't see your file there, your browser might be using a different location for its download files. Many Web browsers provide a "download manager" tool that allows you to locate a downloaded file and open it automatically.

② Mount the Disk Image

If your application is on a CD-ROM or DVD, insert it into the drive. Its icon will appear on the Desktop, or in the Finder's sidebar (if you have configured the Finder to show removable disks in the sidebar).

If the application is an archive file downloaded from the Internet, double-click its file icon. If it's a ZIP or SIT archive, StuffIt Expander launches and expand the file into a folder. If it's a disk image, however, Disk Utility launches and transforms the file into a virtual disk, mounted on your Desktop or in the Finder's sidebar.

③ Locate the Installer or Installation Instructions

At this point, you have the application source disk mounted— whether it's an inserted disc or a disk image. Navigate to the disk's contents in the Finder or double-click its icon on the Desktop. A Finder window opens, showing the disk's contents.

It's a good idea to keep the download page open in your browser even after you've downloaded the archive or disk image file; the page often contains useful installation instructions.

The window should contain instructions for installation, a "Read Me" document, or a "package" file (which is an installer application that you must double-click). Each application is distributed differently. The Snapz Pro X disk image, for instance, has clear instructions for what to do next, whereas the installer folder for iTunes contains nothing but a package file. If it's not clear what you need to do, look for a "Read Me" file or other similar instructional document.

4 **Install the Application**

Snapz Pro X's installation instructions are clear enough: simply drag the application icon from the disk image folder to your **Applications** folder. To do this, open a second Finder window by clicking the **Finder** icon at the far left of the Dock or by pressing ⌘N. Then drag the Snapz Pro X folder from the first window to the **Applications** folder icon in the second window.

Many other applications, however, have an installer program. To install iTunes, for instance, double-click the **iTunes.pkg** file icon to launch the installer. Follow the on-screen instructions which direct you to choose an installation disk, accept the user agreement, and restart the computer at the end (if necessary).

5 **Put Away the Disc**

A disk image can be unmounted (or ejected) just like any other disk. Drag its icon to the **Trash** in the Dock (which turns into an "eject" symbol with the label **Eject**), or click the **Eject** button next to its icon in the Finder's sidebar. The original disk image file is still there; you might want to create a special folder to keep it in, in case you need it later (for instance, to reinstall the application). See **12** **Create a New Folder**.

If you're installing from an inserted disc, when you eject it (using the same method) the drive door opens, allowing you to remove the disc.

TIP

Many browsers, such as Safari, automatically expand archive files when they're done downloading. Safari launches StuffIt Expander to unpack SIT archives; if the downloaded file is a disk image (with a **.dmg** extension), or if a SIT archive expands into a disk image, Safari opens the disk image and mounts it as a disk on the Desktop. When downloading an application from the Internet, wait until the browser finishes unpacking it to either an application folder (as with GraphicConverter) or a mounted disk image (as with Snapz Pro X), and then use that item to install the application.

2 Find and Launch an Application

Before You Begin

✔ **1.** Install an Application from Disc or Download

See Also

→ **3** Add an Application to the Dock

NOTE

Old Mac hands might be accustomed to the ⌘N keystroke creating a new folder, not a new Finder window. In Mac OS X, ⌘N is used to create a new instance of whatever the standard window is for the current application—and that applies to the Finder, too. Use ⌘+**Shift+N** to create a new folder.

TIP

You can tell what application you're currently in by the boldfaced menu name to the right of the **Apple** icon in the menu bar at the top-left of the screen. If you aren't in the Finder, click anywhere on the Desktop to switch to the Finder.

TIP

If you know the application's name, try using the **Search** bar at the top of the Finder window. Click on the down-arrow and select **Local Disks** or **Everywhere** to make sure that the Finder is looking throughout the entire disk.

In Mac OS X, applications reside primarily in the **Applications** folder. The most basic way to launch an application is to navigate to that folder and double-click its icon.

1 Open a Finder Window

Click the **Finder** icon at the far left end of the Dock, or press ⌘N while in the Finder to open a new Finder window.

2 Go to the Applications Folder

The Finder sidebar contains a shortcut icon to the **Applications** folder. Click this icon to open the **Applications** folder. Alternatively, select **Applications** from the **Go** menu, or press **Shift**+⌘+**A**. (With this key command, you don't even have to open a Finder window first.)

3 Scroll to the Application You Want

Depending on the view mode you're in, the applications in the folder will be arranged differently—generally alphabetically, but Icon view and List view allow the applications to be sorted by many other criteria. Use the scroll bars to search through the window until you find the application you're looking for.

4 Double-Click the Application Icon

When you double-click the application in the Finder, the application icon appears in the Dock, bouncing up and down. It will keep bouncing until the application has completed launching; after that, a black triangle underneath the icon shows that the application is running.

5 Work with the Application

When the application has launched completely, you can begin to use it. With most applications, you can choose **File**, **Open** from the menu bar to select an existing document with which you want to continue working or editing. To open a new document in most applications, choose **File**, **New**, or press ⌘N.

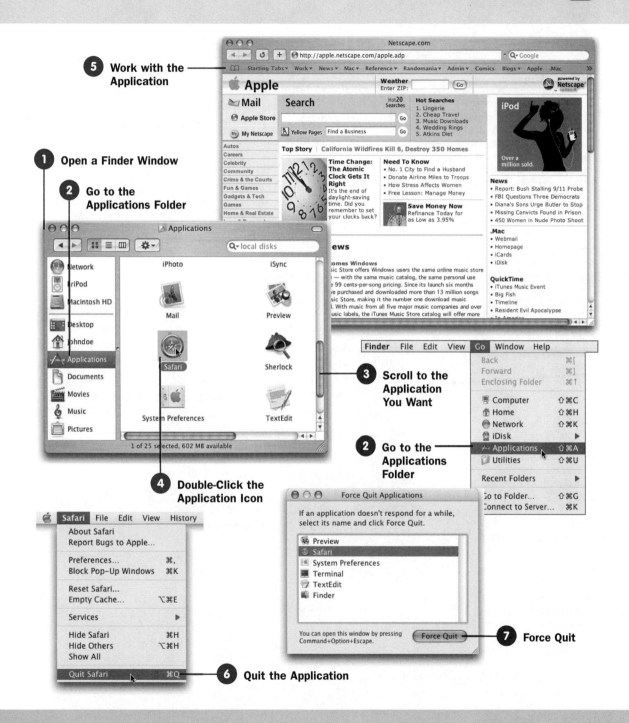

5 Work with the Application

1 Open a Finder Window

2 Go to the Applications Folder

3 Scroll to the Application You Want

2 Go to the Applications Folder

4 Double-Click the Application Icon

7 Force Quit

6 Quit the Application

TIP

Almost every application has **Preferences** you can set. Preferences (which under Windows are often variously called **Options** or **Settings**) control the application's behavior, appearance, and interaction with the rest of your system. By convention for consistency, every Mac application's **Preferences** are accessible from the bold-titled application menu. The keyboard shortcut to reach **Preferences** is typically ⌘, (comma).

6 Quit the Application

In Mac OS X, just because all the application's windows have been closed does not mean the application is no longer running. An application can be running with no windows open; it's still taking up memory and system resources. If you want to quit an application, you must explicitly tell it to quit.

Under the bold application menu, no matter what application you're running, the last option is always **Quit**. Switch to the application you want to quit, open the application menu, and select **Quit**. You may be prompted to save changes in whatever document windows you have open. The standard key combination for the **Quit** command is ⌘Q.

7 Force Quit

Sometimes, an application might misbehave, crash, freeze, or otherwise become unresponsive. Mac OS X is robust enough that if this happens, you can generally switch to another application and continue using the rest of the system; but to stop the misbehaving application and get it to stop using system resources, you might have to force it to quit. This method immediately terminates the application without saving any changes in memory; it's sort of messy, but it gets the job done.

Press ⌘+**Option**+**Escape** or select **Force Quit** from the **Apple** menu. The **Force Quit Applications** dialog box appears, showing a list of all currently running applications. Select the one you want to quit and click the **Force Quit** button. The misbehaving application is immediately terminated.

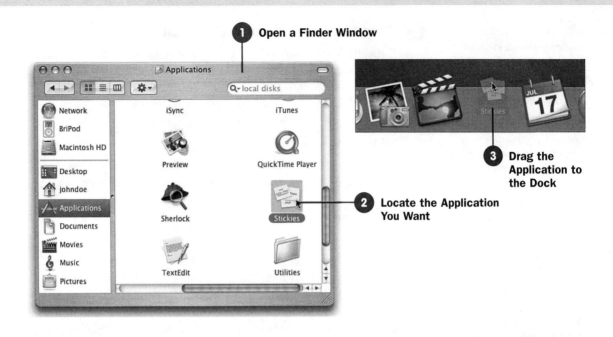

1 Open a Finder Window

3 Drag the Application to the Dock

2 Locate the Application You Want

3 Add an Application to the Dock

Navigating to the **Applications** folder every time you want to launch an application can be tiresome. Fortunately, the Dock is there to act as a combination launch bar and task manager. You can add as many applications as you want to the Dock; after an application is on the Dock, your access to that application is just a single click away.

1 Open a Finder Window

Click the **Finder** icon at the left end of the Dock, or press ⌘N while in the Finder to open a new Finder window.

2 Locate the Application You Want

Navigate to the **Applications** folder using the shortcut in the Finder sidebar, or choose **Go, Applications** from the menu bar at the top of the Desktop. Scroll to the frequently used application icon you're looking for.

Before You Begin

✔ **1** Install an Application from Disc or Download

See Also

→ **4** Control an Application from the Dock

→ **5** Minimize and Restore a Window

→ **134** Change the Dock's Position and Behavior

TIP

You can add all kinds of items to the Dock—not just applications. To the right of the vertical dividing line, you can place documents, folders, aliases, and even whole disks. You just can't put them to the left of the dividing line, and you can't place applications to the right of the line.

 TIP

It's even simpler to add an application permanently to the Dock if the application is already running. Click the application icon in the Dock and hold; after a moment, the contextual menu appears above the icon. Select **Keep In Dock**. The application icon will remain in the Dock even after you quit it.

③ Drag the Application to the Dock

Click the application icon in the Finder; holding down the mouse button, drag the icon into the Dock, to any position left of the vertical divider bar. Move the icon between any two icons you like, and they will separate to make room for the new icon. Release the mouse button, and the icon settles into position. After that, a single click on the Docked icon launches the application.

You can place the application anywhere you like on the left side of the Dock; if you don't like where you put it, drag it to a new position in the Dock. You can also remove it altogether by dragging it upward off the Dock so that it disappears in a puff of smoke.

A translucent "question mark" symbol in the Dock signifies an item that had previously been placed in the Dock, but that no longer exists on the disk. If you see one of these question marks, hover your mouse over it to see what it's labeled; if its name is of an application or document that you know you have on your system and you want to keep in your Dock, locate that item in the Finder and drag it to the Dock again. Then remove the question mark by dragging it off the Dock.

Try adding the entire **Applications** folder to the Dock! Open a Finder window, then select your disk from the sidebar; drag the **Applications** folder icon from the main Finder window down onto the right side of the Dock. Now you can click and hold, **Control**+click, or right-click the **Applications** folder in the Dock and have immediate access to all the applications installed on your system.

---

④ Control an Application from the Dock

Before You Begin

✔ **②** Find and Launch an Application

✔ **③** Add an Application to the Dock

See Also

→ **⑤** Minimize and Restore a Window

→ **134** Change the Dock's Position and Behavior

The Dock gives you the ability to control certain basic behaviors of all applications, whether they're running or not. Some applications are designed so that you can control more specific functions from the Dock without even needing to switch active applications.

① Show an Application in the Finder

Although having an application icon in the Dock is convenient, the icon is just a shortcut to the original application. Sometimes you have to access the original item, for instance if you want to

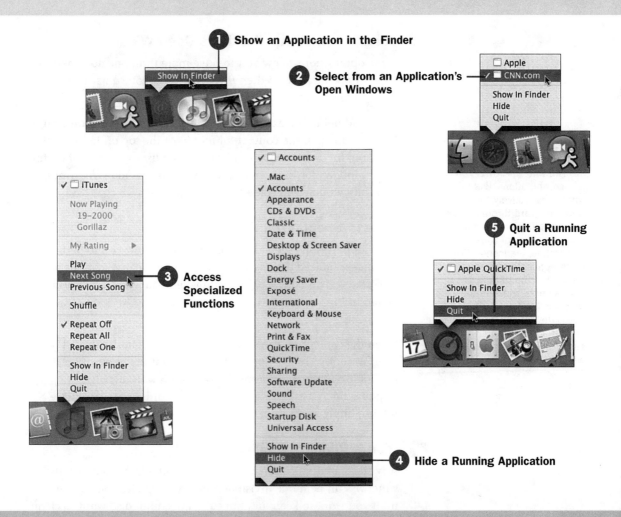

1 **Show an Application in the Finder**

Show In Finder

2 **Select from an Application's Open Windows**

☐ Apple
✓ ■ CNN.com

Show In Finder
Hide
Quit

✓ ☐ iTunes

Now Playing
19-2000
Gorillaz

My Rating ▶

Play
Next Song
Previous Song

Shuffle

✓ Repeat Off
Repeat All
Repeat One

Show In Finder
Hide
Quit

3 **Access Specialized Functions**

✓ ☐ Accounts

.Mac
✓ Accounts
Appearance
CDs & DVDs
Classic
Date & Time
Desktop & Screen Saver
Displays
Dock
Energy Saver
Exposé
International
Keyboard & Mouse
Network
Print & Fax
QuickTime
Security
Sharing
Software Update
Sound
Speech
Startup Disk
Universal Access

Show In Finder
Hide
Quit

5 **Quit a Running Application**

✓ ☐ Apple QuickTime

Show In Finder
Hide
Quit

4 **Hide a Running Application**

view the **Get Info** panel for the application to find information such as its version number. Fortunately, any application in the Dock—whether it's running or not—can be traced back to its original location.

Click and hold the icon in the Dock, or **Control**+click or right-click it. A contextual menu pops up. Every contextual menu for items in the Dock has, at the very least, a **Show In Finder** option. Select this option, and a Finder window appears showing the original item in the folder where it resides.

TIP

You can switch between applications using the ⌘+**Tab** and ⌘+**Shift+Tab** key combinations, which rotate respectively forward and backward through your open applications. When you use either of these keystrokes, the icons of the open applications appear floating in the middle of your screen, and remain there as long as you hold down the ⌘ key. Press **Tab** or **Shift+Tab** repeatedly to select the application you want.

② Select from an Application's Open Windows

Some applications allow you to have more than one document window open at once. When this is the case, you can switch from one window to another using the Dock.

Click and hold, **Control**+click, or right-click the application icon in the Dock to open the contextual menu. At the top of the contextual menu, for any running application, is a list (by name) of all the open windows for that application. Select the window you want, and that window will come to the foreground.

③ Access Specialized Functions

Some applications such as iTunes and Mail allow you to perform certain specialized actions without bringing the applications to the foreground. This can be very useful when you want to perform an action in the background while you continue to work on something else.

Open the contextual menu for the application; under the list of open windows are any special functions that the application has available. iTunes, for instance, has controls that allow you to play or pause the music, skip forward or backward, or toggle shuffle mode. Simply select from the menu to perform these functions.

④ Hide a Running Application

Any running application can be hidden—in other words, all its windows can be made invisible. Hiding an application can be useful if you want to keep an application open but also want to clean up your work environment.

TIP

With the application's contextual menu open, press the **Option** key. The **Hide** option turns into **Hide Others**. Selecting this option allows you to hide all applications *except* the application you're controlling.

Open the contextual menu and select **Hide** from the bottom area of the list of options. All the application's windows will disappear; if the application is currently active, the previously active application becomes active.

5 Quit a Running Application

Quitting an application terminates its execution, closing all its windows and removing it from memory. You can do this by switching to the application and choosing **Quit** from the application menu; you can also quit using the Dock's contextual menu. Open the contextual menu and select **Quit** from the bottom of the list. The black triangle disappears from under the application icon in the Dock as the application quits.

 TIP

If you press the **Option** key while the contextual menu is open, the **Quit** option turns into **Force Quit**. If an application is misbehaving or not responding, the Dock's contextual menu will have a note to that effect at the top, and the **Force Quit** option will be available at the bottom.

5 Minimize and Restore a Window

Minimizing an application's windows shrinks them to thumbnail-sized versions sitting at the right end of the Dock, near the **Trash**. Minimizing windows allows you to get certain windows off the screen while keeping others active. A minimized application is still running; it just takes up none of your Desktop space. You can easily restore a minimized window at any time.

Before You Begin

✔ **2** Find and Launch an Application

See Also

→ **6** Grab the Window You Want

1 Minimize a Window

The yellow control button at the top left of any window minimizes that window. Click the button, and the window shrinks into the Dock using the "Genie Effect"—the window morphs into a flexible shape that condenses as it "flows" into an icon in the Dock.

You can also minimize a window by selecting **Minimize** from the **Window** menu, or by pressing ⌘M.

NOTE

Some kinds of windows, such as QuickTime movies, will continue to play even if minimized into the Dock.

2 Restore a Window

A minimized window can be restored by simply clicking its icon in the Dock.

3 Use a Different Minimize Effect

The Genie Effect looks cool the first few hundred times, but eventually you might want to use a minimize effect that's a little quicker and less ostentatious.

TIP

You can also select the minimize effect from the Dock's contextual menu. **Control+** click (or right-click) the vertical dividing line in the middle of the Dock; from the contextual menu select **Minimize using**, and then choose the effect you want.

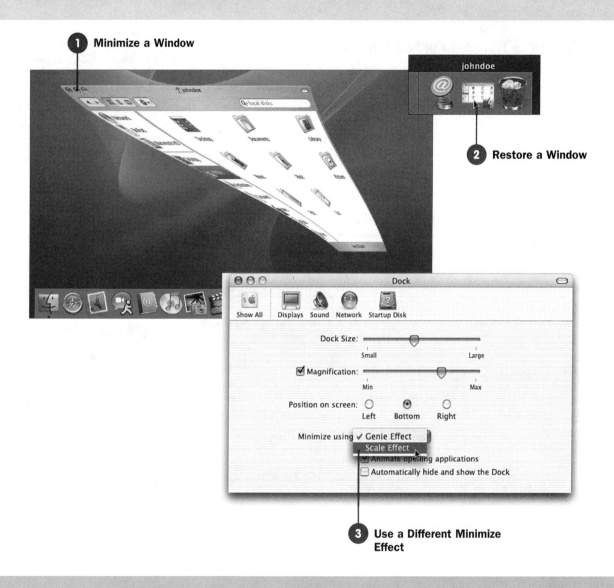

① Minimize a Window

② Restore a Window

③ Use a Different Minimize Effect

TIP

If you like showing off Mac OS X's graphical talents to your friends and co-workers, you can run the Genie or Scale Effect in slow motion by holding down the **Shift** key as you minimize the window.

You can select the minimize effect from the Dock **Preferences**. From the **Apple** menu, choose **Dock**, **Dock Preferences**. In the dialog box that opens, select **Scale Effect** from the **Minimize using** drop-down list. The **Scale Effect** option simply scales the window directly into its Dock position, rather than following the smooth curved path of the **Genie Effect** (which takes a little bit longer).

6 Grab the Window You Want

Exposé is a new Panther feature that allows you to instantly tile all your open windows across your screen—smoothly shrunk so that they all fit—and select the one you want without having to shuffle through hidden applications and windows piled on top of each other. Exposé is set up by default so that certain function keys invoke it, but it can be configured to use other keys or even simple mouse gestures.

Exposé has three modes:

- **All Windows.** All the currently open windows scoot out from underneath each other and tile across the screen so that you can visually pick the application or document you want.

- **Application Windows.** All the open windows in your current application, such as all open images in Photoshop, are tiled; windows belonging to other applications fade into the background.

- **Desktop.** All the windows slide off the screen so that you can see your Desktop and the files on it.

Suppose that you want to embed a picture file in a document you're writing in TextEdit. The picture you want is on the Desktop, but there are so many windows open that you can't see it. Exposé allows you to brush all the open windows out of the way instantly, grab the file, bring all the windows back, and drop the file into TextEdit—all without having to minimize or hide any applications or disrupt your working window layout.

1 Invoke Exposé

Press the **F9** (**All Windows**) key. This key is set up to tile all the open windows in the system, no matter which applications they belong to.

Press the **F10** (**Application Windows**) key to tile only the windows that belong to the current application.

Press **F11** to move all the windows offscreen and show the Desktop (and all its icons, such as that picture file you want for TextEdit) free of window clutter.

Before You Begin

✔ **2** Find and Launch an Application

✔ **5** Minimize and Restore a Window

See Also

→ **131** Select a Screensaver

TIP

In most Mac OS X applications, you can cycle between all the application's open windows by repeatedly pressing ⌘` (backquote). Cycle through your running applications by pressing ⌘+**Tab**.

TIP

If you've accidentally invoked Exposé when you didn't want to, or you want to cancel it, press **Escape**—or press the function key you pressed to invoke Exposé (**F9**, **F10**, or **F11**).

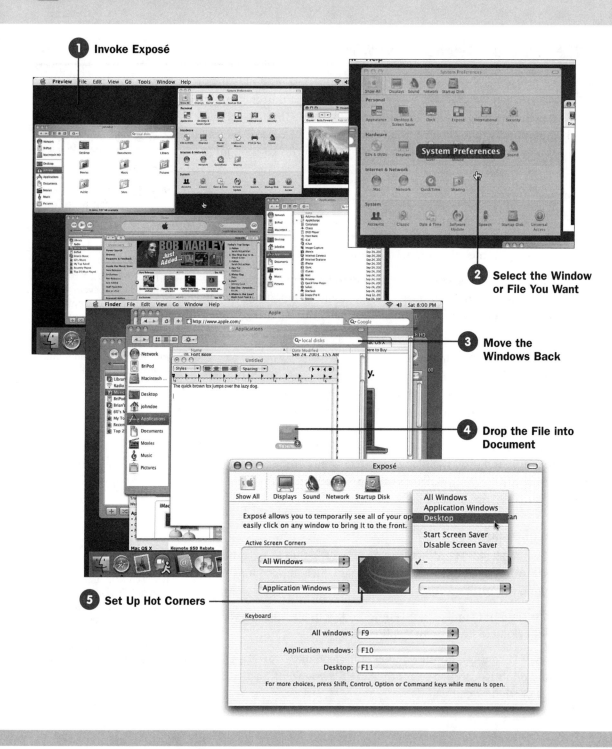

1 Invoke Exposé

2 Select the Window or File You Want

3 Move the Windows Back

4 Drop the File into Document

5 Set Up Hot Corners

2 Select the Window or File You Want

Hover the mouse over each tiled window to dim the window with the window title superimposed over it. Use the **All Windows** or **Application Windows** mode to help you choose which window you want; then click the desired window.

For the picture file/TextEdit example, find the picture file on the Desktop that you want to embed in the TextEdit document. Click and hold the picture file icon, as though you're going to drag it.

3 Move the Windows Back

Without releasing the mouse button, press **F11** again to recall all the offscreen windows back into place (the **Desktop** mode). Your mouse pointer should still be dragging the picture file's icon.

Exposé's tiled windows are "spring-loaded," in much the same way that folders in the Finder behave. If you're dragging a file icon when you invoke Exposé, you can hold the mouse on top of a tiled window until the window flashes and springs to the front. Use this method, for example, to drag a document from a Finder window into Mail or TextEdit.

4 Drop the File into Document

Drag the graphic file icon to wherever in the TextEdit document you want to embed the file, and release the mouse button (**Desktop** mode).

5 Set Up Hot Corners

If you don't like using the **F9**, **F10**, and **F11** keys to access the Exposé tiling modes, select **System Preferences** from the **Apple** menu, then open the Exposé pane. Here, you can choose different trigger keys for the various tiling modes.

Furthermore, you can configure the four corners of the screen to trigger Exposé using "mouse gestures." In other words, you might configure the upper-left corner of your screen so that if you move the mouse into that corner, all the windows will tile; you can specify that if you move the mouse into the lower-right corner of the screen, all the windows will move offscreen.

TIP

Briefly tap one of the function keys (**F9**, **F10**, or **F11**) to tile the windows and leave them tiled until you select the window you want; press and hold a function key to tile the windows only for as long as you hold down the key so that they snap back to position as soon as you release the key.

Use the menus in the **Keyboard** section to choose different function keys or key combinations to invoke the three Exposé modes, if you find them easier than the default settings. For instance, if you want to invoke **Desktop** mode using **Control+Shift+F3**, simply hold down **Control** and **Shift** while opening the menu for **Desktop** mode.

Similarly, if you have a multibutton mouse connected to your Mac, you can configure special mouse clicks to invoke Exposé with almost no physical effort. For example, hold down **Option** while choosing the **Middle Mouse Button** option from the **All Windows** menu in the **Mouse** section to make **Option**+clicking the middle mouse button invoke Exposé's **All Windows** mode. If you don't have a multibutton mouse connected, the **Mouse** section does not appear.

7 Assign an Opener Application to a File

Before You Begin

✔ **1** Install an Application from Disc or Download

✔ **2** Find and Launch an Application

KEY TERM

Opener application—The application you set a document to open with. When you double-click the document, this is the application that will launch to open the document.

Navigating to the **Applications** folder and picking an icon from the Dock aren't the only ways to launch applications. Perhaps even more useful is the fact that you can automatically launch an application simply by double-clicking a document created by that application.

Mac OS X allows you to assign a certain *opener application* to any individual document, or to all documents of a given type. This is the application that will launch when you double-click the document, opening the file so that you can work with it.

1 Find the Document You Want

Open the Finder and navigate to a document to which you want to assign an opener application. For instance, if you want to open a JPEG image file in Adobe Photoshop, first use the Finder to locate the JPEG file in question. Select the JPEG file by clicking it.

2 Get Info

Select **Get Info** from the **File** menu or from the Finder's **Action** menu. Alternatively, press ⌘I, or **Control**+click or right-click the file and select **Get Info** from the contextual menu that appears.

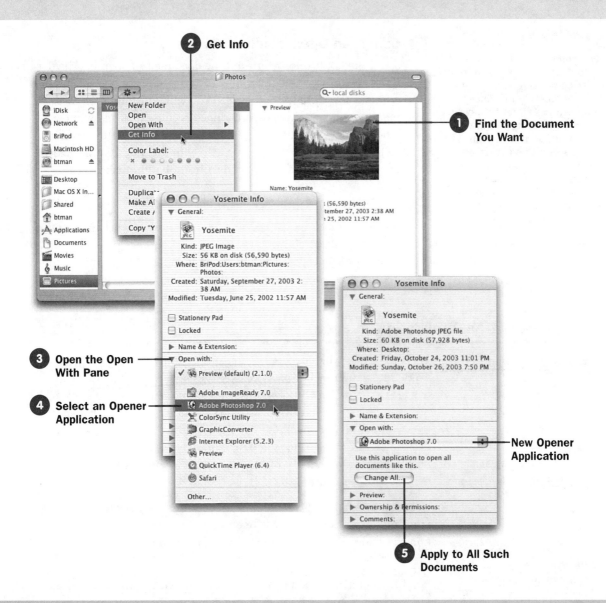

2 Get Info

1 Find the Document
You Want

3 Open the Open
With Pane

4 Select an Opener
Application

New Opener
Application

5 Apply to All Such
Documents

3 **Open the Open With Pane**

In the **Info** panel, click the gray triangle next to the **Open with**
heading. All the applications capable of opening documents of the
same type as the selected document (in this case, a JPEG image)
are listed in the drop-down menu.

TIP

If you want, you can select the opener application for a given document on a one-time basis. In the Finder, **Control**+click (or right-click) the document; from the contextual menu that pops up, select **Open With**. All the installed applications capable of opening the selected document appear in the resulting list. Select the application you want to open the selected file in, and the application will launch.

4 Select an Opener Application

Select the application you want the document to open in. The document is immediately associated with the application you choose, and you can close the **Info** panel. You will know that the document's application has been changed because its icon will now reflect the new application. In the example shown, the **Yosemite** picture file was originally associated with the Mac OS X **Preview** application; now it is associated with **Adobe Photoshop**.

5 Apply to All Such Documents

If you want to open *all* JPEG images in Photoshop, click the **Change All** button. Be careful with this option—if you have previously set up a lot of different JPEG images to open in different applications, that information will be overridden and lost when you click **Change All**.

---

8 Revert an Application to Factory Settings

Before You Begin

✔ **1** Install an Application from Disc or Download

See Also

→ **175** Restore the System to Factory Settings

→ **176** Move Your Data to a New Mac

KEY TERM

Crash—When an application quits unexpectedly (and typically puts up a dialog box explaining that it has done so), it is the result of something in the application happening in a way the programmer didn't intend, and from which the application cannot recover.

There are times when an application simply stops working properly—every time you launch it or try to execute some action, the application will *crash*, freeze, or otherwise misbehave. An operation that worked perfectly fine when you first installed the application might suddenly stop working for good, with no apparent reason. This might be the result of the computer not being shut down properly (as the result of a power outage or a laptop battery running down), or of physical corruption on the hard disk's surface.

It's possible for the entire system to crash; if this happens (a rare occurrence in Mac OS X), the mouse freezes and the screen becomes dimmed and overlaid with an instructional message saying that you must restart the computer using the power on/off button.

Because applications don't "decay" over time, and neither do they malfunction out of spite (although the evidence for this belief might seem overwhelming), there is often a simple explanation for such a malfunction: the application's configuration has become corrupted.

If you have a misbehaving application, the following procedure might help. Because every application is different, this procedure might not work; but the architecture of Mac OS X is such that if you follow this procedure, the application will effectively be returned to its pristine, just-installed state, and should work the same as it did when you first installed it.

---

1 Quit the Application

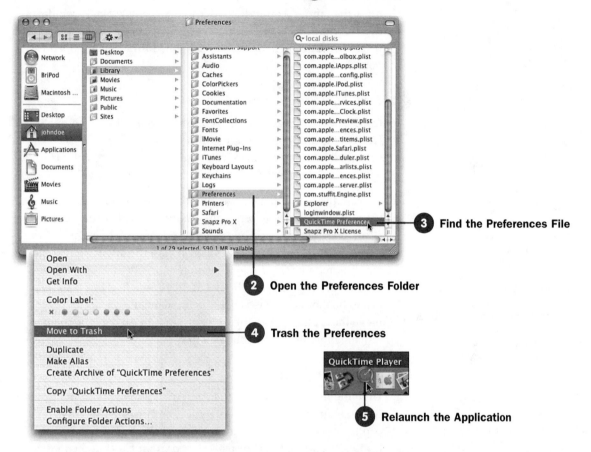

3 Find the Preferences File

2 Open the Preferences Folder

4 Trash the Preferences

QuickTime Player

5 Relaunch the Application

1 Quit the Application

Make sure that the application is not running, if it is capable of running at all. If the crash is related to a certain command you use, but the application otherwise runs properly, you must quit the application if it's running before you can restore it. Choose **File**, **Quit** or press ⌘Q. An application typically writes out its configuration to the **Preferences** folder at the time you quit; so you should quit the application before messing with the Preferences.

TIP

The process of returning an application to its factory settings is typically known in Mac circles as "trashing the Preferences."

2 Open the Preferences Folder

Click the **Finder** icon in the Dock to open a new Finder window; then navigate to your **Library** folder inside your **Home** folder. Inside the **Library** folder is a folder called **Preferences**; open this folder.

3 Find the Preferences File

Inside the **Preferences** folder is a list of documents, each one associated with an application installed on your computer. Every application keeps its preferences in one of these files and writes changes to it as you change the settings of the application.

Some applications' preferences are in the form of an XML "plist" file, with a filename in the form **com.<*company*>.<*application*>.plist**. Other preference files are named more clearly, such as **QuickTime Preferences**. Locate the file associated with the application you're trying to repair. (There might be more than one such file; there might even be a folder with several files inside it. If this is the case, just to be thorough, select all of them. Remember, you can always move these files back to their proper location, so don't be shy about moving more files than you need to.)

 TIP

If you're not sure which Preference file is the one you want, try viewing the **Preferences** folder in List view and sorting the list on the **Last Modified** column. The most recently modified file probably corresponds to the application you most recently quit or that most recently crashed.

4 Trash the Preferences

Drag the file (or files) from the **Preferences** folder onto the Desktop (if you want to experiment safely) or directly into the **Trash**. You can also select **File, Move to Trash** or open the contextual menu for the Preference file (**Control**+click or right-click) and choose **Move to Trash**.

5 Relaunch the Application

Start the application again, and try the operation that was previously misbehaving. If it works, great! You can move the old, faulty preference file from the Desktop into the **Trash** and discard it if you want.

If the application is still misbehaving, you can move the preference files back into your **Preferences** folder (after quitting the application) to restore your old settings.

 NOTE

Because you have reset your Preferences for this application, you will now need to examine the application's settings and adjust them to your liking again.

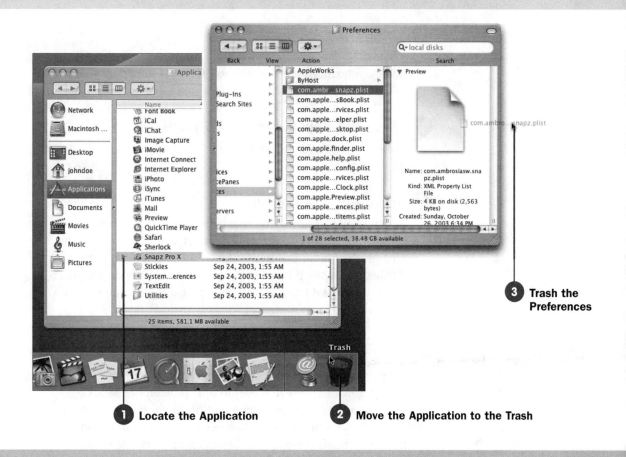

3 Trash the Preferences

1 Locate the Application

2 Move the Application to the Trash

9 **Uninstall an Application**

Removing an application from your computer is one of the easiest things you can do, and one of the nicest advantages of the Mac over Windows. Because Windows operates based on the Registry (a complex database of pieces of data installed by applications), you usually have to run uninstaller programs to remove an application from a Windows machine (even then, it's rarely a clean operation). A Mac OS X application, however, is just a single item you can simply throw away.

Before You Begin

✔ **1** Install an Application from Disc or Download

✔ **8** Revert an Application to Factory Settings

See Also

→ **175** Restore the System to Factory Settings

① Locate the Application

Open a Finder window and navigate to the **Applications** folder. Most applications are found in this folder; if the application you want to remove is in a different location, navigate there instead.

② Move the Application to the Trash

Drag the application icon from the Finder window into the **Trash** in the Dock.

③ Trash the Preferences

If you want to be really thorough, go into your **Preferences** folder (inside the **Library** folder, under your **Home** folder), locate the Preferences file for the application you just deleted, and throw it away too. This step is generally unnecessary, because the preference file won't do any harm if the application it relates to is no longer present on the system.

10 Run a "Classic" Application

Before You Begin

✔ Install an Application from Disc or Download

Most Mac applications are designed to run "natively" in Mac OS X, meaning that they are programmed specifically for the architecture of the Mac OS X operating system. However, some older applications are still in use which were designed to be run on Mac OS 9 or earlier versions, and are therefore very different from Mac OS X applications in a number of key ways.

You can run these so-called "Classic" applications only within an environment called **Classic** (which is, in effect, a copy of Mac OS 9 running inside Mac OS X). If you launch a Classic application, the Classic environment launches automatically, and from then on you can use the application just as you would any other; but you can also launch the Classic environment separately. For example, you can save time by launching the Classic environment at the beginning of your session so that Classic applications can later be launched quickly.

① Open Classic Preferences

Open the **System Preferences** (select it from the **Apple** menu) and open the **Classic** pane.

1 Open Classic Preferences

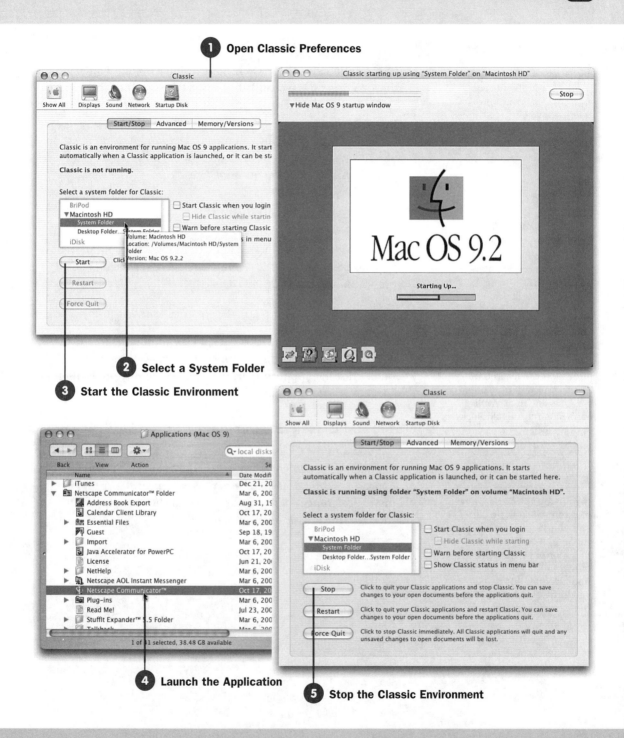

2 Select a System Folder

3 Start the Classic Environment

4 Launch the Application

5 Stop the Classic Environment

NOTE

If you receive a notification that Mac OS X must update some files in the Classic environment before proceeding, allow the OS to do so; this is expected behavior for new installations.

TIP

Applications for Mac OS 9 can be found in the global **Applications (Mac OS 9)** folder. You can navigate to this folder using the standard Mac OS X Finder. A Classic application can often be identified by the way its icon looks. Mac OS 9 supported icons only up to 32×32 pixels in size (Mac OS X icons can be 128×128 pixels and can incorporate 24-bit color with transparency). Thus, a Classic application's icon might look blocky or drab.

NOTE

If you stop the Classic environment while there are still Classic applications running, the applications are shut down. Be sure to quit your Classic applications cleanly, just as you would before shutting down the computer altogether!

② Select a System Folder

Most installations of Mac OS X have a single **System Folder** (the folder containing the complete Mac OS 9 system that comprises the Classic environment). If you have multiple copies of the operating system installed, however, you must select which one to use for Classic. Select a disk or volume (and expand it using the triangular arrow), and select the **System Folder** corresponding to the installation of Mac OS 9 you want to use.

③ Start the Classic Environment

Click the **Start** button to launch the Classic environment. Classic starts up in a window you can expand to show the boot procedure of a Mac OS 9 computer (the one that's effectively being booted from within your Mac OS X system).

④ Launch the Application

Open the Mac OS X Finder by clicking the familiar Finder icon in the Dock and navigate to the application you want to run. Double-click the application icon as you would any application in Mac OS X to start the Classic application.

⑤ Stop the Classic Environment

After you quit the Classic application, it's a good idea to shut down the Classic environment as well, because the environment takes up resources you might need for other tasks. Repeat step 1 to open the **Classic Preferences** dialog box again and click the **Stop** button to shut down the Classic environment.

3

Keeping Things Organized

IN THIS CHAPTER:

→ **14** Make an Alias (Shortcut)

NOTE

Mac OS X gives you the ability to manage these documents and folders, to move them around, change their names, create new ones, and get rid of the ones you don't need anymore. In the context of modern computing hardware, this means that Mac OS X must enable you to manipulate disks—hard disks, CD-ROMs, DVDs, and other such devices that store your documents. In this chapter, you will see how to use the tools that Mac OS X gives you to accomplish these tasks.

Mac OS X, like all operating systems, is designed to help you organize data. This data is represented using the industry-standard "desktop" metaphor, originally pioneered by the first Macintosh and its precursors. In the "desktop" metaphor, any meaningful grouping of data under a single name—a picture, an audio recording, a shopping list—is represented by a *document* (also known as a *file*, a term which will be used interchangeably with *document* in this book). Documents can be sorted into *folders*, which are simply containers for documents. Folders can contain other folders as well as documents, and thus you can organize all your information into a hierarchy that resembles a large, ungainly filing cabinet.

As your computing needs grow, so does the need for Mac OS X to adapt to them. Over time, you will probably feel the need to add memory, new hard disks, and even second displays to keep up with the pace of the technology you interact with at home and at work. This chapter discusses how to add a new hard disk to your system and configure it to hold your expanding data; it also covers how to add a second display and configure it to your liking. Finally, because keeping your Mac's internal clock accurate is so crucial to the internal system functions, as well as to applications such as iCal that keep track of your schedule for you, this chapter discusses how to set the time and date, and how to set up your computer to configure them automatically.

11 Find an Item

See Also

They don't call it the Finder for nothing. In addition to its normal navigational tools, the Finder contains streamlined searching functionality that lets you zero in directly on a document or folder that interests you. Finder windows have their shortcut **Search** bar, but there's a more sophisticated version of it available as well.

The Finder's searching tool lets you define the scope in which to search (which disks, network resources, and folders you want to search in), as well as any number of criteria (such as file name, kind, last-modified date, and so on). The search results appear in a separate window which you can then use to work with the items you find.

 Open the Find Dialog Box

Choose **File**, **Find** or press ⌘F while in the Finder. The **Find** dialog box appears.

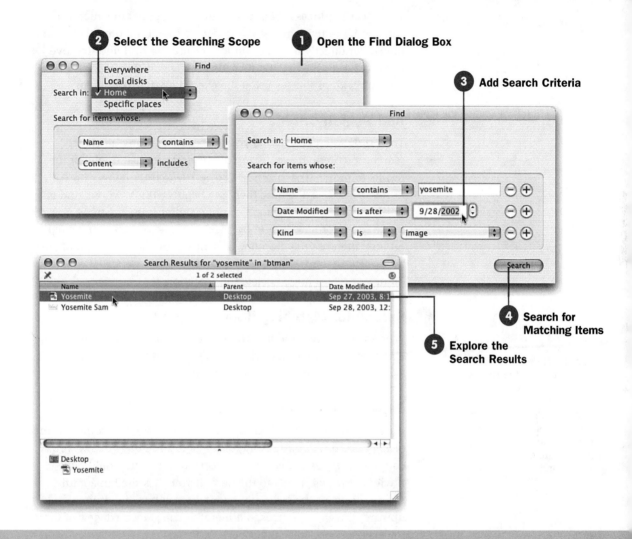

2 Select the Searching Scope

1 Open the Find Dialog Box

3 Add Search Criteria

4 Search for Matching Items

5 Explore the Search Results

2 Select the Searching Scope

Use the **Search in** drop-down menu to define where you want the Finder to look for your items. The **Everywhere** option uses all available disks and network resources; **Local disks** uses only the disks physically attached to (or inside) your computer; **Home** uses only your **Home** folder.

The **Specific places** option brings up a new panel in which you can specify individual disks or folders to search in; drag them from the Finder directly into the window, or use the **Add** and **Remove** buttons to edit the list of data sources. You can then include or omit individual sources using the check boxes next to them.

❸ Add Search Criteria

The **Find** dialog box allows you to specify as many different searching criteria as you want; *all* the criteria must apply for the results to match. For instance, you can search for items whose filename contains **art**, whose filename begins with **A**, whose kind is **audio**, and whose last-modified date is after last Christmas. You make room for new criteria by clicking the + icon after any criterion line; then use the drop-down menus to define what kind of criteria they are and what sort of comparisons to use. Use the – icon on any criterion line to delete that criterion.

❹ Search for Matching Items

TIP

Use the **Refresh** button (the little round button with the circle-arrow) in the upper-right corner of the result window to perform the same search again, in case the disk contents have changed since your first search.

When you're done fine-tuning the search criteria, click **Search**. The Finder will pop up a new window to show the search results, which appear in the listing as they are found.

❺ Explore the Search Results

Click any item in the search results window, and its location on the disk is shown in a path listing at the bottom of the window. You can see the series of folders (in a horizontal layout) you'll have to navigate through to get to the item; if you click the horizontal dividing line just below the horizontal scroll bar and drag it upward, the view changes to a hierarchical, staggered view of the folders.

You can double-click a file anywhere in the search results window to launch it in its opener application; double-click any folder to open it in a Finder window. You can also drag any file or folder from the results window to the Desktop or another Finder window to move it.

12 Create a New Folder

The basic unit of document storage is the folder. A folder can reside in any place on a disk, and folders (and folders within folders within folders) are what make up the hierarchical organization of any Mac OS X system.

Mac OS X provides a number of special-purpose folders inside your **Home** folder for storing certain kinds of documents. You can always create new folders to suit your purposes, and you can keep those new folders anywhere you like. For instance, you might create a folder on your Desktop to hold Word files for a project you're working on, and then move that folder into your **Documents** folder when you're done with it, so that you can easily find it later. The first step in all this organizational wizardry is creating that new folder.

1 Open a Finder Window

Click the **Finder** icon at the far left end of the Dock. Alternatively, click anywhere on the Desktop to switch to the Finder, and then press ⌘N to open a new Finder window.

2 Navigate to Where You Want the New Folder

Using whichever view modes you find most convenient, move through the folders in your **Home** folder until you're at the position where you want to create the new folder.

3 Create the Folder

Select **File**, **New Folder**. Alternatively, press **Shift+⌘N** or select **New Folder** from the **Action** button menu in the Finder window. A new folder appears in the listing, with the name **untitled folder**.

4 Name the Folder

The new folder's name is selected as soon as it's created, so that you can immediately type a new name for it. You can use any name that doesn't duplicate the name of any other item in the current folder. When you're done typing the name, press **Return** to commit the change.

See Also

→ **13** Rename a Folder or Document

→ **15** Change an Icon

→ **16** Set a Color Label

 TIP

Press ⌘ and click the title bar of the Finder window to see the path to your current location.

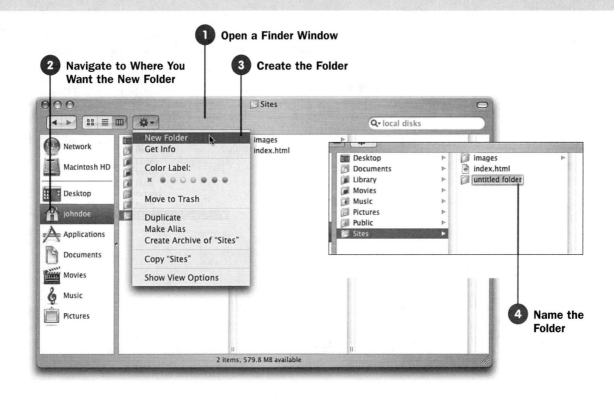

1 Open a Finder Window

2 Navigate to Where You Want the New Folder

3 Create the Folder

4 Name the Folder

13 Rename a Folder or Document

Before You Begin

✔ **12** Create a New Folder

See Also

→ **14** Make an Alias (Shortcut)

→ **16** Set a Color Label

Renaming a folder or document in Mac OS X is a seemingly simple process that hides some surprising complexity. On the face of it, there's really nothing to it: select the item, type the new name, and you're done. However, there are a few hidden complexities to watch out for.

In Mac OS X, filename *extensions* are often (but not always) required to define a document's type—but you don't have to see them. Extensions can be turned off on a per-document basis. If you rename the document in the Finder so that the extension is removed, the extension merely becomes hidden. Similarly, if you add the appropriate extension to a document, it merely becomes "un-hidden."

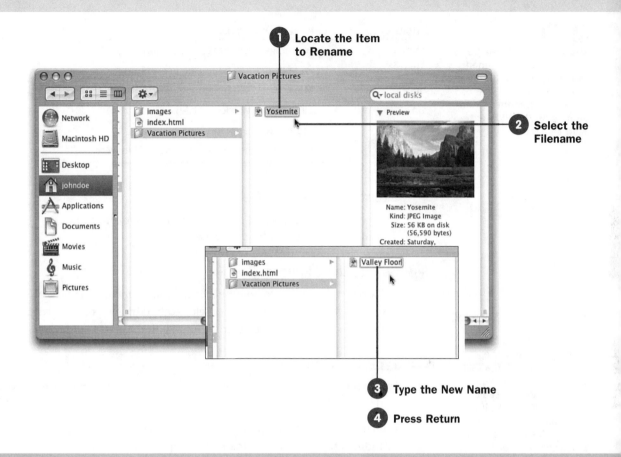

1 Locate the Item to Rename

2 Select the Filename

3 Type the New Name

4 Press Return

By hiding documents' extensions, Mac OS X guarantees that the extension will be there if you transfer the file to a Windows machine, where extensions are required for documents to work properly.

A few common extensions are listed here:

Extension	Kind of Document
.jpg	Picture (Joint Photographic Experts Group)
.gif	Picture (Graphics Interchange Format)
.doc	Microsoft Word document
.rtf	Rich Text document
.txt	Plain Text document
.mov	QuickTime movie

🔍KEY TERM

Extension—The often cryptic final few letters in a filename. Originally popularized by Windows, the extension is a simple way to designate a document as being of a certain type; this way, an application could know what kind of file it is just by looking at the filename.

TIP

Use the Get Info palette to see whether a document has a hidden extension or not. You can also hide or show a document's extension using the **Hide extension** check box.

Extension	Kind of Document
.html	Web page (Hypertext Markup Language)
.pdf	Page layout (Portable Document Format)
.dmg	Mountable Disk Image file
.zip	ZIP archive (Windows-style)
.sit	StuffIt archive (Mac-style)
.cwk	AppleWorks document (originally ClarisWorks)

① Locate the Item to Rename

Open a Finder window and navigate to the folder containing the document or folder you want to rename.

② Select the Filename

For the item you want to rename, click the filename underneath or beside the icon. The item becomes selected (a darkened box appears around it) and the filename turns into an editable text field.

TIP

In Mac OS X, if you click a text field (such as the name of a file in the Finder) and drag the mouse down, all the text to the right of where you clicked becomes selected. Similarly, if you click and drag up, everything to the left of where you clicked becomes selected.

③ Type the New Name

Type whatever name you like into the name field. Filenames can be any length up to 255 characters.

You can use almost any letters, numbers, or symbols in filenames, including characters in Japanese, Russian, and many other languages. However, there are a couple of exceptions to this freedom. Colons (:) are not allowed in filenames because the internal architecture of Mac OS X uses the colon to signify the separation between folders in the path to an item. Similarly, you can't use a period (.) as the first letter of a filename because that character has special meaning for Mac OS X.

Some applications might prevent you from creating files with a slash (/) in the name, or names longer than 31 characters. These are limitations in the applications (caused by the merging of Unix and of the old Mac OS), not in Mac OS X.

TIP

If you've accidentally started renaming an item that you don't actually want to rename, simply press **Escape** (**Esc**) to cancel the operation.

④ Press Return

Press **Return** to commit the change. Alternatively, click anywhere on the Desktop or the folder window to deselect the item and make the name change stick.

14 Make an Alias (Shortcut)

Sometimes you will have need to keep a document (or folder or application) in more than once place at once. You might have a Word document in your **Documents** folder or a song in your **Music** folder, but you might also want to have it on your Desktop for easy access. The Dock provides some of this convenience, but sometimes what you really want is to create an *alias*—a shortcut to a document, folder, or application. This is helpful in situations where an application or another user expects to be able to find a document in a certain folder, but you want to have it in a more convenient place for yourself—but you don't want to make a duplicate that might be changed independently of the original. An alias lets you access one item from two, three, or as many locations in the system as you want, while leaving the original item unmoved.

An alias looks just like the original item, but has no contents of its own; it's just a pointer to the original file. If you double-click the alias, the original item opens. You only ever have to make changes in one place (the original file), rather than having to keep two copies of the document in sync. Unlike shortcuts in Windows, aliases in Mac OS X continue to work even if you move the original item from one place to another.

❶ Select Item to Alias

Open a Finder window and navigate to the folder that contains the item to which you want to create an alias. Click the item so that it becomes selected, with the darkened box around it.

❷ Create the Alias

Select **Make Alias** from the **File** menu. Alternatively, press ⌘L, or select **Make Alias** from the **Action** button menu in the Finder window. A new item appears next to the selected one, with the same name as the original and **alias** appended to the end of the name.

❸ Name the Alias

The new alias becomes the selected item, and the name becomes an editable text field. You can type whatever name you like for the new alias, as long as it doesn't have the same name as any other item in the folder it's in. Press **Return** to commit the name change.

Before You Begin

✔ **11** Find an Item

✔ **13** Rename a Folder or Document

See Also

→ **15** Change an Icon

KEY TERM

Alias—A pseudo-file that, when opened, instead opens a real file, application, or folder elsewhere in the system. An alias can even point to files on external disks or remote servers, and it will mount the disk or server to access the original item.

NOTE

To delete an alias, simply throw it away. Trashing the alias will not damage the original item!

NOTE

The ⌘L key combination seems to have no relation to the term "alias"; however, it is likely named for the Unix "link" concept, which is very similar to the aliases of the Mac OS. Mac OS X introduced the idea of minimizing windows, which was given the old ⌘M key combination that used to be used for **Make Alias**.

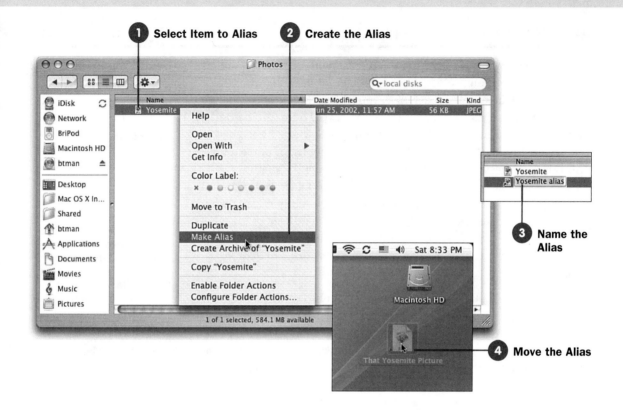

1 Select Item to Alias   **2** Create the Alias

3 Name the Alias

4 Move the Alias

4 Move the Alias

Open another Finder window, navigate to where you want to move the alias, and drag the alias from its original location to the new window. If you want the alias to reside on the Desktop, just drag the newly renamed alias from the original Finder window to the Desktop.

15 Change an Icon

Before You Begin

✔ **12** Create a New Folder
✔ **13** Rename a Folder or Document

See Also

→ **16** Set a Color Label

One of the convenient and unique features of the Mac OS is that you can apply your own custom icons to individual documents, folders, and volumes (disks). You can copy an icon from one item to another, create your own icons from picture files, or remove custom icons from items to return them to their generic appearance.

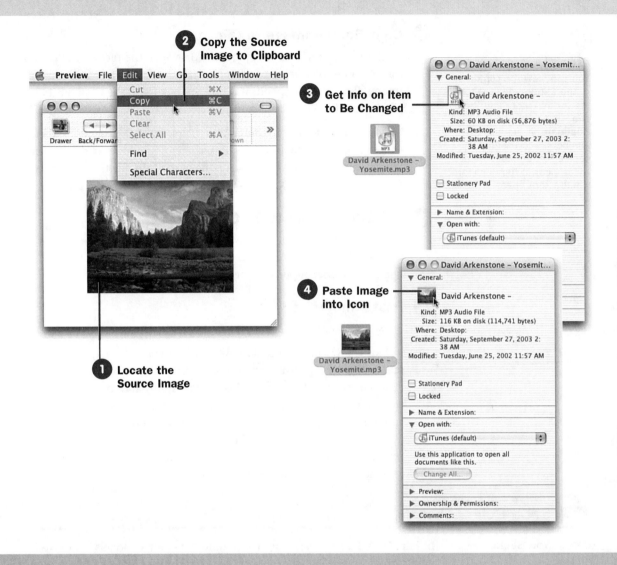

② Copy the Source Image to Clipboard

③ Get Info on Item to Be Changed

④ Paste Image into Icon

① Locate the Source Image

① Locate the Source Image

An icon can come from either of two places: a picture file copied to the Clipboard, or an existing icon copied from another document or folder. Decide where the icon is going to come from; open a Finder window and navigate to where that source item is.

② Copy Source Image to Clipboard

To create an icon from a picture file, first open the picture in Preview (or any other picture-viewing application that allows you to copy image data to the Clipboard). Copy the picture to the Clipboard by choosing **Edit**, **Copy** or pressing ⌘C.

To copy an existing icon from another item, select that item and then choose **File**, **Get Info** (or press ⌘I). Use the mouse to select the icon in the top-left corner of the **General** pane of the **Info** palette, and choose **Edit**, **Copy** or press ⌘C to copy the icon to the Clipboard.

③ Get Info on Item to Be Changed

Select the document or folder whose icon you want to change. Choose **File**, **Get Info** or press ⌘I. Click the icon in the top-left corner of the **General** pane of the **Info** palette.

④ Paste Image into Icon

Press ⌘V to paste the Clipboard's contents onto the item as its new icon.

In Mac OS X, icons can contain 32-bit picture data—red, green, blue, and alpha (transparency) channels. If a part of the icon image is transparent (the alpha channel is at maximum), that part of the icon will not be clickable—clicking that region does not select the icon. If you apply a custom icon that's got a weird shape and not much non-transparent image data, it will be difficult to click the icon in the Finder. For icons in the Dock, the whole square region of an icon responds to a click, whether it's transparent or not.

⑯ Set a Color Label

Before You Begin

✔ ⑬ Rename a Folder or Document

✔ ⑮ Change an Icon

See Also

→ ⑪ Find an Item

In Mac OS X Panther, you can assign different colored "labels" to documents and folders. The meanings of these labels are up to you to define—a blue label might mean "Incomplete projects" or "Items I haven't looked at yet," and red labels might signify "Documents from the Thompson account." Labels appear in the highlight color of an item's name, in an oval around the text. You can sort items in the Finder based on the label color, allowing you to group items conceptually without having to fiddle with their names or put them into folders.

① Select the Item

In a Finder window, select the item you want to label.

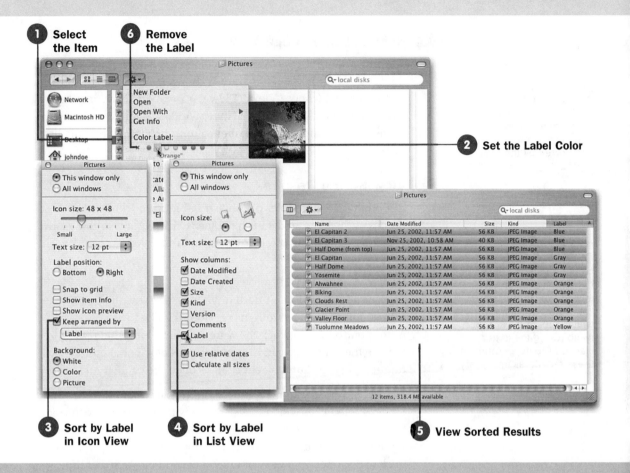

① Select the Item

⑥ Remove the Label

② Set the Label Color

③ Sort by Label in Icon View

④ Sort by Label in List View

⑤ View Sorted Results

② Set the Label Color

From the **File** menu or the **Action** button menu, choose the **Color Label** you want to use. Seven colors are available to choose from; click the appropriate colored dot. You can also set the label by right-clicking (or **Control**+clicking) the item and selecting the label color from the contextual menu.

③ Sort by Label in Icon View

In the Finder's Icon view, you can sort items by label color. After you have set different colored labels for several items within a folder, select **View**, **View Options**. In the **View Options** panel that opens, enable the **Keep arranged by** check box and select **Label** from the drop-down menu to group items by their assigned label colors.

 TIP

You can label multiple items at once. Select as many items as you want, using the **Shift** or ⌘ key in conjunction with mouse clicks, and then set the label color.

TIP

In Icon view, choose **View**, **Arrange** and then choose **by Label** to arrange the contents of a folder imme- diately into a well-organized grid sorted by the files' labels.

 TIP

You can also make use of color labels when finding files. In the **Find** dialog box, create a criterion based on the **Label**; you can then specify which color labels you want to look for or which ones you want to avoid (using the **is not** clause). Create as many of these criteria as necessary.

④ Sort by Label in List View

You can also sort items by label colors in the Finder's List view. First make sure that the **Label** column is shown by opening the **View Options** panel (choose **View**, **View Options**) and enabling the **Label** check box. Then, in the Finder window, scroll to the far right of the window and click the **Label** column heading to sort the list based on the assigned colors.

⑤ View Sorted Results

Although these examples are shown in black-and-white, the names of the label colors in the Finder's List view show how easily you can sort items in a folder based on label colors.

⑥ Remove the Label

To clear a label you don't need anymore, select the item with the colored label you want to remove. From the **File** menu or the **Action** button menu, click the **X** under the **Color Label** option to remove the color. You can also access the **Color Label** options by right-clicking (or **Control**+clicking) to open the contextual menu.

You can assign special meanings to the various color labels. In the **Finder Preferences** window, click the **Labels** tab. Next to each color, type a new name for each label. For instance, you might make red signify "overdue" and yellow signify "in-progress" to help you keep track of documents you're working on over a long period of time.

⑰ Move, Copy, or Delete a Document or Folder

Before You Begin

✔ **11** Find an Item

✔ **13** Rename a Folder or Document

✔ **16** Set a Color Label

Moving a document or folder from one place to another is one of those fundamental tasks that make up the core of using an operating system such as Mac OS X. If you ever decide to organize your files or clean up your system, you've got a lot of folder manipulation and document-moving ahead of you.

When you **duplicate** a document or folder, you create an identical copy of it in the same folder, with all the same properties except for the word **copy** added to its name. You can then use this duplicate to make changes, create a backup, or any number of other uses. Unlike an alias (which is just a link back to the original file), a duplicate is actually a second file that exists separately from the original and shares nothing with the original except for its name.

Because **deleting** a document or folder is by nature a destructive action, Mac OS X makes it a two-step process to protect your files. First you move the item into the Trash; later, you empty the Trash to delete the items in it permanently. You might think this an unnecessary precaution, but sooner or later you will have an experience where you wish you hadn't deleted something. If you haven't yet emptied the Trash, you can easily retrieve the deleted item. The convenience of retrieving items from the Trash is why Microsoft Windows eventually added a Recycle Bin, years after the Mac had been mocked for its Trash.

1 Locate the Item to Move, Copy, or Delete

In a Finder window, navigate to the document or folder that you want to move, copy, or delete. If you're working with an item on the Desktop, you don't have to open this first Finder window.

2 Navigate to the Destination Folder

If you're moving an item, open a second Finder window and use it to navigate to the folder to which you want to move the document or folder. If you're moving an item to the Desktop, you don't have to open a second Finder window.

3 Drag the Item to Move or Delete

To **move** the item, click and drag the document or folder from the first Finder window into the second one.

To **delete** the item, drag the item to the **Trash** can at the right end of the Dock. Alternatively, choose **File**, **Move to Trash**, right-click or **Control**+click the item and select **Move to Trash** from the contextual menu), or press ⌘+**Delete**. The items are now in the Trash, and can be retrieved by clicking the **Trash** icon to open a window that lists all the items in the Trash, and then dragging the items back out again.

4 Duplicate the Item

Choose **File**, **Duplicate** to create a copy of the selected item. Alternatively, select **Duplicate** from the Finder's **Action** menu, press ⌘D, or right-click or **Control**+click the item and choose **Duplicate** from the contextual menu that opens.

NOTE

If you drag an item from one volume or disk to another (such as from a CD-ROM to the hard disk), the item is duplicated rather than moved. The green + icon next to the mouse pointer indicates that the operation will be a duplication. To duplicate rather than move an item directly into another location, hold the **Option** key as you drag a document or folder from one Finder window to another.

TIPS

You can select multiple items at once by dragging a selection box or by using modifier keys—hold down **Shift** to select a contiguous block of files or ⌘ to select multiple individual files. To move or delete these multiple items, click any of the selected items and drag.

You don't necessarily have to open a second, "destination" Finder window. If you have spring-loaded folders enabled, you can drag the item onto any folder, hold it there, and the folder will spring open into a new Finder window. Keep repeating this process—without letting go of the mouse button—until you're at the destination. Then release the button to move the item.

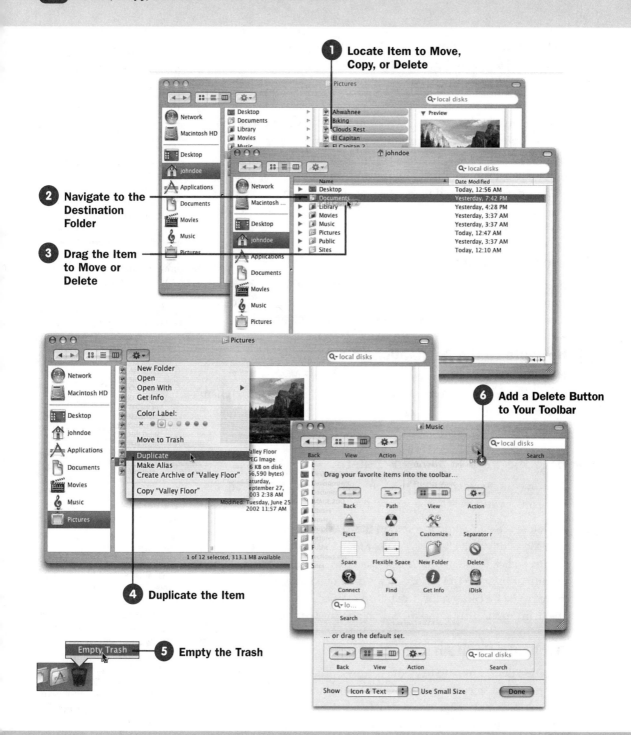

1 Locate Item to Move, Copy, or Delete

2 Navigate to the Destination Folder

3 Drag the Item to Move or Delete

4 Duplicate the Item

5 Empty the Trash

6 Add a Delete Button to Your Toolbar

A new item is created next to the original one; the new item has the same name as the original with the word **copy** appended to it before the extension (if any). This default naming convention allows the duplicate to appear next to the original when you sort by name.

To give the new item a more descriptive name, click the item's name and type a new one. Press **Return** when you're done.

⑤ Empty the Trash

Periodically, you should empty the Trash to clear out the list of items you have thrown away and free up disk space (which is not recovered if you simply throw items away). Emptying the Trash is a permanent, one-way operation; afterwards, items that were in the Trash can't be recovered. Choose **Empty Trash** from the **Finder** menu; alternatively, press **Shift+⌘+Delete**. A confirmation message appears (which you can turn off in the **Finder Preferences** window). After you confirm the operation, the Trash is emptied.

⑥ Add a Delete Button to Your Toolbar

If you want, you can put a button on the Finder toolbar that lets you immediately move all selected items to the Trash with a single click. With a Finder window open, choose **View**, **Customize Toolbar** and drag the **Delete** button from the **Customize Toolbar** dialog box into the toolbar where you want it to appear. Then click **Done** to close the dialog box.

NOTE

If you duplicate a folder, all of the folder's contents are duplicated as well.

NOTE

If you simply empty the Trash, there's a possibility that the deleted items can be recovered by the right kind of special software. If you've thrown away sensitive data that you want to make sure can never be retrieved, Mac OS X provides a **Secure Empty Trash** option. From the **Finder** menu, select **Secure Empty Trash**, and select a level of security (**1**, **7**, or **35 Pass**). Each "pass" is an attempt by the operating system to scramble the disk's data where the deleted items were; the more passes you select, the longer the process takes, but the more certainly the items will not be recoverable.

18 Burn a CD/DVD

Most modern Macs come with drives that can *burn* CD-ROMs, and many can also burn DVDs. If you have such a drive, you can take advantage of the modern physical method for transferring documents from one computer to another: writable optical discs.

Floppy disks used to be the medium of choice for storing or transferring data. With the advent of the iMac, however, floppy drives vanished from the Mac in favor of transferring files over the Internet. Although this provided much of the same functionality as floppies did (without the 1.44-megabyte size limitation), many people still had a need for a way to store large documents, as well as to create better media for installing software. Writable CD and DVD drives, with their versatility and inexpensive media, have stepped into that niche in the computing world.

Before You Begin

✔ **17** Move, Copy, or Delete a Document or Folder

See Also

→ **19** Add a Newly Installed Hard Disk to the System

→ **101** Burn a Custom Audio CD

KEY TERM

Burn—To write documents to an optical disc (a *CD-R*, *CD-RW*, or *DVD-R*).

Mac OS X makes the process of burning a CD or DVD straightforward. You insert a blank disc, move documents to that disc in the Finder, and then drag the disc's icon to the Trash to burn the documents onto it.

❶ Insert a Blank CD or DVD

Most Macs have an optical drive with a tray you must eject before you can insert a disc. Press the **Eject** key on the keyboard, place the blank disc in the tray, and press **Eject** again to close the drive.

Some Macs, such as the PowerBook G4s and the later colored iMacs, have slot-loading drives. On these Macs, simply insert the disc into the slot and wait until the drive pulls the disc in.

❷ Enter a Volume Name and Click OK

Mac OS X automatically tries to mount the disc. When it finds that the disc is blank, the operating system will present you with a dialog box that asks for a name for the disc. Type any descriptive name you like; after the disc is burned, this is the name that will appear under the disc's icon when it's mounted.

For CD-R discs, you can choose whether the disc is intended for documents or for music. To create a disc for music files, select **Open iTunes** from the **Action** drop-down list. You can then use iTunes to burn a music CD that can be played in any CD player, or an MP3 CD that can be played on modern MP3 CD players. To create a disc for documents, choose **Open Finder** (the default) from the **Action** drop-down list. If you mistakenly choose the wrong application, just eject the disc and insert it again.

❸ Move Items to the Disc

You can now fill the disc with documents. The disc appears on the Desktop, like any other mounted volume, and you can drag items to it as you would any other disk. Organize items in folders the way you want them to appear each time you or anyone else inserts the disc; if you try to put more data on the disc than it can hold, you will get an error message.

In this example, I opened the Finder and created a new folder called **Photos** into which I placed many of my latest vacation photos. You can create subfolders within this main folder if you want.

KEY TERMS

CD-R—Writable compact disc. A CD-R can be burned once, and after that its contents cannot be changed. A CD-R or CD-RW can hold 650 or 700 megabytes of data, depending on the format.

CD-RW—Rewritable compact disc. A CD-RW can be burned multiple times, usually up to a few dozen times.

DVD-R—Writable digital versatile disc. A DVD can hold 4.7 gigabytes of data and generally costs significantly more than a writable CD. Data on a DVD is heavily compressed, making the format much more complex than that of a CD. Some DVD formats, such as DVD+RW and DVD-RW, can be written to more than once.

TIP

If you change your mind about the volume name you gave the disc, you can change the name by renaming the disc—just as you would rename a folder, by clicking its name and typing a new one—anytime until you burn the disc.

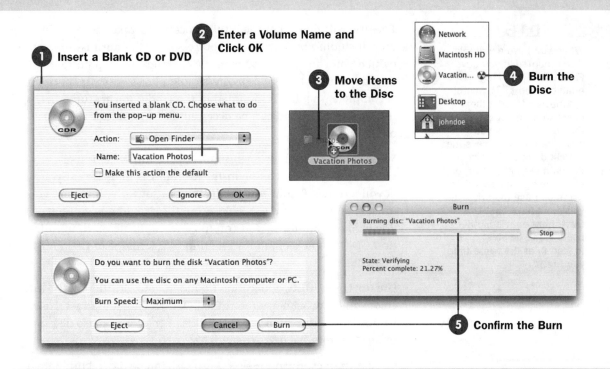

1 **Insert a Blank CD or DVD**

2 **Enter a Volume Name and Click OK**

3 **Move Items to the Disc**

4 **Burn the Disc**

5 **Confirm the Burn**

When the items are arranged as you want them to be, drag the folder from the Finder window and drop it on the disc icon on the Desktop. A green plus sign next to the mouse pointer tells you that you're copying the files to the disc rather than moving them.

4 **Burn the Disc**

When you're happy with the contents of the disc, it's time to burn it. In the Finder, click the **Burn** symbol next to the disc's icon in the sidebar; alternately, drag the disc's icon from the Desktop to the **Trash** can icon (which becomes a **Burn** symbol while you're dragging the disc).

5 **Confirm the Burn**

A dialog box prompts whether you want to eject the disc (discarding all the changes you've made) or burn it. Click the **Burn** button.

NOTE

Make sure that you have enough space on your startup disk to allow the system to create a disk image of all the data you put on the blank disc—up to 700MB for a CD or 4.7GB for a DVD. Mac OS X creates copies of the documents to be burned, in a special temporary location, and will eject the disc if not enough free hard disk space is available.

NOTE

While you have a writable disc mounted, if you have **Fast User Switching** enabled (see **140** Switch to Another User), other users who are logged in at the same time as you won't be able to access the optical drive or the disc in it. You must either burn or eject the disc before other users can use the drive. (If you don't have **Fast User Switching** enabled, other users won't be able to be logged in at the same time you are.)

The disc will now be burned; this process can take several minutes, including the verification process after the burn is complete (which you can skip if you want by clicking the **Stop** button that appears in the **Burn** progress dialog box). After the burn is complete, the disc is mounted in the Finder (or in iTunes, if it's a music CD), and can be accessed like any other CD-ROM or DVD.

Some software, such as open-source operating systems like Linux and FreeBSD, can be installed from CD images that you download free. Before you can install the software, however, you must create an actual CD-ROM using the *disc image* you have downloaded. Similarly, you can make a duplicate of an installation CD (for safekeeping) by creating a disk image of the CD-ROM.

Use the **Disk Utility** application (found in your **Utilities** folder) to create a new disk image. Insert the CD, then choose **Images**, **New**, **Image from** *<disc name>*. **Disk Utility** then creates a *.iso* disk image file from the disc's contents.

Choose **Images**, **Burn** to select a *.iso* disk image file to burn onto a new CD. Be sure to have a blank CD handy!

19 Add a Newly Installed Hard Disk to the System

See Also

→ **20** Partition a Hard Disk

→ **21** Set Up Software RAID

No matter how large your Mac's disk might seem when you first buy it, the computing world has a way of coming up with new ways to use up disk space. Just a few years ago, it was difficult to imagine a 10-gigabyte disk. Now, most people's MP3 collections exceed that size easily. With digital video editing becoming ever more popular, even 60 or 100GB disks are starting to look small.

Tower Macs allow you to install new internal hard drives; even with iMacs and laptops you can hook up new storage devices over USB or FireWire connections. When you buy a new disk, however, you must properly prepare it before it can be used.

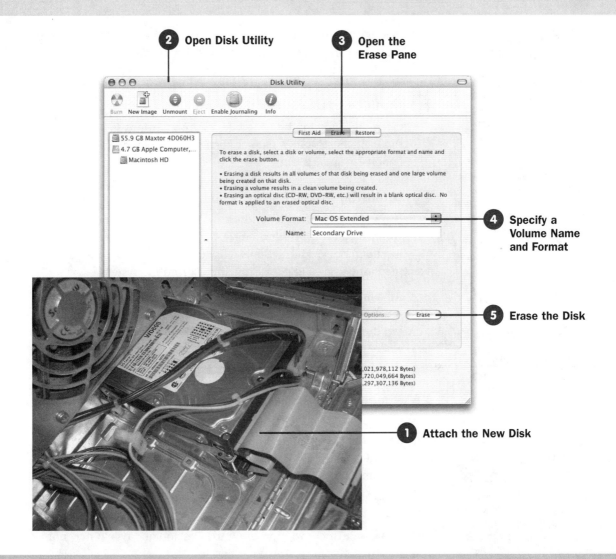

2 Open Disk Utility

3 Open the Erase Pane

4 Specify a Volume Name and Format

5 Erase the Disk

1 Attach the New Disk

1 Attach the New Disk

For an internal hard disk, follow the instructions provided with your Mac for adding a new disk. Generally, you will have to remove your computer's cover (with the power off, of course), remove a metal caddy, mount the drive in the caddy, and replace the cover so that the disk cable and power cords can be attached.

External drives are much easier to connect; they involve little more than plugging them in and turning them on. You can install external drives while the Mac is running.

2 Open Disk Utility

Open the Finder and navigate to the **Applications** folder, then to the **Utilities** subfolder. Launch the **Disk Utility** program by double-clicking its icon.

3 Open the Erase Pane

If you want to make the entire new disk available as one large volume, you will want to "erase" the disk. This process is what most other operating systems refer to as "formatting" the disk—preparing it to hold data within your operating system.

All available disks are shown in the left pane of the **Disk Utility** window. Select the new disk (in this example, it's listed as **55.9 GB Maxtor 4D060H3**), and then click the **Erase** tab. The **Erase** pane is where your disk will be initialized and made available for you to store your additional data.

4 Specify a Volume Name and Format

Select a format for the volume; **Mac OS Extended** is the default and is the best choice for Mac OS X. Don't select any of the other format options unless you intend to use this disk with Windows or Unix machines as well.

Enter a descriptive name for the volume that will be created. You can change this name later if you want; simply click the volume name in a Finder window or on the Desktop and type a new name (as when renaming any other item).

5 Erase the Disk

Click the **Erase** button to erase the disk. This process might take several minutes; after it is done, the new hard disk volume will be mounted in the Finder and ready for use.

20 Partition a Hard Disk

If you've just added a new disk but you don't want it all to be represented as single large volume—but rather to slice it up into several smaller volumes—you can *partition* the disk.

Partitioning provides a number of practical and psychological advantages; you can designate one volume for video editing, another for MP3s, another for random junk, and a fourth for an alternative installation of Mac OS X. Each of these volumes is mounted as a different disk in the Finder and can be navigated separately, with each volume comprising its own unique organizational structure. This arrangement can be much easier to manage than having a single large volume with folders for different uses.

If your disk has multiple volumes, you can put a different custom icon on each one—and let's face it, custom icons are fun. The more, the merrier!

1 Open Disk Utility

Open the Finder and navigate to the **Applications** folder, then to the **Utilities** subfolder. Launch the **Disk Utility** program by double-clicking its icon.

2 Open the Partition Pane

All available disks appear in the listing on the left. Click the disk you want to partition; the **Partition** tab appears. Click this tab. The **Partition** pane appears.

3 Select the Number of Partitions

The displayed disk is most likely represented as a single large, gray pool of storage space. Divide this space in two by clicking the **Split** button; the pool of space is divided in half. Click **Split** again to create a third partition, dividing one of the first two areas in half again.

Alternatively, you can directly select how many partitions you want from the **Volume Scheme** menu above the visual representation of the partitions. You can have as many as sixteen partitions on a single disk.

Before You Begin

✔ **19** Add a Newly Installed Hard Disk to the System

✔ **173** Back Up Your Information

See Also

→ **21** Set Up Software RAID

🔍 **KEY TERM**

Partition—A disk can be uses as a single large volume or be divided into several smaller volumes. This can be done for a variety of reasons, from security to performance to simple organizational preference. Each smaller volume is a *partition*, and to *partition* the disk is to divide it into volumes.

📝 NOTE

Practically speaking, you can't partition a disk without losing all the data that's already on it. If you want to divide an existing disk, or change the sizes of existing partitions on a disk, you'll have to resign yourself to the idea that your data will be erased in the process. Some third-party commercial software allows partitions to be resized without data loss, but most such packages don't support Mac OS X.

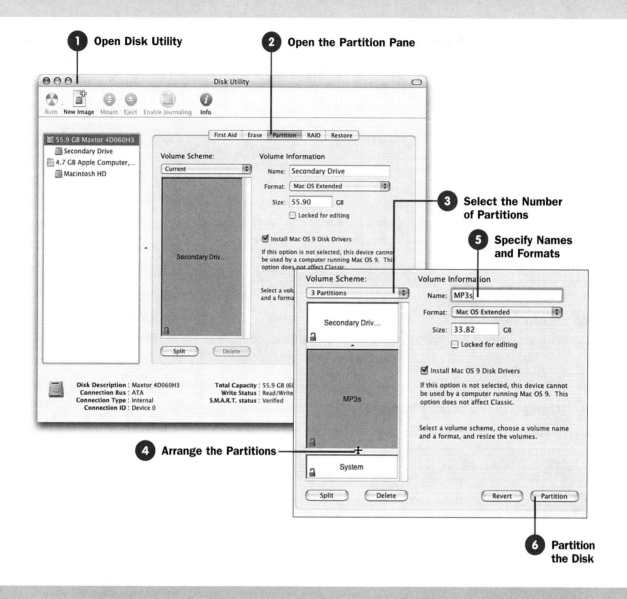

① Open Disk Utility

② Open the Partition Pane

Disk Utility

Burn New Image Mount Eject Enable Journaling Info

First Aid Erase Partition RAID Restore

55.9 GB Maxtor 4D060H3
Secondary Drive
4.7 GB Apple Computer,...
Macintosh HD

Volume Scheme:

Current

Secondary Driv...

Split   Delete

Disk Description : Maxtor 4D060H3
Connection Bus : ATA
Connection Type : Internal
Connection ID : Device 0

Total Capacity : 55.9 GB (60
Write Status : Read/Write
S.M.A.R.T. status : Verified

Volume Information

Name: Secondary Drive

Format: Mac OS Extended

Size: 55.90   GB

☐ Locked for editing

☑ Install Mac OS 9 Disk Drivers

If this option is not selected, this device canno
be used by a computer running Mac OS 9. Thi
option does not affect Classic.

Select a volu
and a forma

③ Select the Number
of Partitions

⑤ Specify Names
and Formats

Volume Scheme:

3 Partitions

Secondary Driv...

MP3s

System

Split   Delete

Volume Information

Name: MP3s

Format: Mac OS Extended

Size: 33.82   GB

☐ Locked for editing

☑ Install Mac OS 9 Disk Drivers

If this option is not selected, this device cannot
be used by a computer running Mac OS 9. This
option does not affect Classic.

Select a volume scheme, choose a volume name
and a format, and resize the volumes.

Revert   Partition

④ Arrange the Partitions

⑥ Partition
the Disk

④ **Arrange the Partitions**

Here's the fun part: To specify how large each partition should be, simply drag the horizontal dividing bar between two areas and move it up or down. The **Size** field in the upper-right portion of the window reflects the size of the selected partition; select another partition to see its size.

To specify a size explicitly, click a partition to select it and type the desired size for that partition into the **Size** field. You can prevent a partition's size from changing as you fiddle with the other partitions' sizes by enabling the **Locked for Editing** check box.

5 Specify Names and Formats

Select each partition in turn and type a name for each one in the **Name** field; the name you specify here is the name for the volume that's created when you partition the disk. You can specify different formats for each partition, too, in case you want to ensure compatibility with other operating systems; for best results, however, stick with the **Mac OS Extended** format option.

6 Partition the Disk

When all the partitions are arranged to your satisfaction, click the **Partition** button. The disk will be erased, formatted, and divided into volumes; after the process is finished, each of the new volumes is mounted in the Finder, ready for you to start using them however you like.

NOTE

You can't partition a volume—you have to select an entire disk from the sidebar. Each volume is, in fact, a partition.

TIP

Always back up your hard disk before partitioning anything! The process is straightforward, but that's no consolation if a disk is inadvertently erased.

21 Set Up Software RAID

For high-performance systems such as Web servers for which disk performance and reliability are paramount, it's important for disks to be available in a redundant and fault-tolerant fashion. This is what *RAID (Redundant Array of Independent Devices)* provides: a scheme by which you can employ multiple hard disks in a set, mirroring or striping the data from each other, enhancing both access speed and reliability. The downside is that you have to buy at least three times as much disk storage as you need if you don't use RAID technology; but for the kinds of high-reliability applications that RAID is designed for, the cost of hardware is a small concern compared to the need for redundancy.

RAID is often managed by a hardware solution (an add-on card in a high-end system) but this solution is unnecessary with Mac OS X's built-in software RAID option. The procedure for setting up software RAID assumes that you have installed at least two separate disks in the system, *in addition to* the startup disk. (Yes, that means you need at least *three* hard drives installed in or attached to your Mac. That's why RAID is intended for high-performance applications only!)

Before You Begin

✔ **19** Add a Newly Installed Hard Disk to the System

✔ **20** Partition a Hard Disk

✔ **173** Back Up Your Information

KEY TERM

RAID (Redundant Array of Independent Devices)—A technology in which multiple hard disks are harnessed in a set so that data can be stored redundantly (for maximum reliability in case one of the disks goes bad) or across multiple disks at once (to maximize the speed of access).

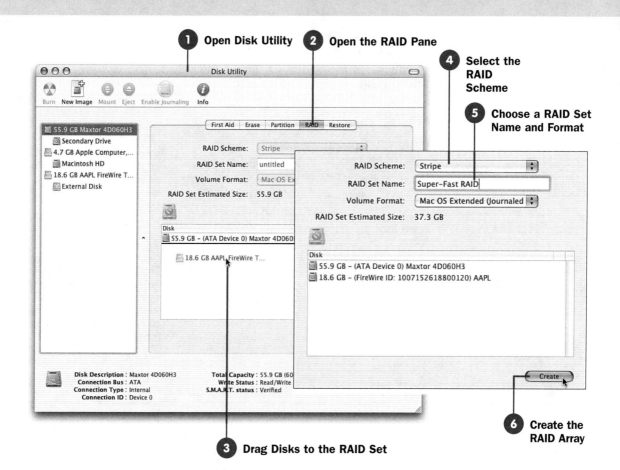

1 Open Disk Utility   **2** Open the RAID Pane

4 Select the RAID Scheme

5 Choose a RAID Set Name and Format

6 Create the RAID Array

3 Drag Disks to the RAID Set

1 Open Disk Utility

Open the Finder and navigate to the **Applications** folder, then to the **Utilities** subfolder. Launch the **Disk Utility** program by double-clicking its icon.

2 Open the RAID Pane

First select an entire disk (not a volume) from the left pane of the **Disk Utility** window. Make sure that you're choosing one of the disks you want to add to the RAID array (and thereby protect its data redundantly or speed up its access with striping), not your Mac's startup disk. Then click the **RAID** tab to open the **RAID** setup pane.

③ Drag Disks to the RAID Set

The left pane of the **Disk Utility** window lists all the available disks; drag the disks you want to use as the redundant disks in the RAID array into the white RAID set box (do not select the same disk you chose in step 2). You can rearrange the disks into priority order by dragging them in the box, or delete disks from the set by selecting them and clicking the **Delete** icon above the box. As you add disks to the set, the estimated usable size of the array (depending on your selected RAID scheme) is updated dynamically.

④ Select the RAID Scheme

You can select **Stripe** or **Mirror** as the RAID scheme. *Striping* is a good scheme for enhancing access speed because it works by storing parts of the same file across different disks so that all the pieces can be read at once; striping also preserves all your combined usable disk space. However, striping doesn't provide redundancy. *Mirroring* copies the files across all the RAID volumes, so it does provide redundancy, but not the speed benefits of striping.

There are "hybrid" RAID schemes that combine the benefits of both striping and mirroring; however, you must connect at least three RAID drives to your system to use this hybrid RAID scheme, and the scheme isn't supported by **Disk Utility** (which is, after all, designed for consumers with desktop Macs, rather than the high-availability server applications that use high-level RAID schemes). Professional data-center administrators might want to look into Xserve RAID, Apple's server-class RAID solution.

⑤ Choose a RAID Set Name and Format

Enter a descriptive name for the RAID array and choose a volume format. The **Mac OS Extended (Journaled)** format is the Mac OS X default and is generally the best way to go. You can select **Mac OS Extended (Non-Journaled)** to obtain a little more speed at the expense of reliability in the case of unexpected shutdowns.

⑥ Create the RAID Array

When everything is set up the way you want it, click the **Create** button. The RAID array is set up and mounted in the Finder as a single new volume, with the name you specified in step 5. You can then use this volume as you would any other disk; all the RAID striping or mirroring takes place under the hood, so you don't have to worry about it any more.

NOTE

You must have at least two disks in the RAID set to create a RAID array; neither of these disks can be your startup disk. Creating a RAID array destroys all the data on all the disks you add to the RAID list. Be absolutely sure that you know what you're doing before creating a RAID array!

KEY TERMS

Striping—A RAID data storage scheme in which parts of each file are stored on different disks so that they can all be read independently at the same time for increased access speed.

Mirroring—A RAID data storage scheme in which all disks in the array are identical copies of each other so that if an error occurs on one disk, the other disks can correct it.

22 Assign a Folder Action

KEY TERM

Folder action—A script (a simple human-readable program) that you attach to a folder. Triggered by certain events, such as when you open or close the folder or add an item into it, the folder action script performs some function.

22 Assign a Folder Action

AppleScript, the built-in application-aware programming language included in Mac OS X, can be harnessed to extend the functionality of the Finder. AppleScript gives you the ability to assign *folder actions* to individual folders in the system. What the script can do is limited only by your imagination.

Apple provides a few sample folder action scripts, in the **Scripts** folder inside the main system **Library**. These include a script which will display the folder's comments in a dialog box when you open the folder in the Finder (useful for making sure that other users are told some useful piece of information if they wander into the folder); one which pops up a dialog box informing you when any new items are added to the folder; and one that, when you close the folder, closes any windows showing subfolders of that folder. If you like, you can modify these scripts or use them as examples for new scripts that you write.

① Enable Folder Actions

Folder actions are controlled from the contextual menu which you open by **Control**+clicking or right-clicking on or inside any Finder window or the Desktop.

Open the contextual menu; select **Enable Folder Actions**. This turns on **Folder Actions** globally and allows you to assign them anywhere in the system.

② Navigate to the Folder You Want to Configure

Open a Finder window and navigate to the folder to which you want to assign an action script. You can set up folder actions either from within the folder in question, or in the folder above it in the hierarchy.

③ Attach a Folder Action

Control+click or right-click the selected folder and select **Attach a Folder Action** from the contextual menu. A file selector window opens, by default starting in the global **Folder Action Scripts** folder in /**Library/Scripts**.

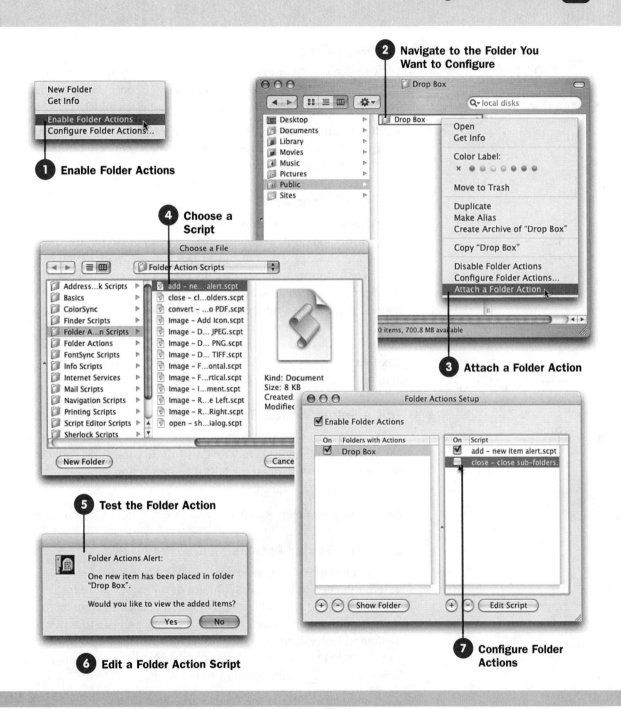

2 Navigate to the Folder You Want to Configure

New Folder
Get Info
Enable Folder Actions
Configure Folder Actions...

1 Enable Folder Actions

Drop Box

Desktop
Documents
Library
Movies
Music
Pictures
Public
Sites

Drop Box

Open
Get Info

Color Label:

Move to Trash

Duplicate
Make Alias
Create Archive of "Drop Box"

Copy "Drop Box"

Disable Folder Actions
Configure Folder Actions...
Attach a Folder Action

0 items, 700.8 MB available

3 Attach a Folder Action

4 Choose a Script

Choose a File

Folder Action Scripts

Address...k Scripts
Basics
ColorSync
Finder Scripts
Folder A...n Scripts
Folder Actions
FontSync Scripts
Info Scripts
Internet Services
Mail Scripts
Navigation Scripts
Printing Scripts
Script Editor Scripts
Sherlock Scripts

add – ne... alert.scpt
close – cl...olders.scpt
convert – ...o PDF.scpt
Image – Add Icon.scpt
Image – D... JPEG.scpt
Image – D... PNG.scpt
Image – D... TIFF.scpt
Image – F...ontal.scpt
Image – F...rtical.scpt
Image – I...ment.scpt
Image – R...e Left.scpt
Image – R...Right.scpt
open – sh...ialog.scpt

Kind: Document
Size: 8 KB
Created:
Modified

New Folder   Cance

5 Test the Folder Action

Folder Actions Alert:

One new item has been placed in folder "Drop Box".

Would you like to view the added items?

Yes   No

6 Edit a Folder Action Script

Folder Actions Setup

☑ Enable Folder Actions

On	Folders with Actions
☑	Drop Box

On	Script
☑	add – new item alert.scpt
	close – close sub-folders.

(+) (−)   Show Folder   (+) (−)   Edit Script

7 Configure Folder Actions

4 Choose a Script

You can choose one of the many sample scripts in this folder or any other script you have written or downloaded. Choose the script file and click **Choose** to assign the script to the selected folder.

Inside the **AppleScript** folder in the **Applications** folder, you'll find another collection of folder action scripts you can attach to folders. Use the built-in navigator to locate these scripts and attach them.

5 Test the Folder Action

Depending on what the script does, it will be triggered by different actions—adding an item to the folder, opening or closing the folder, and so on. Make sure that the folder reacts properly when you trigger it. For instance, if you selected the **open - show comments in dialog.scpt** script, first use the **Get Info** panel to add a comment to the folder. Then open the folder and make sure that a dialog box pops up showing you the comments you entered. In the example shown here, the **add - new item alert.scpt**, attached to the **Drop Box** folder, pops up a notification whenever anybody puts a new item into your **Drop Box** folder.

6 Edit a Folder Action Script

After a script has been attached to a folder, you can edit the script file directly to modify its behavior. **Control**+click the folder to view the contextual menu, open the **Edit a Folder Action** submenu, and select the script you want to edit.

After making your changes, click **Save** and test the folder action again.

7 Configure Folder Actions

You can manage all the folders in the system that have folder actions attached at once. **Control**+click or right-click on or inside any Finder window or the Desktop to display the contextual menu and select **Configure Folder Actions**. A panel opens up that lists all configured folders and all the scripts assigned to each one. You can turn the individual scripts on and off, add or remove configured folders, and add or remove scripts from folders.

Select any script and click the **Edit Script** button to modify the script so that it does exactly what you want. If you have a lot of folder actions to manage, this is the most direct way to control them all.

23 Add a Second Display

Doubling your Desktop's real estate has always been one of the best things about the Mac. Ever since the first color Macs, it's been possible to attach a second monitor and instantly use it to its fullest capacity. For instance, you could hook up a small grayscale monitor in addition to your big color one, and the two monitors would act as one large, oddly shaped screen, and you could drag your icons and windows seamlessly from one monitor to the other (watching them change from color to black-and-white and back).

It's the same today. All Power Mac models come with video cards that support two monitors, and all PowerBooks have video ports for additional monitors as well. You can even add more video cards if you want to plug in more monitors. Mac OS X lets you define where each monitor is in relation to the others, specify which is the primary monitor (the one that gets the menu bar and the Dock), and control each monitor's resolution and color depth.

See Also

→ **130** Change Your Desktop Picture

1 Attach the Second Monitor

Plug in the new monitor's power cord and connect the VGA or DVI cable to the available port on your Mac's video card. Mac OS X immediately recognizes the new monitor and repaints the screen.

2 Open the Displays Preferences

Open the **System Preferences** from the **Apple** menu and click the **Displays** icon to open the **Displays Preferences** window. Notice that a **Displays** window is open on both monitors; each one controls the display on which it appears.

3 Select the Resolution and Color Depth for Both Displays

In the **Display** tab, select the desired resolution (the size of the screen, in pixels) from the **Resolutions** box. The display changes immediately to the selected resolution. Then choose how many colors you want to display on the new monitor, using the **Colors** drop-down menu.

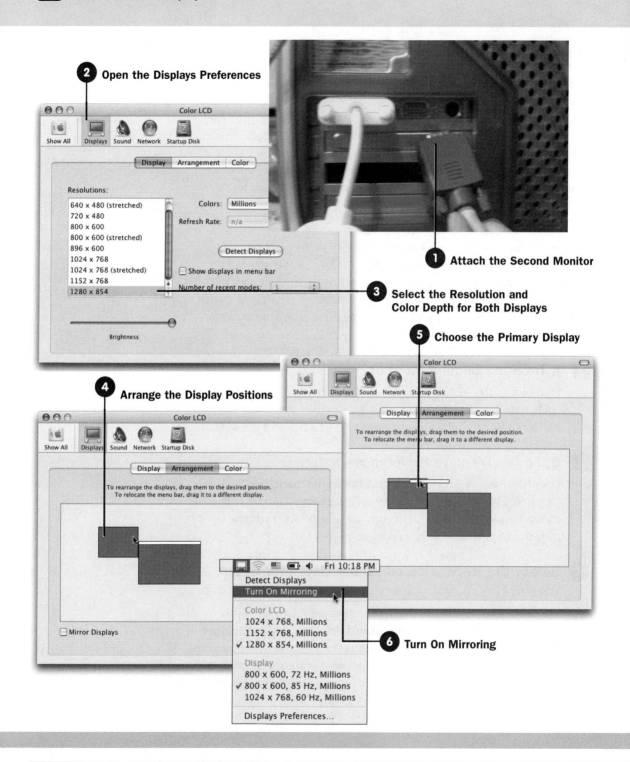

2 Open the Displays Preferences

Color LCD

Show All   Displays   Sound   Network   Startup Disk

Display   Arrangement   Color

Resolutions:

640 x 480 (stretched)
720 x 480
800 x 600
800 x 600 (stretched)
896 x 600
1024 x 768
1024 x 768 (stretched)
1152 x 768
1280 x 854

Colors: Millions
Refresh Rate: n/a

(Detect Displays)

☐ Show displays in menu bar
Number of recent modes: 3

Brightness

1 Attach the Second Monitor

3 Select the Resolution and
Color Depth for Both Displays

5 Choose the Primary Display

Color LCD

Show All   Displays   Sound   Network   Startup Disk

Display   Arrangement   Color

To rearrange the displays, drag them to the desired position.
To relocate the menu bar, drag it to a different display.

4 Arrange the Display Positions

Color LCD

Show All   Displays   Sound   Network   Startup Disk

Display   Arrangement   Color

To rearrange the displays, drag them to the desired position.
To relocate the menu bar, drag it to a different display.

☐ Mirror Displays

🖥 📶 📧 🔋 🔊   Fri 10:18 PM

Detect Displays
Turn On Mirroring

Color LCD
1024 x 768, Millions
1152 x 768, Millions
✓ 1280 x 854, Millions

Display
800 x 600, 72 Hz, Millions
✓ 800 x 600, 85 Hz, Millions
1024 x 768, 60 Hz, Millions

Displays Preferences...

6 Turn On Mirroring

Flat-panel monitors, such as the displays Apple sells, typically have a single "natural" resolution because an LCD has a fixed grid of pixels. Traditional CRT-based monitors can operate at a variety of resolutions because they are analog devices that can place an arbitrary number of lines on the screen. If you select a resolution other than the "natural" resolution for a flat-panel display, the display might appear blurry because Mac OS X has to interpolate the pixels to simulate the specified resolution. Consult the manual for your flat-panel display to determine its natural resolution.

Every display reproduces colors in a slightly different way, which can wreak havoc on a picture file you're trying to get to look right on displays other than your own. When you connect a new display, you should calibrate its colors using the **Calibrate** button found in the **Color** tab of the **Displays Preferences** window. When you do this, you create a *profile* using ColorSync, Apple's industry-standard color-calibration technology. With ColorSync, every picture you create on your computer (using Adobe Photoshop or any other application that uses ColorSync) is embedded with the profile that corresponds to your display's unique color characteristics. When you send the file to another Mac user, that user's ColorSync-calibrated display can adjust itself to match what it knows about your display. The result is that the other user gets to see the picture exactly as you see it on your display, even if that monitor's colors are calibrated differently. Printers, scanners, and other display and output devices can be ColorSync-calibrated as well.

4 Arrange the Display Positions

On your primary display, click the **Arrangement** tab. This screen lets you visually select exactly where you want your two monitors to be positioned relative to each other. The primary display is shown in the center of the screen; click and drag the second display, shown adjacent to it, anywhere around the primary display that you want. You can place the second display to the right or left of the primary, or above or below it.

Wherever you drag the rectangle representing the second monitor is the position Mac OS stores, allowing the monitors to assemble themselves into a virtual "display" of the shape you have defined here. For instance, in this example, you can drag a window from the primary display to the secondary display by moving it to the top left of the screen; keep moving the mouse up and to the left, and the window moves onto the second display.

> **TIP**
>
> Enable the **Show displays in menu bar** check box to put the **Displays** system menu in your menu bar. This menu gives you easy access to the resolution and color depth for any of your connected monitors.

> **NOTE**
>
> Even today, ColorSync doesn't really have an equivalent in the Windows world; this is why the Macintosh is still so popular in the graphics and publishing industry.

5 Choose the Primary Display

You can make the second display into your primary display if you want. Your primary display is the one on which your menu bar, Dock, Desktop icons, and any dialog boxes or messages appear. To select which display is the primary one, drag the white bar at the top of the rectangle representing the current primary display onto the other display. When you release the mouse button, the displays rearrange themselves accordingly.

6 Turn On Mirroring

Mirroring allows you to display the same screen contents to two different displays at once. This is useful for presentations in which you have your laptop hooked up to a projector. Any actions that you perform on your laptop's screen are reflected on the projector.

Enable the **Mirror displays** check box on the **Arrangement** tab to turn on mirroring. (You can also select **Turn On Mirroring** from the **Displays** system menu.) Both displays must have the same resolution for mirroring to work; if you mirror the displays, the second display's resolution is changed to match that of the primary display.

24 Set the Time and Date

See Also

→ **25** Enable Automatic Time Synchronization (NTP)

→ **133** Customize the Menu Bar Clock

→ **135** Adjust the Format of Numbers and Other Notations

It's important for your Mac to be able to keep accurate track of the time. Lots of system functions depend on carefully scheduled execution; for instance, if you have **Software Update** set to check for new updates every week, or **iSync** set to synchronize your data every hour, your Mac must be able to kick off those processes at the correct time. These are just two of the functions you can see at the user level. As a Unix system, Mac OS X runs a number of self-cleaning and bookkeeping tasks every day— late at night, when you're most likely asleep, so that those tasks don't interfere with your work. You don't want to have the disk grinding away mysteriously at noon just because your system's time is set incorrectly.

If you don't have a network connection, you'll have to set the date and time for your computer manually. You use the **Date & Time Preferences** window to do this.

The time zone is an important part of your computer's time setting, especially when it comes to communicating with other computers around the world. If you send an email to someone on the other side of the country, for example, the email headers must be able to convey what time zone you're in, so that when the recipient gets the message, his email program can tell him when, *by his clock*, you wrote the message.

Apple provides a graphical method for choosing your time zone, and also allows you to select a nearby city to use its time zone information.

① Open the Date & Time Preferences

Open the **System Preferences** from the **Apple** menu. Alternatively, you can select **Open Date & Time** from the menu that appears when you click the time display at the far right of the system's menu bar.

Click the **Date & Time** tab, if it isn't already selected. This brings up the manual configuration pane.

② Pick or Enter a Date

Click a date in the graphical calendar to select another date within the current month.

If the date you want is in another month, use the text field above the calendar to numerically specify a month. Click each of the date fields and either type a number or click a date field. You can increment the field using the **Up** and **Down** arrows.

③ Move Clock Hands or Enter a Time

On the graphical clock, click any of the clock hands and drag it to the position you want. Click the **AM** or **PM** display to toggle between them.

If you prefer, you can enter the time manually. Click any of the time fields above the graphical clock and type a number or use the **Up** and **Down** arrows to increment the values.

④ Click a Geographical Region or Select a City Name

Click the **Time Zone** tab to bring up the time zone configuration pane.

On the graphical map, click as close to your geographical location as possible; the time zone for the location you click lights up. The map also shows the location of a city close to where you clicked (from which the system is actually deriving the time zone information).

TIP

The Network Time Protocol (NTP) allows your computer to keep its date and time in sync with a central server (see **25** **Enable Automatic Time Synchronization** for more on NTP). If you don't have a network connection, however, you must check periodically to make sure that your Mac's time is accurate. Computers' clocks can drift over time, losing or gaining seconds or even minutes each week. NTP corrects this for you, but if you aren't networked, you must check the system time manually.

NOTE

The analog clock remains in motion, with the second hand going around, until you start to make changes; if you move any of the hands, the second hand stops so that you can put it in an accurate position and apply it at exactly the right time by clicking **Save**.

NOTE

Don't worry about Daylight Savings Time or other such localized adjustment systems. If your calendar date is set properly, Mac OS X will know what the correct time zone mode is for whatever location you select. When your area "springs forward" or "falls back" for Daylight Savings Time, your Mac will automatically adjust the system time for you.

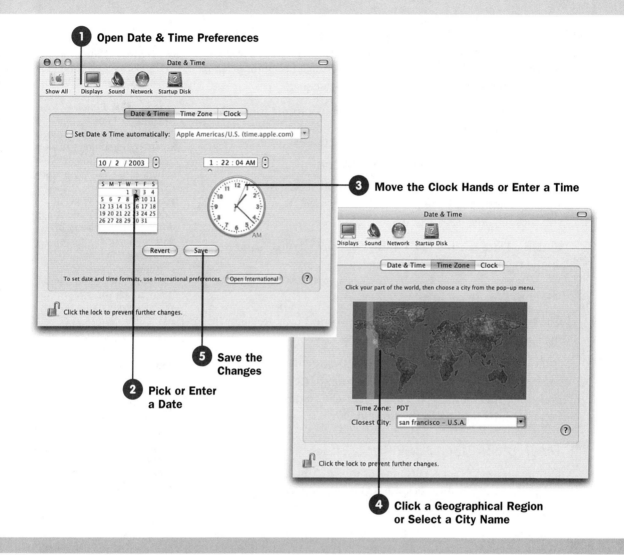

1 Open Date & Time Preferences

2 Pick or Enter a Date

3 Move the Clock Hands or Enter a Time

4 Click a Geographical Region or Select a City Name

5 Save the Changes

If you can't click your location on the map (for instance, if your time zone is really small), you can select a city in your time zone, and the system will adopt it. Use the **Closest City** drop-down menu to locate a nearby city; if you can't find a city in the list, it might be because the list shows cities only in the currently selected time zone. Select the text in the input box and begin typing the name of a major city in your region; the box auto-completes your input to show the nearest match, allowing you to type only as much of the city name as you have to before the system knows where you are.

Press **Return** to accept a city name that has been automatically completed; your time zone will change to match that city.

⑤ Save the Changes

As soon as you make any changes, the **Revert** and **Save** buttons on the **Date & Time** pane become active. If you're not already on the **Date & Time** pane, click the **Date & Time** tab to open that pane. Click **Revert** if you don't want to keep your changes; click **Save** to apply the changes.

> **NOTE**
>
> You are prompted to either **Revert** or **Save** your changes if you quit the **System Preferences** application or try to move to another preference pane before you click **Save**.

㉕ Enable Automatic Time Synchronization (NTP)

The *Network Time Protocol (NTP)* allows your computer to keep its date and time in sync with a central server. If you have a network connection—even an intermittent one, as you might with a laptop—it's absolutely better all around to use network time rather than manually setting the system's time and date. Whenever your computer's network or Internet connection is active, it communicates with the NTP server to ensure that its clock is accurate; if there is any discrepancy, Mac OS X makes the adjustments automatically. Because this checking takes place in the background, the adjustments to be made are never large enough for you to notice—unless it's been a long time since your connection was active and your system clock has drifted a lot.

A lot of NTP servers are active on the Internet, run by organizations such as the U.S. Naval Observatory and various universities. However, Apple runs its own NTP servers as well, in various places around the world, one of which is bound to be close to your location.

① Open the Date & Time Preferences

Open the **System Preferences** from the **Apple** menu; click **Date & Time** to open the **Date & Time Preferences** window. Alternatively, select **Open Date & Time** from the menu that appears when you click the time display at the far right of the system's menu bar.

② Enable NTP

Enable the **Set Date & Time Automatically** check box to enable network time synchronization.

Before You Begin

✔ ㉔ Set the Time and Date

✔ ㉗ Dial Up to the Internet with a Modem (PPP)

✔ ㉙ Configure Networking Manually

See Also

→ ⑫ Create an iCal Event

→ ⑬ Customize the Menu Bar Clock

→ ⑬ Adjust the Format of Numbers and Other Notations

→ ⑯ Schedule Automatic Software Updates

> **KEY TERM**
>
> *Network Time Protocol (NTP)*—A technology in which a computer (such as a Mac) can periodically check with any of a number of central, public servers and receive an accurate reading of the current time. The computer can then calibrate its clock to match the central server, which is often of military precision.

2 Enable NTP   **1** Open the Date & Time Preferences

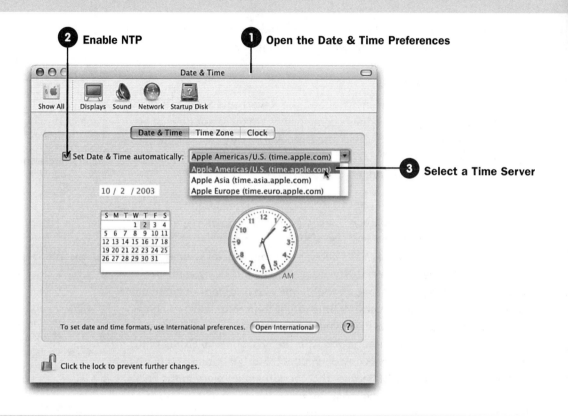

3 Select a Time Server

 NOTE

Some computers' clocks have severe drift problems. If you find that you have to manually set your clock more than once every couple of months—in other words, if your Mac's clock drifts by more than a couple of minutes a month—you should consider having it serviced and getting the clock chip replaced.

3 Select a Time Server

The default time server is **time.apple.com**, located at the Apple campus in Cupertino, California. There are other choices available— **time.asia.apple.com** for Asia, and **time.euro.apple.com** for Europe— that you might want to choose instead if you're not in the Americas. Because NTP operates by a carefully timed exchange of data packets, it's important to choose a time server that's geographically near to you to minimize network latency during the sync process.

If you want to use a different time server (such as **tick.usno.navy.mil**, the United States Naval Observatory's public NTP server), enter its hostname in the input box.

As soon as you select a time server, the time is synchronized. You can then close the window, because no further configuration is needed and no changes must be saved.

PART II

Networking and the Internet

IN THIS PART

4

Networking Your Mac

IN THIS CHAPTER:

TCP/IP—Transport Control Protocol and Internet Protocol. This is the general term for the software architecture that underlies all communication on the Internet.

LAN—Local Area Network. A group of computers directly connected to each other with cables and devices such as hubs or switches. If you have to connect using a long-distance method such as a dial-up modem or DSL connection, it's a Wide Area Network, or WAN.

.Mac—Apple's centralized network service, available for a yearly fee, that allows you to publish the products of your creativity online and make all your Macs operate as one.

Rendezvous—A technology built into Mac OS X that allows applications on your Mac to automatically find network services provided by other computers on the same network, such as shared music, chat partners, and file servers.

No Mac is an island. Computing in the modern world is almost synonymous with Internet connectivity and the ability for one computer to communicate with others, whether down the hall or across the globe. Mac OS X is a thoroughly modern operating system, with professional-grade support for *TCP/IP* (the communication mechanism that runs the Internet) and a suite of full-featured applications that give you the tools you need to make the most of the Internet—use email, browse the Web, and much more. Whether your Mac is connected to the global network using a dial-up modem, or whether you have several computers in your household or office that are connected to each other in a *LAN* (local area network), Mac OS X can handle it all.

Sure, you can do a ton of things with just a single computer—process words, listen to music, edit video, organize photos—but when you plug in an Internet connection, you open up the horizons of a much wider computing world. What's more, when you make the move from a single Mac to several Macs, or add some Windows machines to the household or office, you begin to reap the benefits of Mac OS X's ability to integrate all your machines together seamlessly. You can share files between Macs or between Macs and Windows machines. You can run programs hosted on other computers. With *.Mac*, you can synchronize your computers' Address Books and Web bookmarks so that they're all the same regardless of whether you're using your desktop Mac or your PowerBook on the road. And thanks to *Rendezvous*, Apple's configuration-free network-service discovery protocol, you can connect immediately with chat partners and shared music on any computer on your LAN.

To take advantage of all this technology, however, Mac OS X must be set up to connect properly to your network environment. Whether you connect using *Ethernet* cables, *AirPort*, or a modem dial-up over a phone line, there is a fair amount of configuration involved before you'll be able to communicate with the outside world. This chapter covers the basic procedures to get you up and running on the Internet. Furthermore, it covers what you need to know in joining your computer to a home or office network so that it can take part as a member of an interlinked community of computers.

For more information about TCP/IP and networking, refer to *Sams Teach Yourself TCP/IP in 24 Hours* or *Sams Teach Yourself Networking in 24 Hours*, both published by Sams Publishing.

26 Set Your Network Device Preference Order

Mac OS X allows you to configure multiple different networking devices, such as modems, Ethernet connections, and AirPort cards, and to place them in the order of your preference. With this arrangement, if the primary device is not plugged in or available, Mac OS X tries the next most preferred device.

For instance, you might have an iBook with an *AirPort* card, an *Ethernet* cable you sometimes plug into, and a phone line. However, you don't always have the Ethernet cable plugged in, and the AirPort signal might sometimes be unavailable as well. You want to be able to set up Ethernet as your most preferred connection method, but if you don't have Ethernet plugged into your iBook, you want the computer to use AirPort instead. As a last resort, if neither of the other methods are available, you want to be able to use the modem and phone line to dial up. Mac OS X makes this configuration easy to set up.

1 Open Network Preferences

Open the **System Preferences** from the **Apple** menu; click the **Network** icon to open the **Network Preferences** page.

2 Edit the Network Port Configurations

From the **Show** drop-down menu, which contains entries for each of the network devices in your computer (which you can select to configure those devices directly), select **Network Port Configurations**. A screen appears that contains an editable list of network devices. Each one of these devices is actually a "port configuration," a combination of a network device (port) and a TCP/IP configuration. This allows you to define more than one configuration for a single port—one set of TCP/IP settings for home, and another set for work, but both assigned to your Ethernet port.

3 Drag Devices into Preferred Order

To set up your iBook as described earlier, click and drag the port configurations into the following order:

1. Built-in Ethernet

2. AirPort

3. Internal Modem

Before You Begin

✔ **43** Install an AirPort Card

See Also

→ **29** Configure Networking Manually

→ **47** Create and Configure a Location

KEY TERMS

AirPort—Apple's brand of wireless Internet connectivity devices. Operating over the industry-standard 802.11 protocol (also called Wi-Fi), AirPort and its faster successor AirPort Extreme allow you to connect to the Internet without wires as long as a base station (a device connected physically to the Internet that broadcasts the 802.11 signal that allows computers within range to access the network) is within range. The AirPort Base Station has a range of about 150 feet.

Ethernet—A physical connection to a LAN is done using Ethernet, a low-level communication protocol that involves cables that end in RJ-45 jacks, which resemble large phone jacks. All modern Macs have an Ethernet port, which runs at 10, 100, or (on top-end models) 1000 megabits per second.

Set Your Network Device Preference Order

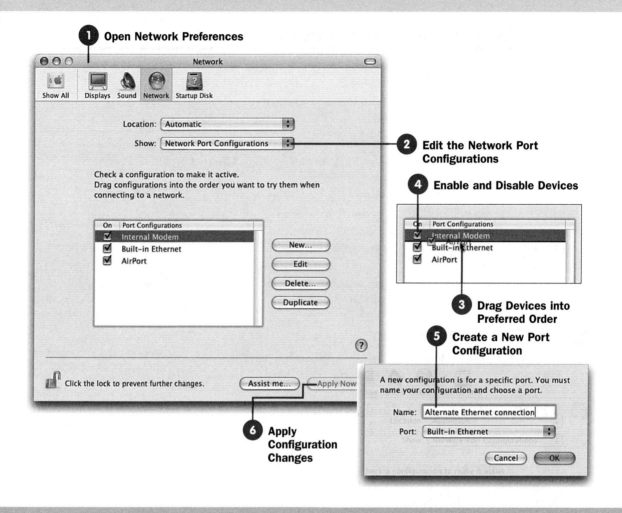

1 Open Network Preferences

2 Edit the Network Port Configurations

4 Enable and Disable Devices

3 Drag Devices into Preferred Order

5 Create a New Port Configuration

6 Apply Configuration Changes

This organization means that your iBook will first try to connect to the network over the Ethernet connection, using the TCP/IP settings you have defined for it. If your Ethernet cable isn't plugged in, the iBook skips that configuration and tries to connect using the wireless AirPort connection. If AirPort isn't available (for instance, if you're out of range of the base station), the computer will fall back to the internal modem dial-up, although even that connection won't be available unless you manually tell the computer to dial the modem.

104   **PART II:** Networking and the Internet

4 Enable and Disable Devices

Your Mac might have network devices you know you'll never use. For instance, you might have a computer without an AirPort card, so you know the AirPort configuration will never be used. You can remove it entirely from the preference list, saving time when your computer tries to connect to the Internet. To remove a device, disable its **On** check box in the configuration list. Turning off a port configuration removes that configuration from the **Show** menu.

5 Create a New Port Configuration

Suppose that you have two different sets of Ethernet settings—one for your home network and another one for your office. Depending on whether you're at home or at work, you want to be able to swap one set of TCP/IP settings for the other, with as little effort as possible.

Click the **New** button. A sheet appears that lets you define what kind of port configuration you want to create. Specify a name for the configuration and select the network device you want to use. You can select from the modem, Ethernet, or FireWire ports.

If you want to make a copy of an existing configuration and make changes to the copy, select the configuration and click **Duplicate**. The **Duplicate** option isn't available for the AirPort device.

After the new configuration has been created, you can then select it by name from the **Show** menu and apply the appropriate TCP/IP settings that allow it to connect to the network. See **28** **Configure Networking Automatically with DHCP or BootP** to configure the device to connect automatically to a network, or **29** **Configure Networking Manually** to configure the device's TCP/IP settings yourself.

6 Apply Your Configuration Changes

After all your configuration changes are complete, click the **Apply Now** button. None of your changes are made active until you click this button.

If you attempt to switch to a different Preferences page or close the **System Preferences** application, a confirmation dialog box appears prompting you to apply your configuration changes.

 NOTE

Every physical network has a different series of settings you must apply to connect your computer to it. Your network at the office, for instance, might provide an Ethernet connection and broadcast its settings to your computer automatically; whereas at home, you might have to configure your TCP/IP settings manually, using a fixed address assigned by your service provider, to connect to a DSL modem. *Locations* allow you to save these configurations and switch back and forth between them with a single command.

TIP

If you're using a less-preferred connection method (for instance, AirPort) and a more-preferred one becomes available (for instance, if you plug in the Ethernet cable), Mac OS X will automatically switch to the Ethernet connection.

NOTE

The TCP/IP settings that allow each of your network devices to connect to the Internet can be obtained from whoever provides your Internet connectivity service. At work or on campus, this person is the network administrator. At home, consult your Internet service provider to find out what settings you need for your Ethernet (or other) connection.

27 Dial Up to the Internet with a Modem (PPP)

Before You Begin

✔ **26** Set Your Network Device Preference Order

See Also

→ **32** Share Your Internet Connection

→ **33** Configure a Secure Tunnel (VPN)

The most common and inexpensive form of connecting to the Internet is to use the internal modem that's built into every Mac. A dial-up PPP (Point-to-Point Protocol) connection can transfer data at up to 56 kilobits per second. A dial-up connection uses a phone line so that it can't be used for other purposes (such as telephone calls) while the modem is connected, so most modem users connect to the Internet only on an as-needed basis. Modems have their inconveniences, but they're still the most popular way for home computer users to get their Internet connectivity.

To set up a dial-up account, you must have subscribed to a dial-up service with an Internet service provider (ISP). The provider will have given you some information to use in setting up your computer, such as an account name and password, a dial-up phone number, and other pieces of important data. Make sure that you have this information handy.

1 Select the Internal Modem Configuration

On the **Network Preferences** page of the **System Preferences** application, double-click the **Internal Modem** option in the configuration list on the **Network Status** page, or select **Internal Modem** from the **Show** drop-down list. The setup panels for the internal modem configuration appear. Because this is the first time you've set up the modem, the fields in the first **PPP** tab are blank.

2 Enter a Service Provider Name

In the **Service Provider** field, type the name of your ISP (for example, **EarthLink**). This name is simply an identifier so that you can tell which dial-up configuration you're using when you connect.

3 Enter Your Account Name and Password

Type in your account name, which is part of the information that came with your dial-up account from your Internet service provider (for example, **johndoe**), and the password for your account. As you type the password, each letter is hidden for security.

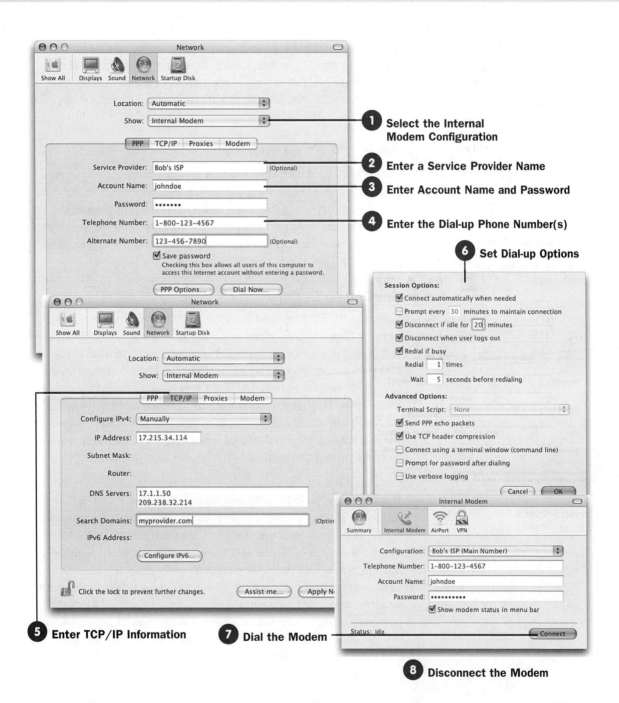

1 **Select the Internal Modem Configuration**

2 **Enter a Service Provider Name**

3 **Enter Account Name and Password**

4 **Enter the Dial-up Phone Number(s)**

6 **Set Dial-up Options**

5 **Enter TCP/IP Information**

7 **Dial the Modem**

8 **Disconnect the Modem**

TIP

Your account password is always saved with your dial-up configuration and is automatically passed to the ISP when your modem dials up. If you enable the **Save Password** check box, and there are multiple users set up on your Mac, all the users will be able to dial up using this modem configuration without having to type in your password. If you disable the **Save Password** check box, each user must have her own dial-up account and configure it in her own login sessions.

Modem Status System Menu

4 Enter the Dial-up Phone Number(s)

Your ISP should have given you an access phone number, and possibly an alternate number as well. Enter these numbers in the appropriate fields. If the modem attempts to dial and finds that the primary number is busy, it will automatically attempt the alternate number.

5 Enter TCP/IP Information

Click the **TCP/IP** tab. Most modern ISPs don't require you to enter any TCP/IP information manually; however, if your ISP gave you such information to enter, such as an **IP Address** or **Domain Name Service (DNS) Servers**, select **Manually** from the **Configure IPv4** drop-down menu and enter that information in the appropriate fields.

6 Set Dial-up Options

Return to the **PPP** tab and click the **PPP Options** button. A sheet appears that contains many options you can enable, disable, or tweak according to your taste. For instance, you can enable the **Connect automatically when needed** check box to set up your PPP configuration so that you don't ever have to manually connect to the Internet; if any application has to access the Internet, Mac OS X will automatically dial your modem for you. You can also set various options for whether and when Mac OS X should automatically disconnect the modem when it's not being used.

Click the **Modem** tab to configure a few extra connection options. You can set up Mac OS X to pop up a notification if you get an incoming phone call while you're connected to the Internet, or to show the modem status in the menu bar. If you enable this latter option, the **Modem Status** system menu (the telephone icon) will appear in the right half of the system's global menu bar (at the top of the screen) and give you the ability to connect the modem with a single click, select between multiple modem configurations (if you have them), or open the Internet Connect application, which lets you manage your modem configurations, dial the modem, and monitor your connection.

7 Dial the Modem

From the PPP tab, click the **Dial Now** button to launch the **Internet Connect** application; select your **Configuration** from the drop-down list at the top of the dialog box if needed, and click **Connect** to dial the modem. You can keep the **Internet Connect** window open to show you your connection status while you're online.

If you've enabled the **Modem Status** system menu (in the upper-right corner of the screen), simply select **Connect** from the menu to dial the modem.

8 Disconnect the Modem

When you're done using your Internet connection, click **Disconnect** in the **Internet Connect** window (the **Connect** button changes to **Disconnect** when the connection is established) or select **Disconnect** from the **Modem Status** system menu.

TIP

You can also launch **Internet Connect** from the **Network Status** page of the **Network Preferences** window; simply click the **Connect** button on that page to bring up the **Internet Connect** window.

28 Configure Networking Automatically with DHCP or BootP

If you connect to the Internet using Ethernet or AirPort, chances are that your Mac is part of a business or home network that is configured to automatically set each computer's *TCP/IP* settings as soon as it connects. If this is the case, you don't have to do any difficult configuration to get online; you just have to set up your Mac to use the *Dynamic Host Configuration Protocol (DHCP)*—the most popular protocol, whereby the computer is automatically assigned an IP address and routing information by a server somewhere on the LAN.

In DHCP (BootP, another similar protocol, is sometimes used instead), as soon as you plug in an Ethernet cable, join an AirPort network, or power-on a computer that's already plugged in, the computer sends out a broadcast message asking for a computer on the network to tell it what to use as an *IP address* as well as other critical TCP/IP information. If a DHCP server is present on the LAN, it sends a reply directly back to your computer with the TCP/IP information it needs. Your computer applies that information to its own configuration, and it can then communicate on the network and with the Internet.

Before You Begin

✔ **26** Set Your Network Device Preference Order

✔ **43** Install an AirPort Card

See Also

→ **29** Configure Networking Manually

→ **44** Hook Up Over the Airwaves

KEY TERM

Dynamic Host Configuration Protocol (DHCP)—A mechanism whereby you plug a computer into a network and have it automatically receive TCP/IP configuration settings from a server somewhere on the network, freeing you from having to type in those settings yourself.

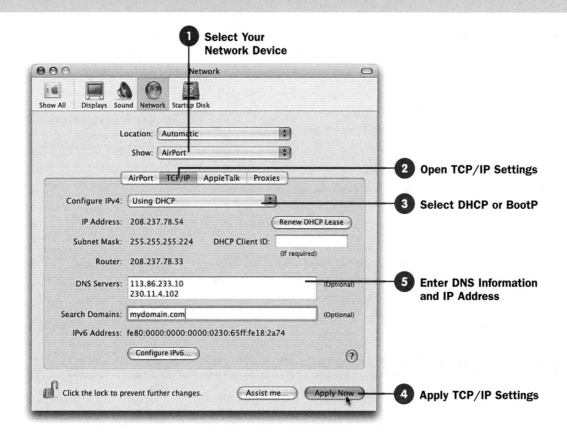

1 **Select Your Network Device**

2 **Open TCP/IP Settings**

3 **Select DHCP or BootP**

5 **Enter DNS Information and IP Address**

4 **Apply TCP/IP Settings**

KEY TERMS

IP address—A unique numeric address that identifies your computer on the Internet. An IP address is of the form **A.B.C.D**, where each letter is any number from 0 to 255—for example, **17.112.152.32**.

Subnet mask—Another set of four numbers, each from 0 to 255, the subnet mask is a numeric string that defines how large the address space is on your local network.

In the *IPv4* protocol, your IP address uniquely identifies your computer on the Internet. This address is a string of four numbers from 0 to 255, separated by dots (periods). Another string of four numbers, the *subnet mask*, defines how large your network's address space is. Common subnet masks are **255.0.0.0**, **255.255.0.0**, and **255.255.255.0**; they correspond to networks with 16.7 million, 65 thousand, and 256 IP addresses, respectively. Finally, the *router*, a device on your local network that enables your computer to communicate with computers on far-flung remote networks around the world, must be present within the address space of the local network defined by the combination of your IP address and your subnet mask.

A further bit of magic is done by *DNS servers*, which provide a mapping between numeric IP addresses and textual hostnames; this mapping is the Domain Name Service, or DNS. When you connect to the hostname **www.apple.com**, a DNS server must supply the IP address associated with that hostname before your computer can connect to it. If you specify a *search domain*, the hostnames you type can be shortened; for instance, if your search domain is **apple.com**, you could simply type **info** to connect to **info.apple.com**. Generally, you use this option on a business network and set it to your company's domain name so that you can connect to internal servers using only their machine names.

1 Select Your Network Device

On the **Network Preferences** page of the **System Preferences** application, select **Network Status** from the **Show** menu. Double-click the network device you want to configure. Alternatively, select the device from the **Show** drop-down menu.

Make sure that your network device is turned on and physically connected to the network. For instance, if you're configuring an AirPort card, make sure that you're within range of the AirPort base station. If you're configuring an Ethernet connection, make sure that the Ethernet cable is plugged in.

2 Open TCP/IP Settings

Click the **TCP/IP** tab to open the screen where you can configure the selected device's TCP/IP settings.

3 Select DHCP or BootP

From the **Configure IPv4** drop-down menu, select **Using DHCP** or **Using BootP**, depending on what protocol your network uses. If you don't know which one to pick, select **Using DHCP** because that protocol is much more common.

4 Apply TCP/IP Settings

Click **Apply Now** to commit the configuration. The Mac sends out a DHCP request; in a few seconds, you should see the information fields become filled in with numeric data. You should now be able to connect to the network using your favorite applications.

KEY TERMS

Router—A device on your local network that enables your computer to communicate with computers on other networks across the Internet.

DNS servers—Computers on the network that provide a mapping between numeric IP addresses and textual hostnames; this mapping is the Domain Name Service, or DNS.

Search domain—Allows you to type shortened versions of hostnames on the Internet.

IPv4—The current and ubiquitous version of IP, the Internet Protocol, is 4. IPv6 is the next-generation version of IP, and you can configure your Mac to use IPv6 if you're on a network that uses it (click the **Configure IPv6** button)—but most networks don't use IPv6 yet.

NOTE

If the IP address that the Mac reports has a subtitle of **Self-assigned**, it means that it got no response to its DHCP or BootP request, and therefore wasn't able to obtain a valid configuration. This could be because the DHCP server is not working properly, or it could mean that your Mac is not connected properly to the network. Check your cabling; if it looks correct, contact your network administrator for assistance or consult the documentation for the device providing DHCP service (such as your AirPort base station).

5 **Enter DNS Information and IP Address**

Normally, you don't have to enter any additional TCP/IP information. However, there are some circumstances under which you might need to enter an IP address or additional DNS information. For instance, you might have a computer that must use a fixed and predetermined IP address, and you must be assured that that IP address will never change; but you still want to be able to get other information, such as the subnet mask and router, automatically through DHCP.

If your DHCP server does not provide DNS information, enter the IP addresses of the network's DNS servers into the **DNS Servers** box—enter the addresses one per line or separate them with commas. (Ask your network administrator or your Internet service provider for the addresses.) If you want, you can enter your company's domain name in the **Search Domains** field to access local servers more quickly.

If you must specify a fixed IP address, use the **Using DHCP with manual address** option in the **Configure IPv4** drop-down menu.

29 Configure Networking Manually

Before You Begin

✔ **26** Set Your Network Device Preference Order

✔ **43** Install an AirPort Card

See Also

→ **28** Configure Networking Automatically with DHCP or BootP

→ **44** Hook Up Over the Airwaves

On many home and corporate networks, you will not be able to get your TCP/IP information automatically from a DHCP server; instead, you will have to enter all the important pieces of networking data yourself, using fixed addresses that won't change unless you change them yourself.

You should have received all the relevant TCP/IP information to set up your Internet connection when you signed up with an Internet service provider. If you don't have it, ask your network administrator or ISP for the *IP address*, *subnet mask*, gateway *router*, and *DNS servers* that you will have to enter; be sure to have this information ready as you set up your Mac's networking.

1 **Select Network Device**

On the **Network Preferences** page of the **System Preferences** application, select **Network Status** from the **Show** menu. Double-click the network device you want to configure. Alternatively, select the device from the **Show** drop-down menu.

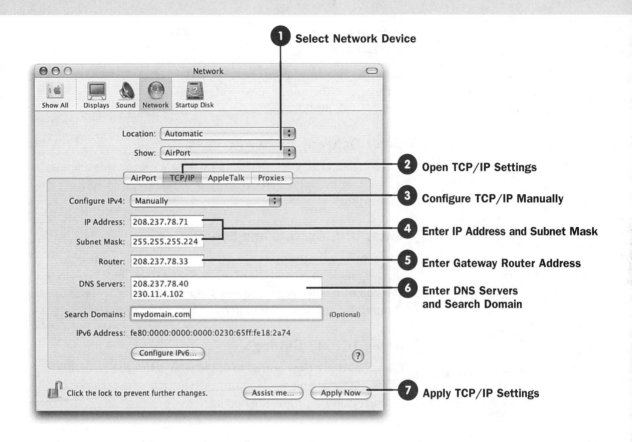

1 Select Network Device

2 Open TCP/IP Settings

3 Configure TCP/IP Manually

4 Enter IP Address and Subnet Mask

5 Enter Gateway Router Address

6 Enter DNS Servers and Search Domain

7 Apply TCP/IP Settings

2 Open TCP/IP Settings

Click the **TCP/IP** tab to open the screen where you can configure the device's TCP/IP settings.

3 Configure TCP/IP Manually

Select **Manually** from the **Configure IPv4** drop-down menu. All the configuration fields become editable.

4 Enter IP Address and Subnet Mask

In the **IP Address** field, replace the default **0.0.0.0** by typing the IP address given to you by your network administrator or ISP. Make sure that you enter the address in the form of four numbers between 0 and 255, separated by periods—for example, **17.112.152.32**.

Enter the **Subnet Mask** as well; depending on your network's architecture, the subnet mask will probably be **255.0.0.0**, **255.255.0.0**, or **255.255.255.0**.

5 **Enter Gateway Router Address**

Enter the address of your network's gateway router. This address must be on the same network as your IP address, as defined by the subnet mask.

6 **Enter DNS Servers and Search Domain**

You should have the addresses of one or more DNS servers; the servers might be on your local network, but they don't have to be. You can also enter your company's domain name if you want to shorten the hostnames you have to type in for local servers.

7 **Apply TCP/IP Settings**

Click the **Apply Now** button to apply your settings. You should immediately be able to communicate with the network and the Internet using your favorite applications.

---

30 **Configure Proxy Server Settings**

Before You Begin

✔ **29** Configure Networking Manually

See Also

→ **32** Share Your Internet Connection

→ **33** Configure a Secure Tunnel (VPN)

KEY TERM

Proxy—An "intermediary" computer that sits between your computer and the outside network, usually to increase access speed to common sites.

In some network configurations, you might have to set up *proxies*, which are intermediary computers that sit between your computer and the outside network.

Proxies can serve many purposes, but the most common is to speed up access to commonly used data. A proxy does this by posing as the server to which you need to connect, and then sending your request on to the remote server itself. The proxy then saves the information that comes back in a cache, as well as passing it on to you. If you (or another computer) tries to access that same information again, the proxy can simply send back the information it already has, rather than sending out another request for the same data from the remote server. This arrangement saves time and bandwidth, particularly on slow Internet connections.

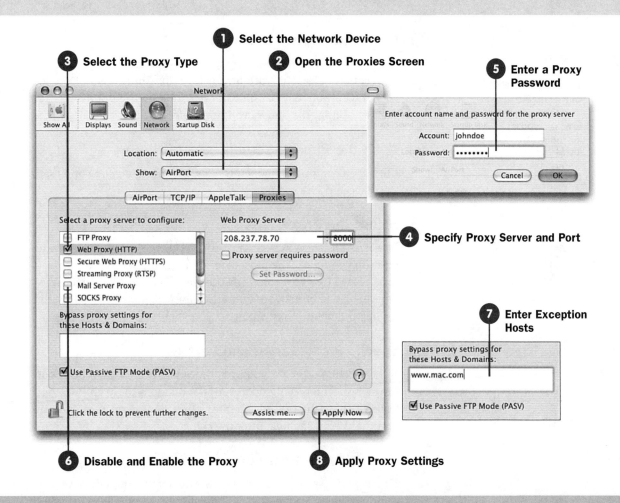

1 Select the Network Device

3 Select the Proxy Type

2 Open the Proxies Screen

5 Enter a Proxy Password

Network

Show All   Displays   Sound   Network   Startup Disk

Enter account name and password for the proxy server

Account: johndoe

Password: ••••••••

Cancel   OK

Location: Automatic

Show: AirPort

AirPort   TCP/IP   AppleTalk   Proxies

Select a proxy server to configure:

☐ FTP Proxy
☑ Web Proxy (HTTP)
☐ Secure Web Proxy (HTTPS)
☐ Streaming Proxy (RTSP)
☐ Mail Server Proxy
☐ SOCKS Proxy

Web Proxy Server

208.237.78.70   : 8000

☐ Proxy server requires password

Set Password...

4 Specify Proxy Server and Port

Bypass proxy settings for these Hosts & Domains:

☑ Use Passive FTP Mode (PASV)

7 Enter Exception Hosts

Bypass proxy settings for these Hosts & Domains:

www.mac.com

☑ Use Passive FTP Mode (PASV)

Click the lock to prevent further changes.   Assist me...   Apply Now

6 Disable and Enable the Proxy

8 Apply Proxy Settings

Most proxies are found in university or corporate networks, for the bene-fit of the students or employees. If your network administrator provides the addresses of proxy servers, you must set up your Mac to use them. You can configure proxies for many different network services, including HTTP, FTP, and email. Each kind of proxy is configured by simply speci-fying an IP address (and, optionally, a port number), as well as a pass-word if the proxy is password-protected.

Configure Proxy Server Settings

 NOTE

You can configure any of your available network devices to use proxies. However, you must configure the proxies for each device separately.

1 Select the Network Device

On the **Network Preferences** page of the **System Preferences** application, select **Network Status** from the **Show** menu. Double-click the network device you want to configure. Alternatively, select the device from the **Show** drop-down menu.

2 Open the Proxies Screen

Click the **Proxies** tab to open the screen where you can configure the device's proxy settings.

3 Select the Proxy Type

The **Select a proxy server to configure** box lists the many proxies you can configure. The most commonly used proxies are **Web Proxy (HTTP)**, **FTP Proxy** (file transfer), and **Mail Server Proxy** (email); ask your network administrator which proxies you should set up, and what proxy addresses you should use for each one.

4 Specify Proxy Server and Port

After selecting a proxy type from the **Select a proxy server to configure** box, enter the IP address of the proxy in the **Web Proxy Server** field to the right. If the proxy uses a numeric port, enter the port number in the field after the colon.

5 Enter a Proxy Password

If your proxy server requires a password, enable the **Proxy server requires password** check box; a sheet appears that prompts you to enter an account name and password for the server. Enter this information and click **OK**.

If you ever have to change the account name and password after you've configured the proxy, click the **Set Password** button to retrieve the password sheet.

6 Disable and Enable the Proxy

After you have configured a proxy, you can disable and enable it without losing its configuration (if, for instance, you need to do some task that doesn't work through a proxy). In the **Select a proxy server to configure** box, enable or disable the check box next to the proxy you want to use or bypass.

7 Enter Exception Hosts

Some hosts on the network might be incompatible with proxies, or you might want to exempt them from using the proxy. You can do this by listing the hostnames in the **Bypass proxy settings for these Hosts & Domains** box at the lower left. List the hostnames one per line or separate them with commas.

8 Apply Proxy Settings

Click the **Apply Now** button to apply the proxy settings; the settings do not take effect until you click this button.

From now on, each time you connect to any of the services for which you have configured proxies (the Web, an FTP site, email, and so on), the computer will connect to the proxy instead of directly to the specified site. On subsequent times that you access the same site, access to the data should be much faster and more reliable than without the proxy.

31 Activate AppleTalk

AppleTalk is Apple's own networking protocol, designed for file sharing and printing over local-area networks before TCP/IP became popular for home or business computing. Most TCP/IP networks in use today no longer explicitly support AppleTalk, which means AppleTalk generally can't be routed from one network (or "zone") to another. Within a LAN, however, AppleTalk operates over just about any networking protocol, and you can still use it to connect to other Macs. Some Mac-based networks are still in use in various places, such as universities, where you can browse different zones and connect to computers across the network using nothing but AppleTalk.

AppleTalk is not active by default; you can easily turn it on, but it can be active for only a single network device at a time. Turning on AppleTalk enables your Mac to access disks on other Macs and for other Macs to access your disks; it also means unwanted visitors might end up browsing your computer, so it's generally a good idea not to activate AppleTalk unless you really have to.

Before You Begin

✔ **28** Configure Networking Automatically with DHCP or BootP

✔ **43** Install an AirPort Card

See Also

→ **34** Share Another Mac's Files

→ **36** Allow Others to Share Your Files

KEY TERM

AppleTalk—Apple's own networking protocol. AppleTalk allows Macs and printers on a LAN to connect directly to one another without any configuration beyond simply turning on the protocol.

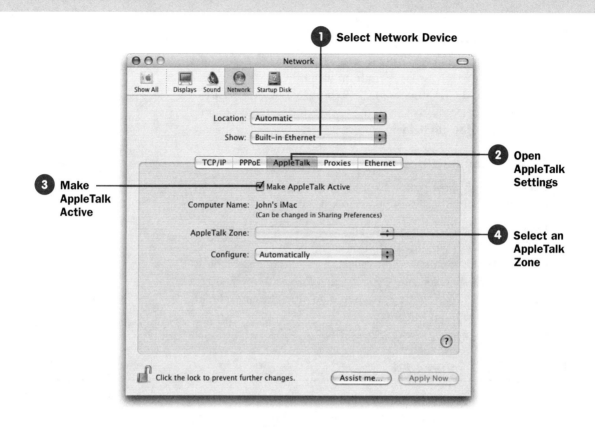

1 Select Network Device

1 **Select Network Device**

On the **Network Preferences** page of the **System Preferences** application, select **Network Status** from the **Show** menu. Double-click the network device you want to configure. Alternatively, select the device from the **Show** drop-down menu.

2 **Open AppleTalk Settings**

Click the **AppleTalk** tab to open the screen where you can configure the device's AppleTalk settings.

3 **Make AppleTalk Active**

Enable the check box to activate AppleTalk. Note that AppleTalk can be active for only one network device at a time; if AppleTalk is

NOTE

Not all devices support AppleTalk, and therefore the AppleTalk tab might not be present for some devices (such as the Internal Modem).

already active on another port, a sheet appears informing you of this and asking whether you want to switch AppleTalk to the current device. Click **OK** if you want to do this.

Click **Apply Now** to activate AppleTalk.

4 Select an AppleTalk Zone

If Mac OS X detects any AppleTalk zones on the network, a list of them appears in the **AppleTalk Zone** drop-down menu. Select which zone you want your Mac to appear in. If there aren't any zones on the network, the **AppleTalk Zone** menu remains disabled.

32 Share Your Internet Connection

Suppose that you have only a single dial-up Internet connection but several computers that all have to be online at once. Normally, you can hook up only one computer at a time, through its own modem connection. But thanks to Internet Sharing, all the computers can be online at once, sharing the same connection.

In this arrangement, one Mac is the central server that shares its connection with all the other computers. That Mac must have a working Internet connection such as the internal modem, Ethernet, or any other network port. That central Mac must also be hooked up to the other computers using an infrastructure such as AirPort or Ethernet. For instance, you might have a Mac with an Ethernet connection to a DSL modem, and an AirPort card with which it can share its connection with other AirPort-equipped computers; or your Mac might have a dial-up modem connection and be plugged in using Ethernet to a hub, with all the other computers likewise plugged into the same hub.

One network port on the central Mac is the active Internet connection, and the other port is the one you use to share the connection. All the other computers on the network need only be configured to use DHCP to obtain their TCP/IP information, and to use the same network device for their Internet connections that you're using to share it. For instance, if you are sharing your connection over AirPort (an optional add-on for most Macs), all the other computers must be using AirPort or compatible *802.11 devices* as well.

Before You Begin

✔ **26** Set Your Network Device Preference Order

✔ **29** Configure Networking Manually

See Also

→ **46** Create a Computer-to-Computer Network

KEY TERM

802.11—A protocol for wireless network connections. Apple's implementation is called AirPort; the same technology is also referred to in the rest of the industry as Wi-Fi. 802.11b, the earlier standard version, runs at 11 megabits per second; 802.11g, the more modern version, runs at up to 54 megabits per second and is called AirPort Extreme by Apple.

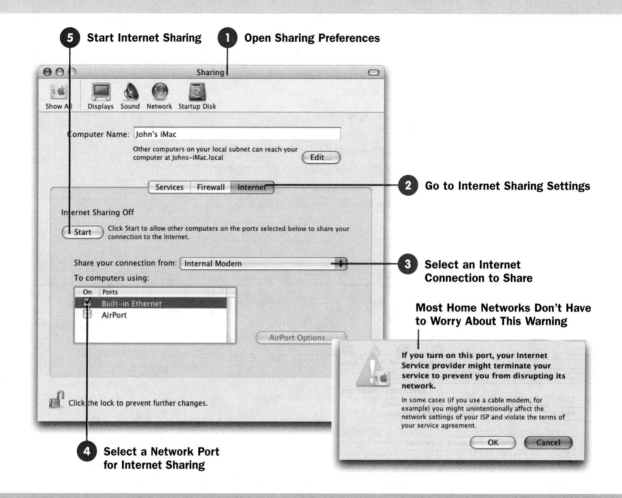

5 Start Internet Sharing   **1** Open Sharing Preferences

2 Go to Internet Sharing Settings

3 Select an Internet Connection to Share

Most Home Networks Don't Have to Worry About This Warning

4 Select a Network Port for Internet Sharing

KEY TERM

Network Address Translation (NAT)—A scheme that allows computers on one side of the router to have different IP addresses in a special range—usually **192.168.2.0** to **192.168.2.255**—and for those computers to all share a single true IP address on the other side of the router.

When your Mac has **Internet Sharing** enabled, the computer is actually acting as a DHCP server and *NAT*-enabled router. This means that external computers can't connect directly to any of the computers sharing their Internet connection from your Mac, because all they can see is the single real IP address that all the computers on your network are sharing.

1 **Open Sharing Preferences**

Open the **System Preferences** application and click the **Sharing** icon to open the **Sharing Preferences** page.

2 ## Go to the Internet Sharing Settings

Click the **Internet** tab to open the **Internet Sharing** configuration panel.

3 ## Select an Internet Connection to Share

All your active network ports are shown in the **Share your connection from** drop-down menu. To share your Internet connection, select the connection you want to share. For instance, if your connection to the outside Internet comes from a dial-up modem, select **Internal Modem**.

4 ## Select a Network Port for Internet Sharing

In step 2, you selected the network device (or port) that represents *your* main Internet connection. Now you must select the port that *other* computers will use to connect to your Mac to share its main connection.

Depending on which network port you have selected as your active connection, the list of available devices in the **To computers using** box at the lower-left changes to show only the devices available for Internet sharing. For instance, the **Internal Modem** option never appears in this box because a modem can't be used to connect a local-area network of other computers to the Internet. AirPort can be used for connecting to the Internet or for sharing the connection to other computers, but not both. Ethernet, however, can be used both to connect to the Internet and to share the connection with other computers.

Enable the check box next to each network port to select the ports you want to use for Internet sharing. You can select more than one network port at once, if (for instance) you want other computers to be able to connect to your Mac with both Ethernet and AirPort to share your Mac's modem connection.

A dialog box appears, warning you that many ISPs do not allow you to "sublet" your Internet connection to other users; for most home networks, this warning should not be a concern, and you can simply click **OK** to dismiss the warning. However, if you have any doubts about your ISP's policy regarding sharing your Internet connection, check with the ISP before enabling this feature.

NOTE

Computers sharing their Internet connections from your Mac don't all have to be Macs. Windows and Unix machines can all share your Internet connection; all they have to do is get their TCP/IP information through DHCP and use the network device you're using to share your Mac's Internet connection.

NOTES

Ethernet can be used both as your main connection method and as the shared port for other computers.

If you select **AirPort** for Internet Sharing, you will want to set up your AirPort options (click the **AirPort Options** button). The sheet that appears allows you to define a name for your network, select an 802.11 channel, or enable WEP encryption (Wired Equivalent Privacy, wherein your AirPort traffic is scrambled so that other wireless users can't intercept it) and set the password required for computers to join your AirPort network.

5 **Start Internet Sharing**

When you have selected at least one network port to use for sharing your connection, you can click **Start** to create the network and begin sharing the connection. You can then connect all the other computers to the network using the same type of device that you're using to share the connection.

---

33 Configure a Secure Tunnel (VPN)

Before You Begin

✔ **29** Configure Networking Manually

✔ **32** Share Your Internet Connection

See Also

→ **34** Share Another Mac's Files

KEY TERMS

Virtual Private Network (VPN)—A virtual "tunnel" that allows you to send and receive scrambled (private) traffic to a secure remote location, such as to your corporate network from home.

PPTP—Point-to-Point Tunnel Protocol; a popular type of VPN architecture.

L2TP/IPSec protocol—Secure IP; a newer and more versatile form of VPN architecture.

One major problem with using the Internet for mission-critical business is that data transmitted over the Internet is subject to being intercepted by malicious eavesdroppers. A confidential document being sent from San Francisco to New York might be captured in transit by someone in Chicago or China; clearly this isn't something that will fill stockholders with confidence.

Fortunately, there's a way of transmitting data so that it can't be usefully intercepted: a *Virtual Private Network (VPN)*. A VPN is a kind of "tunnel" on the Internet, a method for encrypting (scrambling) your transmitted data and sending it to a server at the other end of the tunnel that descrambles it so that it can be read by the intended recipients. If your computer is part of a VPN, it uses a different set of TCP/IP settings from the ones it normally uses on the open, "clear-text" Internet. Other computers in the VPN are also configured as though part of the same virtual network, hence the name.

Many companies use VPNs to connect one office to another, or for employees to gain access to the private internal network protected by a *NAT* gateway. Your Mac can use the *PPTP* or *L2TP/IPSec* protocol to create a VPN tunnel to an appropriate server and join its virtual network, provided that you have a valid username and password for the VPN.

1 **Open Internet Connect**

To create a VPN, you must use the **Internet Connect** application. This utility can be launched a number of ways, the simplest of which is to simply navigate to the **Applications** folder and double-click its icon. You can also open **Internet Connect** from the **AirPort** or **Modem** system menus (if you have enabled them, these menus appear at the far right of the Mac's menu bar), or by clicking the **Connect** button on the **Network Status** pane of the **Network Preferences** page.

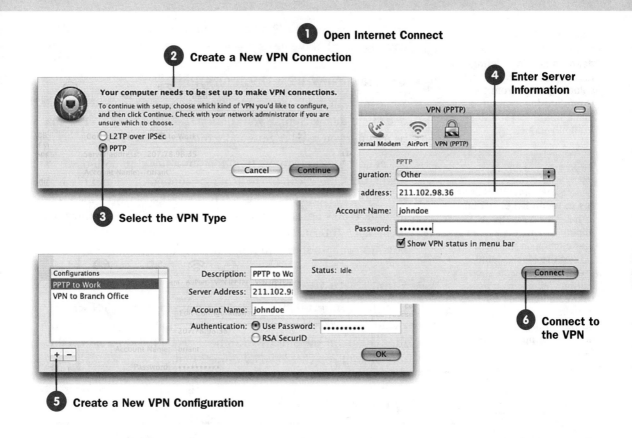

1 Open Internet Connect

2 Create a New VPN Connection

4 Enter Server Information

Your computer needs to be set up to make VPN connections.

To continue with setup, choose which kind of VPN you'd like to configure, and then click Continue. Check with your network administrator if you are unsure which to choose.

○ L2TP over IPSec
◉ PPTP

Cancel   Continue

3 Select the VPN Type

VPN (PPTP)

ternal Modem   AirPort   VPN (PPTP)

PPTP

guration: Other

address: 211.102.98.36

Account Name: johndoe

Password: ••••••••

☑ Show VPN status in menu bar

Status: Idle

Connect

Configurations
PPTP to Work
VPN to Branch Office

Description: PPTP to Wo

Server Address: 211.102.9

Account Name: johndoe

Authentication: ◉ Use Password: ••••••••••
                 ○ RSA SecurID

OK

+ −

6 Connect to the VPN

5 Create a New VPN Configuration

2 Create a New VPN Connection

Choose **File, New VPN Connection**. A sheet appears that prompts you for the type of VPN connection to make.

3 Select the VPN Type

Enable the radio button for either **L2TP/IPSec** or **PPTP**, depending on the kind of VPN you're using to connect. Consult your network administrator if you're not sure which kind of VPN it is. Click **Continue**.

4 Enter Server Information

The menu bar at the top of the **Internet Connect** window now has an icon for the new VPN connection, named either **VPN (L2TP/IPSec)** or **VPN (PPTP)** depending on the type you chose.

TIP

You can always manually define a new VPN configuration without saving it by selecting **Other** from the **Configuration** menu and filling in the server information yourself.

TIP

Enable the **Show VPN status in menu bar** check box to have the VPN status appear among the system menu icons on the right side of the Mac's global menu bar; this icon shows you how long you've been connected, as well as allowing you to select between multiple VPN tunnels and to open **Internet Connect**.

Enter the VPN server's IP address, your account username, and your password in the fields provided.

⑤ Create a New VPN Configuration

You can create more than one VPN configuration, and switch from one to another each time you connect. Having multiple VPNs can be useful if you regularly use more than one VPN.

Select **Edit Configurations** from the **Configuration** drop-down menu. Click the + icon to create a new configuration and fill in the server details. Click **OK** when you're done; this newly defined configuration now appears as the active configuration. From now on, if you open **Internet Connect** and click the **VPN** icon in the toolbar, this configuration will automatically appear.

⑥ Connect to the VPN

Click the **Connect** button. Mac OS X connects to the VPN server, exchanges account information, and sets up the tunnel. You can then communicate directly with the hosts on the other side of the tunnel until you click the **Disconnect** button.

---

34 Share Another Mac's Files

Before You Begin

✔ **29** Configure Networking Manually

✔ **44** Hook Up Over the Airwaves

See Also

→ **36** Allow Others to Share Your Files

→ **37** Share Files from a Windows PC

When your Macs are networked, you no longer have to keep copies of all your files and applications on each individual machine; you can store them all in one central location, and connect to that machine (the server) whenever you need to access those items. You can even create aliases to items hosted on remote servers, and when you try to open them, Mac OS X will mount the remote server automatically and open the item for you.

You can even connect to Macs that aren't on your local network; you can mount a shared resource from a computer in Boston onto your Desktop in San Francisco, as long as you know the remote computer's hostname or IP address.

① Open Finder Window

Create a new Finder window by clicking the **Finder** icon in the Dock or by pressing ⌘N.

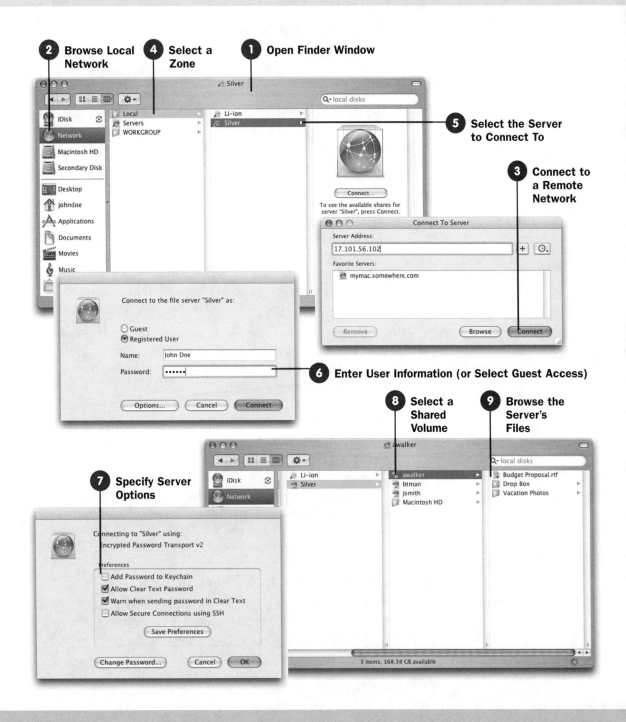

2 Browse Local Network

4 Select a Zone

1 Open Finder Window

5 Select the Server to Connect To

3 Connect to a Remote Network

Li-ion
Silver

To see the available shares for server "Silver", press Connect.

Connect...

Connect To Server

Server Address:

17.101.56.102

Favorite Servers:

mymac.somewhere.com

Remove   Browse   Connect

Connect to the file server "Silver" as:

○ Guest
● Registered User

Name: John Doe

Password: ••••••

Options...   Cancel   Connect

6 Enter User Information (or Select Guest Access)

8 Select a Shared Volume

9 Browse the Server's Files

7 Specify Server Options

Connecting to "Silver" using:
Encrypted Password Transport v2

Preferences

☐ Add Password to Keychain
☑ Allow Clear Text Password
☑ Warn when sending password in Clear Text
☐ Allow Secure Connections using SSH

Save Preferences

Change Password...   Cancel   OK

awalker

Li-ion   awalker   Budget Proposal.rtf
Silver   btman   Drop Box
                jsmith   Vacation Photos
                Macintosh HD

3 items, 168.38 GB available

② Browse the Local Network

Click the **Network** icon in the Finder's sidebar. This icon leads you to all the browseable resources available on the local network.

The Finder can show you only those servers on the local network (LAN). To connect to a server in a remote location on the Internet, or to go directly to a server whose name you know without having to browse, you can enter its network name, Internet hostname, or IP address manually as explained in step 3.

③ Connect to a Remote Network

Press ⌘K or select **Connect to Server** from the Finder's **Go** menu. Type into the **Server Address** box the hostname or IP address of the server you want to connect to, and then click **Connect**. You will then be presented with an authentication dialog box similar to the one you would get if you had browsed to the server on your local network. Type your name and password and click **Connect**.

Use the + button next to the **Server Address** box to add the server to your **Favorite Servers** list, and use the **History** button (the "analog clock face" icon next to the + button) to select from recently used server addresses.

④ Select a Zone

Most Macs today operate without *zones* (logical groupings of computers under descriptive names). Existing Mac-based networks that have always used *AppleTalk* for their in-house networking might have multiple named zones to choose from; click the name of the zone you want. If your network has only newer Macs, however, they will all be found in the **Local** zone. Double-click the zone (or single-click in Column view) to open the zone's server listing.

⑤ Select the Server to Connect To

Each of the available servers appears in the Finder window. Double-click the one to which you want to connect; in Column view, click the **Connect** button that appears in the preview pane. A dialog box appears that prompts you for your name and password, or to opt for guest access.

6 **Enter User Information (or Select Guest Access)**

If you have a registered user account on the Mac you're connecting to, enter your name (either your full name or your short name as specified when you first set up Mac OS X; see **146** **Add a New User** for more on users' full names and short names) and password and click **Connect**. If you don't have an account on that machine, click **Guest**; this will give you limited access to the publicly shared resources on the server to which you're connecting.

If you connect to a server directly, by typing in a machine name or IP address in the **Connect to Server** dialog box instead of by browsing, you can specify some extra options in the connection screen.

7 **Specify Server Options**

Before connecting, click the **Options** button to bring up a dialog box that permits you to set certain default behaviors for when you connect to a Mac server. For privacy and security, you will probably want to disable the **Allow Clear Text Password** option, and enable **Allow Secure Connections using SSH**. Enable the **Add Password to Keychain** option to save the password so that you don't have to remember it the next time you connect.

Be sure to click **Save Preferences** when you're done setting the options, so that they will be in effect the next time you connect to this Mac server.

8 **Select a Shared Volume**

All the server's shared resources (which are thought of as *volumes* in the context of file sharing) are accessible as soon as Mac OS X connects to the server. All these volumes are listed beneath the selected server in the Finder's hierarchy. If you've connected as a **Guest**, each user account appears as a volume; if you have authenticated with a user account instead, you can select from the physical disk volumes attached to the remote Mac as well as from your own **Home** folder.

NOTE

If you connect as a **Guest**, and you select any user's **Home** folder as the volume to mount, you are connected directly into that user's **Public** folder. You cannot browse any of the user's other files or folders.

NOTE

The Finder responds more slowly when you're browsing remote files than files locally mounted. All the information about the remote resources must be transferred to your computer as you browse, and if you open any document, the entire document must be transferred to your computer as well. The circular "progress" icon in the lower-right corner of a Finder window indicates that the system is transferring data.

TIP

You can send files to individual users on remote servers, privately, using the **Drop Box** folder inside each user's **Public** folder. To do this, connect as a Guest and navigate into the volume corresponding to the user's short name. Open the volume; then drag any items you wish to the user's **Drop Box** folder. The owner of the folder can then open the folder and retrieve the items.

9 Browse the Server's Files

If you've connected to the server directly, Mac OS X connects to the server and mounts the selected volume as a new data source in the Finder. The volume appears on the Desktop if you have configured it to do so; the volume also appears in the sidebar of any Finder window that is open. Click the icon for the volume and browse its contents as you would any other mounted volume.

If you've connected by browsing using the **Network** icon in the Finder, the server resources can be browsed using that icon's hierarchy. The server volumes do not appear on the Desktop, nor will they be listed in the Finder's sidebar.

---

 35 Run a Remotely Hosted Application

Before You Begin

✔ **2** Find and Launch an Application

✔ **34** Share Another Mac's Files

See Also

→ **36** Allow Others to Share Your Files

NOTE

Some commercial applications have built-in copy-protection and licensing schemes that prevent you from running the application on multiple computers at the same time. Read the license agreements for your commercial software to make sure that you're allowed to deploy it in this way.

You can simplify the maintenance of multiple computers by installing certain applications on only a single machine and letting the other Macs connect to that machine and run the application remotely. This saves you having to install the application separately on each Mac, although it does mean that it will take a little longer to launch the application remotely.

1 Mount the Remote Volume

Browse to the remote server in the Finder, and connect to the remote volume that contains the application. You will generally have to connect as an authenticated user so that you can access the complete disk volume containing the **Applications** folder. Make sure that you have a user account on the remote server!

2 Navigate to the Application

Use your preferred navigation method to open the **Applications** folder on the remote volume and locate the application you want to run.

Double-click the application to launch it.

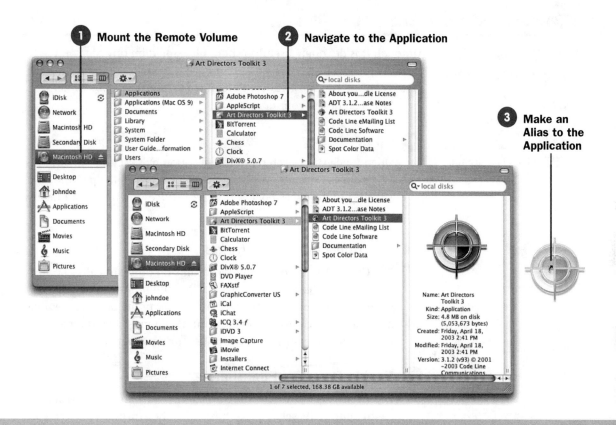

1 Mount the Remote Volume

2 Navigate to the Application

3 Make an Alias to the Application

1 of 7 selected, 168.38 GB available

3 ## Make an Alias to the Application

To gain quick access to a remotely hosted application in the future, make an alias to the application and keep the alias on your own computer. To do this, hold down the **Option** and ⌘ keys and drag the application icon to your own Finder or Desktop; alternatively, while the application is running, open the application's contextual menu from the Dock and select **Keep In Dock**.

When you double-click the alias in the Finder or click the application icon in the Dock, if the remote server isn't mounted, Mac OS X automatically mounts it, prompting you for your password if necessary.

NOTE

Because Mac OS X has no local Registry, as Windows does, and because of the "bundle" style of monolithic application construction on the Mac, most applications can be run from any volume on any computer, without the need for supporting libraries or other additional files to be installed on your computer. However, if the application is installed on one volume and has support information residing on another volume, you might not be able to run it remotely.

36 Allow Others to Share Your Files

Before You Begin

✔ **32** Share Your Internet Connection

✔ **34** Share Another Mac's Files

See Also

→ **37** Share Files from a Windows PC

Although it is definitely useful to share files stored on any Mac on the network, privacy concerns dictate that each Mac be set up by default to share nothing. You must enable **Personal File Sharing** before other computers can access your data.

1 Open Sharing Preferences

Open the **System Preferences** application by selecting **System Preferences** from the **Apple** menu. Click **Sharing** to open the **Sharing Preferences** page. Click the **Services** tab if it's not already selected.

2 Set Your Computer's Name

The **Computer Name** text box contains an automatically chosen name for your computer, based on your full name (for instance, **John Doe's Computer**). Enter a more appropriate or more creative name for your computer if you want; this name is what remote users browsing your network for file-sharing servers will see.

3 Enable Personal File Sharing

Enable the **Personal File Sharing** check box in the **Select a service to change its settings** list box. Click the **Start** button or the corresponding check box in the **On** column to start up Personal File Sharing.

4 Place Files in Your Public Folder

With Personal File Sharing enabled, anybody in the world can connect to your computer—they can browse to it by name on the local network or, if they know your IP address or hostname, they can connect to it directly without browsing. If the remote user doesn't have an account on your Mac, he can only connect using Guest access; but with that level of access, he can mount your **Public** folder (or any other user's **Public** folder) and browse its contents.

Place files in the **Public** folder inside your **Home** folder to make them publicly accessible. Be sure to avoid placing anything in that folder that you wouldn't want the whole world to see!

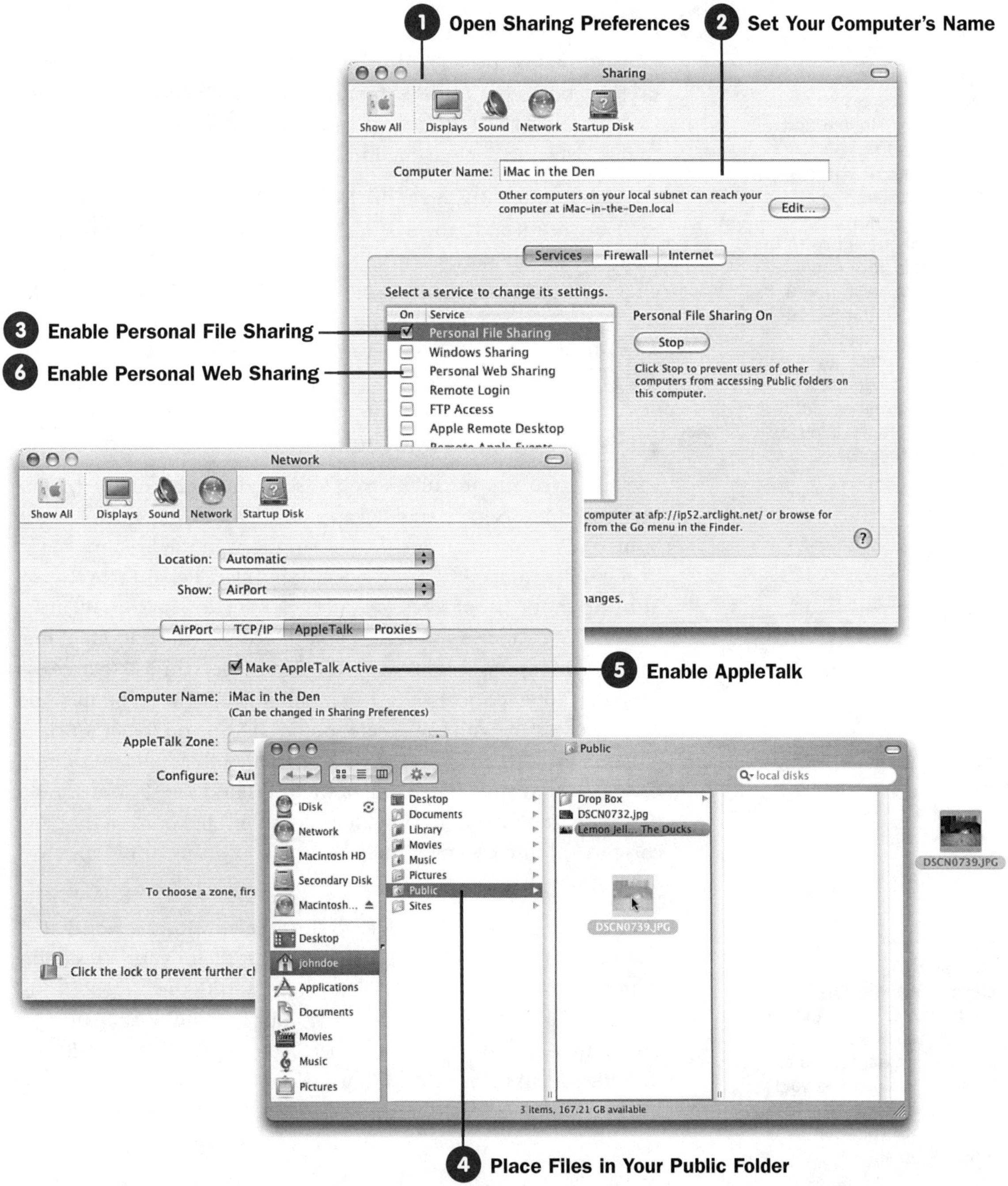
1 Open Sharing Preferences
2 Set Your Computer's Name
3 Enable Personal File Sharing
6 Enable Personal Web Sharing
5 Enable AppleTalk
4 Place Files in Your Public Folder
Sharing
Show All
Displays
Sound
Network
Startup Disk
Computer Name: iMac in the Den
Other computers on your local subnet can reach your computer at iMac-in-the-Den.local
Edit...
Services
Firewall
Internet
Select a service to change its settings.
On
Service
Personal File Sharing
Windows Sharing
Personal Web Sharing
Remote Login
FTP Access
Apple Remote Desktop
Personal File Sharing On
Stop
Click Stop to prevent users of other computers from accessing Public folders on this computer.
computer at afp://ip52.arclight.net/ or browse for
from the Go menu in the Finder.
Network
Location: Automatic
Show: AirPort
AirPort
TCP/IP
AppleTalk
Proxies
Make AppleTalk Active
Computer Name: iMac in the Den
(Can be changed in Sharing Preferences)
AppleTalk Zone:
Configure:
To choose a zone, firs
Click the lock to prevent further cl
Public
local disks
iDisk
Network
Macintosh HD
Secondary Disk
Macintosh...
Desktop
johndoe
Applications
Documents
Movies
Music
Pictures
Desktop
Documents
Library
Movies
Music
Pictures
Public
Sites
Drop Box
DSCN0732.jpg
Lemon Jell... The Ducks
DSCN0739.JPG
3 items, 167.21 GB available

⑤ Enable AppleTalk

Modern Personal File Sharing on the Mac uses AppleShare/IP, a protocol based on the older proprietary *AppleTalk* that is designed to operate over TCP/IP (meaning that it can be used over standard routed networks such as the Internet).

To enable AppleTalk, open the **Network Preferences** page (click the **Network** icon in the **System Preferences** application window). Double-click the network interface you want to use (you can enable AppleTalk on only a single interface at a time), then click the **AppleTalk** tab. Use the options in that screen to make AppleTalk active, select an existing zone, or create your own zone. See **31** **Enable AppleTalk** for details.

⑥ Enable Personal Web Sharing

Personal Web Sharing allows you to share files with anybody who has a Web browser. To enable Personal Web Sharing, open **Sharing Preferences** (click the **Sharing** icon in the **System Preferences**), and click the **Services** tab. Select **Personal Web Sharing** in the list of services, and click the **Start** button. When Personal Web Sharing starts up, text appears at the bottom of the window informing you of two URLs that others can use to access your Mac: one for accessing the global page for the computer, and one for accessing your own **Personal Web Sharing** folder. Click either of the URLs to view the pages to which they refer, or right-click (or **Control**+click) on one of the URLs and select **Copy** from the contextual menu to copy the URL to the Clipboard so that you can paste it into an email message or a text document in another application.

Place files into your **Sites** folder to share them with the world. If you name a file **index.html** and place that file in your **Sites** folder, that file becomes the "default" page for the URL that is reported in the **Sharing Preferences** window for your Personal Web Sharing site; it appears if no filename is specified at the end of the URL. (If no **index.html** file is present, a user can browse the list of files in the folder.)

37 Share Files from a Windows PC

Mac OS X can share files with Windows machines just as easily as it can with other Macs; in fact, it can be more straightforward to network a Mac and a Windows PC together than to network two PCs.

Sharing files with Windows machines is a two-way process; first you must mount a remote Windows machine as a volume on your Mac, and then you have to set up your Mac to share its own files with Windows users.

1 **Browse the Network in the Finder**

Open a Finder window; click the **Network** icon in the sidebar. The available Windows domains and workgroups appear in the column view listing along with any Mac *zones*.

2 **Select a Domain or Workgroup**

Click the name of the *domain* or *workgroup* containing the Windows machine you want to use.

A Windows domain is managed by a *domain controller*, a Windows computer whose administrator controls all the computers in the domain. User accounts on Windows machines that are part of a domain authenticate their passwords with the domain controller, not the client Windows machine itself.

From the Mac standpoint, there is really no practical difference between a workgroup and a domain; both operate the same way to the Mac.

3 **Select the Windows Server to Connect To**

The name of each available Windows server appears in all capital letters. Double-click the one you want to connect to; if you're in Column view, select the server and click the **Connect** button in the preview pane. The server's **SMB/CIFS Authentication** dialog box appears.

4 **Enter User Information**

To connect to a Windows machine, you must have a username and password for that machine. Enter that information in the dialog box and enable the **Add to Keychain** check box if you want to save the password for future connections. Click **OK** to connect.

Before You Begin

✔ **34** Share Another Mac's Files

✔ **36** Allow Others to Share Your Files

🔍KEY TERMS

Zone—A named collection of Macs in an AppleTalk network. AppleTalk zones have no built-in authentication; they're just logical groupings for more convenient access.

Workgroup—In Windows, a workgroup is very similar to an AppleTalk zone—it's simply a name used to group Windows computers together so that they can be browsed more meaningfully.

Domain—Centrally managed groups of Windows computers with centralized password management and administration.

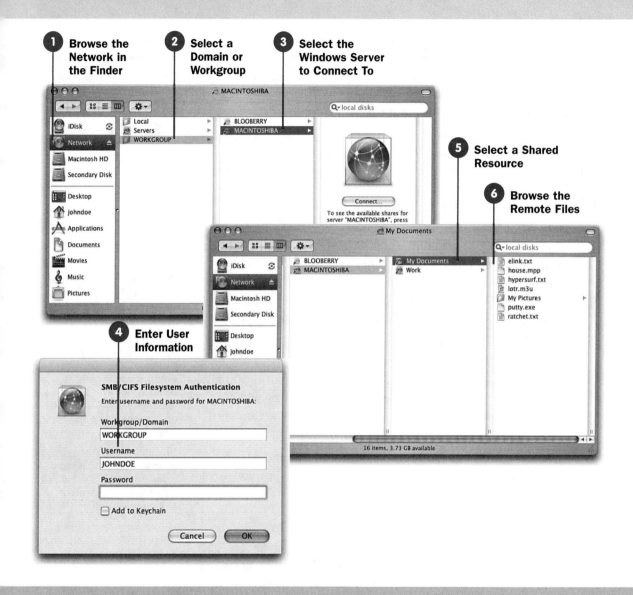

1 Browse the Network in the Finder

2 Select a Domain or Workgroup

3 Select the Windows Server to Connect To

5 Select a Shared Resource

6 Browse the Remote Files

4 Enter User Information

---

5 **Select a Shared Resource**

After your user information is authenticated, the Windows server is mounted in the Finder and shown in the sidebar. You can navigate into it to choose a shared resource (also called a *share*). Shares are individual folders configured on the Windows machine for sharing.

All shared folders configured under the account you used for authentication are available for you to mount.

6 Browse the Remote Files

Navigate into any available share; you can then browse it as you would any other volume.

38 Allow Windows Users to Share Your Files

Setting up your Mac OS X machine to allow Windows users to access it is very similar to configuring it for Mac-based access. The only difference is that because Windows file sharing requires you to authenticate with a real user account and not with Guest access, each Windows user who wants to access your Mac must have a user account on your Mac. See **146** **Add a New User** for how to add a new user on your Mac.

1 Open Sharing Preferences

Open the **System Preferences** application by selecting **Preferences** from the **Apple** menu. Click **Sharing** to open the **Sharing Preferences** page. Click the **Services** tab if it's not already selected.

2 Enable Windows Sharing

Select the **Windows Sharing** option in the **Select a service to change its settings** box and click the **Start** button or enable the corresponding check box in the **On** column to start up Windows Sharing.

If your Mac has been running Mac OS X since version 10.0 or 10.1, you might have difficulty connecting to it from a Windows machine; this is because Windows Sharing requires a separate encrypted password database to be stored on your Mac, and that database did not exist in earlier versions of Mac OS X. If your user accounts were created before that password database existed, Windows users won't be able to connect to your Mac using those accounts.

To solve this problem, open the **Accounts Preferences** page and change each user's password. You can change each password to the same string as the current password, if you want. When you do this, Mac OS X creates the necessary entry in the Windows File Sharing password database, enabling Windows users to connect properly.

Before You Begin

✔ **36** Allow Others to Share Your Files

✔ **37** Share Files from a Windows PC

🔔 TIP

By default, your Mac is a member of the workgroup called **WORKGROUP**. You might want to change this name so that you can browse an existing workgroup of a different name or so that others can connect to your Mac using an existing domain. To do this, open the **Directory Access** application (found in the **Utilities** folder inside **Applications**). Authenticate as an administrator by clicking the lock icon at the bottom. Then double-click **SMB** and type the desired workgroup or domain name in the sheet that appears. You can specify a WINS server as well, if necessary. Click **OK** and then quit **Directory Access**.

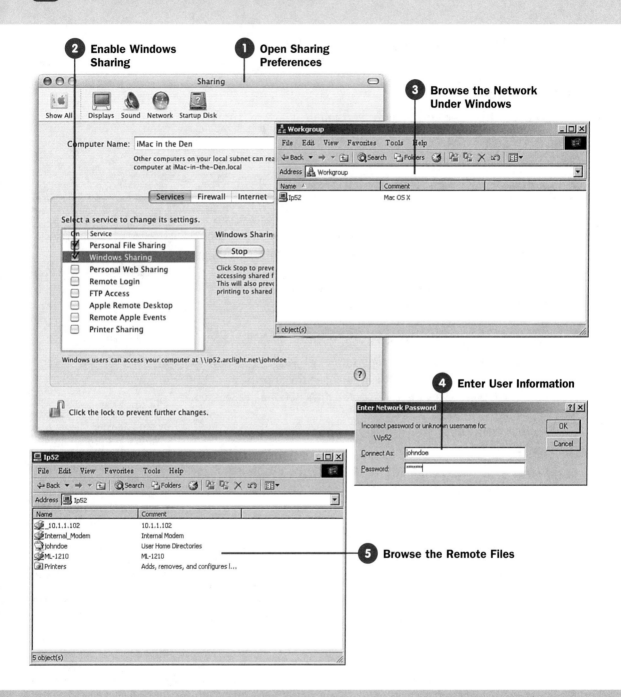

2 Enable Windows Sharing

1 Open Sharing Preferences

3 Browse the Network Under Windows

4 Enter User Information

5 Browse the Remote Files

③ Browse the Network Under Windows

On a Windows machine on the same network as your Mac, open the **My Network Places** window; navigate to **Entire Network**, then **Microsoft Windows Network**. Open the workgroup called **Workgroup**. You should then see the hostnames for your Mac and any other Samba-based machines on your network.

④ Enter User Information

Double-click the entry representing your Mac. A dialog box pops up, prompting you for a username and password. Depending on the version of Windows, this dialog box could report an **Incorrect password or unknown username** error; this is normal. Enter the requested information, matching the account information on the Mac, and click **OK**.

Windows 2000 and later allows you to specify both a username and a password when connecting to a remote server. However, the Windows 95/98 series allows you to enter only a password; the username is derived from your Windows profile name. If you're using one of these older versions of Windows, you must be using a Windows profile with the same name as the short name of the account you're connecting to on the Mac. Consult your network administrator for assistance in finding out or changing your Windows profile name.

If the check box is present (not all versions of Windows have one), click the **Remember my password** check box to save the password for future connections.

⑤ Browse the Remote Files

After authenticating successfully, the available shares on the Mac appear in the window; these include the **Home** folder for the account you've authenticated for, the Mac's built-in modem, and any connected printers. You can navigate these items, create shortcuts to them, and access them as though they were local or served from another Windows machine.

After you have authenticated once, you won't have to do so again for your current Windows session. However, if you log out or reboot the Windows machine, you must authenticate again.

NOTE

If your Mac started life with Mac OS X 10.2 (Jaguar) or later, or if your user accounts were all created using these recent versions, Windows users should be able to access your Mac without difficulty.

NOTE

Your Mac will appear in the Windows network by its hostname as determined by a reverse network lookup (in this example, the hostname is **lp52**). Make sure that the proper hostname is associated with your machine's IP address in order for it to show up correctly in the listing! If it is not, depending on the version of Windows you're using, you might see only a string representing the version of Samba (an open-source Windows file-sharing utility common in the Linux and Unix worlds) your Mac is using (for instance, **Samba** followed by a version number). Contact your network administrator for assistance if this happens.

39 Discover iChat Partners

Before You Begin

✔ **77** Set Up Your AIM or .Mac Account

See Also

→ **79** Add a Buddy

→ **80** Start a Chat Session

With *Rendezvous* technology built into Mac OS X, your home or office network becomes an auto-configured communication switchboard. iChat and Mail, two of the applications included with Mac OS X, take advantage of Rendezvous to take you from the delayed communication of email to the direct and instant communication of text or audio/video chat.

❶ Open iChat

Open a Finder window and navigate to the **Applications** folder; double-click the **iChat** icon. You can also click the **iChat** icon in the Dock to launch the application.

❷ Turn On Rendezvous Messaging

Choose **iChat**, **Preferences** and click the **Accounts** icon. Click the **Enable local Rendezvous messaging** check box, if it isn't already checked. This option allows your version of iChat to discover other iChat users who are on the same local network.

❸ Open the Rendezvous Window

Choose **Window**, **Rendezvous** or press ⌘2. iChat's Rendezvous window appears, showing all the other iChat users who are also on your local network. Double-click any of the user names in the list to begin a chat session.

TIP

Update your Address Book to make sure that the email address for each of your contacts is the same as the one she uses for iChat! Remember that you can enter multiple email addresses in Address Book for each person.

❹ Contact iChat Partners from Mail

From the Dock or the **Applications** folder, launch **Mail** and view your Inbox. If any messages in it were sent to you from someone in your Address Book who is currently using iChat, a green dot appears next to their name in the message listing. Click the dot to begin a direct iChat session with that person. You can also click the down arrow next to the person's name in the message pane to see several more communication options, as well as to start an iChat session.

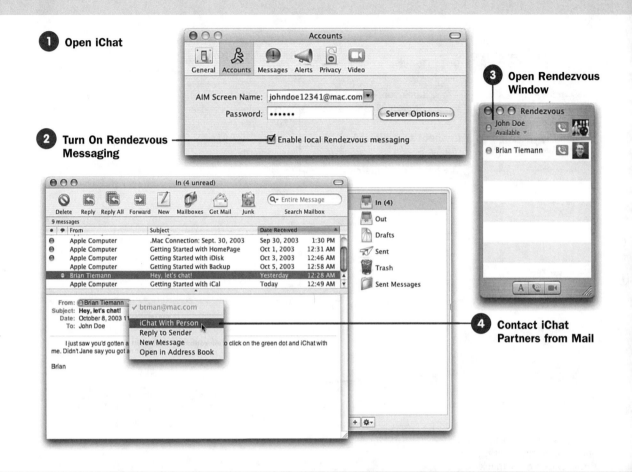

1 Open iChat

2 Turn On Rendezvous Messaging

3 Open Rendezvous Window

4 Contact iChat Partners from Mail

40 Discover Shared Music

Before You Begin

✔ **98** Import or Rip an Audio CD

✔ **100** Create a Playlist

See Also

→ **99** Purchase Music from the iTunes Music Store

With iTunes' Shared Music feature, you no longer have to keep all your music on all your Macs, using up huge amounts of disk space on every one. Instead, you can store all your music on a central Mac and play it from any other machine in the house or office using *Rendezvous*.

If you have music in your iTunes **Library** that you purchased from the iTunes Music Store, you must authorize each computer that you want to use to play that purchased music—and you can authorize only three computers to share that music. Use this power wisely!

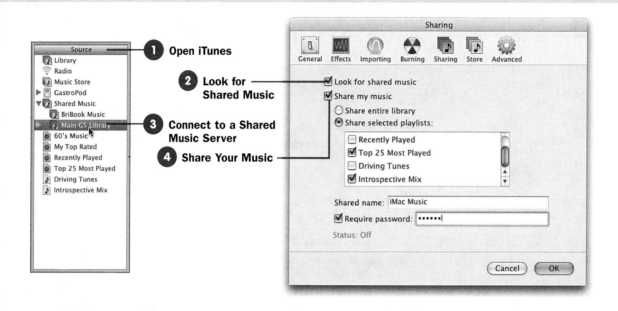

1 **Open iTunes**

2 **Look for Shared Music**

3 **Connect to a Shared Music Server**

4 **Share Your Music**

NOTE

If you have the Mac OS X firewall enabled, you must open a hole in it to allow iTunes **Music Sharing** to occur. Open the **Sharing Preferences** page (click **Sharing** in the **System Preferences** application window) and click the **Firewall** tab; in the **Allow** box, enable the **iTunes Music Sharing (port 3689)** option to allow other users to connect to your copy of iTunes.

TIP

After you select a shared music source, you can browse it as you would your own music **Library**.

1 **Open iTunes**

Open a Finder window and navigate to the **Applications** folder; double-click the **iTunes** icon. You can also click the **iTunes** icon in the Dock to launch the application.

2 **Look for Shared Music**

From the **iTunes** menu, choose **Preferences**; click the **Sharing** icon. In the **Sharing Preferences** page, enable the **Look for shared music** check box (if it isn't already enabled). This option allows iTunes to discover other Macs running iTunes on the local network and to stream their shared music libraries to your Mac.

3 **Connect to a Shared Music Server**

Shared music libraries on the local network appear in the **Source** list in the left pane of the iTunes window, above any playlists you have created and below the **Music Store** and any devices (such as iPods) you have connected. If there are multiple shared music libraries on the network, they are grouped under a **Shared Music** entry; click the triangle to expand the entry and show all the shared music servers.

④ Share Your Music

To allow other Mac users on your local network to share your music, go back to the iTunes **Preferences** window, reopen the **Sharing** pane, and enable the **Share my music** check box (if it isn't already checked). You can choose to either share your entire music library, or share only selected playlists.

In the **Shared name** text box, specify a name for your shared music library; this name is what will appear in other iTunes users' **Source** lists. You can also specify a password, if you want to restrict your music to certain other users.

④① Discover Nearby Web Sites

Mac OS X allows any Mac to be a Web server, hosting files that can be accessed from anywhere in the world using only a browser. However, if you don't know the IP address or hostname for each Mac, the usefulness of this feature is limited.

It's common, though, for individuals in a household or office network to use Personal Web Sharing to make certain files available just to the other members of the household or office. *Rendezvous* makes this possible without requiring anybody to know the hostnames or IP addresses of the Macs that are sharing the files. In **Safari**, Apple's built-in Web browser, you only have to go to the **Rendezvous** section of your bookmarks to see all the Web sites hosted by Macs on the local network along with the status pages for all Rendezvous-enabled printers.

① Open Safari

Open a Finder window and navigate to the **Applications** folder; double-click the **Safari** icon. You can also click the **Safari** icon in the Dock to launch the application.

② Open the Bookmarks Pane

Click the **Bookmarks** icon (at the far left of the **Bookmarks** bar). If the **Bookmarks** bar is hidden, choose **Show All Bookmarks** from the **Bookmarks** menu (or press ⌘+**Option**+**B**). The **Bookmarks** pane opens, showing all your bookmarks in their various collections.

Before You Begin

✔ **69** Keep Track of Web Sites with Bookmarks

See Also

→ **71** Access Your Bookmarks Using .Mac

🎤 TIP

Personal Web Sharing uses your **Sites** folder as its Web root; in other words, the URL **http://your.host.name/ ~johndoe** will show you the contents of John Doe's **Sites** folder, or (if one exists) the **index.html** file inside that folder. The default settings for the built-in Apache Web server (which is what powers Personal Web Sharing) are such that if you don't have an **index.html** file in your **Sites** folder, you will be able to see a file listing of that folder and access every file in your browser. Make sure to put an **index.html** file in your **Sites** folder if you want to hide its contents from other users!

1 Open Safari   **2** Open the Bookmarks Pane   **4** Go to Local Web Site

3 View Rendezvous Locations

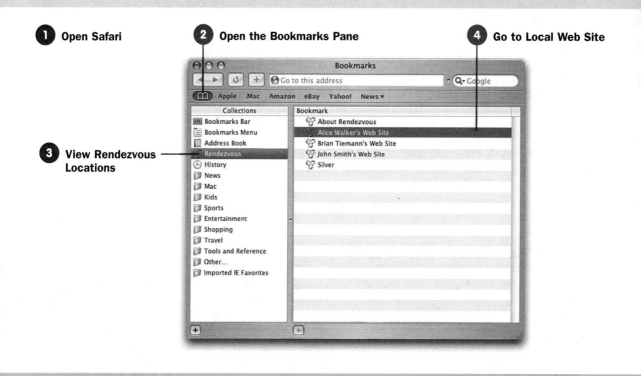

3 View Rendezvous Locations

Click the **Rendezvous** entry in the **Collections** list. All the Web sites served by Macs (or Rendezvous-enabled printers) on the local network appear in the list, named according to the full name of the owner of the account hosting each site.

4 Go to Local Web Site

Double-click any listed site to open it in the same Safari window.

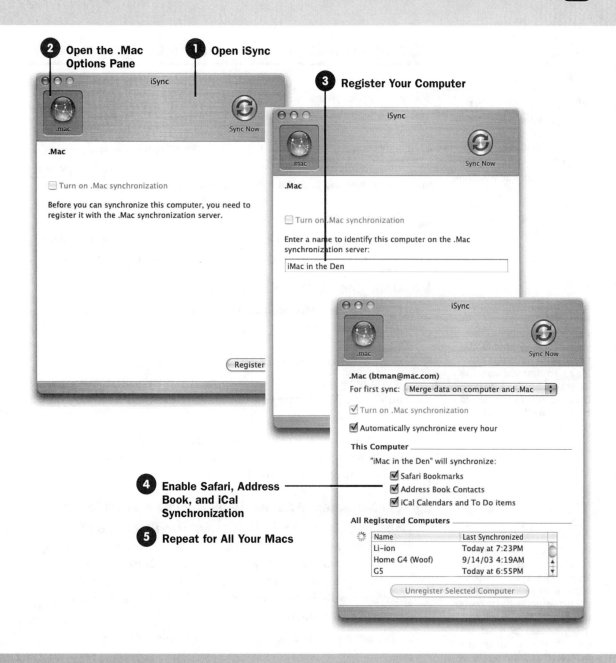

2 Open the .Mac Options Pane

1 Open iSync

3 Register Your Computer

iSync

.mac

Sync Now

.Mac

☐ Turn on .Mac synchronization

Before you can synchronize this computer, you need to register it with the .Mac synchronization server.

Register

iSync

.mac

Sync Now

.Mac

☐ Turn on .Mac synchronization

Enter a name to identify this computer on the .Mac synchronization server:

iMac in the Den

iSync

.mac

Sync Now

.Mac (btman@mac.com)
For first sync: Merge data on computer and .Mac ◆

☑ Turn on .Mac synchronization

☑ Automatically synchronize every hour

This Computer

"iMac in the Den" will synchronize:
  ☑ Safari Bookmarks
  ☑ Address Book Contacts
  ☑ iCal Calendars and To Do items

All Registered Computers

Name	Last Synchronized
Li-ion	Today at 7:23PM
Home G4 (Woof)	9/14/03 4:19AM
G5	Today at 6:55PM

Unregister Selected Computer

4 Enable Safari, Address Book, and iCal Synchronization

5 Repeat for All Your Macs

42 Synchronize Your Information Using .Mac

Before You Begin

✔ **50** Sign Up for .Mac

✔ **69** Keep Track of Web Sites with Bookmarks

✔ **120** Add a Person to Your Address Book

See Also

→ **127** Synchronize Your .Mac Address Book

TIP

The registered name for your computer should distinguish it from your other Macs, so that you can see its status easily in iSync. Good names to use would be **iMac at Work** or **New iBook**.

NOTE

Because each computer must merge its information with what's in the central .Mac database, and then each computer must merge that information back to itself, it could take two or even three sync processes before all your bookmarks have propagated completely to all your Macs.

If you have a .Mac account, it can take all your disparate Macs—your desktop G5, your iBook, your iMac at work—and tie them all together so that you always have your critical information at your fingertips no matter which Mac you're using. **iSync** is the tool to use for this; you need only to register each computer with .Mac using iSync, set it up to synchronize your information automatically using the central .Mac server, and never think about keeping your Address Book and iCal events up-to-date again.

1 Open iSync

Launch iSync by double-clicking its icon in the **Applications** folder, or by selecting **Open iSync** from the **iSync** menu in the menu bar.

2 Open the .Mac Options Pane

Click the large **.Mac** icon at the left side of the iSync window. The .Mac options appear.

3 Register Your Computer

If you have never used iSync before, you must register your computer with .Mac before you can synchronize it. Click the **Register** button to do this.

Type a name that will identify your computer, if you don't like the one that's automatically suggested for you. Click **Continue** after you've entered a name for the computer.

4 Enable Safari, Address Book, and iCal Synchronization

After your computer is registered with .Mac, the options for synchronization appear on the iSync window. Make sure that the check boxes for **Safari Bookmarks**, **Address Book Contacts**, and **iCal Calendars and To Do Items** are all selected. Enable the **Automatically synchronize every hour** check box to have iSync do its work without any input from you.

Click **Sync Now** to kick off the first synchronization process.

5 Repeat for All Your Macs

On each of your Macs, open iSync and register it. After each one has synchronized, all your contacts, bookmarks, and calendar items will be the same across all your Macs.

5

Going Mobile

IN THIS CHAPTER:

Networking takes on a whole new dimension when you unplug the Ethernet cable or phone line and go wireless. Apple's *AirPort* technology introduced the computing world to the freedom of *802.11* wireless networking back in 1999, and it's become one of the great hits of our time. Wireless-enabled coffee shops, restaurants, bookstores, and other public locales are springing up daily, giving patrons the ability to shed the chains of a stationary, hard-coded Internet configuration. It's all dynamic and automatic now, and the future will only be more so, as sales of laptops (both in the Windows world and among Macs) continue to outstrip sales of even the most powerful desktop computers. Mobility is a much-prized commodity these days.

Wireless networking involves two basic pieces of equipment you have to know about: the AirPort or AirPort Extreme card, and the AirPort Base Station.

The AirPort Base Station, sold by Apple for about $200, is a device that broadcasts the wireless network signal to your computer. There might be one (or a compatible device, often referred to as an "access point") installed already at your workplace, or you might choose to buy one to set up a home wireless network. It's a fairly complex piece of networking equipment in that it acts as a wireless hub, media bridge, NAT router, and DHCP server; the details of its operation are beyond the scope of this book and will not be addressed here.

NOTE

AirPort is Apple's term for 802.11b, currently the most common form of wireless networking. 802.11b can transmit data at up to 11 megabits per second, at a signal range of 50 feet. *AirPort Extreme* is Apple's implementation of 802.11g, the next-generation standard for wireless networking. 802.11g is backward-compatible with 802.11b (devices using both can share the same network), but it transmits at up to 54 megabits per second. The signal range is the same as that of 802.11b.

The AirPort card, AirPort Extreme card, and AirPort Base Station make it possible for your Mac to connect to other users without a hard-wired Internet connection.

Many Mac models come with the AirPort card built-in, but you can install such a card in any Mac, whether a desktop or a laptop. Portable computers (PowerBooks and iBooks) are clearly the ones most likely to benefit from the mobility of AirPort, but stationary desktop computers can reap the rewards too—you can wire an entire household for Internet access without stringing any Ethernet cables under carpets or over doors.

True, AirPort is somewhat slower than Ethernet, and there's always the issue of signal strength, especially in larger houses; but because most Internet connections—even broadband—are nowhere near as fast as AirPort is, in real-world terms you're not going to see the disadvantage. Downloading a Web page over AirPort will be just as fast as over Ethernet because the speed bottleneck is in the Internet link itself, not in the LAN. The freedom afforded to you and your computer by AirPort, and the ability to roam freely from home to work to the coffee shop, more than make up for the slight speed penalty wireless networking incurs.

If you have a portable Mac that you frequently take with you from one place to another, chances are that you will often have to switch back and forth between the network configurations that are compatible with each place you go. You might have one set of TCP/IP settings at home, another one at work, and another one at your favorite wireless-enabled coffee shop. It's no fun to have to constantly open up the **Network Preferences** page and enter a new set of TCP/IP settings. Mac OS X makes configuring TCP/IP much more direct than Windows does, but it's still not the best use of several minutes of your time when you've just opened up your PowerBook to show someone a cool Web site.

Fortunately, there's a way to avoid all that tedious configuration: *locations*. All the TCP/IP configuration that you now know how to do is all part of a "location," which is a configuration profile that applies to a certain network environment. If you have other network environments, each of those can have its own location, and its own associated TCP/IP settings. Then, whenever you go from one place to another, you have simply to select which networking location you want to use, and the associated configuration will automatically go into effect.

A location can contain not just TCP/IP settings, but also a profile of which network ports are active. For instance, you might have an Ethernet network at the office, but only AirPort at home; switching from your **Work** location to your **Home** location can disable the Ethernet port

KEY TERM

Location—A set of network configuration settings defined in association with a certain networking environment, such as your home or work network. Switching from one location to another immediately changes your networking settings.

and enable AirPort. A location can also include *VPN* settings, as well as a unique preference list for what network devices you do have available.

Of crucial importance to mobile computing is power management. You must configure your iBook or PowerBook to use its precious battery power efficiently on long airline flights, and yet to be able to take advantage of continuous power through a wall adapter if it's plugged in by increasing its processor speed and keeping the display lit. Because configuring your Mac's power-saving behavior is applicable to all Macs, and not just laptops, power management is covered in Chapter 16, "Managing Power and Accessibility Options."

43 Install an AirPort Card

NOTE

Be sure to buy only a genuine AirPort card made by Apple. Although many companies sell 802.11 wireless cards, only Apple's are certified to be compatible with your Mac. Also, be sure to check whether your Mac supports AirPort or AirPort Extreme; the cards are different shapes, and only one will fit properly in your Mac.

If your Mac didn't come with an AirPort card already installed, you can always buy one off the shelf and install it yourself. Every Mac has a slightly different installation procedure, but it's always printed clearly on the interior where you can find it if you open the computer.

1 Turn Off and Open Your Mac

Caution: Although some Macs can be opened while they're running, don't try to install an AirPort card without turning off your Mac first! If you do, you could damage both the card and the Mac. The interior of your computer contains many sensitive parts, such as the hard drive, memory, and power supply. Some of these components can be damaged easily, and others (such as the power supply) can damage *you.* If you have any doubts at all about how to work inside your computer, consider having the work done by a certified Apple Reseller or Apple Store.

After shutting down the computer, find the *User Guide* that came with it and look up the section that describes the process of installing an AirPort card. If you don't have your *User Guide*, don't despair—all you should have to do is find out how to open the computer, and the instructions for installing an AirPort card will be printed on the inside.

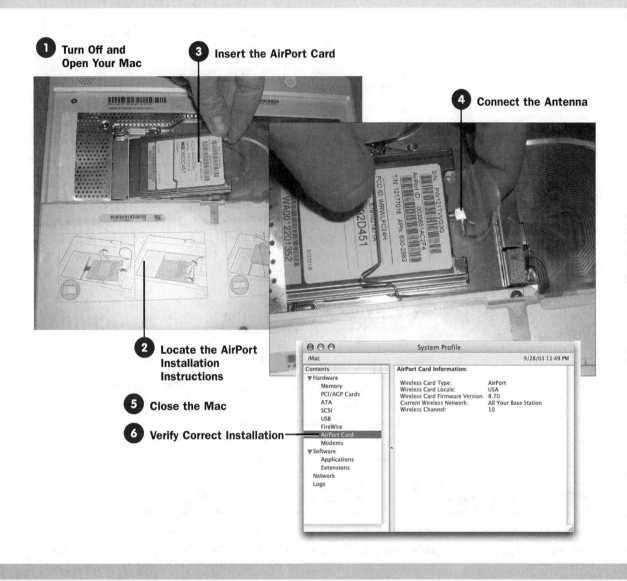

1. **Turn Off and Open Your Mac**

3. **Insert the AirPort Card**

4. **Connect the Antenna**

2. **Locate the AirPort Installation Instructions**

5. **Close the Mac**

6. **Verify Correct Installation**

System Profile

iMac

Contents

AirPort Card Information:

▼ Hardware
   Memory
   PCI/AGP Cards
   ATA
   SCSI
   USB
   FireWire
   AirPort Card
   Modems
▼ Software
   Applications
   Extensions
Network
Logs

9/28/03 11:49 PM

Wireless Card Type: AirPort
Wireless Card Locale: USA
Wireless Card Firmware Version: 8.70
Current Wireless Network: All Your Base Station
Wireless Channel: 10

iBooks can be opened by lifting out the keyboard; PowerBooks generally have a hatch on the bottom that opens. Flat-panel iMacs are opened by unscrewing the round metal plate on the bottom, and eMacs and colored iMacs have a plastic panel on the bottom that lifts out after you insert a coin into the key slot and turn. Power Mac G4s open when you pull the ring on the side, and the Power Mac G5 has a panel on the side that you lift off.

2 Locate the AirPort Installation Instructions

Attached to the inside of the Mac, either in the body or on the inside of the door, is a label that shows how to install an AirPort card as well as additional RAM. Remove the AirPort card from its protective packaging and orient it as shown in the diagram.

3 Insert the AirPort Card

Install the card in the slot as directed in the diagram; if there is a metal bail, lift it over the card to lock it into place.

4 Connect the Antenna

There is a small wire with a metal tip near the opposite end of the AirPort card from the connectors. This is the antenna. Press the tip into the hole on the AirPort card to connect it.

5 Close the Mac

Replace the cover or door of your Mac, and boot it up.

6 Verify Correct Installation

To verify that your AirPort card was installed correctly, choose **About This Mac** from the **Apple** menu, then click **More Info**. The **Apple System Profile** appears. If the AirPort card is installed properly, an **AirPort Card** entry appears under the **Hardware** heading in the left pane.

44 Hook Up Over the Airwaves

Before You Begin

✔ **43** Install an AirPort Card

See Also

→ **45** Set Up AirPort to Automatically Reconnect

→ **47** Create and Configure a Location

You're walking down the street, and you see one of those telltale chalk marks on a building that means "open wireless network." Or you wander into a store in the mall that advertises free wireless Internet access, or you're sitting in the airport terminal with nothing to do but wait for your flight. You see other people with laptops typing happily away. How do you, your Mac, and AirPort join in?

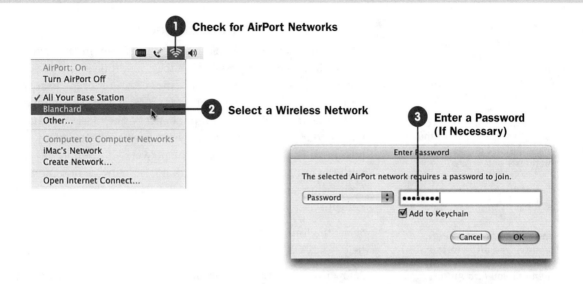

① Check for AirPort Networks

② Select a Wireless Network

③ Enter a Password (If Necessary)

www.warchalking.org

A Web site devoted to the hobo-style chalk marks made on buildings and sidewalks to indicate the presence of a wireless network.

① Check for AirPort Networks

Click the **AirPort Status** system menu icon on the right side of the Mac's menu bar. The resulting menu lists all the public AirPort networks that are within range, displayed by their network names. If no networks are present, a message saying **No AirPort networks within range** appears instead.

② Select a Wireless Network

Choose a network to join, and click its name in the **AirPort Status** system menu. Mac OS X attempts to connect to the network.

"Private" (or "closed") networks do not appear in the **AirPort Status** system menu. You can still connect to them, however. To do this, select **Other** from the menu; a dialog box appears, asking for the name of the network you want to join, and a password (along with several encryption methods if the network uses WEP encryption) if one is required. The network name is case sensitive, so make sure that you know it exactly.

💡 **TIP**

You can't tell from the menu which networks have the strongest signal, but there's a way to check. Click to open and close the **AirPort Status** system menu several times. If some of the networks in the list have a very weak signal, they might disappear and reappear from the list. Try to select a network that stays steadily in the list, or try to discover the location of the base station (if you know who owns it, ask) and move closer to it.

NOTE

If the **AirPort Status** system menu doesn't show on your Mac, turn it on in the **Internet Connect** application, found in the **Applications** folder. Open **Internet Connect**, click the **AirPort** toolbar icon, and enable the **Show AirPort status in menu bar** check box.

TIP

You can turn your AirPort card on and off from the **AirPort Status** system menu. If you turn AirPort off, you can save a fair amount of battery power. It's a good idea to turn off AirPort if you know you're not going to be near a wireless network anytime soon.

③ Enter a Password (If Necessary)

The owner of the wireless network you've chosen might have configured it to require a password. If so, it might be in one of several different forms. Depending on the manufacturer of the base station and whether WEP encryption is enabled, you might have to enter an encrypted string of alphabetical or hexadecimal characters as your password. Other networks might accept a plain-text password. The administrator of the network will be able to tell you both the format and the password; if it's a network in a public area, where you don't know the administrator, then it's a private network that you won't be able to join.

Select the format for the password, and type the password into the field. Click **OK** to join the network.

Allow five to ten seconds for Mac OS X to apply the network settings and for the network to become usable.

Some public networks (such as those in airport terminals) allow you to connect without a password to the wireless network, but then ask you for credit card information as soon as you try to go anywhere on the Web. After you enter this information and purchase some time on the wireless network, your computer can access any Internet resource you want.

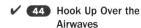**Set Up AirPort to Automatically Reconnect**

Before You Begin

✔ **44** Hook Up Over the Airwaves

See Also

→ **47** Create and Configure a Location

If you frequently go to a certain place with a wireless network that you have to join manually each time you open your laptop, you might find it useful to configure Mac OS X to automatically reconnect to that network. This way, you'll be able to be online as soon as you activate the computer.

① Open Network Preferences

Open the **System Preferences** application by choosing **System Preferences** from the **Apple** menu. Click the **Network** icon to go to the **Network Preferences** page.

If you've set up a *location* for the place where you use the wireless network, select it from the **Location** drop-down menu.

1 Open Network Preferences

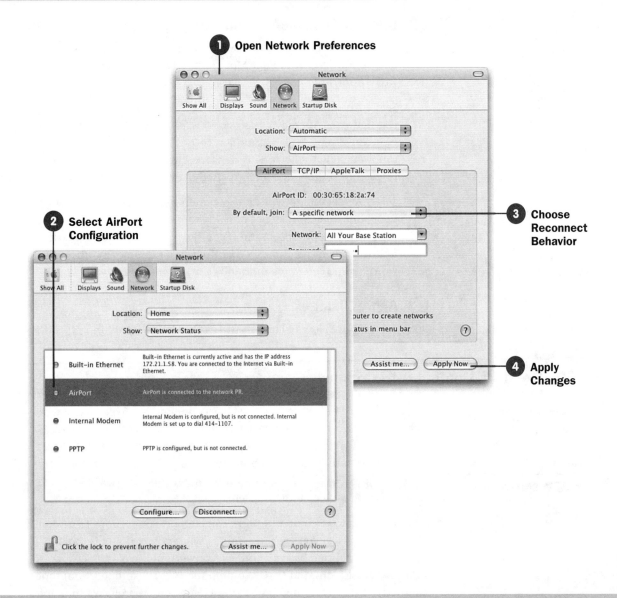

2 Select AirPort Configuration

3 Choose Reconnect Behavior

4 Apply Changes

2 Select AirPort Configuration

Double-click the **AirPort** configuration in the **Network Status** page, or click to select it and then click **Configure**. Then click the **AirPort** tab to configure the AirPort-specific options.

3 Choose Reconnect Behavior

The **By default, join** drop-down list has two options you can choose from for what your Mac should do when you restart or wake from sleep.

Select **Automatic** if you will be using the Mac in a wide-area wireless network with many base stations, such as a university campus or a convention hall. This option causes Mac OS X to connect automatically to the AirPort network with the best signal, giving preference to the most recently used network (if it's available).

Select **A specific network** if there are multiple base stations where you want to be online, but only one of the networks is appropriate for you. This option is useful if you have a home wireless network and so do your neighbors. Enter the network name and the password, typing the name manually if it's a private network.

4 Apply Changes

Click **Apply Now** to commit the AirPort behavior settings.

46 Create a Computer-to-Computer Network

Before You Begin

✔ **43** Install an AirPort Card

See Also

→ **34** Share Another Mac's Files

→ **36** Allow Others to Share Your Files

AirPort isn't just for connecting a mobile computer to a fixed base station—although that's certainly the most useful application for it. You can also connect two AirPort-equipped computers together, so that you can share files or iTunes music, without a base station anywhere in the vicinity. This is what's known as a computer-to-computer network, and you can create many of them at once—up to eleven.

Any computer-to-computer network can support connections to as many other computers as you wish; essentially what you're doing is making your computer into a base station, except without the *NAT* (Network Address Translation) and *DHCP* (automatic *TCP/IP* configuration) that characterize a full-featured base station. Non-routed protocols that operate on a LAN—such as *AppleTalk*—work just fine over a computer-to-computer network.

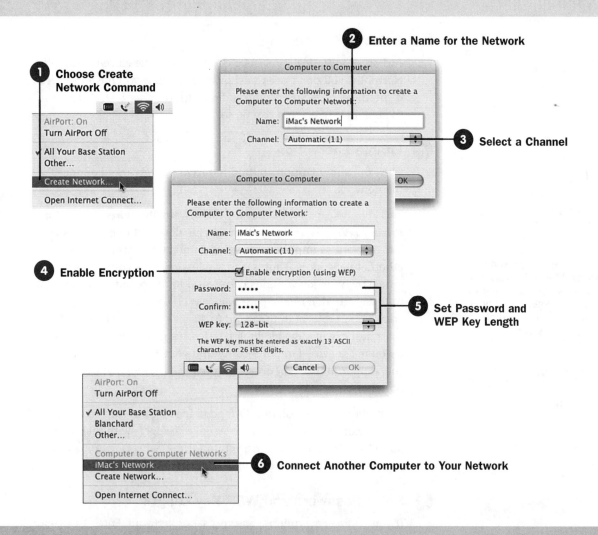

Enter a Name for the Network

Choose Create Network Command

Select a Channel

Enable Encryption

Set Password and WEP Key Length

Connect Another Computer to Your Network

❶ Choose Create Network Command

From the **AirPort Status** system menu at the top of the Desktop, select **Create Network**. A dialog box appears that prompts you for a name and (optionally) a channel for the new network.

❷ Enter a Name for the Network

Enter a descriptive name for your network. The name can be at most 32 characters long. This is the name that will show up on other people's computers when they scan for available wireless networks.

③ Select a Channel

AirPort automatically selects a channel from the eleven available. Normally, you don't need to change this, but if you have to select a specific channel to avoid colliding with another 802.11 device in the neighborhood, you can do so.

④ Enable Encryption

Click the **Show Options** button to reveal the advanced options for the network.

✏️ⓀEY TERM

Wired Equivalent Privacy (WEP)—An encryption scheme that prevents unauthorized parties from eavesdropping on the wireless Internet traffic present anywhere within range of the base station.

Encryption keeps your communications private. *Wired Equivalent Privacy (WEP)* is an encryption scheme designed to make a wireless network as impermeable by unauthorized users as a wired Ethernet network is. That is, the wireless network can be freely joined by anybody who has permission to do so, but is unavailable to those who don't have permission. WEP isn't the most secure encryption protocol in the world (a 40-bit key can be cracked by tools that are readily available), but you can specify a 128-bit key if you're concerned about security and your partners' computers can support it. (All AirPort cards produced after mid-2001 can support 128-bit keys.)

Encryption is optional, but it's a good idea if you want to keep your communications secure from eavesdroppers with their own 802.11 cards. To turn on encryption for the network you are creating, enable the **Enable encryption (using WEP)** check box.

⑤ Set a Password and WEP Key Length

If you enable encryption, you must set a password. Enter it twice to ensure that it's what you want. Select the WEP key length that's right for your situation (40-bit or 128-bit key lengths are available).

Click **OK** to create the network.

⑥ Connect Another Computer to Your Network

On the second computer, open the **AirPort Status** system menu on the right side of the global menu bar and look for available wireless networks. Your newly created network should appear by name in the list. Connect to it just as you would a base station. You can now use one computer to browse the other for file sharing or print-ing through AppleTalk, or use any Rendezvous-enabled services between the two computers, such as iTunes music sharing.

To disconnect the computer-to-computer network, switch your AirPort card back to a different wireless network (using the **AirPort Status** system menu) or turn AirPort off.

47 Create and Configure a Location

Your Mac starts out with a single *location*: **Automatic**. This location is set up to use the most automatic TCP/IP setup methods possible for all available network devices, such as DHCP and automatic connection to the nearest AirPort network. If your Mac is a stationary desktop machine, you can safely change the settings on the default **Automatic** location to match your local network; however, it's best—especially if your Mac is a portable, but even if it isn't—to create a new location and use it to hold your specific connection configuration.

After you've created a new location, you have to set up the networking configuration associated with it. The networking configuration depends on what types of network connectivity are available, what kinds of man-ual options you want to have available, and what role your computer plays in the network. Your laptop might just be an AirPort-connected Web-surfing device while you're at home, but at work it might have to connect to two or three different *Ethernet* networks and a *VPN*. Any number of configurations is possible—each location can have an entire-ly different style of networking from the next.

1 Open Network Preferences

Open the **System Preferences** application (using the **Apple** menu or the **Applications** folder) and click the **Network** icon to open the **Network Preferences** page. Alternatively, open the **Network Preferences** directly from the **Location** submenu of the **Apple** menu.

2 Create a New Location

From the **Location** drop-down menu, choose **New Location**. A sheet appears that asks for a name for the new location.

Before You Begin

✔ **26** Set Your Network Device Preference Order

✔ **44** Hook Up Over the Airwaves

See Also

→ **49** Switch to a New Location

⚓ NOTE

As the sheet points out, your new location is acces-sible by any of the users on your Mac, if you have multi-ple users set up.

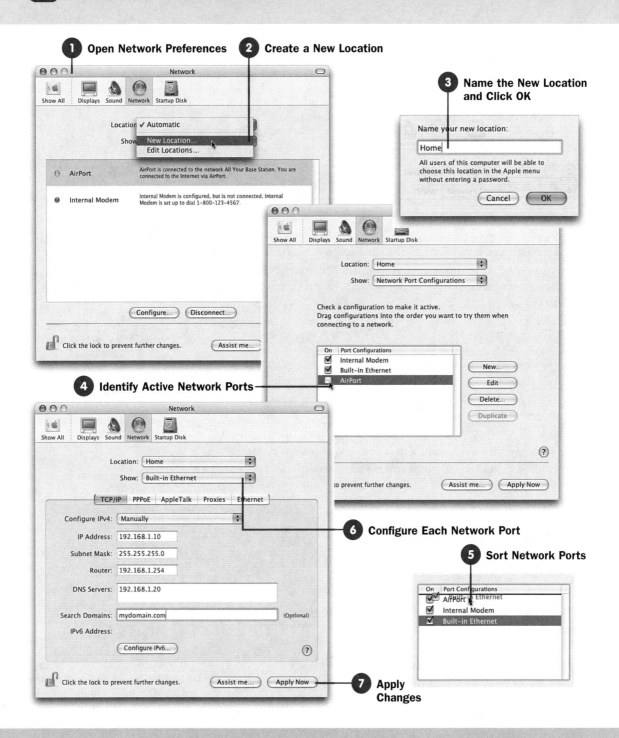

1 Open Network Preferences

2 Create a New Location

3 Name the New Location and Click OK

Name your new location:

Home

All users of this computer will be able to choose this location in the Apple menu without entering a password.

Cancel   OK

AirPort   AirPort is connected to the network All Your Base Station. You are connected to the Internet via AirPort.

Internal Modem   Internal Modem is configured, but is not connected. Internal Modem is set up to dial 1-800-123-4567.

Location: Home

Show: Network Port Configurations

Check a configuration to make it active.
Drag configurations into the order you want to try them when connecting to a network.

On	Port Configurations
☑	Internal Modem
☑	Built-in Ethernet
☐	AirPort

New...
Edit
Delete...
Duplicate

4 Identify Active Network Ports

Configure...   Disconnect...

Click the lock to prevent further changes.   Assist me...

to prevent further changes.   Assist me...   Apply Now

Location: Home

Show: Built-in Ethernet

TCP/IP   PPPoE   AppleTalk   Proxies   Ethernet

Configure IPv4: Manually

IP Address: 192.168.1.10

Subnet Mask: 255.255.255.0

Router: 192.168.1.254

DNS Servers: 192.168.1.20

Search Domains: mydomain.com   (Optional)

IPv6 Address:

Configure IPv6...

6 Configure Each Network Port

5 Sort Network Ports

On	Port Configurations
☑	AirPort Ethernet
☑	Internal Modem
☑	Built-in Ethernet

Click the lock to prevent further changes.   Assist me...   Apply Now

7 Apply Changes

③ Name the New Location and Click OK

Enter a name for the new location. The name can contain any special characters you like, and can be as long as you want. Use a short, descriptive name such as **Home** or **Joe's Coffee**.

Click **OK** to create the new location. The **Network Preferences** page now shows the configuration for this location, but it isn't active until you click **Apply Now** to make your changes take effect. Before you click that button, though, you should adjust the networking settings for your various devices to match the network the location represents.

④ Identify Active Network Ports

From the **Show** menu, select **Network Port Configurations**. On the configurations screen, you can disable any network devices you don't use, duplicate configurations for devices you want to use in different circumstances, or rename your device configurations.

Determine which network devices will be useful in the location you're configuring. If you won't ever have access to an AirPort network in this location, for example, disable the check box next to the **AirPort** entry.

⑤ Sort Network Ports

Click and drag the network devices in the port configuration list into your preferred order. Sort the devices so that the fastest, most flexible devices are at the top of the list, followed by devices that are more reliable and likely to be available. For instance, Ethernet is faster than AirPort, but you might not always have Ethernet plugged in; if you put Ethernet at the top of the list and AirPort below it, Mac OS X will use Ethernet if it's connected, but otherwise will fall back on AirPort (assuming that you're within range of a base station).

⑥ Configure Each Network Port

Select each network device in turn from the **Show** drop-down menu. Using the **TCP/IP** tab for each device, configure the TCP/IP settings according to the environment in the location you're configuring. For instance, configure the device to use DHCP if automatic configuration is available (usually the case in AirPort and

TIP

To add a *VPN* configuration to your active network ports, open **Internet Connect** (from the **Applications** menu) and create a new VPN connection as described in **33** **Configure a Secure Tunnel (VPN)**. After the VPN configuration is complete, the new configuration appears in the **Show** drop-down menu in the **Network Preferences** page.

corporate Ethernet networks—see **28** **Configure Networking Automatically with DHCP or BootP**), or configure the settings manually if necessary (see **29** **Configure Networking Manually**).

7 **Apply Your Changes**

When your configuration is complete, click the **Apply Now** button. The TCP/IP configuration for the network device that's highest in your preference order and that is connected will be applied immediately.

48 Duplicate a Location

Before You Begin

✔ **47** Create and Configure a Location

See Also

→ **49** Switch to a New Location

One easy way to set up a new *location* is to duplicate an existing one. If you have a highly customized setup, and you want to make a new configuration that's different only in some detail so that you can test it, it's very useful to be able to duplicate the custom location and play with the duplicate.

1 **Open Network Preferences**

Open the **System Preferences** application (using the **Apple** menu or the **Applications** folder) and click the **Network** icon to open the **Network Preferences** page. Alternatively, open **Network Preferences** directly from the **Location** submenu of the **Apple** menu.

2 **Select Edit Locations**

Select **Edit Locations** from the **Location** drop-down menu. This action brings up a sheet showing all your locations and several action buttons.

NOTE

If you want to delete a location you don't use any longer, select it from the **Edit your locations** box and click **Delete**. The location is immediately deleted from the list. Click **Done** to dismiss the sheet, and then click the **Apply Changes** button at the bottom of the **Network Preferences** page.

3 **Select Location to Duplicate**

Find the location entry that you want to duplicate; select it by clicking it.

4 **Duplicate the Location**

Click the **Duplicate** button to create a copy of the selected location. The duplicate appears at the bottom of the list, with the same name as the original except with **Copy** appended to it.

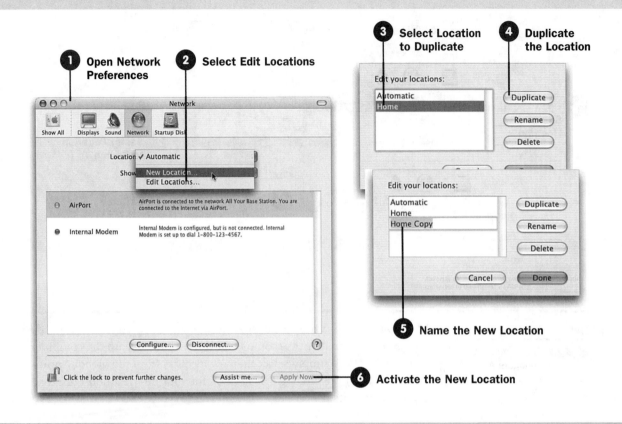

1 Open Network Preferences

2 Select Edit Locations

3 Select Location to Duplicate

4 Duplicate the Location

5 Name the New Location

6 Activate the New Location

5 Name the New Location

The name of the new location is selected; you can immediately type a new name for it.

6 Activate the New Location

Click **Done** to dismiss the sheet. The screen still shows the original configuration, but you can select the new duplicate from the **Locations** drop-down menu. However, the location is not fully active until you click the **Apply Now** button.

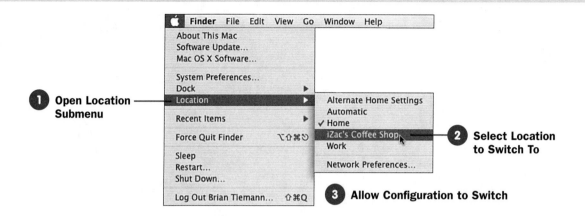

① **Open Location Submenu**

② **Select Location to Switch To**

③ **Allow Configuration to Switch**

49 Switch to a New Location

Before You Begin

✔ **47** Create and Configure a Location

After your *locations* are set up, switching from one to another is a straightforward matter. As soon as you turn on or wake up the computer in a new location, simply select the new location from the global **Apple** menu; the most preferred access method for your new location is automatically activated.

① Open Location Submenu

Open the **Apple** menu and hover the mouse over the **Location** option; a submenu appears, listing all the currently configured locations.

② Select Location to Switch To

Find the location whose configuration matches the place where you are; click the location entry to switch to that location.

③ Allow Configuration to Switch

Depending on the kind of network devices that are configured as part of the selected location, Mac OS X may take several seconds to apply the configuration and activate the most preferred device in your list. Allow five to ten seconds before attempting to connect to the network with your favorite applications.

6

.Mac Services and iDisk

IN THIS CHAPTER:

In the modern computing world, more and more of what we think of as "computing" involves the exchange of data over the Internet. Not only that, but this digital exchange is no longer just the impersonal Web-surfing of the Internet's first explosive years; nowadays, the way we interact with our computers and the Internet is increasingly personalized. Online commerce has reached the level where a great many people are as comfortable shopping on the Web as they are using a catalog or going to a store. An even more infectious phenomenon, though, is the proliferation of personalized services that take advantage of the new digital devices we use in our daily lives. Personal Web publishing, file sharing, photo albums, network storage—these things all have come about only recently as a result both of the ever-decreasing price of data storage and the explosion of digital lifestyle devices on the market—the so-called "Digital Hub" that Steve Jobs announced as Apple's strategy in the year 2000. It was only with the maturation of Mac OS X and its core technologies, and the introduction of .Mac, that the digital hub strategy truly became a reality.

Digital cameras don't just take pictures; they remove a dozen tedious steps from what once was a laborious and technically demanding process standing in the way of anybody who wanted to share those pictures with the world. The same is true of digital camcorders, MP3 players, personal organizers, and Internet applications such as Web browsers and email programs—each one is fun on its own, but its appeal is enhanced by the availability of centralized data services such as .Mac and Microsoft's .NET.

KEY TERM

.Mac—An architecture in which Mac users all over the Internet can store their personal data and preferences on central servers at Apple.

By signing up for .Mac and configuring your computer to use your .Mac account, you raise its capabilities to a whole new level. When you start up your .Mac-enabled Mac, you automatically log in to your *.Mac* account at Apple's servers. A whole host of personalized services becomes available: network disk storage (iDisk), one-click purchasing of photo prints and music downloads, iChat instant messaging, email service, and a lot more. Apple keeps bringing out new features for .Mac users every time we turn around—virus-protection software, data backup tools, synchronization of Address Book contacts and Safari bookmarks, and so on. Some people might find it disconcerting to have their personal information stored at a remote site, and information privacy is certainly not a trivial thing to worry about; but Apple's .Mac services are becoming so rich and so compelling that their benefits outweigh the risks inherent in centralized data management. After a few months on .Mac, it's hard to imagine computing without it.

.Mac costs $99 per year. Apple offers a free 60-day trial account, which you can sign up for directly from Mac OS X. At the end of the trial period, you can either stop using .Mac or pay the yearly fee and upgrade to a full .Mac account.

iDisk is a central feature of .Mac; it's a network disk system that allows you to store data on Apple's central servers. Whenever you use .Mac to host a Web page, synchronize your contacts, or read your email, you're using the disk space on the iDisk system. Every .Mac account comes with 100 megabytes of iDisk space, and you can buy more—up to a gigabyte—for between $60 and $350 extra per year.

Your iDisk is like a remote version of your **Home** folder—it has a **Pictures** folder, a **Movies** folder, and **Documents**, **Sites**, and **Music** folders, just like your local Mac does. Items you put in these folders can be shared with others using applications such as iPhoto, or with the .Mac services that store data in those folders according to their type. But the foremost purpose of iDisk is to let you share your data among multiple Macs; if you put your documents into the **Documents** folder on your iDisk, for instance, you can connect to your iDisk from any Mac and access those documents no matter where you are.

In Mac OS X Panther, iDisk features automatic synchronization: As long as you have an active network connection, your Mac will keep a local copy of your iDisk so that you can access all the items in it quickly. If you make any changes to the items in the local iDisk, the changes are automatically propagated to the central server and then to your other Macs as well, so they all always have the most current copies of your important files.

NOTE

Email storage space is separate from your regular iDisk space. A standard .Mac account has 15 megabytes of email space, but you can buy more of that as well.

TIP

A full description of each of the folders in your iDisk and what they're used for can be found in the document called **About your iDisk**, found in the top level of your iDisk.

TIP

In your iDisk, you'll also find a **Software** folder, which contains copies of many downloadable applications provided by Apple. Browse these pieces of software by category, find one you like, and drag it to your Desktop to download it.

50 Sign Up for .Mac

To use the .Mac services, you must have a .Mac account. The username (also called a "member name") and password associated with this account are specified in your .Mac Preferences. After your account is set up, whenever you want to use any of the .Mac services that tie into any of the applications you use, the account information comes straight out of your computer's preferences; you don't have to type them in.

If you're concerned about your credit card information being stored in a central server where it might be subject to theft or hacking, don't worry. .Mac does not ask for a credit card when you sign up.

Before You Begin

✔ **27** Dial Up to the Internet with a Modem (PPP)

✔ **29** Configure Networking Manually

See Also

→ **52** Create a .Mac Web Page

→ **56** Connect to Your iDisk

1 **Open .Mac Preferences**

2 **Go to the .Mac Sign-up Site**

3 **Enter Your Personal Information**

4 **Choose a Member Name and Password**

5 **Enter Verification Information**

6 **Accept Terms and Conditions**

7 **Announce Your New Email Address**

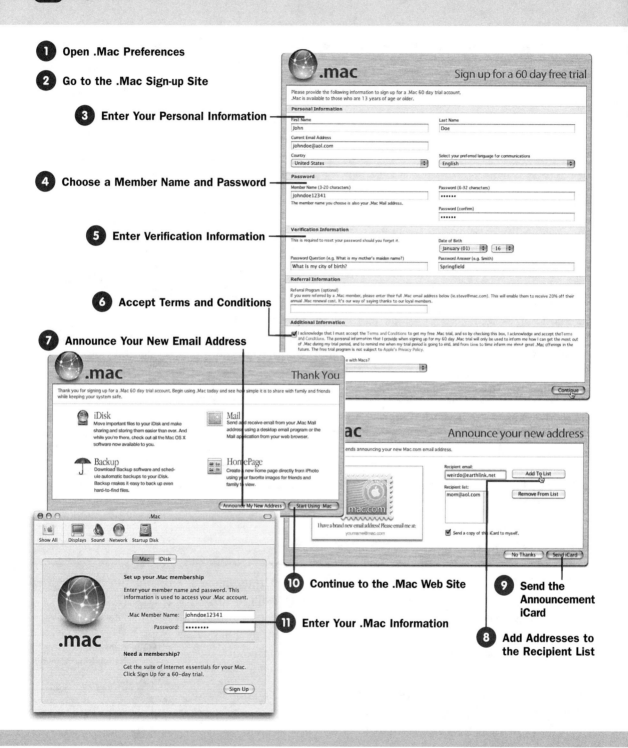

10 **Continue to the .Mac Web Site**

9 **Send the Announcement iCard**

11 **Enter Your .Mac Information**

8 **Add Addresses to the Recipient List**

For certain online purchasing functions, you can enable *1-Click ordering*, which does store your credit card information in a central server. However, for your .Mac account itself, a credit card is not necessary. You must be at least 13 years old to get a .Mac account.

When you first install Mac OS X, or when you first turn on a brand-new Mac, you are guided through an optional procedure to set up a new .Mac account. If you didn't sign up at the time of installation, you can easily sign up for your .Mac account at any time by starting from the **System Preferences**.

1 Open .Mac Preferences

Open **System Preferences** from the **Apple** menu. Click the **.Mac** icon to go to the **.Mac Preferences** page.

2 Go to the .Mac Sign-up Site

Assuming that you don't already have a .Mac account, begin the sign-up procedure by clicking the **Sign Up** button at the bottom of the window. Your Web browser launches and takes you to the sign-up page for .Mac.

Alternatively, go to **http://www.mac.com** and click the **Free Trial** button to sign up for a free 60-day trial .Mac account.

3 Enter Your Personal Information

In the first section of the form, enter your first and last name, your current email address, your country of residence, and your preferred language for using the .Mac services. As of this writing, English and Japanese are the only supported languages.

4 Choose a Member Name and Password

Select a member name. This name can be as short as three letters or as long as twenty, but it can only contain alphanumeric characters (letters and numbers). The password must be between 6 and 32 characters; for maximum security, use a password that's at least 8 characters long, and use non-alphanumeric symbols (!@#%) instead of a word that can be found in the dictionary.

KEY TERM

1-Click ordering—A technology pioneered by Amazon.com that allows you to predefine your credit card information at the server, so that you can later purchase items (on Web sites or in .Mac-enabled applications) with a single click.

NOTE

You must have a working Internet connection before you sign up for .Mac.

TIP

When selecting a member name for your .Mac account, try using your Mac OS X "short name" (**jsmith**, for example). It's always good to keep things simple, and if your .Mac account name can be the same as your account name on your own Mac, that's one fewer name to remember. In case this name is taken, however, make sure that you have a few alternative names in mind.

⑤ Enter Verification Information

Apple requires that you provide a personalized question and answer, and your birth date, for verification purposes. If you forget your password, you will be asked this question, and you must be able to answer it correctly to be reissued your password.

TIP

If you know a friend with a .Mac account, enter her @mac.com email address in the field provided; this referral entitles your friend to a discount on her .Mac services.

⑥ Accept Terms and Conditions

Follow the links to read the .Mac Terms and Conditions and Privacy Policy. Fight the temptation to skip this step; reading these agreements is tedious, but it's an excellent habit to be in, just in case. Click the check box when you're done reading.

From the drop-down menu, select your level of experience with Macs. You can choose **New to computers**, **New to Macs**, or **Experienced Mac user**. If you select either of the first two options, you are given a quick .Mac tour and the opportunity to announce your new email address to a list of your friends. If you selected the third option, you'll skip directly to the .Mac Web site, at step 10.

Finally, click the **Continue** button.

⑦ Announce Your New Email Address

If you selected either **New to computers** or **New to Macs** when asked about your Mac expertise, you are first shown a screen with your account information, to print or write down for future reference. After you have recorded this information, click **Continue**. Next appears a page with links to further information about .Mac services, as well as a button called **Announce My New Address**. Click this button to set up the announcement postcard.

⑧ Add Addresses to the Recipient List

You are shown a preview of the announcement iCard, an electronic postcard. There is a list of addresses, initially empty, that you can fill with the email addresses of as many friends as you like. Enter their addresses one by one in the **Recipient email** field and click **Add to List** to put each address into the recipient list.

9 Send the Announcement iCard

When you've added all the addresses to the list that you want, click the **Send iCard** button. The postcard is sent to all the recipients, and you will be taken back to the .Mac welcome screen.

You can click the various icons on the .Mac welcome screen to view information about certain key .Mac services, or click **Start Using .Mac** to go on to the .Mac Web site.

10 Continue to the .Mac Web Site

The .Mac Web site contains all the services that you'll find useful for your .Mac account, including downloadable premiums, news and tutorials, technical support, and links to external .Mac community sites.

WEB RESOURCE

http://www.mac.com

You'll most likely be automatically logged in at the .Mac site using your new .Mac member name and password; if not, click the **Log in** link to log in.

The .Mac Web site is where you start to access your email and your iDisk space, which come with your .Mac membership.

11 Enter Your .Mac Information

Return to the **System Preferences**. In the same **.Mac Preferences** page you started from, enter your new .Mac member name and password. The settings are immediately saved, and all your .Mac-aware applications can now use your .Mac account.

TIP

Consider setting the .Mac site as your browser's home page, so that it's the first page that opens each time you launch your browser.

51 Share a Slideshow Screensaver

One of the easiest and most fun ways to get into the spirit of .Mac is to create a public slideshow screensaver. Anybody with a Mac can subscribe to your public screensaver and watch your published pictures fade and pan across their screens. Apple provides the infrastructure; you provide the pictures. All you have to do is publish them using a free downloadable application provided as part of your .Mac account.

Before You Begin

✔ **50** Sign Up for .Mac

See Also

→ **105** About iPhoto

→ **131** Select a Screensaver

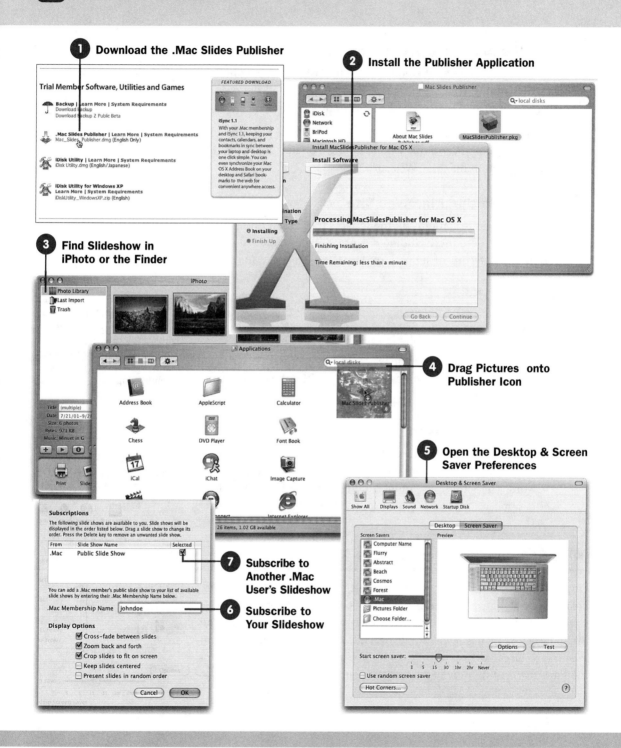

1 Download the .Mac Slides Publisher

Trial Member Software, Utilities and Games

Backup | Learn More | System Requirements
Download Backup
Download Backup 2 Public Beta

.Mac Slides Publisher | Learn More | System Requirements
Mac_Slides_Publisher.dmg (English Only)

iDisk Utility | Learn More | System Requirements
iDisk Utility.dmg (English/Japanese)

iDisk Utility for Windows XP
Learn More | System Requirements
iDiskUtility_WindowsXP.zip (English)

FEATURED DOWNLOAD

iSync 1.1
With your .Mac membership and iSync 1.1, keeping your contacts, calendars, and bookmarks in sync between your laptop and desktop is one click simple. You can even synchronize your Mac OS X Address Book on your desktop and Safari bookmarks to the web for convenient anywhere access.

2 Install the Publisher Application

Mac Slides Publisher

About Mac Slides   MacSlidesPublisher.pkg

Install MacSlidesPublisher for Mac OS X

Install Software

Processing MacSlidesPublisher for Mac OS X

Finishing Installation

Time Remaining: less than a minute

Installing
Finish Up

Go Back   Continue

3 Find Slideshow in iPhoto or the Finder

iPhoto

Photo Library
Last Import
Trash

Title: (multiple)
Date: 7/21/01–9/28
Size: 6 photos
Bytes: 971 KB
Music: Minuet in G

Print   Slide

Applications

local disks

Address Book   AppleScript   Calculator

Chess   DVD Player   Font Book

iCal   iChat   Image Capture

Mac Slides Publisher

4 Drag Pictures onto Publisher Icon

5 Open the Desktop & Screen Saver Preferences

26 items, 1.02 GB available

Subscriptions
The following slide shows are available to you. Slide shows will be displayed in the order listed below. Drag a slide show to change its order. Press the Delete key to remove an unwanted slide show.

From	Slide Show Name	Selected
.Mac	Public Slide Show	☑

You can add a .Mac member's public slide show to your list of available slide shows by entering their .Mac Membership Name below.

.Mac Membership Name johndoe

Display Options
☑ Cross-fade between slides
☑ Zoom back and forth
☑ Crop slides to fit on screen
☐ Keep slides centered
☐ Present slides in random order

Cancel   OK

7 Subscribe to Another .Mac User's Slideshow

6 Subscribe to Your Slideshow

Desktop & Screen Saver

Show All   Displays   Sound   Network   Startup Disk

Desktop   Screen Saver

Screen Savers   Preview
Computer Name
Flurry
Abstract
Beach
Cosmos
Forest
.Mac
Pictures Folder
Choose Folder...

Options   Test

Start screen saver:
3 5 15 30 1hr 2hr Never
☐ Use random screen saver
Hot Corners...

① Download the .Mac Slides Publisher

Go to the .Mac Web site (**http://www.mac.com**). Click the .**Mac Downloads** link in the lower-left pane and then click the link to the .**Mac Slides Publisher** installation file (**Mac_Slides_Publisher. dmg**). The file downloads to your computer, and the disk image mounts automatically in the Finder.

② Install the Publisher Application

Open the newly mounted disk image, if a window for it is not already open. Double-click the installer package, **MacSlidesPublisher.pkg**. The installation program begins; follow the onscreen instructions to install the application.

③ Find Slideshow in iPhoto or the Finder

To make a slideshow, you need a collection of pictures. To make things easy, collect all the pictures you want to use in your slideshow in a single folder so that you can select them all at once. Alternatively, select a group of pictures from within iPhoto.

④ Drag Pictures onto Publisher Icon

After selecting the pictures, drag them into the Finder window containing the .**Mac Slides Publisher** application, and release them on top of the icon. You'll know when your mouse is positioned properly when the application icon darkens to show that it is capable of opening those files.

The **Slides Publisher** launches. Using your stored .Mac account information, the application connects to the .Mac server, processes the picture files one by one, and uploads them to the server. You will see a progress meter and thumbnail versions of each picture as it is processed. After the pictures have all been uploaded, the application quits.

⑤ Open Desktop & Screen Saver Preferences

Now you must do what any other user must do to view your slideshow: subscribe to your .Mac screensaver. To do this, open **System Preferences** (under the **Apple** menu); click the **Desktop & Screen Saver** icon, and then click the **Screen Saver** tab to open the screensaver setup pane. Click the .**Mac** option in the **Screen Savers**

TIP

If the disk image did not automatically mount after downloading, simply go to your Desktop (or wherever you downloaded the file) and double-click its icon to mount it.

NOTE

The pictures you choose must be in JPEG format. JPEG image files can have up to 16.7 million colors, but are compressed to achieve a small file size; this compression can result in degraded image quality. Because the compression/quality tradeoff is so flexible, JPEG is by far the most widely used image format on the Internet.

list; the **Preview** window shows the default .Mac slideshow screen-saver, which is a series of promotional product photos.

NOTE

Your computer downloads all the pictures in the slideshow in the background; if you have a slow connection, it might take several minutes before all the pictures in the slideshow appear.

NOTE

To delete a slideshow, you must delete the pictures from where they are stored on your iDisk. See **56** **Connect to Your iDisk** for more information about using your iDisk. Simply drag the **Public** folder out of the **Slide Shows** folder inside **Pictures** on your iDisk, and put it in the Trash to remove your slideshow.

6 **Subscribe to Your Slideshow**

Click the **Options** button. A sheet appears that lets you subscribe to any .Mac member's slideshow. Type your own .Mac member name into the **.Mac Membership Name** field and enable or disable the check boxes next to the various display options to suit your taste. (You can always reopen this sheet later to tweak the options.) Then click **OK**.

Your slideshow appears in the **Preview** pane on the **Desktop & Screen Saver Preferences** page. To see the slideshow full-screen, click the **Test** button. The next time your screensaver activates, it will use your slideshow.

7 **Subscribe to Another .Mac Member's Slideshow**

You can subscribe to another person's slideshow just as easily as you can your own—if you know his .Mac member name. On the **Desktop & Screen Saver Preferences** page, click **Options** again to reopen the subscriptions sheet and enter the other person's .Mac member name in the **.Mac Membership Name** field. (Notice that your own .Mac member name now appears in the list at the top of the sheet, as another available slideshow from which you can choose.) Click **OK**; your active screensaver is now your friend's .Mac slideshow.

---

52 Create a .Mac Web Page

Before You Begin

✔ **50** Sign Up for .Mac

See Also

→ **57** Keep Your iDisk in Sync

→ **59** Password-Protect Your Public Folder

.Mac is all about personal publishing. Whether you want to display a photo album, write a personal journal or newsletter, share files with other Web users, or post a résumé, .Mac provides ready-made templates you can use to create your online presence quickly, easily, and attractively.

This procedure explains how to create a home page using Apple's pre–defined themes and page structures. If you're an experienced Web designer, though, you can publish your pages in a much more streamlined way: by adding files to the **Sites** folder in your iDisk. Copy an **index.html** file and other pieces of Web-page content to upload them to the .Mac server, and they will be immediately available at **http://homepage.mac.com/** **<***membername***>**.

1 Log In to the .Mac Web Page

2 Go to the HomePage Section

3 Select the Type of Page

4 Choose a Theme

5 Edit the Page

7 Publish

6 Insert a Picture

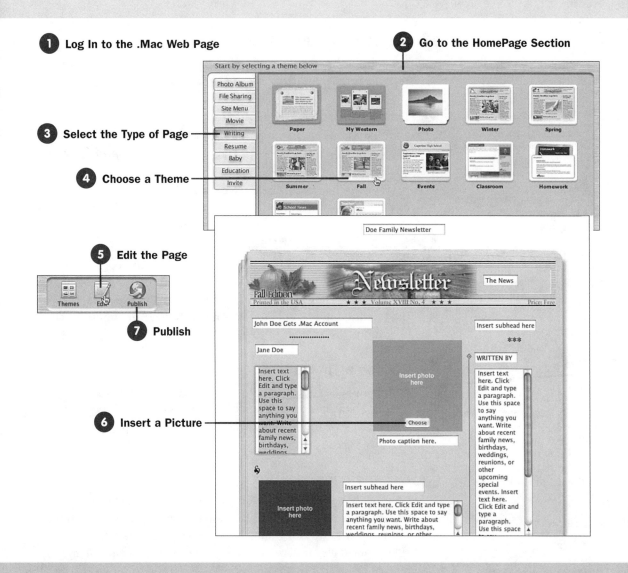

If you use a locally cached copy of your iDisk (see **57** **Keep Your iDisk in Sync** for details on how to do this), publishing is even more straightforward: just copy the items into the **Sites** folder, and they will be automatically synchronized to the server in the background.

1 **Log in to the .Mac Web Page**

Go to **http://www.mac.com** and log in using your .Mac account information if you aren't already logged in.

2 **Go to the HomePage Section**

Click the **HomePage** icon in the menu on the left side of the screen. You are taken to the main screen for your HomePage, where you can create new pages, manage existing pages, view news about the HomePage service, and add special features such as password protection.

3 **Select the Type of Page**

At the bottom of the screen is a vertical row of tabs, each corresponding to a style of Web page. Click the tab that best matches the kind of Web page you want to create. For this example, click the **Writing** tab to create a page on which you can publish personal writings.

4 **Choose a Theme**

Each page style comes with a palette full of ready-made themes designed by Apple; they range from the basic and austere to the flashy and downright gaudy. Click the icon for the page style you like best.

5 **Edit the Page**

After selecting your theme, you are taken to the **Preview** page, where you can view the layout of the page with dummy text and pictures. Click the **Edit** button at the top of the page. All the changeable fields become editable; you can click any of them and type text to your heart's content.

6 **Insert a Picture**

Some types of pages let you place pictures of your choice—selected from the **Pictures** folder on your iDisk, not your Mac hard disk—in certain positions in the layout. (See **56** **Connect to Your iDisk** and **57** **Keep Your iDisk in Sync** for more information on accessing the contents of your iDisk and placing pictures into its **Pictures** folder.) In places where you can put a picture, there is

NOTE

You can always change the theme for your Web page later, even after you've entered all the content, by clicking the **Themes** button at the top of the **Preview** page.

TIP

You can return to the HomePage start page at any time by clicking the **HomePage** title at the top of any page during the editing process. Doing so cancels your in-progress page.

always a **Choose** button; click this button to be taken to the iDisk file browser page. This screen looks similar to the Column view of the Finder, and gives you access to the **Pictures** and **Movies** folders in your iDisk, as well as to the .Mac **Image Library**. You can browse any subfolders that might exist inside these folders to locate a file. The only difference between this screen and a Finder window is that instead of double-clicking a picture file, you must click to select it and then click **Choose**. It is, after all, a Web page, and double-clicking doesn't do anything.

7 **Publish**

When you're done editing the page, click **Preview** to return to the **Preview** screen and see the page with all your modifications. From there (or directly from the **Edit** page), when you're ready to publish the page and make it available to Web surfers, click the **Publish** button. You are given a link in large letters that goes to the newly created page; you can copy the URL and send it to friends, or click the handy **iCard** button to send the link in an electronic postcard.

 TIP

After you've created a page or two, experiment with the options at the **HomePage** start page. You can edit or delete existing pages, add password protection, or even click and drag pages in the list to change the order in which their links are listed (the first page, shown in bold, is the main page that users see when they go to your home page's URL: **http://homepage. mac.com/<membername>**, where **<membername>** is your .Mac member name.

 Use .Mac Webmail

Every .Mac account comes with a free email address: *<membername>*@**mac.com**, where *<membername>* is your .Mac member name. This means you have a .Mac mail account that you can access either using your desktop Mail program in Mac OS X, or the Webmail service provided by .Mac.

.Mac email accounts use *IMAP*, the *Internet Message Access Protocol*. IMAP allows you to store your messages on a central mail server, organize them into server-side folders, and access them using any mail program from any computer. The chief rival to IMAP, the *Post Office Protocol (POP)*, operates by downloading new mail to your desktop machine. POP means faster access to your messages (because they're stored on your own computer), but you can use POP with only one computer, the one to which you download all your messages.

Before You Begin

✔ **50** Sign Up for .Mac

See Also

→ **60** Configure a Server-Based Mail Account (.Mac, Exchange, or IMAP)

→ **127** Synchronize Your .Mac Address Book

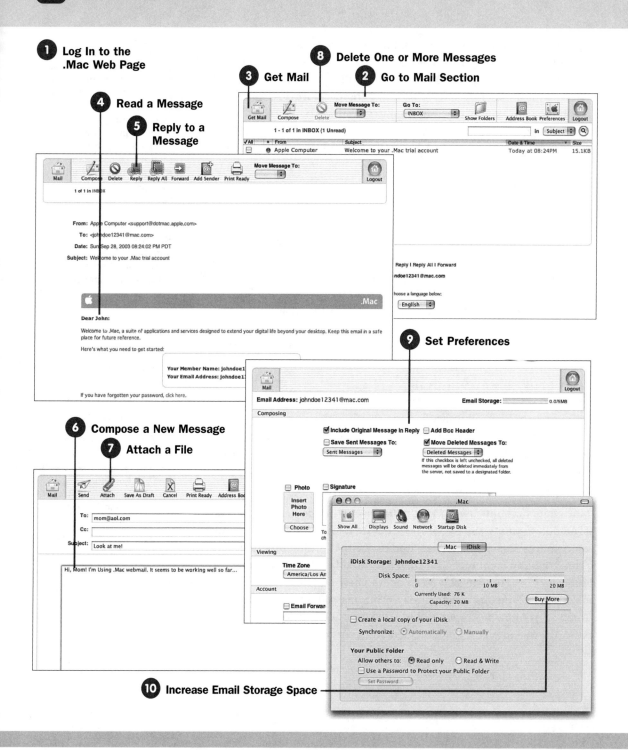

Webmail is a way for you to access your email using a Web browser. After logging in to the .Mac Web site, you simply go to the **Mail** section to view your **Inbox**; click any message to display it as a Web page. You can write messages, organize your mail into folders, and do just about everything in Webmail that you can on your desktop—with the bonus that you can access your mail from any computer in the world instead of just your own. The only downside is that it's a bit slower and has a less sophisticated interface than a dedicated email program. The trade-off, for many people, is more than fair.

1 Log In to the .Mac Web Page

Go to **http://www.mac.com** and log in using your .Mac account information if you aren't already logged in.

2 Go to the Mail Section

Click the **Mail** icon in the menu on the left side of the screen. You are immediately taken to a view of your mail account's **Inbox**, the folder to which all new mail automatically comes.

3 Get Mail

Click the **Get Mail** button at the top left of the screen to refresh the message listing and display any newly arrived messages. New messages, by default, are shown at the top of the list.

4 Read a Message

Click any listed message to read it. If the message has an attachment, a paperclip icon appears next to it in the message listing; when you view the message, all attachments are shown as links at the top of the message. Clicking on the links downloads the attachments as files to your computer.

5 Reply to a Message

When viewing a message, click the **Reply** icon in the toolbar at the top of the screen. If the message was sent to you and several other recipients, you can send your reply to all the original recipients by clicking **Reply All**. The original message appears "quoted"—indented in front of a column of > characters—in a large text-input field; you can add your reply text either above or below the quoted text, and delete any of the quoted material.

KEY TERMS

Internet Message Access Protocol (IMAP)—An email delivery method that allows you to read messages that are stored and managed on the server.

Post Office Protocol (POP)—An email delivery method in which your email application downloads all your messages to store on the local computer.

 TIP

As you can with many other applications, you can sort the messages in your **Inbox** by clicking the column headers. Click a column header twice to reverse its sorting direction.

 TIP

You can turn off quoting in the **Webmail Preferences**, accessible by clicking **Preferences** in the toolbar of the Webmail page that lists your messages; disable the **Include Original Message in Reply** check box.

6 Compose a New Message

To create a new message, click the **Compose** toolbar icon when viewing the message list. You can select contacts (people to whom you want to send the email message) from your Address Book by clicking the **Address Book** icon in the toolbar; select the contacts you want, select a destination (the **To:**, **Cc:**, or **Bcc:** fields), and click **Apply**.

The **Quick Addresses** drop-down lists to the right of the **To** and **Cc** fields contain names from your .Mac Address Book that you have selected to be included in your **Quick Addresses** list. Simply select a name from one of the lists to copy it to the appropriate input field.

When you're done typing your message, click **Send** in the toolbar or at the bottom of the screen to send it.

7 Attach a File

To attach a file, click **Attach** in the toolbar or at the bottom of the screen. You are taken to a page where you can select a document from your computer, click **Attach**, and repeat for as many documents as you want to attach; when you're done, click **Apply** to attach the files to the message.

8 Delete One or More Messages

When viewing the message list, enable the check boxes to the left of the **From** column to select the messages you want to delete. The **Delete** icon in the toolbar becomes active; click it to delete the selected messages.

9 Set Preferences

.Mac Webmail has a number of settings you can adjust to suit your taste; access these options by clicking the **Preferences** icon in the main toolbar (in the message list view). You can choose whether or not to include the original message in a reply, choose whether and where to save copies of your sent mail, add a photo and custom signature to all your messages, and many more behavior switches. Be sure to click the **Save** button (located at the bottom of the page) when you're done changing your preferences.

TIP

To use the .Mac Address Book, you must first synchronize your Mac's own Address Book; see **127** **Synchronize Your .Mac Address Book** for more information.

10 **Increase Email Storage Space**

A standard .Mac account comes with 15MB of storage space for your **@mac.com** email. You can see how much of that allotted space you are currently using by opening the **.Mac Webmail Preferences** page (by clicking **Preferences** on the toolbar on the message list page) and looking at the usage bar at the top. If you find that you need more space, you can purchase more by clicking the **Buy More** button.

Additional email storage is available in varying increments, with prices ranging from $10 per year for 10MB of additional space to $90 per year for a 200MB mailbox ceiling. This storage is separate from your iDisk space, which can be upgraded from the basic 100MB to as much as 1GB for $350 per year.

---

54 **Change Your .Mac Password**

Among the many available account management options that you will want to know about, such as changing your credit card information and personal details, is the ability to change your password. It's always a good idea to change your password periodically; communication with .Mac is secure (using *SSL*, the *Secure Sockets Layer*, for its Web connections), but selecting a new password every six to twelve months is a good general policy in a world of ever-increasing online commerce and risk of identity theft and fraud.

1 **Log In to the .Mac Web Page**

Go to **http://www.mac.com** and log in using your .Mac account information if you aren't already logged in.

2 **Go to the Account Section**

Click the **Account** link at the upper-right corner of the page. This link takes you to your main account management page.

Before You Begin

✔ **50** Sign Up for .Mac

See Also

→ **55** Recover a Lost .Mac Password

KEY TERM

Secure Sockets Layer (SSL)—An Internet transport protocol that encrypts standard traffic, such as Web surfing, so that unauthorized parties can't intercept and read the traffic.

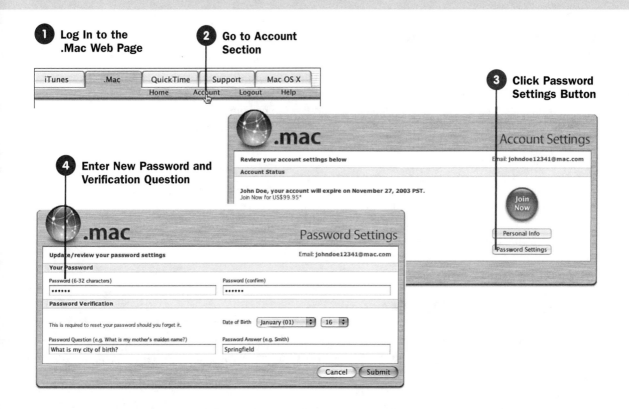

1 Log In to the .Mac Web Page

2 Go to Account Section

3 Click Password Settings Button

4 Enter New Password and Verification Question

TIPS

A .Mac password must be between 6 and 32 characters in length. For maximum security, use a mixture of different capitalization, numbers, and symbols in the password—and you should especially avoid using any word that can be found in the dictionary.

If you ever have to recover a lost or forgotten password (as described in **55** Recover a Lost .Mac Password), you can change your password to anything you like by clicking **Forget your password?** and answering the verification questions.

3 Go to Password Settings

Click the **Password Settings** button located at the right side of the screen to go to the screen where you can enter a new password.

4 Enter New Password and Verification Question

Enter your new password and enter it again to confirm it. If you want to update your verification question (which .Mac asks if you forget your password, so that it can securely reveal your password for you), you can do so in this screen.

Click **Submit** when you're done, and your password will be changed.

55 Recover a Lost .Mac Password

Everyone forgets passwords. Even with the help of *Keychain* (Apple's password-management system, which is described in **164** **Extract a Password from the Keychain**), passwords can get lost—and your .Mac password, because it holds the key to all your .Mac services on which you might come to rely, is an especially bad one to lose.

Fortunately, the procedure for recovering access to your .Mac account isn't difficult. Apple provides two methods for obtaining a new password, which you can choose between depending on your circumstances.

1 **Go to the .Mac Login Screen**

Go to the .Mac Web site at **http://www.mac.com** and click the **Log in** link to attempt to log in. You are presented with the main .Mac login screen.

2 **Click the Forget Your Password? Link**

If you can't remember your password, click the **Forget Your Password?** link below the password field to begin the password recovery process.

3 **Enter Your Apple ID (.Mac Email Address)**

Your Apple ID is the same as your .Mac email address, *<membername>*@mac.com. Enter that into the **Apple ID** field and click **Continue**.

4 **Choose a Recovery Method**

You are given two options for how to reset your password. If you can access your **@mac.com** email (and are therefore only trying to change your password, rather than recover a lost one), use **Option 1**, in which Apple sends you an activation code in an email message to that account. If, however, you don't have access to that account (which is likely the case if you don't know your .Mac password), choose **Option 2**, which asks you for your verification question's answer.

Before You Begin

✔ **50** Sign Up for .Mac

See Also

→ **54** Change Your .Mac Password

→ **128** Recover from a Corrupted iSync Configuration

KEY TERM

Keychain—A technology built into Mac OS X that keeps track of all your passwords for Web pages, applications, or other parts of the system. A single master Keychain password unlocks all your other passwords to be used automatically on request.

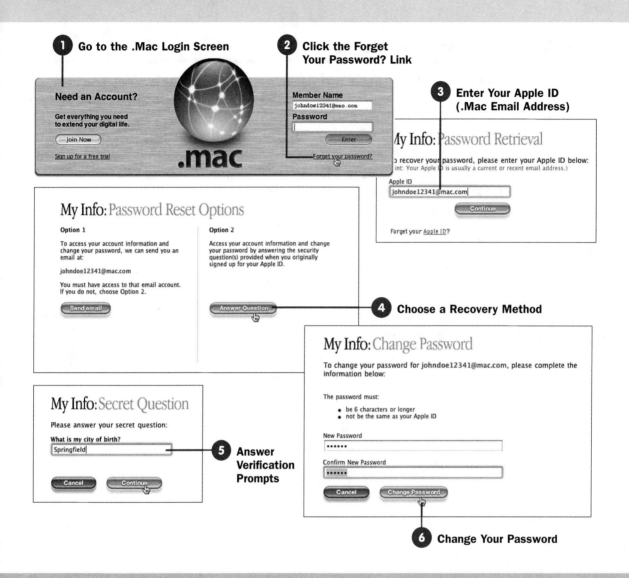

1. **Go to the .Mac Login Screen**

2. **Click the Forget Your Password? Link**

Need an Account?

Get everything you need to extend your digital life.

Join Now

Sign up for a free trial

.mac

Member Name
johndoe12341@mac.com
Password

Enter

Forget your password?

3. **Enter Your Apple ID (.Mac Email Address)**

My Info: Password Retrieval

To recover your password, please enter your Apple ID below:
(Hint: Your Apple ID is usually a current or recent email address.)

Apple ID
johndoe12341@mac.com

Continue

Forget your Apple ID?

My Info: Password Reset Options

Option 1

To access your account information and change your password, we can send you an email at:

johndoe12341@mac.com

You must have access to that email account. If you do not, choose Option 2.

Send email

Option 2

Access your account information and change your password by answering the security question(s) provided when you originally signed up for your Apple ID.

Answer Question

4. **Choose a Recovery Method**

My Info: Change Password

To change your password for johndoe12341@mac.com, please complete the information below:

The password must:
- be 6 characters or longer
- not be the same as your Apple ID

New Password
••••••

Confirm New Password
••••••

Cancel   Change Password

My Info: Secret Question

Please answer your secret question:

What is my city of birth?
Springfield

Cancel   Continue

5. **Answer Verification Prompts**

6. **Change Your Password**

5 Answer Verification Prompts

Apple first asks for your birthday. Provide this date and click **Continue.** You are then asked your verification question. You must provide the exact answer that you specified in your account information. If you do, you will be taken to the screen where you can enter a new password.

6 **Change Your Password**

Apple has a fairly lax policy regarding password "strength," or the alphanumeric complexity of the password string. (A strong password contains mixed uppercase and lowercase letters, numbers, and special characters, and cannot be found in any dictionary.) All Apple requires is that the password be at least six characters long, and that it not be exactly the same as your Apple ID (your .Mac email address). You can use your old password, too, if you have found your way into this procedure accidentally—so don't worry about having to come up with a new and unused password if you only have one password in mind. (.Mac does not tell you what your old password is, as a security measure.)

After changing your password, you are given a set of links to lead you back to the .Mac login page or to various other destinations at Apple's site.

56 Connect to Your iDisk

iDisk is like any other network server—you must connect to it before you can access what's inside it. Fortunately, iDisk is integrated into .Mac, so you don't have to waste time logging in and entering passwords when you want to connect. To connect to your iDisk—after your .Mac member information is entered into the **.Mac Preferences** page of the **System Preferences** application—click the **iDisk** icon in the Finder sidebar.

1 **Open the .Mac Preferences**

Open the **System Preferences** application using the **Apple** menu. Click the **.Mac** icon to open the **.Mac Preferences** page. Click the **.Mac** tab if it's not already selected.

2 **Enter Your .Mac Member Name and Password**

You might have entered your .Mac information already, during the initial setup of the system. If you haven't, however, enter your member name and password into the boxes provided.

Close the **System Preferences** window when you're done entering your .Mac name and password. This action saves the account information you've entered.

Before You Begin

✔ **50** Sign Up for .Mac

See Also

→ **57** Keep Your iDisk in Sync

→ **58** Share Your iDisk Public Folder with Others

NOTE

If you haven't yet signed up for a .Mac account, the **Sign Up** button provides a convenient link to the site where you can do so. See **50** **Sign Up for .Mac** for more information.

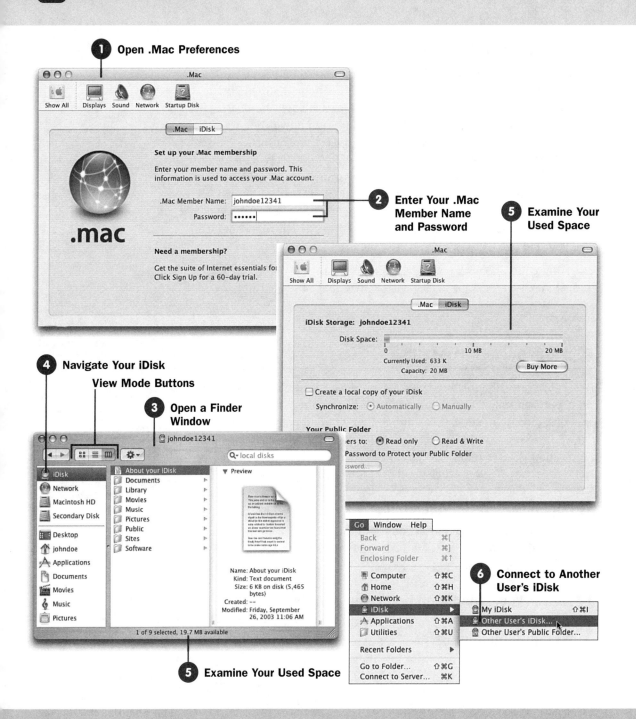

1 Open .Mac Preferences

2 Enter Your .Mac Member Name and Password

5 Examine Your Used Space

4 Navigate Your iDisk

View Mode Buttons

3 Open a Finder Window

6 Connect to Another User's iDisk

5 Examine Your Used Space

3 Open a Finder Window

After you enter your .Mac information, the next time you open a Finder window, you'll see an **iDisk** icon at the top of the Finder sidebar.

4 Navigate Your iDisk

Click the **iDisk** icon to open its contents in the right pane of the Finder window. Switch to the view mode you like and navigate the various folders that are available.

You can add documents, folders, and other items to any of the folders in your iDisk by simply dragging them from the Desktop or from another Finder window into the window showing your iDisk contents.

Dragging items to your iDisk copies the items to the remote iDisk space (just as with any network server) and makes the files available for use in your .Mac Web pages and slideshows. If you want to make files available for other .Mac users to access, drop those files into your iDisk **Public** folder.

You can access your iDisk from as many different Macs as you want, or even from non-Mac computers. If you want certain documents, applications, or other files available to you no matter what computer you're using, iDisk is the perfect solution—it's like having a copy of the same disk attached to every one of your computers. (This is especially true if you turn on local .Mac synchronization, as discussed in **57** **Keep Your iDisk in Sync**.)

5 Examine Your Used Space

There are two ways to see how much of your allotted iDisk space is used up. The quickest is to simply click the **iDisk** icon in the Finder, or navigate to any folder in your iDisk; the readout at the bottom of the Finder window shows how much space is available.

To see a more detailed readout—one that shows you how much space is allocated to your .Mac account, as well as how much space has been used—open the **.Mac Preferences** page of the **System Preferences** application and click the **iDisk** tab. Your iDisk storage is displayed graphically, showing you the overall capacity and how much is currently used. If you decide you need more iDisk space, click the **Buy More** button. You can increase the

> **NOTE**
>
> To delete individual files or folders from your iDisk, navigate to the iDisk (using the Finder) until you find the files you want to delete; then drag them to the Trash. The items are immediately deleted from the iDisk server.

amount of iDisk space you have from the basic 100MB (at no extra cost) to as much as 1GB for $350 per year.

NOTE

Sharing your entire iDisk is advisable only if you completely trust the other person—after all, you're giving away your .Mac password, which means giving away access to your entire .Mac account. Generally, this feature is intended for people who have more than one .Mac account or manage more than one .Mac account in a household or business. The best way to share files using iDisk is to put them in your iDisk's **Public** folder, and then allow others to access that folder (which does not require an access password unless you set one). See **58** Share Your iDisk Public Folder with Others.

6 **Connect to Another User's iDisk**

If you have another .Mac user's member name and password, you can connect to her iDisk—her own personal storage space on Apple's central servers, not her own Mac—and browse its files just as you would your own. To do this, open the **Go** menu in the Finder and choose the **iDisk** option. From the submenu that opens, select **Other User's iDisk**. A **Connect To iDisk** dialog box appears; enter the .Mac user's member name and password and click **Connect**. The user's iDisk appears on the Finder's sidebar as well as on your Desktop, labeled with the user's .Mac member name.

You can connect to your iDisk using any of several different operating systems, including Windows, by using the downloadable **iDisk Utility** (if you're using Windows XP or Mac OS X 10.1 or 10.2). See **58** **Share Your iDisk Public Folder with Others** for details on how to do this. To access your entire iDisk (or that of any other .Mac member) from another operating system, use this URL **http://idisk.mac.com/<*membername*>** (where <*membername*> is the user's .Mac member name) when specifying the server location.

Many applications that are aware of .Mac accounts—such as Address Book—allow you to connect directly to a .Mac user's iDisk. In the user's Address Book card, click the identifier (such as **work** or **home**) next to the **@mac.com** email address and select **Open iDisk** from the menu that pops up.

---

57 **Keep Your iDisk in Sync**

Before You Begin

✔ **50** Sign Up for .Mac

✔ **56** Connect to Your iDisk

See Also

→ **125** Set Up iSync to Synchronize Your Information

iDisk is at its best when you use it to keep all your Macs—if you're fortunate enough to have more than one—in sync with each other. Using this feature of Mac OS X Panther, you can keep a copy of your iDisk on your own computer at all times, making access to it as fast as accessing your own hard disk. Any changes you make to your local iDisk are published to your remote iDisk on the .Mac server in the background, without requiring any effort from you. From your remote iDisk, the changes are propagated automatically to any other Macs that are logged in to your .Mac account. No matter which Mac you use, the files, folders, and applications you've placed into your iDisk are immediately available.

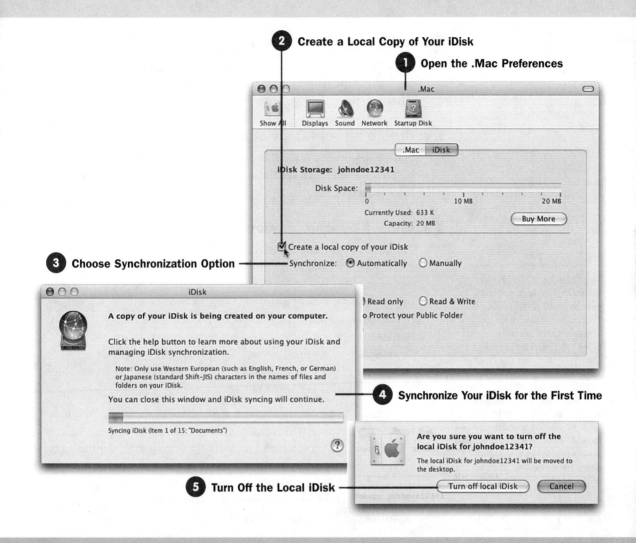

2 Create a Local Copy of Your iDisk

1 Open the .Mac Preferences

iDisk Storage: johndoe12341

Disk Space:
0   10 MB   20 MB
Currently Used: 633 K
Capacity: 20 MB   Buy More

☑ Create a local copy of your iDisk

3 Choose Synchronization Option ——— Synchronize: ⦿ Automatically ◯ Manually

◯ Read only   ◯ Read & Write
○ Protect your Public Folder

iDisk

A copy of your iDisk is being created on your computer.

Click the help button to learn more about using your iDisk and managing iDisk synchronization.

Note: Only use Western European (such as English, French, or German) or Japanese (standard Shift-JIS) characters in the names of files and folders on your iDisk.

You can close this window and iDisk syncing will continue.

4 Synchronize Your iDisk for the First Time

Syncing iDisk (Item 1 of 15: "Documents")

Are you sure you want to turn off the local iDisk for johndoe12341?

The local iDisk for johndoe12341 will be moved to the desktop.

5 Turn Off the Local iDisk ———   Turn off local iDisk   Cancel

You can elect to synchronize your iDisk manually, if you choose. For instance, while you're trying to get work done online, you might not want your Mac to take up precious bandwidth synchronizing with the remote iDisk server. But if you let your Mac synchronize automatically, you can use your iDisk as your primary disk for important files that you need to access a lot—and those files will always be at your fingertips, regardless of which of your Mac computers you're using.

① Open the .Mac Preferences

Open the **System Preferences** application using the **Apple** menu. Click the **.Mac** icon to open the **.Mac Preferences** page. Click the **iDisk** tab to view those options.

② Create a Local Copy of Your iDisk

Enable the **Create a local copy of your iDisk** check box. This option enables iDisk synchronization but does not yet start creating the local iDisk.

③ Choose Synchronization Option

NOTE

The **Backup**, **Library**, and **Software** folders you can see on your local iDisk become aliases to their counterparts on the remote iDisk on the .Mac server so that you can still connect and view them. While you are disconnected from the remote .Mac iDisk, however, the local aliases might appear with the wrong icon. If you click the icons, however, the remote .Mac iDisk mounts and the correct aliases are restored.

The default behavior is for your iDisk to be synchronized automatically, whenever Mac OS X detects that your local or remote iDisk has been changed. The synchronization process can be bandwidth intensive; if you don't want your Mac to be constantly exchanging information with the .Mac server as you use your local iDisk, select the **Manually** option. However, it's recommended that you keep your iDisk synchronization set to **Automatically** at all times, unless you're on a very constricted network connection or an older Mac with limited processor power.

Some iDisk folders from the .Mac server are not copied to your local computer: **Backup**, which holds archives written by Apple's Backup application; **Library**, which keeps application-specific data for .Mac services; and **Software**, which has copies of many pieces of shareware provided for download by Apple. You don't need these folders or their files on your local hard disk, and you wouldn't want to download all those files at once!

TIP

Click the **?** button in the dialog box for further information about how automatic and manual syncing work.

④ Synchronize Your iDisk for the First Time

Close the **System Preferences** application. This action kicks off the first synchronization process, which might take a long time, depending on how much data is in your remote iDisk and how fast your Internet connection is. A dialog box shows you the progress of the initial sync process.

If you have selected to synchronize your iDisk manually, you can start a new sync process by clicking the circular **Sync** button next to the **iDisk** icon in the Finder's sidebar. Alternatively, right-click (or **Control**+click) the **iDisk** icon on your Desktop and select **Sync Now** from the context menu that appears.

Repeat steps 1 through 4 for all your Macs; when all of them have been synchronized for the first time, automatic synchronization will operate efficiently in the background, keeping all your computers up to date.

5 Turn Off the Local iDisk

If you choose, you can turn off the local synchronized iDisk; simply go back to the **iDisk Preferences** page of the **System Preferences** application and disable the **Create a local copy of your iDisk** check box. If you do this, your local iDisk will be converted into a *disk image* and placed on your Desktop. You can keep it in a safe place (double-click it to mount it so that you can access its contents) or dispose of it in the Trash, as you prefer.

NOTE

After the initial sync process is complete, the local iDisk also appears on your Desktop, as a separate volume that you can use as you would any other disk. (You can hide the iDisk on your Desktop by turning off the **CDs, DVDs, and iPods** option in the **Finder Preferences**, on the **General** tab.) Whenever your iDisk is being synchronized, its progress is shown at the bottom of the Finder window when you're looking at the iDisk's contents.

58 Share Your iDisk Public Folder with Others

Although iDisk is most useful in keeping your Macs' files synchronized, that is not by a long shot its only function. Your iDisk can also be used as a quick way to share files with other users—even if they're not using Macs.

The **Public** folder in your iDisk, like the **Public** folder in your **Home** folder on your local Mac, is accessible to anybody on the Internet. Anything you place into that folder can be accessed by Mac OS X users, Windows XP users (using the free **iDisk Utility** for Windows), Mac OS 9 users, or anybody with a Web browser; all they have to know is your .Mac member name.

Before You Begin

✔ **50** Sign Up for .Mac

✔ **56** Connect to Your iDisk

See Also

→ **59** Password-Protect Your Public Folder

1 Place Files in Your Public Folder

Open your **iDisk** (access it remotely or use the local copy) in the Finder; drag files or folders into the **Public** folder inside your iDisk. If you're using a locally synchronized copy of your iDisk, this will be an almost instantaneous process (click the **Sync** button next to **iDisk** in the Finder sidebar to publish the files to the server, if you have chosen to sync your iDisk manually); if you're connecting to your iDisk remotely, it will take a few moments to copy the files to the server.

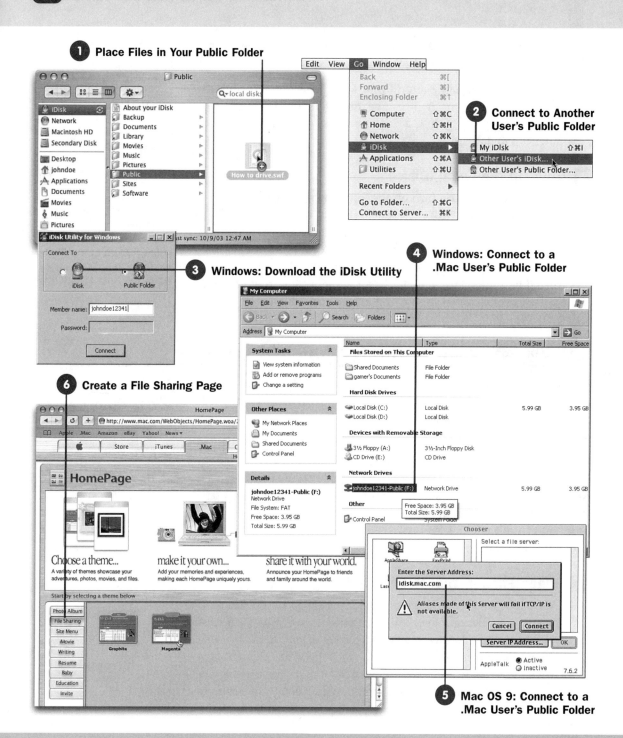

1 Place Files in Your Public Folder

2 Connect to Another User's Public Folder

3 Windows: Download the iDisk Utility

4 Windows: Connect to a .Mac User's Public Folder

5 Mac OS 9: Connect to a .Mac User's Public Folder

6 Create a File Sharing Page

② Connect to Another User's Public Folder

If you know another .Mac user who has placed files in his iDisk's **Public** folder, you can access that folder directly knowing only the user's member name. Open the **Go** menu in the Finder; in the **iDisk** submenu, select the **Other User's Public Folder** option. Enter the other user's .Mac member name in the dialog box that appears and click **Connect.** The other user's iDisk **Public** folder will appear in the Finder's sidebar as well as on your Desktop under the name *<membername>*-**Public** (where *<membername>* is the other user's .Mac member name).

Depending on the other user's iDisk settings, you might be able to copy files into his **Public** folder by dragging them or delete files by ⌘+dragging them; if the user has allowed **Read only** access to the **Public** folder, however, you will not be able to make any changes to the files in that user's **Public** folder.

③ Windows: Download the iDisk Utility

If you have a PC running Windows XP, you can access the files in a .Mac user's **Public** folder using the free **iDisk Utility**, available at the .Mac Web site. Go to **http://www.mac.com**, and log in using your .Mac account information; click the **iDisk** icon, and follow the links to the **iDisk Utility**. Download the ZIP archive for Windows and install the program.

④ Windows: Connect to a .Mac User's Public Folder

Open the **iDisk Utility** and click the radio button next to the **Public Folder** icon. Type the .Mac user's member name whose **Public** folder you want to connect to in the **Member Name:** box.

Click the **Connect** button; if a password is required to open the folder, enter it in the dialog box that appears and click **OK.**

The user's **Public** folder will be mounted as a network drive within Windows, accessible from **Windows Explorer** or **My Computer**; you can browse its contents and place files into it (if the owner has granted **Read & Write** access to others).

NOTE

If the other user has protected his **Public** folder with a password, another dialog box appears, prompting you for that password. Enter it and click **OK.**

TIP

If you're using Mac OS X version 10.1 or 10.2, you also must download the **iDisk Utility** before you can access other users' iDisks or **Public** folders. This functionality is built into Mac OS X Panther (version 10.3), but earlier versions don't have it as part of the system. Download the **Mac OS X** version of the **iDisk Utility** if you have one of these older releases of Mac OS X.

5 Mac OS 9: Connect to a .Mac User's Public Folder

To connect to another user's iDisk **Public** folder from a Mac OS 9 machine, open the **Chooser** (using the **Apple** menu) and click the **AppleShare** icon on the left. Click the **Server IP Address** button and then type **idisk.mac.com** in the **Enter the Server Address** field. Click **Connect**.

You are prompted to enter the person's .Mac member name; if the **Public** folder requires a password, type it in the **Password** field. If the folder doesn't require a password, type the word **public** instead. Click **Connect** to continue.

In the next dialog box, select the shared resource whose name matches the user's .Mac member name (it should be the only one available); when you click **OK**, the iDisk share will appear on your Desktop.

You can connect to a .Mac user's iDisk with other operating systems, too. In Windows 2000, select **Map Network Drive** from the **Tools** menu, then click **Web folder or FTP site** and enter the URL **http://idisk.mac.com/<*membername*>-Public?** (where <*membername*> is the user's .Mac member name).

You can even connect to a user's **Public** folder using Linux or Unix if you have a WebDAV client (iDisk operates using WebDAV). Enter this URL when you are prompted for the server location by the client: **http://idisk.mac.com/<*membername*>-Public?**

NOTE

In Windows 98, open **My Computer** and double-click the **Web Folders** option. Then double-click **Add Web Folder** and enter the URL **http://idisk.mac.com/ <*membername*>-Public?**

6 Create a File Sharing Page

You can create a .Mac Web page to share the contents of your iDisk **Public** folder with anybody who has a Web browser. To do this, go to the .Mac Web site at **http://www.mac.com** and log in using your .Mac account information. Then click the **HomePage** icon. Create a new page using the **File Sharing** theme tab in the lower portion of the screen. Customize the page as you would any other .Mac Web page, giving it a proper descriptive name; then click **Publish**. The .Mac service will then give you the URL for your new File Sharing page.

Use this URL to open a Web page that shows a listing of all the files and folders in your **Public** folder; give the URL to your friends so that they can access those same files. However, people don't even have to know the URL of your File Sharing page, as long as they know your .Mac member name: People can go directly to **http://homepage.mac.com/<*membername*>** (where **<membername>** is your .Mac member name). There will be a link at the top of the page to your File Sharing page, listed by the name that you gave it when you created it.

59 Password-Protect Your Public Folder

Anybody, anywhere, can access whatever is in the **Public** folder on your iDisk—and that includes not just the people to whom you *want* to allow access but also a lot of people you might *not* want to see your files. As a rule of thumb, don't put anything in your **Public** folder that you wouldn't want to show up in the newspaper.

Sometimes it's necessary (or just too convenient) to use your **Public** folder to exchange files of a sensitive nature, or you might want to provide your **Public** folder with a measure of privacy out of principle. Fortunately, iDisk provides that capability.

1 **Open the .Mac Preferences**

Open the **System Preferences** application using the **Apple** menu. Click the **.Mac** icon to open the **.Mac Preferences** page and click the **iDisk** tab.

2 **Choose the Access Level for Others in Your Public Folder**

You can choose what kind of capabilities other users can have within your iDisk's **Public** folder. You can make it so that other users can put files into your **Public** folder (**Read & Write** access), but this level of access also enables users to delete files that are already in the folder. On the other hand, you can give your **Public** folder **Read only** access, which allows others to access existing files but not to add any of their own; this forgoes the convenience of allowing others to put files into your iDisk's **Public** folder, but it's much safer.

Before You Begin

✔ **50** Sign Up for .Mac
✔ **58** Share Your iDisk Public Folder with Others

NOTE

It's important to stress the difference between your iDisk **Public** folder and the **Public** folder inside your **Home** folder on your local Mac. Your local **Public** folder is accessible from other Macs only; it has a **Drop Box** subfolder, which other users can use to send files to you while maintaining your privacy. The **Public** folder in your iDisk, however, doesn't have a **Drop Box** subfolder; you can only choose between **Read only** and **Read & Write** privileges for the iDisk **Public** folder.

1 Open the .Mac Preferences

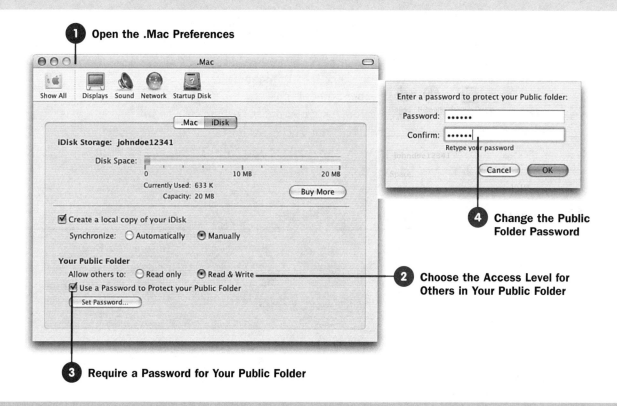

4 Change the Public Folder Password

2 Choose the Access Level for Others in Your Public Folder

3 Require a Password for Your Public Folder

TIP

As with many pages of the **System Preferences** application, you might have to close the **System Preferences** window (or click the **.Mac** tab and then click the **iDisk** tab again) to force the changes to take effect. To remove the password protection, just disable the **Use a Password to Protect your Public Folder** check box.

3 **Require a Password for Your Public Folder**

Enable the **Use a Password to Protect your Public Folder** check box to set a password on your iDisk **Public** folder. A sheet appears that prompts you to enter a password (twice); click **OK** when you've done so.

4 **Change the Public Folder Password**

If you want to change the password on your iDisk **Public** folder, click the **Set Password** button on the **iDisk** tab of the **.Mac** Preferences page. Enter the new password (twice) in the sheet that appears. When you click **OK** and close the **System Preferences** application, the password for your iDisk **Public** folder will be changed.

7

Email

IN THIS CHAPTER:

Arguably the most revolutionary and pervasive part of the Internet (rivaled only by browsing the Web), email is an application whose use has joined the world's lexicon as firmly as television did—and much more quickly. It's easy to understand why: Now, effectively free, a person anywhere on Earth can communicate nearly instantaneously with someone else no matter where she is on the planet. Email has become the *lingua franca* of the Information Age; people use it to send each other everything from brief one-line messages to whole picture albums or installable applications. Email can get you in touch with everybody from a family member down the hall to your Congressman or favorite author. For all that, email is still conceptually one of the simplest of applications: You type in some text, and off it goes into the cloud of flowing bits that is the Internet.

Anybody who has ever used email before, though, will know that there's actually a lot more to it than that. Everybody has their own style for how they use email, from what "signatures" they attach to the ends of messages to how they prefer incoming messages to be listed. Email applications in recent years have become increasingly complex, adding more and more convenience and flexibility so that the user has complete control over the entire experience of interacting with their virtual mailboxes. Applications such as Microsoft Outlook, in particular, have set a new standard for just how complex a concept as simple as email can be made.

Apple's **Mail** application, built into Mac OS X, provides all the flexibility of programs such as Outlook, coupled with the intuitiveness and elegance typical of Apple software. Although .Mac Webmail (covered in **53 Use .Mac Webmail**) offers you rudimentary but convenient access to your .Mac mail account, it can be vastly more intuitive, fast, and flexible to use **Mail** to read the email in that account (and any other email accounts you might have) on your own computer rather than on the Web. All the advanced features of modern email programs are incorporated into Mail—automatic junk-mail filtering, color-based message flagging, automated message organization with user-definable rules, *LDAP* directory integration, and support for *POP* and *IMAP* mail access protocols. Mail's **Preferences** window contains innumerable ways to configure the application to match your work style; this chapter will concentrate on the most important core features of Mail, while pointing out areas where you can customize it to your taste.

Working in tandem with your **Address Book** (a small application that keeps track of all your "contacts," the people you correspond with by email, phone, or any other means) and synchronizing all your information using iSync and .Mac, Mail can turn a formerly austere and potentially confusing form of communication into one that anticipates what you want to say and who you want to say it to. Refer to **120** **Add a Person to Your Address Book** to start making the most of your Address Book.

60 Configure a Server-Based Mail Account (.Mac, Exchange, or IMAP)

If you have a .Mac account, using the @**mac.com** email address that comes with it is the easiest way to use the **Mail** program. The .Mac service email accounts use *IMAP*, the Internet Mail Access Protocol; so do accounts hosted on a Microsoft Exchange server, which is often the type of server used in corporate networks. You can set up many kinds of email accounts to use IMAP, from free hosting services to your own ISP (consult with the provider of your email service to see whether it's capable of using IMAP). If you specify that your email account is a .Mac account, however, **Mail** uses certain default settings to allow you to interact with the .Mac mail servers without any further configuration.

Mail can support many kinds of email accounts, but each account must be configured in the application before you can use it. When you configure the Mail program to use your email account, you'll have to enter a fair amount of information. Be sure that you have all the information you need from your Internet service provider (ISP) or network administrator: The type of email account, your email address, the incoming and outgoing mail servers, and your account name and password.

IMAP operates by keeping all your messages and mailboxes on the mail server at the Internet service provider. When you use Mail to check for new messages, it accesses those messages on the server and downloads copies to your Mac so that you can peruse them at your leisure (even when you're offline). The messages are not deleted from the server until you delete them using Mail; when you do that, messages are moved into the **Trash** folder on your computer's hard drive.

Before You Begin

✔ **29** Configure Networking Manually

✔ **50** Sign Up for .Mac

See Also

→ **61** Configure a Downloaded Mail Account (POP)

→ **62** Find and Read Messages and Attachments

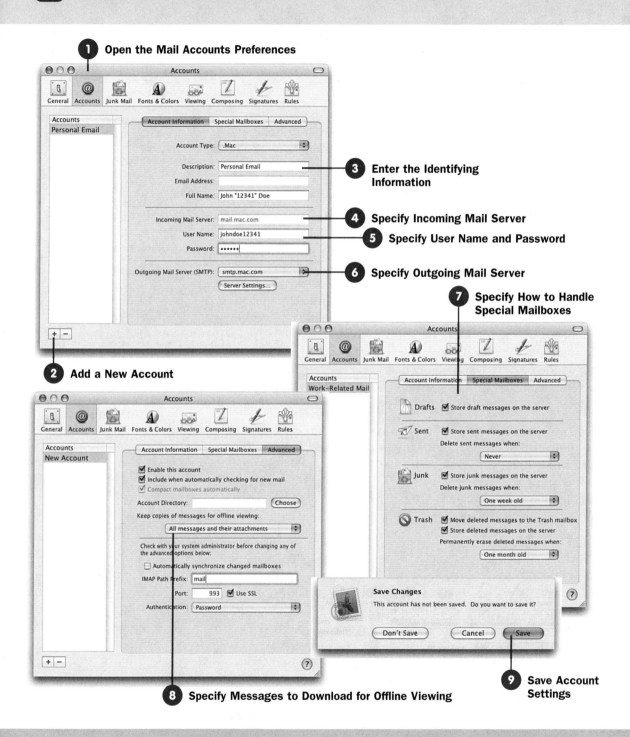

1 Open the Mail Accounts Preferences

3 Enter the Identifying Information

4 Specify Incoming Mail Server

5 Specify User Name and Password

6 Specify Outgoing Mail Server

7 Specify How to Handle Special Mailboxes

2 Add a New Account

8 Specify Messages to Download for Offline Viewing

9 Save Account Settings

This behavior is distinct from *POP* mail accounts, in which Mail downloads all new messages to your computer and removes them from the server. With IMAP, you can always access your mail from any computer; with POP, you can read your mail only from a single computer (unless you configure Mail to leave the messages on the server). Furthermore, IMAP frees you from having to worry about what happens if your Mac crashes and you lose your data; you can simply connect again with a new or freshly rebuilt computer, and your messages are all still there. With POP, unless you've diligently backed up your data, your old mail messages are gone forever if your hard drive crashes. (See **173** **Back Up Your Information** for more on backing up your data!)

❶ Open the Mail Accounts Preferences

Launch the Mail application by clicking its icon in the Dock or by double-clicking its icon in the **Applications** folder. Select **Preferences** from the **Mail** menu and click the **Accounts** icon in the toolbar to open the **Accounts** page, if it isn't already open.

❷ Add a New Account

At the bottom of the list of accounts on the left, click the + icon to create a new mail account. The new account appears in the list, named **New Account**; you must specify some minimal information before you can leave this screen without discarding the new account.

Select **.Mac**, **Exchange**, or **IMAP** from the **Account Type** dropdown menu, depending on the kind of email account your Internet service provider or network administrator has assigned for you.

❸ Enter Identifying Information

Type a descriptive name for the account. This name is what will appear in the **Mailboxes** drawer in Mail; choose a name that adequately describes what the account is for, such as **Work-Related Email** or **My .Mac Account**.

In the fields provided, type your email address and your full name; these are used in constructing the return address on the messages you send out, so make sure that they're accurate!

TIP

Consult your ISP if you're not sure whether you have an IMAP or POP account; if you're configuring your .Mac mail account (*<membername>*@mac. com), select .Mac.

TIP

You can specify either a host-name or an IP address for your incoming mail server. Using a hostname (such as **mail.somecompany.com**) is easier to type and to remember, but because it depends on an extra layer of networking architecture (DNS, the Domain Name System), there is a risk that your email service could be interrupted if DNS service is not available because of a network problem. If you specify an IP address (for instance, **112.113.114.115**), your email service will be a little more fault-tolerant because it no longer depends on DNS.

4 Specify Incoming Mail Server

If you're setting up a .Mac account, the incoming mail server is automatically set to **mail.mac.com**; for an IMAP or Exchange account, type the hostname of the incoming mail server provided by your ISP or network administrator. This server name is usually of a form similar to **mail.somecompany.com**.

5 Specify User Name and Password

In the **User Name** and **Password** fields, type the account name and password associated with the account you have with your ISP.

The user/account name is typically the same as the first part of your email address, before the @ symbol. For instance, if your address is **johndoe@mac.com**, the account name is **johndoe**.

6 Specify Outgoing Mail Server

For the outgoing mail server (or SMTP server—meaning the Simple Mail Transfer Protocol, the delivery mechanism for outgoing mail), a .Mac account automatically has the server **smtp.mac.com** configured. If you're setting up an IMAP account, your ISP might have given you a server name to use; it might, in fact, be the same as your incoming mail server.

If you have an outgoing mail server from your provider, select **Add Server** from the **Outgoing Mail Server (SMTP)** drop-down menu and then enter the server name in the dialog box that appears. Standard outgoing mail servers use port 25 (the default port to which the account is set); if your provider uses a different port for the outgoing mail server, enter it in the **Server Port** field in the dialog box. If the provider supports secure SMTP (using Secure Sockets Layer, or SSL), enable the check box under the port. You can also select an authentication method (such as **Password**) and specify a name and password, if your provider requires authentication for sending mail.

Some kinds of email accounts, notably accounts with free Web hosting services, don't provide SMTP server access. This is a measure intended to fight *spam*, or unsolicited email broadcast through mail servers on the Internet. To defend against spam, many hosting services do not permit remote users to send mail through their

SMTP servers at all. This means that even if you are setting up an account to fetch mail from a remote service on the Internet, you might have to set the account to use an SMTP server provided by your Internet service provider. Your ISP will almost certainly make a usable SMTP server available to you as a customer on its local network.

If your ISP has not given you an outgoing mail server, you can use your .Mac account to gain access to the **smtp.mac.com** server, provided that you have specified your **@mac.com** email address in the account configuration (which you can do even in accounts other than your .Mac email account—think of it as your return address); select **mail.mac.com:<*membername*>**, which uses your .Mac account information for authentication, from the **Outgoing Mail Server (SMTP)** list.

NOTE

Click the **Server Settings** button to change the settings for a server entry that has already been created.

If you're creating an Exchange account, and your network administrator has given you the name of a server for Outlook Web Access (or an Internet Information Services server, or IIS), enter it in the **Outlook Web Access Server** field. (When you select **Exchange** from the **Account Type** drop-down list, the **Outlook Web Access Server** field appears at the bottom of the screen.) This server may be the same as your incoming mail server. If you specify an Outlook Web Access server name, the Mail application will do some extra filtering to make sure that mail coming from that server is formatted properly.

7 **Specify How to Handle Special Mailboxes**

Click the **Special Mailboxes** tab. This brings up the pane where you can fine-tune the behavior of mail that is automatically sorted into your **Drafts**, **Sent**, **Junk**, and **Trash** folders. For any of these mailboxes, you can elect to have their contents stored on the server rather than downloaded permanently to your computer. You can also specify when Mail should automatically delete messages in those folders—after a day, a week, a month, whenever you quit Mail, or never.

By default, Mail downloads messages in these special mailboxes and removes them from the server to save server space. However, if you stick with this default behavior, you can't access the contents of those mailboxes from other computers. If you elect to keep the messages on the server, they will take up more space on the server (as well as being slower to access), but you can browse them from any computer. For instance, if you keep your **Drafts** mailbox on the server, you can begin a message with one computer, save it, and resume working on it in another computer before sending it.

8 Specify Messages to Download for Offline Viewing

TIP

If you're setting up an IMAP account to access mail on a Unix shell system, you will probably have to specify the **IMAP Path Prefix**. On most servers, this prefix is typically **mail**. If you don't set this path, every file in your home directory on the server will appear as a mailbox in Mail!

Click the **Advanced** tab. The **Advanced** tab allows you to configure several additional options, including whether the account is *enabled* (appears in the **Mailboxes** drawer), whether your connections to the incoming mail server are secure (using SSL), and whether Mail should download copies of all your messages automatically so that you can read them even when you're not online. Use the **Keep copies of messages for offline viewing** drop-down menu to select whether Mail should keep all messages or just the ones you've read, and whether it should download attachments or not.

9 Save Account Settings

Close the **Mail Preferences** window when you're done. In the confirmation sheet that appears, click **Save** to create the new account.

---

61 Configure a Downloaded Mail Account (POP)

Before You Begin

✔ **29** Configure Networking Manually

See Also

→ **60** Configure a Server-Based Mail Account (.Mac, Exchange, or IMAP)

→ **62** Find and Read Messages and Attachments

→ **67** Import Mailboxes from Another Email Program

The *Post Office Protocol (POP)* is traditionally the most popular type of email account, although more and more Internet service providers are switching to *IMAP* because of its flexibility. POP accounts are still quite common; if your Internet service provider has set you up with one, it means that whenever you get new mail, the **Mail** application downloads it to your Mac and removes it from the server. You can configure Mail to leave messages on the server for a certain period of time, but after that period expires, you won't be able to access your mail from any computer but the one that downloaded the messages. The upside of this arrangement is that your Mac will always be able to access the messages quickly, whether online or offline, because the messages have already been downloaded completely.

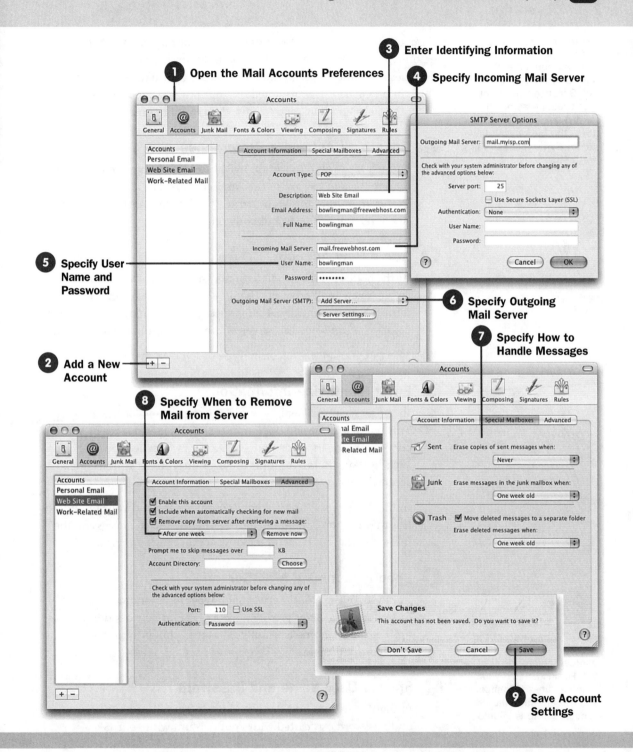

3 Enter Identifying Information

1 Open the Mail Accounts Preferences

4 Specify Incoming Mail Server

5 Specify User Name and Password

2 Add a New Account

6 Specify Outgoing Mail Server

7 Specify How to Handle Messages

8 Specify When to Remove Mail from Server

9 Save Account Settings

Configuring a POP account is similar to configuring an IMAP account; the only major differences are that you only have to decide how long to keep messages in the special mailboxes (such as **Junk**, **Trash**, and **Sent**, which in a POP account are stored on your Mac) before deleting them, rather than electing how long to keep them on the server.

1 Open Mail Accounts Preferences

Launch the **Mail** application by clicking its icon in the Dock or by double-clicking its icon in the **Applications** folder. Select **Preferences** from the **Mail** menu and click **Accounts** to open the **Accounts** page, if it isn't already open.

2 Add a New Account

At the bottom of the list of accounts on the left, click the + icon to create a new mail account. The new account appears in the list, named **New Account**; you must specify some minimal information before you can leave this screen without discarding the new account.

Select **POP** from the **Account Type** drop-down menu.

3 Enter Identifying Information

In the **Description** field, type a descriptive name for the account. This name is what will appear in the **Mailboxes** drawer in Mail; choose a name that adequately describes what the account is for, such as **Work-Related Email** or **Secondary Address (johndoe@ somewhere.com)**.

In the fields provided, type your email address and your full name; this information is used in constructing the return address on the messages you send out, so make sure that they're accurate!

4 Specify Incoming Mail Server

In the **Incoming Mail Server** field, type the hostname of the incoming mail server provided by your ISP or network administrator. This server name is usually of a form similar to **mail. somecompany.com**.

5 Specify User Name and Password

In the **User Name** and **Password** fields, type the account name and password associated with your account with your ISP.

⑥ Specify Outgoing Mail Server

For the outgoing mail server (or SMTP server), your ISP might have given you a server name to use; it might, in fact, be the same as your incoming mail server. If you have an outgoing mail server from your provider, select **Add Server** from the **Outgoing Mail Server (SMTP)** drop-down menu and then enter the server name in the input field in the dialog box that appears.

Some kinds of email accounts, notably accounts with free Web hosting services, don't provide SMTP server access. This measure is intended to fight *spam*, or unsolicited email broadcast through mail servers on the Internet. To defend against spam, many hosting services do not permit remote users to send mail through their SMTP servers at all. This means that even if you are setting up an account to fetch mail from a remote service on the Internet, you might have to set the account to use an SMTP server provided by your Internet service provider. Your ISP will almost certainly make a usable SMTP server available to you as a customer on its local network.

If your ISP has not given you an outgoing mail server, you can use your .Mac account to gain access to the **smtp.mac.com** server, provided that you have specified your **@mac.com** email address in the account configuration (which you can do even in accounts other than your .Mac email account—think of it as your return address); select **mail.mac.com:<*membername*>**, which uses your .Mac account information for authentication, from the **Outgoing Mail Server (SMTP)** list.

⑦ Specify How to Handle Messages

Click the **Special Mailboxes** tab. On this tab, you can fine-tune the behavior of mail that is automatically sorted into your **Sent**, **Junk**, and **Trash** mailbox folders, which reside on your Mac's hard disk. For any of these mailboxes, you can specify when the Mail program should automatically delete messages from those folders—after a day, a week, a month, whenever you quit Mail, or never.

 TIP

Standard outgoing mail servers use port 25, which is the default the account is set to use. If your provider uses a different port, enter it in the **Server Port** field in the **SMTP Server Options** dialog box. If the provider supports secure SMTP (using Secure Sockets Layer, or SSL), enable the check box under the port number. You can also select an authentication method (such as **Password**) and specify a name and password, if your provider requires authentication for sending mail.

TIP

Click the **Server Settings** button to change the settings for a server entry that has already been created.

TIP

The Mail application's default setting is to delete messages from the server after a week; this gives you some insurance time in case you should lose the data on your Mac and need to download your mail again. When you're using POP mail, remember that you can recover only the mail that's less than a week or a month old, depending on how you configured Mail. You should be especially sure to make backups of your hard drive regularly to ensure that your older mail is safe!

8 Specify When to Remove Mail from Server

Click the **Advanced** tab to configure several additional options, including whether the account is *enabled* (appears in the **Mailboxes** drawer), whether your connections to the incoming mail server are secure (using SSL), and how quickly the Mail program should delete new messages from the mail server after it downloads them. Use the **Remove copy from server after retrieving a message** drop-down menu to select whether Mail should delete messages right away or wait for a day, a week, or a month before deleting them.

9 Save Account Settings

Close the **Mail Preferences** window when you're done. In the confirmation sheet that appears, click **Save** to create the new account.

62 Find and Read Messages and Attachments

Before You Begin

✔ 60 Configure a Server-Based Mail Account (.Mac, Exchange, or IMAP)

✔ 61 Configure a Downloaded Mail Account (POP)

See Also

→ 63 Send a Message

→ 64 Filter Junk Mail

It won't be long before you have received your first few email messages. Indeed, chances are that before you know it, you'll be getting more than you can handle (particularly in the form of junk mail, which the Mail program can filter for you—as you see in 64 Filter Junk Mail). The first function of the Mail program is to allow you to read these messages, as well as to open any attached files that might come with the messages.

Within your email account (and each additional account, if you happen to have more than one), you have a number of mailboxes—which can be thought of as "folders" within your email account. The primary mailbox—which each account has—is the Inbox, which in Mail is labeled with the name **In**. The rest of the mailboxes depend on the types of accounts you have; but the most common important mailboxes are **Sent**, **Trash**, and **Junk**, as well as the **Drafts** and **Outbox** (or **Out**) mailboxes. The **Sent** mailbox holds every message you send; the **Trash** mailbox contains all the messages you delete; and **Junk** has the messages that the Mail programs deems junk mail. The **Drafts** mailbox is used to hold partially completed messages while you're composing them, and **Out** keeps a copy of each outgoing message while Mail is attempting to deliver it. Additionally, you can create as many other mailboxes as you want—either stored locally on your Mac or remotely on the server (for IMAP accounts).

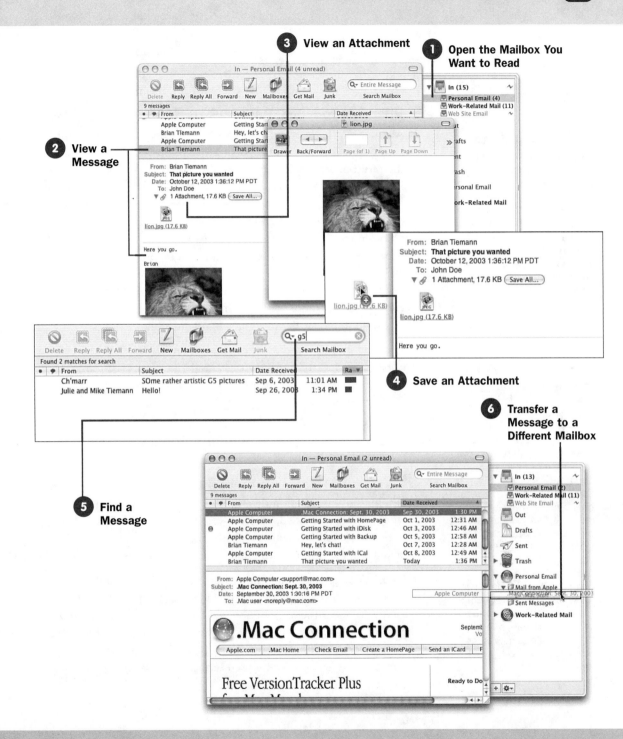

3 View an Attachment

1 Open the Mailbox You Want to Read

2 View a Message

4 Save an Attachment

6 Transfer a Message to a Different Mailbox

5 Find a Message

New messages always appear in your Inbox, unless they are moved else-where by an automated rule, as you will see in **65** **Create a Mailbox**.

① Open the Mailbox You Want to Read

All your available email accounts and all their associated mail-boxes appear in the **Mailboxes** drawer of the Mail application. (If the **Mailboxes** drawer is not currently shown, click the **Mailboxes** icon to show it or choose **View, Show Mailboxes**.) Depending on the types of accounts you have and what options for the special mailboxes you have already specified, the mailboxes are sorted according to their importance and how likely you are to need access to them. Your Inboxes appear at the top of the list, all grouped together into a single unified **In** box; you can either expand the **In** mailbox (using the triangle control to its left) to view each individual account's Inbox, or you can click the **In** mail-box itself to see all the messages in all your Inboxes at once.

Click the mailbox you want to view; the messages in that mailbox appear listed in the Message List pane. The number of total mes-sages in the mailbox appears above the message list.

② View a Message

Click a message's subject to view that message in the Message pane below.

The top part of the message consists of the *headers*, which are sev-eral lines of information describing who sent the message, to whom it was addressed, when it was sent, and the subject (shown in bold), as well as a variety of other optional pieces of data. Then, below a horizontal line, the body of the message itself appears.

Email messages can come in two styles: Plain Text and Rich Text. Rich Text, a designation which includes HTML and inline attach-ments, allows a message to have text in custom colors and fonts and styles; however, these messages are also larger and take longer to download. For this reason, many messages—such as informa-tional messages from Web-based services—are sent as Plain Text.

NOTE

Each mailbox indicates how many unread mes-sages are in it. If there are any unread messages, the mailbox name appears in bold, with the number of unread messages after it in parentheses. If there are no unread messages in the mailbox, no number appears.

TIP

If you prefer, double-click a message in the Message List pane to open the mes-sage in a separate window. Viewing messages in a separate window can be useful if you prefer to see only a list of message sub-jects, so that you can see as many messages as pos-sible, or so that you can control messages without downloading them (for instance, if you're on a very slow network link). Double-click the horizontal divider between the panes to hide the Message pane and cre-ate a larger Message List pane.

Often, Plain Text messages are laid out to organize text into tabular format, such as in billing reports that list line-items and a total. However, for this kind of layout to work properly, you must tell the Mail program to use a monospaced font for Plain Text messages. Otherwise, the letters will all be different widths and won't line up properly. To do this, open the **Mail Preferences** window, click the **Fonts & Colors** icon, and enable the **Use fixed-width font for plain text messages** check box.

❸ View an Attachment

In addition to Plain Text or Rich Text content, an email message can also contain one or more *attachments*—files, folders, or applications that are sent along with the message for you to open and save on your own computer. Email attachments have become the *de facto* standard method for transferring pictures, Word and Excel documents, and Zip archives around the office or across the Internet.

If an email message has an attachment, you will see a line in the headers area noting how many attachments there are, as well as a **Save All** button. Click the triangle to the left of this line to expand the attachments summary; double-click any listed attachment to open it in its default application. You can also right-click (or **Control**+click) the attachment icon to choose which application to open it in, just as you would in the Finder.

❹ Save an Attachment

If you simply view an attachment by double-clicking it, it will open in its associated application; but if you want to save the attachment permanently on your hard disk, move it from the Mail program into the Finder. Click and drag any attachment icon from the expanded header area onto the Desktop or into a Finder window; the green + symbol next to the mouse pointer as you drag indicates that the item will be saved correctly.

❺ Find a Message

You can quickly locate a message if you know any text that appears in its **Subject** line or contents, or if you know to or from whom it was sent. Just type the search text into the **Search**

NOTE

Rich Text messages can have pictures and other types of data embedded directly into the body of the message; to view or save these items, double-click them or drag them from their position in the message to your Desktop or a Finder window (or even straight into another application, such as Preview). However, for both Plain Text and Rich Text messages, all attachments are listed in the header portion of the message, so that you can examine the filename and type of each attachment.

TIP

Click the **Save All** button to choose a location and have the Mail application save all the message's attachments to that location at once.

TIP

Click the gray circled **X** at the right end of the **Search Mailbox** field to clear the contents of the field and go back to viewing your mailbox normally.

TIP

The Mail application supports a form of the "spring-loaded folders" feature used by the Finder: To move a message into a mailbox that's deeply nested within other mailboxes, drag the message to the top mailbox and hover the mouse pointer over that mailbox until the mailbox expands. Repeat for a mailbox inside that one, if necessary, until the target mailbox is visible. Then drop the message into the mailbox where you want it to go.

Mailbox field, and the mailbox you're currently viewing is immediately filtered to show only the messages that match what you've typed.

Click the magnifying glass icon at the left end of the **Search Mailbox** field to select what part of the message to search. By default, Mail searches the entire contents of all your messages; if you want to narrow the results down still further, you can select **From**, **To**, or **Subject** from the magnifying-glass list to limit the searching to those header fields. You can also tell Mail to search messages in all your mailboxes instead of just the mailbox you're currently viewing.

Transfer a Message to a Different Mailbox

To help you organize your communications more efficiently, you can create new mailboxes in any of your accounts, either those on your local hard disk or those on the remote server (for .Mac, IMAP, or Exchange accounts). Mail lets you sort your messages into your various mailboxes by simply dragging and dropping. Click any message and drag it to the mailbox you want to move it to. You can move messages from any mailbox to any other mailbox, including mailboxes in other accounts.

 **Send a Message**

Before You Begin

✔ **60** Configure a Server-Based Mail Account (.Mac, Exchange, or IMAP)

✔ **62** Find and Read Messages and Attachments

See Also

→ **66** Subscribe to a Directory Server

→ **120** Add a Person to Your Address Book

Naturally, email isn't just for receiving messages; you'll also want to send messages of your own. You can send email to anybody whose email address you know, whether they're in your Address Book or not. Note, however, that the more people you add to your Address Book, the easier it is to communicate with the important people in your life.

To reply to a message that someone else has sent to you, simply click the **Reply** or **Reply All** button while viewing the message; you can then type whatever you want to say in response.

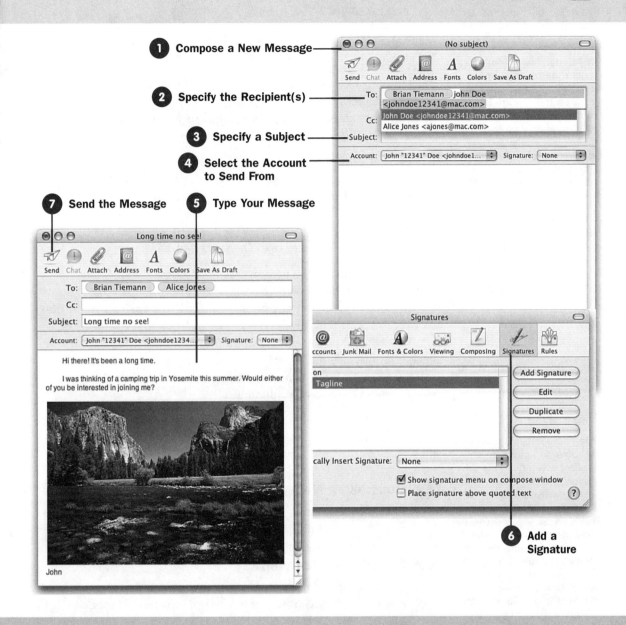

1　Compose a New Message

2　Specify the Recipient(s)

3　Specify a Subject

4　Select the Account to Send From

7　Send the Message

5　Type Your Message

6　Add a Signature

Internet etiquette ("netiquette") dictates that you should always *quote* the message you're replying to—that is, you should include the other person's text in your message, so that she knows what you're talking about. The Mail application automatically quotes the entire message for you when you click **Reply**. You can add your own reply at the top of the

NOTE

If you don't want Mail to quote the other person's message for you, you can turn off this feature by disabling the **Quote the text of the original message** check box in the **Composing** pane of the **Mail Preferences** window. It's probably best to leave this option enabled, however!

Forward

TIP

Mail automatically matches a name no matter which part of it you type: the first name, the last name, or the email address. When you finish specifying a recipient's name and address, the address changes to a colored oval showing the person's full name, which you can then drag from one place to another—from the **To** field to the **Cc** field, for instance, or to any other application that accepts text. When dragged into another application, the recipient's name and address is copied in the form **John Doe <johndoe12341@mac. com>**.

quoted text, at the bottom of the quoted text, or interspersed between the paragraphs in question.

The Mail program's default behavior is that if you have selected a portion of the other person's message when you click **Reply**, only the selected text is quoted. You can turn this feature off as well in the **Composing** tab of the **Mail Preferences**.

Rather than writing a new message or replying to a message that was sent to you, you have a couple of further options. You can forward a message to another recipient—just click the **Forward** button and specify the new recipient's email address in the composition window that appears. Add some message text of your own, if you like, above or below the quoted body of the message. Then click **Send**.

Similarly, you can use the **Redirect** command (found in the **Message** menu) to resend the message to a different email address without quoting the body or changing any of the headers; this is useful if you mistakenly receive a piece of mail and want to pass it on to the proper recipient. Finally, the **Bounce** command (in the **Message** menu) sends a simulated error message back to the sender, making it appear that your email address no longer works (useful if you're trying to shake off a secret admirer or get off a mailing list).

To compose a new message of your own, without replying to or forwarding an existing message that someone sent you, follow these instructions.

1 **Compose a New Message**

Click the **New** button in the toolbar of the main Mail window to begin a new email message.

2 **Specify the Recipient(s)**

In the **To** field of the new email message, enter the name or email address of the person to whom you want to send the message. If the recipient is someone you've emailed before, or if the person is in your Address Book, the Mail program will automatically complete the name or address as you type it; press **Tab** or **Return** to accept the first name that matches, or use the arrow keys or the mouse to scroll through the drop-down menu to select from all the names that match.

Specify more than one recipient by typing a new name as soon as the first one is accepted, or by separating the addresses with commas.

If you don't want Mail to hide the email addresses in recipients that you specify, select **Show Name and Address** (rather than **Use Smart Addresses**) in the **Addresses** submenu of the **View** menu.

The **To** field can accept more than one address, if you want to send the message to multiple people. However, it can often be useful to use the **Cc** (Carbon Copy) field to specify other recipients, instead of listing them all in the **To** field. Typically, **Cc** recipients are included for informational purposes only; if it's a business correspondence, only the recipients in the **To** line are expected to respond. This, however, is all just netiquette, and nothing really compels people to behave according to these rules.

Everybody who receives the message can see all the other recipients in the **To** and **Cc** fields. If you want to send a private copy of the message to another recipient, so that the primary recipients don't know you've sent this person a copy, you can use the **Bcc** (Blind Carbon Copy) field. This field is normally not shown in a Compose window; choose **View, Bcc Header** to create a **Bcc** field.

③ Specify a Subject

Type a descriptive subject for the message. Keep the subject brief and informative; when coming up with a subject, imagine what it would be like to receive a message with the subject you specify. Nobody likes receiving messages with empty or cryptic subject lines—or subject lines that are as long as the message itself!

The Mail program can view messages in *threads*, or groupings of related messages. Mail can also group relevant messages into threads even if the subject line is different, based on other identifiers in the headers. To view your messages in threads, choose **Organize by Thread** from the **View** menu.

When viewing messages in threads, click a collapsed thread to see a list of all the messages in the thread. Click one of the listed messages in the **Message** pane to view that message (and expand the thread).

TIP

Enable the **Mark addresses not in this domain** option in the **Composing** page of the **Mail Preferences** window and specify your company's Internet domain to have Mail use a red color on recipients who are not within that domain. This option is intended to help you distinguish between intra-office correspondence and mail that travels outside the company.

NOTE

If you're replying to a message instead of composing a new one, the text in the **Subject** field begins with **Re:** to indicate that this reply is "regarding" the original message. A long string of email exchanges can generally take place with a single subject line, with every message after the very first one starting with the **Re:** prefix. Most email applications, including Mail, don't add another **Re:** prefix if there's one there already.

KEY TERM

Thread—A single string of correspondence, between any number of people, in which all the messages share the same subject line (barring the absence of the **Re:** prefix in the first message's subject line).

TIP

The Mail application will automatically use the account associated with the mailbox you're currently viewing. **To make sure that you always send using the correct identity, it can be a good idea to be in the habit of selecting the In mailbox for the account you want to use before composing a new message.** Doing so ensures that you use the right account even if you don't check what's shown in the **Account** menu.

4 **Select the Account to Send From**

If you have configured more than one email account, there will be an **Account** drop-down menu above the message input area. Use this menu to select which identity you want to send the message as. Always check this menu to make sure that you're using the right address!

5 **Type Your Message**

Compose your message. You can use whatever style you like—you can make your message massively long, or just a few words; you can style your text with bold and italics and special fonts, or you can make it plain text; you can even add pictures by dragging image files into the message window from the Finder.

Select **Plain Text** from the **Format** menu in the **Composing** tab of the **Mail Preferences** window if you want to compose your messages using plain, unstyled text. A Plain Text message cannot be formatted with text styles, but if you have enabled the **Use fixed-width font for plain text messages** check box in the **Fonts & Colors** tab, the text you type will be laid out using a monospaced font. Using a fixed-width font can be helpful if you want to create a message that contains tabular information, such as a column of numbers.

Any picture or other file that you drag into the message window becomes an attachment; the recipient can view the attachment along with the message, or (if he is using a sufficiently capable email application) he can view the picture inline, right where you placed it in the message.

 TIP

You can define as many signatures as you like; when you compose a new message, you can select the signature you want or allow Mail to automatically insert a certain signature into every message (useful if, for instance, you have to include your business contact information at the end of every message you send). Mail can even choose a signature for you at random from the ones you've defined.

6 **Add a Signature**

The Mail program allows you to define *signatures*, or predetermined bits of text that it can insert at the end of a message with a quick command.

Define your signatures in the **Signatures** tab in the **Mail Preferences** window. Click the **Add Signature** button to create a new signature; type a description (which is what will appear in the **Signature** menu in the Compose window) and the signature text, then click **OK**. Repeat the process to create multiple signatures for different purposes.

Enable the **Show signature menu on compose window** check box. Now, when you compose a message, you can select a signature from the **Signature** menu above the message input area.

7 Send the Message

Double-check your message and proofread it if you want. When you're satisfied with how it looks, click the **Send** button in the toolbar at the top of the Compose window to deliver it to the mail server, and from there to the recipient.

While you are composing your message, it is saved in the **Drafts** mailbox. This arrangement allows you to quit the Mail application and come back to it right where you left off. Also, if you are using a server-based email account and have configured your email account to keep the **Drafts** mailbox on the server, you can come back to your half-composed messages and finish them using a different computer.

When you click **Send**, Mail copies the message to your **Out** mailbox while it tries to deliver it. If the delivery attempt is successful, the message moves to your **Sent** mailbox. If delivery fails, however, the message remains in your **Out** mailbox while Mail keeps trying to send it. Mail will prompt you for a different mail server to try. You can select any properly configured SMTP server from the list Mail gives you, or you can elect to try again later (or edit the message if you made an error in addressing).

TIP

If you want to cancel sending a message, select **Try Again Later** from the sheet that Mail presents, and then go to the **Out** mailbox and delete the pending message.

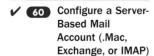
Filter Junk Mail

Before You Begin

✔ **60** Configure a Server-
Based Mail
Account (.Mac,
Exchange, or IMAP)

✔ **62** Find and Read
Messages and
Attachments

See Also

→ **65** Create a Mailbox

If there is a downside to email, it would have to be what is commonly known as *spam*, or junk mail. Anybody who has ever used email has been plagued with junk messages—unsolicited business propositions, pornographic advertisements, get-rich-quick schemes, and even viruses and Trojan horses (malicious programs that sneak onto your computer by innocuous means, such as in an email attachment). Some people get so much junk mail that their real, legitimate email is lost in the shuffle. What's really infuriating is that there's usually no good way to defend against this kind of onslaught. Sure, you could set up a rule to delete messages from a certain sender or with a certain subject, but junk mail always comes from different sender addresses and has constantly changing subject lines and content. What's an email user to do?

Fortunately, Apple's Mail application helps you fight back. Mail contains a heuristics-based junk-mail filtering system that learns with time what kinds of messages you consider to be "junk" and which ones you don't.

When you turn on junk mail filtering, Mail can operate in either of two modes: It can delete messages it determines to be junk, moving them into a special **Junk** folder, or it can simply mark junk messages with a certain color, allowing you to review them later. This latter mode, **Training** mode, is what you can use while Mail is "learning" how to spot junk messages. When the Mail application has gotten good enough at recognizing junk mail, you can put it into **Automatic** mode, keeping junk mail out of your face for good.

❶ Enable Junk Mail Filtering

Open the **Mail Preferences** window and click the **Junk Mail** icon in the toolbar at the top. If it is not already enabled, check the **Enable Junk Mail filtering** check box.

❷ Train Mail to Recognize Junk Messages

Mail begins in **Training** mode, in which it leaves junk messages in your **In** mailbox, but doesn't do anything but mark the messages with a certain color (light brown) and a special symbol in the **Flags** column. This way, you can check which messages it has identified as junk mail and make sure that the program has made the right decision before deleting those messages yourself.

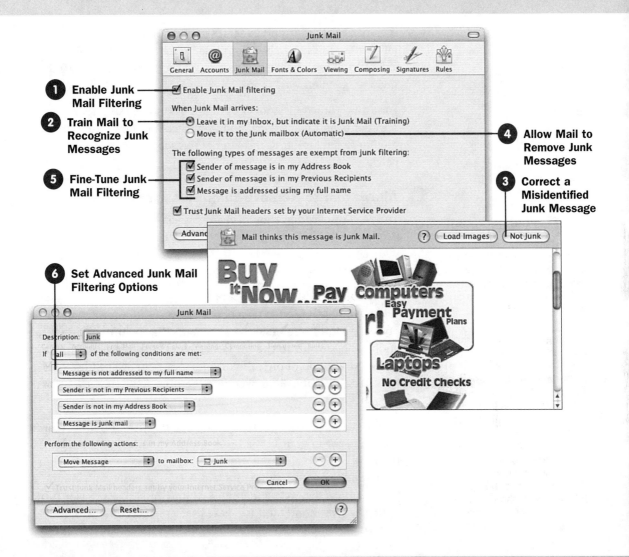

① Enable Junk Mail Filtering

② Train Mail to Recognize Junk Messages

⑤ Fine-Tune Junk Mail Filtering

④ Allow Mail to Remove Junk Messages

③ Correct a Misidentified Junk Message

⑥ Set Advanced Junk Mail Filtering Options

③ Correct a Misidentified Junk Message

While Mail is in **Training** mode, you need to help it correctly iden-tify junk mail and ignore messages that it mistakenly flags as junk.

For a message that Mail incorrectly identifies as junk mail but that you actually want to receive, select or open the message and then click the **Not Junk** button, which appears both in the brown header area of the message and in Mail's toolbar. This action adds an entry into Mail's heuristics database, so that future messages that share the characteristics of this message will have a higher likelihood of being allowed through.

For an unwanted message that didn't get marked as junk mail, select or open the message, and then click the **Junk** button in the toolbar to tell Mail that this kind of message is something it should catch.

④ Allow Mail to Remove Junk Messages

The Mail application should spend at least a couple of weeks in **Training** mode, learning to identify junk mail properly. Judge for yourself when you're ready to let Mail start automatically deleting junk messages on its own instead of just turning them brown for your review.

When you deem Mail to be ready to go into **Automatic** mode, open the **Mail Preferences** window and click the **Junk Mail** icon; enable the **Move it to the Junk mailbox (Automatic)** radio button. From that point on, all messages that Mail determines to be junk are automatically moved into the **Junk** mailbox for that account.

Mail is designed to err on the side of caution—it will sooner leave a junk message in your Inbox than send a legitimate message to the **Junk** mailbox. Just the same, it's a good idea to open up your **Junk** mailbox occasionally and look for "false positives," messages that Mail has incorrectly identified as junk mail. Use the **Not Junk** button to reprimand Mail for these transgressions and, with time, they won't happen any more.

⑤ Fine-Tune Junk Mail Filtering

Mail's junk filtering depends on several exception conditions, which you can control using the check boxes in the **Junk Mail** tab of the **Mail Preferences** window. Mail's default behavior is to ignore messages that come from addresses in your **Address Book** or **Previous Recipients** list, or if the address contains your full name (something that spammers seldom do, because usually all they have are lists of email addresses). Disable these check boxes if you want Mail to be stricter with these kinds of messages.

TIPS

After a couple of weeks in **Training** mode, Mail gives you an informative sheet that reminds you that it might be time to switch to **Automatic** mode.

You might still see unwanted messages in your Inbox, even when Mail is in **Automatic** mode; these are messages that Mail is still not identifying as junk messages. You can continue to train Mail to trap these messages by selecting them and using the **Junk** button, which now moves the messages to the **Junk** folder as well as adding their characteristics to Mail's heuristics database.

6 **Set Advanced Junk Mail Filtering Options**

Click the **Advanced** button to gain access to even finer detail regarding how Mail deals with junk mail. In the sheet that appears, you can define an arbitrary number of criteria for what causes a message to be flagged as junk. For instance, **Message is junk mail** means that Mail's heuristics database determines that the message is likely junk. **Sender is not in my Address Book** ensures that if the message is sent to you by someone you know (who is listed in your **Address Book**, as discussed in **120** **Add a Person to Your Address Book**), Mail's filters will never trap the message.

Use the – button next to any of these criteria to remove them from Mail's junk filtering scheme, or click + in any line to add a new criterion (which you can then specify using the extensively populated drop-down list). Finally, you can choose between whether **all** or **any** of the criteria have to be met for messages to be marked as junk, using the drop-down menu at the top of the sheet; if you change the sense to **any**, Mail will mark far more messages as junk than otherwise.

65 **Create a Mailbox**

Central to a modern email application is the ability to define custom mailboxes, which you can think of as "folders," to hold categorized messages. The Mail application already uses special mailboxes for incoming mail, sent messages, junk mail, and deleted messages; but you can also define your own mailboxes to hold messages related to a certain project, for instance, or for correspondence with a certain person over the years. Mail even lets you define rules that automatically direct new messages into special mailboxes, depending on certain criteria that you can define.

1 **Select the Parent Mailbox**

Open the **Mailboxes** drawer by clicking the **Mailboxes** icon at the top of the main Mail window. Select the mailbox inside which you want to create the new mailbox. For instance, to create a mailbox at the top level in an account, select the icon for that account in the drawer; to create a mailbox inside an existing mailbox in that account, expand the account (using the triangle) and select the mailbox you want to use.

Before You Begin

✔ **60** Configure a Server-Based Mail Account (.Mac, Exchange, or IMAP)

✔ **62** Find and Read Messages and Attachments

See Also

→ **67** Import Mailboxes from Another Email Program

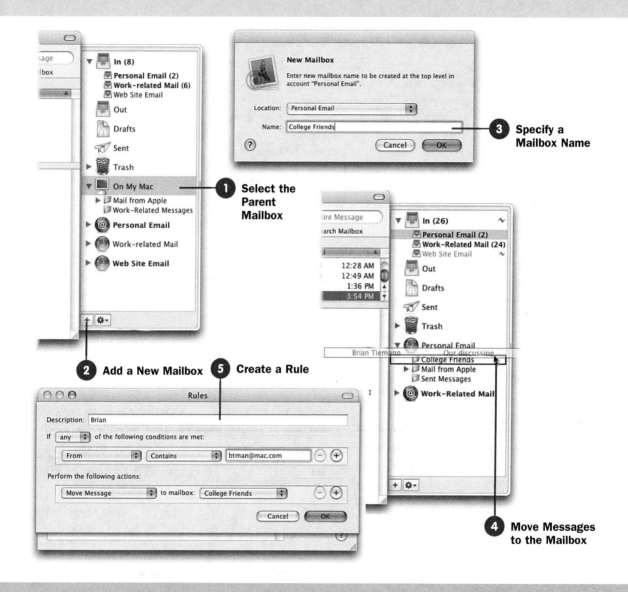

New Mailbox

Enter new mailbox name to be created at the top level in account "Personal Email".

Location: Personal Email

Name: College Friends

Cancel   OK

3 Specify a Mailbox Name

1 Select the Parent Mailbox

2 Add a New Mailbox   **5** Create a Rule

Rules

Description: Brian

If [any] of the following conditions are met:

[From] [Contains] [btman@mac.com]

Perform the following actions:

[Move Message] to mailbox: [College Friends]

Cancel   OK

4 Move Messages to the Mailbox

You can also create mailboxes on your local computer, independent of any account; select the **On My Mac** icon, or any mailbox underneath it, to create a local mailbox. If you don't see the **On My Mac** icon (which appears only if you have server-based mail accounts, such as .Mac or IMAP, instead of POP), don't select any mailbox icon.

2 Add a New Mailbox

Click the + icon at the bottom of the drawer. Carefully read the dialog box that pops up; it tells you where exactly the new mailbox will be created. If it doesn't report the correct location, click **Cancel** and select the correct parent mailbox.

3 Specify a Mailbox Name

Type a short name for the new mailbox.

Mailbox names can't contain slashes (/). If you put a slash in the name of the new mailbox, Mail will actually create a subfolder within the parent mailbox, and put the new mailbox inside the subfolder; the slash separates the name of the subfolder from the name of the mailbox. This can be quite useful, depending on what you want to do. For instance, if you specify **Vacations/2003** as the name of the new mailbox, Mail will create a subfolder called **Vacations**, and a mailbox called **2003** inside it. You can then create further mailboxes inside the **Vacations** folder—even if you're using an IMAP account.

4 Move Messages to the Mailbox

Click and drag any message, or group of selected messages, to the mailbox you want to move them to. You can automatically expand a hierarchical structure of mailboxes by dragging the messages onto the top mailbox and holding them there without releasing the button; as with spring-loaded folders in the Finder, the mailboxes expand so that you can drill down to the mailbox you want.

5 Create a Rule

Open the **Mail Preferences** window and click the **Rules** icon at the top. Click **Add Rule** to create a new rule. Give the rule a descriptive name so that you can find it later.

Use the + and – buttons to add conditions for new messages to match. For instance, if you want Mail to identify all messages from a certain mailing list, all such messages might come from a particular address, or they might all have a certain string in the **Subject** line (such as **[Motor-List]**). The Mail program provides many different kinds of criteria you can define, from substrings of various

NOTES

Different kinds of email accounts support different kinds of mailboxes. For instance, .Mac or Exchange email accounts allow you to create *nested* mailboxes, or mailboxes within mailboxes. IMAP accounts permit you to create only a single layer of mailboxes, just underneath the top level. POP accounts don't let you create mailboxes on the server at all; if you're using a POP account, you have to create all new mailboxes under the **On My Mac** icon, or (if you only have POP accounts) as folders in the **Mailboxes** list.

The only downside to using the slash to create subfolders is that you can't place messages directly into the **Vacations** subfolder (which shows up with a white folder icon instead of a blue one); you can only put messages into the blue **2003** mailbox folder inside the **Vacations** folder.

TIP

Create a rule so that Mail knows what kinds of messages to put in your new mailbox.

header fields to complex conditions, such as whether the sender is in your Address Book. You can specify as many of these conditions as you want, and you can require that new messages match all of these conditions or any single one of them.

In the **Perform the following actions** area of the **Rules** dialog box, select **Move Message** from the first drop-down list and then select the target mailbox from the **to mailbox** drop-down list. Click **OK**.

From this point on, all messages that match the criteria you specified in your rule are moved into the specified mailbox so that you can peruse them at your leisure.

66 Subscribe to a Directory Server

Before You Begin

✔ **60** Configure a Server-Based Mail Account (.Mac, Exchange, or IMAP)

✔ **63** Send a Message

See Also

→ **120** Add a Person to Your Address Book

KEY TERM

Directory server—a centralized service that provides complete and canonical names for all the company's employees, and mappings of full names to email addresses.

In corporate network environments, it's common for there to be a *directory server*. The most common protocol for directory servers is *Lightweight Directory Access Protocol (LDAP)*.

The Mail application allows you to subscribe to an LDAP server so that you can efficiently put every employee's name and address into Mail's memory. Even if these email addresses are not in your Address Book, Mail will be able to look up and automatically complete fellow employee names if you just type in a part of their name or email address.

① Open the Composing Preferences

Open the **Mail Preferences** window and click the **Composing** icon.

② Configure LDAP

Next to the **Automatically complete addresses** check box (which should be checked—enable it if it is not), click the **Configure LDAP** button.

③ Add an LDAP Server

Click the + button at the bottom of the first dialog box that appears to configure a new LDAP server. In the second dialog box that pops up, specify a descriptive name for the server, the server's hostname or IP address, and the "search base" (a string of codes that define how the Mail program should search the server).

2 Configure LDAP

3 Add an LDAP Server

1 Open the Composing Preferences

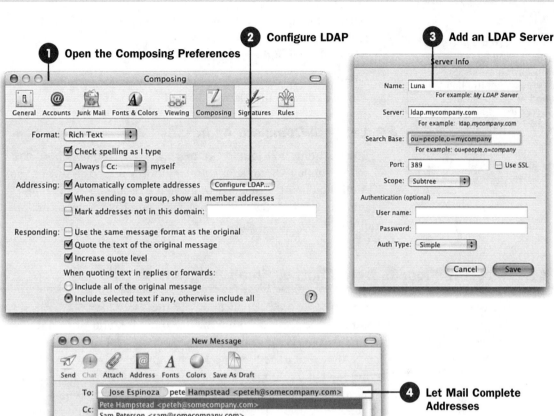

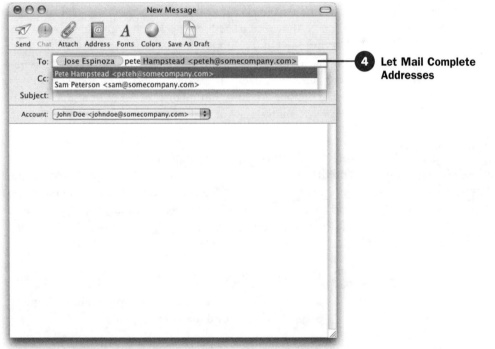

4 Let Mail Complete Addresses

TIP

Because LDAP servers are usually available in corporate environments, the configuration information you need to complete the **Server Info** dialog box is available from the company's IS department. Consult your network administrator for information about your LDAP server.

Enter authentication information if necessary (select **Simple** from the **Auth Type** menu). Again, consult your network administrator to see whether authentication is required.

Finally, click **Save** to close the **Server Info** dialog box. Back in the first dialog box, click **Done**.

4 **Let Mail Complete Addresses**

The next time you compose a message, try typing only part of a fellow employee's name or email address; within a second or two, Mail should automatically complete the recipient's name and address, just as though the employee's name was in your Address Book.

Import Mailboxes from Another Email Program

Before You Begin

✔ Configure a Downloaded Mail Account (POP)

 NOTE

Sadly, Mail does not support importing mailboxes from America Online accounts.

Mail isn't the only email application out there for Mac OS X. True, it's one of the best, and it's certainly the one that's best integrated into the operating system and the one that's most enthusiastically under development. More and more Mac users—even the old-time experts—are discovering Mail and falling in love with its straightforward approach to configuration and its intuitive integration of advanced features. However, nearly every new Mac user has used some email program before in their life, and that means there's a lot of mail built up inside whatever email application the person previously used.

The Mail application provides the capability to import mailboxes from any of a number of different popular email applications: Microsoft Entourage or Outlook Express, Eudora, Netscape, Claris Emailer, or even bare Unix-style "mbox" files. All you have to do is tell Mail where to find these mailbox files, and it will reformat them into its own **Mailboxes** drawer so that you can continue using all your archived mail.

1 **Import Mailboxes**

Select **File**, **Import Mailboxes** from the main Mail menu. The first page of the **Import** dialog box appears.

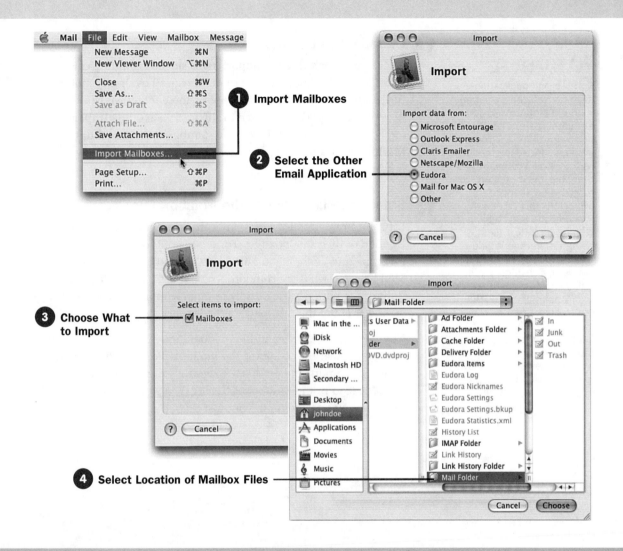

Select the Other Mail Application

Select the email program you used before the Mail program. This is the email program that contains the mailboxes you want to salvage. Click the right-arrow button in the lower-right corner of the dialog box to begin the import process.

③ Choose What to Import

Mail's importer script can import items such as contacts, calendar items, and other pieces of information as well as simply mailboxes (if the other mail application supports these features). However, none of the applications listed in the first page of the **Import** dialog box support any of these items. Simply make sure that the **Mailboxes** option is selected, and then click the right-arrow button.

④ Select the Location of the Mailbox Files

For some email applications, Mail can automatically determine the location of their mailbox files. For other email programs, such as Netscape and Eudora, you must select the mailbox files manually. Mail tells you what the standard location is for these files; click the right-arrow button to go directly to that location in the Finder-like arrangement of the next page of the **Import** dialog box.

Navigate to the location of the mailbox files you want to import; select the folder that contains the mailbox files and click **Choose**. Mail then imports the mailboxes, and they appear under the **On My Mac** icon in the **Mailboxes** drawer. You can now reorganize the mailboxes according to your taste.

8

Surfing the Web

IN THIS CHAPTER:

It's hard to deny that the principal function of a computer in this day and age is to run a Web browser. Surfing the World Wide Web—be it for shopping, banking, business, research, or plain old personal fun—is what has driven the Internet's explosive growth in recent years. Surfing the Web is easy, it's useful, and it's indelibly entered our common consciousness. The Web has changed a lot since its inception, and we can't predict what it will eventually become; however, we're all certainly enjoying the ride.

There are some tricks to Web surfing, though. Mac OS X includes Apple's own browser, *Safari*. Although Safari is a very intuitive and simple application to run, for a user whose only experience has been with Microsoft Internet Explorer on Windows, there are some subtle details about Safari that you might find surprising, as well as some features that might be new to you. The tasks in this chapter focus on using Safari to navigate the Internet.

68 Select Your Default Web Browser

Before You Begin

✔ **2** Find and Launch an Application

✔ **27** Dial Up to the Internet with a Modem (PPP)

✔ **29** Configure Networking Manually

See Also

→ **69** Keep Track of Web Sites with Bookmarks

→ **72** SnapBack to the First Page of a Site

Although Safari is the browser most favored by Apple (understandably, as it's their own application), there are several other popular browsers for Mac OS X that have some of their own advantages. Internet Explorer for Mac, for example, although it is no longer being developed by Microsoft, is sometimes compatible with certain complex Web pages that Safari cannot handle properly. Camino provides fine-grained control over animated GIF images and ad banners. OmniWeb and Mozilla are also popular competitors, each with their own strengths.

The *default Web browser* is what Mac OS X uses to open Uniform Resource Locators (URLs), or Web addresses, that appear in applications such as Mail or Word. You can specify the default browser in Safari's **Preferences** window, choosing one favored browser from all the browsers installed on your Mac.

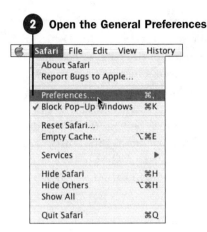

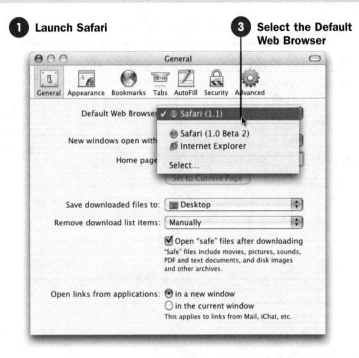

1 Launch Safari

Click the **Safari** icon in the Dock; alternatively, navigate to the **Applications** folder in the Finder and double-click the **Safari** icon.

2 Open Safari Preferences

Select **Preferences** from the **Safari** menu. When the **Preferences** window opens, click the **General** icon at the top to open that page if it's not already shown.

3 Select the Default Web Browser

Use the **Default Web Browser** drop-down menu at the top of the window to select from among the Web browsers already installed on your system. As soon as you click a browser in the list, it is set as your default browser.

If the browser you want to use is not shown in the list, click **Select** at the bottom of the menu, and then use the navigation sheet to locate and select the browser application.

69 Keep Track of Web Sites with Bookmarks

Before You Begin

✔ **29** Configure Networking Manually

✔ **68** Select Your Default Web Browser

See Also

→ **70** Synchronize Your Bookmarks with iSync

→ **71** Access Your Bookmarks Using .Mac

KEY TERM

Bookmark—A reference to a favorite Web site to which you want to return in the future. A bookmark consists of a title and the address of the site; Safari lets you organize them in folders for easy access.

KEY TERM

Google—The most popular "search engine" on the Web. Located at **http://www.google.com**, Google is faster and more accurate than most other search engines available. Safari allows you to perform a Google search without having to go to Google's site first.

Saving a reference to a favorite Web site so that you can quickly access it again later is known as *creating a bookmark* for that site, or *bookmarking the site*. (Internet Explorer uses the term *Favorites* instead of *bookmarks*, but they're effectively the same thing.) Safari allows better bookmark organization than most other browsers, giving you a full-screen bookmark manager page in which you can organize bookmarks into folders and access them by name. You can also use bookmarks that are stored in the *bookmark bar*, shown just below the toolbar; folders of bookmarks in the bookmark bar expand into drop-down menus from which you can select Web sites with a single click.

Safari also provides another advantage over other browsers in bookmark management: It lets you specify a descriptive name for each bookmark at the time you create it. Most browsers automatically use the Web page's title as the name of the bookmark, but this isn't always what you want. Although other programs allow you to edit bookmark names after you create them, that can be tedious. Safari lets you enter an appropriate name right when you create the bookmark.

Safari's bookmark management function, unlike that of many other browsers, is both a full-featured editing utility and a hierarchical catalog for accessing bookmarks directly. From the **Bookmarks Library** page, you can go to any bookmark's address by double-clicking the bookmark in the list.

1 Surf to a Web Site

Launch Safari and enter a URL (Web site address) in the Address bar (the text box) at the top of the screen. You can also search for a Web site that suits your interest by entering search terms into the *Google* search box in the upper-right corner of the screen and pressing **Return**.

2 Click the Bookmark Button

Click the + button to the left of the Address bar. This action brings up a sheet that prompts you for the bookmark name and location.

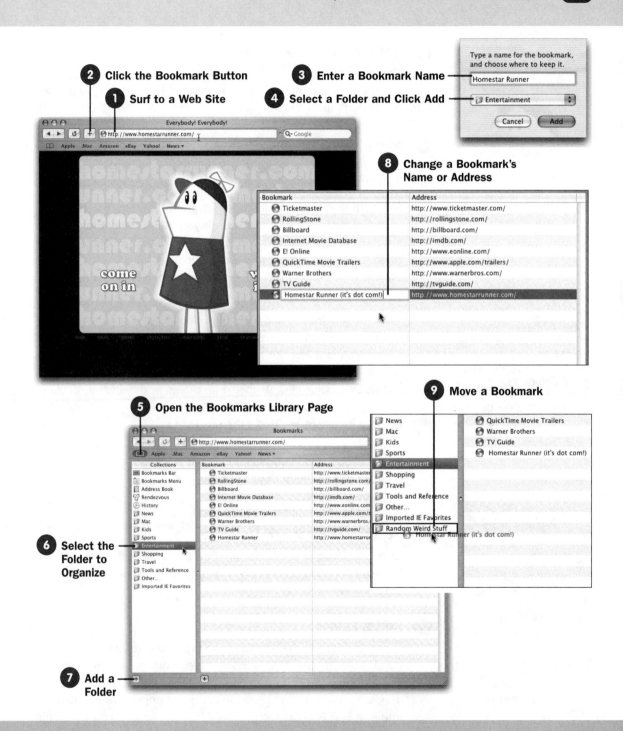

2 Click the Bookmark Button

1 Surf to a Web Site

3 Enter a Bookmark Name

4 Select a Folder and Click Add

Type a name for the bookmark, and choose where to keep it.

Homestar Runner

Entertainment

Cancel   Add

8 Change a Bookmark's
Name or Address

Bookmark	Address
Ticketmaster	http://www.ticketmaster.com/
RollingStone	http://rollingstone.com/
Billboard	http://billboard.com/
Internet Movie Database	http://imdb.com/
E! Online	http://www.eonline.com/
QuickTime Movie Trailers	http://www.apple.com/trailers/
Warner Brothers	http://www.warnerbros.com/
TV Guide	http://tvguide.com/
Homestar Runner (it's dot com!)	http://www.homestarrunner.com/

9 Move a Bookmark

5 Open the Bookmarks Library Page

| News |
| Mac |
| Kids |
| Sports |
| Entertainment |
| Shopping |
| Travel |
| Tools and Reference |
| Other... |
| Imported IE Favorites |
| Random Weird Stuff |

QuickTime Movie Trailers
Warner Brothers
TV Guide
Homestar Runner (it's dot com!)

Homestar Runner (it's dot com!)

Collections	Bookmark	Address
Bookmarks Bar	Ticketmaster	http://www.ticketmaster
Bookmarks Menu	RollingStone	http://rollingstone.com/
Address Book	Billboard	http://billboard.com/
Rendezvous	Internet Movie Database	http://imdb.com/
History	E! Online	http://www.eonline.com
News	QuickTime Movie Trailers	http://www.apple.com/b
Mac	Warner Brothers	http://www.warnerbros.
Kids	TV Guide	http://tvguide.com/
Sports	Homestar Runner	http://www.homestarru
Entertainment		
Shopping		
Travel		
Tools and Reference		
Other...		
Imported IE Favorites		

6 Select the
Folder to
Organize

7 Add a
Folder

③ Enter a Bookmark Name

The default name for the bookmark is the Web page's title; that name is selected, though, so if you don't like it, simply type a name that's more to your liking.

④ Select a Folder and Click Add

Click the drop-down menu to show all your bookmark folders. Select the folder where you want to save your new bookmark.

Safari, in its default configuration, comes with a few folders with some bookmarks already defined for you: **News**, **Mac**, **Kids**, **Sports**, and so on. As you add more folders for your bookmarks, those folders will appear in a hierarchical list (all folders are shown, even folders inside other folders) when you add a new bookmark.

Click the **Add** button to add the new bookmark to your list. You can now access the bookmark by clicking the **Bookmarks** icon at the left end of the bookmark bar (the icon looks like an open book) to open the **Bookmarks Library** page and then opening the correct folder; double-click the bookmark to go to the site.

⑤ Open the Bookmarks Library Page

Any bookmark-organizing efforts you might want to make begin on the **Bookmarks Library** page. Open the **Bookmarks Library** page by clicking the Bookmarks icon at the far left end of the bookmarks bar.

⑥ Select the Folder to Organize

Click any folder in the **Collections** list on the left side of the **Bookmarks Library** page. The contents of that folder appear in the pane on the right.

⑦ Add a Folder

Click the + icon at the bottom of the right pane to create a new folder inside the currently selected folder. Click the + icon at the bottom of the **Collections** pane to create a new top-level folder to appear in that list. The default folder name appears as **untitled folder**; it is selected as soon as the folder is created, so that you can immediately type a new name for the folder.

TIP

To delete a bookmark from the **Bookmarks Library**, select the bookmark and press **Delete**. You can undo a deletion by selecting **Undo** from the **Edit** menu.

TIP

Bookmark folders can contain other folders. In the right pane of the **Bookmarks Library** page, you can open and browse folders the same as you can in List view in the Finder. Note the triangles that indicate whether the folder is expanded or collapsed.

8 Change a Bookmark's Name or Address

Click to select a bookmark in the right pane of the **Bookmarks Library** page, pause briefly, and then click the name or address field again to select that field's contents for editing. Alternatively, right-click or **Control**+click the bookmark and choose **Edit Name** or **Edit Address** from the context menu. Type the new name or the new URL and press **Return**.

9 Move a Bookmark

To move a bookmark, drag it from one folder to another or to another position within the same folder. To navigate down into a subfolder, hover the mouse (while still dragging the bookmark) over the folder you want to expand; after a moment, it will open automatically.

TIP

The bookmarks bar is special. You can drag bookmarks into it and off it from the **Bookmarks Library** page, or you can drag an address into it straight from the Address bar. The bookmarks bar is represented as its own collection/folder in the **Bookmarks Library** page; you can move bookmarks into it as you would into any other folder. Click and drag to change how bookmarks are positioned in the bookmarks bar; you can also delete a bookmark from the bar by dragging it off the bar.

---

70 Synchronize Your Bookmarks with iSync

If you have a .Mac account and multiple Macs, you can take advantage of one very handy feature of Safari: the ability to have your bookmarks synchronized across all your computers. This way, you'll never have to worry about being unable to remember a bookmark address on your laptop because you'd only added it to your bookmarks on your desktop machine. Using your .Mac account and iSync, the same bookmarks are always available on all your machines.

Before beginning this task, make sure that you have an active Internet connection; otherwise, your Mac won't be able to contact the .Mac server.

1 Open iSync

Launch iSync by double-clicking its icon in the **Applications** folder or by selecting **Open iSync** from the **iSync** system menu (a circle formed by two arrows "chasing" each other clockwise) in the menu bar.

2 Open the .Mac Options Pane

Click the large **.Mac** icon at the left side of the iSync panel. The .Mac options appear.

Before You Begin

✔ **50** Sign Up for .Mac

✔ **69** Keep Track of Web Sites with Bookmarks

See Also

→ **71** Access Your Bookmarks Using .Mac

→ **125** Set Up iSync to Synchronize Your Macs

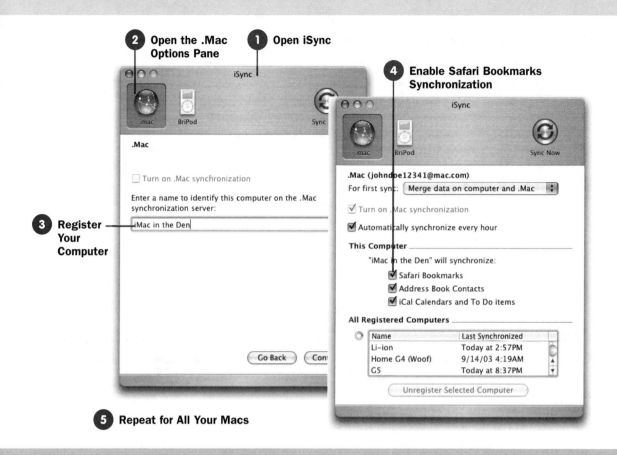

2 Open the .Mac Options Pane

1 Open iSync

4 Enable Safari Bookmarks Synchronization

3 Register Your Computer

5 Repeat for All Your Macs

③ Register Your Computer

If you have never used iSync from this computer before, you must register your computer under your .Mac account before you can synchronize it. The .Mac service "knows" whether your computer has been registered and reminds you that you must register your computer with the .Mac synchronization server; click the **Register** button provided to do this.

Type a name by which to identify your computer, if you don't like the one that's automatically suggested for you. Click **Continue** when you've entered a name.

TIP

The registered name for your computer should distinguish it from your other Macs, so that you can see its status easily in iSync. Good names to use include **iMac at Work** and **New iBook**.

4 Enable Safari Bookmarks Synchronization

After your computer is registered with .Mac, the options for synchronization appear in full. Make sure that the **Safari Bookmarks** check box is enabled. Enable the **Automatically synchronize every hour** check box to have iSync do its work without any further input from you.

Click **Sync Now** to kick off the first synchronization process. iSync exchanges information about your bookmarks with the .Mac server, compares the bookmarks on your Mac with the ones stored in the .Mac account, and combines them into a single large collection that's identical on your Mac and on the .Mac server. From now on, each time iSync synchronizes your data (every hour, as long as your Mac is connected to the Internet), any changes you make to your bookmarks are copied to the server, and from there to any other Macs you have registered with iSync.

5 Repeat for All Your Macs

On each of your Macs, open the iSync application and register your computer with the .Mac service. After each computer has synchronized with the .Mac server, all your bookmarks will be the same across all your Macs.

> **NOTE**
>
> Because each computer must merge its information with what's in the central .Mac database, and then must merge that information back to itself, it might take two or even three sync processes before all your bookmarks have propagated completely to all your Macs.

71 Access Your Bookmarks Using .Mac

Another handy feature for .Mac users is the ability to access the bookmarks that are synchronized with .Mac—whether you're using a computer that's synchronized with your other Macs or not. In fact, you can even access your .Mac bookmarks from a Windows PC.

This feature is particularly useful if you frequently need access to your bookmarks when you're accessing the Internet from coffee shops or libraries, where you might not have access to your own Mac and instead have to use a public computer. The .Mac service allows you to be productive even if you have to use Windows!

Before You Begin

✔ **50** Sign Up for .Mac

✔ **70** Synchronize Your Bookmarks with iSync

See Also

→ **73** Remove a Cookie

→ **127** Synchronize Your .Mac Address Book

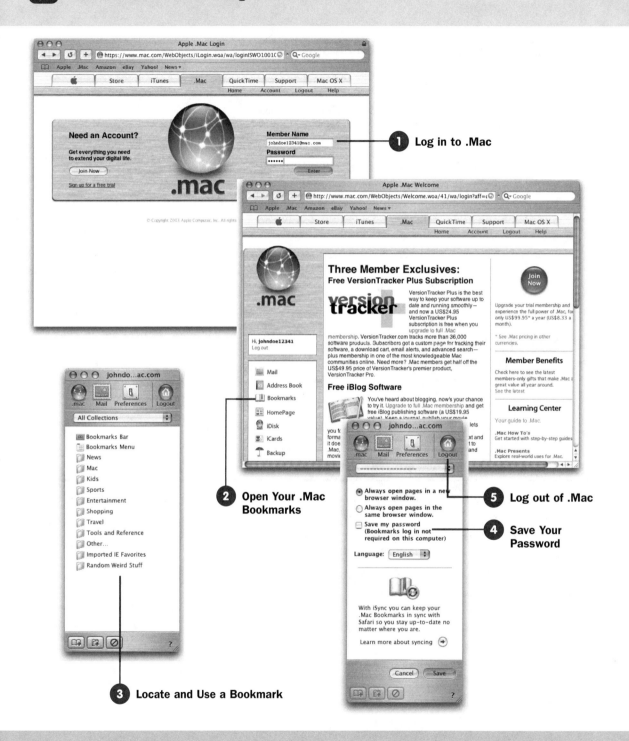

1 Log in to .Mac

2 Open Your .Mac Bookmarks

3 Locate and Use a Bookmark

4 Save Your Password

5 Log out of .Mac

When accessing your bookmarks on a public computer, you should be very careful about what kind of data you are exposing to the public. Some Web addresses, for instance, can contain encoded passwords to services that you access. Always assume the worst about the security of a public computer: Would you feel safe about the prospect of the next person sitting down at that same computer from which you have just accessed your bank account online?

If you have any doubts at all about the security of the computer from which you're accessing the Web, don't go to any sites in your bookmarks that might reveal sensitive information. This doesn't just apply to your .Mac bookmarks, either. Any time you use a public computer for anything, always clean up after yourself: empty the Trash (or Recycle Bin), clear the browser's cookies and caches, and close down all browser windows before you leave the computer.

 TIP

Before you can access your Safari bookmarks through the .Mac service, you must turn on synchronization using iSync. Refer to **70** **Synchronize Your Bookmarks with iSync** for information on how to do this.

❶ Log in to .Mac

Surf to the .Mac Web site at **http://www.mac.com**. If you are not already logged in, click the **Log in** link and enter your .Mac member name and password when prompted.

❷ Open Your .Mac Bookmarks

Click the **Bookmarks** icon in the left pane. .Mac opens a **Welcome** window to inform you that your bookmarks are available; click the **Open Bookmarks** button to pop them up in a small, palette-sized external window.

❸ Locate and Use a Bookmark

The floating **Bookmarks** window lists all your bookmark folders, the same as in the sidebar of the **Bookmarks Library** page in Safari. Click any of the listed folders to move into that folder, and use the drop-down menu above the folder list to select a folder to jump to.

When you find the bookmark for the site you want to visit, click it. The site will open in a new browser window.

4 **Save Your Password**

The .Mac Web site prompts you to enter your password every few screens as you move through the site to ensure the security of your account. If you want to always be able to open your bookmarks from the computer you're using without having to enter your .Mac password, click the **Preferences** icon at the top of the palette-sized external window .Mac provides for your use and enable the **Save my password** check box. Click **Save** to preserve your changes.

5 **Log out of .Mac**

When you're done using any public computer, always be sure to log out of any services that might provide access to your personal information—including .Mac. Don't forget to end your session by clicking the **Logout** link at the top of the palette-sized external window .Mac provides for your use.

NOTE

If the computer you're using is a public terminal (such as a computer in a public library), don't have .Mac automatically save your password for that computer! Remember, anybody in the world could be next to sit down at that computer; if you've enabled this option from that computer, that person would have complete access to your bookmarks.

---

72 SnapBack to the First Page of a Site

Before You Begin

✔ **69** Keep Track of Web Sites with Bookmarks

See Also

➡ **73** Remove a Cookie

KEY TERM

SnapBack—A Safari feature that returns the user to the entry point of a Web site, regardless of how far into the site—or subsequently linked sites—the user has wandered.

Safari has a feature that is absent from other browsers: **SnapBack**. This feature allows you to navigate Web sites more efficiently by letting you jump instantly to the entry point of any site, lifting you out of the site's inner pages.

When you visit a bookmark or enter a Web address manually, Safari "marks for SnapBack" the page where you arrive at a site. This means that no matter how many subsequent pages you visit by clicking links found on the site—even if those links take you to entirely different sites—you can always find your way immediately back to the first page where you were taken by the bookmark or the manually entered address, simply by clicking the orange SnapBack icon in the Address bar.

The *Google* search box in the upper-right corner of the Safari screen makes use of the SnapBack feature as well. If you use the box to do a Google search, you can prowl through the sites that Google returns, looking for what you want. When you decide that the site you've been looking in doesn't have what you're after, simply click the SnapBack icon to return to the page of Google results.

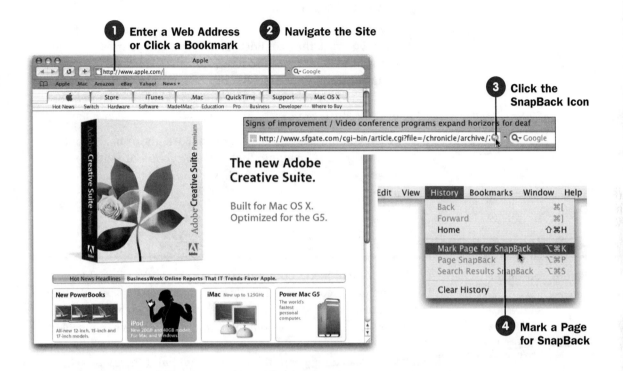

1 Enter a Web Address or Click a Bookmark

2 Navigate the Site

3 Click the SnapBack Icon

4 Mark a Page for SnapBack

1 Enter a Web Address or Click a Bookmark

Type a Web address (URL) into the Address bar and press **Return**; alternatively, select any bookmark to travel directly to a favorite site.

2 Navigate the Site

Click links within the site to move from page to page. As soon as you browse to a new page, the orange **SnapBack** icon appears in the Address bar to signify that you can now use the SnapBack feature to return to the original page.

3 Click the SnapBack Icon

Click the orange **SnapBack** icon in the Address bar, and you are taken back to the first page you visited.

NOTE

Safari immediately jumps back to the entry point as cached in its own history; you can then navigate either forward or backward through the pages in the browser's history.

④ Mark a Page for SnapBack

You can manually define any page as the destination point for when you click the SnapBack icon. If you find yourself at a site that you know you want to return to, select **Mark Page for SnapBack** from the Safari **History** menu. You can then surf the links in the site and return immediately to the starting page using the **SnapBack** icon.

When you mark a new page for SnapBack, the orange SnapBack icon disappears, meaning that the page you're currently on is where you will SnapBack to. Click a link, and the orange icon will appear again.

73 Remove a Cookie

Before You Begin

✔ **69** Keep Track of Web Sites with Bookmarks

✔ **71** Access Your Bookmarks Using .Mac

See Also

→ **74** Report a Safari Bug to Apple

KEY TERM

Cookie—A piece of information that some Web sites store on your computer to store your preferences for the site or your username and password.

Cookies are small pieces of information that some Web sites store on your computer. A cookie is generally nothing to worry about; it's usually used for convenience, storing your preferences for how to view a given site, for instance. There is seldom anything more sensitive in a cookie than a username or password for a certain site, and that information can be exchanged only with the Web site that put it there.

However, cookies can also be used in nefarious ways—to track Web users' surfing habits, to try to harvest your passwords, and so on. There have even been documented cases of malicious sites using "cross-site scripting" tactics to harvest credit card information or other personal data submitted to another, legitimate site. Regardless of how seldom or frequently you use the Web, it's a good idea to know how to remove a cookie (or all your browser's accumulated cookies) and thereby "clean" your computer of sensitive information on a regular basis.

Although it might be tempting to simply remove all your cookies, be careful—doing so can mean the loss of good cookies, the ones that store your personalized profile information for sites you use frequently. It's a good idea to look carefully at the domain or hostname for each of your cookies and remove only those you don't recognize.

① Open the Security Preferences

Select **Preferences** from the **Safari** menu. Click the **Security** icon to bring up the security options.

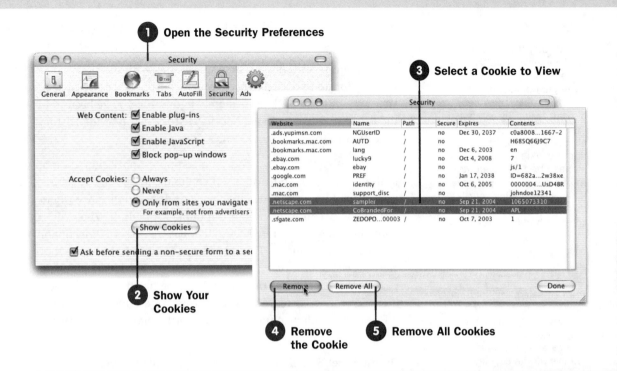

1 Open the Security Preferences

3 Select a Cookie to View

2 Show Your Cookies

4 Remove the Cookie

5 Remove All Cookies

---

2 **Show Your Cookies**

Click the **Show Cookies** button to display a sheet listing all the cookies currently stored on your computer, what sites created them, when they're set to expire, and what information is stored in them.

3 **Select a Cookie to View**

Click any cookie to select it.

4 **Remove the Cookie**

Click **Remove** to delete the selected cookie or cookies from your browser.

5 **Remove All Cookies**

To completely clean your browser of all cookies and return it to its original, pristine condition, click **Remove All**. Be aware, however, that any preferences you might have stored for certain Web sites

 NOTE

Removing all your cookies can be exactly the feature you need if you're trying to clean up the computer so that you can give it to someone else. For more about returning the computer to its factory condition, see **175** **Restore the System to Factory Settings**.

NOTE

Don't worry if the **Contents** column shows what seems to be incomprehensible garbage. Cookies aren't meant to be read by people, but rather by computers; sometimes you'll be able to tell what information a cookie is storing, but just as often the contents will be a mystery. You never know when seeing your cookies' ingredients might come in handy, however.

TIP

You can select multiple cookies by holding down ⌘ or **Shift** as you click. You might want to select several cookies if you want to remove all the cookies for a given site.

are also reset, and you'll have to set them up again if you return to those sites.

Safari keeps records of your browsing history—all the sites you've visited—for up to a week. This can be very convenient because it enables you to go back immediately to any site you've been to in the last seven days, using either the **History** menu or the **History** collection in the **Bookmarks** page.

However, if you're using Safari on a computer that's shared among multiple users (and particularly if you're using a public machine), it might not be a good idea to leave your browsing history where just anybody can come in and rummage through it. When you're done browsing on a shared computer, use the **Reset Safari** option under the **Safari** menu. This option not only clears out your complete browsing and Google-searching history, it also deletes all your cookies, clears out the browser's cache (local copies of Web files the browser stores for quicker access), and removes sensitive information such as names and passwords from AutoFill form fields.

On the **Reset Safari** dialog box that appears, be sure to click the **Reset** button instead of the **Cancel** button—for safety, **Reset** is the default action button in the dialog box.

74 Report a Safari Bug to Apple

Before You Begin

✔ **69** Keep Track of Web Sites with Bookmarks

TIP

If you find that you have a lot of Safari bugs to report to Apple, you can enable the **Bug** toolbar button, which lets you open the **Bug Report** dialog box with a single click. Select **Bug** from the **View** menu to enable this button.

Safari is a new browser. It is based on the open-source KHTML rendering engine, which itself is very fast and feature rich, but yet unproven by much time in the field. Safari still has a number of bugs that have yet to be fixed by Apple. As a Safari user, you might find a Web site that renders incorrectly, some operational behavior that seems wrong, or a problem with the application itself (such as a crash). Apple provides a mechanism in Safari that lets you report these problems directly to the Safari development team so that they can develop better future versions of the browser.

1 **Open the Bug Report Sheet**

Select **Report Bugs to Apple** from the **Safari** menu. The **Bug Report** dialog box appears in the browser window.

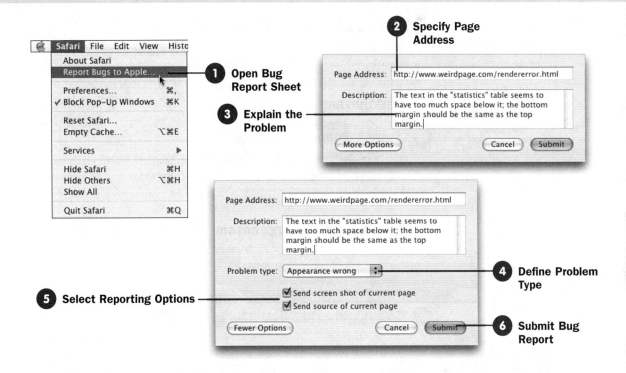

② Specify the Page Address

The current site's URL is shown in the **Page Address** input box. If your bug report is about a different Web site, enter the URL of that site in this text box.

③ Explain the Problem

Type as much text as necessary to succinctly and helpfully explain what the problem is. If it's a page that doesn't look right, explain what Safari is doing wrong. If a feature of Safari itself is misbehaving, describe what it should be doing and what it's doing instead.

Click the **More Options** button to provide additional details about the bug.

4 **Define the Problem Type**

Use the **Problem type** drop-down menu to specify what kind of problem you're experiencing. This information helps the Safari team categorize your bug report so that it can be addressed most efficiently.

5 **Select Reporting Options**

If the problem is with how a certain Web page is being rendered, it might be helpful to select one or both of the **Send screen shot of current page** and **Send source of current page** check boxes. These options allow the Safari team to see for themselves how the browser is rendering the page, and to have a copy of the HTML source code so that they can try to track down the problem. Use these options if the rendering problem is too difficult to explain adequately in words alone.

6 **Submit the Bug Report**

Click **Submit** to send the bug report to Apple, along with any relevant screen shots and source files. You will not receive any feedback from Apple's developers, but be aware that every bug report is read carefully and acted on—and that you've helped make Safari a better browser, benefiting you and all other Mac users.

---

75 **Connect to an FTP Server**

Before You Begin

✔ **29** Configure Networking Manually

See Also

→ **30** Configure Proxy Server Settings

→ **76** Seek Information with Sherlock

The *File Transfer Protocol (FTP)* is a venerable form of Internet communication still widely used today. When you download a piece of software from its publisher's Web site, you might well be downloading it from an FTP server. This is because FTP is well suited to transferring large binary files (such as application installers), rather than the many short text transactions that make up navigation on the Web (which typically are done using HTTP, the Hypertext Transfer Protocol).

Another key feature of FTP is that you can upload files as well as download them. If you have a Web site or Unix shell account on a remote server, you can use FTP to upload your Web pages and image files.

Mac OS X integrates FTP into the Finder, and when you encounter an FTP link in Safari, Safari passes the FTP connection into the Finder so that you can navigate the FTP server as you would any network server.

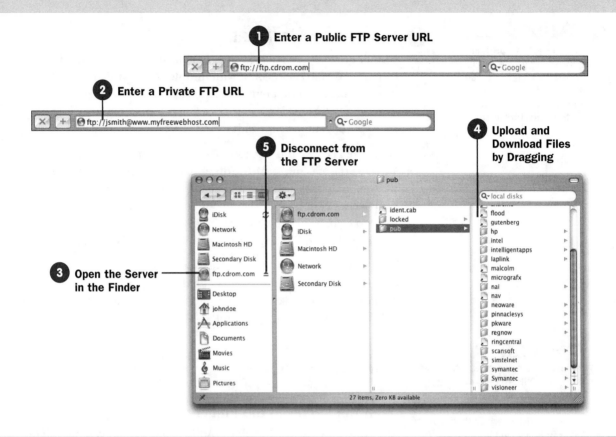

1 Enter a Public FTP Server URL

2 Enter a Private FTP URL

5 Disconnect from the FTP Server

4 Upload and Download Files by Dragging

3 Open the Server in the Finder

1 Enter a Public FTP Server URL

In Safari, enter the URL of the FTP server or click the link to the FTP server if such a link is presented in a Web page.

A public FTP URL (as offered, typically, by shareware sites) is of this form **ftp://ftp.hostname.com/path/to/directory**. Optionally, you can add a trailing slash (which does not affect the system's behavior) or a filename. If you specify the filename, Safari downloads the file directly and transparently, using the **Downloads** pane. If you specify only the path to a directory, Mac OS X connects to the server and opens that directory as a folder in a Finder window.

KEY TERM

File Transfer Protocol (FTP)—A method of transferring files from one computer to another, dating back to the earliest days of the Internet and still in use today for downloading large files (such as software installers).

NOTE

Of course, Mac OS X is Unix—so if you're a Unix expert and prefer to use the traditional command-line **ftp** program, just fire up the Unix Terminal.

② Enter a Private FTP URL

Not all FTP sites are public; some, such as the one you might have as part of a Web site account with an Internet service provider, are private—meaning that only you can access it, and only after you provide a valid username and password combination (which are also part of your account with the service provider).

A private FTP URL is of the form **ftp://username<:password>@ftp.hostname.com/path/to/directory**. The password is optional, as is the path. For instance, if your username on the FTP server **somewhere.com** is **jsmith** and your password is **abc123**, and you want to connect directly into the home directory of your account, use the following URL: **ftp://jsmith:abc123@somewhere.com**.

If you'd rather not specify your password so that it can't be seen over your shoulder, you can leave it out: **ftp://jsmith@somewhere.com**. If you do this, you will be prompted with a dialog box to provide the password for the account.

WEB RESOURCE

Get information and obtain the Panic Transmit FTP program from this Web site. Transmit provides a more user-friendly and feature-rich interface than does FTP in the Finder.

http://www.panic.com/transmit/

③ Open the Server in the Finder

After you type the URL in Safari's Address bar and press **Return** (or click an equivalent FTP link), a dialog box appears showing that Mac OS X is connecting to the FTP server. After the connection is established (which might take a few moments), a Finder window appears showing the contents of the target folder specified in the URL. The FTP server is listed in the Finder's sidebar as a standard network server.

NOTE

Standard FTP does not provide for a secure connection method. Whether or not you specify your password as part of the URL, the password is transmitted over the network in clear text. An eavesdropper snooping on the network can obtain your password this way. Be aware of this security risk when using private FTP; you might want to look into a more full-featured FTP program, such as Panic's Transmit.

④ Upload and Download Files by Dragging

Navigate the FTP server as you would any hierarchical folder system. When you find a file you want to download, drag it to your Desktop or to another target in the Finder. A dialog box appears to show the progress of the download.

Uploading files—transferring them from your computer to the FTP server—is just as easy; drag a file or folder from your Desktop or a Finder window into the window showing the FTP server. However,

unless it is an authenticated private FTP session, you might not
have permission to upload files. An error message appears if you
try to upload a file to a server that does not permit it.

5 **Disconnect from the FTP Server**

When you're done transferring files, click the **Eject** icon next to the
FTP server in the Finder sidebar; alternatively, drag the server's
icon from the Desktop into the Trash, which becomes an **Eject** icon
while you're dragging the icon.

76 Seek Information with Sherlock

There's more to the Web than just surfing with a browser. When you've
become accustomed to using certain services online, such as searching
for movie listings or looking up maps, it becomes apparent that the flexibility of a Web browser can be limiting rather than liberating.
Specialized tasks such as obtaining formatted results from database-
driven Web resources demand more specialized client applications.
Fortunately, Apple provides *Sherlock* for just that purpose.

Sherlock is an application that operates on *channels* rather than URLs;
a channel is a customized interface to a certain data resource, such as a
search engine, a flight-info database, a stock-quote engine, or a translation service. Rather than making you navigate a confusing, ad-beset
Web page with generic form elements to get the information you want,
Sherlock presents you with specialized input fields and controls that take
your queries and return exactly the results you're looking for, with a
minimum of fuss.

Sherlock comes with a variety of useful channels, but its extensible
framework allows third parties to submit their own channels, such as
those designed for iCalShare (a site dedicated to cataloging users' iCal
calendars) and VersionTracker (which keeps comprehensive listings of
Mac OS X software updates, both shareware and commercial). Every
third-party channel is available directly through Sherlock under the
Other Channels collection, which queries the public **dmoz** directory (at
http://www.dmoz.org), a part of the Mozilla organization. More third-
party Sherlock channels are being added to the directory all the time,
giving you more tools and toys to experiment with.

Before You Begin

✔ **29** Configure
Networking
Manually

EY TERMS

Sherlock—A built-in application that communicates
with specialized databases
on the Internet for stock
quotes, text translations,
yellow-pages listings, movie
information, and a lot more.

Channel—Any of the
dozens of specialized service screens available in
Sherlock, such as stock
quotes, yellow pages, or
movie listings.

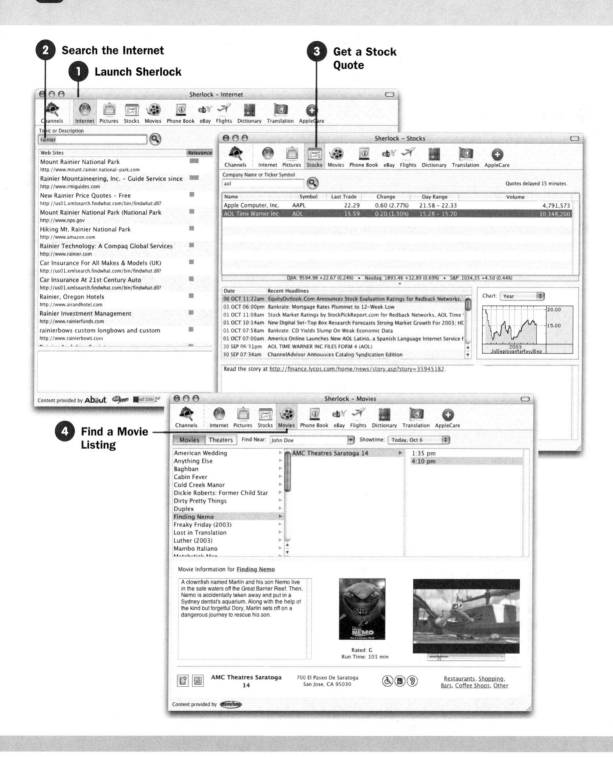

2 Search the Internet

1 Launch Sherlock

3 Get a Stock Quote

4 Find a Movie Listing

5 Look Up a Business or Person

6 Translate Text

7 Create a Channel Collection

8 Add Third-Party Channels to the Toolbar

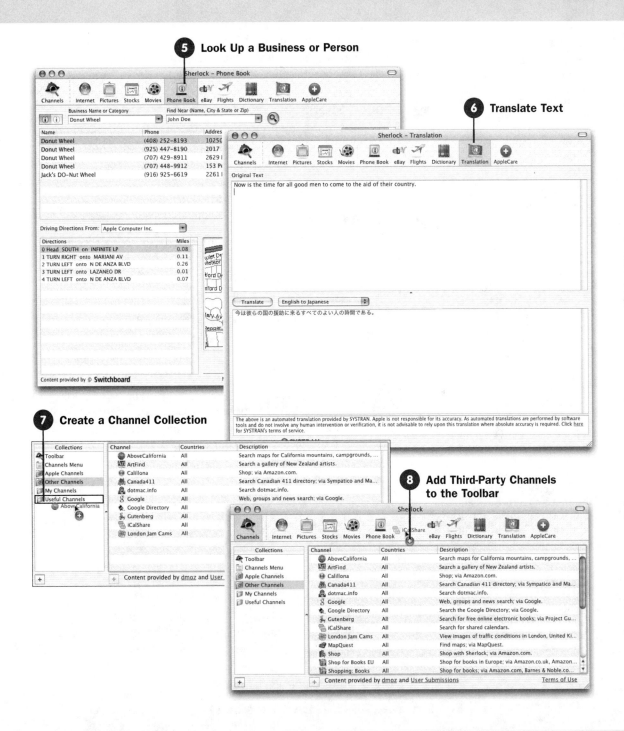

NOTE

An application that's similar to Sherlock in concept and design, but with a somewhat different set of available channels, is Watson, by Karelia Software (**http://www.karelia.com**). Watson lets you do many of the same things that Sherlock does, but additionally has channels that allow you to do such things as track packages, browse the Meerkat news service, get TV listings, and find sports scores. If you find Sherlock useful, you might find Watson an agreeable piece of software to have on hand as well.

TIPS

Click any site in the results list to see a brief description of the site in the pane at the bottom of the window.

You can copy a stock performance chart for use in documents or presentations if you want. Click and drag the chart to your Desktop to create a picture clipping of the chart. Double-click the picture clipping icon and press ⌘C to copy it to the Clipboard. You can then paste the chart into any application that accepts image data, such as TextEdit.

Sherlock contains far too many channels for this book to cover; you can, however, explore all the channels (whether supplied by Apple or by third parties) and see for yourself how useful each might be to you.

① Launch Sherlock

Navigate to the **Applications** folder and double-click the **Sherlock** icon to launch the program. The application starts in the **Channels** menu screen, where you can select any available channel or customize which channels you can use.

② Search the Internet

Click the **Internet** icon in the toolbar. Type your search terms in the **Topic or Description** box and press **Return** (or click the **Search** button). Search results from a variety of sources appear in the list window, listed according to relevance.

Double-click any site in the results list to open that site in your Web browser.

③ Get a Stock Quote

Click the **Stocks** icon in the Sherlock toolbar. Type a company name or stock trading symbol into the **Company Name or Ticker Symbol** box and press **Return** (or click the **Search** button). Apple's stock numbers—under the symbol AAPL—appear in the results by default (you can remove it); the company you search for is added to the list of results.

Select a duration from the **Chart** menu to view a chart of the stock's performance over that period. You can also click entries in the **Recent Headlines** box to see company news.

④ Find a Movie Listing

Click the **Movies** icon in the Sherlock toolbar. If you entered your home address during initial setup of Mac OS X, Sherlock uses that address (listed under your name) as the default one for determining the theaters nearest to you. If you didn't provide that information to Mac OS X, type any city name into the **Find Near** box. Sherlock auto-completes city names for you.

Select whether you want to search by movie or by theater.

Whichever method you select, a primary listing appears at the left. Click any movie or theater in the list to navigate (using a mechanism very much like Column view in the Finder) to narrow the results down to a showtime and theater you like.

To add a selected theater to your Address Book, click the **Add** button in the lower-left corner of the window; click the **Map** button next to it to fetch a map to the theater in the **Phone Book** channel.

⑤ Look Up a Business or Person

Click the **Phone Book** icon in the Sherlock toolbar. This channel allows you to find the location and phone number of any business or person you enter. First, select whether you're looking for a business or person, using the **i** buttons at the top-left of the screen. Then enter the name of the person or business in the fields provided; use the **Find Near** or **Find In** field (which auto-completes your input) to specify a city or location to help narrow down the search.

Driving directions from your current location and a map appear in the lower part of the screen. Use the **Zoom** slider to adjust the zoom level of the map; click the **Print** button to get a printout to take with you in the car.

⑥ Translate Text

Click the **Translation** icon in the Sherlock toolbar. Sherlock uses the Systran service to translate between any of twelve different languages; not all the combinations of these languages are available in Sherlock, but all the most popular ones are present in the selection menu.

Type the text you want to translate into the upper box, or paste it in from another application. Select the language pair you want to translate from and to and click **Translate**. The translated text appears in the lower pane, for you to copy back out into your other applications.

⑦ Create a Channel Collection

Sherlock operates in much the same way as Safari, in that you can create collections of channels to organize them for quick access just as you can with Safari's bookmarks. When you open Sherlock,

NOTE

If a trailer video for the selected movie is available, it begins downloading and playing automatically. This can be hard on a low-bandwidth connection; to stop downloading a trailer, click a different Sherlock channel after you've obtained the movie information you want.

click the **Channels** icon in the toolbar. In the **Collections** pane on the left, click the collection from whose channels you want to select. Double-click a channel in the list on the right to open that channel.

To create a new collection, click the + icon at the bottom of the **Collections** pane. A new untitled collection appears in the list, with its name selected; you can immediately type a more meaningful name for the collection and press **Return**.

Add channels to the new collection by selecting the **Apple Channels** or **Other Channels** collection, and then dragging channels from that list into your collection.

8 Add Third-Party Channels to the Toolbar

You can add any of the available third-party channels to your Sherlock toolbar. To do this, select the **Other Channels** collection; examine the available channels, using their descriptions to determine whether you'd be interested in them.

Drag channels from the list into the **Toolbar** collection to add them to the toolbar. You can also drag channels one by one directly to the toolbar itself, dropping the channel wherever in the toolbar you want it to go.

Select **Customize Toolbar** from the **View** menu to rearrange the icons that appear in your toolbar. With the customization sheet visible, you can click and drag icons to new positions, drag them off the toolbar to remove them, or add new icons from the sheet.

Drag the entire "default set" of icons to the toolbar to reset the toolbar to its original state.

9

Communicating with iChat

IN THIS CHAPTER:

iChat is Apple's integrated chat client, compatible with the AOL Instant Messenger (AIM) and incorporating all the networking and graphics technologies that make Mac OS X itself streamlined and attractive. Paired with a FireWire video camera, such as Apple's iSight, you can chat not only with the traditional instant text messages made so popular with AIM, ICQ, Yahoo! Messenger, and MSN Messenger, but with audio and full-motion video as well. Because iChat is integrated into Mac OS X itself, finding chat partners, receiving messages, and exchanging files is often as simple as dragging an icon or selecting a globally available menu option.

There are a lot of little details to using iChat, such as sending hyperlinks, setting chat background pictures, configuring your chat text's appearance, tuning your privacy options, and using smileys; this chapter explains some of the features that are most immediately useful, allowing you to explore the rest at your leisure.

77 Set Up Your AIM or .Mac Account

Before You Begin

✔ **29** Configure Networking Manually

✔ **50** Sign Up for .Mac

✔ **60** Configure a Server-Based Mail Account (.Mac, Exchange, or IMAP)

See Also

➜ **78** Set Up Your Picture

➜ **80** Start a Chat Session

🔍 KEY TERM

AOL Instant Messenger (AIM)—One of the leading instant-messaging applications used by millions of people (who may or may not be subscribers to the America Online service). iChat users can communicate with AIM users and vice versa.

The first step in using iChat is to set up your account. iChat supports both .Mac accounts and *AIM* screen names; if you already have an AIM name, you can continue to use that as your identification in iChat, and you won't have to create a new identity when you first start iChat. If you have a .Mac account, however, you might want to use it for your identification in iChat because it stores more information about you than an AIM identification does. You can add all your AIM buddies to your iChat Buddy List just as they appear in AIM.

Make sure that you have either a .Mac account or an existing AIM screen name before you launch iChat for the first time. If you don't have an account name or a screen name, follow the **Get an iChat Account** link (a button on the account information screen) during iChat's initial setup.

➊ Launch iChat

Click the **iChat** icon in the Dock; alternatively, navigate to the **Applications** folder and double-click the **iChat** icon.

If this is the first time you have run iChat, you will be taken through the initial setup screens. Click **Continue** after reading the information on the first screen.

1 Launch iChat

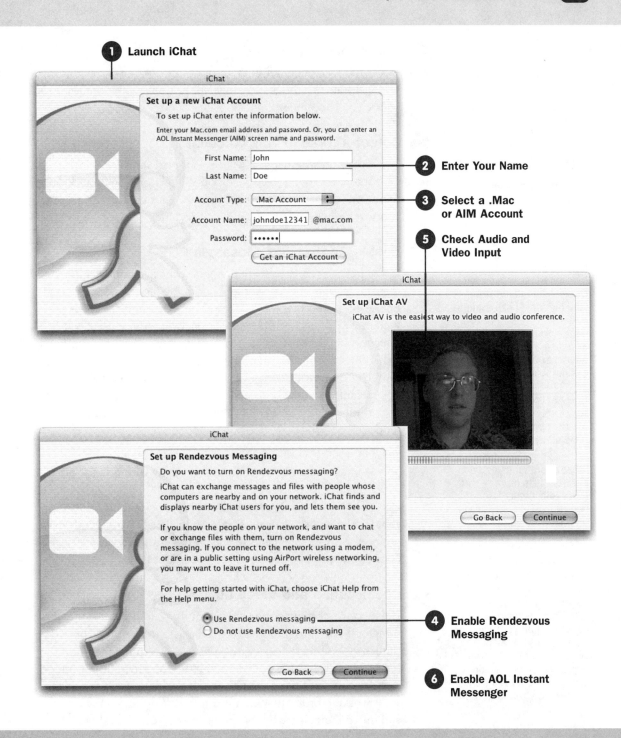

iChat

Set up a new iChat Account

To set up iChat enter the information below.

Enter your Mac.com email address and password. Or, you can enter an AOL Instant Messenger (AIM) screen name and password.

First Name: John

Last Name: Doe

2 Enter Your Name

Account Type: .Mac Account

Account Name: johndoe12341 @mac.com

Password: ••••••

(Get an iChat Account)

3 Select a .Mac or AIM Account

5 Check Audio and Video Input

iChat

Set up iChat AV

iChat AV is the easiest way to video and audio conference.

(Go Back) (Continue)

iChat

Set up Rendezvous Messaging

Do you want to turn on Rendezvous messaging?

iChat can exchange messages and files with people whose computers are nearby and on your network. iChat finds and displays nearby iChat users for you, and lets them see you.

If you know the people on your network, and want to chat or exchange files with them, turn on Rendezvous messaging. If you connect to the network using a modem, or are in a public setting using AirPort wireless networking, you may want to leave it turned off.

For help getting started with iChat, choose iChat Help from the Help menu.

⦿ Use Rendezvous messaging
○ Do not use Rendezvous messaging

(Go Back) (Continue)

4 Enable Rendezvous Messaging

6 Enable AOL Instant Messenger

CHAPTER 9: Communicating with iChat

2 Enter Your Name

In the next screen, enter your account information. Type your first and last name in the boxes provided. You must enter both names before you can proceed.

3 Select a .Mac or AIM Account

Depending on whether you will be using a .Mac or an AIM account with iChat, select the account type from the drop-down menu. Fill in the remaining blanks with your account name and password. Click **Continue** when you're done.

4 Enable Rendezvous Messaging

In the next screen, select whether you want to enable *Rendezvous* messaging. Rendezvous, Apple's automatic service-discovery technology built into Mac OS X, allows you to see and chat directly with other iChat users on your local network; those users will appear automatically in your iChat window without your having to add them yourself. Chatting with Rendezvous partners is faster than chatting with users in your Buddy List; the text you type appears immediately on the other person's screen as you enter it, rather than waiting for you to finish typing before each message is sent.

You can disable Rendezvous messaging if you choose. If you disable Rendezvous, you can communicate only with other iChat and AIM users on the Internet using the Buddy List window, and you won't have direct and automatic access to the other iChat users on your local network. You might choose to disable Rendezvous messaging if your Mac is the only one on the local network—Rendezvous would be of no use to you in this case.

5 Check Audio and Video Input

The next iChat setup screen shows you the current status of your camera, if you have one connected. Be sure to open the camera's shutter (as you have to do with Apple's iSight camera) so that the camera is active. iChat will show you the camera's current image, as well as the audio input level. This lets you ensure that the camera is working properly. When you're satisfied that your camera and microphone are working correctly, click **Continue**.

NOTES

AOL Instant Messenger (AIM) is a part of the America Online service (AOL), but it can be used by people who aren't AOL subscribers. If you're an AOL customer, the Instant Messenger service is automatically configured for you, just as iChat's setup is streamlined if you have a .Mac account; but millions of people use the stand-alone version of AIM who are not AOL subscribers, and iChat can use either a true AOL screen name or a separately created AIM name, if you don't have a .Mac account.

iChat operates using two different lists of chat partners: your Buddy List (which lists users with AIM and .Mac accounts, to which you add chat partners manually), and your Rendezvous list (which shows all iChat users on your local network). You can choose to show one list, the other, or both, depending on your circumstances. To display or switch to one of the two lists, select either **Buddy List** or **Rendezvous** from the **Window** menu in iChat.

With the exception of the Power Mac G4 and G5 (which have a port for an external microphone), all Macs have a built-in microphone that can be used for audio input. The microphone is a little pinhole next to the screen on most Mac desktop and laptop models.

If your camera has a built-in microphone, you can choose whether to use this microphone or the one built into your Mac, using the drop-down menu that appears.

6 Enable AOL Instant Messenger

If you entered information for a .Mac account, you might be prompted to enable AOL Instant Messenger access. Click **Enable** to do this.

You are now set up to use iChat. You can communicate immediately with other iChat users on the local network who appear in the **Rendezvous** window or add .Mac or AIM buddies to your **Buddy List** (see **79** **Add a Buddy**) .

78 Set Up Your Picture

After you've set up your iChat account, it's time for the most critical part of all: choosing your picture. This picture is what represents you visually in a chat with another person, so you should choose something that accurately depicts your personality, your likes and dislikes, and your usual mood. Or you'll just want to find something nice and silly to use.

iChat starts you out using the picture from your card in Address Book, if you have defined one, or your login picture. You can tell iChat to use a different picture by simply dragging it into iChat from the Finder (or even straight from a Web page).

1 Drag in a Picture

Launch iChat using the icon in the Dock or in the **Applications** folder. Make sure that one of your iChat windows is visible—either your **Buddy List** or the **Rendezvous** list (select one from the **Window** menu if one is not visible). Either window shows your picture in the upper-right corner of the window.

Before You Begin

✔ **77** Set Up Your AIM or .Mac Account

See Also

→ **120** Add a Person to Your Address Book

→ **149** Set Your Login Picture

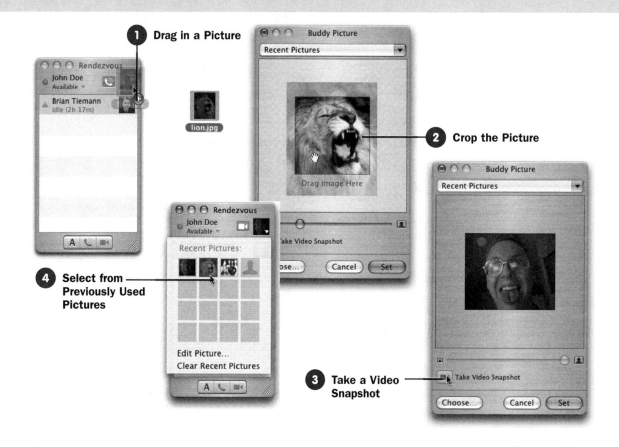

① **Drag in a Picture**

lion.jpg

② **Crop the Picture**

④ **Select from Previously Used Pictures**

③ **Take a Video Snapshot**

 TIP

Try to choose a picture that's "facing right"—that will look good at the left side of a chat window. Although on your side of a chat, your picture appears on the right side of the window, your chat partners see your picture on the left side of their windows. For aesthetic reasons, the picture you choose to represent you should show you facing right (towards your text) rather than left.

Open the Finder and locate the picture you want to use. Drag it to the square containing your current picture in iChat. You can even drag an image from a Safari window, if you find a picture on the Web that you'd like to use.

② **Crop the Picture**

The **Buddy Picture** picture-editing screen appears, showing the picture you've dragged into iChat. Use the slider below the picture to set the "aperture" size, or the size of the square that defines your iChat picture relative to the whole picture you've dragged in. You can scale down the entire picture to fit into the square, or you can select only a small portion if you prefer. Click and drag in the picture window to set where the square is centered, and click **Set** when you're satisfied with how it looks.

③ Take a Video Snapshot

If you have a digital video camera hooked up to your Mac with FireWire, the **Take Video Snapshot** button at the bottom of the **Buddy Picture** window becomes active. Click the button; the output from your video camera appears in the picture-editing window. A series of beeps sounds, becoming progressively quicker; as the beeps speed up, aim the camera at yourself (or at anything else you want to take a picture of), and in a few seconds iChat will freeze-frame an image, using whatever is on the camera at the time. You can then edit the image using the aperture and drag tools in the **Buddy Picture** window.

Just about any kind of digital video camera will work with the login picture selector; any FireWire camera that iChat recognizes will activate the feature. Apple's iSight and other FireWire Webcams are ideal, but you can also use a standard digital camcorder; just connect it to your computer, put it in standby mode, and the video signal will automatically be picked up by the system and used in the video snapshot.

If you don't like your snapshot, you can immediately take another one by clicking the **Take Video Snapshot** button again. Keep trying until you have a picture you like.

④ Select from Previously Used Pictures

While you're using iChat, you can change your picture immediately to any picture you've used in the past. Click your current picture in either the Buddy List or Rendezvous list window, and a sheet showing all your recently used pictures appears. Click the picture you want to switch to, and it becomes your active picture.

NOTE

G3-based Macs slower than 600MHz cannot use iChat's video capabilities, and thus the **Take Video Snapshot** option is also unavailable (iChat will say that video-conferencing is not supported on this computer).

TIP

To invoke the picture-cropping window directly without dragging in a new picture, select **Change My Picture** from the **Buddies** menu.

79 Add a Buddy

Before You Begin

✔ **77** Set Up Your AIM or .Mac Account

✔ **120** Add a Person to Your Address Book

✔ **125** Set Up iSync to Synchronize Your Information

See Also

→ **39** Discover iChat Partners

→ **80** Start a Chat Session

→ **82** Set a Custom Status Message

Rendezvous lets you see all the iChat users on your local network immediately; but when it comes to talking with people who are elsewhere on the Internet, Rendezvous won't help you. In those situations, you have to rely on your Buddy List, and the .Mac and *AIM* users listed there, to connect you with them across large Internet distances.

iChat lets you select "buddies" from your Address Book or specify them manually. To add a buddy manually, you must know the .Mac or AIM account name they're using.

1 Open the Address Book Sheet

Launch iChat using the icon in the Dock or in the **Applications** folder; open the **Buddy List** window, if it is not already open (choose **Buddy List** from the **Window** menu). Make sure that you are connected to the Internet.

Click the + button in the lower-left corner of the **Buddy List** window. This brings up a sheet that shows a simplified version of your Address Book, with your Groups at the left and the individual addresses on the right.

2 Select a Person from Your Address Book

If the buddy you want to add is in your Address Book already, simply find her name in the list and double-click it.

3 Add a New Person

To add a buddy manually to your Buddy List, click the **New Person** button at the bottom of the Address Book sheet. A new sheet appears, with form fields that allow you to specify the person's name and other information. This information adds the person to your Address Book as well as to your Buddy List in iChat.

You must know what kind of chat account the other person has—an AIM name or a .Mac account. The account name and type is the minimum information you must have to add a new person.

TIP

You can filter the names by typing a partial name into the **Search** box at the top of the Address Book sheet.

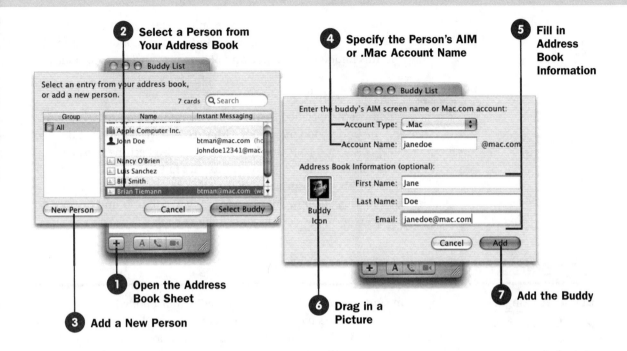

2 Select a Person from Your Address Book

4 Specify the Person's AIM or .Mac Account Name

5 Fill in Address Book Information

1 Open the Address Book Sheet

3 Add a New Person

6 Drag in a Picture

7 Add the Buddy

4 Specify the Person's AIM or .Mac Account Name

From the **Account Type** drop-down list, select the type of account the person you want to add to your Buddy List has (.Mac or AIM), and then type the account name for that person.

5 Fill in Address Book Information

If you leave the rest of the fields blank, this buddy will appear in your Buddy List with a generic picture icon and with her account name instead of a full name. To make the person's entry appear a little more streamlined in the Buddy List window, specify a first and last name and an email address here. This information will be added to the person's new address card, which is automatically created in your Address Book.

6 Drag in a Picture

If this person has already specified a picture in her copy of iChat, that picture will appear next to the person's name in your Buddy

List as soon as the person appears online. However, if you want, you can drag any picture into the **Buddy Icon** well to use instead, and this image will override any picture provided by your buddy.

7 Add the Buddy

When you've specified all the pertinent information for the buddy you are adding to your Buddy List, click **Add**. The information sheet closes and your Buddy List updates to reflect the person's online status; if the person is online, her full name and picture will appear if they are specified by the other person. In addition to finding the person in your Buddy List, you will also find this person listed in a new card in your Address Book.

80 Start a Chat Session

Before You Begin

✔ **77** Set Up Your AIM or .Mac Account

✔ **79** Add a Buddy

See Also

→ **81** Send a File

→ **82** Set a Custom Status Message

TIP

You must enable chat transcripts for them to be saved automatically; you can do this by enabling the **Automatically save chat transcripts** check box in the **Messages** pane of iChat's **Preferences**, which are accessible through the **iChat** menu.

You can start a chat session with anybody in your Buddy List or Rendezvous list who's available—in other words, anybody who has a green dot next to their name in the list. (You cannot send messages to people who are offline.) When you send a message to an online user, and the other person replies, a chat has begun.

The difference between a *direct message* and an *instant message* (either of which you can send to any online user in your Buddy List) is that an instant message is relayed through a central server on the Internet, whereas a direct message is sent straight from your computer to the other person's computer. Use a **Direct Message** (choose it from the **Buddies** menu) if you are concerned about the risk to privacy that comes with sending your messages through the central server.

You can start chatting using plain text (which appears in your iChat window surrounded by glossy balloons), audio (using your Mac's built-in microphone or the microphone in your video camera), or video (using an external FireWire camera, such as a DV camcorder or Apple's iSight camera).

If you choose, you can have your text chats saved as transcripts; each time you chat with another person, the entire session is saved in a file in the **iChats** folder inside the **Documents** folder in your **Home** folder. Simply double-click a chat file (named for the person you were chatting with) to open it for review.

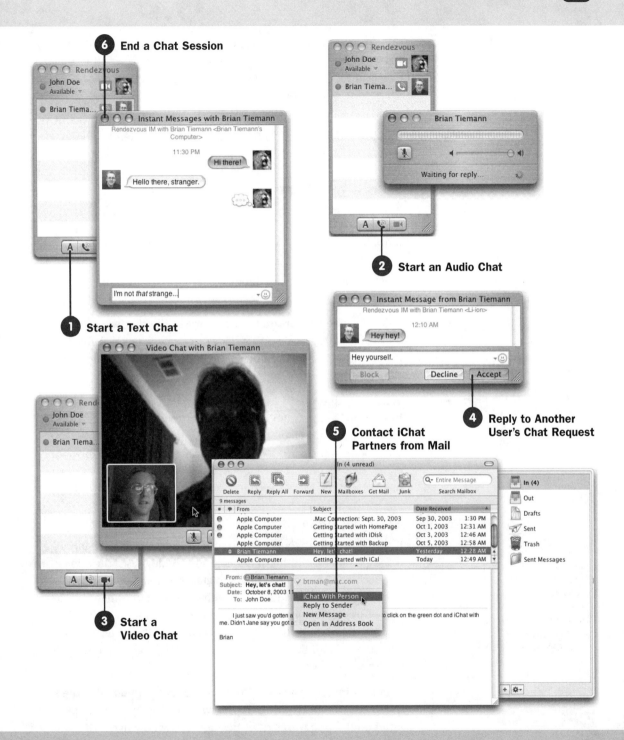

6 End a Chat Session

Rendezvous
John Doe
Available ▾

Brian Tiema...

Instant Messages with Brian Tiemann
Rendezvous IM with Brian Tiemann <Brian Tiemann's Computer>

11:30 PM

Hi there!

Hello there, stranger.

I'm not *that* strange...

1 Start a Text Chat

Rendezvous
John Doe
Available ▾

Brian Tiema...

Brian Tiemann

Waiting for reply...

2 Start an Audio Chat

Instant Message from Brian Tiemann
Rendezvous IM with Brian Tiemann <Li-ion>

12:10 AM

Hey hey!

Hey yourself.

Block   Decline   Accept

**4 Reply to Another
User's Chat Request**

**5 Contact iChat
Partners from Mail**

Video Chat with Brian Tiemann

Rend...
John Doe
Available ▾

Brian Tiema...

**3 Start a
Video Chat**

In (4 unread)

Delete Reply Reply All Forward New Mailboxes Get Mail Junk   Q▾ Entire Message
                                                                              Search Mailbox

9 messages

•	🏴	From	Subject	Date Received	▲
●		Apple Computer	.Mac Connection: Sept. 30, 2003	Sep 30, 2003 1:30 PM	
●		Apple Computer	Getting Started with HomePage	Oct 1, 2003 12:31 AM	
●		Apple Computer	Getting Started with iDisk	Oct 3, 2003 12:46 AM	
●		Apple Computer	Getting Started with Backup	Oct 5, 2003 12:58 AM	
●		Brian Tiemann	Hey, let's chat!	Yesterday 12:28 AM	
		Apple Computer	Getting Started with iCal	Today 12:49 AM	

In (4)
Out
Drafts
Sent
Trash
Sent Messages

From: ● Brian Tiemann   ✓ btman@mac.com
Subject: **Hey, let's chat!**   iChat With Person
Date: October 8, 2003 11   Reply to Sender
To: John Doe   New Message
                             Open in Address Book

I just saw you'd gotten a ... to click on the green dot and iChat with
me. Didn't Jane say you got a ...

Brian

+ ⚙▾

You can start a chat immediately with any active person on your Buddy List by using the **iChat** system menu, a cartoon word balloon in the menu bar; simply select the name of the person under **Available Buddies** to send a message.

You can turn the **iChat** system menu on and off using the **Show status in menu bar** check box in the **General** page of the iChat **Preferences** application, which is accessible through the **iChat** menu.

① Start a Text Chat

The simplest kind of chat, a text chat, can be initiated simply by double-clicking the name of the buddy you want to chat with in either the Buddy List or Rendezvous window. (Alternatively, select the buddy from the list and click the **A** button at the bottom of the window.) An **Instant Messages** window appears in which you can type your message; press **Return** to send the text you've typed.

TIPS

To insert a carriage-return into your message (that is, to break one line and start typing on the next line) without sending the message, press **Option+Return**.

Your message appears on the right side of the chat window. When your chat partner replies, his messages appear on the left side of the window. A cartoon bubble with an ellipsis (…) in it indicates that your partner is typing a response.

When chatting with a Rendezvous partner, the text you type is sent immediately as you type it without waiting for you to press **Return** (your buddy can see all the typos you make and when you Backspace over them). If you'd rather iChat wait until you've fully composed your message before sending it, you can turn off this behavior in the **Messages** pane in iChat's **Preferences** window.

② Start an Audio Chat

If the other user is capable of an audio chat, a green "telephone" icon appears next to her picture in your Buddy List. Click this icon or select the user from the list and click the **Telephone** button at the bottom of the window. If the other user doesn't have a microphone, you can still set up a one-way audio chat, in which she will be able to hear you, but not vice versa. To do this, select the user from the list and then choose **Invite to One-Way Audio Chat** from the **Buddies** menu.

A small window appears, with the name of the buddy you are trying to contact in the title bar. The window displays your audio input gain along with status messages showing whether the audio chat is properly set up yet. When the chat is initiated correctly, the status messages disappear and you should be able to talk and hear the other person.

To monitor the quality of your connection, use the **Connection Doctor** (available in the **Audio** menu). The **Connection Doctor** panel shows you the frame rate and bandwidth (bit rate) used by the connection, as well as a meter showing the connection's quality. This information can be useful in diagnosing network problems that arise.

③ Start a Video Chat

If the other user has a video camera hooked up and turned on, you can start a video chat (assuming that you have a video camera, too). Click the green camera icon next to the user's picture, or select the user and click the **Camera** button at the bottom of the window.

A window appears showing your moving image as your camera sees it, and a connection status bar at the top showing whether the chat is set up or not. When the chat starts, the status bar disappears, and the other user's image takes up the whole window. Your image shrinks to a small "picture-in-picture" view, which you can drag to another position in the window or change its size (by dragging its corner).

You might have difficulty starting a chat with other users on your local network using Rendezvous if your firewall is enabled. To allow iChat traffic to get through the firewall, open the **Firewall** tab in the **Sharing Preferences** window (click **Sharing** in the **System Preferences** application), then enable the exception rule for **iChat Rendezvous** (ports 5297 and 5298). For more information on working with the firewall, see **163 Add or Remove Firewall Rules**.

④ Reply to Another User's Chat Request

If another person invites you to a text, audio, or video chat, you will see a message pop up in the upper-right corner of the screen telling you about the invitation. (A sound effect plays, too; for text chats, it's a soft "pop" sound, whereas for audio and video chats, it's a "ring" sound.)

Click the translucent message to turn it opaque and see its contents; the window also has buttons you can use to accept the chat,

NOTE

If the other user doesn't have a camera, you can still set up a one-way video chat, in which he will be able to see and hear you, but not vice versa. To do this, select the user and then choose **Invite to One-Way Video Chat** from the **Buddies** menu.

refuse it, or block the user from contacting you in the future. If you click **Accept**, the chat session will start.

To end any chat session, simply close the chat window.

TIPS

To make sure that incoming messages can't reach you, choose **Offline** from the **iChat** system menu (or from the menu under your name within iChat if it's running). You will now appear "offline" to other iChat and AIM users, and they won't be able to send messages to you.

Update your Address Book to make sure that the email address for each of your contacts is the same as the one that she uses for iChat! Remember that you can enter multiple email addresses in Address Book for each person.

To turn off iChat altogether, quit the application. However, iChat still launches to accept incoming messages even if the application isn't running, unless you enable the **When I quit iChat, set my status to Offline** check box in the **General** tab of the iChat **Preferences** window.

⑤ Contact iChat Partners from Mail

Open the **Mail** application (click its icon in the Dock) and view your Inbox. If any messages in it were sent to you from someone in your Address Book who is currently using iChat, a green dot appears next to their name in the message listing. Click the dot to begin a direct iChat session with that person. Alternatively, click the down arrow next to the person's name to access the **iChat With Person** command as well as several other communication options.

⑥ End a Chat Session

When you're done chatting with the other person, simply click the **Close** button on the chat window to end the session.

Set your status to **Offline** (using the menu under your name) if you want to stop receiving new messages from other users.

---

81 Send a File

Before You Begin

✔ **77** Set Up Your AIM or .Mac Account

✔ **79** Add a Buddy

✔ **80** Start a Chat Session

See Also

→ **34** Share Another Mac's Files

→ **82** Set a Custom Status Message

You can use iChat to transfer files instantly between users. You can send a file directly to anybody in your Buddy List or Rendezvous list simply by dragging the file to that person's entry in the list; similarly, anybody can send you a file, which will appear as a document in a text message.

① Find the File to Send

Use the Finder to locate the file you want to send to the other person.

PART II: Networking and the Internet

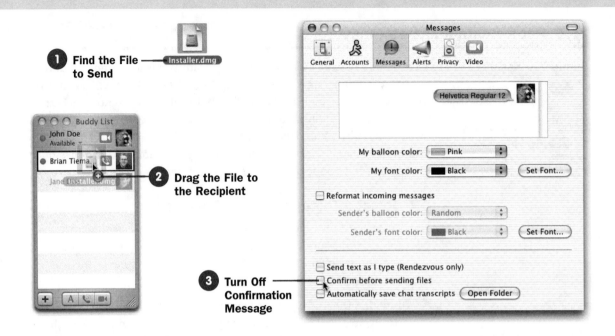

1 Find the File to Send

2 Drag the File to the Recipient

3 Turn Off Confirmation Message

Drag the File to the Recipient

Make sure that the Buddy List or Rendezvous window containing the user's name is open and that the user is online (a green dot appears next to the user's name if she is online). Drag the file to the user's name in the list and drop the file on the recipient's name. A dialog box opens, prompting you to confirm that you want to send the file; click **Send** to send it.

Turn Off Confirmation Message

If you don't want iChat to confirm whether you want to send a file before you send it, click the **Don't ask again** check box in the confirmation dialog box. Alternatively, open the iChat **Preferences** window and click the **Messages** icon to display the **Messages** pane. Disable the **Confirm before sending files** check box.

TIP

If you're already in a chat with a user, a common mistake is to drag the file into the chat window. The result of this action can be surprising, especially if the file you're trying to send is a picture—this is how you set the background picture for the chat window. Make sure that you drag the file to the user's name in the Buddy List or Rendezvous window, not into the chat window.

82 Set a Custom Status Message

Before You Begin

✔ **77** Set Up Your AIM or
.Mac Account

See Also

→ **78** Set Up Your Picture

→ **80** Start a Chat
Session

By default, you can select from only two status messages that iChat displays to other users under your name: **Available** and **Away**. Your status changes to **Idle** if you have been idle (that is, if you have not touched your keyboard or mouse) for ten minutes. You can set your status to **Away** to let others know that you're not at your computer to answer instant messages; but if you want others to see a more detailed message to explain what you're doing, it's easy to set one.

1 Select a Custom Status Message

Launch iChat using the icon in the Dock or in the **Applications** folder. Make sure that either the Rendezvous or Buddy List window is open; select one from the **Window** menu if neither of the windows is present.

In either the Buddy List or Rendezvous window, click the down arrow next to your status message to open the menu of selectable status messages. Select the **Custom** option under either **Available** or **Away**; the status message in the window's title bar turns into a text input box.

2 Type a Temporary Custom Message

Type a new message of your choice in the text box and press **Return**. The new message appears under your name in others' Buddy Lists, until you change it or log out of iChat.

TIP

To cancel entering a new message, leave the text entry field blank and press **Return**.

3 Add a Permanent Custom Message

From the status message menu, select **Edit Status Menu** to bring up the custom message definition sheet. Click the + icon under either the **Available** or **Away** column; a new message blank becomes selected in the appropriate column. Type a message that you want to keep so that you can select it at opportune times. This message, along with any others that you define, appears under either **Available** or **Away** in the status message menu under your name or in the **iChat** system menu. Click the message you want to set as your new status message.

You can define as many custom messages as you want, to match the myriad different ways you can be "available" or "away."

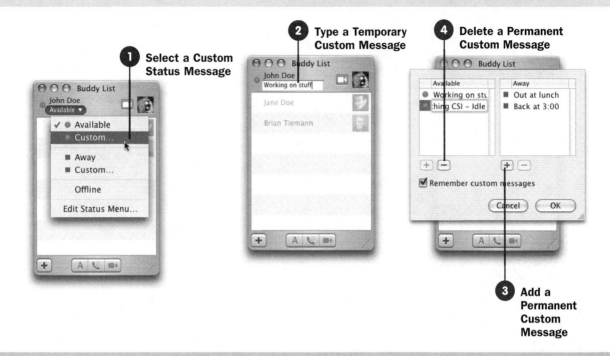

2 Type a Temporary Custom Message

1 Select a Custom Status Message

4 Delete a Permanent Custom Message

3 Add a Permanent Custom Message

4 **Delete a Permanent Custom Message**

To remove a custom status message from the list, open the custom message definition sheet (select **Edit Status Menu** from the status message menu). Select the message you want to delete and click the – (minus sign) button under the column in which the message is listed.

TIP

You can delete multiple messages at the same time: Hold down **Shift** or ⌘ while clicking the messages you want to delete. Then click the – (minus sign) button to delete all the selected messages. Be careful—there is no "undo" function, and if you delete any custom messages, they're gone for good.

PART III

Making It Work Together

IN THIS PART

10

The Home Office: Word Processing, Drawing, and Creating Presentations

IN THIS CHAPTER:

When discussing what kinds of things the Mac does well, most people usually mention graphics, video, music, and other such multimedia disciplines. Something that often escapes notice, though, is the Mac's usefulness as a tool for standard office productivity—word processing, diagrams, presentations, spreadsheets, and other such applications that have come to be thought of as strictly the domain of Windows computers and Microsoft software.

Microsoft Office for Mac OS X is a fine piece of software, and it's the best way to achieve complete compatibility with your Windows-using co-workers. However, Microsoft Office is expensive, and you might find that you can get by with the Office compatibility that's built into Mac OS X. This chapter looks at a few of the built-in capabilities the Mac has for accomplishing the same tasks your co-workers do in Windows. Even without additional software, Mac OS X gives you the tools to create text documents, read and write Microsoft Word files, process your handwriting into text using a graphics tablet and pen, and manage fonts. Adding AppleWorks or Keynote—both available as commercial packages for $100 or less—gives you many additional capabilities, including many that Windows users can't match.

83 Create a New Text Document

Before You Begin

✔ **2** Find and Launch an Application

✔ **17** Move, Copy, or Delete a Document or Folder

See Also

→ **16** Set a Color Label

→ **85** Write Using a Tablet

Text files are even today the bread and butter of computing. Whether you use your computer for video editing, email, gaming, or photography, you've most likely also found indispensable the ability to enter some quick textual notes into a document—a shopping list, a phone number, a description of the dream you had last night—and while there are specialized applications designed to handle each of these situations, nothing is more versatile than the good old-fashioned text file.

Text documents can take two forms: *plain text* and *rich text*. A plain text document has nothing in it but the letters, numbers, and other characters you type—no special formatting, pictures, defined fonts (typefaces), or other complications. A rich text document, however, can have styled text (text in bold, in italics, underlined, or in different fonts), special paragraph formatting, pictures, page layout information, and much more.

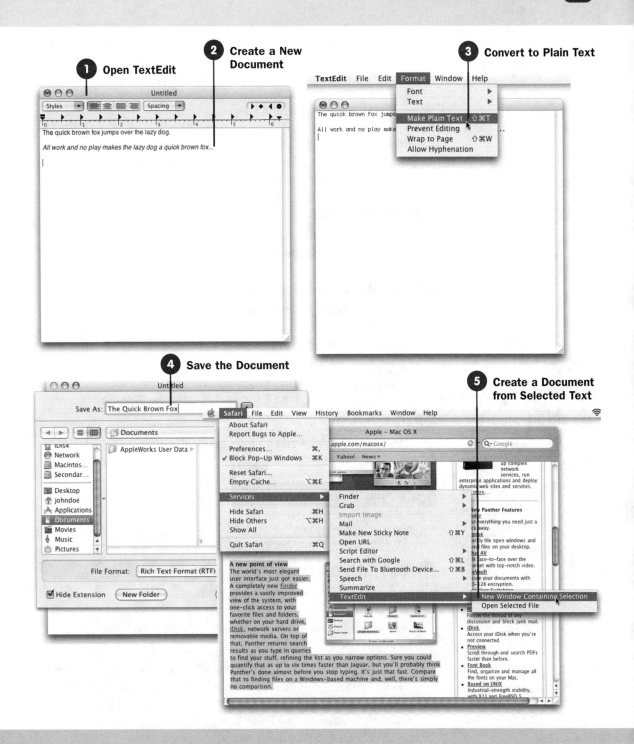

1 Open TextEdit

2 Create a New Document

3 Convert to Plain Text

4 Save the Document

5 Create a Document from Selected Text

Mac OS X lets you create documents in either of these two formats, using the built-in TextEdit application, a handy little word-processing program with some surprising capabilities. Plain text files are more versatile in many ways—you can transfer them from one platform to another, open them in very simple applications (such as Notepad in Windows), serve them from a Web server to be shown natively in a browser, and so on. But rich text documents—which Mac OS X can save in either RTF (Rich Text Format) or Microsoft Word format—must be opened in more specialized software, such as Word.

1 Open TextEdit

Open a Finder window, navigate to the **Applications** folder, and double-click the **TextEdit** icon.

2 Create a New Document

TIP

To create a new document from scratch, choose **New** from the **File** menu.

When TextEdit launches, a new blank document window appears, with simple formatting controls and tab markings at the top. (The presence of these controls means that TextEdit is in rich text mode.)

You can now type text into the window, format it using the displayed controls and the **Format** menu, print the file's contents, and so on.

3 Convert to Plain Text

TIP

Double-click a word in any selectable block of text in any Mac OS X application, and the whole word will become selected. Triple-click, and the entire paragraph will be selected.

At any point while the document is open, you can convert it to plain text mode. You might choose to do this if you want to use the document in a Web page, at the Unix Terminal command line, or another such application that can only handle plain text.

To convert the open document to plain text, choose **Format**, **Make Plain Text**.

4 Save the Document

Before you invest too much time in creating a text document, you should save the file to your hard disk. Saving files periodically as you're working on them is an excellent habit to get into.

Select **Save** from the **File** menu. The **Save** dialog box appears. Type a filename, select a location for the document, and (if it's a rich text document) choose which format—RTF or Microsoft Word format—to save it in. You can also choose whether or not to hide the filename extension; the **Hide Extension** check box is automatically enabled and disabled depending on the filename you type.

Whatever you enter in the **Save As** box is how the filename will be displayed. If you don't type the extension, an appropriate one is added automatically to the filename and hidden.

5 **Create a Document from Selected Text**

If you already have some text in another application that you want to turn into a text document, there's a quick one-step way of doing it. Select the text you want to save and open the application menu (in the example shown here, I'm saving a chunk of text I found on a Web page with Safari). From the **Services** submenu, select **TextEdit**, and then select **New Window Containing Selection**. A new TextEdit window will appear with the selected text in it. You can then save the text as a new file, print it, or do whatever else you want.

NOTE

The standard extensions are **.txt** for plain text documents, **.rtf** for Rich Text Format documents, and **.doc** for Microsoft Word documents.

84 Type §¶éçïå£ ¢hÁràcṫérs

The Macintosh has a history of being especially adept at handling special characters—accented letters, punctuation marks, mathematical or scientific symbols—in an intuitive and efficient manner. The **Option** key is what makes this possible; pressing **Option** along with any of the regular keys either creates a special symbol (such as the copyright symbol, ©) or a *combining character*, which is an entity that combines with the next character you type. For example, to create an accented e (é), you first press **Option+E** to create the acute accent combining character (′); then you press **E** again, and the letter would combine with the acute accent to create the desired character. After pressing **Option+E**, you can also press **A**, **I**, or any of several other letter keys to get an accented version of that letter.

Every alphanumeric key on the keyboard is bound to a special **Option** key character, including a second special character binding that you get if you hold the **Shift** key as well as the **Option** key. The bindings were created in a carefully designed manner. Rather than making you hunt through a table for special characters or remember symbols by their ASCII number, the Mac is designed to let you memorize the intuitive built-in bindings for immediate access to commonly used symbols. Some key combinations are suggested by the shape of the character, for instance the Japanese yen character (¥), which you get by pressing **Option+Y**, or the lowercase delta (∂), which is summoned with **Option+D**.

Before You Begin

✔ **2** Find and Launch an Application

✔ **83** Create a New Text Document

See Also

→ **85** Write Using a Tablet

→ **136** Change the System's Language

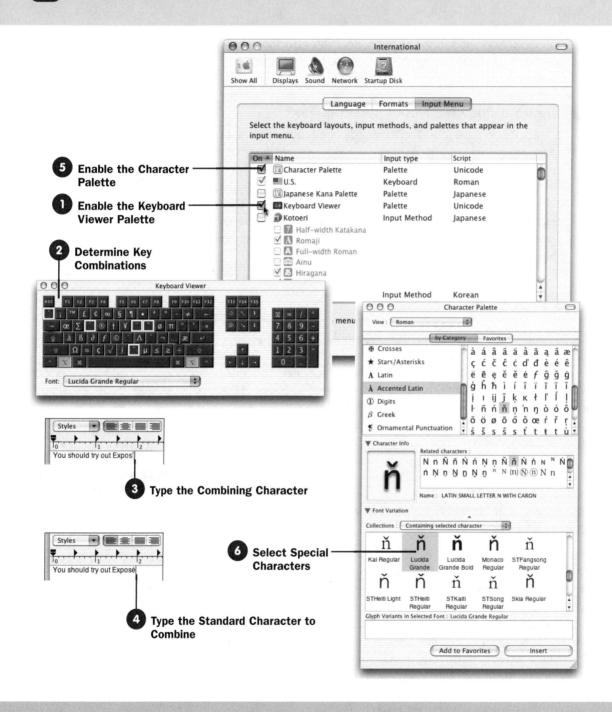

5 Enable the Character Palette

1 Enable the Keyboard Viewer Palette

2 Determine Key Combinations

3 Type the Combining Character

4 Type the Standard Character to Combine

6 Select Special Characters

It can be interesting to try to figure out the reasoning behind each key binding and to explore what each key does when combined with the **Option** key; fortunately, however, trial and error isn't the only way to figure out what keys you have to press. There are two input palettes at hand that assist in this investigation: **Keyboard Viewer**, which gives you a visual map of what each key does, and the **Character Palette**, which lets you select a character from a unified grid and copy it directly into your document.

❶ Enable the Keyboard Viewer Palette

Open the **International Preferences** window (click **International** in the **System Preferences** application, available from the **Apple** menu). Click the **Input Menu** tab and then enable the **Keyboard Viewer Palette** check box. The **Keyboard Viewer** is now available in the **Keyboard Input** system menu, a "flag" icon on the right side of the Mac's menu bar that indicates the current keyboard layout mode (for example, an American flag for the **U.S.** standard layout).

❷ Determine Key Combinations

Select **Show Keyboard Viewer Palette** from the **Keyboard Input** system menu. The palette that appears lets you explore **Option**-key bindings visually; you can press and hold **Option** to see what each key's meaning becomes. Press and hold **Shift+Option** to see the second, alternative meanings. From the **Font** drop-down list, select a font for the key caps so that you can see exactly what the symbols will look like when you type them.

❸ Type the Combining Character

In a TextEdit window (or in any other application where you can enter text, including changing filenames in the Finder), press the **Option** key combination you want. For instance, to create a capital O with a circumflex, press **Option+I** to invoke the circumflex combining character (^). The symbol appears in your text, highlighted in yellow, to indicate that the next character you type—if such a combined character exists—will be combined with the circumflex to create an accented character.

TIP

Other bindings are based on the most common usage of a combining diacritic—for instance, the E key generates the acute accent because the acute-accented é is so common, and the umlaut (¨) is generated with **Option+U**; the tilde diacritic (~) is generated with **Option+N** because of the common ñ character, but it can also combine to form ã and õ. Still other bindings are suggested, loosely, by the pronunciation of the natural key and the symbol, as with the trademark symbol (™) which is generated with **Option+2**.

TIP

The **Keyboard Viewer** can show you a lot of the most commonly used special characters, but to access all the character sets that Mac OS X supports, you must use the **Character Palette**. Fortunately, most Mac OS X applications that deal with text (such as TextEdit) have a handy option in the **Edit** menu: click **Special Characters** to pop up the **Character Palette** and browse for just the right character.

4 Type the Standard Character to Combine

Press the key that creates the "standard" version of the character to combine with the combining character. For instance, press **O** to enter a lowercase **o**, or press **Shift+O** to enter a capital **O**. The character combines with the preceding circumflex to form the desired character, Ô. You can now continue typing as usual.

Use this same procedure to create any common accented character. For example, to create the â character, press **Option+I**, then **A**. To create Ü, press **Option+U**, then **Shift+U**.

5 Enable the Character Palette

If you're having difficulty using the **Keyboard Viewer** (some people have trouble translating the special characters shown there to the correct key on their physical keyboard), you can insert special characters into your text by using the **Character Palette**. You might have to do more scrolling in the **Character Palette** window than in the **Keyboard Viewer**, but the **Character Palette** lets you see exactly what you're selecting.

Open the **International Preferences** window (click **International** in the **System Preferences** application). Click the **Input Menu** tab and then enable the **Character Palette** check box to add it to the listing under the **Keyboard Input** system menu, if it is not already enabled.

6 Select Special Characters

Click the input menu icon (if you're using **U.S.** keyboard options, it's the American flag icon on the right side of the Mac's menu bar) and choose **Show Character Palette**. All characters in the vast Unicode spectrum are available in this palette. From the **View** menu at the top of the palette, select the class of characters you want (such as **Roman**); depending on which class you select, a variety of different organizing categories are available. (For instance, select **Japanese** from the **View** menu if you want to browse characters by radical, by category, or by code table.)

Browse until you find the character you want; then either double-click it or select it and click **Insert** to copy the character into your current document.

85 Write Using a Tablet

Ink is what Apple calls its handwriting technology, borrowed from the old Newton handheld computer, now incorporated natively into Mac OS X. Using Ink, you can plug in a graphics tablet (a pointing device with a flat sensitive surface and a stylus or mouse, such as Wacom's popular Graphire) and use the stylus to write words in your natural handwriting. Mac OS X learns over time to recognize your lettering style and becomes more and more accurate the more you use Ink.

When a tablet is connected and Ink is enabled, you can start writing anywhere on the tablet pad, and the text you write—phrase by phrase—is sent directly into the current application. There is also a floating control strip you can use to summon the Ink window and a floating input pad in which you can write larger amounts of text and refine it before sending it to your application (these tools appear when Ink is enabled). The Ink window is useful for training Ink's handwriting recognition and for selecting among word variants; you can also use the Ink window to draw pictures and send them to applications that support images.

1 Install the Tablet's Drivers

Most graphics tablets require that you first install a driver. Follow the installation instructions that came with your graphics tablet before proceeding with these steps; the Ink program might not work properly if you don't correctly install your tablet.

2 Plug In the Tablet

Connect the tablet to your Mac using any available USB port, if it's not already plugged in.

3 Open the Ink Preferences

Open the **System Preferences** window using the **Apple** menu. As long as the tablet is plugged in to the Mac, the **Ink** icon appears among the **Hardware** preference pane icons; click **Ink** to open the **Ink Preferences** window.

4 Turn On Handwriting Recognition

Click the **Handwriting recognition is: On** radio button to turn on handwriting recognition. The floating Ink control strip appears on the screen.

Before You Begin

✔ **83** Create a New Text Document

See Also

→ **87** Create a Drawing in AppleWorks

KEY TERM

Ink—Apple's handwriting-recognition technology, adapted from the Newton handheld computer and incorporated into all levels of Mac OS X. Ink lets you write text by hand into any Mac OS X application using a tablet.

TIP

Even without Ink turned on, Mac OS X immediately recognizes the tablet as a pointing device; you can use the tablet's stylus or mouse to navigate the operating system if you like.

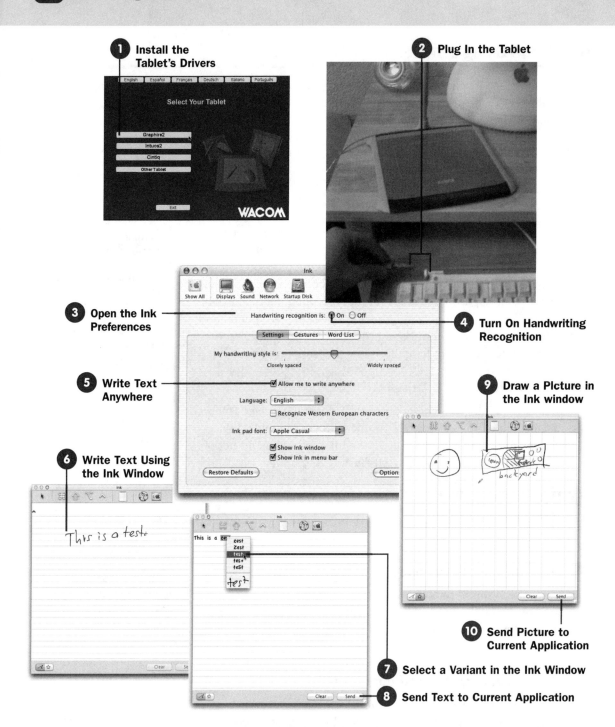

1 Install the Tablet's Drivers

2 Plug In the Tablet

3 Open the Ink Preferences

4 Turn On Handwriting Recognition

5 Write Text Anywhere

6 Write Text Using the Ink Window

7 Select a Variant in the Ink Window

8 Send Text to Current Application

9 Draw a Picture in the Ink window

10 Send Picture to Current Application

❺ Write Text Anywhere

If you have enabled the **Allow me to write anywhere** check box in the **Ink Preferences** window, you can write text immediately anywhere on the tablet's input area (which corresponds to any place on the screen), whatever application you're using. As soon as you begin moving the stylus, a floating sheet of yellow lined paper appears with your pen lines on it.

Write a short phrase, then lift the stylus. The yellow sheet disappears, and your text is interpreted and inserted into the active application.

❻ Write Text Using the Ink Window

Click the notepad icon in the Ink control strip to expand the Ink window. Use the input area to write your text. As you write each word or phrase and lift the stylus or pause, the words you've written are interpreted into formal text. You can use the stylus to tap a location in the Ink window where you want to begin writing, or you can double-tap existing text to select it and overwrite it.

Enable the **Show Ink in menu bar** check box in the **Ink Preferences** window to gain one-click access to the **Ink** system menu (the icon on the right side of the Mac's menu bar looks like an old-fashioned pen nib); this menu lets you show or hide the Ink window, or to switch handwriting recognition modes from letting you write anywhere (on the yellow lined paper) or only in the Ink window.

❼ Select a Variant in the Ink Window

If Ink interprets one of your words incorrectly, you might be able to select a variant from among the possibilities the program has identified. To bring up the menu of variants, double-tap and hold the incorrect word, or hold down the button on the stylus while you tap to select the incorrect word. Ink displays a context menu of possible variations along with the word as you wrote it on the tablet; tap to select the correct word.

Careful control of the stylus is essential to making Ink work well. To select text, press and hold for a moment before moving the stylus to expand the selection area. A short stroke from right to left erases the previously written character. Most tablets work using the same methods and have similar buttons to those described here; refer to your tablet's documentation for details on how to use it with Mac OS X.

TIP

You can move the Ink control strip anywhere onscreen that's convenient for you. It's best to keep it near the top of the screen, however, because when you open the Ink window, it expands downward from the control strip to form the drawing and writing pad area.

TIP

Writing text anywhere is most useful when Mac OS X has already learned your handwriting well. If your words are not being interpreted correctly, consider using the Ink window for a while until Ink's recognition is more accurate.

TIP

If Ink is adding space between your letters or crunching your letters together, adjust the **My handwriting style is** slider in the **Ink Preferences** window to tell Mac OS X whether your writing is spaced out or close together.

8 **Send Text to Current Application**

When you're done writing text in the Ink window, click in the current application where you want the text to be inserted; then click **Send** in the Ink window. The text is copied into your application.

9 **Draw a Picture in the Ink window**

Click the star icon in the lower-left corner of the Ink window to put the Ink window into drawing mode. You can use the stylus or mouse to draw pictures, diagrams, sketches, or anything else you might want to insert into a document (for instance, an illustration in TextEdit or Word).

10 **Send Picture to Current Application**

When you're done drawing in the Ink window, click in the current application where you want the picture to be inserted; then click **Send** in the Ink window. The picture is copied into your application as a pre-rendered image (it can no longer be modified using the Ink tablet, but it is included as part of the document when you save it).

86 Use Microsoft Word Documents Without Word

Before You Begin

✔ **2** Find and Launch an Application

✔ **7** Assign an Opener Application to a File

✔ **83** Create a New Text Document

See Also

→ **87** Create a Drawing in AppleWorks

→ **89** Save a Keynote Presentation for Use in Microsoft PowerPoint

Mac OS X has built-in support for Microsoft Word documents; TextEdit, the workhorse text-editing application, can read documents that were created in most versions of Word, and it can write documents that Word users can open.

TextEdit can handle basic rich-text word processing; however, many features of Word documents, such as tables, collaborative editing, Web links, and so on require additional software, such as *AppleWorks*—or Microsoft Word itself.

1 **Open a Word Document in TextEdit**

If you don't have Word installed, TextEdit is the default opener application for Word documents (identified by their **.doc** file extensions). Simply double-click a **.doc** file to open it in TextEdit.

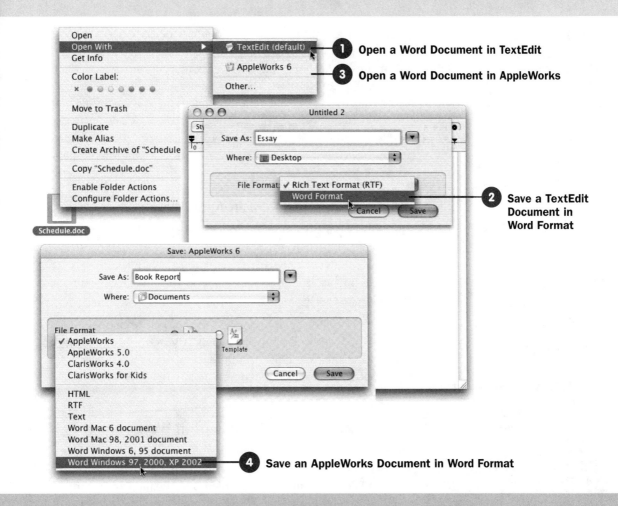

1 Open a Word Document in TextEdit

3 Open a Word Document in AppleWorks

2 Save a TextEdit Document in Word Format

4 Save an AppleWorks Document in Word Format

2 Save a TextEdit Document in Word Format

After you've finished typing a text document in TextEdit, you can save the document as a Microsoft Word document. Choose **Save** or **Save As** from the **File** menu; in the **Save** dialog box that opens, choose **Rich Text Format (RTF)** or **Word Format** from the **File Format** drop-down menu. Select **Word Format** to create a **.doc** file that Microsoft Office users can open without ever knowing that it was created on a Mac—and a Mac that didn't even have Office installed, at that.

Microsoft Word can read RTF documents; RTF is, indeed, a Microsoft-developed format. However, if you have included pictures, tables, or

KEY TERM

AppleWorks—A commercial application sold by Apple for about $80. AppleWorks is a suite of productivity tools, including a word processor, a spreadsheet program, a drawing program, and more components designed to provide most of the functions of Microsoft Office.

other complex items in an RTF document, Mac OS X uses a somewhat different format for storing the document's contents. An RTF document with pictures and other objects gets the extension **.rtfd**, or Rich Text Format Directory. The file is not a single file at all, but a *bundle* (or *package*)—a folder that masquerades as a file. Inside this folder are all the included pictures and objects, as well as the document's text, in standard RTF. You can right-click or **Control**+click a **.rtfd** file and select **View Package Contents** to see the various items inside the document.

③ Open a Word Document in AppleWorks

AppleWorks is a suite of applications sold by Apple that incorporates many of the features of Microsoft Office, although by no means all of them. AppleWorks can read many different types of Word documents; if TextEdit can't open a Word file, try opening it in AppleWorks instead.

You can select **File**, **Open** in AppleWorks, browse to the Word file you want to work with, and click **Open.** Alternatively, right-click or **Control**+click the Word file; from the contextual menu, select **Open With**, and then select **AppleWorks** to open the file directly in AppleWorks.

④ Save an AppleWorks Document in Word Format

You can save an AppleWorks word processing document in any of several different versions of Word format. Select **Save** or **Save As** from the **File** menu; in the **Save** dialog box, use the **File Format** drop-down menu to choose which format you want to use. For best results, use the most recent version of Word that's listed in the menu.

---

⑧⑦ Create a Drawing in AppleWorks

AppleWorks, if you have it installed, includes a full-featured vector-based drawing program you can use for laying out publishing pages, creating diagrams, making charts or presentations, or just doodling.

You can save your drawing in any image format that *QuickTime*—the underlying multimedia architecture within Mac OS X—understands, and that includes just about every popular format in use today, from JPEG to TIFF to BMP. You can also open nearly any image file in AppleWorks and modify it further.

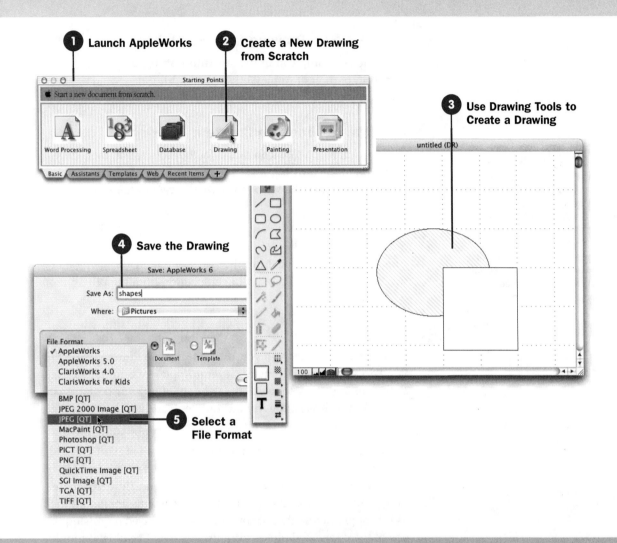

1 Launch AppleWorks

2 Create a New Drawing from Scratch

3 Use Drawing Tools to Create a Drawing

4 Save the Drawing

5 Select a File Format

1 Launch AppleWorks

Open a Finder window and double-click the **AppleWorks** icon in its folder inside the **Applications** folder. Alternatively, single-click the **AppleWorks** icon if it's in the Dock. The **Starting Points** palette appears, offering several basic templates you can use for creating different kinds of documents.

② Create a New Drawing from Scratch

Click the **Drawing** icon in the **Starting Points** palette. The **Drawing** portion of AppleWorks opens, with a new window showing a grid, and a floating toolbar with the available drawing tools.

③ Use Drawing Tools to Create a Drawing

Click any drawing tool icon in the toolbar to select it, then click and drag in the drawing window to use that tool to create a shape. You can then click the shape to resize, move, or alter its appearance.

NOTE

After you use a tool once, the arrow pointer tool becomes selected again (the arrow pointer tool is the default state for your mouse pointer). Use the arrow pointer to click an existing shape; the shape is surrounded by a bounding box. You can click the control points on the bounding box to manipulate them.

④ Save the Drawing

Choose **Save** or **Save As** from the **File** menu. Enter a filename in the **Save As** field and select a folder location from the **Where** drop-down list.

⑤ Select a File Format

Select the format in which you want to save the drawing from the **File Format** drop-down menu. Several AppleWorks formats appear at the top of the list, followed by a variety of popular portable image formats. Select the format that best suits your needs and then click **Save** to save the picture.

The popular image formats shown in the menu—JPEG, TIFF, Photoshop, and so on—can be freely exchanged with Windows users and opened in many different applications. However, these formats are *rendered*, meaning that their contents are just defined as lists of pixels and their colors. After you've saved a drawing in one of these rendered image formats, you won't be able to manipulate the individual shapes anymore if you reopen the file in AppleWorks.

To make sure that you can always go back and edit the drawing's component shapes using the AppleWorks Drawing application, save the drawing file in **AppleWorks** format. Note that files saved in AppleWorks format can't be usefully exchanged with people who don't have AppleWorks.

88 Create a Keynote Presentation

Designed to replace and yet to interoperate with Microsoft's PowerPoint, Keynote is Apple's full-featured presentation application. It's a commercial product, retailing for about $100; if you have it, you can create presentations that not only are compatible with PowerPoint and can be sent to all your co-workers using Windows PCs, but you can use all of Mac OS X's graphics technologies to create slides that leave PowerPoint presentations in the dust.

This task cannot provide a complete tutorial of Keynote; rather, it touches on the highlights of how the program operates so that you can explore the rest on your own.

1 Launch Keynote

Open a Finder window and navigate to the **Applications** folder; double-click the **Keynote** icon to launch the program.

2 Select a Presentation Theme

Keynote opens with the theme selection screen. You can choose from a variety of predefined themes, and you can create your own theme as well by modifying the text defaults and background images.

From the **Presentation Size** drop-down list, select the screen size for your resolution. Most digital projectors today support **1024×768**, the most common screen size; if you will be using an older projector, however, select **800×600**.

When you have selected the theme and size you want, click **Choose Theme** to build the theme and start working on your presentation.

3 Edit the Default Text

Each theme starts out with a single slide with a few default text fields. These are easy to identify—the text in them says **Double-click to edit** or **Double-click to enter text**. Double-clicking in these fields makes them editable, with a bounding box and control points you can use to resize the text field; click outside the bounding box to stop editing the field.

Before You Begin

✔ **1** Install an Application from Disc or Download

✔ **2** Find and Launch an Application

See Also

→ **38** Allow Windows Users to Share Your Files

→ **89** Save a Keynote Presentation for Use in Microsoft PowerPoint

NOTE

If this is your first time running Keynote, you are prompted to register the software with Apple. Enter your name and email address and click **Register Now**. If you prefer, you can click **Register Later** to avoid sending your registration information.

TIP

You can always change your theme later, if you decide you don't like the one you've picked. To change the theme, click the **Themes** button in the Keynote toolbar.

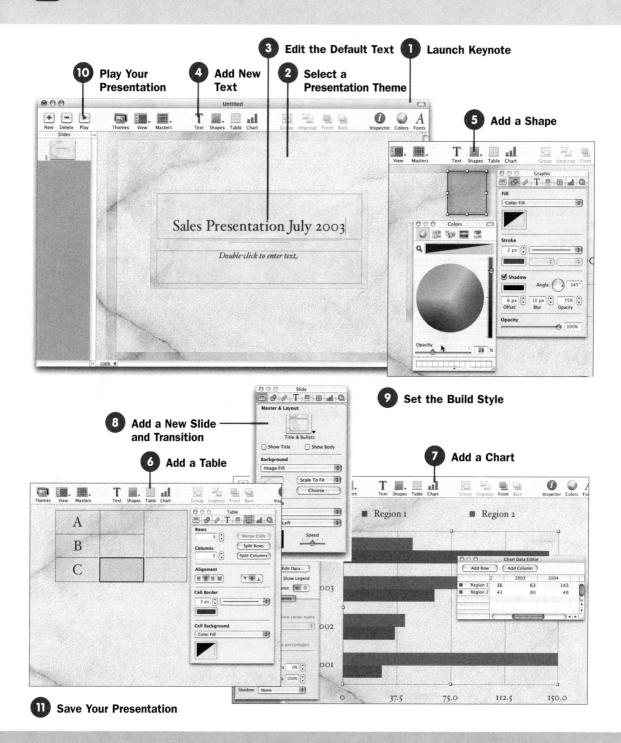

③ **Edit the Default Text** ① **Launch Keynote**

⑩ **Play Your Presentation** ④ **Add New Text** ② **Select a Presentation Theme**

⑤ **Add a Shape**

Sales Presentation July 2003

Double-click to enter text.

⑨ **Set the Build Style**

⑧ **Add a New Slide and Transition**

⑥ **Add a Table**

⑦ **Add a Chart**

A

B

C

■ Region 1   ■ Region 2

⑪ **Save Your Presentation**

Some of the objects in the slide (pictures, for instance) are not editable; if you double-click one of these, you will get a message stating that these objects can only be edited in the *master slide*. The master slides are what define the overall look of the slides, with a variety of predefined layouts for each theme. Each time you add a new slide (using the **New** button in the toolbar), you can pick a layout for the slide by selecting from the menu that pops up when you click the **Masters** icon in the toolbar. You can modify the master slides by selecting **Show Master Slides** from the menu under the **View** icon in the toolbar; click a master slide to work with all the objects in it. All slides using the master slide you modify are adjusted according to the changes you make.

④ Add New Text

Click the **Text** button in the toolbar to create a new text field (with the word **Text** in it) in the middle of the slide. Click and drag the text object to the position where you want it, and double-click to edit its text. You can also click and drag the control points to change the field's size and shape.

⑤ Add a Shape

Click and hold the **Shapes** button in the toolbar, then select a shape from the menu that pops up (a line, a circle, a rectangle, or any of several others). The shape appears in the middle of the slide, using default colors and fill patterns. Drag it to the position where you want it, and use the control points to change its size and shape.

⑥ Add a Table

Click the **Table** icon in the toolbar. The default table starts with three rows and three columns; open the **Table Inspector** to change the dimensions of the table.

Click in a table cell to type text into it, or click and drag to select multiple cells to change all their properties. You can drag pictures from the Finder into table cells to set their background.

⑦ Add a Chart

Click the **Chart** icon in the toolbar. A default chart appears in the slide; the **Chart Data Editor**, another floating palette, appears in

TIP

As you move a text field or other object, vertical and horizontal lines (*alignment guides*) appear to help you line up the object with other objects in the slide. By default, the guides appear only when the center of the object you're moving lines up with the center of another object in the slide; but you can have the guides appear when the edges line up as well, by enabling the **Show guides at object edges** check box in the **Keynote Preferences** window (available under the **Keynote** menu).

TIP

To change the colors, fonts, and fill patterns of a shape, text field, or other object, select it and then click the **Inspector** icon in the tool-bar. The **Inspector** is a floating palette that lets you define the properties of all kinds of objects in Keynote; to modify the appearance of a shape, for instance, click the **Graphic** icon in the **Inspector** (hover the mouse over each icon to see a tooltip that explains what each icon is) to access the controls for the shape.

 NOTE

Some build styles have more controls, such as the direction and speed; some types of objects have more options as well, such as bulleted lists in which you can define the "delivery" method, or how and when each bullet should appear.

the upper-right corner of the window. Use this palette to enter the row and column data series for the chart to use. You can summon this palette by clicking **Edit Data** in the **Chart Inspector**.

Use the **Chart Inspector** to select the style of chart, the format of the axes, and the appearance of the data.

⑧ Add a New Slide and Transition

Click the **New** icon in the toolbar to add a new slide. Choose a master slide format for it by selecting from the menu under the **Masters** icon.

Open the **Slide Inspector**. For each slide, you can define the transition—the style in which the current slide changes to the next one. Select from a variety of 3D and 2D effects; the transition is shown in the preview box below the **Transition** menus.

⑨ Set the Build Style

Open the **Build Inspector**. This palette allows you to choose how the objects in the current slide "build in" (appear) and "build out" (disappear) as you move from slide to slide. Use the **Build In** and **Build Out** tabs and the **Build Style** menu to select what kind of transitions to use for each object in the slide.

⑩ Play Your Presentation

At any point while you're working on your presentation, you can preview how it will look, whether on a computer monitor or on a projector screen. Click the **Play** button to start playing the presentation from the beginning. Click or press the **Spacebar** to advance each slide or build element.

⑪ Save Your Presentation

Choose **File**, **Save** to save your presentation. Enter a name and select a folder location, then click **Save**.

89 Save a Keynote Presentation for Use in Microsoft PowerPoint

Perhaps Keynote's most important feature—above and beyond its flashy graphics—is that the presentations it creates can be opened in Microsoft PowerPoint. Granted, they won't look as good in PowerPoint—Windows doesn't support all the graphical gymnastics that Keynote presentations can do—but the data and pictures will all be faithfully preserved, and the flashy transitions and build effects will be replaced with more modest ones that match what PowerPoint can handle.

If someone sends you a PowerPoint presentation (a **.ppt** file), simply double-click it to open it in Keynote. The presentation will look pretty austere compared to what you're used to in Keynote, but it will work just like a natively created Keynote presentation.

However, if you make changes to the presentation and try to save them, you must choose whether to save it in Keynote format and preserve all your Keynote effects—or export it back to PowerPoint format to interoperate with your Windows co-workers.

1 Export the Presentation

Select **Export** from the **File** menu.

2 Select the Presentation Format

From the sheet that appears, select what format to use. You can save the presentation in **PowerPoint** format (for interoperability with Windows users), **QuickTime** (to create a movie of your presentation which Mac and Windows users alike can view), or **PDF** (to make a document showing each of the slides that can be browsed using *Preview* or the Adobe Acrobat Reader).

Select **PowerPoint** format and click the **Next** button.

3 Enter a Name and Location

Specify a name and location for the exported file.

4 Save the Presentation

Click **Export** to export the presentation into PowerPoint format. This conversion might take several moments; when you're done, you'll have a **.ppt** file that you can email to your co-workers.

Before You Begin

✔ **88** Create a Keynote Presentation

See Also

→ **38** Allow Windows Users to Share Your Files

🔍 **KEY TERM**

Preview—Mac OS X's built-in image-viewing application, which can read picture files of almost any format, including Adobe Acrobat (PDF) files.

✏ **NOTE**

If you select **QuickTime** or **PDF**, you won't be able to import the presentation back into Keynote in an editable format; these aren't editable presentation formats at all, but rather alternatives you can use in a pinch.

✏ **NOTE**

If you selected **QuickTime** format, you are given another sheet with further options for how the QuickTime movie will behave. You can make the movie into an interactive slideshow (requiring the user to press a key to advance the slide) or to advance automatically; you can also adjust the compression options to achieve better compression or better quality.

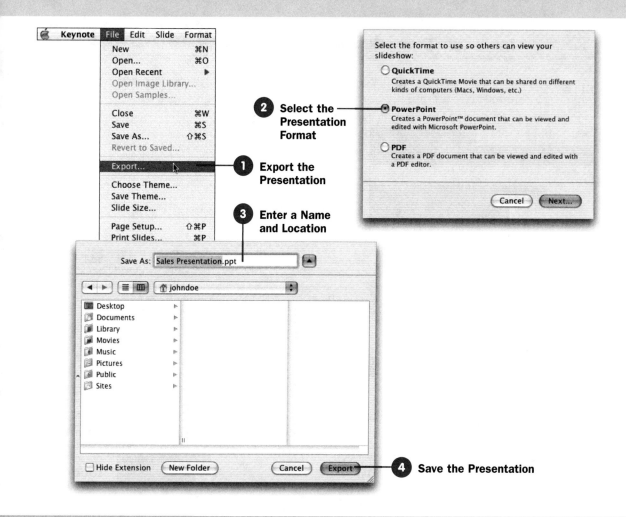

2 Select the
Presentation
Format

1 Export the
Presentation

3 Enter a Name
and Location

4 Save the Presentation

Mac OS X comes with a large variety of *fonts*, or typefaces, to use in your
applications. However, nobody who has used computers for any length
of time has ever been satisfied with their system's default font selections.
Fortunately, there are hundreds of sites on the Web from which you can
download new fonts, and catalogs of commercial fonts from which you
can order if you do professional layout work.

Before You Begin

✔ **83** Create a New Text
Document

See Also

→ **91** Create a Font
Collection

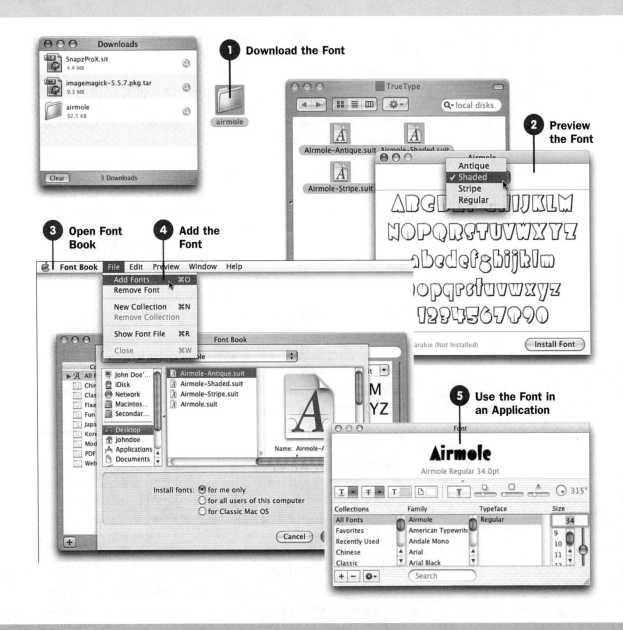

1 Download the Font

2 Preview the Font

3 Open Font Book

4 Add the Font

5 Use the Font in an Application

Fonts available for download are generally available in either "Windows" or "Mac" format. Both Windows and Mac OS X can use *TrueType* or *PostScript* Type 1 fonts; however, there are subtle differences in formats, such as between the Windows and Mac versions of "TrueType" (originally an Apple technology, but popularized in a reduced format by Windows). Because Mac OS X can read Windows TrueType fonts without trouble, don't worry too much about whether to download the Mac or Windows version, if you have a choice. In fact, it might be easier to simply download the Windows version, as the Mac version is often designed for use in Mac OS 9 and earlier, in which fonts were distributed either as "suitcases" (unified files containing multiple styles) or with multiple files for the "outline" and "bitmap" font definitions. These conventions are largely obsolete with Mac OS X's smooth font technology, so you can save yourself a headache by simply downloading the unified Windows versions of fonts—but if a Mac version is available at the Web site where you have found a good font, try downloading both versions to see which one is higher quality and better packaged.

Mac OS X lets you install new fonts so that all users of your computer can have access to them, or you can install the font just for your own use. Using the built-in **Font Book** application, you can preview and install fonts directly from the Finder.

❶ Download the Font

Download the font from the Web, or insert a disc containing new fonts in your CD-ROM drive. Downloaded fonts are usually in an archive, such as a **.zip** or **.sit** file; Safari should automatically expand the archive into a folder on your Desktop. If it does not, locate the archive file and double-click it to unpack it.

❷ Preview the Font

Double-click the font file. A panel appears showing you all the letters, numbers, and symbols in the font. Many fonts come in folders that contain several style variants (bold, italic, shadowed, striped, and so on) on the font; if you select more than one font file and then double-click one of them, all the variants are available using the drop-down menu in the panel.

A valid font file is recognizable by its icon, which is of a document with the **Font Book** icon on it, or (for native TrueType fonts) a capital italic letter **A**. The label of the icon can be one of many different types (for instance, TTF, DFONT, LWFN, or FFIL, among others); Mac OS X can use any font file whose icon has the **Font Book** logo (or a large italic **A**) on it. If you have a choice between TrueType and PostScript (Type 1) fonts, go for TrueType.

③ Open Font Book

With the font preview window open, you're already in the **Font Book** application; select **Font Book** from the **Window** menu to open the main Font Book window.

④ Add the Font

Select **File**, **Add Fonts**. A sheet appears allowing you to navigate to the location of the new font file. Select the valid font file you were just previewing (files that aren't valid font files or folders are grayed out). Select whether to install the font for yourself only or for all users in the system; then click **Open** to add the font.

In this example, several valid font files for the Airmole font appear in the **TrueType** subfolder inside the newly downloaded **airmole** folder. The different font variants are well labeled by their file-names here, but often this is not the case, as with Windows fonts that are packaged with short filenames. For example, if you had downloaded the Windows version of the Airmole font, inside its folder would be files with much more inscrutable filenames than those seen here. However, if you double-click each file in the Finder, the preview panel that appears tells you (in its title bar) the font's full name. For instance, **airmole.ttf** is simply Airmole; **air-molea.ttf** is Airmole Antique; **airmoleq.ttf** is Airmole Stripe; and **airmoles.ttf** is Airmole Shaded. You can install all of these variations, or just the ones you like.

Every font site packages fonts differently; some archives are more confusing to navigate than others. The ease with which you can install a free font to your system depends a great deal on the individual font and the site that packaged it. This is one reason why commercially sold fonts are popular: ease of installation.

NOTE

When you install a font, the font file is *moved* (not copied) to the appropriate **Fonts** folder—the one in your own **Library** if you're installing it just for yourself, or the one in the global **Library** if you're installing it for all users.

TIP

You can also install a font using the **Install Font** button in the font preview window. This button installs the font into your personal **Library** and makes it available for you only.

TIP

Click and drag the control button in the top middle of the **Font** palette to open the **Preview** pane, showing you the font's name in the selected style. The **Font** palette changes its format to show more options and information as you make it bigger.

⑤ Use the Font in an Application

In any application that supports multiple fonts, select **Format, Font, Show Fonts**. This command brings up the **Font** palette, which floats over your application window and lets you choose fonts visually. You can also use the **Font** palette to tune the font's display style, including its foreground and background colors, underlines and strikethroughs, and even drop shadows.

---

91 Create a Font Collection

Before You Begin

✔ **83** Create a New Text Document

✔ **90** Install a New Font

TIP

You can disable individual fonts as well; click any font in the **Font** column and then click the **Disable** button underneath that column.

TIP

You might have to enlarge the **Font** palette (using the grip in the lower-right corner) until the **Action** button appears; the palette changes its format to show more options and information as you make it bigger.

Font Book acts as an organizer for your fonts, allowing you to sort your installed fonts into functional groupings according to what you're likely to use them for. Mac OS X comes with predefined font collections such as **Fun, Modern,** and **Web,** which appear in the **Font** dialog box and help simplify the process of searching for the right font to use in your application. If you're writing a Web page, for instance, you might want to limit yourself to the fonts in the **Web** collection, to make sure that you don't use any fonts that Web viewers won't have.

You can also disable font collections or individual fonts; disabling a font collection can help further narrow down the fonts you have to search through in the **Font** panel. You can disable the **Chinese** collection, for example, if you're sure that you won't be using any Chinese text in your word processing application.

① Open Font Book

Open the **Font Book** application by double-clicking **Font Book** in the **Applications** folder. If you're working in another application, open the **Font** palette by choosing **Format, Font, Show Fonts**; then click the **Action** button in the lower-left corner of the **Font** palette and choose **Manage Fonts** to open **Font Book.**

② Create a New Font Collection

Click the + icon under the **Collection** pane of the Font Book window to create a new collection. The name of the collection is selected, so that you can immediately type a new name for the collection.

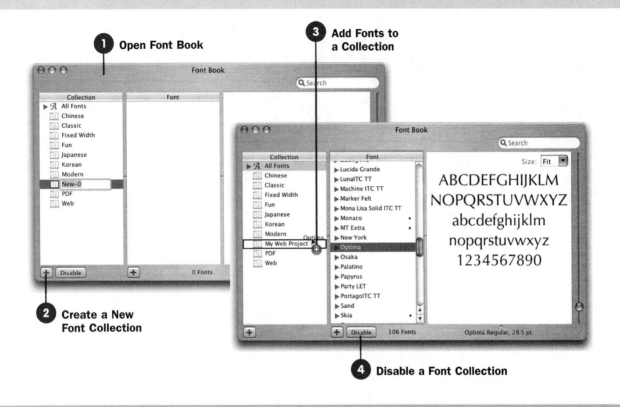

1 Open Font Book

3 Add Fonts to a Collection

2 Create a New Font Collection

4 Disable a Font Collection

3 Add Fonts to a Collection

Populate your new font collection by dragging fonts from the **Font** column onto the collection's entry. Click the **All Fonts** entry in the **Collection** column to list all the fonts in your system; expand the **All Fonts** entry (using the triangle) to list only globally available fonts or fonts that are available only to you.

 TIP

To rename any font collection, double-click it in the **Collection** pane, type a new name, and press **Return**.

4 Disable a Font Collection

Select a collection to disable and then click the **Disable** button. A sheet appears warning you that the collection will no longer appear in the **Font** panel; assuming that this is the whole point of what you want to do, click **Disable**. You can also use the check box to tell Font Book not to ask you for confirmation when you disable fonts in the future.

 TIP

If you ever want to re-enable a disabled font or collection, select it. The **Disable** button at the bottom of the column becomes an **Enable** button. Click it to re-enable the font or collection.

11

Printing and Faxing

IN THIS CHAPTER:

No home office—or real office, for that matter—is complete without the ability to print your documents. It might be an electronic world, but nothing quite beats having a piece of paper in your hand that you can mark up with a red pen.

Mac OS X, with its strong pedigree in the printing and publishing industries, has an advanced printing architecture that allows every application in the system to share a unified printing setup and execution system. Every application you'll use on the Mac has **Page Setup** and **Print** commands in the **File** menu, and each application's command leads to the same dialog boxes and preview screens—and each one takes its settings from the centralized printer queue, in which you can set up as many different printers as you like. Mac OS X supports printers hooked up directly to your computer with a USB connection; network printing using AppleTalk, IP, or Rendezvous; and even Windows print queues. What's more, the printing system in Mac OS X can be used to send and receive faxes over your phone line—just as easily as printing documents.

92 Add a New Printer

Before You Begin

✔ **2** Find and Launch an Application

✔ **83** Create a New Text Document

See Also

→ **93** Configure Printer Options from Any Application

→ **94** Print to a PDF File

Before you can print anything, you have to add your printer to the system. You might have an inkjet printer connected to your Mac with a USB cable, a laser office printer that's accessible by IP, or a *Rendezvous*-capable network printer that requires no setup. Mac OS X lets you configure any of these printers, add them all to your Mac's printer list, and set one of them as the default printer used by your applications.

Mac OS X comes with drivers for hundreds of popular printers. Many printer models, however, require you to download a driver and install it before it will work in Mac OS X. Most popular printer manufacturers have Mac OS X versions of their printer drivers available on their Web sites.

1 Connect and Turn On the Printer

Mac OS X automatically detects most printers you connect directly to the computer through USB (the most common method). Plug the printer in and connect its USB cable to your Mac; then turn the printer on and wait for it to finish its self-test cycle, which for most printers is no longer than about ten seconds.

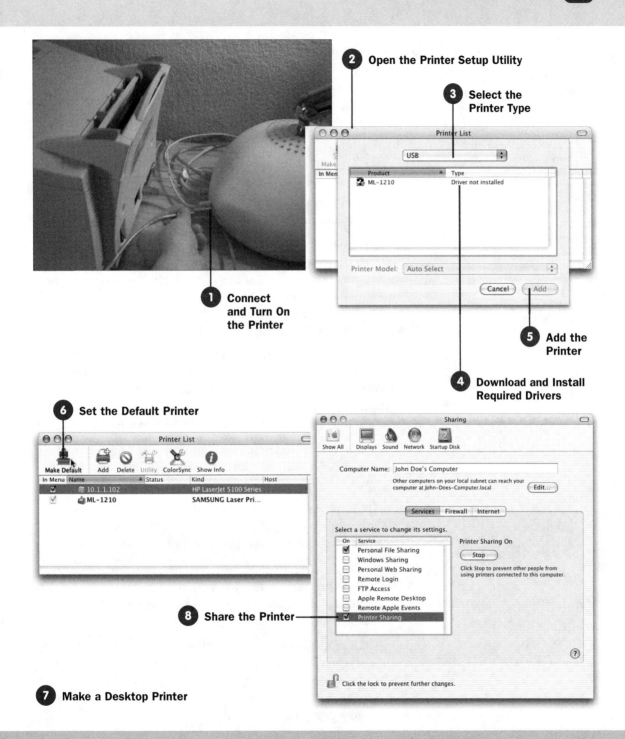

2 Open the Printer Setup Utility

3 Select the Printer Type

1 Connect and Turn On the Printer

5 Add the Printer

4 Download and Install Required Drivers

6 Set the Default Printer

8 Share the Printer

7 Make a Desktop Printer

NOTE

If you have a network printer, make sure that it is available on the network; Mac OS X won't be able to autodetect it, unless it's a Rendezvous or AppleTalk printer. Most networkable printers traditionally support AppleTalk, and many of the newer printers from Epson, Hewlett-Packard, Lexmark, and other manufacturers support Rendezvous technology. Consult the specifications for your printer (or on any printer you're planning to buy) to see whether it supports Rendezvous or AppleTalk.

② Open the Printer Setup Utility

Open the **Applications** folder, then the **Utilities** folder; double-click the **Printer Setup Utility** icon to launch the Printer Setup program. Alternatively, choose **File**, **Print** from any application that can print, and select **Edit Printer List** from the **Printer** drop-down menu.

A third way to launch the Printer Setup utility is by opening the **Print & Fax Preferences** window (click the **Print & Fax** icon in the **System Preferences** application), and click the **Set Up Printers** button on the **Print** tab.

If you have not set up any printers before, a sheet stating **You have no printers available** automatically prompts you to add to your printer list; click **Add**. If this sheet does not appear, click the **Add** button in the toolbar.

③ Select the Printer Type

In the sheet that appears, select the type of printer you will be adding. Each type of printer has its own set of configuration options; some types (such as Rendezvous printers) are all but self-configuring, while others (particularly IP Printing printers) require you to enter a fair amount of information manually.

- **AppleTalk** printers appear automatically by name and usually provide their own drivers. Just select the printer from the list.

- **IP Printing** requires that you specify the printer's IP address or hostname, the printing protocol (**LPD/LPR** is most common), the queue name, and the printer model. Consult your network administrator for details on IP printers.

- **Open Directory** and **Rendezvous** printers are self-discovering; all available printers appear automatically in the list. Just click the one you want.

- **USB** printers appear listed by their model number; if a printer is connected to your Mac but a driver is not available, the message **Driver not installed** appears in the **Type** column. You'll have to download and install the appropriate driver before that printer will work.

- **Windows Printing** allows you to select a domain or work-group and then navigate to a machine to choose from the printers connected to that machine. Use the **Network Neighborhood** menu option to see all the available domains.

4 Download and Install Required Drivers

If the Printer Setup utility reports that the driver for your printer is not installed, you must install the driver from the printer's installation disc, or download the driver from the company's Web site. Follow the instructions in the CD or the downloaded installation program to install the driver.

You might be requested to restart your Mac after installing the printer driver. If you do, reopen the Printer Setup utility after you've restarted and click the toolbar **Add** button again to verify that the printer's **Type** is reported correctly in the configuration sheet. (The Printer Setup utility might detect that there are new printer drivers available, and prompt you to reload the browser; click **OK** on this dialog box.)

Select the appropriate driver from the **Printer Model** menu, if it is not already selected. Be aware that many printer drivers have odd names, such as **GDI For Jaguar 1.0**. In most cases, the correct driver is what is automatically selected when you click the printer in the list.

5 Add the Printer

Click **Add** when you have successfully selected the printer you want to add. The printer appears in the **Printer List** dialog box, showing its model name and driver. The printer is also available in the **Print** dialog box in any application from which you can print.

6 Set the Default Printer

If you have multiple printers configured, use the **Make Default** button to specify which printer should be the default for your Mac (the default printer is the one that is automatically used when you print a document).

TIP

If you have to restart the computer after installing the driver, the Printer Setup utility might cancel the restart process if its configuration sheet is open. Be sure to quit the Printer Setup utility before installing the new printer driver, just to be safe.

TIP

Use the **In Menu** check box on the **Printer List** dialog box to specify whether the printer should appear in the **Printers** menu of applications' printing dialog boxes.

TIP

If you'd rather clutter up your Dock than your Desktop, you can add your desktop printer to the Dock. You *could* simply drag the desktop printer icon itself into the Dock; but the desktop printer is itself just an alias to an item in the **Printers** folder inside your **Home** folder's **Library**. Navigate to that folder and drag the printer icon to your Dock from there. You can then throw away the desktop printer icon.

7 **Make a Desktop Printer**

A *desktop printer* is an icon of one of your printers that sits on your Desktop (or in your Dock); double-clicking the icon brings up the queue viewer for that printer. Desktop printers make printing a drag-and-drop process: You can print a document simply by dragging it onto the printer icon.

From the list of printers in the **Printer List** dialog box, click the printer you want to add to the Desktop. From the **Printers** menu, choose **Create Desktop Printer**. Enter a name for the printer icon when prompted and click **Save**. The icon for the printer is added to your Desktop.

To print a document, drag the document icon directly onto the desktop printer icon.

8 **Share the Printer**

Open the **System Preferences** application from the **Apple** menu; click the **Sharing** icon to open the **Sharing Preferences** window. On the **Services** tab, enable the **Printer Sharing** check box to allow other people on the network to print using the printers connected to your Mac.

Another way to enable printer sharing is to open the **Print & Fax Preferences** window (click the **Print & Fax** icon in the **System Preferences** application), click the **Print** tab, and then enable the **Share my printers with other computers** check box.

With printer sharing enabled, other Macs on the network will automatically list your computer's printers in their Printer Setup Utility lists and **Print** dialog boxes. (This is accomplished using the Rendezvous technology built into every Mac, which allows each computer to see all the printers—whether they support Rendezvous or not—that are attached to any Mac with **Printer Sharing** enabled.)

Every Mac OS X application uses the same printing setup screens. There's typically a **Page Setup** dialog box, in which you define how the application should handle fitting your document to a given paper size; and then there's the **Print** dialog box, where you can specify dozens of options specific to your printer before sending the document to be printed. You can configure everything from the number of copies to print to the Quartz and ColorSync post-processing to apply. If you frequently use complex configurations, you can save your configuration as a printing preset.

Before You Begin

✔ **2** Find and Launch an Application

✔ **92** Add a New Printer

See Also

→ **94** Print to a PDF File

→ **108** Print Photos

① Open Page Setup

From TextEdit, Word, or any other application that can print, choose **File, Page Setup**. This command brings up the **Page Setup** dialog box, in which you define the document's layout relative to the style and size of paper that you'll be using.

② Select the Paper Size and Orientation

Select the size of paper you'll be printing on from the **Paper Size** drop-down menu. Among other things, this option defines how the margins and rulers behave in your application. Then select the **Orientation** you want, using the icons to choose between landscape and portrait configurations.

Many other options are available in the **Page Setup** dialog box; explore the various **Settings** pages to see what other levels of control you have over how your applications' pages are laid out. Click **OK** when you're done.

③ Prepare to Print

When you're ready to print the document, select **File, Print** to bring up the **Print** dialog box, in which you can set any of several dozen printer-specific options for how the job should be printed.

④ Select the Printer

Select the printer you'll be using from the **Printer** drop-down list. Many of the other options on the page depend on which printer you select and what it's capable of, so make sure that you select the correct printer.

TIP

The **Page Setup** options often affect how the application itself displays your document, so setting up your page should be one of the first things you do when putting together your document or project.

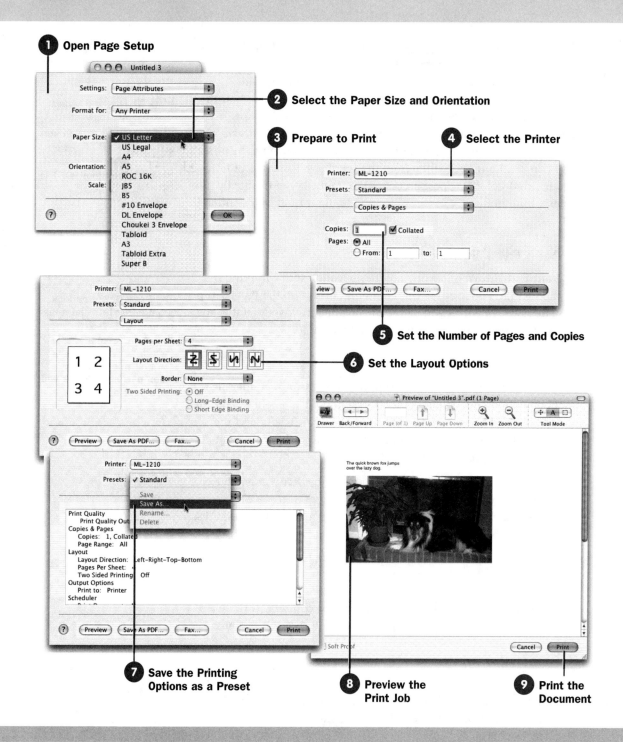

1 Open Page Setup

2 Select the Paper Size and Orientation

3 Prepare to Print

4 Select the Printer

5 Set the Number of Pages and Copies

6 Set the Layout Options

7 Save the Printing Options as a Preset

8 Preview the Print Job

9 Print the Document

PART III: Making It Work Together

⑤ Set the Number of Pages and Copies

Select **Copies** & **Pages** from the selector menu in the middle of the dialog box, if it's not already selected. Specify how many copies of the document you want, as well as which pages to print; you can print all the pages or specify a range from one page number to another.

⑥ Set the Layout Options

Select **Layout** from the selector menu in the middle of the **Print** dialog box. For multipage documents, you can have Mac OS X print more than one page worth of data on a single sheet. From the **Pages per Sheet** drop-down list, select the number of pages you want to print on a single sheet of paper.

Use the visual **Layout Direction** icons to specify the order in which the pages should be printed. You can also separate the printed pages with a single or double outline using the **Border** drop-down list. A preview of the layout on the left shows you what the page output will look like.

Explore the many other option pages using the selector menu; define the options that need to be changed from their default settings.

NOTE

For quick proofs, you can print "four-up" (meaning four pages of data on a single sheet of paper), or from two to as many as 16 pages per sheet of paper.

⑦ Save the Printing Options as a Preset

After you've finished setting up your printing options, you might want to save them in a "preset" so that you can use them again in the future. Select **Save As** from the **Presets** drop-down list at the top of the **Print** dialog box; enter a name for the preset and click **OK**. You can then select this preset from the **Presets** drop-down list in future print jobs, or create other presets and switch easily between them.

⑧ Preview the Print Job

Click the **Preview** button to see what the final printed output will look like. The preview is generated in PDF and displayed in the Preview application (which should come as no surprise).

TIP

Some applications, such as Mail and Microsoft Word, have a **Print** icon that appears in the toolbar (or that you can place there using the **Customize Toolbar** command, under the application's **View** menu). Click this icon to send a single copy of the document directly to the default printer.

⑨ Print the Document

Whether you're in **Preview** mode or still viewing the **Print** dialog box, you can click **Cancel** to dismiss the print job or click **Print** to send it directly to the printer.

94 Print to a PDF File

Before You Begin

✔ **92** Add a New Printer

✔ **93** Configure Printer Options from Any Application

See Also

→ **104** Convert Between Image Formats

→ **63** Send a Message

🔍 KEY TERM

Portable Document Format (PDF)—A popular printer-ready document format developed by Adobe. PDF documents are totally self-contained and do not depend on any particular application or operating system. Mac OS X uses PDF technology as a key part of its graphics engine.

📝 NOTE

Remember that many of the options in the **Print** dialog box are printer specific. Not only do some of these options not apply to saving to a PDF file, they might be incompatible with another person's printer who tries to print your PDF file. It's best to use the default settings for your printer if you're going to save the print job as a PDF file.

Adobe's *Portable Document Format (PDF)* has become one of the most widely used document formats on the Internet, allowing printer-ready documents to be transmitted and distributed easily over the Web or through email. Mac OS X uses the built-in PDF technology to create its characteristic graphic effects, such as the transparency on menus and the smooth scaling when you magnify the Dock. One of the other nice things about PDF being integrated so tightly into Mac OS X is that it's a trivial matter for the operating system to create PDF files out of anything being sent to the screen or the printing subsystem. The upshot of this is that even if you don't have a printer connected to your computer, you can print your document to a **PDF** file, which is an exact copy of the document as it is sent into the printing queue. It's like freezing a print job for future repeated use; you can email the PDF file to a colleague, for instance, so that she can print it for you.

1 Prepare to Print the Document

From the **File** menu of an application such as TextEdit or Word, select the **Print** option to bring up the **Print** dialog box.

2 Specify the Printing Options

Specify the output options for your print job, using a saved preset or by going to each of the individual configuration screens (using the selector menu in the middle of the **Print** dialog box) and adjusting the controls to match your needs. For instance, you might want to specify a "four-up" page layout in the **Layout** screen, or define a cover page in the **Cover Page** screen.

3 Save as a PDF

Click **Save as PDF** at the bottom of the **Print** dialog box. In the **Save to File** dialog box that appears, specify a name for the PDF file and a location where it should be saved. Click **Save** to create the PDF file.

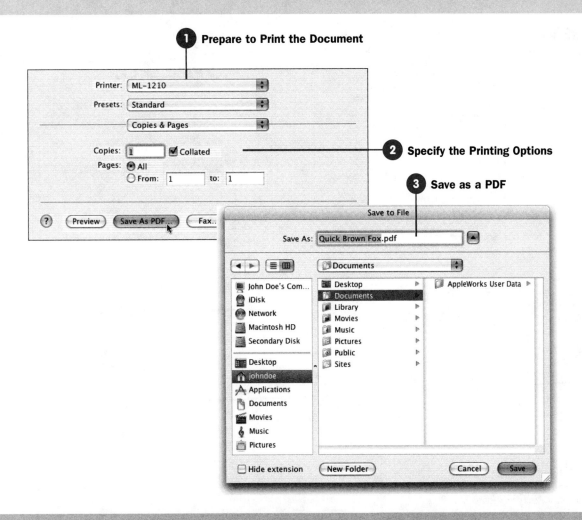

1 Prepare to Print the Document

Printer: ML-1210

Presets: Standard

Copies & Pages

Copies: 1 ☑ Collated

Pages: ⊙ All
○ From: 1 to: 1

(?) (Preview) (Save As PDF...) (Fax...)

2 Specify the Printing Options

3 Save as a PDF

Save to File

Save As: Quick Brown Fox.pdf

Documents

John Doe's Com...
iDisk
Network
Macintosh HD
Secondary Disk

Desktop
johndoe
Applications
Documents
Movies
Music
Pictures

Desktop ▶   AppleWorks User Data ▶
Documents ▶
Library ▶
Movies ▶
Music ▶
Pictures ▶
Public ▶
Sites ▶

☐ Hide extension   (New Folder)   (Cancel) (Save)

95 Send the Print Job as a Fax

What's a fax machine but a remote printer to which you connect over a phone line? That's the reasoning behind the ability to send a print job as a fax to a remote recipient in Mac OS X. To send a fax, go through the same procedure as you would to print a document to a local or networked printer; instead of printing, however, a couple of extra steps allow you to specify the fax recipient, cover sheet, and other fax options before sending the job out using your Mac's internal modem.

Before You Begin

✔ **92** Add a New Printer

✔ **93** Configure Printer Options from Any Application

See Also

→ **94** Print to a PDF File

→ **103** Convert Between Image Formats

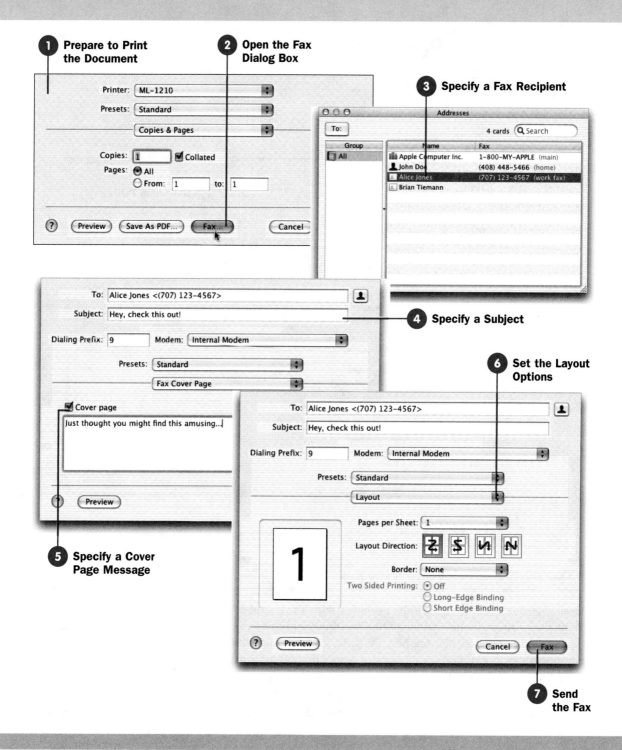

1 Prepare to Print the Document

2 Open the Fax Dialog Box

3 Specify a Fax Recipient

4 Specify a Subject

5 Specify a Cover Page Message

6 Set the Layout Options

7 Send the Fax

① Prepare to Print the Document

From the **File** menu of an application such as TextEdit or Word, select the **Print** option to bring up the **Print** dialog box.

② Open the Fax Dialog Box

At the bottom of the **Print** dialog box, click the **Fax** button. This action brings up a new dialog box that allows you to set the options for faxing the print job.

③ Specify a Fax Recipient

In the **To** field, type the fax number to which you want to send the document.

④ Specify a Subject

Type a descriptive subject for the fax into the **Subject** line. This line is used in constructing the fax cover page.

⑤ Specify a Cover Page Message

Enable the **Cover page** check box to create a cover page that is sent before the main fax job. In the text box provided, type a message to be printed on the cover page.

⑥ Set the Layout Options

Use the selector menu in the middle of the **Fax** dialog box to select the **Layout** options; as you do for a regular print job, use the provided controls to specify how many pages should be condensed onto a sheet of paper, and in what direction they should be laid out.

NOTE

Make sure that your Mac is hooked up to an active phone line using the modem port before trying to send a fax. A cable or network Internet connection won't work for a fax.

TIP

You can select one or more fax recipients from your Address Book; click the "person" icon to the right of the **To** field to bring up the **Addresses** palette. Locate the fax recipient using your contact groups and the **Search** bar to narrow down the list; click to select the recipient, making sure that you select the person's fax number if you have more than one number listed for that person. Click the **To** button to copy the recipient's name and fax number to the **Fax** dialog box and close the **Addresses** palette.

TIP

You can use external modems or other devices to send faxes, as well as your Mac's internal modem. Select **Show Fax List** from the **Modem** drop-down list in the **Fax** dialog box to open the Printer Setup utility, with its secondary window that shows faxing devices. These devices can be set up and managed in much the same way as your printers can be; you can even create a desktop printer of your faxing device so that you can send faxes by dragging-and-dropping. See **92** **Add a New Printer** for more about desktop printers.

Many of the other options available for standard printing are also available as fax options. Refer to **93** **Configure Printer Options from Any Application** for more information on these options. Use the selector menu to set these options, and the **Presets** menu to save a preset for future fax jobs.

7 **Send the Fax**

When you're satisfied with your fax job's settings, click **Fax**; Mac OS X dials your modem, connects to the remote fax machine, sends the job, and then disconnects.

12

Living with iLife

IN THIS CHAPTER:

If you're a music lover, a digital photographer, or a video or movie buff with a Mac, you can already count yourself lucky—you've got a computer that comes preloaded with some of the best software and tools for finding, obtaining, playing, and storing all these kinds of media.

KEY TERMS

DVD (digital versatile disc)—The increasingly popular CD-sized medium for commercial movies as well as home videos and computer data.

iLife—The Mac OS X packaged combination of iTunes, iMovie, iPhoto, and iDVD.

The first technology for you to understand as part of this topic is *QuickTime*, the underlying multimedia software subsystem embedded throughout Mac OS X. Far from being a simple "video player" application (as it might appear to Windows users), QuickTime is at the heart of all the star applications that ship with new Macs: iTunes (for digital music), iPhoto (for digital photography), iMovie (for digital video editing, and—if you're lucky enough to have a Mac with a DVD-writing drive (a SuperDrive, in Apple's parlance)—iDVD, for writing your digital video and photography projects onto *DVDs* (digital versatile discs) that you can then play on any commercial DVD player. These four applications, along with QuickTime at their core, form *iLife*—Apple's packaged suite of free digital-media applications that turn your Mac into what Steve Jobs called the "digital hub": the computer at the center of your digital lifestyle.

This chapter begins with a tour of QuickTime, including how to set up the QuickTime player application for best performance on your network, and how to watch a DVD movie on your Mac. From there, it takes you on a tour of iLife itself: iTunes, iPhoto, iMovie, and iDVD. Each of these applications, although designed for simplicity rather than feature richness, makes for a very complex subject; for more in-depth coverage of all of them, pick up a copy of *iLife in a Snap* from Sams Publishing.

96 About QuickTime

KEY TERM

QuickTime—The multimedia subsystem embedded in Mac OS X that plays back all music, image, and video data.

Apple was one of the first pioneers of video playback on computers; the *QuickTime* technology dates back to the early 1990s, when it was the subject of many breathtaking demonstrations. In one, for example, Apple engineers displayed a movie showing a cube rotating in space, six different QuickTime movies playing on each of its sides, all composited together in real time. All this before the Internet even existed.

It's small wonder, then, that Apple—whose CEO, Steve Jobs, is also a major player in the animation world, what with his other company, Pixar, making so much noise on the big screen—is still in the forefront of consumer and professional video technology. Apple's high-end video offerings, such as Final Cut Pro, affordably bring digital video production to the desktop computer for the first time and are rapidly becoming the *de facto* standard in many segments of television and feature content production. And those same technologies that have turned Apple into a powerhouse in the professional market are also present in Apple's free, consumer-oriented software, included with every Mac: QuickTime, iMovie, and iDVD.

QuickTime is the underlying video and multimedia engine incorporated throughout Mac OS X. Whenever any application has to display a picture, sound, or movie file, it calls QuickTime to handle it. QuickTime understands a vast variety of media formats and is being expanded with each new release. New codecs—encoding and compression algorithms—are continually released, allowing users to create movie files with better quality and lower file size, the better to transmit them over the Internet. You can watch movies on DVD that you rent or purchase from video stores, using the built-in DVD Player application, itself built upon the QuickTime technology. iMovie serves as the creation side of the Mac video equation; it allows you to take footage from your DV (digital video) camcorder or any other FireWire video source, edit it, add effects, set it to music, and create a compact QuickTime movie to send to your friends and family. iDVD rounds out the suite, allowing you to create DVDs of your movies that can be played in nearly any standard DVD player.

Video editing and DVD creation are both complex topics. Each can involve a full artistic discipline if you are to use them to their fullest extent. This book cannot hope to cover all the techniques you might need. It will, however, describe the basics of operating QuickTime, iMovie, and iDVD so that you can hone your skills working with the content itself, without having to worry about how to use the applications.

Adjusting the System Volume and Sound Options

Perhaps the most fundamental multimedia operation you can do on any computer is to change the sound volume. Most applications that produce sound—for instance, audio players such as iTunes or apps such as video games—have their own volume controls that affect that application and nothing else. But the master system volume, which is indicated by an icon in the system menu bar, controls the sound volume of all applications throughout the system.

NOTE

The free version of QuickTime that comes with every Mac includes a player for movie files, but that's about it. QuickTime Pro, however, which QuickTime nags you to buy each time you run it, is an enhanced version that provides a full-fledged suite of tools for editing and processing video. QuickTime Pro lets you convert between movie formats and codecs, composite audio and video tracks, create custom player skins, and much more. The Pro version is enabled by entering a key code that you can obtain from Apple for about $30.

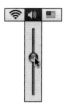

💡 TIP

You can turn off the "splat" sound you hear each time you press a volume control key by going to the **Sound Effects** tab in the **Sound Preferences** window and disabling the **Play feedback when volume keys are pressed** check box.

You can adjust the volume of any of the sounds the computer makes using the **Volume** icon among the system menu icons at the top right of the screen. The number of curved lines that appear to the right of the speaker icon show how loud the master system volume is set. Click the icon to access the master system volume control slider. Drag the blue indicator up and down to your desired level (drag the indicator all the way to the bottom to mute the system). Alternatively, you can use the volume-control keys present on all Mac keyboards: **Mute**, **Decrease**, and **Increase**. Press the **Increase** or **Decrease** key to raise or lower the master system volume by small increments; each time you press one of these keys, a volume indicator appears in the middle of the screen to show you the current volume level. Press the **Mute** key to immediately turn off all sound; press the **Mute** key a second time to return the volume to its previous level.

To obtain more control over your computer's sound output, open the **System Preferences** application (from the **Apple** menu) and click the **Sound** icon.

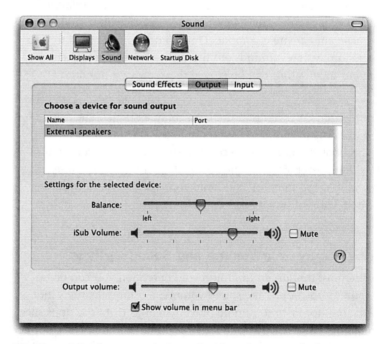

The Sound Preferences window, showing the controls for various audio output options.

Use the **Output** tab in this window to set the balance between speakers, the output device (if you have multiple sets of speakers connected), and the independent volume settings for certain kinds of speakers, such as the iSub subwoofer. The **Sound Effects** tab lets you select a different error beep sound and set its volume relative to the master system volume. Finally, the **Input** tab lets you select a microphone (most Macs have built-in microphones) and input gain level for sound input (such as you would use in iChat, which is discussed in detail in **80** **Start a Chat Session** and related tasks).

Setting Up the QuickTime Player

Most of the time, when you see the word *QuickTime,* it will be in relation to the QuickTime Player, an application that allows you to view movie files—short video clips that you might download from the Internet, in any of a variety of formats. The QuickTime Player can also open music files (such as MP3 and AAC files) and pictures, but its primary use is for viewing movies. Common movie file formats that you might encounter are QuickTime (Apple's native format, which uses a **.mov** extension), Flash (with a **.swf** extension), AVI or WMV (Windows Media, with **.avi** or **.wmv** extensions), or MPEG (using a **.mpg** or **.mpeg** extension). QuickTime can play any of these kinds of movie files, although newer AVI or WMV movies often require a separate codec to be downloaded.

WEB RESOURCE

http://www.divx.com

Home of the DivX codec, one of the most widely used algorithms in movies found on the Internet, and a necessity for viewing modern AVI or WMV movies.

The QuickTime Player can also view "streamed" movie content (video that plays instantly in your Web browser or QuickTime Player window without your having to wait for a large download to complete). To do this, you must set up your QuickTime preferences and tell your Mac what kind of Internet connection you have.

Open the **QuickTime Preferences** window by clicking the **QuickTime** icon in the **System Preferences** application (found under the **Apple** menu).

On the **Connection** tab, select what kind of Internet connection you have. Be sure that you don't overestimate your connection speed; if you do, QuickTime might request streamed data at a rate faster than your connection can handle, resulting in choppy video and a poor viewing experience. Choose the highest speed that is realistic for your Internet service.

NOTE

One common type of movie file that QuickTime cannot open is Real Media, usually using a **.rm** extension. To view Real movies, download the RealOne Player from **http://www.real.com.**

*In the QuickTime Preferences window, specify your type of internet
connection so that you can view streaming video.*

Viewing a Movie File

After you have set up your QuickTime preferences, you can double-click
any movie file's icon to open it in the QuickTime Player.

Use QuickTime to play movie files.

Use the scrub bar—the long horizontal slider-like control, which represents the time line of the movie's duration—to skip to any point within the movie by dragging the knob left or right. The other buttons let you play and pause the movie, fast-forward or rewind, or jump to the beginning or the end—as well as adjusting the volume for the movie (this does not affect the master system volume, but rather controls the movie's sound level relative to the master setting).

To play an audio file in the QuickTime Player, or to use it to view pictures, simply drag the files you want to open to the **QuickTime Player** icon in the Dock. Audio files (such as MP3 or AAC files) can be controlled the same way you would control a movie file; there just won't be any video shown above the scrub bar.

Watching a DVD Movie

You can view almost any commercial DVD movie on your Mac, if it's equipped with a drive that can read DVDs. To do this, simply insert the DVD as you would any CD-ROM. The DVD Player application automatically launches, presenting you with a controller similar to a normal DVD remote. The onscreen controller is actually much simpler than your typical DVD remote control, in fact; it has only the controls you're most likely to need to use: To control the volume, use the slider provided—rather than hunting down the separate remotes for your TV and sound system!

Click areas of the viewer window as you would use a DVD remote to select "hot spots" in the DVD menu. You can also control the size of the viewer window—from postage-stamp size to full-screen—using the **Video** menu. Many other special features are available, from control buttons available in a slide-out "drawer" in the controller to closed-captioning and floating progress readouts, which are available in the **Controls** and **Go** menus.

When you're done watching the movie, click the **Eject** button on the controller to eject the DVD, and then quit the DVD Player application (select **Quit** from the **DVD Player** menu).

TIP

To access streamed video content, such as music videos, movie trailers, and propaganda—excuse me, make that keynote speeches from Apple—click the **Q** button in the lower right of the QuickTime Player window.

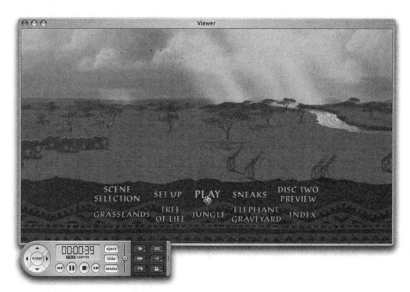

Use the DVD Player application to play DVD movies; you can use the simple controller to make menu selections, control volume, and advance the movie playback.

97 About iTunes

The iPod.

One of Apple's most legitimate claims to fame today is the music management system formed by the jukebox application iTunes, the industry-defining iPod music player, and the media-handling capabilities of Mac OS X.

iTunes and the iPod together form a total music management system that lets you acquire new music, organize it into playlists, burn it onto CDs, and (using the iPod) put it in your pocket to take wherever you go. The music in question, and the reason for this revolutionary new kind of listening experience, is digital audio. This medium takes the form of either MP3 or AAC audio files that are formed by copying the raw audio data from a digital source (such as a music CD) and compressing it so that each song takes up much less space on your hard disk—generally between two and six megabytes, as opposed to twenty to sixty megabytes in raw form—while retaining most, though not all, of its sound quality.

The world has accepted *MPEG-1 level 3 (MP3)* as the *de facto* standard for digital audio; it's versatile, ubiquitous, and mostly free. MP3 files can be played just about anywhere and by anything, from PDAs to cell phones to car stereos. Best of all, they have no *digital rights management (DRM)* technology. Or, perhaps (depending on whom you ask), that's the worst aspect of MP3 files. MP3s have been the scourge of the commercial music industry in recent years, enabling music enthusiasts to trade songs freely and amass huge collections of commercial music without paying for it. The large record labels demanded a form of MP3-like digital audio that allowed copyright holders to protect their property by only allowing users to make a limited number of copies of the files; they got it in *Advanced Audio Coding (AAC)*, which is a component of the MPEG-4 standard brought to life in part by Apple.

AAC files can be as unfettered as MP3 files; for instance, you can use AAC to encode tracks from CDs that you own. However, AAC also provides copyright holders the capability to control who can play them and where; keyed to a centralized database of users and protected with passwords, AAC files can't be copied from one person's computer to another without the files becoming unusable.

Fortunately, AAC brings more to the table than just DRM restrictions; AAC files are smaller and clearer than MP3 files under most circumstances, with true separate stereo tracks and a more efficient codec (encoding and decoding) algorithm. *Windows Media Audio (WMA)* provides similar features and benefits over MP3, although the DRM infrastructure used in WMA files is more restrictive than what is found in AAC.

The downside of AAC files is that they're not as widely used as MP3 or even WMA files. Nearly all digital audio players can play MP3 files, and many can now handle WMA files as well. Currently, however, only the iPod—the world's most popular portable digital music player—can play AAC files.

iTunes is Apple's star performer, a "jukebox" (MP3 song file player) application that has set the direction for how such applications should appear and behave. Its clean design and ease of use in accomplishing otherwise complex tasks have won it great respect in the computer industry. However, there are a few things you should understand about how iTunes works, which you might find confusing—especially if you're used to working with Windows.

KEY TERMS

MPEG-1 level 3 (MP3)—The most widely used format for digital music, MP3 files sound pretty good but have no copy protection built in.

Digital rights management (DRM)—Software algorithms that provide "copy protection" for digital music, usually enforced with digital "keys."

Advanced Audio Coding (AAC)—A new digital audio format co-developed by Apple as part of the MPEG-4 definition; AAC has better quality than MP3, as well as built-in DRM.

Windows Media Audio (WMA)—Microsoft's competitor format to AAC, WMA files are similarly higher-quality than MP3s, but their DRM is more restrictive.

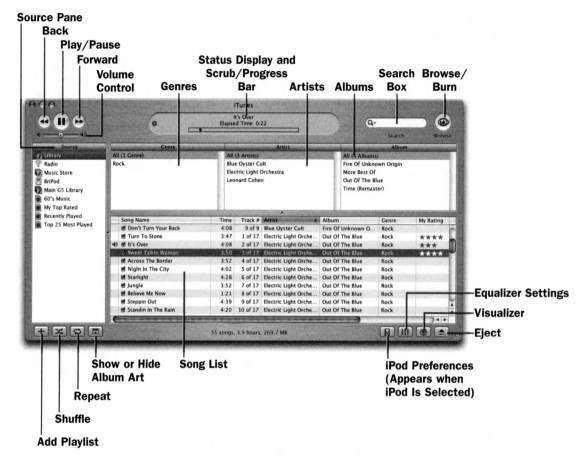

Source Pane
Back
Play/Pause
Forward
Volume
Control
Genres
Status Display and
Scrub/Progress
Bar
Artists
Albums
Search
Box
Browse/
Burn

Equalizer Settings
Visualizer
Eject

Show or Hide
Album Art
Song List
iPod Preferences
(Appears when
iPod Is Selected)

Repeat

Shuffle

Add Playlist

The main iTunes window provides many features associated with recording and playing back audio files.

First of all, iTunes does not operate in conjunction with MP3 files in the Finder; rather, it is a separate, specialized interface for your music. iTunes doesn't use the traditional "documents and folders" computing metaphor for organizing music; instead, it treats each individual MP3 file as a *song*, and organizes songs on the basis of their *artists*, *albums*, and *genres*, as well as in the custom *playlists* you can define. You don't "open an MP3 file" in iTunes. Rather, you select a song from iTunes' internal music **Library** and play it. The song you select corresponds to an MP3 or AAC file in a folder on your disk, and the folder it resides in is organized according to the artist and album—but you ideally never have to deal with the files themselves in the Finder in the course of your daily musical enjoyment.

Playing and controlling music in iTunes is much the same as you do in the QuickTime Player: The **Play/Pause** button starts and stops the music, the *scrub bar* lets you skip immediately to a specific place in a song by dragging the playhead, and the **Back** and **Forward** buttons skip from song to song in the current listing. Play a song by double-clicking it in the song list or by selecting it and clicking **Play**. There's nothing revolutionary about that. Where iTunes shines is in how it organizes your massive music collection and gets you to exactly the music you want.

You can browse immediately to an artist to see all the songs in that artist's albums, or to an album directly, by using **Browse** view (click the **Browse** button to reveal the navigation lists). You can zoom straight to a song by typing part of its title into the **Search** box. By sorting the song list by its visible columns of data, you can put all your music in exactly the order you want to play it.

Songs in iTunes' **Library** all have numerous pieces of data associated with them: Aside from the artist and album and genre, each song (potentially) has a track number, a "star" rating that you assign, a date when it was last played, and other such fields—all specified in what are known as *ID3 tags* embedded within the file itself. iTunes is really just a big database, managing songs by their ID3 tags, which you can use to sort your songs into playlists, filter them to your preference, and track how often you play them.

KEY TERM

Scrub bar—A long, horizontal control with a sliding knob that allows you to skip directly to specific point in the timeline of a music or video file, as well as showing you your current position in the timeline.

 TIP

If you hold down the **Back** or **Forward** button, it will "fast-forward" or "rewind" the song, the same as with most personal music players.

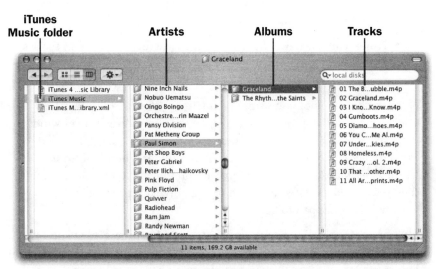

The hierarchical structure of the iTunes Music folder.

NOTE

Mac OS X uses the HFS+ file system, which assigns a "Unique File ID" to each file in the system. Files can be tracked and addressed directly by applications using this ID, rather than by relying on the path through the folders to a file's location. This means that if you add a file to the iTunes Music **Library**, iTunes keeps track of the file by its Unique File ID, not by its path; you can therefore move an MP3 file from one folder to another, as many times as you want, and iTunes won't ever lose track of it.

TIPS

If you elect to let iTunes use MP3 files wherever they are in the system, you can later decide to copy all your MP3 files into the organized **iTunes Music** folder; do this by selecting **Consolidate Library** from the **Advanced** menu. This is a one-way operation; it can't be undone. However, it won't change iTunes' behavior for music files you add in the future.

Click the **Browse** button in the upper-right corner of the iTunes window to show or hide the lists that allow you to browse and filter songs by artist and album. You can browse by genre too, if you enable that option in the iTunes **Preferences** window on the **General** page.

Behind the scenes, iTunes keeps all its MP3 (and AAC) files in a special **iTunes Music** folder, inside the **Music** folder in your **Home** folder. Inside the **iTunes Music** folder are folders for every artist in the **Library**, and inside those folders are folders for each album by each artist. MP3 files are sorted into those folders, with filenames kept in sync with the ID3 tags you specify for the song name, track number, artist, and album. This way, you can always find your music files quickly using the Finder if you have to. iTunes can also keep track of MP3 files that aren't in its **iTunes Music** folder, but those files won't be automatically organized if you change their ID3 tags.

Chances are that you've used MP3 files at some point in your life—whether you obtained them commercially, or through (*ahem*) other means. Any MP3 files you might have collected can be used in iTunes, and you can fill in any missing ID3 tags right in iTunes' interface to organize the files better. However, before you can do any of that, you must add your MP3 files to the iTunes Music **Library**. And before you can add MP3 files to the **Library**, you must decide how you want iTunes to treat the MP3 files. You have two choices:

- iTunes can automatically copy any newly added MP3 file to the managed **iTunes Music** folder; thereafter, the song file that iTunes uses will be the one inside its special folder. If you change the file's ID3 tags, iTunes renames it accordingly and refiles it in the properly named folders. You can do anything you like with the original MP3 file; iTunes won't be using it.

- iTunes can use newly added MP3 files wherever they are in the system. If you change their ID3 tags within iTunes, the files are not reorganized or renamed.

To select the behavior you want, open iTunes (it's in the **Applications** folder, or click its icon in the Dock); open the iTunes **Preferences** window (choose **Preferences** from the **iTunes** menu) and go to the **Advanced** tab. Enable the **Copy files to iTunes Music folder when adding to library** check box if you want iTunes to manage its own copies of your files; disable the box if you want it to use only your original MP3 files wherever they happen to be.

MP3 and AAC files, by default, are set to open in iTunes. Locate an MP3 or AAC file in the Finder and double-click it; the file opens and plays in iTunes, and a reference to the file appears in the iTunes **Library**. (Note that if you double-click uncompressed AIFF and WAV audio files in the

Finder, the files open in the QuickTime Player.) If the ID3 tags for the song name, artist, and album are set, their contents appear in the song list in the iTunes window.

To add an MP3 file to the iTunes **Library** without going through the Finder, you can select **File, Add to Library**. A navigator window pops up; use this window to locate and select the file you want to add. Click **Open** to select the file and add it to your iTunes **Library**.

The quickest way to add a file to the iTunes **Library** is to drag it from the Finder into the iTunes application window, or to the **iTunes** icon in the Dock. When you release the mouse button, the file is added to your **Library**.

You can add a whole folder full of MP3 files in this way, too—even a hierarchical folder full of other folders. Provided that the ID3 tags are set correctly, the files immediately become organized by their artists and albums in iTunes, rather than by their folders and filenames, as they are in the Finder.

MP3 files you obtain from random sources on the Internet probably don't have all the ID3 tags filled in properly—and this will prevent you from being able to take full advantage of iTunes' navigation methods to find these songs. While the song is selected or playing, simply click in the blank fields in its entry line to type in the proper values. Alternatively, press ⌘I to bring up the **Song Info** dialog box for the current song; in the **Info** tab, you can fill in all the ID3 tags directly. Click **OK** when you're done.

Songs from "compilation" albums—where each track is by a different artist—should have the **Part of a compilation** check box enabled in the **Song Info** dialog box. This option doesn't affect how the songs are listed in iTunes; rather, it ensures that the MP3 files are placed in a single folder named for the album itself, in a folder called **Compilations** inside **iTunes Music** (rather than each song being listed on its own in a different folder for each artist). The **Part of a compilation** option is purely a convenience feature for if you want to access your music files in the Finder and have them organized similarly to how you'd access them in real life.

 TIP

Select any song in the iTunes **Library** and choose **File, Show Song File** (or choose the command from the contextual menu you get if you **Control**+click or right-click the song) to open a Finder window showing the folder containing the song file itself. You can then copy or transfer the file, or do anything else that requires you to access the file in the Finder view.

NOTE

iTunes does not create duplicate entries in its database for the same MP3 files. You can drag a file into iTunes as many times as you want, but it will not create an additional entry or lose track of the file. This means you can add a whole folder full of MP3s, even if you've already added some of the individual MP3 files to the iTunes **Library**. The **Date Added** field for those files won't even be updated.

 TIP

Note that this automatic reorganization only takes place if you have enabled the **Keep iTunes Music Folder Organized** check box in the **Advanced** pane of the **iTunes Preferences** window.

98 Import (or Rip) an Audio CD

Before You Begin

✔ **29** Configure Networking Manually

See Also

→ **99** Purchase Music from the iTunes Music Store

→ **101** Burn a Custom Audio CD

NOTE

Before importing music from a CD, make sure that you're connected to the Internet! It's possible to import successfully without an Internet connection, but if you do, the music tracks you import will not have any titles or other useful organizing information embedded in them, and you will have to enter the track names and artist information manually. If you have an Internet connection, however, iTunes can download this information automatically from the central database.

KEY TERMS

Ripping—Creating new MP3 or AAC audio files for use in iTunes by copying them in raw form from a CD and compressing them.

CD Digital Audio (CDDA)—The raw, uncompressed digital audio format in which music is stored on audio CDs.

The proper way to obtain new *MP3* or *AAC* files, of course, is to import them from audio CDs you already own—a process usually known as *ripping*. To rip a track from a CD, iTunes must copy the uncompressed *CD Digital Audio (CDDA)* data from the disc, convert the audio stream to the compressed MP3 or AAC format, apply the track names and other data to the new file's ID3 fields, and add them to the iTunes **Library**. Before iTunes, this was usually a process that involved three or four laborious steps; now, however, it's ideally a one-button operation.

1 Insert a CD

Find the CD from which you want to import music and insert it into your Mac's CD drive. Wait for it to spin up and mount, a process that could take up to twenty seconds.

2 Wait for Track Listing to Download

If you're connected to the Internet, iTunes will query the centralized CD track database at **www.cddb.com**. If the CD is found there, iTunes downloads the track names, album title, and artist name, and applies them to the tracks that appear in the iTunes window when the CD is selected in the **Source** pane.

If you're not connected to the Internet, the CD's tracks will appear with generic names (**Track 1**, **Track 2**, and so on). You will have to change these names yourself, either before or after importing, by clicking on the field showing the name and typing the correct title.

3 Make Necessary Edits to Track Names

Although the track information from the central CD database is usually accurate (it contains information for nearly every CD ever produced), there is always the possibility of typos and other errors. Check the track names for spelling errors and inconsistencies; to edit any field, simply click it and edit it as you would a filename in the Finder. You can edit the fields after importing, of course, but it's better to edit the information before importing so that Mac OS X will remember the CD's information as accurately as possible in the future.

1 Insert a CD

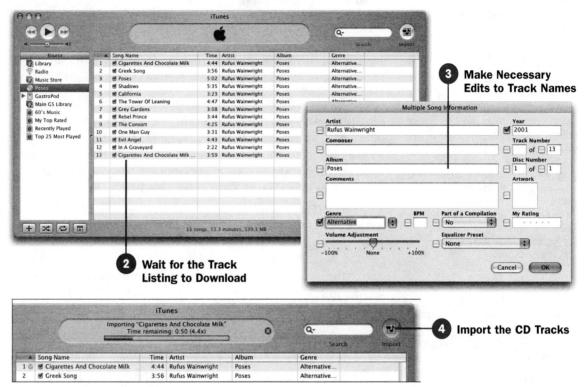

3 Make Necessary Edits to Track Names

2 Wait for the Track Listing to Download

4 Import the CD Tracks

If you were unable to connect to the Internet, you can manually enter the track names here as well. To enter the artist and album name for all the tracks at once, select them all (press ⌘**A**) and then open the **Info** dialog box with ⌘**I**. Enter as much common information as you want and click **OK**.

4 **Import the CD Tracks**

When you're satisfied with the appearance of the track data, click the **Import** button at the top-right corner of the iTunes window. The songs begin importing; depending on the speed of your computer, this can take anything from a tiny fraction of the time it would take to play back the CD in real time (1/20th of the time or

After the CD has been mounted and the track information downloaded, the CD appears in the **Source** pane at the left side of the iTunes window. Select the album and click the **Play** button to play audio tracks from the CD directly or double-click the CD to open its track listing in a separate window. This separate track listing can be helpful if you want to work in the main iTunes window and listen to your existing music while you import the CD's songs in the background.

less) to as much as one-fourth of the time. When the CD has finished importing, the songs appear in your **Library** listing.

If you want to import only certain songs, rather than the entire disc, use the check boxes next to the song names to select the songs you want to import. By default, all the check boxes are enabled; disable check boxes for individual songs to exclude them.

Use as many of the ID3 tags as possible in your song files. Click a song and select **Get Info** from the **File** menu to see all the available fields you can set. The more fields you fill in, the better you will be able to organize your music. If you have a multiple-CD set, the query that iTunes makes to the **cddb.com** database might assign album names with suffixes such as **(Disc 1)** or **(1/3)**. Consider removing these suffixes (so that all the discs share the same album name), and instead use the **Disc Number** field to define which tracks belong to which discs. This will allow iTunes to sort the tracks in the correct order, from the beginning of the first disc to the end of the last, while keeping your album list clean and organized.

99 Purchase Music from the iTunes Music Store

Before You Begin

✔ **29** Configure Networking Manually

✔ **50** Sign Up for .Mac

See Also

→ **101** Burn a Custom Audio CD

→ **102** Synchronize with an iPod

In April 2003, Apple opened the iTunes Music Store—the first online music purchasing system that allows customers to buy whole albums or individual tracks, at 99 cents a track or $9.99 an album, with no further obligation or monthly fees. Imitators have already appeared, but Apple's offering is still the one that has the most consistent and least restrictive terms of use—and it's available in the Windows version of iTunes, too. You can burn individual songs to CD as often as you like; you can burn unaltered playlists up to ten times; you can play purchased music on up to three computers; and you can copy the downloaded AAC files to your iPod or any other MP3 player that handles such files (only the iPod currently supports AAC files, however). The selection of available music is quite strong, and Apple adds dozens of new albums each Tuesday.

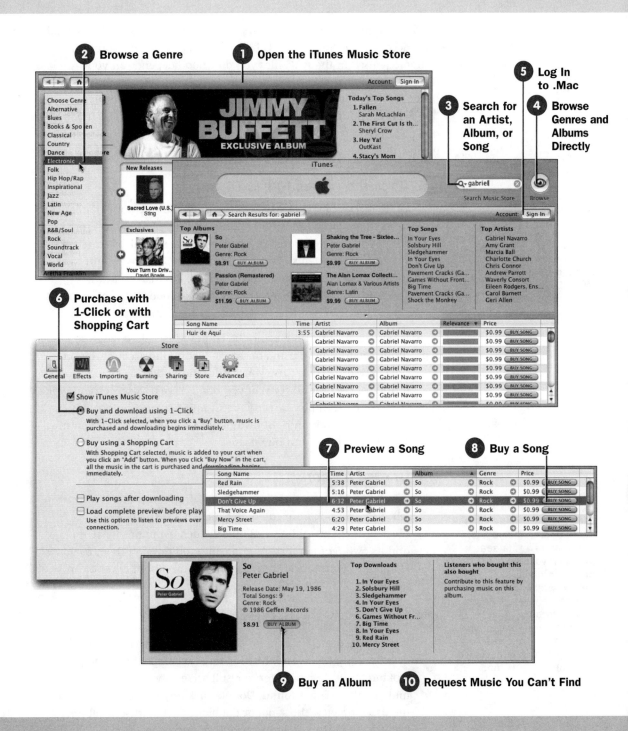

2 Browse a Genre

1 Open the iTunes Music Store

5 Log In to .Mac

3 Search for an Artist, Album, or Song

4 Browse Genres and Albums Directly

6 Purchase with 1-Click or with Shopping Cart

7 Preview a Song

8 Buy a Song

9 Buy an Album

10 Request Music You Can't Find

Purchasing music through the iTunes Music Store requires either a paid .Mac account or a free Apple ID because the *DRM*, or copy-protection, technology used in the AAC files you download depends on your Apple ID (or your .Mac account's email address) and password to unlock the music for listening. Be sure that you've signed up for a .Mac account (see **50** **Sign Up for .Mac**) before using the iTunes Music Store! If you don't want to buy a .Mac membership, you can create a free Apple ID using iTunes' built-in sign-up process.

1 **Open the iTunes Music Store**

Open iTunes and click **Music Store** in the **Source** pane. iTunes connects to the online Music Store and loads its main page. From there, you can navigate the listed genres or special pages (such as the **Just Added** items), or page through the featured albums listed in the various categories (**New Releases, Exclusives, Staff Favorites**), or view the most popular downloads listed at the right side of the screen.

If this is your first time using the iTunes Music Store, you are prompted to sign in using an Apple ID or .Mac account. If you have a .Mac account, use your .Mac email address (for example, **johndoe12341@mac.com**); if you don't have a .Mac account, you can create an Apple ID using the **Create Account** button. If you don't want to sign in right away, click **Cancel**. Note that you must sign in before you can buy music.

2 **Browse a Genre**

Select a genre from the **Choose Genre** drop-down menu at the top left. You can pick from categories such as **Classical, Rock, Electronic, Jazz,** and several others. Each genre has its own page and its own featured artists; you can scroll through them as you would the main Music Store page. Click an album cover or artist name to go to its download page.

3 **Search for an Artist, Album, or Song**

If you have a specific song or artist in mind, you can search for it directly using the **Search Music Store** box. Type the name you're looking for and press **Enter**; a result screen shows you all the matches that iTunes found. Double-click any of the song titles in the list to preview the song, or double-click the artist or album name in the list to go to its own download page.

NOTE

Click the **Just Added** link on the Music Store main page to see lists of music that has been added to the Music Store in each of the last several weekly updates.

TIP

Click the magnifying glass in the **Search Music Store** box to narrow your search to match your input only in **Artists, Albums, Composers,** or **Songs.** Alternatively, select **Power Search** to bring up a screen where you can type more specific and customized search terms, such as a specific artist and song name.

④ Browse Genres and Albums Directly

Click the **Browse** button at the top right of iTunes to put it into the direct Browser mode. This mode works like the Finder's Column view. The Browser mode is austere but practical, and allows you to quickly navigate down through the genres to the artists, albums, and songs. Double-click any artist or album name to go to its download page.

⑤ Log In to .Mac or Enter Your Apple ID

Click the **Sign In** button. If you've used the Music Store before, simply enter your Apple ID (or .Mac member name) and password in the box that appears. If this is the first time you've used the Music Store, however, you are taken to a series of screens where you enter your .Mac information (if you have an account) and set up your purchasing options. Follow the onscreen instructions to enter your credit card information and other data that the system requires.

⑥ Purchase with 1-Click or with Shopping Cart

Open the **iTunes Preferences** window (choose **Preferences** from the **iTunes** menu) and click the **Store** icon to open the **Music Store Preferences** page. A radio button allows you to select whether to use *1-Click*, which means that songs and albums you buy will be downloaded immediately; or with a shopping cart, which means that instead of **Buy** buttons you will see **Add** buttons, and you can purchase and download all your shopping cart's contents at once. The **Shopping Cart** option is often better if you have a slower Internet connection. Click **OK** when you're done.

⑦ Preview a Song

In any screen where song files are shown, such as an album page or a search result listing, you can get a thirty-second preview of any song by double-clicking the song title (or by selecting the song and clicking iTunes' **Play** button). The preview is selected from the middle of each song so that you get a good idea of the main sound of the song, rather than just its first thirty seconds.

8 Buy a Song

Each song in a listing page has a **Buy Song** button next to its price in the listing. Click the **Buy Song** button to buy the track. A dialog box appears to confirm whether you want to buy it; the download begins when you click **Buy**.

9 Buy an Album

On nearly every full album page, there is a **Buy Album** button at the top next to the cover art. Click this button to download the entire album at once. A dialog box appears to confirm whether you want to buy it; the download begins when you click **Buy**.

10 Request Music You Can't Find

Chances are that you'll be looking for some specific song or artist that doesn't seem to be in the iTunes Music Store. You can request it, however, by using the built-in feedback form available from the Music Store's main page.

Click the **Requests & Feedback** link, in the upper-left corner of the Music Store window. In the form that appears, type the name of the song, artist, or album that you're looking for. Click **Send**, and your request is sent to Apple. The Music Store is constantly being updated, with new additions made every Tuesday; if enough people request the music you're looking for, it will likely be added to the Music Store and appear in one of the weekly updates.

TIP

Click the **My Account** link or the **Account** button to access your online account options. Among the things you can do in this area are reviewing your purchase history, requesting technical support, and selecting whether you want Apple to send you email notifications when the Music Store is updated. Enable the weekly notification option to get a message each Tuesday showing you what new music has been added.

100 Create a Playlist

Before You Begin

✔ 98 Import/Rip an Audio CD

✔ 99 Purchase Music From the iTunes Music Store

See Also

→ 40 Discover Shared Music

→ 101 Burn a Custom Audio CD

Although iTunes makes it easy to locate and play any individual song or album, sometimes you'll want to mix and match your music. It's one thing to be able to select a single artist and simply play through all the songs that artist ever produced; it's quite another to pull together a selection of your personal favorite thirty songs, a choice collection for working out at the gym, a soothing set of songs to fall asleep to, or your most highly rated rock songs from the 70s. These kinds of specialized, personalized groupings are what's known as *playlists*.

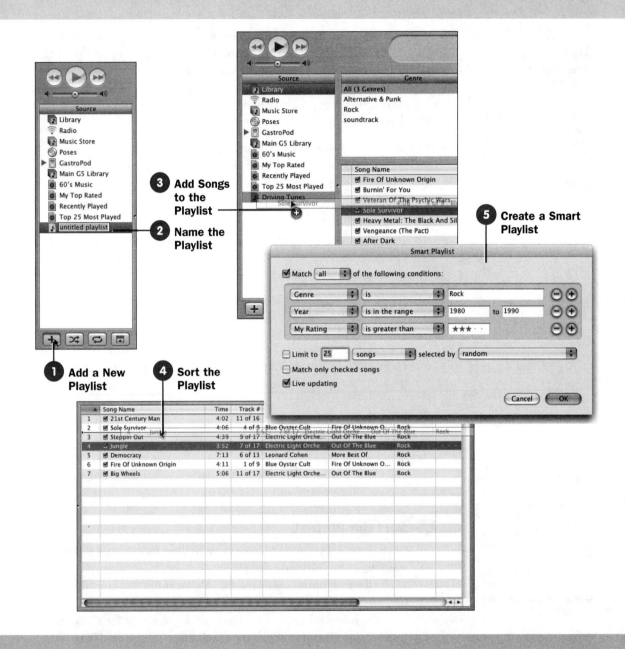

3 Add Songs to the Playlist

2 Name the Playlist

5 Create a Smart Playlist

1 Add a New Playlist

4 Sort the Playlist

Playlist—A grouping of songs that you create by dragging songs into it in whatever order you please.

Smart playlist—A playlist that is automatically created according to criteria you specify, updating itself as you add new music that matches those criteria.

NOTE

When you drag songs from your **Library** into a playlist, you're not removing them from the **Library**; you're merely creating a list of references to selected songs. You can always access each song in its original location in the **Library**. You can add the same song to multiple playlists.

iTunes can create two kinds of playlists: standard ones, in which you simply make a new list and then manually add songs to it; and *smart playlists*, which are in fact sophisticated database queries that automatically select songs that match criteria you specify. Smart playlists have near-infinite versatility; how they can be configured is limited only by your imagination.

Whether a playlist is standard or smart, you can play its contents by selecting the playlist from the **Source** pane on the left side of the iTunes window and then clicking **Play**.

① Add a New Playlist

To create a new playlist, click the + button below the **Source** pane, at the bottom left of the iTunes window. A new playlist appears in the **Source** list, with the name **untitled playlist**.

② Name the Playlist

The name of the new playlist is selected so that you can immediately type a new name, such as **Driving Tunes** or **Hair Band Classics**. Press **Return** after typing the perfect title for your collection.

③ Add Songs to the Playlist

Click the **Library** option in the **Source** pane to view all the songs available in iTunes; navigate to each song you want to add to the playlist and drag it to the playlist in the **Source** pane. Each new song is added to the end of the list.

④ Sort the Playlist

Click the playlist in the **Source** pane to view its contents in the song list area. Click and drag individual songs to different places in the list to manually sort the list to your taste. You can also click any of the column headers to sort the playlist on that column; click the column header again to reverse the sort order. Click the first column, showing the entry numbers, to return the list to your manual sort order.

❺ Create a Smart Playlist

To create a smart playlist, hold down the **Option** key and click the + button; its icon changes from a + sign to a sprocket, indicating the automated mechanism underlying smart playlists. Alternately, select **New Smart Playlist** from the **File** menu.

A **Smart Playlist** dialog box appears to give you access to the specifications of the list. Various check box options are available, such as limiting the list to a certain number of songs. You can add as many organizational criteria as you want by clicking the + button after the single shown criterion. You can filter songs using any of the available ID3 tags, as well as comparison operators such as **contains** or **starts with** for textual entries, **is** or **greater than** for numeric entries, or **is after** or **is in the range** for date entries. You can, for instance, create a list composed of all songs in the **Rock** genre that were made in the years **1966–1974**, and whose track number is 1. The details are all up to you.

Smart playlists are especially useful in conjunction with the **My Rating** and **Play Count** columns. For instance, you can create a smart playlist that consists only of songs you've rated three stars or higher, or to which you've listened at least five times, or both conditions at once. As you listen to your music, rate each song by giving it anything between one and five stars. Do this by **Control**+clicking the song and then picking a rating from the **My Rating** submenu or by selecting a rating from the contextual menu on iTunes' Dock icon. You can also configure iTunes to show the **My Rating** column and then simply click in that column to set the appropriate number of stars. As you rate your songs and listen to the ones you like best, a Smart playlist that you might have set up to include only highly rated or frequently played songs automatically becomes populated with music.

 TIP

iTunes becomes more and more useful the more you use it; it hones itself to match your listening habits.

101 Burn a Custom Audio CD

Before You Begin

✔ **18** Burn a CD/DVD

✔ **100** Create a Playlist

See Also

→ **102** Synchronize with an iPod

"Rip, Mix, Burn," said Apple's ad when iTunes was released. The whole idea of digital music management is that you can take the music you already own, import it into your computer, organize it according to your own likes and dislikes, and then make your own "mix" CDs of your favorite music arranged just the way you want them.

iTunes makes creating your own mix CDs nearly as simple as importing the music in the first place. Simply create a playlist containing the music you want to burn onto a CD; then insert a blank writable CD into the CD-ROM drive, and let iTunes do the rest. You can then play the CD in your car, on your portable stereo, at a dance, wherever your fancy strikes.

 TIP

iTunes can burn playlists that are longer than will fit on a single CD, if you have multiple blank CDs to use. See step 5 for details.

1 Create a Suitable Playlist

The first step in creating a custom mix CD is to make a playlist containing the songs you want on the disc. Drag the songs from the **Library** to the playlist, keeping in mind that typical CD-R discs can hold up to either 71 or 74 minutes of music. Don't make the playlist any longer than this! Use the statistics shown at the bottom of the iTunes window to determine how many minutes your playlist will last.

2 Click the Burn Disc Button

When you're viewing the playlist, the **Browse** button in the top-right corner of the iTunes window becomes a **Burn Disc** button; click it to begin the creation of the new disc.

TIP

You can also insert the CD before you click the **Burn Disc** button; if you do, Mac OS X will prompt you asking whether to prepare the disc for use as an audio CD (by switching to iTunes) or a data CD (by mounting it in the Finder). If you choose to open iTunes, iTunes can then burn a playlist immediately without prompting you to insert a disc.

3 Insert a Disc

In its display oval, iTunes prompts you to insert a blank disc. If your Mac has a CD tray, it is automatically ejected so that you can insert the disc. When you retract the tray, iTunes recognizes the blank disc and automatically changes the message in the display oval to a prompt telling you to click the **Burn Disc** button again (it is now throbbing gently) to begin burning the playlist to the disc.

If you don't click **Burn Disc** within about ten seconds, iTunes cancels the operation and ejects the disc.

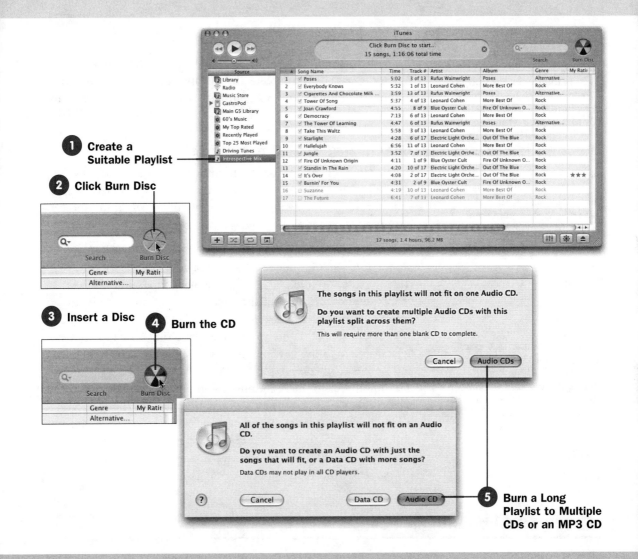

1 Create a
Suitable Playlist

2 Click Burn Disc

3 Insert a Disc **4** Burn the CD

The songs in this playlist will not fit on one Audio CD.

Do you want to create multiple Audio CDs with this playlist split across them?

This will require more than one blank CD to complete.

Cancel   Audio CDs

All of the songs in this playlist will not fit on an Audio CD.

Do you want to create an Audio CD with just the songs that will fit, or a Data CD with more songs?

Data CDs may not play in all CD players.

Cancel   Data CD   Audio CD

5 Burn a Long
Playlist to Multiple
CDs or an MP3 CD

NOTE

The difference between an MP3 CD and a data CD (or DVD) is that in an MP3 CD, all songs are converted to MP3 format to be compatible with as many music devices as possible. A data CD or DVD is designed purely for use in a computer, where you can mount the disc and work with the individual music files on it. A data disc can contain some songs that can't be converted to MP3 format, such as Internet Radio streams, purchased AAC tracks, and MIDI music files.

TIP

You can set iTunes to create audio CDs, MP3 CDs, or data CDs/DVDs by default in the **iTunes Preferences** window on the **Burning** page. You can also use that page to set various options for audio CDs, such as the length of the gap between tracks.

④ Burn the CD

Click **Burn Disc** for the second time to begin the burn process. When the process is complete, the CD appears in your **Source** pane to show the tracks you've just burned. Eject the disc to use it in any CD player.

⑤ Burn a Long Playlist to Multiple CDs

If your playlist contains too much music to fit on a CD, iTunes automatically detects this when you click **Burn Disc**. iTunes asks whether you want to burn the entire playlist to multiple CDs, or to cancel the burn process and trim the playlist down to fit on a single disc.

Yet another option you have is to burn the music to an MP3 CD or a data disc, leaving the songs as MP3 or AAC files. Normally, iTunes creates an audio CD, which involves expanding each MP3 or AAC audio track into its uncompressed form and then writing it onto the disc as raw CDDA data—just like a regular music CD. An MP3 CD, on the other hand, is essentially a data disc full of MP3 files, identical to the ones on your hard disk. A CD can hold only 74 minutes of uncompressed CDDA, but it can hold about 12 times that amount of compressed music. Additionally, an MP3 CD can preserve all your ID3 tags for the benefit of devices that can read them and display them during playback. The downside is that although devices that can read MP3 CDs are becoming more common, they are still nowhere near as numerous as standard audio CD players, which can't handle MP3 CDs.

---

102 Synchronize with an iPod

Before You Begin

✔ **98** Import (or Rip) an Audio CD

✔ **99** Purchase Music from the iTunes Music Store

✔ **100** Create a Playlist

See Also

➔ **126** Synchronize Your Palm PDA and Other Devices

The iPod is Apple's own MP3 and AAC music player. With its capacious internal hard drive, its small size, and its intuitive button-and-wheel interface, it has defined the field of digital audio players and spawned a horde of imitators. None of these, however, integrates so well with iTunes as the iPod does—which should not come as a surprise.

An iPod is designed to synchronize with your iTunes **Music Library** simply through the act of plugging it in. However, a few complicating factors can arise, such as when you have more music in your iTunes **Library** than can fit on your iPod's hard disk. For these situations, a few alternative operating modes are available.

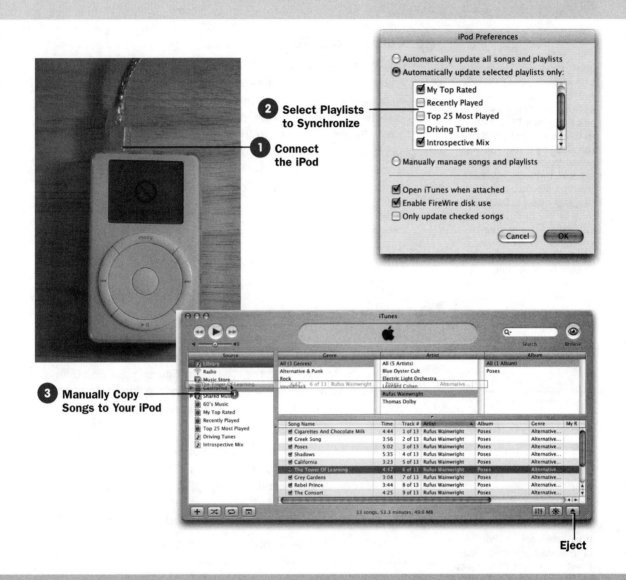

2 Select Playlists to Synchronize

1 Connect the iPod

3 Manually Copy Songs to Your iPod

iPod Preferences

○ Automatically update all songs and playlists
◉ Automatically update selected playlists only:

☑ My Top Rated
☐ Recently Played
☐ Top 25 Most Played
☐ Driving Tunes
☑ Introspective Mix

○ Manually manage songs and playlists

☑ Open iTunes when attached
☑ Enable FireWire disk use
☐ Only update checked songs

Cancel   OK

Eject

1 Connect the iPod

If your iPod has a dock, place the iPod into it. If it has no dock, plug the FireWire cable directly into the iPod's socket. In a few seconds, Mac OS X recognizes the iPod and iTunes automatically launches. The iPod appears in the **Source** pane, and iTunes automatically synchronizes with it, replacing the iPod's contents with your current iTunes **Library**. All the songs in the **Library** are transferred to the iPod; this process can take ten or twenty minutes, depending on how large your music collection is.

When iTunes and the iPod's screen report that it is safe to disconnect the iPod, feel free to do so. Do not disconnect the iPod while songs are being transferred—this can result in lost data. It's a good idea to leave the iPod plugged in as long as possible because doing so keeps the battery charged.

2 Select Playlists to Synchronize

If your iPod doesn't have enough capacity to hold all the music in your **Library**, a dialog box tells you so. Open the **iPod Preferences** window (to do this, select the iPod in the **Source** pane and then click the **iPod** button at the bottom right of the iTunes window). Enable the **Automatically update selected playlists only** radio button.

In the scroll box, select the playlists you want to synchronize with your iPod. Every time you connect your iPod to your Mac, these playlists and all their contents are copied to your iPod.

3 Manually Copy Songs to Your iPod

You can configure your iPod so that it doesn't automatically synchronize with your iTunes **Library** at all. If you select the **Manually manage songs and playlists** radio button in the **iPod Preferences** window, you can select and manipulate the songs on your iPod within iTunes as you can any other music source. You can then drag songs and playlists from your iTunes **Library** directly to the iPod option in the **Source** list. This way, you can specify exactly which songs to put on it. This method is laborious but exact.

103 Convert Between Image Formats

One of the seemingly unnecessarily complex things that all computer users have to deal with, even in this day and age, is image formats. Picture files that we encounter on the Web, in publishing, in digital photography, and in any of the numerous other digital graphics arenas can come in any of a dozen different popular *formats*—JPEG, GIF, BMP, and so on. A *format* is the internal structure of a file on the disk, which every application did differently, in its own way, back when the computer world was young. Each of these formats is subtly different only in its underlying structure; if you double-click a picture to view it, you likely won't be able to tell what format it's in. But different formats all have different capabilities and limitations, and they're not interchangeable. Here's a list of the most popular image formats:

Before You Begin

✔ **2** Find and Launch an Application

✔ **11** Find an Item

See Also

→ **63** Send a New Message

- **JPEG.** The Joint Photographic Experts Group format, JPEG is by far the most common image format on the Internet. It supports 16.7 million colors (24 bits worth), and a JPEG file can be saved with a "quality" or "compression" setting—the higher the compression, the smaller the file size, but the lower the visual quality. JPEG is best for photographs and smoothly digitally colored images that don't have sharp edges between their color areas. If the definition of individual pixels is important, as with mouse-drawn line art, try GIF instead.

- **GIF.** The Graphics Interchange Format, popularized by CompuServe, is the other common image format on the Web. GIF files are 8-bit, meaning that they can only contain 256 separate colors; but GIF files can also support features such as transparency and animation, and they are small without losing image quality (as occurs with JPEG). Mac OS X can view GIF files, but it does not allow you to export images into GIF format because of patent disputes with Unisys, the format's original patent holder.

- **PDF.** The Portable Document Format, developed by Adobe, is Apple's native image format in Mac OS X. PDF files are flexible and can contain millions of colors, as well as separate text and multiple pages. However, PDF files are not generally supported as "images" on the Internet.

- **BMP.** The native Windows format, BMP or "bitmap" files are uncompressed and can contain up to 24 bits of color data. Because they're not compressed, BMP files can be extremely large and are unsuitable for use on the Internet.

1 Open the Picture in Preview

2 Export the Picture

3 Select the Target Image Format

4 Set the Image Options

5 Save the Picture

- **TIFF**. The Tagged Image File Format is the industry standard for high-quality, 24-bit images in publishing applications. TIFF files can support compression, layers, and different embedded codecs (encoding and decoding algorithms).

- **PNG**. The Portable Network Graphics format was developed as an open standard to replace GIF and JPEG. It supports "lossless" compression (reducing the file size without losing image clarity, as happens with GIF), transparency, alpha channels, and other advanced formats. However, the PNG format is still not well supported in most popular browsers, and file sizes are still prohibitively large for widespread adoption on the Web.

- **PICT**. The old Mac Picture format, PICT dates back to the days of the original Macintosh. PICT files can support JPEG compression and complex QuickTime functions embedded into the pictures. However, PICT is becoming less well supported in publishing, and TIFF is supplanting it as the industry standard.

Some applications, such as Photoshop, have their own proprietary image formats; this allows the application to save data into the file that you can't see when you're viewing the file, but that is meaningful to Photoshop (such as layers, ColorSync profiles, paths, and other such "metadata"). In most cases, though, the most popular image formats—GIF, JPEG, BMP, and a handful of others—are ubiquitous because they create small, portable files and use open standards. GIF and JPEG images make up the bulk of the pictures you encounter on the Internet; they are the *de facto* standard. Most Web browsers, in fact, do not support any other image formats but those two.

However, there might come a time when you need to convert a picture from one format to another. This might be because you have a screenshot in PICT or TIFF format, and you need to make it into a JPEG so that you can post it on the Web; or you might have to take a BMP picture that was created in Paint on a Windows machine and turn it into a TIFF or PNG. Mac OS X allows you to perform these conversions, using **Preview** (the built-in picture viewing application) and only a few steps.

① Open the Picture in Preview

Locate the picture file you want to view by navigating to its location in a Finder window. Double-click the picture file to open it in

Preview. You can also launch Preview separately (by double-clicking its icon in the **Applications** folder), and then drag the picture onto Preview's icon in the Dock.

2 Export the Picture

Select **Export** from the **File** menu. The **Export** dialog box opens.

3 Select the Target Image Format

In the **Save As** field, specify a filename; in the **Where** field, specify a location for the new file you will be creating. (Use the **Where** drop-down list to navigate to the folder you want.)

From the **Format** menu, select the format to which you want to convert the picture.

Because Unisys—the patent holder for the GIF format—is exercising its right to collect royalties for the use of GIF images, Preview does not allow you to export images into GIF format. For most purposes, PNG or JPEG can do the job of GIF; but if you need GIF's unique features, such as transparency or animation, or if you have to take advantage of GIF's ubiquitous compatibility, you can obtain third-party applications to do the conversion.

 WEB RESOURCE

Visit this Web site to look into the excellent GraphicConverter application by Lemke Software if you want a program that converts picture files to the GIF format, as well as dozens more formats than Preview supports.

http://www.lemkesoft.com/en/graphcon.htm

4 Set the Image Options

Click the **Options** button to activate a small dialog box that allows you to specify options specific to the image format you selected in step 3. Most formats allow you to choose the color depth (grayscale or color, and anything from 2 to 16 million levels). TIFF, for instance, lets you choose a compression method and a "byte order" (for use on different platforms); JPEG has a slider you can use to specify the quality and compression. Remember, the higher the quality, the larger the file size, and the lower the compression.

Click **OK** when you're done specifying the options.

5 Save the Picture

Back in the **Export** dialog box, click **Save** to save the new file.

104 Capture a Screenshot

Whether you're publishing a picture of your desktop so that others can see what you're doing, capturing an image of an application you're running so that you can demonstrate a bug to a developer, or writing a book full of screen images, the ability to snap a picture of your screen at any given moment is endlessly useful. Mac OS X, like every version of the Macintosh since 1984, provides a simple keystroke that captures the entire screen or a selected portion of it. Additionally, the **Grab** utility lets you capture a "timed" screen, taking a snapshot several seconds after you request it.

The built-in screen-capture functions in Mac OS X will likely address most of your needs; but if you want an even more elegant solution, allowing you to capture the drop-shadows and smooth rounded edges that are so characteristic of Mac OS X windows, look into Snapz Pro X by Ambrosia Software. This gem of an application runs in the background and can be summoned with a user-defined key combination; it can select from any of the distinct objects on the screen, from a Finder window to the menu bar to the Dock.

See Also

→ **103** Convert Between Image Formats

🌐 **WEB RESOURCE**

http://www.ambrosiasw.com/utilities/snapzprox

Visit the Ambrosia Software site for more information about the Snapz Pro X program.

❶ Capture the Entire Screen

To capture the entire screen at any time, no matter what you're doing, press ⌘+**Shift+3**. A "camera" sound effect plays, and then a file (in PDF format) named **Picture 1** appears on your Desktop. If you capture more screens, the files are created as **Picture 2**, **Picture 3**, and so on.

❷ Capture a Selected Area

If you want to capture only a certain selected part of the screen, press ⌘+**Shift+4**. The mouse pointer turns into a crosshair, and you can then click and drag a rectangle to specify the area of the screen you want to capture. When you release the mouse button, the selected area is saved to a **Picture 1** file on your Desktop.

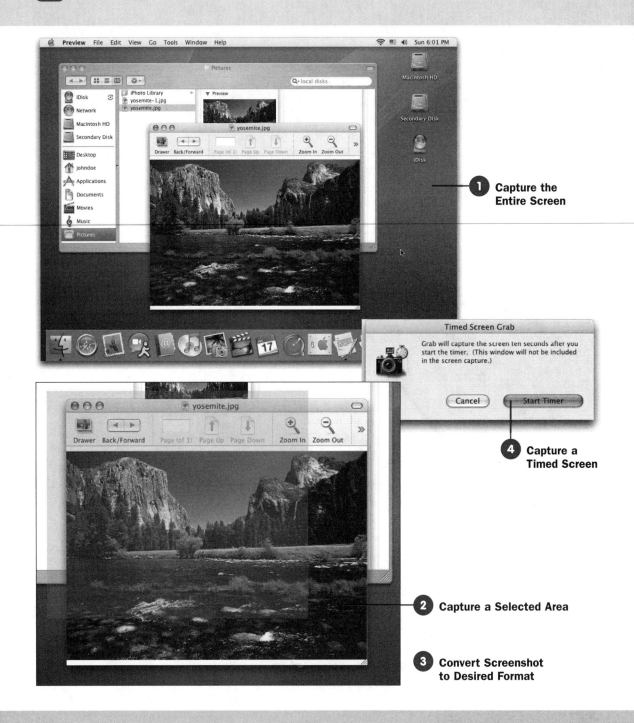

1 Capture the Entire Screen

Timed Screen Grab

Grab will capture the screen ten seconds after you start the timer. (This window will not be included in the screen capture.)

Cancel   Start Timer

4 Capture a Timed Screen

2 Capture a Selected Area

3 Convert Screenshot to Desired Format

3 **Convert Screenshot to Desired Format**

Double-click the new picture file to open it in Preview. Export the picture to convert it into whatever format you like, for publishing on the Web or for emailing to a correspondent. See **103** **Convert Between Image Formats** for more information about changing image formats in Preview.

4 **Capture a Timed Screen**

It can be useful to capture a screenshot several seconds after you trigger the capture. For instance, if you want to capture an application that requires a lot of mouse and keyboard input (such as a game), and you can't press the screen-capture key commands at the proper time, you can use the Grab application that comes with Mac OS X.

Launch **Grab** from the **Utilities** folder, inside **Applications**. From the **Grab** menu bar, choose **Capture**, **Timed Screen**. In the **Timed Screen Grab** dialog box that opens, click the **Start Timer** button; from that moment, you have ten seconds to get the screen to the state where you want it. At that point, Grab will take a snapshot and open it in a window inside Grab itself.

Save the file by selecting **Save** from the **File** menu. The resulting file will be in TIFF format, and you can use Preview to convert it to whatever format you like.

105 About iPhoto

The graphics and imaging portion of the iLife suite of applications is iPhoto. Apple has focused on digital photography as the primary reason for home users to get into image processing, and they have designed iPhoto accordingly—acting as an organizer for all the photographs you've ever taken with your digital camera. And that's not where its capabilities end.

Photo Information
Photo Album
Photo Sources
Photo Thumbnails
(Contact Sheet)

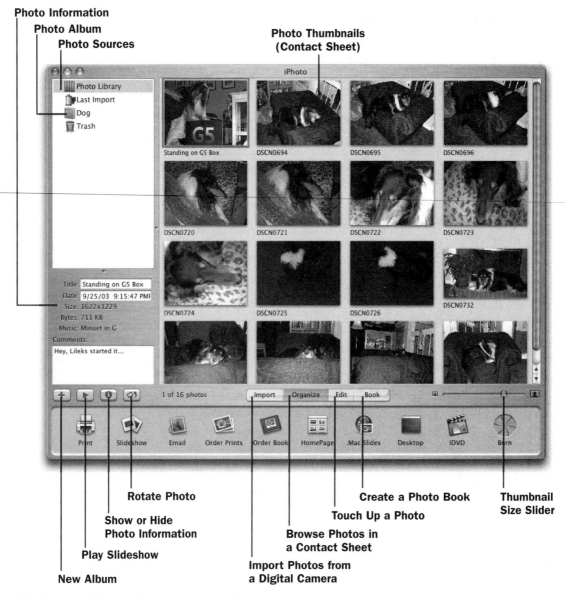

Rotate Photo

Show or Hide
Photo Information

Play Slideshow

New Album

Import Photos from
a Digital Camera

Browse Photos in
a Contact Sheet

Touch Up a Photo

Create a Photo Book

Thumbnail
Size Slider

iPhoto, the digital photographer's best friend.

Digital photography, as anybody who owns a digital camera knows, provides a great many benefits over traditional film photography. Not only do you get to take as many pictures as will fit on your camera's memory card, and delete bad pictures immediately after you take them instead of having to wait until they come back from the developer, but the camera can store all kinds of interesting information about each picture: the date and time when it was taken, the flash and shutter settings, even the model of camera that was used. After the photos have been downloaded to your computer, you can retouch them using your favorite graphics tools, instead of having to rely on the skills of the person at the photo lab. The only thing that digital photography is missing is a way to get the digital photographs onto nice heavy paper so that you can send them to your relatives. That's where iPhoto comes in.

iPhoto lets you view all the special information your camera associates with your pictures. It also revolutionizes the process of organizing your photos. You can scroll through them by *thumbnails* or by name, browse them by "film rolls" (each batch of photos you import from your camera is a "film roll"), assign descriptive names to them, and organize them into "albums" to group them by content or your own artistic pleasure.

When you double-click any photo in iPhoto, the image opens in **Edit** mode so that you can use iPhoto's built-in retouching tools. These tools are limited to cropping the photo, reducing red-eye, and several others that can reduce blemishes (the **Retouch** tool applies a soft blur effect to what you click), sharpen the contrast and color saturation (the **Enhance** button and **Brightness/Contrast** tools), or change the color photo to black-and-white.

You can assign a different editing program, such as Adobe Photoshop, to launch when you want to retouch a photo. Assign this third-party application by selecting the **Opens in other** option in the **iPhoto Preferences** window and then use the navigation screen that appears to find the retouching application you want to use.

When you crop, rotate, or edit photos in iPhoto, you aren't actually making any changes to the picture files themselves—iPhoto is merely changing how it displays them to you. If you export or share the photos, iPhoto applies your crops, rotations, and color processing to them in the process of exporting them. This allows you to revert back to the original state of any photo, exactly as it first left your camera, if you want to back out of your changes.

This technique is very similar to how iMovie operates—it keeps the original, unedited digital video clips in their pristine form and merely keeps track of pointers to the edits and rendered transitions you make so that

NOTE

Sometimes, when you open a photo in iPhoto's Edit mode, it first shows up looking blocky and low resolution; it takes a few seconds for it to resolve to the full-resolution picture. Give iPhoto a few seconds to display a picture properly when you open it in Edit mode.

EY TERM

Thumbnail—A small version of a picture, useful when you're browsing for the picture you want.

you can always revert to the original media. See **112** **About iMovie** for more about the digital video portion of the iLife suite.

When you're satisfied with how your photos look, iPhoto steps up to the plate by giving you a whole palette full of ways you can export or share them. These range from computerized methods for the tech-savvy—such as sending them by email, creating an online photo album on the Web, publishing them to your .Mac account so that others can use them as a slideshow, and burning them onto a CD or DVD—to methods that are much more familiar to traditional photographers: creating *contact sheets*, ordering prints on photographic paper, or creating a hardbound photo book that Apple prints and mails to you as a beautiful keepsake.

The sharing methods that iPhoto provides are listed here:

- The **File**, **Export** command lets you extract regular image files from iPhoto, which you can then process using whatever external tools you like. This option also lets you create a Web page full of thumbnails you can place in your **Sites** folder, or make a QuickTime slideshow of the selected photos.

- The **Print** option at the bottom of the iPhoto window lets you print your photos using a color or black-and-white printer, either one per sheet or in contact sheets.

- The **Slideshow** option allows you to display a group of photos in sequence, along with any selection of music you choose from your iTunes **Library**.

- The **Email** option opens a new email message with the selected photos in it, ready to address to an unsuspecting friend or relation.

- The **Order Prints** option allows you to place an order through Apple for professional photo prints of the selected photos, on whatever size paper you like. You must have a .Mac account (or a free Apple ID) to order prints online with this option.

- The **Order Book** option lets you place an order for a hardcover linen-bound coffee-table book, printed to your specifications for about $30—after you have composed a photo book using the **Book** editing tab.

- The **HomePage** option publishes the selected photos to a Web page on the .Mac service's servers, using any of the decorative templates and layouts provided by .Mac.

KEY TERM

Contact sheet—A group of thumbnail images gathered together onto a single sheet so that you can see them all at a glance.

- The **.Mac Slides** option lets you upload the selected photos as a slideshow that other .Mac users can subscribe to as a screensaver. They must enter your .Mac account name in the .Mac option in their **Desktop & Screen Saver Preferences** window.

- The **Desktop** option creates a selection of photos that are placed in your **Desktop Preferences** window (under the name **Screen Effects**), which you can then enable as a rotating Desktop background picture.

- The **iDVD** option (if you have a Mac equipped with a DVD-burning SuperDrive) adds the selected photos as a slideshow in your current iDVD project, or creates a new iDVD project containing the slideshow.

- The **Burn** option allows you to burn the selected photos to a CD or DVD.

The full range of iPhoto functionality is covered in *iLife in a Snap* (published by Sams Publishing). The next few tasks look at some of the highlights of iPhoto to get you started using your digital camera to its fullest potential.

106 Import Photos from a Digital Camera

When you plug a digital camera into your Mac, iPhoto launches automatically; you don't have to install any drivers. iPhoto goes into **Import** mode so that it can report how many photos you've taken and are stored on your camera, what kind of camera it is, and other such information. The **Import** button is the only thing you have to click to get your photos from your camera onto your computer and into your iPhoto **Library**.

● Connect Your Camera and Launch iPhoto

Plug your camera into your Mac using the USB cable that came with it. Most cameras connect directly to the computer—all you have to do is plug it in and turn it on, and then wait a few seconds for iPhoto to launch. Other kinds of cameras have a cradle that you rest the camera in and press a button to download the photos; with other cameras, you remove the memory card and put it in a USB card reader to download the photos from it. Consult the instruction manual for your camera to determine the appropriate way to connect your camera to the Mac.

See Also

→ **107** Create an iPhoto Album or Slideshow

→ **109** Order Photo Prints Online

1 Connect Your Camera and Launch iPhoto

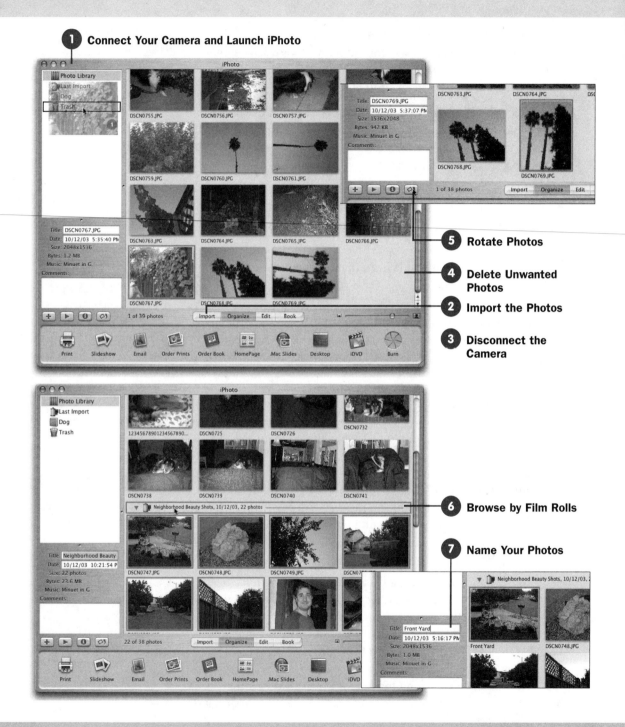

5 Rotate Photos

4 Delete Unwanted Photos

2 Import the Photos

3 Disconnect the Camera

6 Browse by Film Rolls

7 Name Your Photos

② Import the Photos

iPhoto launches as soon as it detects that the camera is connected and turned on. It switches to **Import** mode and reports the model of camera (if it can be determined) and how many photos are available to import.

Click the **Import** button to copy the photos from your camera into iPhoto.

③ Disconnect the Camera

As soon as iPhoto has completed importing the photos (it will beep to let you know it's done), you should disconnect the camera from your Mac. If you forget to do this, your camera's battery can waste away while you edit your pictures!

In most cases, when you plug a camera into your Mac, the camera (or its memory card) appears on the Mac's Desktop as an external disk. Before you simply unplug your camera from the USB cable, you should properly *unmount* this disk to make sure that there is no damage done to the memory card, the camera, or the Mac. Drag the icon representing the external disk (the camera) to the **Trash** or eject the camera "disk" using the **Eject** icon next to the camera "disk" in the Finder's sidebar. Then you can disconnect the USB cable.

④ Delete Unwanted Photos

Now that your camera is unplugged, you can edit your photos at your leisure. Scroll through the contact sheet in iPhoto's right pane to browse your newly imported photos. Use the **Thumbnail Size** slider to select a comfortable size for viewing the thumbnails.

Not all your photos will be masterpieces; it's best to admit that right away and delete the ones you aren't likely to show off to all your friends. Click any photo and press **Delete** or drag it to the Trash to delete it.

Select **Empty Trash** from the iPhoto **File** menu to permanently delete all the photos you have moved to the Trash. Until you empty the Trash, all photos in the Trash can be safely moved back into the iPhoto **Library** if you change your mind.

💡 TIP

If you enable the **Erase camera contents after transfer** check box, all the photos are deleted from your camera after iPhoto has finished importing them. This is the simplest way to keep your camera's memory card clean and ready for you to take more photos. If you want to leave the photos on the camera after importing them into iPhoto, disable the check box.

👆 NOTE

A key difference between USB (as is used on most digital cameras) and FireWire (as used on external hard disks and the iPod) is that FireWire is designed to carry enough electricity to power and charge devices such as iPod. USB connections provide enough power to run only very low-power devices such as mouse devices and keyboards. USB devices that rely on batteries for power are not recharged by a USB connection. Some variants of FireWire (such as Sony's iLink) do not carry any power at all, and devices such as camcorders that use unpowered FireWire cables can run out of battery power when connected, just as they can with USB.

By default, when you double-click a photo in **Organize** view, that photo appears in iPhoto's **Edit** view. To return to **Organize** view, click the **Organize** button below the thumbnails. You might find it less constraining to have iPhoto open the picture in a separate editing window instead of in Edit view in the main iPhoto window. Select **Opens in separate window** in the **iPhoto Preferences** window to set this as the default double-click behavior.

You can expand or collapse film rolls in the Photo **Library** view for easier browsing. If you don't want to see all the photos you've ever taken, you can collapse the film rolls you don't want by clicking the triangle icon next to each one.

Although the title for a photo can be just about as long as you want, certain exporting and sharing features—such as HomePage and the Photo Book—limit the **Title** field to only 20 or 40 characters. It's best to keep the name of each photo as short as possible while still being descriptive. If you want to add a longer description to a photo, such as notes about when and where it was taken or under what circumstances, click the **Photo Information** button (the *i* in a circle at the bottom of the left pane) repeatedly until the **Comments** field appears. Type whatever notes you want into this field.

5 Rotate Photos

Chances are that you will have taken some pictures with the camera in a vertical orientation. iPhoto lets you rotate any photo 90 degrees in either direction, repeatedly if necessary.

Select any photo and then click the **Rotate** button to rotate the photo 90 degrees counter-clockwise. To rotate the photo clockwise, hold down the **Option** key while you click.

6 Browse by Film Rolls

Normally, iPhoto keeps every photo you've ever taken in a single large Photo **Library** that you can scroll through visually. It can be useful for organizational purposes, however, to divide this huge mass of photos—as huge as it will inevitably become—on the basis of "film rolls," which is how iPhoto refers to a single imported batch of photos. Obviously there's no film involved in digital photography, but it does make sense to group your photos as though they *were* part of an actual developed film roll—of which the digital equivalent is a batch of photos downloaded at once from the camera.

Select **View**, **Film Rolls** to allow iPhoto to divide its Photo **Library** by film rolls. When you have done this, each film roll is delineated by a horizontal line and a "film roll" icon along with a generic name (such as **Roll 3**) and the date and time when the batch of photos was imported. Give a film roll a name by clicking the "film roll" icon and then typing a name in the **Title** field on the left side of the iPhoto window and press **Return**.

7 Name Your Photos

After you import them, each of your photos will have a nondescript, numeric name, such as **DSCN0724** (although this name varies depending on the manufacturer of your camera). Give your photos more descriptive names; this will be very helpful in the future when you order prints or create a photo book.

Click any photo to view its information in the pane on the left. Type a title for the selected photo in the **Title** field and press **Return** to set a name for the photo.

107 Create an iPhoto Album or Slideshow

iPhoto was designed to operate much in the same way that iTunes does—data sources in the pane on the left, media on the right, organized according to the intrinsic searching and sorting criteria in the media itself. Just as music in iTunes is organized by artist, album, and genre, photos in iPhoto are browsed by their thumbnails or by film roll. And just as you can create playlists of your favorite songs in iTunes so that you can play them back or burn onto a CD, in iPhoto you can create their equivalent: photo albums.

An album is like a playlist of pictures. You can drag as many photos as you want into an album, and you can sort them any way you want. An album can consist of photos from as many different film rolls as you want. This means you can create albums for landscape photography, family friends, holidays, Little League games, baby pictures—anything you fancy.

A photo album is also a convenient way to group photos for a slideshow. iPhoto allows you to start a slide presentation at any time, using the photos that are selected (if any) or all the photos in the current iPhoto window. You can start a slideshow using your entire Photo **Library** or by manually selecting the photos you want before starting the presentation. But the simplest way is to create a photo album containing just the photos you want to display, and then simply click the **Play Slideshow** button.

1 **Create a New Album**

Click the **New Album** button at the bottom of the left pane in the iPhoto window.

2 **Name the New Album**

In the **New Album** dialog box that appears, enter a name for the new album. Click **OK** to create the album in the left pane.

3 **Drag Photos into the Album**

Populate the album with photos from your Photo **Library**. Drag photos one by one to the album icon in the left pane; you can also select multiple pictures (press ⌘ or **Shift** while clicking), and drag them in groups to the album. This is much easier than using those little sticky-corner doodads, isn't it?

Before You Begin

✔ **50** Sign Up for .Mac

✔ **106** Import Photos from a Digital Camera

See Also

→ **110** Create an iPhoto Book

→ **111** Create an Online Photo Album

TIP

You can rename an album at any time by double-clicking its title, typing a new name, and pressing Return.

3 Drag Photos into the Album

2 Name the New Album

New Album

Please enter a name for the new Album:

Neighborhood

Cancel   OK

1 Create a New Album

4 Customize Slideshow Settings

Slideshow Settings

Slides

Play each slide for 2 ÷ seconds

☐ Display photos in random order

☑ Repeat slideshow

☑ Music

iTunes Library

Song	Artist	Time
Don't Turn Your Back	Blue ...Cult	4:08
Turn To Stone	Elect...stra	3:47
The Return of the King (1/16)	J.R....kien	1:12:57
The Return of the King (2/16)	J.R....kien	1:13:39
The Return of the King (3/16)	J.R....kien	1:13:57
The Return of the King (4/16)	J.R....kien	1:13:50
The Return of the King (5/16)	J.R....kien	1:10:24
The Return of the King (6/16)	J.R....kien	1:13:59
The Return of the King (7/16)	J.R....kien	1:13:30
The Return of the King (8/16)	J.R....kien	1:13:59
The Return of the King (9/16)	J.R....kien	1:13:49
The Return of the King (10/16)	J.R....kien	1:12:41
The Return of the King (11/16)	J.R....kien	1:13:57

turn   ⊗   15 of 145 items

Cancel   Save Settings   Play Slideshow

5 Play a Slideshow

4 **Customize Slideshow Settings**

Click the **Slideshow** button at the bottom of the iPhoto screen to display the **Slideshow Settings** dialog box. Here you can define the global settings for how any slideshow is played in iPhoto. After you save the settings in this dialog box and you click the **Play Slideshow** button with any group of photos selected, iPhoto will use these global settings to display the slideshow.

Specify how many seconds you want each photo to be displayed, whether you want the photos to be shown in a random order, and whether you want to repeat the presentation when it's done.

Your entire iTunes Library, as well as all your iTunes playlists, are shown under the **Music** heading. Select a song to use in the background while the slideshow is playing. You can preview any song by selecting it and clicking the **Play** button; you can also search for a specific song by typing part of its name in the **Search** box.

When you're satisfied with your global slideshow settings, click **Save Settings**. From now on, whenever you click the **Play Slideshow** button in iPhoto, the slideshow plays using these custom settings.

5 **Play a Slideshow**

Select an album, or several photos within an album. Click the **Play Slideshow** button at the bottom of the left pane in the iPhoto window. The screen fades to black, and then the slideshow begins, featuring all the selected photos or the entire album you're viewing.

Press **Escape** to quit the slideshow.

> **NOTE**
>
> When you add photos to an album, you're not actually moving the photos out of your **Library**—as with playlists in iTunes, you're just creating a list of references to pictures in your **Library**. The original picture remains in your **Library** so that you can add it to multiple albums if you want. You can't add the same photo multiple times to an album; if you're not sure whether or not you've added a photo into an album already, go ahead and drag it—it will just snap back into place if it's already in the album.

> **TIP**
>
> If you don't want any music to play along with your slideshow, disable the **Music** check box.

108 Print Photos

It's all well and good to have your photos in your computer so that you can browse them in iPhoto and show them off in slideshows. But something is missing from digital photography: the ability to hold a physical photograph in your hands, turn it around in the light, and look at it along with a stack of other photos you hold in your hand while you sit with a loved one on the couch.

Before You Begin

✔ **92** Add a New Printer

✔ **93** Configure Printer Options from Any Application

✔ **106** Import Photos from a Digital Camera

See Also

→ **109** Order Photo Prints Online

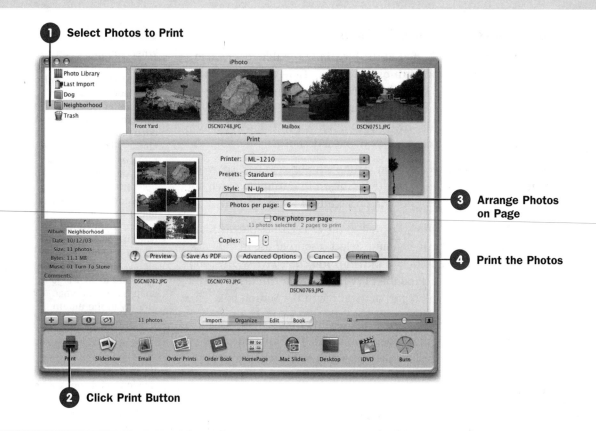

1 Select Photos to Print

3 Arrange Photos on Page

4 Print the Photos

2 Click Print Button

You might be one of those lucky souls who owns a photographic printer, one that can print digital images directly onto heavy photo paper. But even if you're not, you can make printouts of your photos that do a reasonably good job of re-creating the experience of physical photographs, without having to order any professional prints. All you need is a good inkjet or laser printer, preferably with color capability. iPhoto does the rest.

1 Select Photos to Print

Select a photo album or a group of photos in the Photo **Library**. If you don't select any photos, all the photos in the current view are printed. To select multiple photos, press ⌘ or **Shift** while clicking photo *thumbnails*.

2 Click Print Button

Click the **Print** button at the bottom of the iPhoto window. The **Print** dialog box opens, in which you define how you want your photos to be printed.

3 Arrange Photos on Page

iPhoto provides a number of useful ways to print your photos, all accessible using the **Style** drop-down list in the **Print** dialog box:

- **Contact Sheet.** Prints all the selected photos in a grid in thumbnail form. A slider lets you select how many photos are shown on a single page, and thus how many pages iPhoto has to print.

- **Full Page.** Uses the entire 8.5"×11" sheet size to print a single photo. A slider lets you define how wide the margins should be.

- **Greeting Card.** Prints each photo on a single page, using half the sheet so that the page can be folded over and a message written on the inside.

- **N-Up.** Lets you print a certain number of photos on each page. You can select anything from 2 to 16 photos per page, as well as whether iPhoto should print **One photo per page**— in other words, if there are six photos printed on each page, iPhoto will print six copies of the first photo on the first page, then six copies of the second photo on the second page, and so on.

- **Sampler.** Prints multiple photos on each page, in varying sizes according to which of two templates you select. You can also choose the **One photo per page** option with this mode.

- **Standard Prints.** Lets you select a standard print size, such as 4×6 inches or 8×10 inches, and prints the photos to match those sizes. Unless you enable the **One photo per page** check box, iPhoto prints the photos using as little paper as possible. **Standard Prints** mode is especially useful if you have a photo printer.

Select the printing options that match your needs. You can click the **Preview** button in the **Print** dialog box to open the sequence of printed pages in Preview.

NOTE

iPhoto automatically rotates each photo to maximize the useful space on the page. For instance, in **N-Up** mode, all photos are printed in either horizontal or vertical orientation, depending on how they fit best.

④ Print the Photos

Click the **Print** button in the **Print** dialog box or in the Preview window, and the print job will start.

109 Order Photo Prints Online

If you aren't satisfied with how your photos look when they come out of your inkjet printer, never fear—iPhoto isn't done closing the loop of digital photography yet. Apple has partnered with the Kodak Print Service, an online photo printing company, to take orders from iPhoto users and print their photos—exactly as they have digitally cropped, enhanced, and retouched them—and send them back in the mail. With today's fast shipping, you can have physical photographs on genuine photo paper in your hands in nearly as little time as it takes the drug store to process and return your film photos to you.

When you've finished retouching your photos and are ready to print them, use the **Order Prints** button at the bottom of the iPhoto window. After you sign in using an Apple ID (which you can obtain for free), you can specify exactly what kind of photo prints you want and how many of each. When you place your order, the high-resolution photos are processed by iPhoto and uploaded to the Kodak Print Service, where they are transferred to photographic paper and mailed back to you using the shipping service you specify. The end result is just like using film—except that you never have to leave your house!

① Select Photos to Order as Prints

Select a photo album or a group of photos in the **Photo Library**. If you don't select any photos, all the photos in the current view are included in the order form.

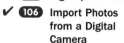

NOTE

You must be connected to the Internet before you can order photo prints. Also, the Kodak Print Service (and iPhoto's online ordering capability) is available only in the United States and Canada.

② Click Order Prints Button

Click the **Order Prints** button at the bottom of the iPhoto window in **Organize** mode. This brings up the **Order Prints** form, in which you specify how many of each photo you want printed, and at what sizes.

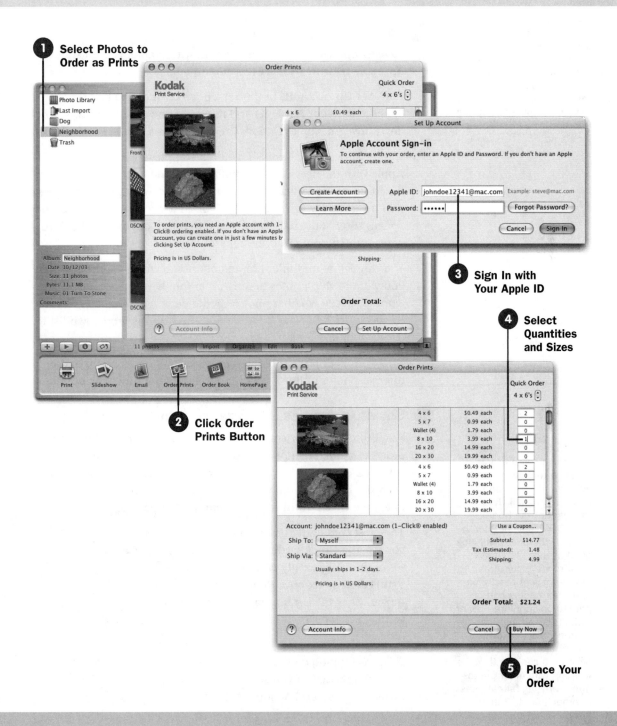

1 Select Photos to Order as Prints

2 Click Order Prints Button

3 Sign In with Your Apple ID

4 Select Quantities and Sizes

5 Place Your Order

TIP

If you have a .Mac account, you can use your **@mac.com** email address as your Apple ID. You might, however, have to fill in your shipping and billing information as prompted by iPhoto.

3 Sign In with Your Apple ID

To use Apple's online ordering system with iPhoto, you must have an Apple ID with 1-Click ordering turned on.

Click **Set Up Account**. In the **Set Up Account** dialog box that opens, enter your Apple ID and password and click **Sign In**. If you don't have an Apple ID, click **Create Account** to sign up for one.

A three-step process begins if you haven't previously provided Apple with the necessary shipping and billing information. Fill out the forms as requested. In the first screen, answer the security question associated with your Apple ID or .Mac account. On the second screen, enter your credit card billing information; and in the third, enter your shipping information.

You can define multiple shipping addresses, which can be useful if you want to ship photos to a friend or family member, or if you want to specify whether photos should be sent to you at work or at home. Select **Add New Address** from the **Address** drop-down list to define additional addresses.

After completing the three-step process, you are signed up and able to order photos online with a single click of the **Buy Now** button.

NOTE

If any of your selected photos are too small to print at a certain size or larger, a yellow triangular "warning" sign displays on the photo thumbnail. This means that the Kodak Print Service can't guarantee that the photo will look good at these large sizes. Most modern cameras have sufficient resolution that their photos can be printed on very large paper without becoming unacceptably blocky. However, low image resolution can become a concern if you're working with older photos from early digital cameras or other, low-resolution image sources.

4 Select Quantities and Sizes of Prints

Scroll through the pricing options for each of the photos in your order selection. Each photo is available in any of six sizes, ranging from wallet-sized up through poster-sized. Enter the quantities of each size of each photo you want to order; with each number you enter, the **Order Total** price is dynamically updated.

The most commonly ordered photo print size is 4×6 inches. You can use the **Quick Order** button to request copies of all your photos at that size; simply click the **Up** arrow at the top of the **Order Prints** dialog box once to request one copy of each photo at 4×6 inches. Click the **Up** button again for each additional copy you want. Click the **Down** arrow to reduce the number of copies ordered.

Select a shipping destination and a shipping method from the menus at the left. If you select **Express** shipping, the **Order Total** is increased by several dollars.

5 **Place Your Order**

When you're satisfied with your order, click **Buy Now**; the order is placed, your photos are uploaded to the Kodak Print Service (this might take several minutes, depending on the speed of your connection), and your credit card is charged. You will receive your photos in a few days, depending on the shipping method you selected.

110 Create an iPhoto Book

Apple's not content with making digital photography merely the equal of film photography; they had to come up with something additional, some feature that was compelling in its own right, that was possible only with digital photography and iPhoto. That feature is the iPhoto Book.

Using iPhoto, you can take any selection of photos and compose them into a book. This book can take on any of a number of different styles (or "themes"), and you can lay out the photos on the pages according to various different artistic schemes. The books include text derived from the **Title** and **Comments** fields on each photo in iPhoto, and you can adjust the text until you've got a professional-looking sequence of pages just the way you want them to look. Finally, with a couple of clicks, you can send these pages to Apple, where the book will be professionally printed and bound in hardcover, printed on acid-free glossy paper with a linen binding and a cover color that you choose. This book is then delivered to you using the shipping information defined in your Apple ID account. The whole process costs no more than $30 or $40, depending on the shipping options you choose, or if you use more than the baseline ten pages.

1 **Select an Album to Make into a Book**

To make a book, you must first select an album. Click any album in the left pane of the iPhoto window to select the photos you want to turn into a book.

2 **Choose a Book Style**

Click the **Book** button under the right pane to switch iPhoto into **Book** mode.

Before You Begin

✔ **50** Sign Up for .Mac

✔ **106** Import Photos from a Digital Camera

✔ **107** Create an iPhoto Album or Slideshow

See Also

→ **111** Create an Online Photo Album

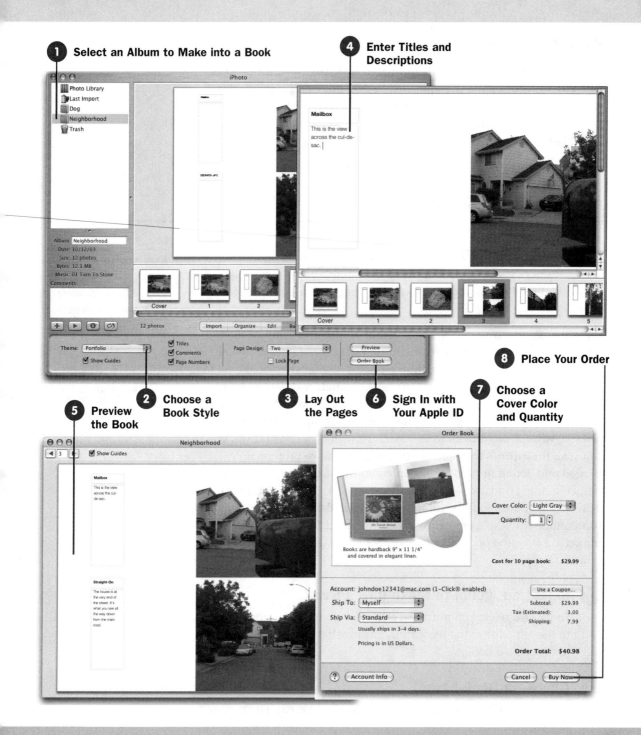

1 Select an Album to Make into a Book

4 Enter Titles and Descriptions

5 Preview the Book

2 Choose a Book Style

3 Lay Out the Pages

6 Sign In with Your Apple ID

7 Choose a Cover Color and Quantity

8 Place Your Order

From the **Theme** drop-down list, choose a layout style for your book. Click each of the options in turn to see what each style looks like. The **Story Book** theme, for instance, uses rotation and overlaps to create a "fun" theme; whereas **Classic** and **Portfolio** create dignified, elegant layouts maximizing the use of the paper. **Picture Book** uses full-bleed printing to extend the photos to the very edges of the pages, and has no text. Pick the style that best matches the kind of book you want to create.

③ Lay Out the Pages

The first photo in your selected album is used for the cover of the book. If you want this photo to appear in the interior of the book as well, select the first photo and choose **Duplicate** from the **File** menu. A copy of the photo appears at the end of the album; drag the copy to wherever in the album sequence you want it to appear.

Next comes the pleasantly absorbing task of deciding which photos to place on which pages, and how many photos should be displayed on each page. Use the **Page Design** drop-down menu to select what kind of layout each page should have. Work from the first page onward; as you finish getting each page into the layout you want, click **Lock Page** to prevent that page from being reformatted as you edit the layout of other pages.

④ Enter Titles and Descriptions

Most book styles provide areas for you to enter titles, comments, and page numbers. The titles and comments come from the contents of those fields on each of the pictures in the **Organize** view; now do you see why it was a good idea to assign titles and comments to all your photos?

You can change the titles and comments for each of your pictures in **Book** view. Click a **Title** or **Comments** field on any of the layout pages; iPhoto zooms in to allow you to type in those fields. Click any area of white space to zoom back out to the layout view.

⑤ Preview the Book

When you're done composing your book, click the **Preview** button at the bottom-right of the iPhoto window. This brings up a viewer window that lets you page through the book, screen by screen, to

TIP

If you want to rearrange the order in which the photos are presented in the book, go back to **Organize** view; rearrange the photos in the album you're using until they're in the right order. The settings for your book are preserved, so if you click the **Book** button to return to **Book** view, you'll be right back where you left your book—only the order of the pictures will be changed.

NOTE

If you change the titles or comments on pictures in **Book** view, those fields are updated in **Organize** view as well.

see just how it will look. Click the green **Zoom** button in the title bar to maximize the preview window, to get the most detail possible.

6 Sign In with Your Apple ID

Click the **Order Book** button at the bottom of the window. Your book is assembled digitally into an uploadable package, which can take a few moments; then you are presented with an order form screen, similar to the one you get when you order photo prints.

To order a book, you must have an Apple ID with 1-Click ordering turned on. If you have not set up an Apple ID account, refer to **109** **Order Photo Prints Online** for the procedure for setting up your account and billing information.

7 Choose a Cover Color and Quantity

You can select from four different cover colors: black, burgundy, light gray, or navy. The preview image shows you what the book will look like in each color.

Use the **Up** and **Down** arrows next to the **Quantity** field to select how many copies of the book you want to order. The **Order Total** price is updated dynamically as you adjust the **Quantity** field. Select the shipping destination and method from the menus at left; if you select **Express** shipping, it will cost a few dollars extra.

8 Place Your Order

Click **Buy Now** when you're ready to order your book. The image data is uploaded to the server; this might take a few moments, depending on the speed of your connection. Your credit card is charged, and the book will be delivered to your shipping address in a few days.

111 Create an Online Photo Album

The synthesis of digital and traditional photography comes in the ability of iPhoto to take your photos and transform them instantly into an online album that everybody can view, no matter where they are. With an online album in the form of a Web page, your photos can reach all your friends and family in the comfort of their own desks or laptops; you don't have to show them a slideshow in iPhoto, nor do you have to physically send them photographs in an envelope. All you have to do is email them a URL.

To create a HomePage photo album, you must have a .Mac account. Use the **.Mac Preferences** window to sign up for a .Mac account if you don't have one (see **50** **Sign Up for .Mac**) or to enter your .Mac account information if you have already signed up.

Before You Begin

✔ **50** Sign Up for .Mac

✔ **106** Import Photos from a Digital Camera

✔ **110** Create an iPhoto Book

See Also

→ **51** Share a Slideshow Screensaver

→ **52** Create a .Mac Web Page

1 Select a Group of Photos to Publish

Select a group of photos, either in the main **Photo Library** or in an album; if you don't select any photos, the HomePage function uses all the photos in the current view. Be careful—if you have hundreds of photos in your **Photo Library**, you could end up publishing a photo album page with hundreds of pictures on it!

For best results, try to keep your album limited to 20 or 30 pictures at most.

2 Click the HomePage Button

Click the **HomePage** button at the bottom of the iPhoto window. This brings up the **Publish HomePage** dialog box in which you can configure your online album page before uploading it to your .Mac account.

3 Enter Titles and Descriptions

The album page provides several editable text fields—the title at the top, a block of descriptive text for the whole page, and titles for each of the pictures on the page. Click to edit each field, being careful to keep the text limited to the size that iPhoto enforces. The descriptive text field for the entire page, for example, can be no more than 150 characters in length.

🖍 **NOTE**

You must be connected to the Internet to create an online album.

1 Select a Group of Photos to Publish

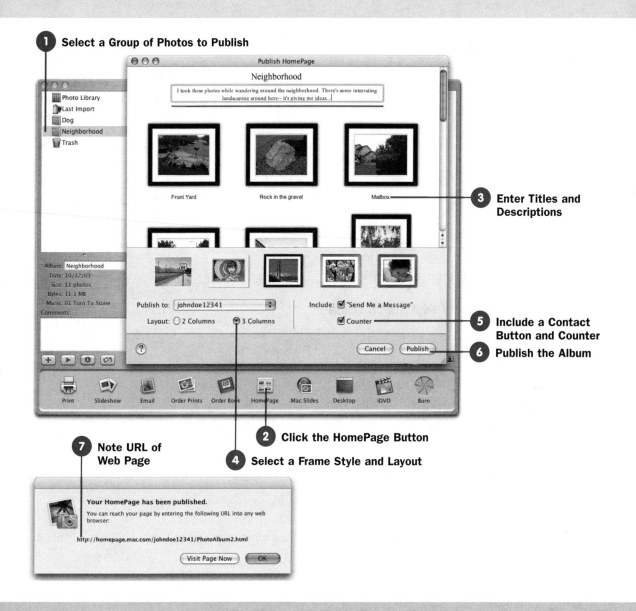

3 Enter Titles and Descriptions

5 Include a Contact Button and Counter

6 Publish the Album

7 Note URL of Web Page

2 Click the HomePage Button

4 Select a Frame Style and Layout

4 Select a Frame Style and Layout

In the pane at the bottom of the **Publish HomePage** dialog box, click any of the five frame styles to choose a theme for the page. Each of the frames changes the font to a common typeface appropriate to the page style.

Use the radio buttons to choose whether the page should have two or three columns of pictures.

⑤ Include a Contact Button and Counter

Apple provides a couple of useful options you can enable if you want: a **Send Me a Message** button, which people can use to contact you by email; and a page **Counter**, which lets you keep track of how many people have viewed your page. Enable one or both of these check boxes.

⑥ Publish the Album

When you're done fixing the page the way you want it, click **Publish**. The pictures are scaled down appropriately and thumbnails are created; the images and the Web page are then uploaded to the .Mac server.

⑦ Note the URL of the Web Page

When the album has uploaded successfully, iPhoto reports to you the URL for the online album. Copy this URL into an email message so that you can send it to all your friends and family!

TIP

.Mac's **HomePage** function provides many more themes than what is available in iPhoto. If you want, you can visit the .Mac Web site (**http://www.mac. com**) and log in to edit the iPhoto online album, which is listed among your other HomePage pages. Select one of the other themes available through .Mac to spruce up your album page even more.

⑪⑫ About iMovie

A major plank in Apple's digital hub platform is the company's commitment to digital video (DV) editing—giving everyday people the ability to import the video they shoot with a common DV camcorder into their computers and edit it into a movie with just a few easily understood procedures. iMovie is the free digital video editing application that comes bundled with every Mac. Although its feature set is quite limited compared to the professional-level editing suites the big-time studios use (such as Adobe Premiere and Final Cut Pro), iMovie is designed to give you the features you need to turn your raw footage into the kind of finished product you want with an absolute minimum of hassle and confusion.

The process for creating a movie in iMovie usually follows a fairly standard pattern: First you import your footage; then you arrange your clips in the order you want them, cutting out the parts you don't want; then you add transitions between clips, digital effects, a soundtrack, and

See Also

→ ⑪⑬ Import Digital Video Footage into iMovie

→ ⑪⑱ Export the Movie to Videotape or QuickTime

overlaid titles. Finally you export the movie to a QuickTime file you can
send to all your friends, whether they're using Windows machines or
Macs. If you prefer, you can export the movie back to videotape so that
you can play it back on a TV—or transfer it to the iDVD application so
that you can burn it to a DVD for your family and friends to enjoy.

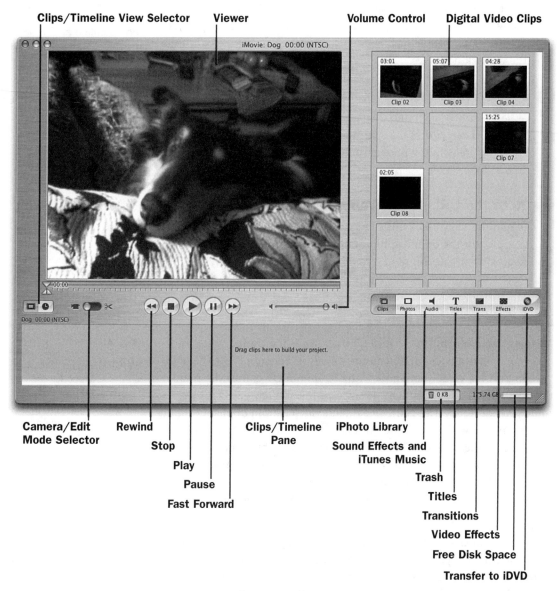

The iMovie application lets you create a movie using digital video clips, add transitions between
clips, and add a soundtrack.

iMovie operates in one of two modes: Camera mode or Edit mode, selectable using the blue switch below the viewer window. When you connect a digital camcorder, iMovie is in Camera mode; you can use the playback control buttons in iMovie to control your camera through the FireWire interface, rewinding and fast-forwarding until you're at the right spot where you want to begin importing your video data.

As you import the video data from the tape, iMovie stores each individual clip—each time you pressed the Record button—as a separate piece of video in the Clips palette. You don't have to worry about splitting apart all your different "takes" so you can edit them together; iMovie knows where each recording break occurs, what time it happened, and how long it is. All you have to do is switch to Edit mode, and then take each of the clips and drag it into the Timeline pane, arranging them until they fit your directorial vision. Then you can spruce them up by adding transitions, titles, video effects, and a soundtrack. Finally, you can save (or "export") the movie in any of dozens of different formats—including, if you have a Mac equipped with a DVD-burning SuperDrive, a DVD project that appears ready-to-edit in iDVD.

iMovie is a rudimentary application as digital video editing tools go; but it's a true "lossless" video editor, as are the best professional tools—meaning that as you make your edits to the video, applying effects and transitions and leaving heaps of bits and bytes on the virtual cutting-room floor, you're not actually making any changes to the imported digital video files at all. Effects and transitions are rendered as new video clips, and iMovie simply keeps track of when to show each clip during playback and export, rather than modifying each clip on the disk and showing them all linearly (as some video editing applications do). This feature allows you to back out any changes you make, returning to the original, pristine video source exactly as it came off your camera, any time you like. This kind of lossless operation is what makes digital video editing so attractive even for seasoned film veterans—it's hard not to like a system where you can instantly cover up a bad directing decision!

The only downside to digital video editing is that it eats up tons of hard disk space. An hour of digital video, for example, takes up 13.3 gigabytes of space—the equivalent of 2,500 songs in iTunes, or 10,000 full-resolution digital photos. Make sure that you have plenty of empty storage on your hard disk before beginning an ambitious iMovie project; if you have an older Mac with a small hard disk, you might want to invest in a new disk (if one can be installed) as scratch space for your iMovie projects. Armed with a digital camcorder and iMovie, soon you'll be turning your daily exploits into QuickTime movies you can email to all your friends or post on the Web for the whole world to see. The digital filmmaking revolution has begun—so don't be left behind!

113 Import Digital Video Footage into iMovie

See Also

→ **19** Add a Newly Installed Hard Disk to the System

→ **114** Arrange Video Clips in the Timeline

Naturally, the real first step in making a digital home movie is to actually take the footage, using any camcorder that can record to digital video tape (MiniDV is the standard format) and connect to the computer using FireWire. (If the camera claims to connect using iLink or IEEE 1394, those are both equivalent to FireWire, although you might have to get a FireWire cable that changes from six pins at one end to four pins at the other, where there are no power pins.)

After you have your equipment and your footage, however, the next step—getting the footage into your computer—is a hands-off and straightforward procedure. Just plug in the camera, find where your footage starts, and click **Import**.

1 Launch iMovie

Click the **iMovie** icon in the Dock to open the program; alternatively, navigate to the **Applications** folder and launch iMovie from there.

2 Create a New Project

If this is the first time you have run iMovie, the program prompts you to either open an existing project or create a new one. Click the **Create Project** button.

If you have used iMovie before, the application will launch using the project you were most recently working on. To create a new project, select **New Project** from the **File** menu.

In the sheet that appears, type a name for the new movie project (which will automatically be created in your **Movies** folder). This name is used only as an identifier, as the name of the folder where the movie is stored while you work on it. This doesn't have to be a title suitable for the Sundance Festival. Click **Save** to begin your project.

TIP

iMovie operates best when it can occupy the entire window. If the iMovie window overlaps under the Dock, click the green **Zoom** button in the title bar to resize it automatically to the available screen space; if you prefer, you can instead hide the Dock so that iMovie can use the space otherwise occupied by the Dock.

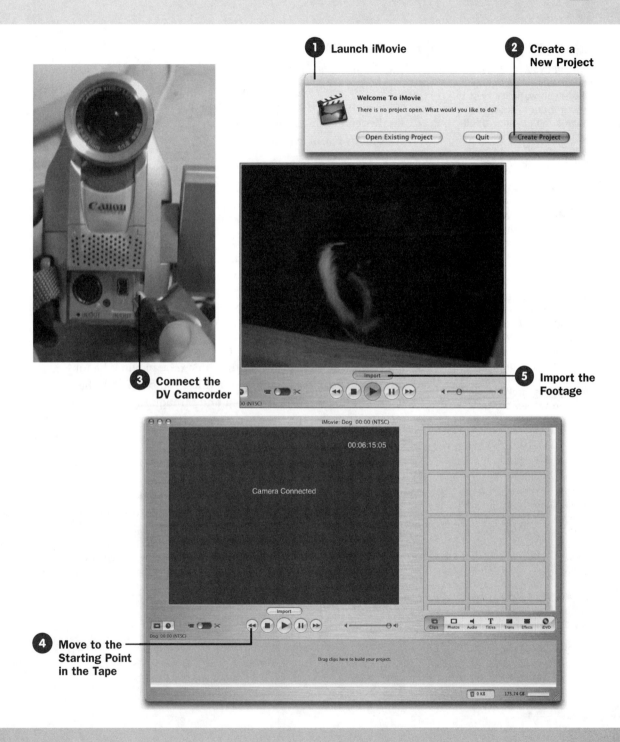

1 Launch iMovie

2 Create a New Project

Welcome To iMovie
There is no project open. What would you like to do?

Open Existing Project   Quit   Create Project

3 Connect the DV Camcorder

5 Import the Footage

iMovie: Dog 00:00 (NTSC)

00:06:15:05

Camera Connected

Import

Clips Photos Audio Titles Trans Effects iDVD

4 Move to the Starting Point in the Tape

Drag clips here to build your project.

0 KB   175.74 GB

3 Connect the DV Camcorder

Your digital video (DV) camcorder probably came with a FireWire cable (also referred to as i-Link for Sony devices, or IEEE 1394); this cable allows you to connect the camera to your Mac. Connect the smaller end to the camera's DV port, and the larger end to one of your Mac's FireWire ports.

Turn the camera to **Play** (or **VCR**) mode. iMovie switches to Camera mode and reports **Camera Connected** in the blue viewscreen.

4 Move to the Starting Point in the Tape

Use the iMovie controls (or your camera's own controls) to move the tape to the position where you want to start importing—where the important footage begins.

5 Import the Footage

Click the **Import** button under the main viewscreen. iMovie starts importing video footage from the camera by playing the tape through the camera's FireWire interface. You can watch the footage in the iMovie viewscreen and through the camcorder's viewfinder as it is imported.

DV camcorders record their footage in distinct "clips," or recorded scenes, each one corresponding to a time when the **Record** button was pressed on the camera. Each clip is marked digitally on the tape exactly where it begins and ends; as iMovie imports the footage, it stores each distinct clip in a separate slot in the **Clips** pane.

When you're done importing video (for instance, when there's no more recorded footage on the tape that you want to import), stop importing by clicking the **Import** or **Play** button in iMovie. The camera stops playing.

114 Arrange Video Clips in the Timeline

After you've imported your footage, you can go ahead and disconnect the camcorder from your Mac—you won't need it anymore. The video clips you'll be working with are all laid out in the **Clips** pane on the right side of the iMovie window. You'll be trimming these clips down to the proper size and arranging them into the right order in the **Timeline** pane at the bottom of the screen.

Each video clip is stored in uncompressed DV format in the **Media** folder within the folder you created when you first began your iMovie project. When you edit a clip by trimming it or splitting it into separate clips, the underlying DV files aren't actually modified; instead, iMovie keeps track of all the edits by pointing to specific points within the raw video files. Similarly, video effects, titles, and transitions you apply to your clips are rendered as new raw video clips and saved as separate media files, spliced into your Timeline at the appropriate points. This means that you can always back out any edit you make, or restore your video footage to its original pristine state, just as it came out of the camera.

1 Switch to Edit Mode

Use the **Camera/Edit Mode** selector (the blue toggle switch under the viewer window) to put iMovie into **Edit** mode, where the central controls no longer control the camcorder, but rather control the playback of the movie project itself.

2 Review a Clip

Click any clip in the **Clips** pane. The clip appears in the viewscreen, with an active scrub bar underneath it; use the **Play** button to play and pause the clip, the **Volume** slider to adjust the sound output level, and the playhead (the blue downward-pointing arrow on the scrub bar) to move manually back and forth through the footage.

3 Drag a Clip to the Timeline

Click and drag any clip from the **Clips** pane into the **Timeline** pane. Putting a clip on the Timeline makes the clip part of the main movie sequence. The clip is *moved* from the **Clips** pane rather than copied; each clip can exist in only one place: in the Clips pane or in the Timeline. (To create a duplicate of a clip, hold down the **Option** key as you drag the clip to an empty slot in the **Clips** pane.)

Before You Begin

✔ **113** Import Digital Video Footage into iMovie

See Also

→ **117** Add a Soundtrack

→ **118** Export the Movie to Videotape or QuickTime

TIP

To better keep track of them, you can give names to all of your video clips. Simply click the automatically assigned label in a clip (such as **Clip 03**) in the **Clips** pane or in the Timeline and type a more descriptive name. Press **Return** to assign the name.

NOTE

The **Volume** slider controls the level of the sound that goes to your speakers while you're working in iMovie; it has no effect on the sound levels recorded within the clips themselves. In **117** Add a Soundtrack, you will see how to adjust the actual sound levels of clips within the movie project.

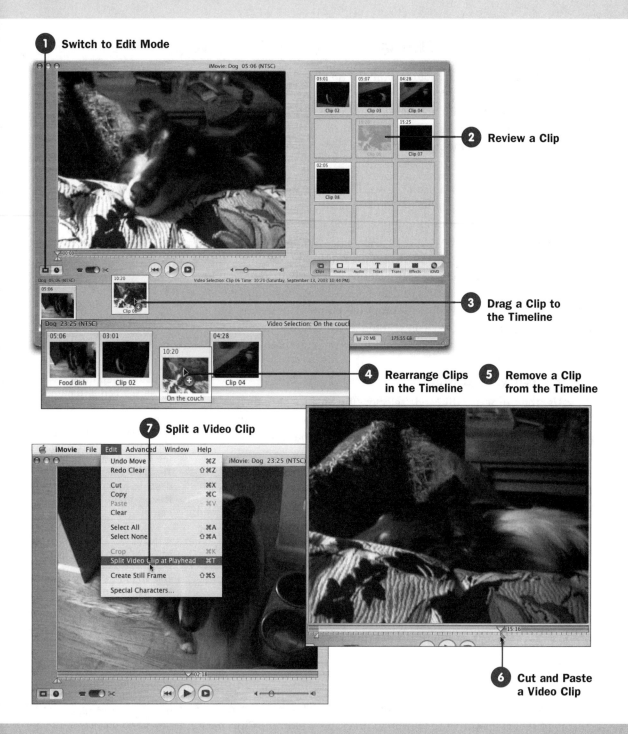

1 Switch to Edit Mode

iMovie: Dog 05:06 (NTSC)

03:01 Clip 02
05:07 Clip 03
04:28 Clip 04

Clip 06
15:25 Clip 07

2 Review a Clip

02:05 Clip 08

Dog 05:06 (NTSC)   Video Selection: Clip 06 Time: 10:20 (Saturday, September 13, 2003 10:44 PM)

05:06

10:20 Clip 06

3 Drag a Clip to the Timeline

Dog 23:25 (NTSC)   Video Selection: On the couch

05:06 Food dish
03:01 Clip 02
10:20 On the couch
04:28 Clip 04

4 Rearrange Clips in the Timeline

5 Remove a Clip from the Timeline

7 Split a Video Clip

iMovie File Edit Advanced Window Help

iMovie: Dog 23:25 (NTSC)

Undo Move   ⌘Z
Redo Clear   ⇧⌘Z

Cut   ⌘X
Copy   ⌘C
Paste   ⌘V
Clear

Select All   ⌘A
Select None   ⇧⌘A

Crop   ⌘K
Split Video Clip at Playhead ⌘T

Create Still Frame ⇧⌘S

Special Characters...

15:16

6 Cut and Paste a Video Clip

02:18

④ Rearrange Clips in the Timeline

After you have dragged all the desired clips into the **Timeline**, you can rearrange them if they're not in the right order. Simply click the clip you want to move and drag it into the right position.

⑤ Remove a Clip from the Timeline

To remove a clip from your project, drag it from the **Timeline** back into the **Clips** pane. Make sure that the **Timeline** is in Clips mode before you drag the clip to an empty slot in the **Clips** pane.

Video clips you remove from the Timeline are not deleted; they can always be reused if you change your mind later. If you want to delete a clip permanently (for instance, if you're sure that you won't use the clip's contents and you want to recover the disk space it takes up), drag it to the Trash at the bottom of the iMovie screen or select the clip and press **Delete**. The amount of data in the Trash is reflected next to the **Trash** icon. This disk space is not freed, however, until you click the **Trash** icon to tell iMovie to empty the Trash, or you select **File**, **Empty Trash**.

Because of the way the original video clips are kept pristine while iMovie keeps track of pointers within the raw clips, if you empty the Trash, you will no longer be able to undo any of the post-processing actions (effects, titles, transitions, and so on) that you have done up to that point. You will also no longer be able to restore the original media for clips moved to the Trash. Be sure that you're happy with your progress so far before emptying the Trash!

⑥ Cut and Paste a Video Clip

Under the scrub bar are two upward-facing playhead markers. Use these to define a selection area in the current clip or the complete timeline; drag the left marker to the beginning of the selection, and drag the right marker to the end of the selection. The selected portion changes to a yellow color. You can then select **Cut**, **Copy**, or **Clear** from the **Edit** menu to trim the selection out of the clip or copy it to the Clipboard, as you would with text. You can then move the playhead anywhere in the Timeline and select **Edit**, **Paste**, which will create a new clip with the cut or copied video inserted at the playhead.

NOTE

You can only rearrange clips when the Timeline is in Clips mode, as selected by the **Clips/Timeline View Selector** buttons (indicated by a "film clip" rectangle and a "time" circle) at the far left. If you're in Timing mode, each clip is shown to scale based on its length; clicking and dragging a clip in Timeline mode only creates black space between clips—it won't rearrange clips.

TIP

If you're viewing a single clip (or several consecutive clips, selected by holding down ⌘ while clicking), you can switch to viewing the entire movie project by clicking anywhere in a blank part of the Timeline or on any inactive part of the iMovie window.

7 **Split a Video Clip**

You might often find it useful to split a video clip into two parts; this allows you to create "cut-away" scenes by inserting new clips into the middle of existing ones, or to define the length of a digital effect you want to apply.

When viewing a clip or the whole Timeline, move the playhead to the point where you want to create the division and choose **Edit**, **Split Video Clip at Playhead** to divide the clip in two. You can then move the clips around separately.

Use the left and right arrow keys on your keyboard to move the playhead back and forth one frame at a time. Remember that in DV footage, there are 29.97 frames per second; the numbers next to the playhead show you which second and which frame you're looking at.

115 Add Transitions and Video Effects

Before You Begin

✔ **113** Import Digital Video Footage into iMovie

✔ **114** Arrange Video Clips in the Timeline

See Also

→ **116** Add a Still Photo

→ **117** Add a Soundtrack

🔍 **KEY TERM**

Transition—A video effect that softens the visual jump from one clip to the next, by using wipes, dissolves, fades, and so on.

iMovie comes with a number of digital video effects you can apply to your clips. The video effects range from simple color adjustments to intricate and flashy Hollywood effects such as **Fairy Dust**, **Electricity**, and **Rain**. An effect can be added to any clip or selection; simply trim the clip to the right length, select the effect you want, adjust it to your liking, and apply it. Effects that once would have cost millions on the silver screen can now be a part of your home movies for free.

Transitions are video effects that allow you to soften the jump from one clip to another, as well as to add an artistic flair to the progress and composition of the movie. Some types of transitions (such as a **Cross Dissolve**) let you suggest a passage of time within a scene; others (such as **Circle Closing** or **Push**) let you exaggerate a jump from one scene to the next; still others (such as **Fade In/Out** and **Wash In/Out**) let you mark major beginning and ending points in the movie.

To create a transition, you need only select the kind of transition you want, define a couple of parameters for how it should look, and then drag it into place between the two clips you want to connect.

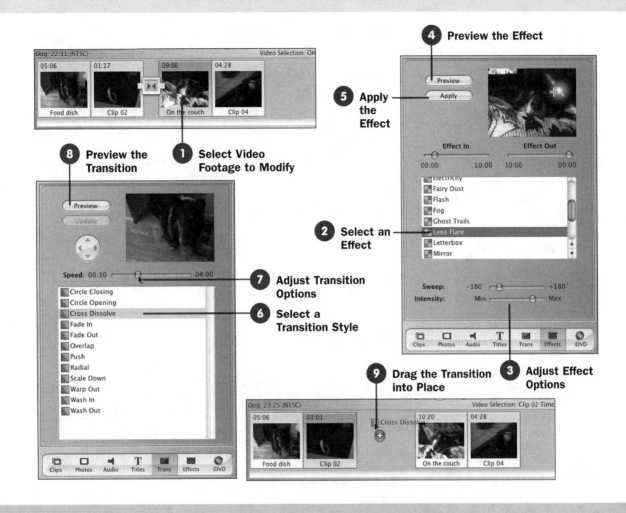

① Select the Video Footage to Modify

A video effect can be applied to an entire clip or to a selected piece of a clip. Click a clip in the **Timeline** to apply the effect to the entire clip; drag the selection markers in the scrub bar to define the footage (indicated in yellow between the markers) you want to modify.

② Select an Effect

Click the **Effects** button under the right pane in the iMovie screen to open the **Effects** pane. Select an effect style from the list. The Preview window at the top right shows you how the effect will look.

③ Adjust Effect Options

Different types of effects have different kinds of options you can set. The **Black & White** effect, for instance, allows you to set only how quickly or slowly the effect should fade in and out (from instantly up to ten seconds). But the **Fog** effect is more complex; it also lets you specify how much fog to show, which direction the "wind" should push it, and how bright it should be. The **Fairy Dust** and **Electricity** effects even allow you to click in the Preview window to select visually where the effect should focus.

④ Preview the Effect

Click the **Preview** button to create a quick-and-dirty preview of the effect in the main iMovie viewscreen. This preview will be choppy and uneven compared to the final, fully rendered effect because it's being created in real time; but it will give you an idea of what the effect will look like when it's done.

⑤ Apply the Effect

When you're satisfied with how the effect looks, click the **Apply** button to apply it to the selected footage. A small red progress bar appears in the **Timeline** underneath the clip, which becomes split from its parent clip if necessary; this progress bar shows you iMovie's progress in rendering the effect. You can play the movie and continue with your work while the effect is rendering, but until the red progress bar has disappeared, you won't be able to see the effect in its final smooth form.

⑥ Select a Transition Style

To adjust the visual sense of how one clip changes into another, you must create a transition. Click the **Trans** button under the right pane on the iMovie window to open the **Transitions** pane. Select a transition style from the list. The Preview window at the top right shows you how the transition will look.

NOTE

If you are applying an effect to a clip that has a transition at its beginning or end, iMovie must rerender the transition to make it blend in smoothly with the new video effect. Click **OK** on the confirmation dialog box that pops up to allow iMovie to do this.

TIP

You can apply multiple effects on top of each other. To layer the **Sepia Tone** and **Aged Film** effects together, for instance, first apply one effect then do the same with the other. Each effect is rendered internally as a new piece of raw footage, spliced into the movie project seamlessly by iMovie. You can revert back to the original footage by selecting any clip to which you've applied an effect and selecting **Restore Clip** from the **Advanced** menu.

The Preview window shows how the transition will look when transitioning to the first clip selected in the Timeline. If no clips are selected (if you're viewing the entire project in the viewscreen), the Preview window shows a transition between the last two clips in the Timeline.

7 Adjust the Transition Options

Different types of transitions have different kinds of options you can set. The **Cross Dissolve** transition, for instance, allows you to set only how fast or slow the transition should be (from ten frames to four seconds). The **Push** transition is more complex—it lets you select the direction in which the "push" effect should move.

8 Preview the Transition

Click the **Preview** button to create a quick-and-dirty preview of the transition in the main iMovie viewscreen. This preview will be choppy and uneven compared to the final, fully rendered transition because it's being created in real time; but it will give you an idea of how the transition will look when it's done.

9 Drag the Transition into Place

When you're satisfied with how the transition looks, click the transition's name or icon in the transition list and drag it into the Timeline between the two clips you want to join. The transition will appear as a "ligature" between the two clips, with a small red progress bar underneath. The progress bar shows you iMovie's progress in rendering the transition. You can play the movie and continue with your work while the transition is rendering, but until the red progress bar disappears, you won't be able to see the transition in its final smooth form.

To remove a transition, simply click to select it and then press **Delete**. The joined clips are immediately restored to their original states.

TIPS

Be aware that when you add a transition, the overall length of the movie is reduced by the configured length of the transition. The transition works by overlapping the two clips so that one fades out while the other fades in. The two clips share the length of time that the transition takes, so that length is cut from the movie's overall length.

You can make changes to a transition after it's been created. Click the transition in the Timeline; in the **Transitions** pane, make the changes you want to the options and click **Update** to re-render the transition.

116 Add a Still Photo

Before You Begin

✔ **106** Import Photos from a Digital Camera

✔ **113** Import Digital Video Footage into iMovie

✔ **114** Arrange Video Clips in the Timeline

See Also

→ **117** Add a Soundtrack

→ **118** Export the Movie to Videotape or QuickTime

 TIP

Use the drop-down menu to select the iPhoto source; you can browse either your complete iPhoto **Photo Library** or any of the albums you have created in iPhoto. The source drop-down list can make it much easier to find the picture you're looking for.

iMovie integrates with iPhoto to allow you to include your photos in your movie—either by including a simple still-frame for a few seconds, or by using the **Ken Burns Effect** (named for the PBS documentarian who used the technique with such success in bringing old Civil War photos to life) to pan and zoom across the picture. All the photos you have imported into iPhoto are immediately available for you to use, accessible from the **Photos** pane in iMovie.

1 Switch to the Photos Pane

Click the **Photos** button under the right pane of the iMovie window to open the **Photos** pane.

2 Select a Photo from iPhoto

Your iPhoto **Photo Library** is shown in the browser panel, with scrollbars that allow you to browse through the thumbnails of all your pictures. Select the photo you want to add to your movie.

3 Select the Duration and Zoom Level

Above the photo browser window are two sliders that allow you to specify how long the photo should appear (in seconds), and how far in the image should be zoomed (in magnification multiples). Use the sliders or enter the numbers manually.

4 Pan and Zoom with the Ken Burns Effect

If you enable the **Ken Burns Effect** check box, you can have iMovie pan across the photo, changing its zoom level as it goes. First select **Start** or **Finish** to specify which end of the effect you want to define; then click and drag the photo in the Preview window to the position where you want the effect to begin or end. Use the **Zoom** slider to set the zoom level at the start and finish of the effect. The **Reverse** button is a handy way to swap the beginning and end behaviors you've specified.

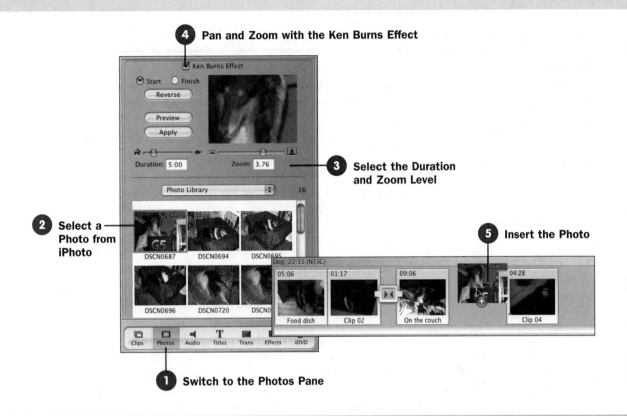

4 Pan and Zoom with the Ken Burns Effect

3 Select the Duration and Zoom Level

2 Select a Photo from iPhoto

5 Insert the Photo

1 Switch to the Photos Pane

5 Insert the Photo

If you're using the **Ken Burns Effect**, click **Apply** to insert the photo into the iMovie Timeline; the photo is rendered into a new clip of its own at the end of your project. You can then drag the new clip to the proper position in the Timeline.

Alternatively, drag the photo directly from the photo browser panel into the Timeline. A red progress bar on the clip shows iMovie's progress in rendering the photo into video.

> **TIP**
>
> You can update the settings for any imported photo. Click the clip of the photo in the Timeline and then adjust the settings in the right Photo pane; click **Update** to apply the new settings to the clip.

117 Add a Soundtrack

Before You Begin

✔ **98** Import (or Rip) an Audio CD

✔ **99** Purchase Music From the iTunes Music Store

✔ **113** Import Digital Video Footage into iMovie

✔ **114** Arrange Video Clips in the Timeline

See Also

→ **118** Export the Movie to Videotape or QuickTime

TIP

It's especially useful to sort your songs based on the **Time** column. Doing so allows you to pick a song that matches the length of the video clip you want to set to music.

The finishing touch on your movie is a good soundtrack. iMovie integrates with iTunes, allowing you to import songs directly from your iTunes Music **Library** into your movie. iMovie also comes with a portfolio of studio-quality sound effects by Skywalker Sound. You can even record a voice-over to use in your movie with the Mac's built-in microphone.

① Switch to the Audio Pane

Click the **Audio** button under the right pane in the iMovie window to open the **Audio** pane.

② Select a Song from Your iTunes Music Library

Select **iTunes Library** from the drop-down list at the top of the **Audio** pane. The browser panel shows a list of all the songs in your iTunes Music **Library**. You can sort the songs by the column headings, or you can zero in on a particular song that you have in mind by typing its name into the **Search** box, which will filter the displayed songs in real time as you type. Click the **Play** button under the **Audio** pane's browser list to preview the song.

③ Drag the Song to an Audio Track

When you have a song that's to your liking, drag it from the browser list to the Timeline. Alternatively, move the playhead in the movie scrub bar to the point where you want the song to start, select the song from the browser list, and then click **Place at Playhead**.

iMovie gives you two audio tracks to work with; you can enable them separately (using the check boxes at the far right) for isolation during playback (for instance, you can use one track for music and the other for voice-overs). When importing a song or sound effect, drag it into whichever audio track you prefer to use. You can move an audio clip from one track to the other simply by dragging the clip up or down to the other track.

If you're in **Clips** mode (select it using the **Clips/Timeline View Selector** buttons at the far left), dragging the sound effect into the Timeline switches iMovie to the Timeline mode so that you can view your various compositing tracks.

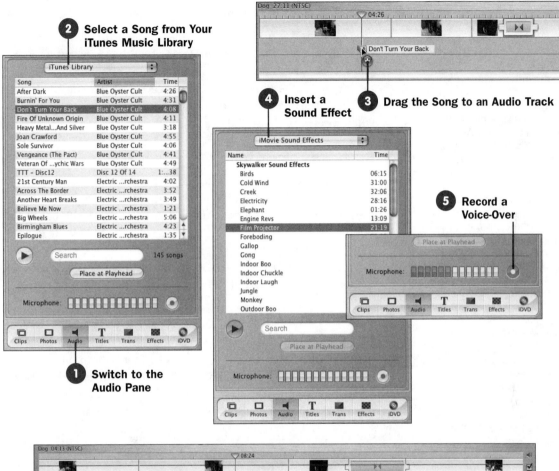

2 Select a Song from Your
iTunes Music Library

4 Insert a
Sound Effect

3 Drag the Song to an Audio Track

5 Record a
Voice-Over

1 Switch to the
Audio Pane

6 Adjust Volume Levels

If you have to adjust the position where an audio clip appears in the Timeline, simply click the clip and drag it to the left or right on the audio track. This allows you to sync up the beginning of an audio clip with a certain point in the video. As you add video clips and transitions, however, the overall length of the movie will change, and your audio might become desynchronized from the point in the video where you initially put it. To avoid this, select the audio clip and then choose **Lock Audio Clip at Playhead** from the **Advanced** menu to ensure that the audio clip stays associated with a certain point in the video stream, even if you change the video content.

You can tell iMovie to play only a certain segment of a song or sound effect, or to trim the audio clip to excise the beginning or end of the sound. To do this, click the triangular "beginning" and "end" markers on the audio clip and drag them left or right. The position where you leave the left marker is where the sound begins, and the right marker is where the audio clip ends.

4 Insert a Sound Effect

Select **iMovie Sound Effects** from the drop-down list at the top of the **Audio** pane to see a list of iMovie's built-in sound effects. You can sort this list and search the titles as you can with the iTunes **Library**; click the **Play** button to preview the sound effect. When you have the one you want, drag it into the Timeline at the point where you want the sound to play.

5 Record a Voice-Over

You can add a voice-over track to your project using the input level meter and the **Record** button located under the browser list in the **Audio** pane. First move the playhead in the movie scrub bar to the point where you want the voice-over to start; then click the **Record** button and begin speaking into the microphone. The voice-over track starts recording immediately and continues until you click the **Record** button again to stop it.

6 Adjust Volume Levels

You can fine-tune the volume levels of the audio clips in your movie project by using the visual curve editor built into the audio tracks in the Timeline. First enable the **Edit Volume** check box located under the audio tracks to display a horizontal line through the audio clips, representing the clips' respective volume levels.

Click a clip and use the **Volume** slider at the bottom of the screen to adjust the clip's constant volume up or down.

To create smooth volume level transitions within a clip, click the volume line in the clip and drag the line up or down; the line warps according to your mouse movement, adjusting the volume level after a brief transition, using a round yellow control knob that appears under your mouse pointer as you drag. To adjust how long the transition to the new level takes, click and drag the purple square at the left side of the transition curve to a new position.

118 Export the Movie to Videotape or QuickTime

When you're finished tweaking your movie project and you're ready to show it off, you have several options ahead of you: Do you create a QuickTime movie to send with email? Do you create a DVD? Do you simply drag everyone over to the computer so that you can play the movie in full-screen mode in iMovie?

The simplest answer, in many cases, is to export the movie straight back out to DV tape using the video camera as a VCR. You can then hook up the camera to a TV using standard video cables and play the movie in the same uncompressed quality it had when you first recorded the clips.

If you want to send your masterpiece to a friend on the Internet (either through email or on the Web using Personal Web Sharing, .Mac's hosting service, or your own Web site), you must export your movie to QuickTime format. You can compress the movie using one of many different codecs supported by QuickTime so that the resultant file is only a few megabytes in size (as opposed to the several gigabytes worth of uncompressed video data that comprise your raw footage from the camera). iMovie provides several prepackaged QuickTime compression formats from which you can choose, based on what you expect to do with the movie file. The quality and size of the resulting QuickTime file aren't as good as the movie looks in iMovie, but you can download or transfer the movie over the Internet in a reasonable amount of time.

Before You Begin

✔ **114** Arrange Video Clips in the Timeline

✔ **117** Add a Soundtrack

See Also

→ **58** Share Your iDisk Public Folder with Others

→ **119** Put Your Movie on a DVD

❶ Connect the Camcorder

Put the DV camcorder in **Play** (or **VCR**) mode and rewind the tape inside, making sure that the tape is one that's safe to record over. Get the tape to the position where you want to record the movie.

Connect the camcorder to your Mac using the FireWire cable, as you did when you imported the footage in the first place (see **113** **Import Digital Video Footage into iMovie**).

❷ Export the Movie to Camera

Select **Export** from the iMovie **File** menu. The **iMovie: Export** dialog box appears and gives you several options for exporting the movie; the default option in the **Export** drop-down list is **To Camera**. If you're exporting the movie to a camera, select this option if it isn't already selected.

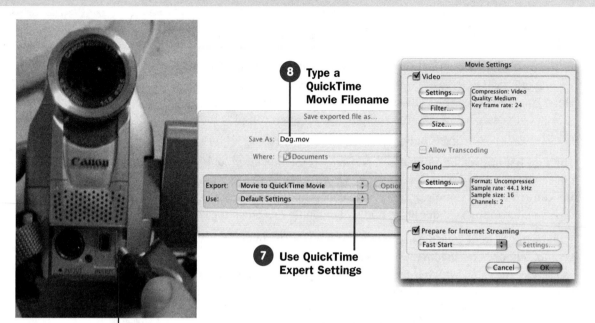

8 Type a QuickTime Movie Filename

Movie Settings

☑ Video

Settings... Compression: Video
Filter... Quality: Medium
Size... Key frame rate: 24

☐ Allow Transcoding

☑ Sound

Settings... Format: Uncompressed
Sample rate: 44.1 kHz
Sample size: 16
Channels: 2

☑ Prepare for Internet Streaming

Fast Start ▾ Settings...

Cancel OK

Save exported file as...

Save As: Dog.mov

Where: 📁 Documents

Export: Movie to QuickTime Movie ▾ Option

Use: Default Settings ▾

7 Use QuickTime Expert Settings

1 Connect the Camcorder

4 Adjust Camera Options   **2** Export the Movie to Camera

3 Export the Movie to QuickTime

5 Select QuickTime Video Format

iMovie: Export

Export: To QuickTime ▾

Formats ✓ Email
Web
Web Streaming
CD-ROM
Full Quality DV

Expert Settings...

Your mo
appropri
in width
operatio
complet

Cancel Export

iMovie: Export

Export: To Camera ▾

Wait 5 ⬍ seconds for camera to get ready.

Add 1 ⬍ seconds of black before movie.

Add 1 ⬍ seconds of black to end of movie.

Please make sure your camera is in VTR mode and has a writable tape in it.

Cancel Export

6 Begin Export

③ Export the Movie to QuickTime

If you want to create a QuickTime movie file from your iMovie project, choose **To QuickTime** from the **Export** drop-down list at the top of the **iMovie: Export** dialog box. The settings in the dialog box change to provide you with QuickTime options.

④ Adjust Camera Options

If you're exporting to a camera, iMovie sends a signal to wake up the camera before it begins sending data and waits five seconds to allow the camera to get ready. Adjust this **Wait** period if your camera takes longer (or shorter) before it's ready to record.

If you want, you can also adjust the amount of black space iMovie adds before and after the movie during export.

⑤ Select QuickTime Video Format

If you're exporting to a QuickTime movie, the dialog box shows a **Formats** drop-down list, which contains several prepackaged export formats. Each format has audio and video compression settings that correspond to a different kind of file use. As you go down the menu, the formats increase in video quality as well as in file size. For instance, if you choose **Email**, the movie file is highly compressed so that you can send it in an email message, but it won't look particularly good. If you choose the **CD-ROM** format, however, the video and audio quality are quite high, suitable for burning onto a CD or keeping in your **Movies** folder for later viewing.

The final option in the **Formats** drop-down list is **Expert Settings**, which allows you to explicitly pick audio and video codec settings and define the output dimensions. If you choose this option, after you click the **Export** button in step 6, a **Save exported file as** dialog box prompts you for the QuickTime settings you want to use. These settings can be useful if you want to fine-tune the codecs you use to maximize video quality and minimize file size; however, for most uses, the prepackaged export formats work fine.

NOTE

If you are ever prompted with a choice between a "movie" and a "self-contained movie," the difference is that a self-contained movie is a single monolithic file that contains all the video content for complete playback. This kind of file is suitable for transfer over the Internet. A plain "movie" has the potential to be created as simply a wrapper with internal pointers to video content elsewhere on your disk. The plain movie file itself can be very small (only a few kilobytes), but it can't be transferred over the Internet without being useless to the recipient (because she won't have access to the actual video data the movie points to). Except in certain special circumstances known to video experts, make your movies self-contained.

6 Begin Export

When you're satisfied with the options you've selected for either the QuickTime movie or the camera, click **Export**.

If you're exporting to a camera, iMovie starts the camera recording and begins playing the movie so that the camera records it. When the export process is done, disconnect the camera and rewind the tape; it's now ready to show on the big screen.

7 Use QuickTime Expert Settings

If you selected **Expert Settings** from the **Formats** drop-down list in step 5, a **Save exported file as** dialog box opens after you click **Export**. You have to specify a few more options before your QuickTime movie is created. Choose a target export format from the **Export** drop-down list. The most useful formats are likely **Movie to QuickTime Movie** and **Movie to MPEG-4**. Click the **Options** button to display the **Movie Settings** dialog box that lets you choose the video and audio compression codecs and the output size. **Sorensen Video 3** and **MPEG-4 Video** are both very good compression codecs, as is the third-party **DivX** format.

The **Use** drop-down list in the **Save exported file as** dialog box allows you to select a target download speed for the movie. The option you select affects the internal settings used by the audio and video codecs.

WEB RESOURCE

Visit this Web site to download the DivX video codec, which provides excellent audio/video compression without sacrificing quality.

http://www.divx.com

8 Type a QuickTime Movie Filename

In the **Save as** text box, type a filename for the QuickTime movie file; from the **Where** drop-down list, select a location for the file. Click **Save** to begin the export of your QuickTime movie. This process might take several minutes or even hours, depending on the speed of your system and the length of the movie.

Put Your Movie on a DVD

The flashiest way to share your video masterwork is to create a fully functional DVD that can be played in just about any DVD player. Apple's iDVD application, which is shipped with any Mac that has a SuperDrive (the optical drive that can burn DVDs), does for DVD authoring what iMovie does for video editing—namely, it makes it easy, straightforward, and fun.

iMovie integrates directly with iDVD, as it does with the other iLife applications (iTunes and iPhoto). After you've defined DVD *chapter markers* so that viewers can skip easily from one scene to another, a single click prepares your movie for DVD authoring.

When you're done putting your DVD presentation together, you can create, or *burn*, a DVD. This is the simplest part of the process; all you really have to do is click the **Burn** button and insert a blank disc in the SuperDrive. When the burn process is finished, you'll have a finished disc you can mail to your friends and family.

1 **Switch to the iDVD Pane**

Click the **iDVD** button at the bottom-right of the iMovie window to open the **iDVD** pane.

2 **Create DVD Chapter Markers**

If you're planning to put your iMovie masterpiece on a DVD, it's a matter of convenience—not to say common courtesy—to create chapter markers to define major scenes in your movies, especially if it's a long stream of video. Chapter markers allow the person watching the DVD to skip from one scene to the next, or to skip directly to an interesting scene, using a standard DVD remote. iDVD picks up all the chapter markers you define and integrates them into the DVD project you create.

Move the playhead on the scrub bar under the movie viewscreen to the spot where you want to create a chapter marker. Click the **Add Chapter** button; the chapter marker appears in the list box above the button. The default name for the marker is selected; type a more descriptive name for the chapter marker.

Before You Begin

✔ **113** Import Digital Video Footage into iMovie

✔ **114** Arrange Video Clips in the Timeline

See Also

→ **18** Burn a CD/DVD

KEY TERMS

Chapter marker—Within a single movie stream on a DVD, a chapter marker is the point to which the DVD player skips if you press the "skip forward" button. A DVD menu may contain clickable links to internal chapter markers within a movie, but it doesn't have to.

Burn—Creating a DVD by writing data to it is known as *burning*, just as with writable CDs.

2 **Create DVD Chapter Markers** 3 **Create an iDVD Project** 1 **Switch to the iDVD Pane**

7 **Insert a Blank DVD-R** 4 **Navigate the Movie with the Chapter Markers**

5 **View Background Encoding Status**

6 **Click the Burn Button**

You can create as many chapter markers as you want, or select any marker and click **Remove Chapter** to clear it. The chapters are listed in the order in which they appear in the Timeline.

❸ Create an iDVD Project

Click the **Create iDVD Project** button; iMovie prompts you to save your changes if necessary, and then launches iDVD with your movie project displayed in one of the premium *motion menus*— menu screen layouts that feature moving visual elements, prede- fined music, and even custom-rendered video effects such as overlays and artificial aging. (In this example, the movie appears in the **Theater** theme, with moving curtains framing a picture or movie clip that you can drag into position.) You can then use iDVD to fine-tune the details of how your DVD presentation will look.

NOTE

The project created in iDVD has the same name as the one you chose for your iMovie project. You can change it afterwards if you desire by choosing **Project Info** from the **Project** menu and changing the title in the **Disc Name** field.

❹ Navigate the Movie with the Chapter Markers

If you have defined chapter markers for your movie, each of them appears by name in the submenu named **Scenes 1-*n*** (where *n* is the number of chapter markers you defined).

Click the **Preview** button. iDVD goes into Preview mode, simulat- ing a DVD player with a floating "remote" controller that lets you navigate your DVD menus. Click the titles or buttons to move into new submenus and view the movies to which each links. While a movie is playing, you can skip to the next chapter marker using the **Forward** button, or return to the menu with the **Menu** button.

To exit Preview mode, click the **Exit** button on the floating con- troller. You can then double-click menu titles to change their text.

You can customize any menu theme that has an area marked **Drag photos or movies here.** Simply drag a photo or a movie (from the **Photos** or **Movies** tab in the drawer that appears when you click **Customize**) into the indicated zone and position it exact- ly the way you want using the mouse. If you drag a movie into one of these "drop zones," the movie will play in a continuous loop while the DVD remains on that menu screen.

TIP

There are a great many ways to customize your iDVD project. For more information on using iDVD to its fullest potential, check out *iLife in a Snap* (Sams Publishing).

5 View Background Encoding Status

iDVD encodes its video data in the background as soon as there's new content to encode. If you select a new motion menu theme, add a new video clip, or rearrange your menus, iDVD automatically begins encoding the compressed video in the background so that it can be written quickly to disc.

Background encoding saves time when you go to burn a disc, but it also eats up processing power while you're working on your project. If your Mac is limited in resources, you might want to turn off background encoding. You can do this by opening the **iDVD Preferences** window (from the **iDVD** menu) and disabling the **Enable background encoding** check box on the **General** page.

To see how much of the project has been encoded and how much space on the DVD it will take up, click the **Status** button in the drawer that appears when you click the **Customize** button; the **Project size** statistics show how large the project is compared to the available disc space. Select **Encoder Status** from the drop-down list to see all the separate pieces of video content that are being encoded. The further along the encoding processes are, the less time you'll have to wait for iDVD to finish encoding before it can start burning the disc.

6 Click the Burn Button

To begin the burn process, click the **Burn** button in the lower-right corner of the iDVD window. The "shutter" icon opens and shows an active **Burn** icon, pulsing gently; click this icon a second time to confirm that you want to burn a disc. The DVD drive tray ejects, and iDVD prompts you to insert a blank disc.

7 Insert a Blank DVD-R

Place a blank DVD-R disc in the tray (or feed it into the slot, if you have a slot-loading drive) and close the drive by pressing the **Eject** button. As soon as iDVD detects a viable blank disc in the drive, it begins the burn process, which might take up to about an hour, depending on how fast your computer is and how much video data is in your DVD project.

When iDVD finishes burning the disc, it ejects it from the drive automatically.

NOTE

Background encoding takes place only after you have saved your DVD project. Save your work right after you create the project so that iDVD can begin encoding in the background.

TIP

You can now take the resulting DVD, label it appropriately, and send it to whomever you think would enjoy seeing it—all they need is a DVD player!

13

Data Management: Address Book, iCal, and iSync

IN THIS CHAPTER:

Modern computing involves a lot more than simply running applications and browsing the Web. These days, the Internet lifestyle includes not just the computer on your desk, but your laptop, your other computer at work, your Personal Digital Assistant (PDA), your iPod, your cellular phone—a whole belt full of devices that all serve to organize the ocean of digital information that washes around you. Hundreds of names, email addresses, phone numbers, fax numbers, scheduled events, Internet bookmarks, and other pieces of assorted data flood through your head as well as your computer—and every one of your devices, including multiple computers if you have them, can all use the same kinds of data. Your cell phone and PDA can both store directories of contacts and scheduled items—and wouldn't it be great if those directories could match what's stored in your computer?

Address Book, iCal, and iSync are three of the utilities that allow you to manage your data and keep the contents of your digital devices synchronized, with a minimum of effort on your part. These utilities work in conjunction with larger applications such as Mail and Safari, corralling your contacts and *bookmarks* and transmitting them from device to device while you work. Address Book keeps track of all your email correspondents, friends, family, and business associates; iCal allows you to schedule events and To Do items. Finally, iSync works in the background, along with your .Mac account if you have one, using Apple's central servers to keep your computers' data synchronized at all times. iSync also keeps all your devices—Palm-compatible PDAs, iPods, and cell phones—synchronized whenever they're connected to your Mac so that you can grab them at any time and access the most up-to-date versions of all the pieces of data that make up your online life.

NOTE

iSync can synchronize your computer with your iPod, PDA, and cell phone whether or not you have a .Mac account (or even an Internet connection). However, to keep multiple Macs synchronized with each other, you must have a .Mac account. See ⑳ **Sign Up for .Mac** for more information.

120 Add a Person to Your Address Book

Email deserves its reputation as an instant, easy-to-understand communication system—but without a simple way for you to keep track of people's email addresses, email is all but useless. Who has the memory to keep an entire catalog of cryptic, frequently changing addresses straight?

The answer, of course, is *a computer.*

Address Book is a small application that works as an adjunct to Mail but that is integrated throughout Mac OS X so that all its contents—names, phone numbers, email addresses, home page URLs—are available to any application capable of using that information. As you use Mail, you can continually add names and addresses into Address Book with a single click, so that sending messages to the people you know becomes faster and easier all the time.

Each entry in Address Book is known as a *card.* A card can contain nearly a dozen different kinds of information about a person, including a picture. A card can be for a person or a business (you make the distinction using a check box). At any time, you can edit a card by selecting it in Address Book and clicking the **Edit** button at the bottom of the window.

You can add contacts to Address Book from the Mail application, or you can enter all of a person's contact information manually. Either way, that information is immediately available to Mail and to the rest of your online applications.

1 **Open Address Book**

Navigate to the **Applications** folder in the Finder and double-click on **Address Book**. Alternatively, you can click the **Address Book** icon in the Dock.

2 **Create a New Contact**

There are + buttons underneath both the **Group** column on the left and the second **Name** column (which by default shows all the contacts in the **All** group). Click the + button under the **Name** column to create a new contact.

Before You Begin

✔ **60** Configure a Server-Based Mail Account (.Mac, Exchange, or IMAP)

See Also

→ **121** Synchronize with an Exchange or Directory Server

→ **125** Set Up iSync to Synchronize Your Macs

TIP

An additional way to organize your contacts is to use groups. Create a new group in Address Book by clicking the + button at the bottom of the **Group** column and enter a name for the new group that appears. You then populate the group by dragging cards into it. Now you can quickly send email to an entire group of people by simply typing the name of the group into the **To** field in Mail. The names in the group are automatically resolved, and the message is addressed to all the members of the group at once.

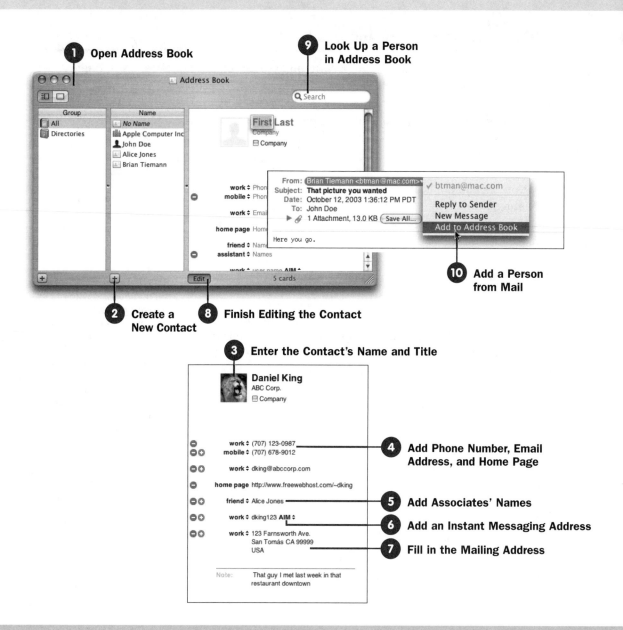

1 Open Address Book

9 Look Up a Person in Address Book

10 Add a Person from Mail

2 Create a New Contact

8 Finish Editing the Contact

3 Enter the Contact's Name and Title

4 Add Phone Number, Email Address, and Home Page

5 Add Associates' Names

6 Add an Instant Messaging Address

7 Fill in the Mailing Address

❸ Enter the Contact's Name and Title

In the right pane, a blank contact card appears. The name of each field appears in gray so that you know what is supposed to go in the fields.

Type the person's first and last name. If the person is a business contact, enter their company name and business title as well. Use the **Tab** key to move between fields. Be sure to put the first and last name in the two separate fields provided for them rather than simply typing the whole name into the first field. Separating the contact's name helps Address Book sort the names properly; you can tell Address Book to alphabetize your contacts based on their first or last names in the **General** page of the Address Book **Preferences** window.

❹ Add a Phone Number, Email Address, and Home Page

Each contact in your Address Book can have as many phone numbers, email addresses, and home pages associated with it as you want. The default template, which you are using now, has space for work and mobile phone numbers, a work email address, and a home page. You can add more of any of these pieces of information if you want or change the label on each field. For instance, you can change the **work** email address to a **home** address by selecting the new label from the drop-down list (click the up/down arrow icon next to the label to access the list of label options). When you have entered text into one of the fields, a + button appears next to the entry; click the + button to create space for a second entry of the same type. This way, you can create dozens of contact addresses for each person.

After you have finished specifying the information for a person, you can use Address Book to quickly access a person's home page, phone number, or email address. Click the label for one of these entries to see a contextual menu of appropriate options. An email entry gives you access to commands for sending email to the person or sending an automatic email with your new contact information if you should change it. If the person is a .Mac user, you can iChat with the person, visit his home page, or open his iDisk right from Address Book.

💡 TIPS

You can assign a custom picture to any person's card in Address Book. Simply find a picture file in the Finder and drag it into the square picture area next to the person's name. You can do this whether or not you're in Edit mode. (You can tell whether you're in Edit mode by whether the Edit button below the card information is pressed.)

If the card you're entering is for a company rather than a person, enable the **Company** check box next to the picture and under the company name. This option reverses the positions of the person's name and the company name, placing the company name in large bold letters.

Select **Custom** from the label menu on any entry to type a custom label for the entry.

Click the label for a person's phone number and select **Large Type** from the contextual menu to show the address in huge letters across your screen; this can be very useful if you need to dial a phone that's across the room from your computer.

5 Add Associates' Names

You can add the names of the person's friends, family members, assistants, managers, or any of several other relationships. Select the relationship you want to add from the list of label options, and type that person's name.

If the associate's name that you type matches any card in Address Book, you will later be able to jump to that associate's Address Book card by clicking the label and selecting the **Show "John Doe"** option from the contextual menu.

6 Add an Instant Messaging Address

Address Book allows you to specify the Instant Messaging address or user ID for any contact. You can enter an AIM, Jabber, MSN, ICQ, or Yahoo! address. Only if you enter an AIM address will you be able to contact the person using iChat, if you click the location label next to the Instant Messaging entry in the Address Book card, or if you click the green dot next to the person's picture (which indicates that he is online in iChat or AIM).

TIP

You can use different countries' mailing address styles, if you want. Click the mailing address label and choose **Change Address Format** from the contextual menu; from the submenu, select the country for the format you want to use for that card. To change the format that is used globally for all cards, open the Address Book **Preferences** window and click the **General** tab; select the country you live in from the **Address Format** menu.

7 Fill in the Mailing Address

Enter the information for the person's mailing address, using all the available fields that you know: street address, city, state, ZIP, and country.

Clicking the mailing address label later in Address Book and selecting **Map Of** from the contextual menu when you're in Safari pops up a map (using the MapQuest service) of that address.

8 Finish Editing the Contact

When you're done editing the person's card, click the **Edit** button to exit Edit mode. This contact's card is added to the Address Book and the contact's name appears in the **Name** column in the Address Book screen.

9 Look Up a Person in Address Book

You can browse for a person's name alphabetically in the **Name** column in Address Book. Alternatively, if you know the person's first or last name (or, indeed, any other piece of information, such as the person's phone number or mailing address), type it into the **Search** box. As you type, only the cards with contents that match what you've typed appear in the **Name** column. When you've narrowed it down to a single card, that card appears in the right pane.

10 Add a Person from Mail

Click the down arrow next to any person's name in the headers of an email message in Mail. Select **Add to Address Book** from the contextual menu to automatically create a new card with that person's name and email address. You can then select **Open in Address Book** from the same menu to go to the new card and add any further contact information you might know.

121 Synchronize with an Exchange or Directory Server

If you're in a corporate network environment, chances are that you and all your co-workers have Windows Networking user names and passwords that you use to access the Windows-based network—and there is equally likely a Microsoft Exchange server or *Lightweight Directory Access Protocol (LDAP)* server available, making it a breeze to access the contact information for any of your co-workers. You don't even have to enter their information yourself—all you have to do is tell Address Book where the server is, and it will do all the work for you.

There are subtle differences between an Exchange server and a directory server. With an Exchange server, Address Book must connect to the server every so often (generally once per hour) and synchronize its cards with the ones on the server. A directory server, on the other hand, doesn't insert its contents into your Address Book; rather, you browse the contents of the directory as you would a group in your Address Book.

Before configuring Mac OS X to synchronize your Address Book with the Exchange server, make sure that your computer is connected to the corporate network and that you know your Windows Networking user name and password. Consult your company's network administrator for assistance if you don't know this information.

Before You Begin

✔ **29** Configure Networking Manually

See Also

→ **60** Configure a Server-Based Mail Account (.Mac, Exchange, or IMAP)

→ **66** Subscribe to a Directory Server

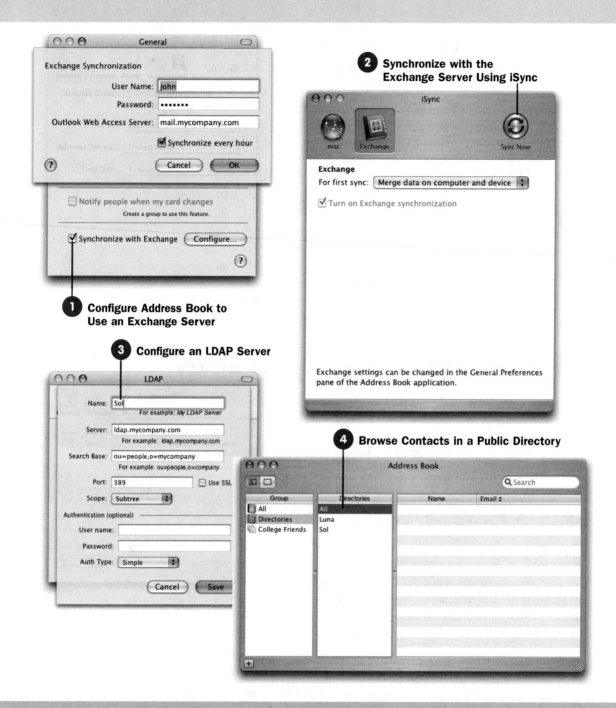

2 Synchronize with the Exchange Server Using iSync

1 Configure Address Book to Use an Exchange Server

3 Configure an LDAP Server

4 Browse Contacts in a Public Directory

1 Configure Address Book to Use an Exchange Server

Open the Address Book **Preferences** window; select the **General** tab. Enable the **Synchronize with Exchange** check box and then click the **Configure** button to specify the Exchange server.

Enter your Windows Networking user name and password. Then put the server's hostname or IP address in the **Outlook Web Access Server** box. Enable the **Synchronize every hour** check box to keep your Address Book in sync at all times, and then click **OK**.

2 Synchronize with the Exchange Server Using iSync

iSync launches in the background, and a new **Exchange** button is added to the toolbar at the top of the iSync window. The settings panel is expanded, allowing you to specify how iSync should perform the first synchronization operation. The best option to choose is **Merge data on computer and device** from the **For first sync** drop-down list. (The "device" in this case is the Exchange server.)

Click the **Sync Now** button. iSync connects to the Exchange server, downloading all the contacts and incorporating them into your Address Book. You might be prompted to approve a large number of additions to your Address Book; click **Proceed** to allow these additions.

After the sync process is complete, your Address Book is populated with all your co-workers' names, email addresses, and phone numbers. iSync will check the server every hour for changes; this way, you will always have the most accurate information at your fingertips.

3 Configure an LDAP Server

You can also subscribe your Mac to a directory server, also known as an LDAP server. Use the **LDAP** pane of the Address Book **Preferences** window to configure an LDAP server, using the server information provided to you by your network administrator.

Click the + button to add a new directory server. In the sheet that appears, enter a descriptive name for the server, the hostname or IP address, and the "search base"—a string that your network administrator will be able to provide for you.

NOTE

When you configure Address Book to synchronize itself with an Exchange server, Address Book is actually passing off the synchronization duties to iSync. While you update contacts in Address Book, iSync operates in the background, finding new and changed entries in the Exchange server and propagating them into your Address Book.

NOTE

If you configured an Exchange email account in Mail, Address Book takes its Exchange server settings from that account. See **60** Configure a Server-Based Mail Account (.Mac, Exchange, or IMAP) for details on accessing an Exchange server.

Click **Save** to close the configuration sheet and then close the **Preferences** window.

④ Browse Contacts in a Public Directory

Back in the Address Book, select the **Directories** entry in the **Group** column; all your configured directory servers appear in the second column. Click a directory to browse the names inside it.

122 Create an iCal Event

Before You Begin

✔ **24** Set the Date and Time

See Also

→ **123** Subscribe to a Shared iCal Calendar

→ **125** Set Up iSync to Synchronize Your Macs

It's one of the great modern ironies: As you work with your Mac in a business or home environment, your time will likely become still more of a precious resource than it was before—even though computers are supposed to be time-*saving* devices! Inevitably, you'll have the need for a way to manage your time in a more elegant and automatic fashion than simply relying on your memory or Post-It notes.

iCal, Apple's calendaring system, is engineered to be a hassle-free and intuitive way to schedule important events in your life and notify you when they're approaching so that you never have to miss an appointment or meeting.

① Launch iCal

Navigate to the **Applications** folder in the Finder and double-click the **iCal** icon. Alternatively, click the **iCal** icon in the Dock.

② Select the Time for the New Event

iCal opens into the Week view, showing you each day in the current week as a column, with the hours of the day shown as horizontal lines. Create a new event by clicking on the day and time when the event starts, and dragging to the point where the event ends. In this example, I've dragged into existence an event that starts on Thursday at 1:00 and ends at 3:45.

③ Name the Event

The name for the new event is selected so that you can immediately type a new descriptive name. Press **Return** when you've done this; the new event is registered in iCal.

✎ NOTE

iCal's icon in the Dock dynamically updates to reflect the current date. Because the automatic update happens only while iCal is running, you might choose to leave iCal running at all times to keep the display accurate.

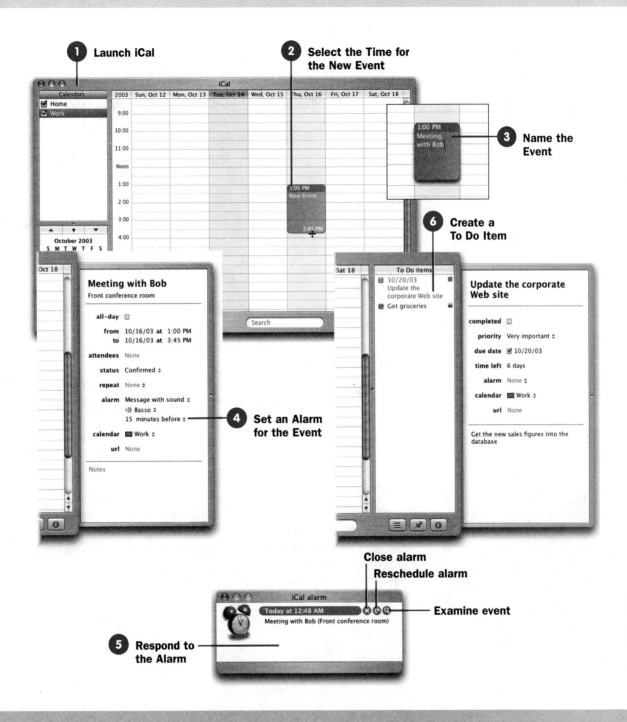

1 Launch iCal

2 Select the Time for the New Event

3 Name the Event

6 Create a To Do Item

4 Set an Alarm for the Event

5 Respond to the Alarm

Close alarm

Reschedule alarm

Examine event

iCal window (step 1):

2003 | Sun, Oct 12 | Mon, Oct 13 | Tue, Oct 14 | Wed, Oct 15 | Thu, Oct 16 | Fri, Oct 17 | Sat, Oct 18

Calendars
☑ Home
☑ Work

9:00
10:00
11:00
Noon
1:00
2:00
3:00
4:00

1:00 PM
New Event

3:45 PM

October 2003
S M T W T F S

Search

1:00 PM
Meeting with Bob

Event detail (step 3/4):

Meeting with Bob
Front conference room

all-day ☐

from 10/16/03 at 1:00 PM
to 10/16/03 at 3:45 PM

attendees None

status Confirmed ↕

repeat None ↕

alarm Message with sound ↕
◁) Basso ↕
15 minutes before ↕

calendar ■ Work ↕

url None

Notes

To Do items panel (step 6):

To Do items

☐ 10/20/03
Update the corporate Web site

☐ Get groceries

To Do detail:

Update the corporate Web site

completed ☐

priority Very important ↕

due date ☑ 10/20/03

time left 6 days

alarm None ↕

calendar ■ Work ↕

url None

Get the new sales figures into the database

iCal alarm (step 5):

● ● ● iCal alarm

Today at 12:48 AM ⊗ ⊙ ⊙

Meeting with Bob (Front conference room)

NOTE

iCal doesn't have to be running for it to send you alarms when your events approach. Feel free to set up your events and then quit iCal; your alarms will appear as scheduled whether iCal is running or not.

4 **Set an Alarm for the Event**

Click the **Info** button in the lower-right corner of the iCal window to open the information drawer for the new event. Set an alarm on the event by clicking the up/down arrows to access the **alarm** drop-down list. You can select from a number of different types of alarms, from a simple pop-up message on your screen a specified number of minutes or hours before or after the event, to a message with a sound effect, or even an email message sent to an address of your choice from your card in Address Book.

Click the various parts of the specification to the right of the alarm label to configure the alarm to your exact specifications.

5 **Respond to the Alarm**

When the alarm goes off, if you've set it to pop up a message before the event, you will be given options to close the window, reschedule the alarm to go off again in a few minutes, or examine the event.

6 **Create a To Do Item**

Another kind of scheduled item in iCal is a To Do item. These are not scheduled events, but rather free-form notes to yourself that relate to tasks you have to accomplish. A To Do item doesn't have to have a due date associated with it, but it can; you can also (optionally) assign a priority level that helps you sort your To Do items according to their importance.

TIP

Click the **Info** button in the lower-right corner of the iCal window to open the information drawer; for To Do items, this drawer lets you set the priority or due date for a To Do item, as well as a few other options.

Click the thumbtack button in the lower-right corner of the iCal window to show the To Do list. To create a new To Do item, double-click anywhere in the To Do list pane. A new item named **New To Do** appears, and you can immediately type in a more descriptive name for the item.

123 Subscribe to a Shared iCal Calendar

Because iCal is part of Apple's networked data management suite of utilities, you can publish the events on your calendar to a central server, subscribe to other people's iCal calendars so that you can see their schedules, and even seek out public calendars that are published as services for the iCal-using community.

① Display the Subscribe Configuration Dialog Box

Select **Subscribe** from the iCal **Calendar** menu to display the **Subscribe** configuration dialog box.

② Enter the Calendar URL

Enter the URL of a calendar that's published on .Mac or a *WebDAV server*. If the calendar was published by a fellow .Mac user, she will be able to give you the URL for the calendar (the URL will have been reported to the person when the calendar was published).

WEB RESOURCE

http://www.icalshare.com

Alternatively, visit Apple's iCal calendar library at **http://www.apple.com/ical/library/** or iCalShare at **http://www.icalshare.com** to find an interesting public calendar to subscribe to. These sites present links you can simply click; when you do this, the URL of the calendar in question appears in the **Subscribe** configuration dialog box.

③ Automatically Refresh the Calendar

You can have iCal automatically query the iCal server periodically to check for updates. Enable the **Refresh** check box and select a refresh interval—anything from 15 minutes to once a month. The more frequently you have iCal refresh its calendars, the more accurate they'll be—but the more frequently your work might be interrupted by iCal's background sync process (or any error messages that might result from it).

Before You Begin

✔ **29** Configure Networking Manually

✔ **122** Create an iCal Event

See Also

→ **60** Configure a Server-Based Mail Account (.Mac, Exchange, or IMAP)

→ **124** Publish Your iCal Calendar

→ **125** Set Up iSync to Synchronize Your Macs

iCalShare is a site dedicated to allowing iCal users to publish their calendars to a browseable directory. You can seek out and subscribe to a calendar of events in which you're interested, no matter whose iCal it's actually part of.

NOTE

iCal uses the industry-standard ICAL format (no relation) when publishing or exporting its calendar data. This means that you can share calendars with Exchange/Outlook users, as well as with any other application that uses the ICAL format.

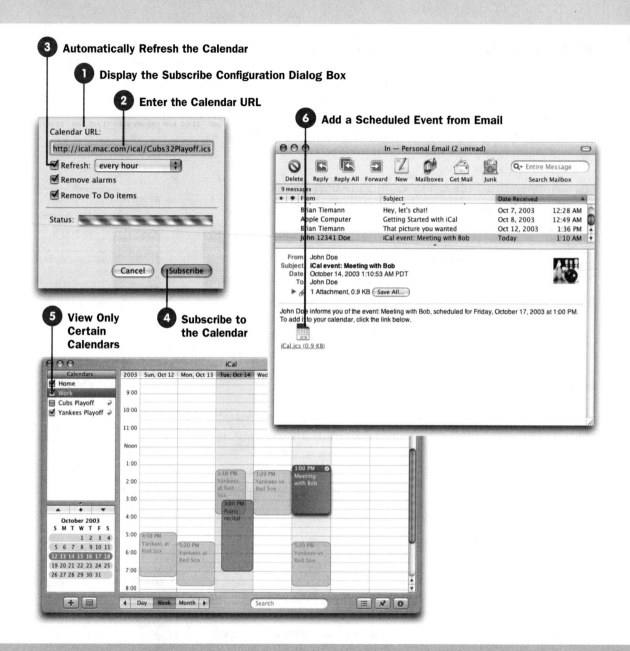

3 Automatically Refresh the Calendar

1 Display the Subscribe Configuration Dialog Box

2 Enter the Calendar URL

6 Add a Scheduled Event from Email

Calendar URL:

http://ical.mac.com/ical/Cubs32Playoff.ics

☑ Refresh: every hour

☑ Remove alarms

☑ Remove To Do items

Status:

Cancel   Subscribe

5 View Only Certain Calendars

4 Subscribe to the Calendar

In — Personal Email (2 unread)

Delete | Reply | Reply All | Forward | New | Mailboxes | Get Mail | Junk | Search Mailbox

9 messages

•	♦	From	Subject	Date Received	▲
		Brian Tiemann	Hey, let's chat!	Oct 7, 2003	12:28 AM
		Apple Computer	Getting Started with iCal	Oct 8, 2003	12:49 AM
		Brian Tiemann	That picture you wanted	Oct 12, 2003	1:36 PM
		John 12341 Doe	iCal event: Meeting with Bob	Today	1:10 AM

From: John Doe
Subject: **iCal event: Meeting with Bob**
Date: October 14, 2003 1:10:53 AM PDT
To: John Doe
▶ 1 Attachment, 0.9 KB Save All...

John Doe informs you of the event: Meeting with Bob, scheduled for Friday, October 17, 2003 at 1:00 PM. To add it to your calendar, click the link below.

iCal.ics (0.9 KB)

iCal

2003	Sun, Oct 12	Mon, Oct 13	Tue, Oct 14	Wed

Calendars
☑ Home
☑ Work
☐ Cubs Playoff
☑ Yankees Playoff

9:00
10:00
11:00
Noon
1:00
2:00
3:00
4:00
5:00
6:00
7:00
8:00

1:18 PM Yankees at Red Sox
1:20 PM Yankees vs Red Sox
1:00 PM ✓ Meeting with Bob
3:00 PM Piano recital
4:50 PM Yankees at Red Sox
5:20 PM Yankees at Red Sox
5:20 PM Yankees vs Red Sox

October 2003
S M T W T F S
          1 2 3 4
5 6 7 8 9 10 11
12 13 14 15 16 17 18
19 20 21 22 23 24 25
26 27 28 29 30 31

+ | ◀ Day Week Month ▶ | Search

4 **Subscribe to the Calendar**

Click the **Subscribe** button at the bottom of the configuration dialog box to add the specified calendar to your **Calendars** pane in iCal. The new calendar is assigned a unique color, and the events in it are overlaid with your existing personal calendar events.

5 **View Only Certain Calendars**

Use the check boxes in the **Calendars** pane to select which calendars you want to see. Hide the calendars (disable their check boxes) that don't interest you at a given time to reduce clutter in your iCal window and let you see how much free time you really have.

6 **Add a Scheduled Event from Email**

Someone can send you an iCal event by email. If you receive an iCal event as an attachment in an email message, simply double-click its link to import it into your iCal.

iCal will prompt you about which of your calendars to put the new event into; select the calendar you want to use and click **OK**. The new event is added into the selected calendar.

KEY TERM

WebDAV server—A type of server, often found on a corporate network, that provides certain kinds of information upload and download services (such as iCal publishing). iDisk also operates over WebDAV.

TIP

To send an iCal event to another person in an email attachment, right-click or **Control**+click the event in your calendar and select **Mail event** from the contextual menu. A new Mail message opens, with the iCal event packaged into it as an attachment.

---

124 **Publish Your iCal Calendar**

iCal lets you publish any one of your calendars to a central server so that others can see what your schedule is and plan their own events accordingly. You can publish your calendar to .Mac if you have a .Mac account; other .Mac users can then subscribe to your calendar on the .Mac server. If you have a *WebDAV server* on your corporate network, you can publish your iCal calendar to that server, eliminating the need for .Mac in your calendaring.

.Mac even provides the ability for you to publish your calendar to a static Web-based calendar. This form of the calendar is visible to anybody with a Web browser, whether they're on a Mac or not. When you publish a calendar to .Mac, iCal tells you both the URL that others must use to subscribe to your calendar in iCal, and the URL for viewing the calendar with a standard Web browser.

Before You Begin

✔ **29** Configure Networking Manually

✔ **50** Sign Up for .Mac

See Also

→ **125** Set Up iSync to Synchronize Your Macs

---

1 Display the Publish Configuration Dialog Box

2 Specify Calendar Name

3 Select Where to Publish the Calendar

5 Note the URL of the Published Calendar

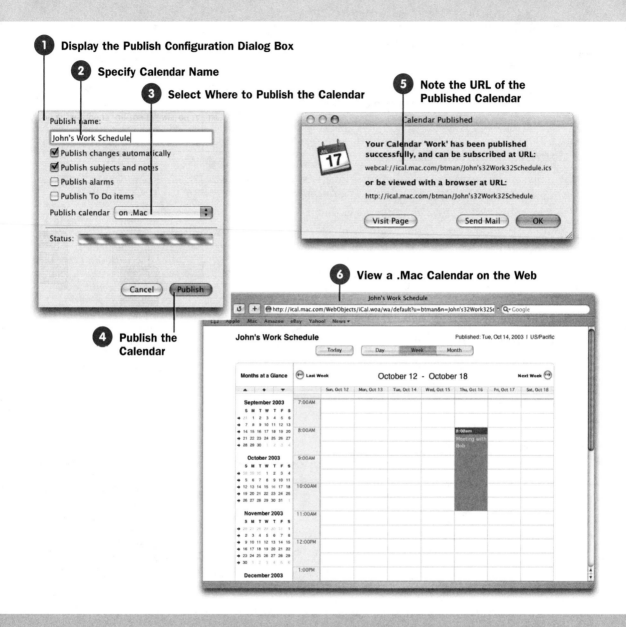

Publish name:

John's Work Schedule

☑ Publish changes automatically
☑ Publish subjects and notes
☐ Publish alarms
☐ Publish To Do items

Publish calendar [on .Mac ▼]

Status:

(Cancel) (Publish)

○ ○ ○ Calendar Published

Your Calendar 'Work' has been published successfully, and can be subscribed at URL:

webcal://ical.mac.com/btman/John's32Work32Schedule.ics

or be viewed with a browser at URL:

http://ical.mac.com/btman/John's32Work32Schedule

(Visit Page) (Send Mail) (OK)

4 Publish the Calendar

6 View a .Mac Calendar on the Web

John's Work Schedule

http://ical.mac.com/WebObjects/iCal.woa/wa/default?u=btman&n=John's32Work32Sc

John's Work Schedule   Published: Tue, Oct 14, 2003 I US/Pacific

(Today)   (Day Week Month)

Months at a Glance ← Last Week   October 12 - October 18   Next Week →

1 Display the Publish Configuration Dialog Box

Select **Publish** from the iCal **Calendar** menu to display the **Publish** configuration dialog box.

2 Specify Calendar Name

Enter a descriptive name for your published calendar. You can leave it as the default (the same name as the calendar has in your local iCal window), or you can give it a more specific or appropriate name for the benefit of others.

3 Select Where to Publish the Calendar

You can publish the calendar either to .Mac or to any WebDAV server to which you have access. Select the destination for your calendar from the **Publish calendar** drop-down list.

4 Publish the Calendar

Click the **Publish** button at the bottom of the configuration dialog box to send your calendar to the specified server.

5 Note the URL of the Published Calendar

iCal will report two URLs for the calendar you just published: the URL other users must use to subscribe to the calendar, as well as the URL for viewing the calendar in a Web browser.

Click **Send Mail** on the **Calendar Published** dialog box to create a new mail message that automatically includes both these URLs in it; all you have to do is fill in the recipients' names and click **Send** to mail these URLs to the people who need to view or subscribe to your published calendar.

6 View a .Mac Calendar on the Web

Click the **Visit Page** button on the **Calendar Published** dialog box to open the static version of the calendar in your Web browser.

Alternatively, right-click or **Control**+click the name of a calendar in the **Calendars** pane in the iCal window and select **View Calendar on .Mac** from the contextual menu to open the calendar in your Web browser.

TIPS

You can send another email message later as well, if you want to tell more people about the location of your calendar. Select **Send publish email** from the iCal **Calendar** menu to bring up a new Mail message containing the calendar URLs.

iCal lets you publish more than one calendar if you want—each calendar you create (using the + button at the bottom-left of the window) can be shared at your discretion. A shared calendar is denoted in the **Calendars** list by a "broadcast" icon to the right of the calendar's name.

125 Set Up iSync to Synchronize Your Macs

Before You Begin

✔ **29** Configure Networking Manually

✔ **50** Sign Up for .Mac

See Also

→ **57** Keep Your iDisk in Sync

→ **127** Synchronize Your .Mac Address Book

TIP

Because iSync depends on each Mac being set to the correct date and time so that it can tell which computer's information is the most up-to-date, you must make sure that all your Macs' clocks are accurate. See **25** Enable Automatic Time Synchronization (NTP) for instructions on ensuring that each of your Macs always has the correct time.

iSync is the real workhorse of Apple's location-agnostic computing concept. It works behind the scenes, gathering your data together from disparate locations such as Address Book, Safari, and iCal, and constantly compares it against your contacts, bookmarks, and calendar events that are stored on the .Mac server. Whenever it finds any discrepancies, it automatically makes the change in whichever system is more out-of-date.

If you have multiple Macs, iSync really comes into its own. If you add a person or a *bookmark* on one Mac, iSync publishes that change to .Mac. On your second Mac, iSync notices that there are newer changes on .Mac than on that Mac. It downloads and incorporates the changes from .Mac, thereby propagating your most current information from the first Mac to the second. And the best part is that this is all done transparently, in the background—you don't ever have to know that it's happening. All that matters to you, the user, is that all your most current information is always available on all your Macs.

Before iSync can do this service for you, however, you must set it up. This involves registering each of your Macs with the .Mac server, so that each copy of iSync knows how many other Macs it's negotiating with and how recently each one's information has been synchronized.

1 **Launch iSync**

Navigate to the **Applications** folder in the Finder, and double-click **iSync**. Alternatively, you can click the **iSync** icon in the Dock.

2 **Add iSync to the System Menus**

Open the **iSync Preferences** window by choosing **Preferences** from the **iSync** menu. Enable the **Show iSync in menu bar** check box to position the **iSync** system menu in the upper-right corner of the Desktop. Now you can view at a glance when your computer was last synchronized with .Mac and also run a manual sync process whenever you choose.

3 **Register Your Computer with .Mac**

If you've never synchronized your Mac with your .Mac account, you must first register the computer in iSync. Your .Mac account

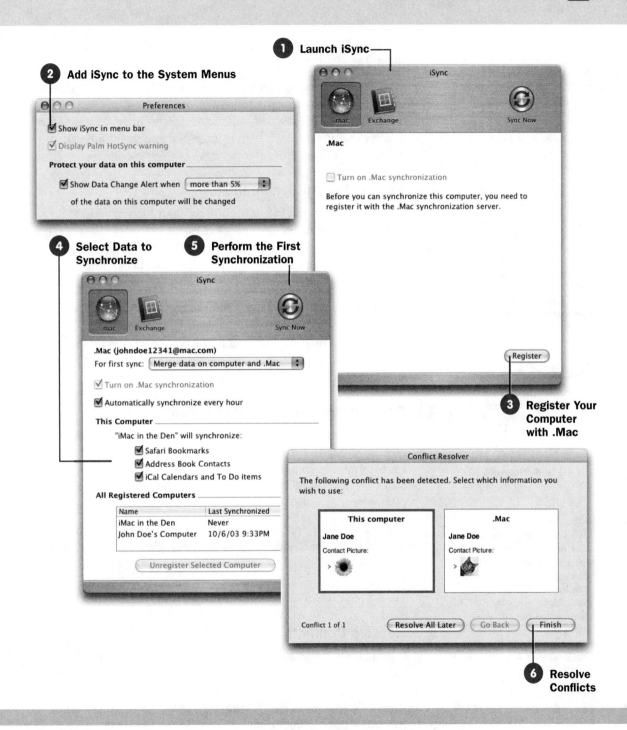

1 Launch iSync

2 Add iSync to the System Menus

4 Select Data to Synchronize

5 Perform the First Synchronization

3 Register Your Computer with .Mac

6 Resolve Conflicts

TIP

Even if you have only a single Mac, synchronizing your information with .Mac is a good thing to do because it protects your valuable data in case it's lost from your own computer. If, for instance, your Mac crashes or you get a new computer, you can immediately restore all your contacts and calendar events by simply subscribing the new computer to .Mac and synchronizing the data. Make sure that you choose **Erase data on computer then sync** from the **For first sync** drop-down list, as shown in step 5.

NOTE

iSync attempts to synchronize with the .Mac server only when you have an active network connection. To set up iSync or register your Mac, you must be connected to the Internet.

TIP

If you don't care about the data on your computer and want to populate it entirely with the data that's in your .Mac account, choose **Erase data on computer then sync** from the **For first sync** drop-down list; if you want to keep the data that's on your computer exactly the way it is and publish it to your other Macs in identical form, select **Erase data on .Mac then sync**.

keeps track of all the Macs you use and marshals the data between them, keeping them all up-to-date.

Click the **.Mac** icon in iSync; this expands the iSync window to show the .Mac settings screen. Click the **Register** button to register your computer. In the next screen, enter a descriptive name for your Mac and click **Continue**. iSync then registers the computer and adds it to the list of registered Macs at the bottom of the iSync window.

4 **Select Data to Synchronize**

iSync now shows you the status and configuration of your .Mac synchronization. Using the check boxes, choose what kinds of data you want iSync to keep updated. You can enable or disable your Safari bookmarks, the contact cards in Address Book, or the events and To Do items in iCal.

Enable the **Automatically synchronize every hour** check box to tell iSync to attempt to connect to .Mac every hour, and if successful, to synchronize all your data in the background. With this option enabled, you should never have to worry about your personal data being out-of-date again.

5 **Perform the First Synchronization**

From the **For first sync** drop-down list at the top of the iSync window, select **Merge data on computer and .Mac**. This setting means that iSync will take the contents of both your .Mac account and your own computer and add them together, thus preserving all the data in both.

When your iSync options are configured to your liking, click the **Sync Now** button. iSync will close the configuration pane and connect to the .Mac server. It will download the data that's in your .Mac account, compare it to what's in your computer's Address Book, iCal, and Safari, and add any new entries into them.

6 **Resolve Conflicts**

If iSync finds *conflicts*—similar but not identical cards on both your computer and .Mac—it shows you the relevant details of the two items that are causing the problem. Click to select the version you want to keep and then click **Finish**. iSync will have to sync again to finalize the resolved conflicts. Click **Sync Now** in the confirmation dialog box to kick off this cleanup-duty sync process.

Quit iSync. Your Mac will now synchronize your data automatically every hour, in the background, as long as you have a network connection.

126 Synchronize Your Palm PDA and Other Devices

iSync is designed to keep your data synchronized not only across all the Macs you use, but also with any other digital devices you use to keep track of things and communicate—Personal Digital Assistants, cellular phones, and iPods. iSync can talk to all these devices and keep their data in sync whenever they're connected to your Mac. All you have to do is set them up.

For cell phones and iPods, the process of registering them with iSync is a simple one: Just plug it in and use the **Device**, **Add Device** command to scan for it so that iSync can automatically pick it up. But to use a Palm OS-based PDA with iSync, the process to set it up is rather more complicated.

1 Add an iPod or Cellular Phone to iSync

Whether you want to add an iPod or cellular phone to iSync, the process is the same. First, plug in the device using FireWire or USB cables as necessary or Bluetooth if your device and Mac both support it. Open iSync and select **Add Device** from the **Devices** menu.

In the **Add Device** dialog box that opens, click the **Scan** button to scan for connected devices. Any iPods or cellular phones connected to the computer appear in the window. Double-click the icon for each device to add it to iSync.

iPods and different models of cellular phones differ in what kinds of data they can synchronize, but the configuration pane contains controls that let you select from whatever types of data are applicable. Enable the check boxes for the data you want to synchronize—contacts, calendars, and other items—and use the **Automatically synchronize when <device> is connected** check box to tell iSync to launch a sync process whenever you connect the device to the computer. With this option enabled, you never have to open iSync to ensure that your latest data is present on your device; just plug it in, and the data is synchronized in the background. To synchronize the new device with the data on your Mac and .Mac server for the first time, click **Sync Now**.

Before You Begin

✔ **120** Add a Person to Your Address Book
✔ **122** Create an iCal Event

See Also

→ **102** Synchronize with an iPod
→ **125** Set Up iSync to Synchronize Your Macs

NOTES

Although you need a .Mac account to synchronize your Macs, you don't have to be a .Mac member—or even have an Internet connection—to synchronize your devices with a single Mac.

If you have multiple Macs, you should choose a single Mac to which you will synchronize your PDA, iPod, or cell phone. In other words, don't synchronize the device to your Mac at home, and then again to your Mac at work; the different copies of iSync might become confused, and you could lose data. Instead, make sure that your multiple Macs are synchronized (see **125** Set Up iSync to Synchronize Your Macs) and then choose one Mac to use any time you want to synchronize your digital device.

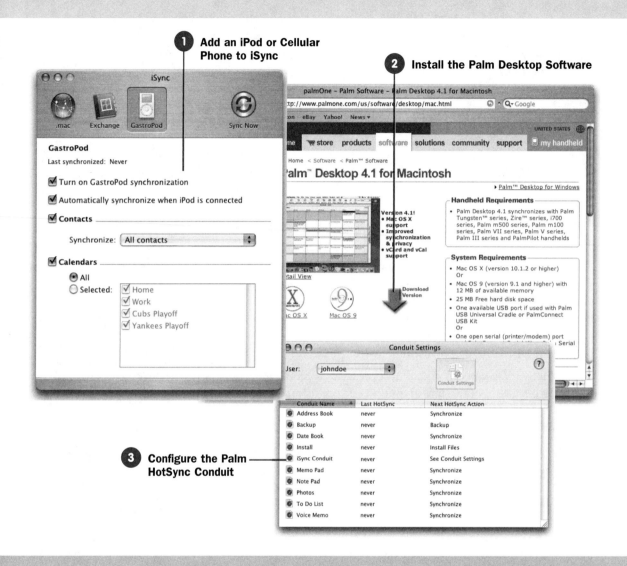

1 Add an iPod or Cellular Phone to iSync

2 Install the Palm Desktop Software

3 Configure the Palm HotSync Conduit

Palm Desktop
Installer

2 Install the Palm Desktop Software

To add a Palm device to iSync, you must first download the Palm Desktop application suite. Visit the Palm Web site at **http://www.palmone.com/software** to locate the Mac OS X version of the Palm Desktop. Register with the Web site and download the software.

Double-click the **Palm Desktop Installer** icon to install the Palm software. The installer creates the **Palm Desktop** and **HotSync**

Manager applications on your computer, and then presents a brief series of panels that set up your user account, using your Mac OS X user information. When the installation procedure is complete, restart your computer.

3 Configure the Palm HotSync Conduit

After restarting your Mac, navigate to the **Applications** folder and double-click the **HotSync Manager** icon. The HotSync Manager launches. From the **HotSync** menu, select **Conduit Settings** to bring up the window where you configure the various *conduits*, or mini-applications that transmit data between your Palm device and the Mac.

Double-click the **iSync Conduit** entry in the list in the **Conduit Settings** window. In the dialog box that appears, select the **Enable iSync for this Palm device** check box and click **OK**. iSync will now show the Palm device in the palette at the top of the iSync window. Whenever you connect the Palm device to your computer from now on (either by directly connecting a USB cable or by pressing the **Synchronize** button on the Palm's cradle), iSync will launch a sync process and update the information on the Palm device, just as it does with .Mac and any other devices to which it is connected and registered.

KEY TERM

Conduit—A piece of software hiding under the surface of Mac OS X that transfers a certain kind of information, such as Address Book contacts or iCal events, to and from a digital device such as a PDA.

NOTE

If the **Conduit Settings** window doesn't show an **iSync Conduit** entry, you might have to get a newer version of the Palm Desktop software. HotSync Manager version 3.0.1 and earlier might not work properly with iSync 1.2.1 or Panther.

127 Synchronize Your .Mac Address Book

In a final flourish, Apple has made it so that if you have a .Mac account, you don't even have to be using your own Mac to access your Address Book contacts; all you need is a computer with a Web browser (even if that computer is running Windows)—and iSync will keep your Mac's Address Book contacts in sync with the Address Book available at the .Mac Web site.

This online version of your Address Book can be used in conjunction with .Mac Webmail (which handles only your **@mac.com** email account, not any other accounts you might have) so that you can have access to all your email correspondents no matter where you're doing your computing.

Before You Begin

✔ **50** Sign Up for .Mac
✔ **120** Add a Person to Your Address Book
✔ **125** Set Up iSync to Synchronize Your Macs

See Also

→ **71** Access Your Bookmarks Using .Mac

1 Log In to the .Mac Web Site

2 Open the .Mac Address Book

3 Turn on .Mac Address Book Synchronization

4 Use Your Address Book with .Mac Webmail

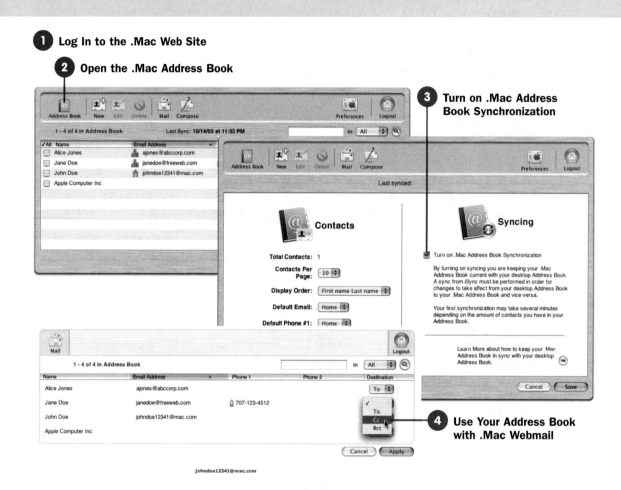

Before beginning this task, make sure that you have synchronized your computer's information with the .Mac server. Instructions for doing this, even if you have only a single Mac, are in **125** Set Up iSync to Synchronize Your Macs.

① Log In to the .Mac Web Site

Using any computer (not necessarily your own Mac), go to the .Mac Web site at **http://www.mac.com**. Log in using the links on the left side of the page.

② Open the .Mac Address Book

Click the **Address Book** icon to display the online version of your Address Book, which starts out its life pretty much empty. Even if you have already synchronized your Mac's information with .Mac, the Web-accessible .Mac Address Book is not made available until you enable it, as a security and privacy measure.

③ Turn on .Mac Address Book Synchronization

Click the **Preferences** icon in the toolbar. In the following screen, enable the **Turn on .Mac Address Book Synchronization** check box and click the **Save** button. .Mac now begins the sync process (which takes place on the Apple servers, and doesn't depend on any contact with your own Mac), accessing your Address Book as saved in your .Mac account and copying it to the Web-accessible front end.

④ Use Your Address Book with .Mac Webmail

After your .Mac Address Book has been successfully synchronized, test-drive it by using .Mac Mail, which you can also access using any Web-capable computer. Click the **Mail** icon in the toolbar to go to your Webmail account, or click **Compose** to immediately start writing a new email message.

Click the **Address Book** icon in the .Mac Mail toolbar to access the contacts in your Address Book. You can select which headers in the email message you want each address to go into by selecting it from the menu in the **Destination** column. Click **Apply** to use the selected addresses in your email message.

NOTE

The synchronization process might take a few minutes. It might even time out and give you a message saying that you should come back later after .Mac has finished synchronizing your data. Give it about ten minutes before trying to access your contacts.

TIP

In the .Mac Address Book, you can add contacts to your Quick Address list by enabling the check boxes at the right and then clicking **Save**. Then, when you use .Mac Mail, you can select these names from the drop-down list next to each header field to import them still more quickly.

128 Recover from a Corrupted iSync Configuration

Before You Begin

✔ **125** Set Up iSync to Synchronize Your Macs

✔ **126** Synchronize Your Palm PDA and Other Devices

See Also

→ **173** Back Up Your Information

→ **176** Move Your Data to a New Mac

NOTE

Before beginning this task, make sure that you have successfully synchronized your information with .Mac (see **125** Set Up iSync to Synchronize Your Macs) and that .Mac has a current copy of your data. If you haven't done that and you throw away the information on your local computer, you'll have thrown away the only copy of your information.

Keeping all your data synchronized isn't an easy task, even for a computer. When you consider just how much work iSync is doing behind the scenes—dealing with multiple computers with conflicting pieces of information, handling intermittent network connections, taking into account differences in system time, and handling cases where software failures might cause one computer to lose track of its synchronization status—it's easy to imagine how your Mac might occasionally lose its footing.

There might come a time when you find that iSync is repeatedly failing in its attempts to synchronize your data. It might pop up a message warning you that synchronization failed, giving long and cryptic error messages as a reason. Until this situation is resolved, your data is no longer being synchronized. You need a way to solve this problem.

Fortunately, there's a fairly easy solution. All you have to do is throw all your data away.

Don't panic! It's not as bad as it sounds. Because all your data is kept in its most recent condition on the .Mac server, if you delete all your Address Book and iCal items from your Mac, the next time you synchronize with .Mac, everything will be repopulated into your computer from the .Mac servers. The iSync configuration will be cleaned up, and you'll be as good as new.

1 Quit Address Book and iCal

If the Address Book and iCal applications are running, quit them. This is necessary because when you quit these applications, they write their configuration data to the disk; if you erase the configuration before quitting, the applications will simply write out what's in memory, returning the same data to the disk that you just deleted—and your work will be for nothing.

2 Throw Away the AddressBook and Calendars Folders

In the Finder, navigate into the **Library** folder inside your **Home** folder. Go into the **Application Support** folder. Drag the **AddressBook** folder into the Trash (or to your Desktop if you want to be safer about it).

Additionally, throw away the **Calendars** folder inside the **Library**.

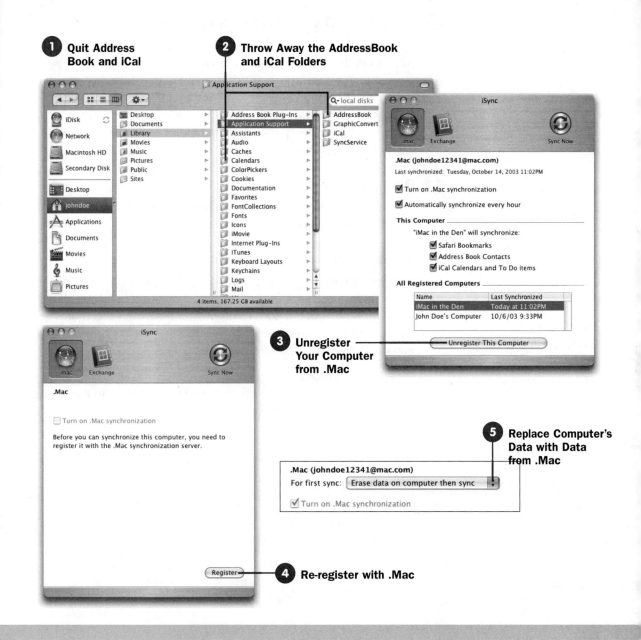

1 Quit Address Book and iCal

2 Throw Away the AddressBook and iCal Folders

3 Unregister Your Computer from .Mac

5 Replace Computer's Data with Data from .Mac

4 Re-register with .Mac

③ Unregister Your Computer from .Mac

Launch iSync. Open the **.Mac** configuration pane, select your computer from the **All Registered Computers** box, and then click **Unregister This Computer**. Click **Unregister** in the confirmation dialog box that appears. Your iSync configuration is now reset to its original condition, and the .Mac settings pane in iSync changes to show you only the sparse screen reminding you to register your computer with .Mac.

④ Re-register with .Mac

Click the **Register** button to register your computer with .Mac again, using a fresh configuration.

⑤ Replace Computer's Data with Data from .Mac

When your Mac is registered with .Mac, select **Erase data on computer then sync** from the **For first sync** drop-down list. Then click the **Sync Now** button to launch a synchronization process that replaces all the Address Book, iCal, and Safari data on your computer with fresh information from .Mac.

When the synchronization process is complete, you should be able to go back to letting iSync keep your data synchronized in the background without hassle or mishap.

PART IV

Making It Work for You

IN THIS PART

14

Customizing Mac OS X

IN THIS CHAPTER:

Any good operating system exists to be customized. To provide a comfortable operating environment for the user, the system must be flexible enough so that the user can tailor its behavior to suit not just his needs, but his tastes and fancies as well.

Apple has made a business out of the art of user-interface consistency—designing an operating environment in which every application behaves more or less the same way, where (for example) pressing ⌘**P** does the same thing no matter what you're doing when you press it. This kind of consistency is the cornerstone of Apple's vaunted ease of use, but it also means that the Mac OS is a user environment that's harder to customize than a system that imposes no restrictions on the behaviors of component utilities and third-party applications. Windows is supremely customizable—for instance, you can apply *skins* and complete interface overhauls to virtually the entire system—but that's as much a side effect of Windows' flexibility, and therefore its potential to be confusing and unstable, as a virtue in itself.

Mac OS X is not anywhere near as customizable as Windows is. Panther comes with only a single *theme*, or color and decoration scheme. Apple tightly controls the rules that dictate which applications should use the "brushed metal" look, and which ones should opt for the traditional white-with-pinstripes color scheme. Every Mac application window has the same shape, with the rounded top corners and the consistent drop shadow. Some third-party tools exist to let you tinker with the interface elements, but such tools are "hacks" at best—usually not comprehensive in what they do, and they often pose the risk of destabilizing your system. For most Mac users, the reality is that customizing Mac OS X is limited to what Apple explicitly allows you to do.

The good news is that what features Apple does permit you to customize are very highly developed. You can do things to your Mac that Windows users can't; if you can't apply a *Lord of the Rings* skin to the *Aqua* interface, so what? You can have your desktop background change smoothly and randomly every five minutes. Customizing the Mac involves some tradeoffs from what you might be used to in Windows; but you can have plenty of fun with what you can do.

129 Change General Color and Appearance Settings

The most basic kinds of customizations you can make to the operating system are the ones that affect the appearance of the entire system (for your login sessions only): fonts, interface element colors, and the items that go into the global **Apple** menu that always appears at the top of the screen no matter what application you're using.

1 Open the Appearance Preferences

Open the **System Preferences** application using the **Apple** menu and click the **Appearance** icon to open the **Appearance Preferences** window.

2 Select an Appearance Color

Mac OS X has two general color schemes: **Blue** (the standard Aqua color scheme, with blue scroll and progress bars and red, yellow, and green window control buttons) and **Graphite** (which turns all these colored elements gray). Select **Graphite** if you dislike the vivid colors in Mac OS X; this color option makes for a much more subdued user environment.

3 Select a Highlight Color

By default, when you select text in applications, it is highlighted in blue. You can change the highlight color to any of seven predefined tones, or you can select your own highlight color by picking **Other** from the **Highlight Color** drop-down menu and then using the color picker to choose a custom color.

4 Customize Scrollbars

You can choose to have the arrows on the scrollbars in windows placed at opposite ends of the scrollbar, or together at the bottom or right side of the bar. Arrows are placed together by default; this is usually more comfortable for most users because it involves less mouse movement.

You can also customize what happens when you click in a part of a scrollbar. Select whether you want Mac OS X to jump directly to the part of the window that you clicked on, or to move closer to that position by a single page with each click.

See Also

→ **90** Install a New Font
→ **130** Change Your Desktop Picture
→ **133** Customize the Menu Bar Clock

TIP

When selecting a custom color, bear in mind that the black text in most text applications has to show up on top of the color you choose when text is selected. If the color you pick is too dark, the text will be hard to read. Pastel colors work best.

1 Open the Appearance Preferences

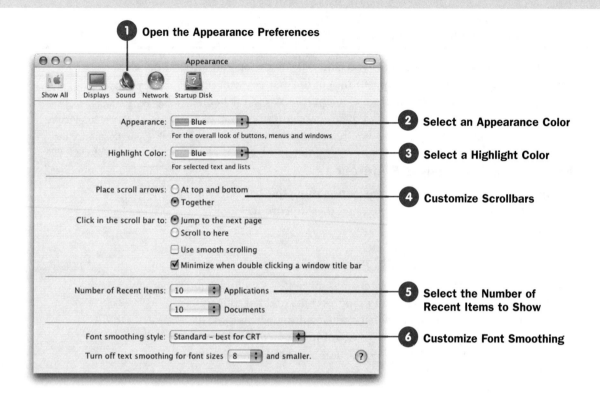

2 Select an Appearance Color

3 Select a Highlight Color

4 Customize Scrollbars

5 Select the Number of Recent Items to Show

6 Customize Font Smoothing

🔍 **KEY TERM**

Antialiasing—The technical term for "smoothing," as with fonts or diagonal lines. Sharp differences—aliasing—between the colors of neighboring pixels (dots on the screen) are "softened" visually by changing the colors of intermediate pixels to colors somewhere in between. This has the effect of making text look smoother (and readable at much smaller sizes), pictures more appealing, and individual pixels on the screen virtually invisible.

5 **Select the Number of Recent Items to Show**

By default, the **Recent Items** submenu of the **Apple** menu shows the ten most recently launched applications, and the ten most recently opened documents. You can configure the menu to show between zero and fifty of each.

6 **Customize Font Smoothing**

Depending on what kind of display (monitor) you have, you might want to modify the style of text smoothing (*antialiasing*) that Mac OS X uses. If you have a CRT display (a large, deep, heavy monitor) or a Mac that uses one (such as an eMac or older iMac), choose the **Standard** option. If you have an LCD (flat panel), choose **Medium** smoothing. You can also make the smoothing sharper (**Light**) or fuzzier (**Heavy**), depending on how you like your text to appear.

Text smaller than a certain size is not smoothed; you can define that threshold size, between 4 and 12 points, using the **Turn off text smoothing for font sizes** <*n*> **and smaller** drop-down list.

130 Change Your Desktop Picture

The Desktop picture, which in the Windows world is usually known as "wallpaper," is the largest and most obvious piece of customization available for your computer—aside from putting fins or racing stripes on the case. Very few people leave their desktop looking the way it does when you first boot up the computer. It's really easy to change the background to any picture you want and give your computer an immediate personal flavor.

1 Open the Desktop & Screen Saver Preferences

Open the **System Preferences** application using the **Apple** menu and click the **Desktop & Screen Saver** icon to open the **Desktop & Screen Saver Preferences** window. The **Desktop** tab opens by default.

2 Choose a Picture Source

Several items appear in the list at the left. Each item is a source for desktop pictures; Apple provides some bundled pictures, available in the **Apple Background Images** source. You can also choose from several solid colors, or from folders containing collections of picture files.

The **Nature** and **Abstract** folders contain themed pictures bundled by Apple. You can also select your own **Pictures** folder; this folder, directly inside your **Home** folder, is where you will normally place image files; choosing it as your picture source lets you select from any of the pictures you've collected.

At the bottom of the list are two picture sources that allow you to choose pictures from iPhoto. **Photo Library** shows you all the pictures in your entire iPhoto Library; **Last Import** lists only the images in the last "film roll" you imported into iPhoto.

Before You Begin

✔ **129** Change General Color and Appearance Settings

See Also

→ **106** Import Photos from a Digital Camera

→ **131** Select a Screensaver

→ **132** Customize a Folder Window

NOTE

As you add more photo albums in iPhoto (see **107** Create an iPhoto Album or Slideshow), each album is added to the list of sources you can use for selecting your desktop picture.

2 Choose a
Picture Source

1 Open the Desktop & Screen
Saver Preferences

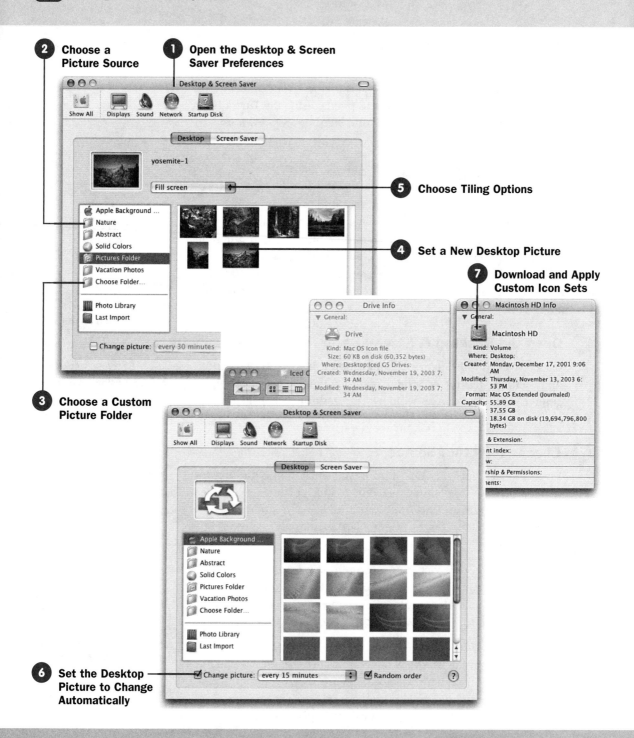

5 Choose Tiling Options

4 Set a New Desktop Picture

7 Download and Apply
Custom Icon Sets

3 Choose a Custom
Picture Folder

6 Set the Desktop
Picture to Change
Automatically

③ Choose a Custom Picture Folder

You can also define a new custom picture source, a folder other than your **Pictures** folder. This is useful if you have a special folder where you keep your desktop pictures. Click **Choose Folder** and use the navigator window that pops up to find the folder you want to use. Click **Choose** after selecting any folder or an item inside it, and the folder will appear among the picture sources.

④ Set a New Desktop Picture

To set a new desktop picture, simply click the one you want to use in the pane on the right. Your computer's Desktop is immediately updated.

⑤ Choose Tiling Options

For pictures from any source but the Apple-bundled ones or iPhoto, a drop-down list appears next to the well to let you select how an odd-shaped picture should be displayed. Select **Fill screen** to stretch the picture proportionally to fit the entire screen; select **Stretch to fill screen** to stretch it anamorphically (scaling each dimension by a different amount as necessary to make the picture completely fill the screen in both dimensions). Select **Center** to place the picture in the middle of the screen, or **Tile** to place multiple copies of it all over the screen.

⑥ Set the Desktop Picture to Change Automatically

You can have Mac OS X automatically change to another picture in the selected source folder after a certain period of time. Enable the **Change picture** check box and then select a time period (or an event, such as logging in or waking from sleep) from the drop-down list.

⑦ Download and Apply Custom Icon Sets

Because Mac OS X lets you set custom icons on files and folders (and even applications), customizing your system can involve collections of custom icons created as "themes." Many Web sites store massive collections of icon sets; from *Star Trek* to Tolkien to *Tintin*, and with hundreds of abstract design styles to choose from, you'll be able to find icon sets that match your personal tastes.

NOTE

Alternatively, if the picture you want is not available in any of the folders or picture sources shown in the list, you can use any picture file anywhere in the system. Simply find the picture file you want to use in the Finder and drag it into the well near the top of the **Desktop Preferences** window (the recessed box showing the current Desktop picture).

TIP

Enable the **Random** order check box to randomize how the picture is selected; if you don't check this box, the pictures are displayed in alphabetical order, using their filenames.

After you download an icon set, you can apply any icon inside it to an item in your system by using the standard method for copying icons: Open the **Get Info** panes for both the source and the target items, select and copy the icon from the source, and then select and paste it onto the icon in the target pane. (See **15 Change an Icon** for details.) You can do this for folders, hard disks, and any documents or applications in the system.

Many icon sets also allow you to set the default or "generic" icons for items such as folders and disks; to do this, however, involves changing the files within the system itself, and these changes will not survive a system upgrade. If you're adventurous, you can try using any of the various third-party tools that are available for changing your generic icons—but under the same caveats as with "theme" utilities, be aware of the risks to your system's stability.

 WEB RESOURCE

One of the most popular sources for custom Mac OS X icons on the Web, featuring hundreds of user-contributed icon sets, including the **Iced G5 Drives** set by Steve Smith.

http://www.xicons.com

---

131 Select a Screensaver

Before You Begin

✔ **130** Change Your Desktop Picture

See Also

→ **51** Share a Slideshow Screensaver

→ **152** Set the Computer's Sleep Time

Some traditions die hard.

Back in the early days of high-resolution color monitors, the concept of a "screensaver" was popularized with the After Dark package, the first widespread piece of software designed to save your monitor from "burn-in" effects resulting from leaving it turned on and showing the same image for hours at a stretch. Simple floating logos and starfields, and goofy animated scenes such as flying toasters, kept the screen from ever showing the same thing from one moment to the next when not in use, lengthening the monitor's useful life. As computing power increased, screensavers became more and more lavish, until the present day, where now our idle monitors show fish tanks that are all but indistinguishable from the real thing, crunch numbers in a distributed effort to find intelligent life in space, and download ads for you to read when you come back to your computer after lunch.

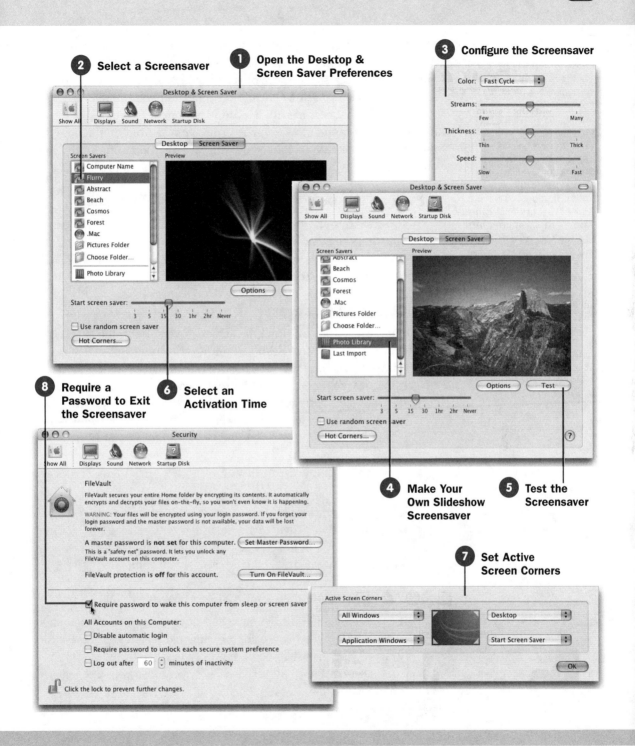

1 Open the Desktop & Screen Saver Preferences

2 Select a Screensaver

3 Configure the Screensaver

4 Make Your Own Slideshow Screensaver

5 Test the Screensaver

6 Select an Activation Time

7 Set Active Screen Corners

8 Require a Password to Exit the Screensaver

TIP

Many third-party developers have published their own screensavers for Mac OS X; you can add these to your system by moving them (each screensaver has the extension **.saver** on its filename) into the **Screen Savers** folder inside the **Library** folder in your **Home** folder. If you don't have a **Screen Savers** folder inside your Library, create it. After moving the **.saver** files into the **Screen Savers** folder, go back to the **Desktop & Screen Saver Preferences** window; the new screensavers should appear in the list.

Monitor technology has come a long way since the first screensavers; not just LCD screens, but even the latest CRT monitors are highly resistant to burn-in effects. Screensavers are thus an outdated concept, except for the small fact that they're *cool*. Whether the image on your monitor needs to be kept in motion or not, it's hard to resist configuring a flashy display for your computer to show when you're not in front of it. It doesn't hurt that the screensavers that come with Mac OS X are some of the best and most visually pleasing examples of the craft ever yet produced.

① Open the Desktop & Screen Saver Preferences

Open the **System Preferences** application using the **Apple** menu and click the **Desktop & Screen Saver** icon to open the **Desktop & Screen Saver Preferences** window. The **Desktop** tab opens by default; click the **Screen Saver** tab.

② Select a Screensaver

Choose a screensaver from the **Screen Savers** list on the left. The choices range from the simple **Computer Name** (which displays an Apple logo and the computer's name in various places around the screen) to the beautiful **Abstract**, **Beach**, **Cosmos**, and **Forest** slideshows, and the mesmerizing **Flurry**. When you click any screensaver in the list, a preview of it appears in the **Preview** panel on the right.

③ Configure the Screensaver

Most screensavers have several controls and options you can adjust. Click **Options** to open these controls in a sheet; click **OK** when you're done. Generally speaking, because these options don't affect anything but how the screensaver behaves, you can feel perfectly free to tweak any of them however you want.

④ Make Your Own Slideshow Screensaver

If you like the bundled slideshow screensavers (**Forest** and **Beach** and so on) but you get tired of the same old pictures, you can easily create your own slideshows that work just like them. Mac OS X can automatically create a slideshow screensaver from any folder full of picture files.

Select **Choose Folder** from the **Screen Savers** list and then navigate to the folder containing the pictures you want to use. Click **Choose** when the folder you want is selected. All the pictures in that folder now become part of a smoothly cross-fading and panning slideshow, subject to the options you select in the **Options** sheet.

5 Test the Screensaver

To see how the screensaver will look using the full screen, click **Test**. Don't move the mouse after clicking the button; moving the mouse or pressing a key quits the screensaver and returns you to whatever screen was active before the screensaver kicked in.

6 Select an Activation Time

You can have the screensaver kick in automatically after a specified period of inactivity, from three minutes up to two hours (or never). Drag the slider to select the time period that must elapse before the selected screensaver is activated, or drag the slider to **Never** to prevent the screensaver from ever activating.

7 Set Active Screen Corners

You can configure *Active Screen Corners* to allow you to start the screensaver immediately, or to prevent the screensaver from activating while you're not moving the mouse or typing (for instance, if you're watching a long QuickTime movie). Click the **Hot Corners** button; use the sheet that appears to define what happens when you move the mouse into each corner of the screen. You can configure some corners to activate *Exposé* functions (see **6** **Grab the Window You Want**), and other corners to control the screensaver.

8 Require a Password to Exit the Screensaver

To protect your computer from the prying eyes of people who walk by after your screensaver has kicked in, you can tell Mac OS X not to allow anybody to reactivate the computer unless they type your account password (see **150** **Change a User's Password** for information on how to manage the account password, which is what a user enters to start a Mac OS X login session). To do this, go to the **Security Preferences** window (click **Security** in the **System Preferences** application). Enable the **Require password to wake this computer from sleep or screen saver** check box.

NOTE

At the bottom of the **Screen Savers** list are entries for your **Photo Library** and **Last Import**, which let you create slideshow screensavers from your iPhoto Library, just as you can do from the **Desktop** tab (see **130** **Change Your Desktop Picture**). Also, as is true for the **Desktop** tab, additional iPhoto albums that you create appear in the list below these entries.

KEY TERMS

Active Screen Corners— Also known as "Hot Corners," this feature allows you to trigger certain functions by moving the mouse pointer into different corners of the screen. Such functions include starting the screensaver or invoking Exposé.

Exposé—A feature that allows you to shrink all your windows to fit on the screen so that you can immediately click to choose the window you want.

132 Customize a Folder Window

Before You Begin

✔ **12** Create a New Folder

See Also

→ **15** Change an Icon

→ **16** Set a Color Label

NOTE

You'll only see your customized folder view if you open a folder directly in a new window—for example, if you have an alias to a folder on your Desktop or in the Dock, or if you double-click the folder in the Finder in Icon view. If you navigate down into a folder using the Finder using List or Column view, the view mode does not change.

TIP

If you change the view mode for a folder and then use that same folder window to navigate to another location, the view mode you selected is not saved for the folder you opened. Changes to the view mode are saved when you close the window; if you want to change the view mode for a folder window you open directly, close the window after selecting the desired view mode. This action saves the setting for that folder.

Because you will be spending a lot of time navigating through the folders in your system and opening the documents in them, it's only natural to want to customize those various folders to reflect your personal tastes. For instance, you might want to navigate the filesystem primarily in the austere but highly functional Column view; but you might want to have your **Pictures** folder be shown in Icon view with each icon cranked up to its maximum size, organized in a grid, sorted alphabetically, and with a special background picture. Mac OS X lets you customize each and every folder in your system if you so desire.

1 **Open the View Options Palette**

While viewing any Finder window or the Desktop, select **Show View Options** from the **View** menu. The **View Options** palette appears and floats along with the Finder window (it becomes invisible if you switch applications).

With the **View Options** palette visible, you can still click items in the Finder window; if you switch to a different Finder window, the **View Options** palette updates to show the options for the folder shown in the new window.

2 **Select the View to Customize**

Click the **view selection buttons** at the top of the Finder window to choose the view mode you want to use for that folder if you open it directly. Note that each view mode has different options shown in the **View Options** palette.

3 **Customize This Window Only or All Windows**

At the top of the **View Options** palette, no matter what the view mode, are two options that let you choose between setting the options for just the folder window you're customizing, or globally configuring all windows in the system at once.

4 **Customize List View Columns**

In List view, you have the option to use large or small icons, to select the font size for document names, and to choose which informational columns you want to show. In the **View Options** palette, enable the check box for each column of information you want to see in List view.

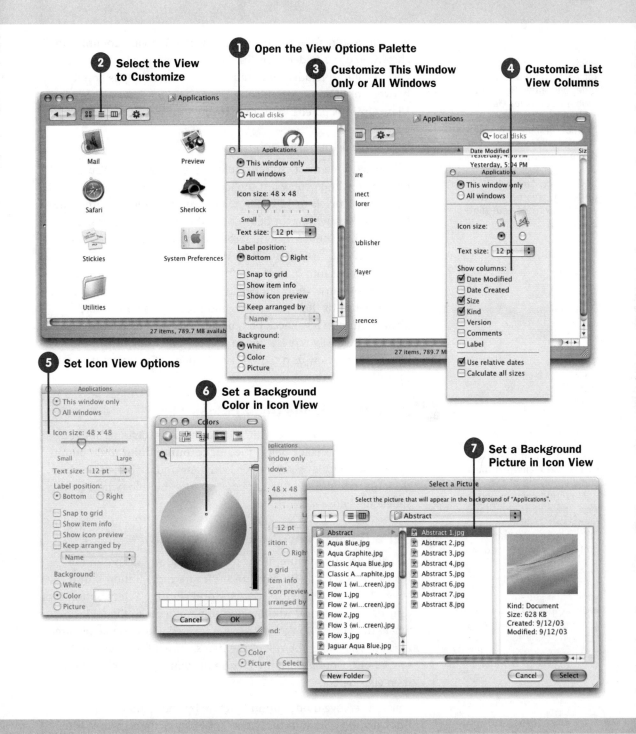

1 Open the View Options Palette

2 Select the View to Customize

3 Customize This Window Only or All Windows

4 Customize List View Columns

5 Set Icon View Options

6 Set a Background Color in Icon View

7 Set a Background Picture in Icon View

Each view mode's options for each window is set independently; if you set global options for List view, folders that have been set to open in Icon view will still open in Icon view; but if you then switch to List view, the global options take effect. Any specific options you've set for that window override your global settings.

NOTE

Remember that the black text of the filenames must show up on top of the background color or you won't be able to read the filenames. Light pastel colors work best as backgrounds for folder windows.

You can also reorganize the order in which List view columns are shown on a per-folder basis. In the Finder window for the folder, click a column header and drag it left and right to position it between a different pair of columns. You do not have to have the **View Options** palette open to rearrange the column order.

⑤ Set Icon View Options

Icon view is the most customizable of the folder views. You can choose how large you want the icons to be (on a smooth scale from 16×16 pixels to 128×128 pixels); you can select whether the filenames should appear below or to the right of the icons, and whether they should include secondary information about the items' contents (using the **Show item info** check box); you can force the icons into a strict grid formation, and you can make them sort themselves alphabetically or according to various other criteria (such as the time of last modification). If you enable the **Show item preview** check box, documents such as picture files that can be easily represented in a "preview" form are shown using that preview as a custom icon instead of the default icon for that document type.

⑥ Set a Background Color in Icon View

Icon view windows have white backgrounds by default, but you can change this color. Select the **Background: Color** radio button in the **View Options** palette for Icon view and click the color box that appears; the color picker pops up. Use the color wheel and sliders to choose a color.

⑦ Set a Background Picture in Icon View

You can use any picture file as a folder window background in Icon view. Select the **Background: Picture** radio button in the **View Options** palette for Icon view and click the **Select** button that appears. A navigator window pops up; navigate to the folder where the picture you want to use is located. Only usable picture files are selectable; the rest of the items, except for folders, are grayed out. Double-click the picture file you want, or click it and then click **Select**.

You can remove a background picture by changing the **Background** option in the **View Options** palette back to **White**.

133 Customize the Menu Bar Clock

Nearly everybody agrees that a clock is a useful thing to have as part of an operating system. Few people, however, agree as to exactly what form that clock should take. Everybody has different preferences: analog or digital, 12-hour or 24-hour, with the seconds or without. Mac OS X lets you customize your clock to suit whatever your tastes dictate.

1 Open the Date & Time Preferences

Open the **System Preferences** application using the **Apple** menu and click the **Date & Time** icon to open the **Date & Time Preferences** window. Click the **Clock** tab to view the clock options.

2 Select a Menu Bar or Floating Clock

A menu bar clock appears in the upper-right corner of the screen, in a small and unobtrusive format; you can choose a larger version that floats in front of all your windows by selecting the **Window** version. You can move the Window clock anywhere you want by clicking and dragging it. Use the **Transparency** slider at the bottom of the **Preferences** window to choose how transparent you want the floating clock to be. The clock's appearance immediately changes with each control you modify so that you can see the results of your customization instantly.

3 Select a Digital or Analog Clock

Displaying the time digitally is something computers do easily; showing an analog clock, with a rotary dial and hands, is a bit more complicated—but you might prefer an analog clock's more traditional look. Whether you're showing the time in the menu bar or as a floating object, selecting **Analog** creates a round clock with hands that update smoothly each second.

4 Set the Clock Display Options

You can specify a few other options as well. Choose whether you want the seconds displayed (with another set of numbers or with a second hand, depending on the clock style), whether you want to use a 24-hour clock (digital clocks only), whether you want to show the day of the week, and whether the clock should show the AM and PM suffixes. Select **Flash the time separators** if you want the colon in the digital menu bar clock to flash slowly; this can be useful in giving you a visual cue that the system is still responsive if it's doing some intense processing.

Before You Begin

✔ **24** Set the Time and Date

✔ **25** Enable Automatic Time Synchronization (NTP)

See Also

→ **135** Adjust the Format of Numbers and Other Notations

→ **136** Change the System's Language

🔋 TIP

Open the **International Preferences** window (click **International** in the **System Preferences** application) and select **Time** to choose among various standardized time formats as used in different countries. In this dialog box, you can manually set what text is used for AM, PM, or the colon separator between numbers.

2 Select a Menu Bar or Floating Clock

1 Open the Date & Time Preferences

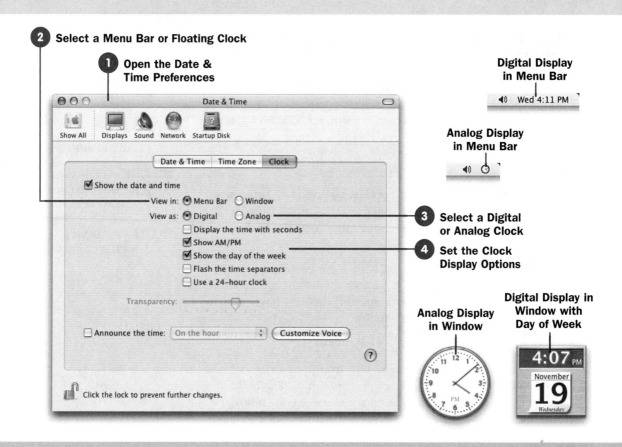

Digital Display in Menu Bar

Analog Display in Menu Bar

3 Select a Digital or Analog Clock

4 Set the Clock Display Options

Analog Display in Window

Digital Display in Window with Day of Week

---

134 Change the Dock's Position and Behavior

Before You Begin

✔ **3** Add an Application to the Dock

✔ **5** Minimize and Restore a Window

See Also

→ **4** Control an Application from the Dock

The Dock is the centerpiece of Mac OS X, the flexible and accommodating control center for your documents and applications. Its ease of use is unprecedented; but it's also configurable in a number of key ways, a fact which you might find very welcome as you try to make the Dock work most efficiently for you.

1 Open the Dock Preferences

Go directly to the **Dock Preferences** window by **Control**+clicking or right-clicking the vertical separator bar in the middle of the Dock; select **Dock Preferences** from the contextual menu that pops up. You can also open the **Dock Preferences** window by clicking **Dock** in the **System Preferences** application, or by choosing **Dock Preferences** from the **Dock** submenu of the **Apple** menu.

2 Change the Dock's Size

Use the **Dock Size** slider to change the size of the Dock. Note that you won't be able to make the Dock larger than the largest size where all icons in the Dock can be shown at once. The Dock's size immediately changes as you move the slider, letting you see the results of your customizations right away.

3 Configure Magnification

One of the Dock's neat features is that even if you make the Dock itself very small, you can still see the individual icons in much larger sizes—because of magnification. If you move your mouse over the icons in the Dock with magnification on, the icon you're moving over and its immediate neighbors appear much larger—up to the size specified by the Magnification slider.

4 Turn On Dock Hiding

Enable the **Automatically hide and show the Dock** check box to hide the Dock from view and regain Desktop space. If the Dock is hidden, it reappears when you move the mouse down to the bottom of the screen.

5 Change the Minimize Effect

There are two minimize effects available in Mac OS X: Genie and Scale. The **Genie Effect** is the default; it's where a minimized window curves and slides into its place in the Dock. The **Scale Effect** simply zooms the window down to its minimized position; you might prefer the **Scale Effect** because of its faster operation.

6 Place the Dock on the Left or Right

By default, the Dock appears at the bottom of your screen. You might not like having the Dock at the bottom; you might prefer it to use up the more plentiful horizontal margin space along the left or right side of the screen (particularly if you have a widescreen display) than the comparatively scarce vertical space at the bottom of the screen. To do this, select either the **Left** or **Right** radio button.

 TIP

Most of these Dock controls can also be accessed from the Dock itself. Some of the options, such as automatic hiding and left or right positioning, can be selected from the pop-up menu that appears if you **Control**+click (or right-click) the vertical divider bar in the middle of the Dock. You can change the Dock's size by clicking the vertical bar and dragging up and down.

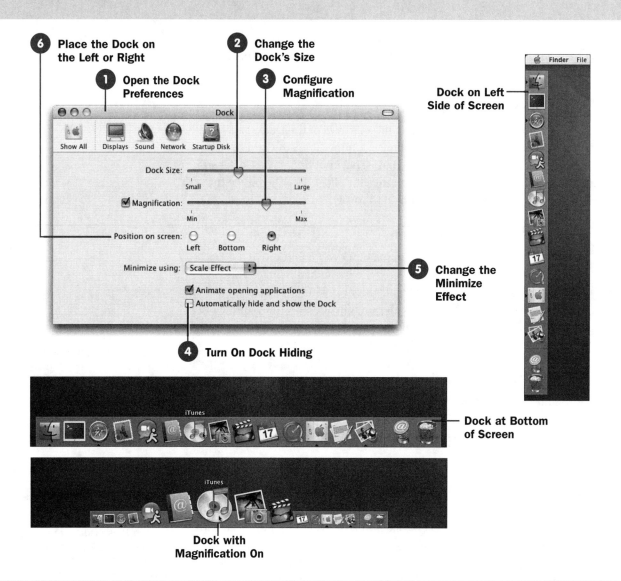

6 Place the Dock on the Left or Right

2 Change the Dock's Size

1 Open the Dock Preferences

3 Configure Magnification

Dock on Left Side of Screen

Finder   File

Dock   Show All   Displays   Sound   Network   Startup Disk

Dock Size: Small   Large

☑ Magnification: Min   Max

Position on screen: ○ Left   ○ Bottom   ◉ Right

Minimize using: Scale Effect

☑ Animate opening applications
☐ Automatically hide and show the Dock

5 Change the Minimize Effect

4 Turn On Dock Hiding

iTunes

Dock at Bottom of Screen

iTunes

Dock with Magnification On

135 Adjust the Format of Numbers and Other Notations

If you're not in the United States, Mac OS X's default behaviors when it displays numbers or dates might appear odd. The operating system supports many different countries' preferred notation formats, and lets you define your own as well (for instance, if you're a U.S. resident who prefers the metric system). Date, time, and number formats can all be changed in the **International Preferences** dialog box.

① Open the International Preferences

Open the **System Preferences** application using the **Apple** menu and click the **International** icon to open the **International Preferences** window. Click the **Formats** tab to open the pane where you can configure the formats of dates, times, and numbers.

② Configure Date Formats

Click the **Customize** button in the **Dates** section. The sheet that appears lets you control how a "long date" (using both full and abbreviated weekday and month names, such as **Thursday, January 2, 2003**, and **Thu, Jan 2, 2003**) and a "short date" (such as **1/2/03**) are displayed. Weekday and month names are predefined; you can't change the name of **Thursday** or its abbreviation **Thu**.

For the long date, you are given four positions in the date string to which you can assign either the day, weekday, month, or year, as well as a suffix you can place after it. These options let you arrange the various parts of the date into whatever order you want, placing commas, periods, or other plain-language separators into the date format.

For the short date, select from any of several predefined numeric orders from the drop-down menu, and choose a separator (such as a slash, hyphen, or period). Choose to show leading zeros if you want; if you enable **Show Century**, a year such as **03** is shown as **2003** to avoid Y2K-like confusion.

Change options as desired and click **OK** to go back to the **International Preferences** window.

Before You Begin

✔ **24** Set the Time and Date

✔ **133** Customize the Menu Bar Clock

See Also

→ **136** Change the System's Language

TIP

The **Customize** buttons let you manually specify the formats for dates, times, and numbers to match your personal taste. If you prefer, however, you can choose a format profile that matches your country's standard usage from the **Region** drop-down list at the top of the **Formats** page of the **International Preferences** window.

NOTE

Note that if you set any two of the fields to be the same, the first one will turn into **None** and be removed from the format string.

① **Open the International Preferences**

② **Configure Date Formats**

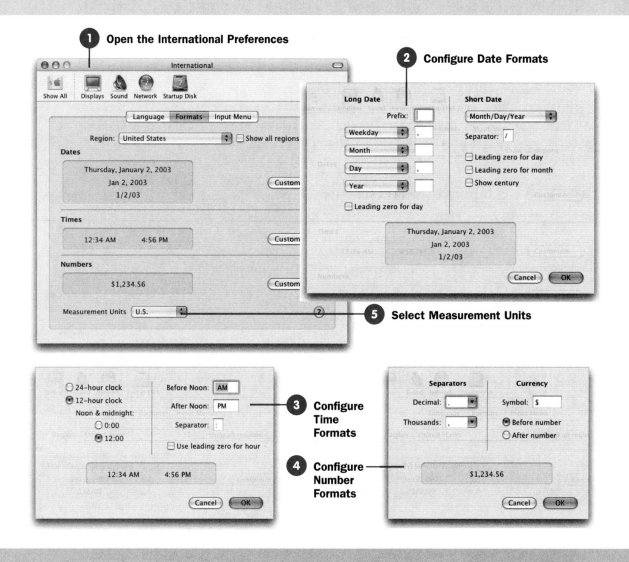

⑤ **Select Measurement Units**

③ **Configure Time Formats**

④ **Configure Number Formats**

③ Configure Time Formats

Click the **Customize** button in the **Times** section. In the sheet that appears, you can configure various aspects of how times are displayed beyond what can be configured in the **Date & Time Preferences** window. For instance, you can choose whether noon and midnight appear as **12:00** or **0:00**; you can have a leading zero placed before one-digit hours (such as **02:00**); and you can enter your own suffixes instead of AM and PM.

Change options as desired and click **OK** to go back to the **International Preferences** window.

4 Configure Number Formats

Click the **Customize** button in the **Numbers** section. In the sheet that appears, you can configure the number separators (such as a comma or period) and the currency symbol and its location.

Change options as desired and click **OK** to go back to the **International Preferences** window.

5 Select Measurement Units

Back in the **International Preferences** window, use the **Measurement Units** drop-down list to specify your preferred measurement system (**U.S.** or **Metric**).

136 Change the System's Language

Mac OS X supports 83 different languages, all in their own native writing systems, thanks to the massive Unicode character set. Also, because of a unique preference-based cascading localization scheme, you can control which languages are used to run your system. You define what languages are your most preferred; then, whenever you run an application, Mac OS X looks inside it for what *localizations* it supports. A Mac application generally contains several different localizations, defining the contents of text strings and menu options in as many different languages as the application's developer chose to include. Mac OS X goes down your list of preferred languages until it finds one that the application supports, and then it launches the application using that language; this way, you can strike the optimal balance between what languages you want to use and the languages each application has been written to support. All you have to do is set up your **Language Preferences** once.

1 Open the International Preferences

Open the **System Preferences** application using the **Apple** menu and click the **International** icon to open the **International Preferences** window.

See Also

→ **84** Type §¶éçïå£ ¢hÁràc†érs

→ **90** Install a New Font

→ **135** Adjust the Format of Numbers and Other Notations

KEY TERM

Localization—Mostly a fancy name for "language," a localization also contains definitions for how sort order, numeric formats, and other written styles behave in a given region.

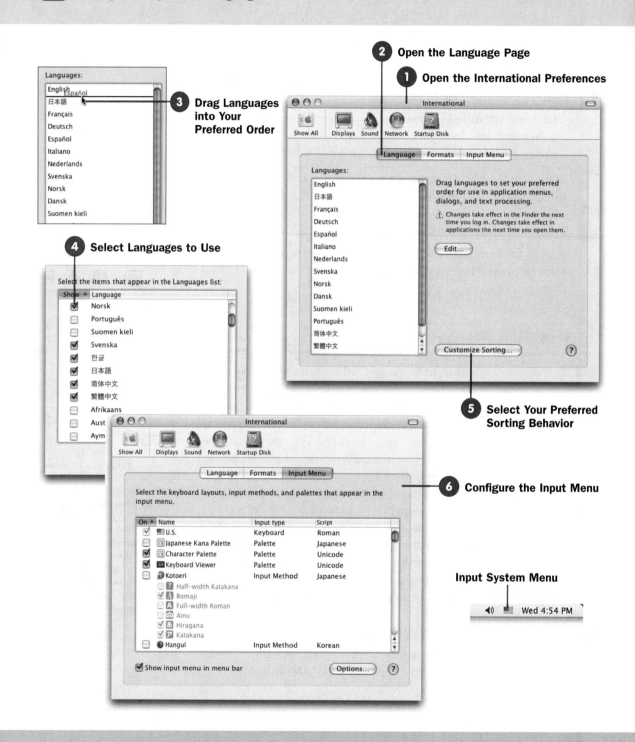

2 Open the Language Page

1 Open the International Preferences

3 Drag Languages into Your Preferred Order

Languages:
- English
- Español
- 日本語
- Français
- Deutsch
- Español
- Italiano
- Nederlands
- Svenska
- Norsk
- Dansk
- Suomen kieli

International

Show All   Displays   Sound   Network   Startup Disk

Language   Formats   Input Menu

Languages:
- English
- 日本語
- Français
- Deutsch
- Español
- Italiano
- Nederlands
- Svenska
- Norsk
- Dansk
- Suomen kieli
- Português
- 简体中文
- 繁體中文

Drag languages to set your preferred order for use in application menus, dialogs, and text processing.

⚠ Changes take effect in the Finder the next time you log in. Changes take effect in applications the next time you open them.

(Edit...)

(Customize Sorting...)   (?)

4 Select Languages to Use

Select the items that appear in the Languages list:

Show ▲	Language
☑	Norsk
☐	Português
☐	Suomen kieli
☑	Svenska
☑	한글
☑	日本語
☑	简体中文
☑	繁體中文
☐	Afrikaans
☐	Aust
☐	Aym

5 Select Your Preferred Sorting Behavior

International

Show All   Displays   Sound   Network   Startup Disk

Language   Formats   Input Menu

Select the keyboard layouts, input methods, and palettes that appear in the input menu.

On ▲	Name	Input type	Script
☑	U.S.	Keyboard	Roman
☐	Japanese Kana Palette	Palette	Japanese
☑	Character Palette	Palette	Unicode
☑	Keyboard Viewer	Palette	Unicode
☐	Kotoeri	Input Method	Japanese
☐	Half-width Katakana		
☑	Romaji		
☐	Full-width Roman		
☐	Ainu		
☑	Hiragana		
☑	Katakana		
☐	Hangul	Input Method	Korean

☑ Show input menu in menu bar   (Options...)   (?)

6 Configure the Input Menu

Input System Menu

◀) ▦ Wed 4:54 PM

2 Open the Language Page

Click the **Language** tab to open the **Language** configuration page, if it is not already displayed.

3 Drag Languages into Your Preferred Order

In the **Languages** box, click and drag the displayed language names into the order you prefer to use them. The topmost language is used first if it's available in the application; if not, the second language is used, and so on.

4 Select Languages to Use

Although Mac OS X supports 83 languages, only 15 are shown in the **Languages** box. If the language you want to use is not shown there, click the **Edit** button to bring up the dialog box that shows all 83 languages Mac OS X knows about.

Only the languages with the check box enabled appear in the **Languages** box. Click the check boxes next to whatever languages you want to appear in the box; you can also disable languages you know you won't be using. Click **OK** when you're done.

5 Select Your Preferred Sorting Behavior

Click the **Customize Sorting** button. In the sheet that appears, select the *script* you use to write your preferred language. For instance, English, French, German, Spanish, and many other European languages use the **Roman** script. Polish, Hungarian, and Slovenian use the **Central European** script. Japanese, Chinese, and Korean each have their own scripts—in fact, Chinese has two. Japanese has three, but only one—**Kanji**—is supported by Mac OS X for the purpose of defining text behaviors.

A list of regional text behaviors for languages that use your selected script is available in the **Behaviors** drop-down list. You can select a different language from the list to make Mac OS X and your applications behave according to that language's rules for alphabetization, case conversion, word definitions, and other minutiae of usage.

NOTE

When you change your language preference order, you are defining what language should be used when each application launches. Because currently running applications have already launched and chosen a language, you'll have to quit and relaunch these applications before they can use your preferred languages. This includes the Finder, so you must log out and log back in before the Mac OS X itself switches languages.

KEY TERM

Script—A general style of writing and set of symbols or letters often shared by many languages. The Roman alphabet is a script, as is Cyrillic, Kanji, or the Arabic alphabet.

TIP

You can define a behavior for every script you will be using if you have languages that use different scripts near the top of your **Languages** list.

6 Configure the Input Menu

Click the **Input Menu** tab to view the list of input styles. Keyboard layouts for many different languages and regions, as well as palettes for all Unicode characters, for Japanese Hiragana/Katakana, or for the **Keyboard Viewer** are available. You can also choose the **Hangul** (Korean), **Kotoeri** (Japanese), or **Simplified** or **Traditional** Chinese input methods, which let you input native characters using special key commands on a U.S.-style keyboard. Many other simple keyboard-based input methods and regional key remappings are available as well. See **84** **Type §¶éçïä£ ¢hÁràc†érs** for more information on these special input palettes.

Every input style that you select in the list under the **Input Menu** tab appears in the **Input** system menu, on the right side of the system's main menu bar, to the left of the clock (if you're using the U.S. keyboard layout, the menu appears as an American flag). When only a single *input menu* option is selected in the **International Preferences** window (for instance, the U.S. keyboard layout), the **Input** system menu does not appear. However, if you enable other options using the check boxes, the **Input** icon appears among the system menu icons, and its icon shows the current input method or layout. You can switch from one layout or method to another quickly by using the menu.

For instance, to enable the Dvorak keyboard layout, select it using its check box and the input menu appears at the top-right corner of the screen. Select **Dvorak** from the input menu, and your keyboard will now operate in Dvorak mode.

EY TERM

Input menu—A tool that lets you quickly open a palette or switch to a special input method to enter special characters or non-Latin languages. The **Input** menu appears among the system menu icons on the right side of the menu bar.

137 Set Applications to Launch Automatically at Login

Before You Begin

✔ **2** Find and Launch an Application

See Also

→ **138** Enable and Disable Automatic Login

→ **142** Automatically Log Out

One final way to customize your Mac OS X user environment is to have one or more applications launch themselves automatically as soon as you log in (or boot the computer, if you have automatic login enabled). You'll find this very useful as you become more familiar with Mac OS X and with the applications you want to have running to be more productive. For instance, in the course of writing this book, it's necessary for me to have Snapz Pro X (the premier screen-capture application for Mac OS X) running at all times. Rather than hunting it down and launching it every time I start the computer, I can have it launch automatically.

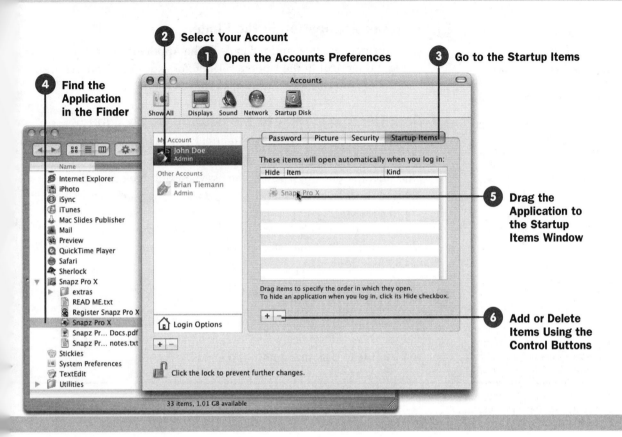

2 Select Your Account

1 Open the Accounts Preferences

3 Go to the Startup Items

4 Find the Application in the Finder

5 Drag the Application to the Startup Items Window

6 Add or Delete Items Using the Control Buttons

1 Open the Accounts Preferences

Open the **System Preferences** application using the **Apple** menu and click **Accounts** to go to the **Accounts Preferences** window.

2 Select Your Account

Your account is the topmost one shown in the list, and is probably already selected. If not, select it. Your account options display, such as your full name and password options.

3 Go to the Startup Items

Click the **Startup Items** tab.

TIP

You can add items other than just applications to your **Startup Items** list. You can add a document, and it will launch at startup in the application that it's set to open in; or you can add a folder, and the folder window will open at startup.

NOTE

To delete an item from the **Startup Items** list, select it and then click the – button. (This action only removes the item from the **Startup Items** list; it doesn't delete it from the computer.)

4 Find the Application in the Finder

Open a Finder window and navigate to the **Applications** folder (using the shortcut in the Finder's sidebar, for example). Find the application you want to launch at startup or login.

5 Drag the Application to the Startup Items Window

Click and drag the application from the Finder window into the **Startup Items** list. If there are already items in the list, you can place the new one anywhere in the list you want; the order of the items in the list determines the order in which they are launched. This order might be important, in case some of the items depend on other items already having been launched. If you want to change the order of the listed applications, just drag them into the desired positions.

6 Add or Delete Items

If you'd rather not drag applications to the **Startup Items** list, you can use the + button below the list box to pop up a navigator sheet you can use to pick the application to add.

15

Working with Other Users on One Computer

IN THIS CHAPTER:

As a true multiuser operating system, Mac OS X gives you and the other members of your household, classroom, or business a great deal of flexibility in how you all share the computer among yourselves. It also, however, introduces complexities that a single-user operating system lacks.

Security and convenience, it has been said, are mutually exclusive concepts. To make software easier to use and more convenient, software companies sometimes have to sacrifice the security of that software; the reverse is also true. For instance, an email program that automatically opens newly received messages is very convenient, but it is inherently insecure in that it can very easily execute a virus in one of those messages without you lifting a finger.

This principle is especially true when it comes to multiuser operating systems such as Mac OS X. This kind of system allows you to create multiple user environments, each tailored to the tastes of each person who uses the computer, and each secure from all the others on the same machine. But to properly take advantage of this added security and privacy, the users of the computer have to individually log in—instead of simply booting the computer into a single, common working environment as in the Windows and Mac OS systems of old. Indeed, many computer users even in the present day find the task of logging in and out to be too tedious—and they don't use the multiuser features of their computers at all, allowing everybody to share a single user account and working environment. However, this practice—beyond simply lacking security and privacy for the computer's multiple users—misses out on many of the coolest parts of Mac OS X, which was designed to make the process of switching from user environment to user environment pain free and convenient.

This chapter discusses the various features of Mac OS X that ease the necessary discomforts associated with a multiuser operating system, allowing users of a single computer to share its resources, exchange files and information with each other, and switch quickly from one login session to another and back. It also discusses the administrative tasks that you, as the owner of the computer, will need to perform—and exactly what makes an "administrator" so special.

138 Enable and Disable Automatic Login

Automatic login is an option that lets your computer act as though it has only one user on it—the user that primarily uses the computer. It's a useful feature if you're the only person who ever uses the machine; it eliminates the need for you to log in to your account when you boot up the Mac, and it logs you directly in to your working environment.

If multiple people use your computer, automatic login can be a detriment; after all, you don't want someone else booting up the computer and automatically being dumped into *your* account. He then has to log out and log in to his own account, or he might decide to just use yours— and you'll come home to find all your icons rearranged and a bunch of new music in iTunes that you don't listen to.

In short, enable automatic login if you are the only one who uses your Mac; disable it if the Mac is shared among several users.

1 ### Open the Accounts Preferences

Open the **System Preferences** using the **Apple** menu. Click **Accounts** to open the **Accounts Preferences** window.

2 ### Select the Login Options

Click **Login Options** at the bottom of the list of users on the left side of the window. The global options for the system's login behavior appear.

3 ### Select the User to Log In As

Enable the check box next to **Automatically log in as** and open the drop-down list; all the users on the system are in the list. Pick the one you want the system to automatically boot into instead of presenting the login screen.

4 ### Enter the User's Password

In the sheet that appears, enter the selected user's password and click **OK.** The next time you restart the computer, it will boot directly into that user's working environment.

Before You Begin

✔ **146** Add a New User

See Also

→ **137** Set Applications to Launch Automatically at Login

→ **140** Switch to Another User

KEY TERM

Automatic login—When you start up a Mac with this option enabled, the computer enters a predetermined user's login session automatically; you don't have to type your password to log in.

NOTE

You must be logged in as an Admin user to open the **Login Options** pane. See **145** About Administrative Responsibilities for more information.

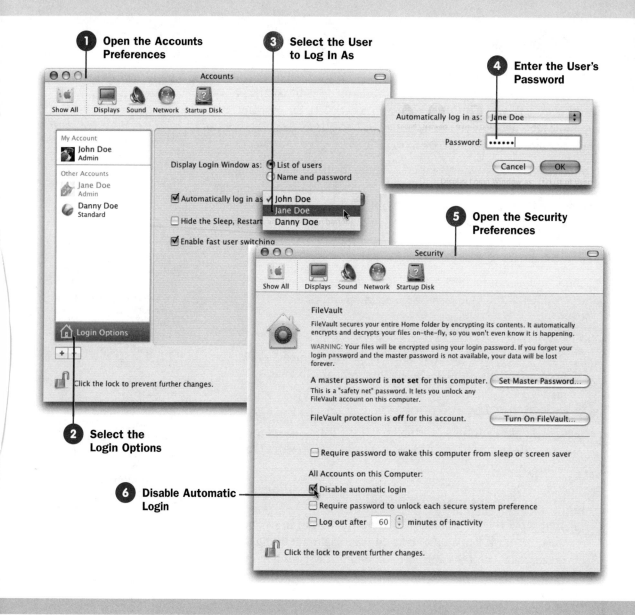

1 Open the Accounts Preferences

2 Select the Login Options

3 Select the User to Log In As

4 Enter the User's Password

5 Open the Security Preferences

6 Disable Automatic Login

5 Open the Security Preferences

If you're an Admin user, you can also disable automatic login and force the computer to present the login screen when it boots up. To do this, open the **System Preferences** from the **Apple** menu and click **Security** to open the **Security Preferences** window.

6 **Disable Automatic Login**

Click the **Disable automatic login** check box. Automatic login is immediately disabled. To re-enable it, return to the **Accounts Preferences** window and follow steps 2, 3, and 4 of this task.

139 Log In from the Login Window

With *automatic login* disabled, one screen that you will become very familiar with is the login window. This screen features a box in the middle with a list of all the available users in the system, each with a personalized picture. Any of these users can log in by clicking their name and entering their password when prompted. At the end of your session, when you log out from the **Apple** menu (or if you have Mac OS X set to log you out automatically), you return to the login window.

You can even return to the login window without ending your session. If you enable **Fast User Switching** (see **140** **Switch to Another User**), you can call up the login window at any time, log in as another user, or return to your session that's been running in the background.

1 **Restart the Computer or Log Out**

First make sure that automatic login is turned off (see **138** **Enable and Disable Automatic Login**) to ensure that the computer will present the login window rather than booting automatically into a certain user's account.

Restart the computer; alternatively, select **Log Out** <*Your Name*> from the **Apple** menu and click **Log Out** to confirm the action. When the computer is ready for your input, it will be at the login window.

2 **Select the User to Log In As**

From the list of users, scroll to the user you want to log in as if necessary, and click the user's name or picture. The window shifts slightly to give you a password box. Click **Go Back** if you have mistakenly selected the wrong user.

Before You Begin

✔ **138** Enable and Disable Automatic Login

✔ **146** Add a New User

See Also

→ **137** Set Applications to Launch Automatically at Login

→ **142** Automatically Log Out

💡 TIP

Security-conscious administrators may choose a different style of login window— one that, instead of a list of available users, presents two text input boxes: a name and a password. You can enter either your full name or your short username; but without the list of users to choose from visually, someone trying to sneak into the system will have a much harder time trying to guess a valid username.

1 **Restart the Computer**

2 **Select the User to Log In As**

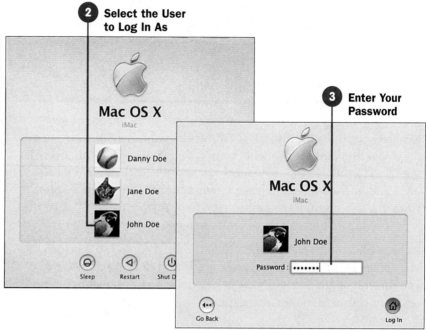

3 **Enter Your Password**

4 **Log Out**

3 **Enter Your Password**

Type your password into the box and click **Log In**. You are logged in to your user environment; in a few moments, after your Dock and Desktop have been set up, you will be ready to use the computer normally.

4 **Log Out**

When you're done using the computer, choose **Log Out <*Your Name*>** from the **Apple** menu. Click **Log Out** in the confirmation dialog box that appears to quit your applications and log out immediately; if you don't click that button, Mac OS X automatically shuts down all your applications and logs you out after two minutes (120 seconds). After you log out, the Mac returns to showing the login window.

140 Switch to Another User

Suppose that you're in the middle of typing an important email or working on a movie in iMovie, when your spouse comes in and asks to use the computer "just for a minute." Do you have to quit all your applications, log out, log into the other account, wait around until it's your turn again, and then log back in using your own account—only to spend another five minutes relaunching all your applications and getting your user environment back the way you like it? Perish the thought.

The **Fast User Switching** feature lets you immediately switch directly between user environments without the laborious process of logging out and logging in as another user. When the feature is enabled, you can select any of the system's users from the **User** menu at the top-right of the screen; when you enter that user's password, you are taken directly to that user environment.

This means that any number of users can be logged in at the same time, all concurrently running their own applications. You can see which users are logged in at any time by opening the **User** menu and seeing which ones are marked with a green check mark. If many users are logged in at once and all running their own applications, the system can become sluggish or run out of memory. It's best to keep simultaneous logins to a minimum, and to avoid using **Fast User Switching** while you're running resource-hungry applications.

1 Enable Fast User Switching

Open the **Accounts Preferences** window (open **System Preferences** from the **Apple** menu and click **Accounts**). Click **Login Options** and then click the **Enable fast user switching** check box (if it isn't enabled already). The menu bar changes to show your name in bold in the upper-right corner. You can open this **User** menu to switch immediately to any other user.

2 Select the User to Switch To

Click the **User** menu to see the list of available users. If any user is marked with a green check mark, that user is already logged in. Click the user to which you want to switch.

A login dialog box similar to the login window appears in the middle of the screen, with the selected user's name and a password input box. You can click **Cancel** if you change your mind about switching users.

Before You Begin

✔ **146** Add a New User

See Also

→ **141** Use the Shared Folder

→ **142** Automatically Log Out

NOTE

You must have administrative privileges to enable **Fast User Switching**; see **145** About Administrative Responsibilities for more information. However, after the feature is enabled, any user can switch to any other user.

TIP

Switching to a user that is already logged in is faster than switching to a user that isn't. If the user is not currently logged in, the computer must perform a complete login operation, starting up any applications the new user has configured to start at login and setting up the user environment with all its trimmings (such as the Dock). This generally takes ten to twenty seconds. However, if the user is already logged in, switching to her user environment should take only one or two seconds.

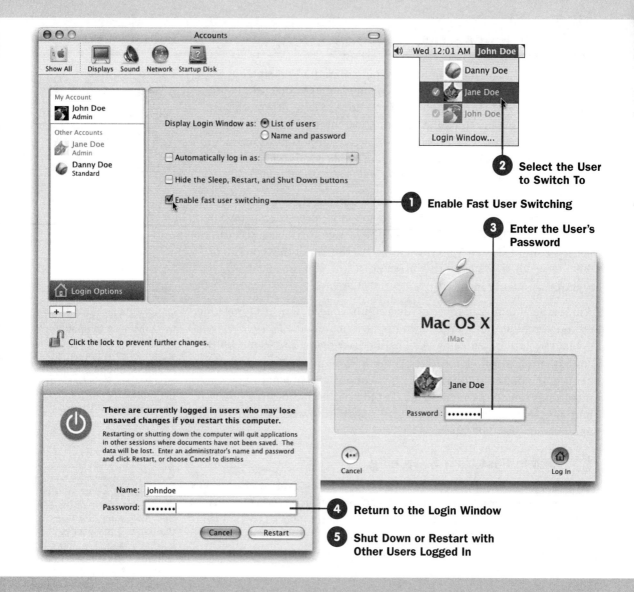

Enable Fast User Switching

2 Select the User to Switch To

1 Enable Fast User Switching

3 Enter the User's Password

4 Return to the Login Window

5 Shut Down or Restart with Other Users Logged In

3 **Enter the User's Password**

Type the user's password; if you're letting another person switch to his account from within yours, let him sit down and type it. It is, after all, best for each user to keep his password secret!

If the password is entered correctly, the screen rotates out of sight and is replaced with the new user's login session.

4 **Return to the Login Window**

A common scenario might be that you want to take a break from your work and leave the computer running, but you don't want to quit all your applications and log out; neither, however, do you want to lock the screen using a screensaver, preventing others from using the computer. Instead, you can use **Fast User Switching** to simply return to the main login window, leaving your session logged in, but allowing others to log in to their own sessions while you're gone.

From the **User** menu, select **Login Window** (the last entry). The screen rotates out of view and is replaced with the login window. Your user session is not suspended or terminated—your applications are still running. You can see this by the green check mark next to your name in the login window. Click your name and enter your password to switch back to your user session.

 TIP

When you wake the computer from sleep or from a screensaver, if it is configured to prompt you for the current user's password, the dialog box also contains a **Switch User** button. Click this button to log in as another user, leaving the current user logged in in the background.

5 **Shut Down or Restart with Other Users Logged In**

If there are multiple users logged in at once, they might lose unsaved data in their applications if you shut down or restart the computer. To shut down or restart the computer while multiple users are logged in, you must be able to *authenticate* as an Admin user so that you can override the other users' login sessions. Standard users can't force other users' sessions to end.

Select **Restart** or **Shut Down** from the **Apple** menu; a dialog box appears informing you that there are other users logged in. Type the full name or short username of any Admin user, as well as her password; then click **Shut Down** or **Restart**, depending which you're doing. If the Admin user information is entered correctly, all login sessions are terminated without saving their data.

 TIP

Naturally, it's best to log out of each user's login session properly before shutting down or restarting. If this is at all possible, switch to each logged-in account and select **Log Out** *<User's Name>* from the **Apple** menu before shutting down the Mac. You should perform step 4 in this task only if there is no other option—if you don't know the other users' passwords, for example.

141 Use the Shared Folder

Normally, one user cannot rummage around the folders inside another user's **Home** folder. If there are multiple users on the same machine, you can use the Finder to navigate to another user's **Home** folder (all **Home** folders are inside the **Users** folder at the top level of the startup disk), but with the exception of the **Desktop**, **Public**, and **Sites** folders, all the user's personal folders are closed to view to others.

Before You Begin

✔ **146** Add a New User
✔ **17** Move, Copy, or Delete a Document or Folder

See Also

→ **140** Switch to Another User

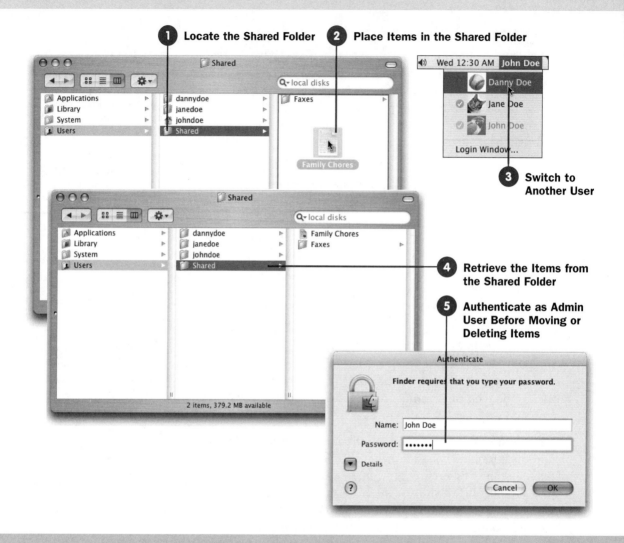

1 Locate the Shared Folder **2** Place Items in the Shared Folder

3 Switch to Another User

4 Retrieve the Items from the Shared Folder

5 Authenticate as Admin User Before Moving or Deleting Items

So how does one user share documents, folders, and applications with another user on the same machine? How can you publish a file so that everybody on the system can access it equally? Using the **Shared** folder, located inside the **Users** folder at the same level as all the **Home** folders. The **Shared** folder has permissions such that any user can place items into it and access items that other users have put there, but only the user who put an item there (or an Admin user) can delete it from the folder.

1 Locate the Shared Folder

Open a Finder window and navigate to the **Shared** folder. The easiest way to do this is to click the computer's hard disk icon, switch to Column view, and click the **Users** folder. The **Shared** folder is there inside **Users**.

2 Place Items in the Shared Folder

Drag documents, folders, or applications into the **Shared** folder.

3 Switch to Another User

Either use **Fast User Switching** if it is enabled (see **140** Switch to Another User) to switch to another user or log out and log in as the other user.

4 Retrieve the Items from the Shared Folder

Navigate to the **Shared** folder. You can access any items placed in that folder, open them in applications, or copy them to your own Desktop simply by dragging (as though they are stored on a different volume).

5 Authenticate as Admin User Before Moving or Deleting Items

If you are an Admin user, you can move other users' items out of the **Shared** folder (by holding down the ⌘ key as you drag it) to your Desktop or the Trash. To make sure that you have the permissions to do this, Mac OS X prompts you for an Admin user's password before it commits such an action.

> **NOTE**
>
> If you create an alias to some item in your **Home** folder and put the alias in the **Shared** folder, note that the original item has to be in a publicly accessible folder (your **Desktop**, **Public**, **Sites**, or any folder you have created yourself) for other users to be able to use the alias.

142 Automatically Log Out

If you have a shared computer with multiple users, and you're not sure you trust the other users not to mess with your stuff (for example, if the computer is shared at a school or with an inquisitive little brother), it might be a good idea to configure Mac OS X to log out automatically after a certain period of keyboard or mouse inactivity. This ensures that if you get up and walk away from the Mac without properly logging yourself out, a mischievous interloper can't come by an hour later and start pawing through your settings and personal documents. After a period of inactivity that you set, your session will automatically end, and the Mac will return to the login window so that only valid users can access the computer by logging in properly.

Before You Begin

✔ **138** Enable and Disable Automatic Login

✔ **139** Log In from the Login Window

See Also

→ **140** Switch to Another User

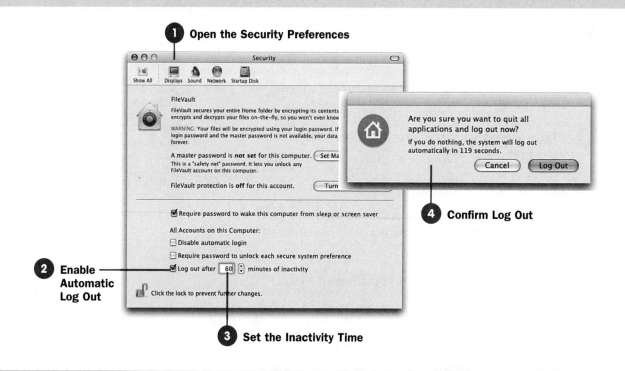

1 Open the Security Preferences

2 Enable Automatic Log Out

3 Set the Inactivity Time

4 Confirm Log Out

1 Open the Security Preferences

Open the **System Preferences** using the **Apple** menu. Click **Security** to open the **Security Preferences** window.

2 Enable Automatic Log Out

Enable the **Log out after** check box to allow Mac OS X to log you out after the default period of 60 minutes of inactivity.

3 Set the Inactivity Time

To adjust how long you want Mac OS X to wait before logging you out, use the up and down arrows to change the period one minute at a time. Alternatively, type a number of minutes by first selecting the existing number and then typing. The value you enter must be a number between 5 and 960. If you enter a larger or smaller number, the value is automatically adjusted to the nearest valid value.

④ Confirm Log Out

When the specified period of inactivity elapses, you will get a dialog box that gives you 120 seconds to cancel logout (or immediately confirm it). If you are running any applications with unsaved data, they will prevent Mac OS X from logging you out. Always make sure that all your data is saved before you get up and walk away!

143 Require a Password When Reactivating the Computer

In a public working environment, it's always a good idea to make sure that your screen will lock itself if you step away. If you don't want to be automatically logged out after a certain period of inactivity, Mac OS X gives you another option: You can have the system prompt you for a password before it rouses the Mac from sleep or disengages a screensaver that has kicked in.

Before You Begin

✔ **131** Select a Screensaver

See Also

→ **144** Lock the Screen

→ **152** Set the Computer's Sleep Time

① Open the Security Preferences

Open the **System Preferences** using the **Apple** menu. Click **Security** to open the **Security Preferences** window.

② Require a Password to Wake the Computer

Enable the **Require a password to wake this computer** check box. When this option is enabled, Mac OS X prompts you with a username and password input dialog box if you try to wake the computer from sleep or from a screensaver.

③ Set an Active Screen Corner

Open the **Desktop & Screen Saver Preferences** window (click **Desktop & Screen Saver** in the **System Preferences** window); in the **Screen Saver** tab, click the **Hot Corners** button. In the sheet that appears, pick an unassigned corner and choose **Start Screen Saver** from the list. From now on, moving the mouse to that corner of the screen immediately starts the screensaver; to reactivate the computer, you (or an intruder) must enter your username and password.

📍 TIP

The password you use to rouse the computer from sleep is the same as your login password.

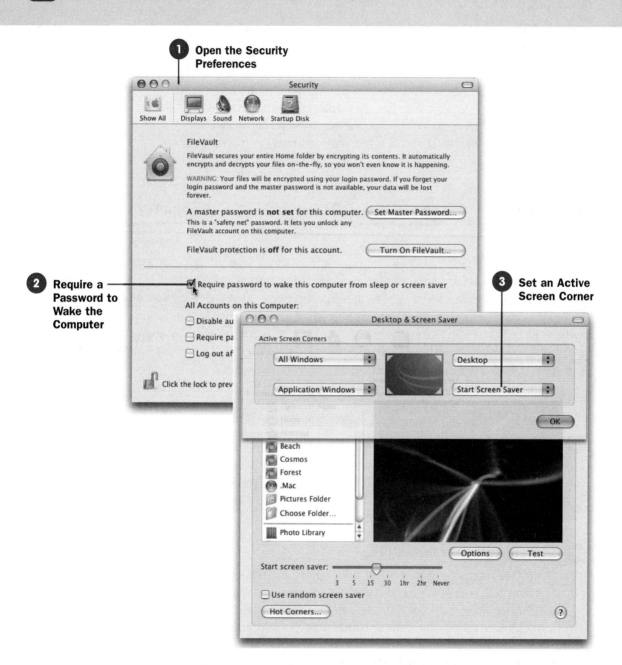

1 Open the Security Preferences

2 Require a Password to Wake the Computer

3 Set an Active Screen Corner

144 Lock the Screen

An alternative way to lock your screen and to gain access to a number of other security features as well (using *Keychain*) is to enable the **Keychain Status** system menu and use it to launch a locked screen-saver. This system menu has many other and more subtle uses, as does the **Keychain Access** utility itself (see **164** **Extract a Password from the Keychain** for more information). This task, however, looks only at how to lock the screen using this mechanism.

1 **Launch Keychain Access**

Navigate to the **Utilities** folder inside the **Applications** folder and launch the **Keychain Access** utility.

2 **Enable the Keychain Status System Menu**

From the **View** menu, select **Show Status in Menu Bar**. The **Keychain Status** system menu appears among your other system menus at the top-right corner of the screen. This menu gives you quick access to the **Keychain Access** utility, as well as one-click shortcuts to locking your current login keychain and the overall system keychain.

3 **Lock the Screen**

From the **Keychain Status** system menu, select **Lock Screen**. The screensaver immediately starts, using the screensaver you most recently selected. When you want to wake the computer by moving the mouse or pressing a keyboard key, you are prompted for a username and password before the screensaver will disengage.

See Also

→ **142** Automatically Log Out

→ **143** Require a Password When Reactivating the Computer

→ **164** Extract a Password from the Keychain

KEY TERM

Keychain—Mac OS X's built-in password manager utility. The Keychain keeps track of all your passwords that you use in various applications, and enters them automatically when called for.

① **Launch Keychain Access**

② Enable the Keychain Status System Menu

③ Lock the Screen

145 About Administrative Responsibilities

There are two kinds of users in Mac OS X: Standard users and *Admin users* (or *administrators*). Standard users have limited capabilities; they cannot change global preferences for the computer, modify system files, or install applications. (They can, however, read and burn CDs, play games, and do many other things that non-administrative users on Windows cannot do.) Admin users, however, have total control over the system's behavior and can change anything they want.

The first account that was created on your computer, at the time when you first started it up, is an Admin user; unless you have created any other users, this is the account you're using now. You can also grant Admin status to Standard users, or revoke it from other Admin users.

The power associated with an Admin user account naturally comes with the responsibility to use that power wisely, which means using it only where necessary. Because an Admin user can change system files and global settings that a Standard user can't modify, such a user also has the potential to wreck the entire system by deleting critical files or mangling system settings. For this reason alone, it's generally desirable to make sure that most of the time the Mac is being used, it's done under a Standard user account. Standard users can't install applications or change global settings, but that also means they can't inadvertently leave the system in ruins.

Under some circumstances, giving up Admin power for the sake of safety during daily computing is an acceptable tradeoff. You might have a public computer in your living room that anybody can use, for instance; on this computer, you might have a single Admin account (that you use only on those rare occasions when you need to install new software or update Mac OS X) and several other Standard accounts for each of the other members of the household that they use to run their applications and store their personal files.

However, because of the way Mac OS X is designed, it's generally safe to use the computer routinely no matter what kind of account you use. The reason for this is that Mac OS X's security architecture allows any user— even a Standard user—to accomplish administrative tasks, provided that the user has the name and password of an Admin user. Mac OS X prompts for this information, in what is known as *authentication*, whenever a user tries to perform a task that requires administrative power (such as changing a global system setting, deleting a file owned by another user, or shutting down while other users are logged in). Thus, as long as there's at least one Admin account on the computer, you can create a Standard account for yourself to use on a routine basis and still be able to accomplish Admin tasks using that account.

Similarly, even Admin users must authenticate before certain actions can be executed. The reason for this is that the system must ensure that it's actually a user with Admin privileges requesting the action, not just some random person who sat down at the computer while the real Admin user was away. Admin users can directly manipulate system files (in the global **Library** folder, for example) and change all **System Preferences** without authenticating; but they must enter their passwords at other critical times, such as when installing new system software. Thus the dangers inherent in routinely working as an Admin user are mitigated, and you generally won't have to worry if your Mac has only a single user account on it (an Admin account) that you use every day.

> ## KEY TERM
> *Authentication*—When you enter the name and password for an Admin user, you're authenticating as an administrator. If you do so correctly, the system lets you perform administrator-level tasks. Authentication is usually triggered by clicking a "lock" icon that's labeled as preventing or allowing changes (as is the case in many **System Preferences** windows).

> ## NOTE
> After you authenticate for any secure task, you have five minutes of free administrative capability (you can do just about anything without entering your password again) before Mac OS X will again require authentication.

The security-conscious Mac user might want to extend Mac OS X's cautiousness about installing system software and overriding file ownership to cover the **System Preferences** as well. Open the **Security Preferences** window (click **Security** in the **System Preferences** application) and enable the **Require password to unlock each secure system preference** check box. With this option enabled, every time you want to modify any of the locked **System Preferences** windows, you must click the lock icon in the lower-left corner of the **System Preferences** window to authenticate as an admin user.

You must authenticate as an Admin user when you attempt to perform certain tasks.

If you create additional user accounts, create them as Standard user accounts, unless you want the other users to have the same administrative powers you do. Creating additional Standard accounts ensures that while these other users must rely on you to install new applications or keep the system updated, you're also the only one who can really do any damage to the computer. The other users can use the system free of worry, leaving the administrative tasks in your capable hands. Aside from the security and privacy benefits discussed earlier in this chapter, having multiple users on a Mac also makes a system a lot easier to administer and keep organized. Particularly thanks to the division of privileges between Standard users and Admin users, you can tightly control what kind of important actions take place in the computer, while giving each of your users the freedom to use it according to their own tastes and preferences.

Standard users can change their own full names, passwords, and login pictures. They can't, however, change any other user's information.

If you are the system administrator, you can create, delete, and modify all the other user accounts from your own Admin account, including their passwords and login pictures (which appear in the login window and in the **Fast User Switching** menu). All this functionality occurs in the **Accounts Preferences** window.

146 Add a New User

It's a good idea to create a separate user account for each person who will be using the computer—each member of your family, each student in your class, each employee in your office. It doesn't matter how many accounts your system has; each account's impact on the computer's resources is minimal, consisting of one more **Home** folder hierarchy in the **Users** folder. But making sure that each person has to log in separately into a separate user environment keeps each person's activities from affecting anyone else's documents and settings.

Each user must be created in a separate action. To create a user account, you must have the user's full name, his short name (or username), his password, and (optionally) a hint that the person can use if he forgets his password. Ask the person what short name, password, and password hint should be used in creating his new account—or, if you prefer, make them up yourself. Mac OS X will supply a default short name derived from the full name; as a practical matter, this short name only appears as the name of the user's **Home** folder.

1 Open the Accounts Preferences

Open the **System Preferences** using the **Apple** menu; click **Accounts** to bring up the **Accounts Preferences** window.

2 Add a New User Account

Click the + icon at the bottom left to create a new user account. The user's account is immediately partially created and appears in the list on the left with no name and a randomly chosen login picture. The right pane contains fields in which you must enter the user's full name, short name, password, and a password hint before the account is fully created.

3 Enter a Name

Type the user's full name. This text entry can contain spaces, apostrophes, and other special characters; it should match how the user naturally writes his full name.

Before You Begin

✔ **145** About Administrative Responsibilities

See Also

→ **147** Grant Admin Capabilities to Another User

→ **148** Restrict Another User's Capabilities

→ **149** Set Your Login Picture

→ **151** Delete a User

 TIP

It's good security practice for every user's password to be as secret as possible— and that means that ideally, even *you* shouldn't know the new user's password. The best way to proceed is to have the other person nearby while you create his account; have him type in his password and hint so that you don't have to know what it is. Alternatively, set a temporary password (such as **ChangeThis**) and tell the user that he must change his password as soon as possible. See **150** Change a User's Password for more information.

NOTE

You must be logged in as an Admin user, or be able to authenticate as one using the lock icon in the **Accounts Preferences** window, to create a new user account.

---

① Open the Accounts Preferences

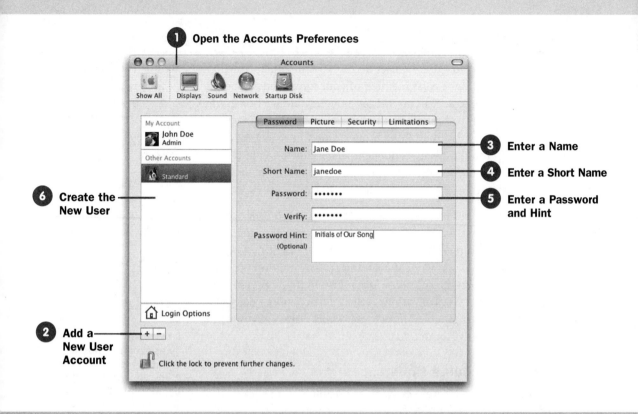

③ Enter a Name

④ Enter a Short Name

⑤ Enter a Password and Hint

⑥ Create the New User

② Add a New User Account

④ Enter a Short Name

NOTE

Short names are generally in all lowercase letters by convention, but you can use capital letters if you want. Logging in using the short name is not a case-sensitive operation, but many of the more advanced Unix features *are* case-sensitive regarding the short name. It's generally best to just stick with all lowercase letters when typing the short name.

The *short name* is what's used at the lower Unix level to identify each user and to provide an easy-to-type user ID (such as **jsmith**). The short name is also used as the name for the user's **Home** folder. You won't often have a need to use the short name in Mac OS X (unless you use some of the more advanced Unix features), but if you're logging in at the login window (and you've configured it to require each user to type his name and password rather than picking his picture from the list), you can use either the full name or the short name to identify yourself.

After you enter the user's full name in step 3, Mac OS X automatically chooses a short name, created by removing any special characters and spaces from the **Name** field and converting it all to lowercase. You can accept the short name that the system picks for you, or you can type any short name that isn't already used by an account in the system. The short name can be as long as you want, but try to keep it under 10 or 12 characters to make it easy for the user to type.

❺ Enter a Password and Hint

Type a password for the new user. A good password should be about six to eight characters in length, should not be any word that can be found in the dictionary (or be the same as the short name or anything else that can be guessed easily by someone trying to break in), and should contain at least one special punctuation or symbolic character (such as @, #, or !). A good password scheme might be to pick all the first letters from the title of a favorite song, or to pick a name of a pet and change the occurrences of **S** to **$**, **A** to **@**, and so on.

Enter the chosen password twice—once in the **Password** field, and again in the **Verify** field. Entering the password twice helps ensure that the password is entered correctly, because it's hidden as you type it.

To assist the user in remembering his password, you can enter a "hint," which is text that appears if the user tries several times to enter the password unsuccessfully. The hint should suggest what the password is to the user, but shouldn't make it too obvious to the uninformed. For instance, if your password is **C@mpbell**, you can make the hint **Mother's maiden name with @ for A**. You can also elect not to enter a hint at all.

❻ Create the New User

After you've entered a full name, short name, and password, click anywhere else in the **Preferences** pane—on another user in the user list, on the **Picture** tab, or on the **Login Options** icon, for instance. When you do this, the new account is created, along with its **Home** folder.

If you make a mistake or change your mind about creating the new user account, click the – button under the user list to cancel the operation.

 TIPS

If you are adding a large number of accounts (such as in a business environment), it's a good idea to develop a plan for assigning unique, short, and predictable short names to users. A standard username form might include the first five letters of the last name, followed by the first and middle initials, as in **doejq** for John Q. Doe.

Each user can change her password at will (see **150** Change a User's Password); but you might want to at least educate users about what makes a good password.

147 Grant Admin Capabilities to Another User

Before You Begin

✔ **145** About
Administrative
Capabilities

✔ **146** Add a New User

See Also

→ **148** Restrict Another
User's Capabilities

→ **151** Delete a User

NOTE

You must be logged in as an Admin user or be able to authenticate as one using the lock icon in the **Accounts Preferences** window, to grant Admin capabilities to another user.

Your own account, created at the time you first started up your Mac, is an *Admin* account; it has the inherent capabilities necessary to change any of the **System Preferences**, install software, and many other system-modifying actions. Every new user account you create begins life as a Standard user, without any of those administrative capabilities. However, you can grant Admin status to any other users you select if you want to share that administrative authority. When you do so, the other users you empower can modify other user accounts, install software, and change pretty much anything about the system.

You should not grant Admin status lightly. Allow only those people you trust completely with the computer to be administrators. Granting Admin status to a user of your computer is equivalent to giving them your house or car keys and the permission to do whatever they want with them.

1 Open the Accounts Preferences

Open the **System Preferences** using the **Apple** menu and click **Accounts** to bring up the **Accounts Preferences** window.

2 Select the User to Promote

From the list of users on the left, select the user you want to promote to Admin status. Then click the **Security** tab to show the security options for that user.

3 Grant Admin Capabilities to the User

Enable the **Allow user to administer this computer** check box. The user is immediately promoted to Admin status, and the **Limitations** tab becomes disabled (because Admin users have no limitations).

1 Open the Accounts Preferences

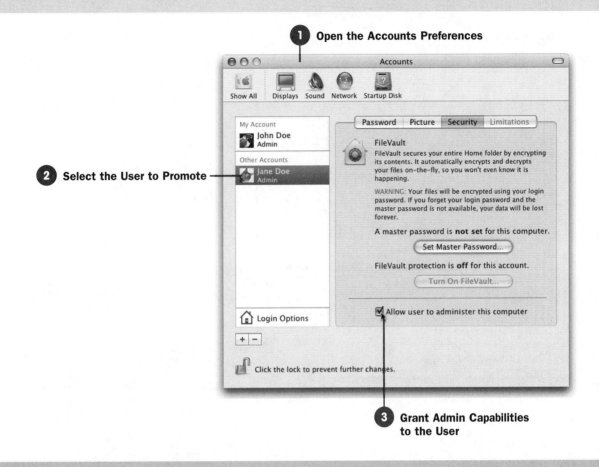

2 Select the User to Promote

3 Grant Admin Capabilities to the User

---

148 **Restrict Another User's Capabilities**

Under some circumstances, you might want to configure a user account to have even more than the standard limitations on what can be done with the computer. For instance, you might have your Mac acting as a public computer for a classroom of unruly kids. In such a case, you might want to restrict them to pick from only a few approved applications, or to prevent them from downloading hundreds of MP3 files to fill up your disk. Mac OS X lets you apply these kinds of limitations to specific users. You can also require any user to use the Simple Finder, a simplified version of the Finder that uses large icons and single clicks to make the system more accessible to younger (or vision-impaired) computer users.

Before You Begin

✓ **145** About Administrative Responsibilities

✓ **147** Grant Admin Capabilities to Another User

See Also

→ **151** Delete a User

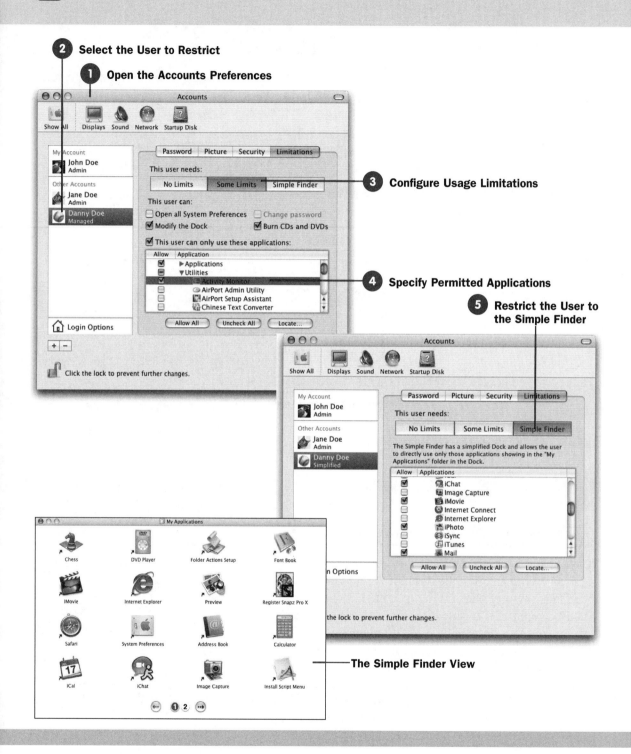

2 Select the User to Restrict

1 Open the Accounts Preferences

3 Configure Usage Limitations

4 Specify Permitted Applications

5 Restrict the User to the Simple Finder

The Simple Finder View

❶ Open the Accounts Preferences

Open the **System Preferences** using the **Apple** menu and click **Accounts** to bring up the **Accounts Preferences** window.

❷ Select the User to Restrict

From the list of users on the left, select the user whose privileges you want to modify. Then click the **Limitations** tab to reveal the various options for restricting the user's privileges.

❸ Configure Usage Limitations

Standard users, by default, have the **No Limits** option selected. This means that a typical user can use any applications in the system and perform any action that is not specifically "locked" and accessible to only Admin users.

You might want to restrict only some of a user's capabilities, depending on your computer's situation. In a classroom setting, for example, you might want to permit users to burn CDs and DVDs, but not to rummage around in the **System Preferences** application or to change which items appear in the Dock.

Click the **Some Limits** button to reveal these options. Use the check boxes to specify which capabilities you want to grant to the user.

❹ Specify Permitted Applications

Enable the **This user can only use these applications** check box if you want to allow the user to be able to use only those applications you define. All the applications installed in the system are organized in this box; you can open one of the collections (**Applications, Utilities,** and so on) to enable only certain applications, or you can use the check boxes to enable or disable whole collections of applications. By default, for example, all applications in the **Applications** collection (which corresponds to the global **Applications** folder) are enabled for the user, but **Utilities** and the other collections are disabled.

If a Managed user tries to run an application that you haven't designated as an allowed application for the user, a dialog box informs her that she doesn't have permission to run it.

 **NOTES**

You must be logged in as an Admin user, or be able to authenticate as one using the lock icon in the **Accounts Preferences** window to restrict another user's capabilities.

You cannot restrict the privileges of an Admin user; only standard users have an active **Limitations** tab.

NOTE

If you restrict which applications a user can run or otherwise limit her capabilities with the **Some Limits** option, the user's status changes from **Standard** to **Managed**. If you don't permit a user to open all **System Preferences** windows, the user will not be able to change her password (because the user has to access the **Accounts Preferences** window to change a password). A user who is restricted in this way can open only those **Preferences** windows that manage how her own login experience behaves, not any of the panes that affect the system.

5 **Restrict the User to the Simple Finder**

 TIP

Effectively, a **Simplified** user can run only the applications you specify, save documents only in the **Documents** and **Shared** folders, and log out.

The **Simple Finder** option is a heavily restricted user mode you can use to give certain users a very simplified, easy-to-use view of the system. It's especially tailored for younger users. When a **Simplified** user (one configured to use the Simple Finder) logs in, only the applications you administratively specify are available. When the user clicks the **My Applications** folder icon in the limited Dock, the applications are presented in a large window in the middle of the screen. The only other Dock items are the **Documents** and **Shared** folders, in which the user can save files. Applications can save files to other folders, but the **Simplified** user won't be able to access them.

149 Set Your Login Picture

Before You Begin

✔ **146** Add a New User

See Also

→ **78** Set Up Your Picture

→ **120** Add a Person to Your Address Book

→ **150** Change a User's Password

The login picture is what appears next to each user's name in the login window and in the **User** menu when **Fast User Switching** is enabled. The login picture is also used in creating the initial picture for a user's iChat profile and in certain other places throughout the system where personalized user information is reflected.

Each user can set his own login picture to anything he wants, either using a picture from Apple's built-in collection or by dragging in any picture from his own folders. The user can then edit the picture (to zoom in on a certain part of the picture), or even grab a snapshot from a digital video camera such as Apple's iSight.

As an Admin user, you can control every other user's login picture as well as your own; however, if you're logged in as a Standard user, you cannot change any other user's picture but your own. You change login pictures in the **Accounts Preferences** window, whether you're an Admin or a Standard user.

1 **Open the Accounts Preferences**

Open the **System Preferences** using the **Apple** menu and click **Accounts** to bring up the **Accounts Preferences** window.

2 **Select the User to Modify**

From the list of users on the left, select the user whose login picture you want to modify. (If you're changing your own picture, click your account name at the top of the list, under **My Account**.) Then click the **Picture** tab to reveal the pane where you can set the login icon.

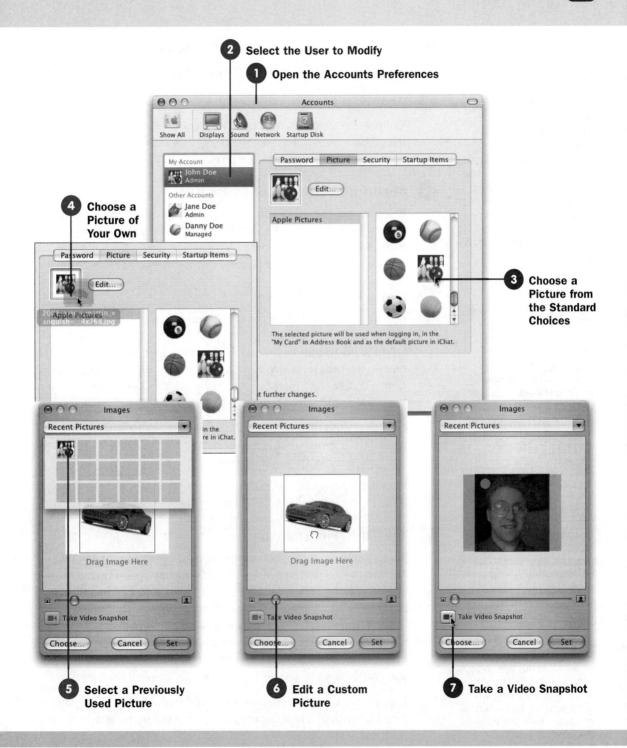

2 Select the User to Modify

1 Open the Accounts Preferences

4 Choose a Picture of Your Own

3 Choose a Picture from the Standard Choices

5 Select a Previously Used Picture

6 Edit a Custom Picture

7 Take a Video Snapshot

❸ Choose a Picture from the Standard Choices

From the pane on the right, click any picture to make it your login icon.

❹ Choose a Picture of Your Own

You can use any picture you want as your login icon. To do this, find the picture file in the Finder and drag it into the well (the recessed box showing the current login picture).

❺ Select a Previously Used Picture

If you've used several login pictures in the past, they're all available for you to reuse. Click the **Edit** button next to the current login picture and then use the **Recent Pictures** drop-down list to browse the palette of previously used pictures. Click the one you want to use.

❻ Edit a Custom Picture

Let's say that you want to crop a custom picture so that you're using only a small portion of the picture you've selected. You can do this by selecting the picture to use and then clicking **Edit** next to the login picture. In the **Images** dialog box that opens, use the slider below the picture to choose the "aperture" size. The portion of the image that's inside the black aperture square is what will be used as the login picture.

Click and drag the picture in the window to adjust where it is centered; you can also drag a new picture from the Finder to replace the one you're currently working with.

Click **Set** when you're satisfied with your adjustments. The edited image is fixed as your login picture.

❼ Take a Video Snapshot

If you have a digital video camera hooked up to your Mac with a FireWire connection, the **Take Video Snapshot** button becomes active. Click the button, and the output from your video camera will appear in the preview window. A series of beeps will sound, becoming progressively quicker; as the beeps speed up, aim the camera at yourself (or at anything else you want to take a picture of), and in a few seconds Mac OS X will freeze-frame, using whatever is on the camera at the time. You can then edit the image using the aperture and drag tools.

If you don't like your snapshot, you can immediately make another by clicking **Take Video Snapshot** again. Keep trying until you have a picture you like.

TIP

Alternatively, you can choose a picture by clicking the **Edit** button next to the current login picture and then using the **Choose** button in the pop-up window that appears to select a picture using the built-in navigator.

NOTE

The slider defines how much of the selected image appears as your login picture, and how much it should be scaled up or down. You can pick any scaling factor between squeezing the entire picture down to the login icon size, and using only a 48×48 pixel section of the picture.

NOTE

Just about any kind of digital video camera will work with the login picture selector. Any FireWire camera that iChat recognizes will activate the feature. Apple's iSight and other FireWire Webcams are ideal, but you can also use a standard digital camcorder. Just put the camcorder in standby mode, and the video signal will automatically be picked up by the system and used in the video snapshot.

150 Change a User's Password

All users can change their own passwords. This is an essential part of conscientious computer usage. As a rule, you should change your password every six months or so, just as a precaution (and more frequently, such as every 30 days, in a business environment in which the information on your computer is more sensitive). And as an Admin user, it will be your task to change users' passwords on a fairly regular basis, often because the users have forgotten them.

To change your own password, you have to re-authenticate to make sure that you are the person who is currently logged in. Making you *authenticate* as the signed in user is a precaution against someone sitting down at your login session and changing your password so that you can no longer log in. However, if you're an Admin user, you can change other users' passwords without authenticating.

Before You Begin

✔ **145** About Administrative Responsibilities

✔ **146** Add a New User

See Also

→ **151** Delete a User

1 Open the Accounts Preferences

Open the **System Preferences** using the **Apple** menu and click **Accounts** to bring up the **Accounts Preferences** window.

2 Select the User to Modify

From the list of users on the left, select the user whose password you want to change. Then click the **Password** tab to reveal the name and password configuration pane.

3 Begin Typing the New Password

Click in the **Password** field to select the current password; begin typing the new password. If you're an Admin user and you're changing someone else's password, you can type the new password directly. If you're changing your own password, however, a sheet pops up that prompts you to enter your own current password.

4 Enter Your Current Password to Authenticate

Type your own current password and click **OK** to authenticate yourself. After you have authenticated as the legitimate user of this account, you can change your own password multiple times, until you quit the **System Preferences** application.

NOTE

If you start typing a new password, you must complete it and type it again in the **Verify** field. You can't simply quit the **System Preferences** application and revert to the previous password.

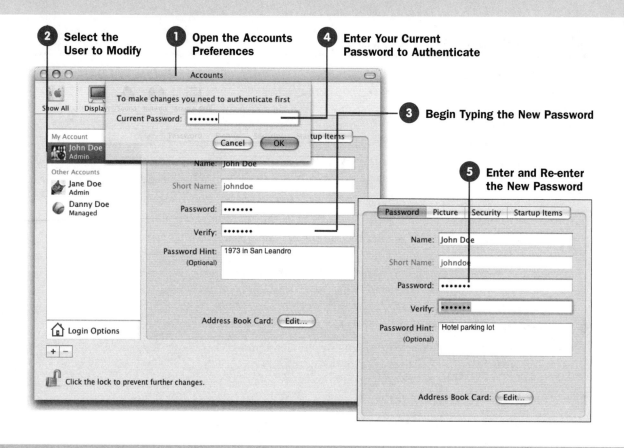

2 Select the User to Modify

1 Open the Accounts Preferences

4 Enter Your Current Password to Authenticate

3 Begin Typing the New Password

5 Enter and Re-enter the New Password

5 Enter and Re-enter the New Password

After you have authenticated, type your new password in the **Password** and **Verify** fields. Click another user or tab to save the new password.

You are prompted with a reminder that your *Keychain* password will be changed to the newly set password. If the Keychain is locked, you'll have to use your old password to unlock it before the password can be changed.

TIP

If you're an Admin user who's changing another user's password, however, the user's Keychain password cannot be changed automatically. That user must change his own Keychain password the next time he logs in, or else continue to use his old password to unlock his Keychain. See **164** Extract a Password from the Keychain for more information about the Keychain.

151 Delete a User

Deleting a user is an essential housekeeping duty. You'll have to remove user accounts that are no longer used, delete accounts as a punitive measure against abusive users, or clean out user accounts to return the system to a pristine state if you sell your computer to someone else.

Mac OS X lets you delete any user account except for your own. When you delete a user, you can also either delete the user's account immediately (removing the user's **Home** folder and everything in it) or package the user's **Home** folder into a disk image you can then browse later.

1 Open the Accounts Preferences

Open the **System Preferences** using the **Apple** menu and click **Accounts** to bring up the **Accounts Preferences** window.

2 Select the User to Delete

From the user list on the left, select the user you want to delete from the system.

3 Remove the User

Click the – icon at the bottom of the list of users.

4 Preserve the User's Home Folder

A sheet appears asking whether you want to delete the user immediately or archive the user's **Home** folder. Click **Delete Immediately** if you want the user's complete account, including the **Home** folder, to be immediately deleted. Click **OK** if you want the user's **Home** folder to be packaged into a disk image.

If you choose this second option, the user is removed from the system's user database, but the archive of the **Home** folder will appear in a folder called **Deleted Users** inside the **Users** folder. You can mount this disk image by double-clicking it; you can then browse through it to retrieve any important files that the user might have had.

Before You Begin

✔ **145** About Administrative Responsibilities

✔ **146** Add a New User

See Also

→ **175** Restore the System to Factory Settings

NOTE

You must be logged in as an Admin user or be able to authenticate as one using the lock icon in the **Accounts Preferences** window to delete another user.

NOTE

Don't try to delete a user that's currently logged in. Doing so can result in an "orphaned" user account that can no longer log out until the computer is restarted.

2 Select the User to Delete

1 Open the Accounts Preferences

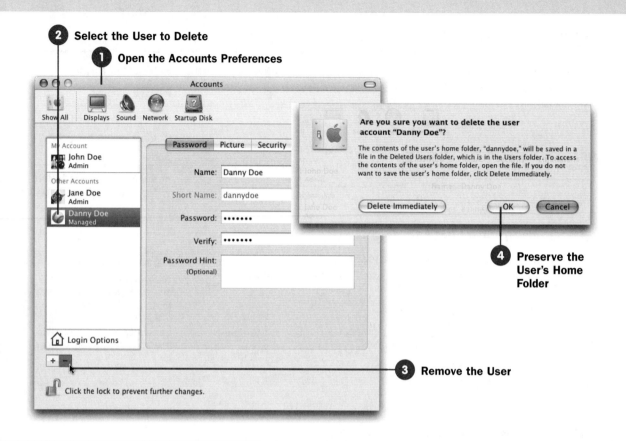

4 Preserve the User's Home Folder

3 Remove the User

16

Managing Power and Accessibility Options

IN THIS CHAPTER:

"One size fits all" is a statement that never applies to computer users. We all need our computers to do something different, and not just because our tastes in desktop backgrounds vary. Sometimes, our own practical constraints—mobile energy needs, physical accessibility challenges, and so on—dictate that our computers must adapt to us or be useless.

Whether your Mac is a laptop or a desktop machine, the practical fact is that you can't just leave it running all the time. Electricity costs money, and besides, you probably instinctively know that the lifetime of your screen and your hard drive can be extended if they don't have to be running all the time.

Nobody, however, wants to have to boot up their computer from scratch every time they sit down. That's why Mac OS X supports *sleep*, a suspended-activity mode in which the computer uses almost no power, but can be awakened almost instantly by pressing a key or moving the mouse. You already know how to put your computer to sleep or wake it up (choose **Sleep** from the **Apple** menu, or—if your computer is a laptop—simply close the lid); this chapter will discuss some of the finer points of power management, enabling you to tune how your computer automatically deals with inactivity and variable power conditions.

Beyond simple power management, Mac OS X has a number of features designed to make life easier for everybody who uses a Mac, under whatever circumstances. Apple has had a long history of making computers that are usable not just by the fully physically capable, but by people who have any of the disabilities or challenges that made traditional computing difficult. The Mac was first to market with text-to-speech synthesis, for example, and there have almost always been ways to control the computer using only the keyboard, rather than relying on the mouse.

Mac OS X, with its many graphical and architectural advances, introduces even more accessibility features that depend more heavily on sophisticated graphics processing: Zoom lets you immediately magnify the screen to any level you choose; Sticky Keys lets you press multiple modifier keys in sequence rather than at the same time, displaying their floating icons in the upper-right corner of the screen. And you can make the computer read alert messages to you, with a high degree of customizability.

152 Set the Computer's Sleep Time

One of the first and simplest energy-saving things you can do with your Mac is to configure it to put itself to sleep after a certain period of inactivity. If you don't touch your keyboard or mouse for that length of time, the computer will automatically go to sleep; you can then wake it up by pressing a key or moving the mouse.

You can also configure separate sleeping behaviors for your display and your hard disk. You might want your screen to turn off after an hour of inactivity, for instance, or for your hard drive to spin down, without allowing your computer to fully go to sleep until another hour has passed. These things are all configurable in the **Energy Saver Preferences** window.

1 Open the Energy Saver Preferences

Open the **System Preferences** using the **Apple** menu and click **Energy Saver** to bring up the **Energy Saver Preferences** window. Click the **Sleep** tab if it's not already selected.

If you have a desktop Mac (an iMac, eMac, or Power Mac), the **Energy Saver Preferences** window will simply show the three tabs for configuring power management behavior: **Sleep**, **Schedule**, and **Options**. However, if you have a laptop (an iBook or PowerBook), the **Energy Saver Preferences** window has an **Optimize Energy Settings** drop-down menu that lets you select from several predefined energy-saving profiles (optimized for various styles of computer usage) or create your own profile, and a second **Settings for** drop-down menu that lets you configure the settings separately for whether your computer is plugged in or using battery power. You can also show or hide the details of the window, using the **Show Details** or **Hide Details** button in the lower-right corner; when the details are hidden, the only controls that are visible are the ones that let you select an energy profile for your different power sources.

2 Set the Sleep Time

Use the **Put the computer to sleep when it is inactive for** slider to select a sleep time. Mac OS X in its default configuration never automatically sleeps, so the slider is in the **Never** position at the far right; you can disable automatic sleep by moving the slider back all the way to the right.

Before You Begin

✔ **24** Set the Date and Time

✔ **25** Enable Automatic Time Synchronization (NTP)

See Also

→ **142** Automatically Log Out

→ **143** Require a Password When Reactivating the Computer

🔍 NOTES

There are a few conditions under which your computer won't go to sleep, even if you haven't touched your keyboard or mouse. If a QuickTime movie or a DVD is playing, for instance, Mac OS X will recognize that something's going on and will not dim the screen or put the computer to sleep.

The illustrations for this task show the **Energy Saver Preferences** window for a laptop (an iBook, to be precise).

1 Open the Energy Saver Preferences

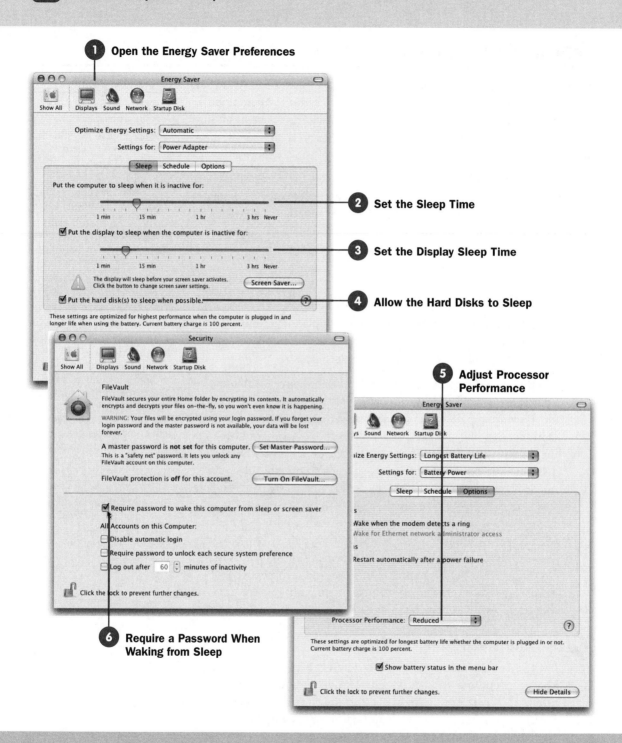

2 Set the Sleep Time

3 Set the Display Sleep Time

4 Allow the Hard Disks to Sleep

5 Adjust Processor Performance

6 Require a Password When Waking from Sleep

③ Set the Display Sleep Time

Normally, your whole computer will go to sleep at once, after the inactivity period you specify has elapsed. However, you can choose to set your Mac to put only its display to sleep, but to keep the computer itself running. This can be useful if you like to keep certain programs running all night long while you sleep, but you don't want to waste energy keeping the screen lit if nobody's looking at it.

Your display will dim (to about half its normal brightness) when the computer has been inactive for half the time it takes to go to sleep or if you have enabled a separate display sleep time. This is useful primarily for laptops, in which the screen is one of the biggest consumers of power; dimming the screen helps reduce power usage.

Enable the **Put the display to sleep when the computer is inactive for** check box to enable a separate display sleep time and use the second slider to set the inactivity period. This period must be less than the period for system sleep; you won't be able to move the slider farther to the right than the first slider is set. Similarly, if you move the system sleep slider farther left than your display slider is set, both sliders will move in unison to keep their values synchronized.

④ Allow the Hard Disks to Sleep

Use the **Put the hard disk(s) to sleep when possible** check box to specify whether you want the hard disk to spin down whenever the system determines it's not being used (usually after a few minutes of inactivity). If you allow the hard disk to sleep, its lifetime will be increased; however, it will take several extra seconds for the system to become responsive, as it spins the disk back up again, if you suddenly need to access the disk.

⑤ Adjust Processor Performance

Click the **Options** tab. Use the **Processor Performance** drop-down menu to select how fast you want your computer's processor to run. With the processor set to **Highest** performance, the computer will run at full speed, but power consumption will be higher than if you select **Reduced**, which causes the processor to run at a slightly slower speed.

NOTES

Notice that the slider's numbering is not linear. At the far left, individual minutes are far apart, so that you can easily select between four and five minutes; but as you move the slider to the right, the numbers increase faster so that you can select up to three hours of inactivity.

If you have a screensaver enabled, Mac OS X warns you if you try to set the system to sleep earlier than how long it takes for the screensaver to kick in. If you set the system to sleep automatically after a certain period of inactivity, visit the **Desktop & Screen Saver Preferences** window to ensure that the screensaver will activate at an appropriate time. See **131 Select a Screensaver.**

6 **Require a Password When Waking from Sleep**

If you have a laptop, especially one with sensitive information on it, it's a good idea to configure Mac OS X to require your password when the Mac wakes from sleep. To do this, open the **Security Preferences** window (click **Security** in the **System Preferences** application). Use the **Require password to wake this computer from sleep or screen saver** check box to make it so that a thief who makes off with your laptop won't be able to access your sensitive documents. (See **165** **Secure Your Files with FileVault** for an additional precaution you can take if your laptop's data is *really* sensitive: encrypting your entire **Home** folder.)

153 Schedule Automatic Startup and Shutdown

Before You Begin

✔ **24** Set the Date and Time

✔ **25** Enable Automatic Time Synchronization (NTP)

See Also

→ **142** Automatically Log Out

NOTE

The settings you specify here are automatically applied; there is no button that you have to click to commit your changes.

To make your computer go to sleep, shut down, or start itself up, you don't have to rely on a certain period of inactivity. If you prefer, you can have the computer turn itself off or on at a specific time of day. While the computer is off or sleeping, it's still keeping time and can react according to your needs so that you don't have to remember to put it to sleep at the end of the day or to wait for it to boot up in the mornings.

1 **Open the Energy Saver Preferences**

Open the **System Preferences** using the **Apple** menu and click **Energy Saver** to bring up the **Energy Saver Preferences** window. Click the **Schedule** tab to access the scheduling options.

2 **Enable Automatic Startup**

Enable the **Start up the computer** check box to enable the computer to start up (or wake itself) automatically at a given time. Then, from the drop-down menu, select whether you want the computer to activate at a certain time every day, on all weekdays, on weekends, or on a single certain weekday.

Finally, set the activation time using the time input fields. Click each number to adjust it, or use the **Tab** key to move between fields; then use the arrow keys, Up/Down buttons, or the number keys to set the appropriate time for the computer to activate.

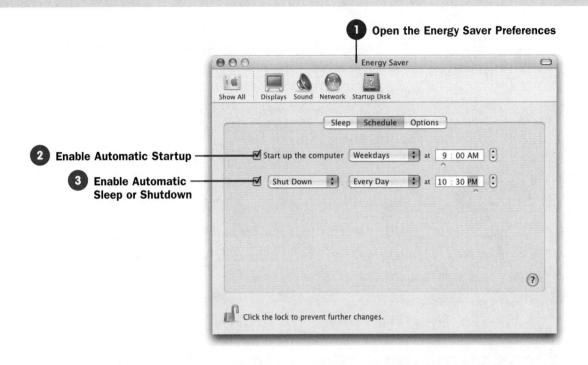

1 Open the Energy Saver Preferences

2 Enable Automatic Startup

3 Enable Automatic
Sleep or Shutdown

3 Enable Automatic Sleep or Shutdown

If you want the computer to automatically shut itself down, first
enable the second check box that lets you set the shutdown time. From
the drop-down list, select whether you want the computer to shut itself
down completely or to simply sleep. Then you can select a day scheme
and a time just as you did with the automatic startup settings.

154 Choose a Power-Saving Profile

If your Mac is a laptop, you will have a variety of different conditions
under which you can run it: You might run it off of battery power on an
airplane while you watch a DVD, or you might have it plugged into
wall power while you play a graphics-intensive game, or you might be
stuck in a long meeting taking notes for the whole two-hour duration.
Each of these activities places different kinds of demands on the computer and its components, and each scenario is affected by what kind of
power is available.

See Also

→ **47** Create and
Configure a
Location

→ **155** Enable the Battery
Status System
Menu

Choose a Power-Saving Profile

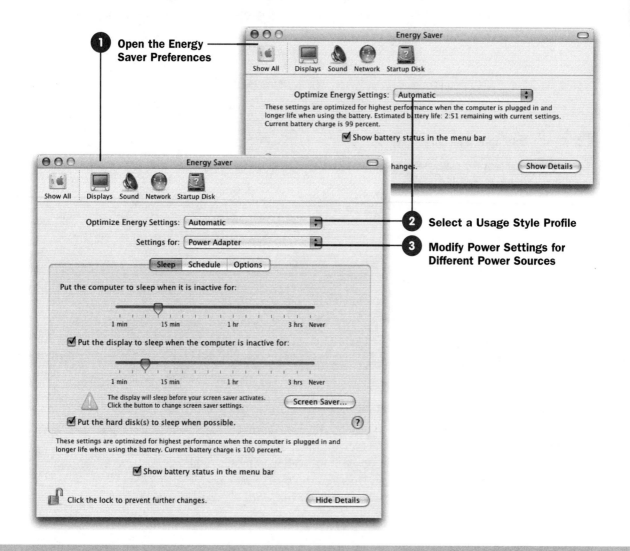

1 Open the Energy Saver Preferences

2 Select a Usage Style Profile

3 Modify Power Settings for Different Power Sources

The **Energy Saver Preferences** window lets you select from several usage profiles that correspond to different styles of how you stress the computer and use its available power. Some profiles are designed for high performance; others are designed for long battery life; still others provide a balance between performance and battery life for specific uses. You can also define your own custom-tuned power usage profile if necessary.

❶ Open the Energy Saver Preferences

Open the **System Preferences** using the **Apple** menu and click **Energy Saver** to bring up the **Energy Saver Preferences** window. Click the **Show Details** button to show the complete set of Energy Saver controls.

❷ Select a Usage Style Profile

From the **Optimize Energy Settings** drop-down menu, select one of the predefined usage profiles, one that corresponds to the kind of computing you will be doing. Explanatory text at the bottom of the window describes what each profile does:

- **Highest Performance** prevents the computer from sleeping and uses the processor at its fastest speed regardless of whether the computer is plugged in (using the power adapter) or not.

- **Longest Battery Life** takes the opposite approach, putting the display and hard disk to sleep after only a couple of minutes of inactivity and running the processor at reduced speed.

- **DVD Playback** prevents the display from going to sleep, but allows the hard disk to spin down, reserving all the battery power for the DVD drive and the display.

- **Presentations** ensures that the computer never goes to sleep, so if you have a projector hooked up to the computer's video output port, the image it shows never disappears.

- **Automatic** optimizes the computer for high performance when it's plugged in, and for long battery life when it's on battery power.

❸ Modify Power Settings for Different Power Sources

To create your own custom power usage profile, adjust the sliders to achieve the sleep behavior you want; the profile name changes to **Custom** as soon as you change the settings from one of the predefined profiles.

You might want to define different usage settings for whether the computer is plugged in or not. Select the power source from the **Settings for** drop-down list at the top of the window and customize the sliders and options according to the power source selected.

NOTE

If your Mac is a desktop model—an iMac, eMac, or Power Mac—the **Energy Saver Preferences** window does not show the power-saving profile options described in this task. This is because desktop Macs only have a single power source: the wall plug. If your desktop Mac is asleep, don't unplug it— even sleep mode requires some power! Laptops get their power during sleep from the battery. To shut down your desktop Mac, first awaken it from sleep, and then shut it down using the **Apple** menu.

TIP

Remember that you can select any of the different configuration tabs after having selected one of the power sources; all the tabs and their controls pertain to whichever power source and usage profile is currently selected.

155 Enable the Battery Status System Menu

Before You Begin

✔ **154** Choose a Power-Saving Profile

See Also

→ **49** Switch to a New Location

→ **57** Create and Configure a Location

If you have a laptop, a crucial piece of status information for you to have available at all times is the **Battery Status** system menu. This icon appears at the top right of the screen and shows your battery's current level and whether the computer is plugged in or not. The icon also gives you access to a menu that shows the battery's status in more detail. You can also use the menu to jump directly to the **Energy Saver Preferences** window.

❶ Open the Energy Saver Preferences

Open the **System Preferences** using the **Apple** menu and click **Energy Saver** to bring up the **Energy Saver Preferences** window.

❷ Enable the Battery Status System Menu

Enable the **Show battery status in the menu bar** check box to enable the battery icon among the system menus in the upper-right corner of the screen.

❸ Select the Battery Level Display Format

Click the **Battery Status** system menu to view the current battery status. The menu shows how much longer the battery will last at current power consumption levels, or how much longer it will take for the battery to become fully charged if the computer is plugged in.

The textual readout next to the **Battery Status** system menu icon can show either the time remaining until the battery is depleted (or fully charged), or the percentage the battery has of its full charge. Select **Show Time** from the menu to display the time remaining, **Show Percent** to show the battery's charge level, or **Show Neither** to show no label at all.

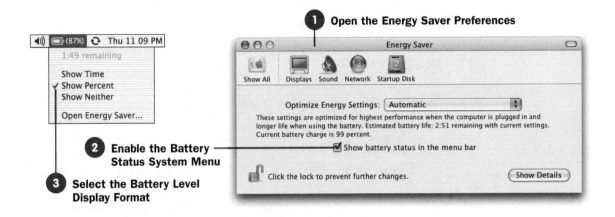

① **Open the Energy Saver Preferences**

② **Enable the Battery Status System Menu**

③ **Select the Battery Level Display Format**

156 **Talk to Your Computer and Have It Talk Back to You (Voice Recognition)**

Users with difficulty reading small text might find it useful to configure Mac OS X to use its built-in text-to-speech synthesis (originally called MacInTalk) to speak the text of alert dialog boxes. There are a lot of configurable options in the **Speech Preferences** window for this; you can adjust them all to taste after you have examined the behaviors of the various controls.

While you're working in the **Universal Access Preferences** window, the **Talking Alerts** option is automatically enabled to read the text under the mouse just for that preference pane. This feature can assist users in finding the options they need, which might include visibility features that are difficult to enable using the normal interface without spoken enhancements. Thus, if you hover your mouse over any control with a text label, Mac OS X speaks the text using the currently selected voice. This is to ease first-time configuration for users who might have difficulty making their way among the controls.

You can turn this behavior off by disabling the **Enable text-to-speech for Universal Access preferences** check box at the bottom of the **Hearing** tab in the **Universal Access Preferences** window.

See Also

→ **158** Choose How the Computer Alerts You

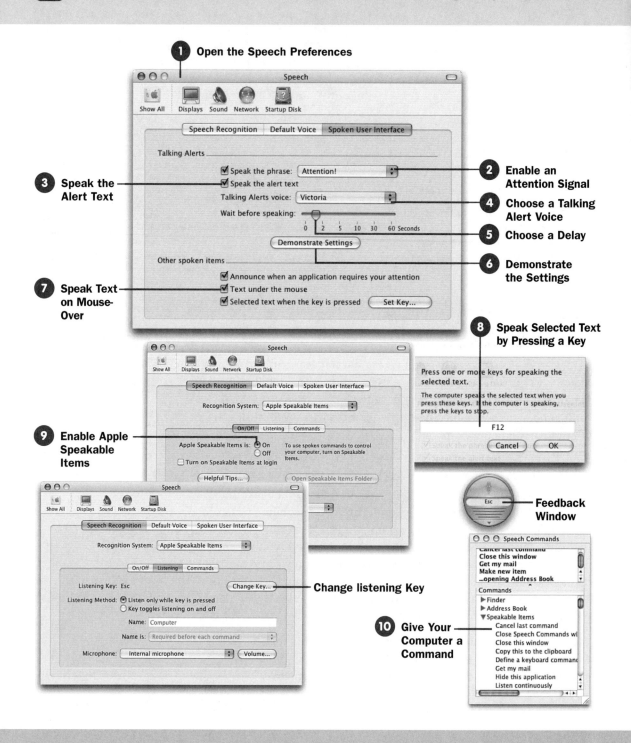

1 Open the Speech Preferences

3 Speak the Alert Text

2 Enable an Attention Signal

4 Choose a Talking Alert Voice

5 Choose a Delay

6 Demonstrate the Settings

7 Speak Text on Mouse-Over

8 Speak Selected Text by Pressing a Key

9 Enable Apple Speakable Items

Feedback Window

Change listening Key

10 Give Your Computer a Command

❶ Open the Speech Preferences

Open the **System Preferences** from the **Apple** menu and click **Speech** to open the **Speech Preferences** window. Click the **Spoken User Interface** tab.

❷ Enable an Attention Signal Phrase

To have Mac OS X alert you with a certain spoken word or phrase whenever an alert box or sheet appears, enable the **Speak the phrase** check box and then choose the phrase for it to speak from the drop-down menu. You can select a single specific phrase, choose a random or sequential phrase, or even add new phrases of your own.

> ## 🎤 TIP
>
> This is text-to-speech synthesis, so you can specify a new phrase by clicking the **Add** button in the **Edit Phrase List** pop-up window and typing the phrase. Mac OS X reads the text you type in the voice you've selected.

❸ Speak the Alert Text

Enable the **Speak the alert text** check box to make Mac OS X read the major text of an alert dialog box when one appears. Mac OS X will read the text of the alert after it reads the alert phrase (if you've configured it to speak an alert phrase).

❹ Choose a Talking Alert Voice

Mac OS X comes with many different "voices" you can use to read your text; **Victoria**, the default, is probably the most natural-sounding one. You can experiment with many others, however; some are "joke" voices, but many are designed to be as natural-sounding as possible. Pick your favorite from the **Talking Alerts voice** drop-down menu.

❺ Choose a Delay

Use the **Wait before speaking** slider to specify a delay that should precede any spoken alert. You can make the system wait for anything between zero and sixty seconds before it reads the alert text; this way, if you dismiss the dialog box quickly, the system will not speak its text (which can be distracting if you're hard at work).

❻ Demonstrate the Settings

Click the **Demonstrate Settings** button to see what it will be like when an alert dialog or sheet appears using your Talking Alerts settings.

7 Speak Text on Mouse-Over

Enable the **Text under the mouse** check box to make Mac OS X speak any line of text if you hover the mouse over it. Mac OS X will use the voice you select in the **Default Voice** pane, not the voice you selected from the **Talking Alerts voice** drop-down menu.

When you enable the **Text under the mouse** check box, a dialog box tells you that you must activate the **Enable access for assistive devices** check box in the **Universal Access Preferences** window; click the **Universal Access** button provided to be open the pane where you can enable that check box.

8 Speak Selected Text by Pressing a Key

Enable the **Selected text when the key is pressed** check box to allow the system to read any selected text aloud when you press a certain key. Click the **Set Key** button; a dialog box appears that allows you to press the key you want to use to trigger speech; a good key to use is one of the unused function keys, such as **F12**. Press the key you want to use and click **OK**.

9 Enable Apple Speakable Items

Imagine telling your computer—in your own natural voice—"Get my mail." Imagine the computer firing up Mail, checking for new messages, and waiting for your next voice command, whether it be "Quit this application" or "Tell me a joke." Sound like science fiction? Well, it's not—it's just life with a Mac.

Click the **Speech Recognition** tab in the **Speech Preferences** window. Turn on **Apple Speakable Items**—Mac OS X's voice recognition system—by clicking the **On** radio button. A round, floating feedback window appears, with the word **Esc** in its display oval; this indicates that you must press and hold the **Escape** key on your keyboard to make the computer listen to you. You can change this default behavior under the **Listening** tab, where you can select a different listening key, choose whether the listening key toggles listening on and off or acts as a "push-to-talk" button, or even define a spoken preamble to make sure that the computer knows you're talking to it. "Computer, get my mail," you might say. You can even define a different name for your computer—the Mac will recognize the name as long as you speak it in a clear voice. Just type the name in the **Name** field, if you have selected to have the listening key toggle listening on and off.

⑩ Give Your Computer a Command

Click the down arrow in the round listening window and select **Open Speech Commands window** from the menu that appears. The **Speech Commands** window lists all the built-in speakable commands and shows you the history of your previous commands.

Hold down the **Escape** key (if you are still using the default "push-to-talk" configuration) and speak the text of any command listed in the **Commands** box. If the Mac recognizes your command, its text appears in the history box, and the command is executed. If the Mac didn't recognize the command, nothing will happen; just try again, speaking as clearly as you can.

 NOTE

The **Speech Commands** window need not be open for voice recognition to work. Because the window shows you all the available speakable commands, it's a good idea to keep the window open for reference until you've memorized the commands you want to use.

TIP

Tell the computer to "tell me a joke," if you like knock-knock jokes.

157 Zoom In

Zoom is a feature that lets you instantly magnify the area of the screen in which your mouse pointer is located. The Zoom feature lets you immediately clarify small text or point to detailed areas of the screen, which can be very useful for users with limited sight (as well as being a cool feature for anyone to try out). When Zoom is enabled, press the ⌘+**Option**+= key combination to zoom in to the configured maximum zoom level. You can keep pressing those keys to zoom in further. Press ⌘+**Option**+ – to zoom out to the minimum zoom level, which is most usefully set to the normal non-zoomed display size.

See Also

→ **23** Add a Second Display

→ **158** Choose How the Computer Alerts You

① Open the Universal Access Preferences

Open the **System Preferences** from the **Apple** menu and click **Universal Access** to open the **Universal Access Preferences** window. Click the **Seeing** tab, if it's not already selected.

② Turn On Zoom

Click the large **Turn On Zoom** button to enable Zoom using its default settings. You can now press ⌘+**Option**+= to zoom in on the mouse pointer's location.

 NOTE

While you're working in the **Universal Access Preferences** window, the **Talking Alerts** option is automatically enabled to read the text under the mouse just for that window. This feature can assist users in finding the options they need, which might include visibility features that are difficult to enable using the normal interface without spoken enhancements.

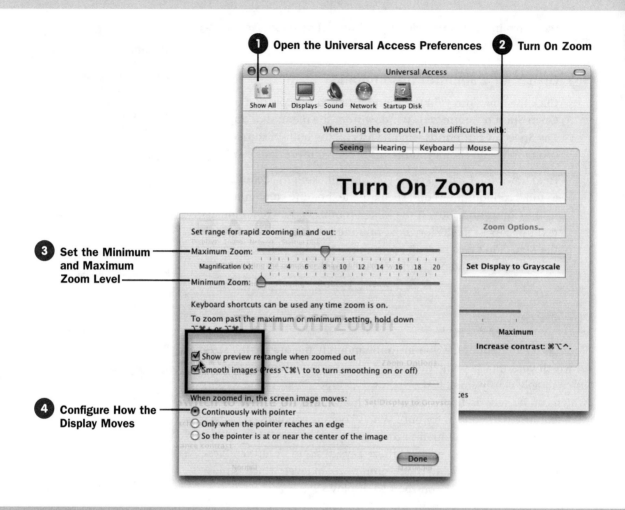

① Open the Universal Access Preferences **②** Turn On Zoom

③ Set the Minimum and Maximum Zoom Level

④ Configure How the Display Moves

TIP

The **Show preview rectangle when zoomed out** check box allows you to see the area of the screen that will be magnified, before you zoom in.

③ Set the Minimum and Maximum Zoom Level

Click the **Zoom Options** button to display a sheet of Zoom configuration options. The **Maximum Zoom** and **Minimum Zoom** sliders at the top allow you to set how far Zoom should magnify the screen when you press ⌘+**Option**+=, and to what level it should back off when you press ⌘+**Option**+ –. Experiment with the sliders until you're happy with the Zoom behavior.

4 **Configure How the Display Moves**

Use the radio buttons at the bottom of the sheet to specify how you want the screen to move when you move the mouse in a zoomed-in window. Normally, the mouse pointer moves in the display area to reflect what part of the screen you're in. You can also set it to move the display only when you push the mouse against the side of the zoomed-in screen, or to keep the mouse pointer at the center of the screen.

Click **Done** when you're happy with your Zoom settings.

TIP

If the **Smooth images** check box is enabled, the zoomed-in screen image will be softened to make graphics appear better and text even easier to read. If this option is not enabled, each pixel of the normally sized screen is simply made larger, without any smoothing or interpolation. Press **Option**+⌘+\ to toggle between smooth and sharp mode while you're zoomed in.

158 Choose How the Computer Alerts You

Mac OS X comes with 14 alert sounds, which are short sound effects that play each time an "alert" event occurs. Alerts happen for a variety of reasons: An application might generate an alert if it needs your attention and it's in the background, or if it pops up a dialog box that requires you to enter some information. The system might sound an alert if you enter invalid input or ask it to do something it can't do. Depending on your tastes, you can have these events signaled by a soft watery echo (the **Submarine** alert sound), a short ringing sound (the **Glass** alert sound), a reedy woodwind (**Blow**), or numerous other sounds. You can even use a sound effect that you provide yourself. When customizing your system, what sound the system makes when something goes wrong is just as important as your desktop picture or the position of your Dock— although tastes, of course, differ.

Before You Begin

✔ **96** About QuickTime

See Also

→ **130** Change Your Desktop Picture

→ **157** Zoom In

If you have difficulty hearing, you might not be able to detect audio alerts that occur when Mac OS X notifies you of some important event. One way to work around this problem is to have the system flash the screen in addition to sounding the audio alert. When the flash feature is enabled, the screen goes suddenly white, then fades quickly back to the normal display level.

1 **Open the Sound Preferences**

Open **System Preferences** using the **Apple** menu; click the **Sound** icon to open the **Sound Preferences** window. Click the **Sound Effects** tab if it isn't already selected.

1 Open the Sound Preferences

2 Select a Sound Effect

3 Add Your Own Sound Effect

4 Set the Alert Volume

6 Enable the Alert Flash

5 Open the Universal Access Preferences

7 Test the Flash Effect

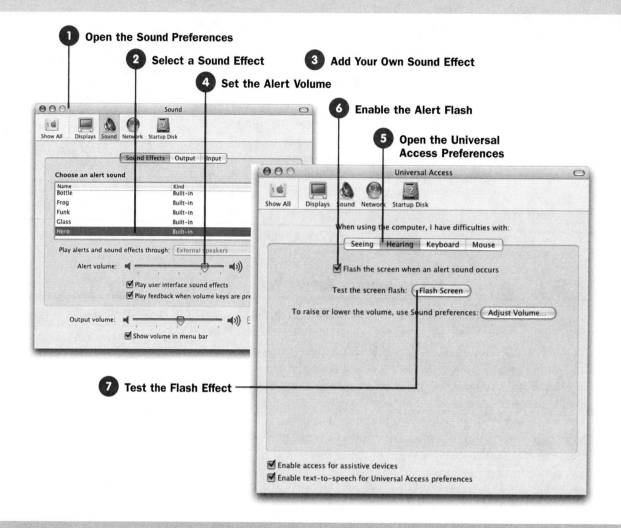

2 **Select a Sound Effect**

You are given a list of the built-in alert sound effects in the system. Click the name of one to hear it played. If you like it, simply close the **Preferences** window; the alert sound is changed as soon as you click it.

3 **Add Your Own Sound Effect**

If you have a sound effect file you want to add to the system, first make sure that it's in AIFF format; then place it in the **Sounds** folder inside the **Library** in your **Home** folder. The next time you open the **Sound Preferences** window, your sound effect will appear in the list for you to select.

4 Set the Alert Volume

Use the **Alert volume** slider to define how loudly the alert sound will play. The alert will never play louder than the master system volume.

5 Open the Universal Access Preferences

To have the Mac flash the screen in addition to playing the alert sound, open the **System Preferences** from the **Apple** menu and click **Universal Access** to open the **Universal Access Preferences** window. Click the **Hearing** tab.

6 Enable the Alert Flash

Enable the **Flash the screen when an alert sound occurs** check box. This option enables the flash effect for whenever the system would normally emit an alert sound. (The sound still plays even if the screen is set to flash.)

7 Test the Flash Effect

Click the **Flash Screen** button to see what the screen will look like when the alert flash occurs.

159 Use Sticky Keys

Sticky Keys let you use key combinations that involve two or more keys that must be pressed at the same time. If you can press only one key on the keyboard at a time, the Sticky Keys feature lets you use such key combinations by enabling a "stack" of pressed modifier keys that are all applied to the next regular key you press. For instance, with Sticky Keys turned on, you can simulate the ⌘+**Option**+M key combination by pressing first ⌘, then **Option**, and then M; the symbols for ⌘ and **Option** appear floating on the screen to tell you that they will be applied to the first "regular" key you press—in this case, the **M**.

TIP

Sound files created on Windows machines are often in WAV format; you can use any of a number of different software tools, including iTunes, to convert a WAV file to AIFF. In iTunes, first add the sound file to your **Music Library**; then change your preferences to use the AIFF Encoder (under **Importing**). You can then select the sound file in the Library and choose **Convert Selection to AIFF** from the **Advanced** menu. Select the AIFF file, then choose **Show Song File** from the **File** menu to access it in the Finder and move it to your **Sounds** folder.

See Also
→ **157** Zoom In
→ **160** Control the Mouse Pointer Using the Keyboard

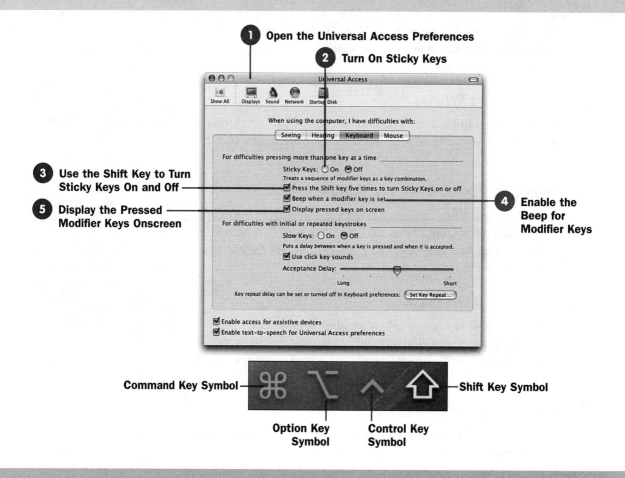

① Open the Universal Access Preferences

② Turn On Sticky Keys

③ Use the Shift Key to Turn Sticky Keys On and Off

⑤ Display the Pressed Modifier Keys Onscreen

④ Enable the Beep for Modifier Keys

Command Key Symbol — Shift Key Symbol

Option Key Symbol

Control Key Symbol

TIP

To remove a pressed modifier key from the displayed list, press that key twice in succession.

① Open the Universal Access Preferences

Open the **System Preferences** from the **Apple** menu and click **Universal Access** to open the **Universal Access Preferences** window. Click the **Keyboard** tab.

② Turn On Sticky Keys

Enable the **Sticky Keys: On** radio button. From now on, icons for the modifier keys you press will appear in the upper-right corner of the screen until you press a regular key.

❸ Use the Shift Key to Turn Sticky Keys On and Off

The **Press the Shift key five times to turn Sticky Keys on or off** check box lets you turn Sticky Keys on and off by pressing **Shift** five times in a row. Because this key sequence is very unlikely to be used for any other purpose, it's assigned to the Sticky Keys feature and is pretty safe to enable.

❹ Enable the Beep for Modifier Keys

When enabled, the **Beep when a modifier key is set** check box tells the system to make a soft "key press" sound effect when you press any modifier key. Disable the check box if you want the modifier keys to be silent.

❺ Display the Pressed Modifier Keys Onscreen

If you don't want the pressed modifier keys to be displayed floating in the upper right of the screen, disable the **Display pressed keys on screen** check box.

160 Control the Mouse Pointer Using the Keyboard

If you don't have a mouse or have trouble using one, you can set up Mac OS X to let you use the numeric keypad instead. This feature, called Mouse Keys, lets you navigate up, down, sideways, or diagonally using the number keys and to use the central **5** key to simulate a click. You can opt to turn the Mouse Keys feature on and off by pressing the **Option** key five times in a row.

❶ Open the Universal Access Preferences

Open the **System Preferences** from the **Apple** menu and click **Universal Access** to open the **Universal Access Preferences** window. Click the **Mouse** tab.

❷ Enable Mouse Keys

Enable the **Mouse Keys: On** radio button to turn on the Mouse Keys feature. This option reassigns the numeric keypad's keys so that they control the mouse pointer's movement. Press **5** to click the "mouse."

Before You Begin

✔ **159** Use Sticky Keys

See Also

→ **156** Talk to Your Computer and Have It Talk Back to You (Voice Recognition)

→ **161** Add a Keyboard Shortcut

1 Open the Universal
Access Preferences

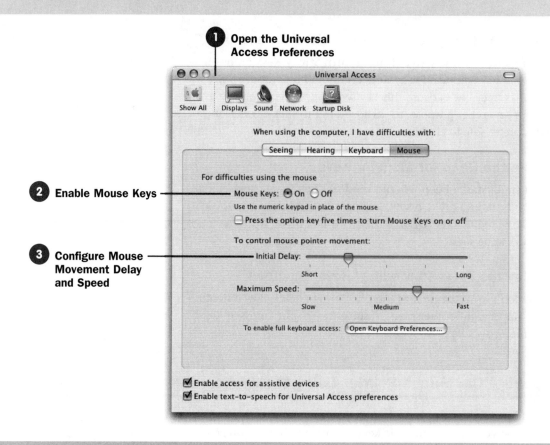

2 Enable Mouse Keys

3 Configure Mouse
Movement Delay
and Speed

3 Configure Mouse Movement Delay and Speed

You can specify a delay before the system responds to the numeric
keys and moves the cursor; this keeps the cursor from moving
immediately if you accidentally touch the numeric keypad's keys.
Use the **To control mouse pointer movement** and **Maximum
speed** sliders to specify how long the system should wait between
the time you press a keypad button and when the pointer begins
to move, and to specify how fast the pointer should move when
you press a button. The mouse keys' behavior changes immediately when you adjust the sliders so that you can experiment to find
where they're most comfortable for you.

161 Add a Keyboard Shortcut

Mac OS X is well instrumented with keyboard shortcuts for most of the popular commands in most applications. However, you may use some actions frequently that aren't bound to any keyboard shortcuts. Fortunately, you can assign new key commands to certain menu options in any application you like. Keyboard shortcuts are controlled in a registry of key combinations you can configure from the **Keyboard & Mouse Preferences** window.

See Also

→ **159** Use Sticky Keys

→ **160** Control the Mouse Pointer Using the Keyboard

1 Open the Keyboard & Mouse Preferences

Open the **System Preferences** from the **Apple** menu and click **Keyboard & Mouse** to open the **Keyboard & Mouse Preferences** window. Click the **Keyboard Shortcuts** tab.

2 Enable Full Keyboard Access

Enable the **Turn on full keyboard access** check box if you want to navigate the Mac OS X system using the **Control** key in conjunction with various function keys (F-keys).

3 Add a New Keyboard Shortcut

Suppose that there's a menu option in a certain application to which you want to bind a new keyboard shortcut. To do this, click the + button under the list of keyboard shortcuts to bring up the configuration sheet.

4 Specify the Application to Control

The **Application** menu lists all the applications currently installed on the computer. Select the application you want to control, or select **All Applications** to create a shortcut that applies to a common menu command that appears in lots of different applications.

5 Specify the Menu Option to Link to a Key Combination

Type the name of the menu item to which you want to bind the key combination. This name is the text of the item in the menu itself; it must be entered *exactly as it appears in the menu*, including the ellipsis (trailing dots), if present. Don't include the name of the menu that contains the menu item.

🔆 TIP

In the list of keyboard shortcuts, you can see which function keys are used for which functions under the **Shortcut** column. In addition to the keyboard shortcuts that control Mac OS X functions and various applications, you can use the key combination for the **Turn full keyboard access on or off** option (by default, **Control+F1**) to turn full keyboard access on and off.

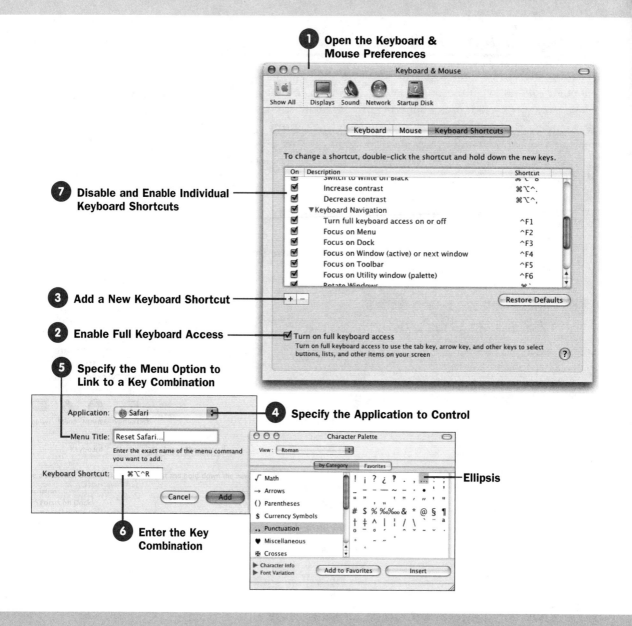

1 Open the Keyboard & Mouse Preferences

7 Disable and Enable Individual Keyboard Shortcuts

3 Add a New Keyboard Shortcut

2 Enable Full Keyboard Access

5 Specify the Menu Option to Link to a Key Combination

4 Specify the Application to Control

Ellipsis

6 Enter the Key Combination

6 Enter the Key Combination

Click in the **Keyboard Shortcut** input field and then press the key combination you want to bind to the specified menu item. The combination appears in symbolic notation in the field. You can press another combination to replace the one shown in the box.

Click **Add** to create the new keyboard combination. Back in the **Keyboard Shortcuts** tab of the **Keyboard and Mouse Preferences** window, the shortcut will appear under the application's name under the **Application Keyboard Shortcuts** heading (scroll down to the bottom of the list of shortcuts to see this heading, which contains all the shortcuts you define for your applications in a hierarchical structure).

7 Disable and Enable Individual Keyboard Shortcuts

You can use the check boxes in the list to enable and disable individual key combinations. Click the check box next to an application's name to disable all key combinations assigned to that application; click the check box next to a heading (such as **Application Keyboard Shortcuts** or **Keyboard Navigation**) to disable all the keyboard shortcuts underneath it in the hierarchy.

If an application has more than one keyboard combination assigned to it, you can disable one of them, and the application's global check box will change to a – symbol to signify that some of the application's keyboard shortcuts are enabled and some aren't. This symbol propagates up the hierarchy to higher levels as well.

Click **Restore Defaults** to reset the check boxes for all the keyboard shortcuts except for the ones you've set for individual applications.

TIPS

An ellipsis (…) is actually a single character, and you must enter it using the **Character Palette**. You can quickly access the **Character Palette** by choosing **Edit, Special Characters**, or by selecting **Show Character Palette** from the **Keyboard Input Menu** in the menu bar (if you have it displayed—see **136** Change the System's Language). Find the ellipsis character under the **Punctuation** category and double-click it (or selected it and click **Insert**) to copy it to the current input field. A much quicker way to enter an ellipsis is by pressing **Option+;** (the semicolon).

To reassign a key combination, double-click the shortcut bound to it in the list; then enter the new key combination. You can also double-click the menu item text in the **Description** column of a custom-defined application shortcut to change the menu item bound to that key combination.

PART V

Administering the System

IN THIS PART

17

Security, Boot Volumes, and Updating the System Software

IN THIS CHAPTER:

As the owner of a computer with a multiuser operating system that's connected to the Internet, you must sooner or later face the unpleasant fact that you are responsible for certain administrative duties that rest on the shoulders of every conscientious computer user. It's the age of viruses, worms, Trojans, and any number of malicious Internet denizens whose sole purpose in life is to make life miserable for the rest of us by breaking into unguarded systems and generally taking advantage of the goodwill of anybody who doesn't keep his system well cared for. Because most of the well-publicized attacks are almost exclusively directed at Windows computers, you're all but immune because Macs are not vulnerable to these kinds of shenanigans.

TIP

Use the **Secure Empty Trash** command instead of the plain **Empty Trash** command in the **Finder** menu if you want to delete your files in such a manner that they can't be recovered even using disk recovery applications. **Empty Trash** deletes files by simply removing the references to them from the disk catalog, leaving their contents intact on the disk; but **Secure Empty Trash** writes random data all over the disk where the old files were, so that there's no way a thief can retrieve sensitive deleted documents from your disk.

However, Mac OS X is based on Unix, and the only thing keeping most Unix systems on the Internet secure is their ever-watchful system administrators staying on top of all the latest vulnerabilities in Samba, Sendmail, BIND, OpenSSH, and the other unsung components of Unix. Now that every Mac is effectively a Unix system, Unix-style exploits threaten the consumer computing world, and every Mac user must assume some of the responsibilities of a full-fledged Unix guru. The free ride will end someday, and it's the casual computer users who haven't been keeping a close eye on their computers' security who will pay the highest price.

The tasks in this chapter explain some of the security features of Mac OS X, features that allow you to operate with transparency and ease while keeping the system buttoned up against possible attacks. You will also learn techniques for booting the computer from alternative volumes such as external disks, which might come in handy if you're managing a complex installation or if you have to troubleshoot a potential security problem; finally, you will learn how to keep your system software as up-to-date as possible, sealing potential security breaches as soon as Apple and the vigilant Internet security community discover them.

162 Enable or Disable the Firewall

Before You Begin

✔ **29** Configure Networking Manually

See Also

→ **163** Add or Remove Firewall Rules

Mac OS X comes with a *firewall* to protect it from unwanted network traffic. For data to be able to travel from your Mac to a host elsewhere on the Internet, that data must match certain criteria. The data must *originate* from your Mac—in other words, it must be a data transaction that *you* initiate—or, if the data is coming from another computer to your Mac, the data must be one of a few specific types that the firewall knows about, such as Web traffic (HTTP).

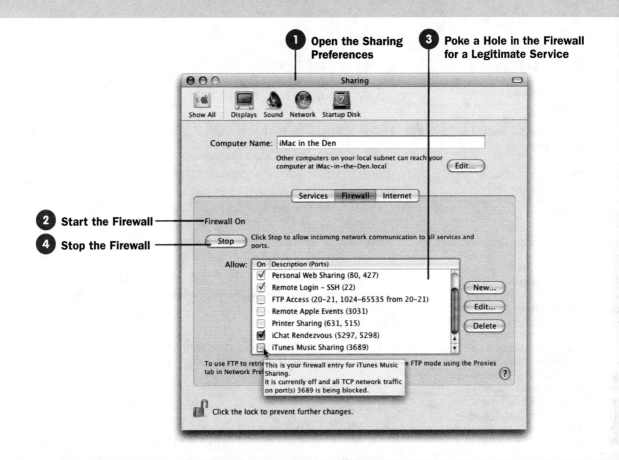

① Open the Sharing Preferences

③ Poke a Hole in the Firewall for a Legitimate Service

② Start the Firewall

④ Stop the Firewall

By default, Mac OS X ships with the firewall turned off. This means that anybody can send traffic of any kind to your Mac, and the Mac's software must either deal with it or throw it away according to what kind of traffic it is. When you turn the firewall on, all the traffic but those few exempt types is simply discarded, and your software doesn't have to deal with it at all. This can improve your system's performance, as well as protect it against unsavory characters probing your computer for a weak spot in its defenses.

🔍 KEY TERM

Firewall—A piece of software that runs at the very innermost level of the operating system (the *kernel*) and serves as a traffic cop for all the Internet communications that travel in or out of your Mac.

① Open the Sharing Preferences

Open the **System Preferences** from the **Apple** menu and click the **Sharing** icon to open the **Sharing Preferences** window. Click the **Firewall** tab.

NOTES

You must be logged in as an Admin user or be able to authenticate as one using the lock icon in the **Sharing Preferences** window to enable or disable the firewall.

The Internet address space for DSL, cable, and corporate network links uses well-known IP ranges; if you are on such a connection, the automated scripts that "script kiddies" use to probe for holes such as the Code Red or Nimda vulnerabilities (which are still being exploited whenever anybody finds an unpatched Windows machine) constantly hit your Mac. Fortunately, Mac OS X is not vulnerable to these Windows-specific attacks; but running a firewall can definitely help you keep them from becoming a drain on your resources.

KEY TERM

Rule—An entry in the firewall's configuration that tells it to allow or disallow a certain kind of traffic.

② Start the Firewall

To turn on the firewall and begin shielding your computer from attack, click the **Start** button. The button's label immediately changes to **Stop**.

③ Poke a Hole in the Firewall for a Legitimate Service

To allow traffic through for the various kinds of online sharing that you can do with your Mac, Mac OS X must create a "hole" in the firewall for each sharing service that you enable. For instance, if you turn on **Personal Web Sharing**, the *ports*—the numeric identifiers for certain well-known services, such as HTTP, or Web traffic—associated with the Personal Web Sharing service are opened so that traffic using those ports can reach your computer. For instance, in the case of the **Personal Web Sharing** service, ports 80 and 427 are made exempt from the firewall so that remote users can connect to your computer with a Web browser and view your public documents. One of these "holes" in the firewall is generally known as a *rule*, and your firewall can have any number of rules that describe which kinds of traffic are allowed through and which are prohibited.

For all the sharing services that are available in the **Services** tab in the **Sharing Preferences** window, the corresponding "holes" in the firewall are opened automatically when you turn on each of the individual services. However, there are a couple of extra rule entries in the **Allow** list box you might find useful to enable.

Enable the check box for **iChat Rendezvous** to allow other people on your local network to send you iChat requests. If you don't enable this exemption, other people won't be able to contact you for voice or video chats in iChat.

Enable the check box for **iTunes Music Sharing** to allow other people to browse your shared music in iTunes.

④ Stop the Firewall

If you are having trouble making a connection to some remote host or online service, as might happen with instant-messaging services such as ICQ, your firewall might be getting in the way. It might be a one-time or uncommon occurrence for you to try to use the service in question; in many cases, it can be easier for you to simply turn off the firewall temporarily to allow a file transfer or other transaction to go through, rather than finding out which specific ports you need to use to allow the traffic through the firewall on a permanent basis.

To turn the firewall off, click **Stop** in the **Firewall** tab of the **Sharing Preferences** window. Remember to turn it back on by clicking **Start** when you're done making the transactions!

163 Add or Remove Firewall Rules

Not every network service in the world is available in the standard list of *rules* in the **Firewall** configuration pane for you to enable and disable at will. A great many more commonly used services won't work properly unless you "poke a hole" in the firewall for them.

Mac OS X's firewall is designed to let you add new exception rules so that certain services can be allowed to contact your machine, even when every other unauthorized form of traffic is blocked.

1 Open the Sharing Preferences

Open the **System Preferences** from the **Apple** menu and click the **Sharing** icon to open the **Sharing Preferences** window. Click the **Firewall** tab.

2 Add a New Firewall Rule

Click the **New** button to the right of the list of services. This brings up a sheet where you can select from a list of commonly used network services with well-known port numbers, or define your own service that isn't in the list.

3 Select a Well-Known Service to Allow

If the service you want to allow to reach your computer is in the **Port Name** drop-down list, select it and click **OK**. The service is now immediately allowed to access your machine through the firewall.

Before You Begin

✔ **29** Configure Networking Manually

✔ **162** Enable or Disable the Firewall

See Also

→ **80** Start a Chat Session

→ **97** About iTunes

▶ NOTE

You must be logged in as an Admin user or be able to authenticate as one using the lock icon in the **Sharing Preferences** window to add or remove firewall rules.

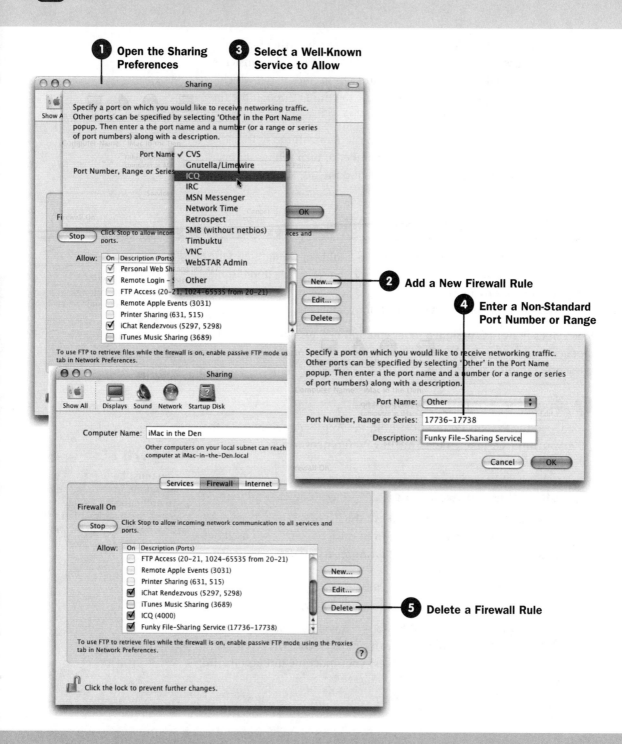

1 Open the Sharing Preferences

3 Select a Well-Known Service to Allow

Sharing

Specify a port on which you would like to receive networking traffic. Other ports can be specified by selecting 'Other' in the Port Name popup. Then enter a the port name and a number (or a range or series of port numbers) along with a description.

Port Name ✓ CVS
Gnutella/Limewire
Port Number, Range or Series ICQ
IRC
MSN Messenger
Network Time
Retrospect
SMB (without netbios)
Timbuktu
VNC
WebSTAR Admin
Other

OK

Stop   Click Stop to allow incoming ...ices and ports.

Allow: On Description (Ports)
✓ Personal Web Sha...
✓ Remote Login – S...
☐ FTP Access (20-21, 1024-65535 from 20-21)
☐ Remote Apple Events (3031)
☐ Printer Sharing (631, 515)
✓ iChat Rendezvous (5297, 5298)
☐ iTunes Music Sharing (3689)

New...
Edit...
Delete

2 Add a New Firewall Rule

4 Enter a Non-Standard Port Number or Range

To use FTP to retrieve files while the firewall is on, enable passive FTP mode us... tab in Network Preferences.

Specify a port on which you would like to receive networking traffic. Other ports can be specified by selecting 'Other' in the Port Name popup. Then enter a the port name and a number (or a range or series of port numbers) along with a description.

Port Name: Other
Port Number, Range or Series: 17736-17738
Description: Funky File-Sharing Service

Cancel   OK

Sharing

Show All   Displays Sound Network Startup Disk

Computer Name: iMac in the Den

Other computers on your local subnet can reach computer at iMac-in-the-Den.local

Services   Firewall   Internet

Firewall On

Stop   Click Stop to allow incoming network communication to all services and ports.

Allow: On Description (Ports)
☐ FTP Access (20-21, 1024-65535 from 20-21)
☐ Remote Apple Events (3031)
☐ Printer Sharing (631, 515)
✓ iChat Rendezvous (5297, 5298)
☐ iTunes Music Sharing (3689)
✓ ICQ (4000)
✓ Funky File-Sharing Service (17736-17738)

New...
Edit...
Delete

5 Delete a Firewall Rule

To use FTP to retrieve files while the firewall is on, enable passive FTP mode using the Proxies tab in Network Preferences. (?)

Click the lock to prevent further changes.

4 Enter a Non-Standard Port Number or Range

For services that aren't in the menu of popular applications, you can enter your own firewall exception rule if you know the port numbers used by the application or service you want to allow.

Select **Other** from the **Port Name** drop-down list. In the **Port Number, Range, or Series** field, type either a single port number, a range of ports (separated by a dash), or a list of ports separated by commas. Then enter a name for the firewall rule in the **Description** field. Click **OK** when you're done. Any application whose traffic matches the ports you specified can now reach your computer from a remote source.

5 Delete or Disable a Firewall Rule

To remove a firewall rule that you don't need anymore, select it and click **Delete**. If you prefer, you can simply disable the firewall rule, without deleting it permanently. To disable a rule, just disable the check box next to the service's name in the list of services to deselect that service.

TIP

To find out what ports a certain application uses, check the application's documentation or customer support service. Another way to find a well-known port number for a common Internet application is to look in the **/etc/services** file: Open the **Terminal** and type `pico /etc/services` to browse the list of well-known services.

164 Extract a Password from the Keychain

Anybody who has been on the Internet for any length of time knows what it's like to work with account passwords. Every Web site, every cooperative application, every email account, every online service has a password for you to remember. And your accounts don't even have the decency to all use the same usernames and passwords, because although your favorite username might have been available at one Web site, at another it might have been taken, forcing you to come up with a new variation on your name. Different Web sites have more or less stringent requirements for secure passwords, forcing you to think of multiple different passwords for different sites.

Who can possibly keep all these passwords and usernames straight? Mac OS X can, using a feature called the *Keychain*. When you use the Keychain feature, you don't have to remember a single one of your passwords. All you have to remember is a single master password for your Keychain itself. After you've unlocked your Keychain, it will unlock all your individual logins on its own. Handily enough, the Keychain is automatically unlocked by the act of your logging in to your Mac OS X account.

Before You Begin

✔ **69** Keep Track of Web Sites with Bookmarks

See Also

→ **150** Change a User's Password

→ **165** Secure Your Files with FileVault

KEY TERM

Keychain—A Mac OS X feature that keeps track of all your usernames and passwords, wherever you encounter them (in applications, in Web forms, anywhere), filling them in automatically for you whenever they're needed.

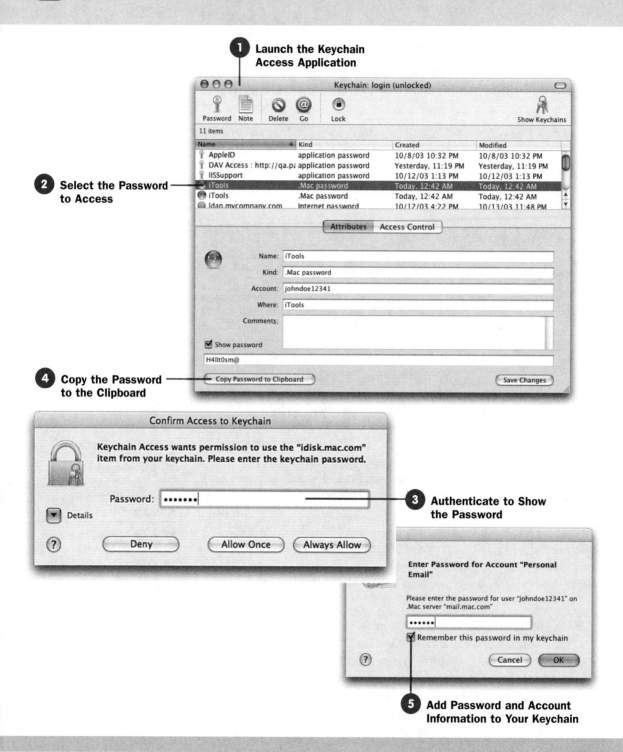

1 Launch the Keychain Access Application

2 Select the Password to Access

4 Copy the Password to the Clipboard

3 Authenticate to Show the Password

5 Add Password and Account Information to Your Keychain

As you use Mac OS X, certain applications and Web sites will ask for passwords. When you enter a password in such a situation, a sheet appears in your browser that contains a **Remember this password in my keychain** check box. This option offers to add the password information to the Keychain for you. If you enable this check box before logging in, the Keychain will fill out the password information for you the next time you open that application or site.

However, you might later have to find out what your password for a given site or application is. You might have to change your password periodically, for example—and everybody forgets passwords. It's just a fact of life. Fortunately, Mac OS X gives you access to the contents of your Keychain, using an application called **Keychain Access**.

① Launch the Keychain Access Application

In the Finder, navigate into the **Applications** folder and then into the **Utilities** folder; double-click the **Keychain Access** icon to launch the application.

② Select the Password to Access

All the authentication keys that have been added to your Keychain are visible in the upper pane. Scroll through them until you find the one you want; you can view the details of an item by clicking it.

All different kinds of authentication keys are listed in the Keychain Access window; each is listed by its **Kind**, such as **Internet password** or **application password**. Use the **Kind** column to zero in on the item you want to examine. When you find it, select it; information about that key appears in the fields at the bottom of the Keychain Access window when the **Attributes** tab is selected.

③ Authenticate to Show the Password

While viewing the item information, click the **Show password** check box at the bottom of the window. A dialog box appears, prompting you for authentication. This is a security measure, ensuring that you are the rightful owner of this Keychain, and not someone who just came in and sat down at your computer while you were logged in already.

Enter your Keychain password, which is usually the same as your Mac OS X login password (unless your login password was changed by an Admin user).

TIPS

There's a lot more you can do with the **Keychain Access** utility than simply extracting forgotten passwords; you can lock the system, customize which applications are explicitly allowed to access certain passwords (also called "keys"), delete keys, change passwords, or create secure text notes that can be unlocked and read only if you know the Keychain password. Feel free to explore all the features in the **Keychain Access** utility!

In Keychain authentication windows like the one that appears here, you are given three options: **Deny**, **Allow Once**, and **Always Allow**. Click **Deny** to cancel the authentication, denying access to your Keychain to the application requesting it. Click **Allow Once** to authenticate the password for just this one instance (if you try to access the same information again in ten seconds, you'll have to provide your password again). Click **Always Allow** to give the requesting application permanent access to your Keychain, until the computer is turned off or restarted.

When you have successfully authenticated and unlocked the Keychain, the password for the account is shown in the field at the bottom of the window.

④ Copy the Password to the Clipboard

It can often be easier, especially with cryptic passwords made up of numbers and special punctuation characters, to copy and paste a password rather than having to key it in manually. Click the **Copy Password to Clipboard** button to copy the password into memory. If you then switch to another application and select **Paste** from the **Edit** menu (or press ⌘**V**), the password is copied into the application as though you'd typed it yourself.

⑤ Add Password and Account Information to Your Keychain

As you're using any application that accesses protected services on the Internet—such as Safari or Mail—you might be prompted on occasion to enter your password. In the dialog box or sheet where you type the password, you will usually see a check box labeled **Remember this password in my keychain**, or some similar variation. Enable this check box to save the password in the Keychain when you click **OK**. The next time the application tries to access the protected resource, it will be able to get the password automatically from the Keychain instead of having to bug you for it.

If you enter an incorrect password, it is not included in the Keychain.

165 Secure Your Files with FileVault

Before You Begin

✔ **146** Add a New User

See Also

→ **143** Require a Password When Reactivating the Computer

→ **150** Change a User's Password

New in Mac OS X Panther, FileVault is a feature that encrypts all the files in your **Home** folder so that they can be accessed only by someone who knows your login password. When you have FileVault turned on, you won't notice any difference in how the system works—by the act of logging in, you've unlocked the FileVault and gained access to your files for the duration of your login session. But if someone else comes along and tries to access your files—even by tearing the computer apart and prying into the hard disk itself—without your password to unlock the files, they'll be beyond the reach of those with ill intent.

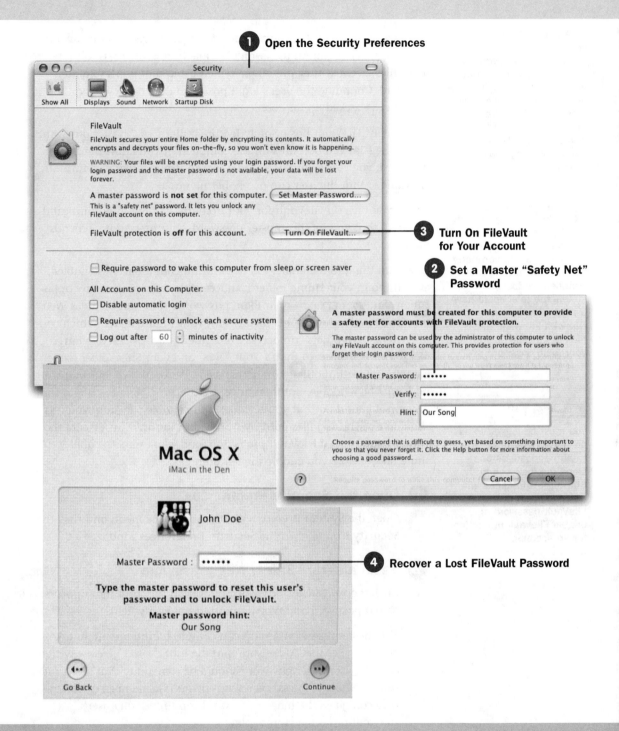

1 Open the Security Preferences

3 Turn On FileVault
for Your Account

2 Set a Master "Safety Net"
Password

4 Recover a Lost FileVault Password

NOTE

Remember that even with FileVault enabled, someone who knows your login password can still access your files. Always be sure to keep your password secret and unguessable—and change it every few months!

 TIP

FileVault is designed with corporate laptop users in mind; if a laptop computer full of trade secrets and confidential documents is stolen, the thief could have a gold mine on his hands. But with FileVault, those files are locked up without your login password available to access them.

NOTE

You must be logged in as an Admin user or be able to authenticate as one using the lock icon in the **Sharing Preferences** window to set a master FileVault password or enable FileVault protection for an account.

The tricky part about FileVault is that if any user forgets her password, even the system's Admin user won't be able to restore access to that user's files, because they are all encrypted using that user's forgotten password. Changing the user's login password does not re-encrypt the files; they're locked up for good.

Fortunately, FileVault has a safety feature built in: a "master password" for all the FileVault accounts on the computer. If you know the master password, you can regain access to a locked **Home** folder and turn off FileVault so that the user can access her files again.

Before you turn on FileVault for your account, it's very important (and required) that you set this master password. Your users' data depends on it!

One final thing to remember about FileVault is that once it's enabled, everything in your **Home** folder is inaccessible to anyone or any application that doesn't know your login password—and that includes Web browsers or other Macs. This means that your **Public** folder (which contains items that others can access from other Macs, as described in
36 **Allow Others to Share Your Files**) and your **Sites** folder (which contains items that others can access using Personal Web Sharing) will no longer be readable. But then, if you're concerned enough about the privacy of your data that you're choosing to enable FileVault, you shouldn't be sharing files publicly from your Mac anyway. Be sure that you absolutely need FileVault protection, and won't miss the ability to share files, before you enable the feature!

❶ Open the Security Preferences

Open the **System Preferences** from the **Apple** menu and click the **Security** icon to open the **Security Preferences** window.

❷ Set a Master "Safety Net" Password

Click the **Set Master Password** button. In the sheet that appears, type a password and type it again in the **Verify** field.

The master password setting can contain a hint; be sure to take advantage of this. Make sure that the hint doesn't give away the game! Your master password should be something that an intruder won't be able to guess, even with the hint. Remember, anybody who can guess the master password can unlock any user's FileVault-protected **Home** folder!

③ Turn On FileVault for Your Account

After a master password has been set by an **Admin** user, you can turn on FileVault for your account by clicking the **Turn On FileVault** button in the **Security Preferences** window. If you are not an Admin user, you will be prompted to enter the name and password of an Admin user before you can proceed.

Enter your login account password when prompted to verify that you are who you say you are. Mac OS X gives you a final warning, reminding you that if you lose your password and can't remember the system's master password, you will never again be able to access your files—ever.

Save all your open files and quit all your applications. When you're ready, click **Turn On FileVault**.

Mac OS X logs you out of your account and encrypts your **Home** folder. After the process is complete, you can log back into your account and use the system as you normally would.

④ Recover a Lost FileVault Password

If you try three times to log in at the login window and can't remember the correct password for your account, Mac OS X presents you with your password hint, as well as a **Reset Password** button. If the hint doesn't help you remember your password, click the button to be given the opportunity to enter the master system password and unlock your account by entering a new login password for the account.

Only the administrator of the computer should know the master system password. If you've forgotten your password for a FileVault-protected account, ask the computer's administrator to enter the master password for you.

After you enter the master password correctly and set a new password for your account, you will see a notice that your *Keychain* is still locked using your old login password. You won't be able to access your Keychain unless you remember your old password, but the original Keychain still exists in the new FileVault-protected **Home** folder, in case you remember the old password and want to extract its contents. Otherwise, a new Keychain is started using your new account password.

NOTES

Because the act of turning on FileVault involves changing all of your files as they are written on the disk, the process must take place while you're logged out of your account so that you don't touch any files that Mac OS X is working on. For the same reason, any other users must be logged out as well, or Mac OS X will not allow you to turn on FileVault. When you give the command to turn on FileVault for your account, Mac OS X logs you out and prevents you from logging in until all your files have been encrypted. The process might take an hour or longer, depending on how much data you have in your **Home** folder.

After your **Home** folder has been secured with FileVault, the icon for it in the Finder changes from a regular house to the "safe house" icon representing FileVault. Furthermore, other users can no longer browse the contents of your **Home** folder at all—not even your **Public** folder.

166 Run Software Update

Before You Begin

✔ Install an Application from Disc or Download

See Also

→ 167 Ignore an Update

→ 169 Schedule Automatic Software Updates

 NOTE

You must be logged in as an Admin user or be able to authenticate as one when prompted to install new software obtained by Software Update.

 TIP

Just to make sure that you don't miss it, Software Update is also available in a button link from the **About This Mac** window.

 NOTE

If the separate Software Update utility does not launch, it means there were no updates available. The **Software Update Preferences** window informs you of this condition as well.

Software Update, accessible either from **System Preferences** or from the **Apple** menu, is Apple's utility for checking the central Apple servers for available updates to Mac OS X, its component utilities, and Apple applications such as iTunes, iMovie, and Keynote. These updates, which generally appear two or three times a month, range in importance from minor revisions to esoteric components like Bluetooth and Java, all the way up to patches for critical security vulnerabilities and new versions of Mac OS X itself that address flaws in the software that impair its operation.

When Software Update detects an update that applies to your system, you can install that update with a couple of clicks. Software Update also gives you the option to ignore updates that don't apply to you, or to schedule automatic checking for updates.

1 Open Software Update Preferences

Select **Software Update** from the **Apple** menu, or click **Software Update** in the **System Preferences**. The **Software Update Preferences** window opens, which allows you to configure the **Software Update** utility and launch a check.

2 Check for New Updates

Make sure that you're connected to the Internet. (The **Software Update** utility can't find any updates if you can't reach the Apple servers.) Then click **Check Now**. (The button's label changes immediately to **Cancel**.) Software Update examines your Mac OS X system and its core applications and compares their version numbers to the updates available on the server. All the applicable updates that the utility finds are listed in the separate Software Update window that appears.

3 Select the Updates to Install

Click an update in the results list to read its description and to decide whether you want to install it. For each update you decide to install, enable the **Install** check box to the right of the update's name. (Updates are typically selected for installation automatically.)

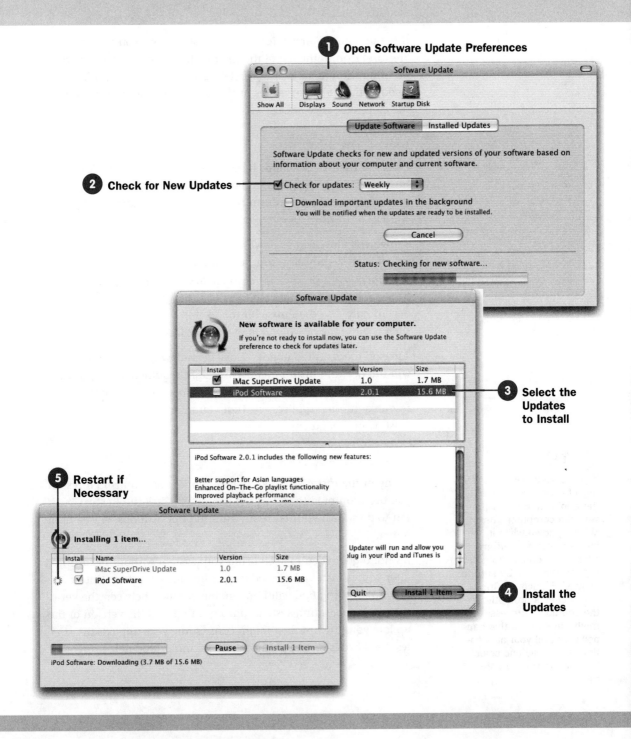

1 Open Software Update Preferences

2 Check for New Updates

3 Select the Updates to Install

5 Restart if Necessary

4 Install the Updates

If the update requires a restart after installation, you will see a "restart" icon to the left of the **Install** check box (it's a leftward-pointing triangle in a small circle). You can install multiple updates that require restarts at the same time and have to restart the computer only once.

④ Install the Updates

Click the **Install** *<n>* **Items** button to install all the updates you have selected. If necessary, a dialog box appears that prompts you to authenticate as an **Admin** user. Enter the username and password of an **Admin** user to continue.

Software Update begins downloading the selected updates. An update can be any size from several hundred kilobytes to a hundred megabytes or more; refer to the **Size** column to determine how large your total download will be and plan the download accordingly. Use the **Pause** button to stop the download; you can then resume the download later without losing your place.

After all the required updates have been downloaded, Mac OS X will unpack and install them. This might require a lot of processor power and system resources, so now is a good time to quit any resource-hungry applications that you might be running, or at least go and get a cup of coffee.

⑤ Restart if Necessary

If any of the installed updates were marked as requiring a restart, you are prompted to restart the computer. Click the **Restart** button to do so. All your currently running applications will be terminated.

It's not a good idea to keep using your system without restarting it after you've installed an update that requires a restart. Chances are that nothing bad will happen, but conflicts between the version of the operating system that's running and the version of the update you just installed might cause some very unpleasant results. Always restart promptly after a major update!

🕯 TIP

If you have unsaved data in any of your applications, the application might prevent the computer from shutting down while it waits for you to confirm whether to quit without saving the changes. Be sure to answer all such confirmation requests promptly or the shutdown process might time out. If this happens, quit all your applications manually and select **Restart** from the **Apple** menu.

167 Ignore an Update

Sometimes the **Software Update** utility will find software that can be installed on your computer, but that you're not interested in. For instance, there might be an update to iMovie, but you don't use iMovie and don't want to spend the time downloading 80 megabytes of software you won't benefit from. To prevent this iMovie update from appearing in your update list every time you check, you can tell Software Update to ignore it.

Before You Begin

✔ **166** Run Software Update

See Also

→ **168** Browse Previous Updates

→ **169** Schedule Automatic Software Updates

1 Check for Updates

Use the **Software Update** utility to check for updates as set out in **166** **Run Software Update**. Review the detected updates to decide which ones you want to install and which ones aren't relevant to you.

2 Select the Update to Ignore

Click to select one of the updates you want to ignore. You can ignore only one update at a time.

3 Ignore the Update

Select **Ignore Update** from the **Update** menu and click **OK** on the confirmation dialog box that appears. The update disappears from the list, and won't ever trigger a Software Update launch in the future.

4 Reactivate Ignored Updates

If you want to see your ignored updates again (for instance, if you suddenly develop an interest in video editing and want to try iMovie after all), select **Reset Ignored Updates** from the **Software Update** menu. Any updates that you had previously ignored will appear in the list again.

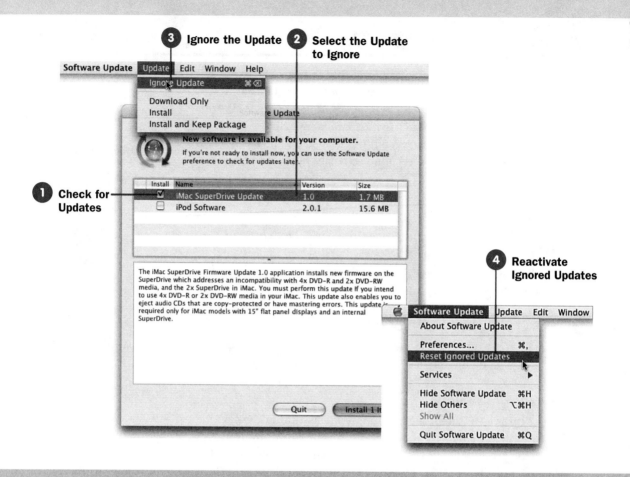

3 Ignore the Update **2** Select the Update to Ignore

1 Check for Updates

4 Reactivate Ignored Updates

168 Browse Previous Updates

Before You Begin

✔ **166** Run Software Update

See Also

→ **169** Schedule Automatic Software Updates

Knowing which updates you've already installed is a big part of knowing how secure and up-to-date your system is. The **Software Update** utility keeps a log of all the updates it installs so that you can review previous updates. The utility also keeps archives of the downloaded update packages so that you can reinstall them at a later date (for instance, if you have to reinstall the operating system and then apply patches that were released after the system was).

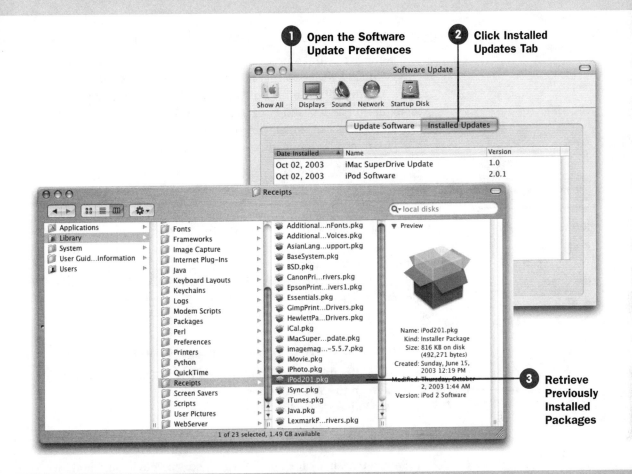

1 Open the Software
Update Preferences

2 Click Installed
Updates Tab

3 Retrieve
Previously
Installed
Packages

1 Open the Software Update Preferences

Select **Software Update** from the **Apple** menu or click **Software
Update** in the **System Preferences** application to open the
Software Update Preferences window.

2 Click the Installed Updates Tab

Click the **Installed Updates** tab to see a list of all previously
installed updates, their version numbers, and the dates on which
they were installed.

③ Retrieve Previously Installed Packages

If you need to find a previously installed package and reinstall it, open a Finder window and navigate to the **Receipts** folder inside the **Library** folder in the hard disk's top level. All installed updates are in that folder, with a **.pkg** extension. These files are generally installable package files, which you can install again (or on a different machine) simply by double-clicking them.

169 Schedule Automatic Software Updates

Before You Begin

✔ **166** Run Software Update

See Also

➜ **167** Ignore an Update

➜ **168** Browse Previous Updates

The **Software Update** utility can run in the background, performing its maintenance tasks on a periodic basis so that you don't have to worry about it. Better yet, when the utility detects available updates, it can download them in the background while you're busy with other tasks. When the package is finished downloading, Software Update notifies you that there's an update ready to install. This can be a big time-saver.

① Open the Software Update Preferences

Select **Software Update** from the **Apple** menu or click **Software Update** in the **System Preferences** application. This action brings up the **Software Update Preferences** window.

② Enable Automatic Checking for Updates

Enable the **Check for updates** check box to enable automatic checking on the default interval, **Weekly**.

③ Select a Checking Interval

Use the drop-down menu to select a checking interval of **Daily**, **Weekly**, or **Monthly**. Whichever period you select counts from the time the last check was performed. For instance, if you last checked for updates at 4:13 P.M. on Tuesday, the next **Weekly** check will occur at 4:13 P.M. the following Tuesday.

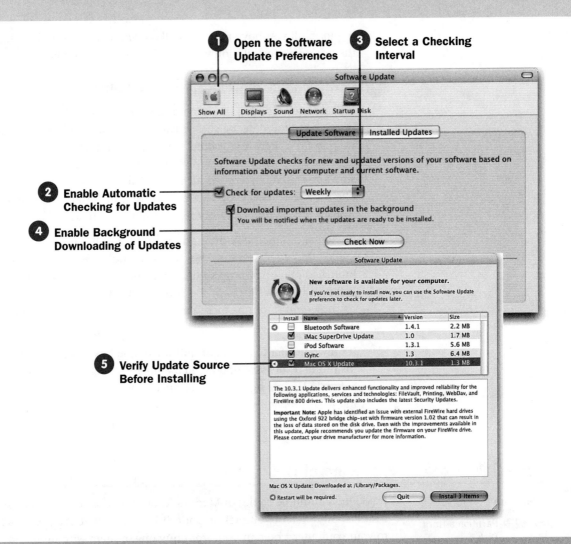

1 Open the Software Update Preferences

3 Select a Checking Interval

2 Enable Automatic Checking for Updates

4 Enable Background Downloading of Updates

5 Verify Update Source Before Installing

4 **Enable Background Downloading of Updates**

If you want to enable background downloads, enable the **Download important updates in the background** check box. This lets Mac OS X download crucial security updates for you. Applying these patches as soon as they become available is so important that Apple has allowed the operating system software to get that much closer to updating itself automatically. With all these options

NOTE

Large and optional updates, such as revisions of iTunes and iMovie, are not downloaded in the background. The background download option is intended only for the most important and critical system updates.

in place, all you have to do—ideally—is authenticate and confirm the package's installation when Mac OS X prompts you.

5 Verify Update Source Before Installing

If you do see a dialog box prompting you to allow Mac OS X to install a new update, be sure to confirm that the update is in fact coming from Software Update! An easy way for a virus or Trojan to install itself on your system is to pose as a legitimate message from Software Update. However, such a malicious program cannot actually use the **Software Update** mechanism; the utility is tied into Apple's servers and can only report legitimate updates from Apple.

If you get a dialog box prompting you to install a newly downloaded update, make sure that the **Software Update** utility has launched and open it up so that you can view what the update is. If the update isn't listed in the **Software Update** window, then beware—you might be facing a program with malicious intentions.

It's always safer to cancel or quit the dialog box instead of installing a software update. Remember that you can always run Software Update again. If there are any legitimate updates remaining to install, Software Update will ask for permission to install them.

170 Select the Boot Volume at Boot Time

If you have multiple copies of Mac OS X (or other operating systems) installed on different volumes on your disk, or on different disks attached to your computer, you can boot from any one of them without having to configure anything in software. This is done through the use of the **Option** key while booting.

1 Restart the Computer

Select **Restart** from the **Apple** menu to restart your computer. If the computer is powered off, start it up.

2 Hold Down the Option Key

Immediately after the "bong" sound, press and hold the **Option** key. Hold the key down until the boot volume selection screen appears.

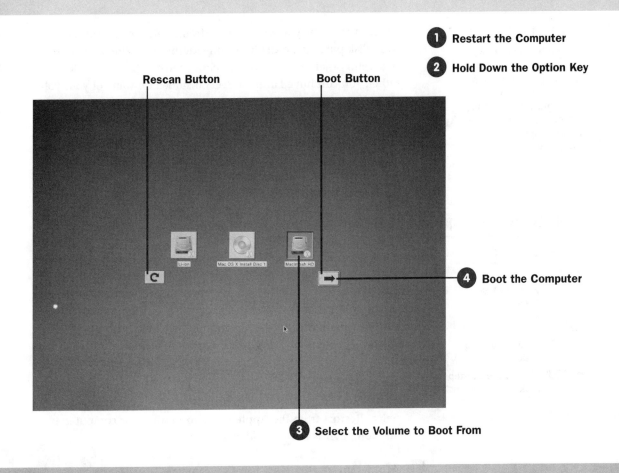

Rescan Button

Boot Button

1 Restart the Computer

2 Hold Down the Option Key

4 Boot the Computer

3 Select the Volume to Boot From

3 ## Select the Volume to Boot From

The Mac scans all available disks for bootable volumes. Each such volume that it finds appears as a button-style icon on the screen, along with two buttons for rescanning and booting. The default boot volume—usually the primary partition on the built-in hard disk—is selected by default. If you click the **Boot** button (with a right arrow symbol), the Mac boots from that partition as it normally does.

To boot instead from a different available volume, wait several moments for the computer to finish scanning for boot volumes (the mouse pointer changes from a stopwatch to a pointer), and then

 TIP

If you want to boot from an external disk that isn't currently plugged in, and you didn't plug it in in time for the Mac to recognize it during the scan, plug it in now and click the Rescan button. The Mac should recognize the disk this time.

select the volume you want to boot from. This volume can be a hard disk partition, a CD-ROM, an external FireWire drive, or any of several other devices—and it doesn't have to be Mac OS X, either. You can have Linux or BeOS installed on some of your volumes, and you can select these volumes as well from this screen.

④ Boot the Computer

After you have selected the boot volume you want, click the **Boot** button. The Mac will boot using that volume.

171 Boot from Different Disks Using Keystrokes

Before You Begin

✔ **170** Select the Boot Volume at Boot Time

See Also

➜ **20** Partition a Hard Disk

➜ **172** Change the Startup Disk

By holding down certain special key combinations at boot time, you can force the Mac to boot from specific devices. These special key combinations can also cause a number of other interesting effects to happen. These key combinations are poorly documented and the subject of folklore, but some are more well-known than others. Memorize the ones you're likely to need, considering your hardware configuration and your work patterns.

① Restart the Computer

Select **Restart** from the **Apple** menu to restart your computer. If the computer is powered off, start it up.

② Hold Down the Key for the Device You Want

Immediately after the "bong" sound, press and hold one of the following key combinations, depending on the effect you want.

Key Combination	Effect
C	Boot from CD
D	Boot from Internal Hard Disk
N	Boot from Network Server
T	Boot into FireWire Target Disk Mode
⌘+Option+Shift+Delete	Boot from External Disk
⌘+Option+Shift+Delete+<# *key*>	Boot from SCSI ID Number Specified
⌘V	Show Console Messages (Verbose Mode)

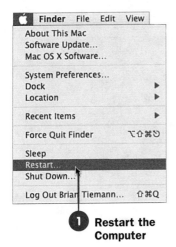

Finder   File   Edit   View
About This Mac
Software Update...
Mac OS X Software...

System Preferences...
Dock ▶
Location ▶

Recent Items ▶

Force Quit Finder ⌥⇧⌘⌫

Sleep
Restart...
Shut Down...

Log Out Brian Tiemann... ⇧⌘Q

1 **Restart the Computer**

2 **Hold Down the Key for the Device You Want**

WEB RESOURCE

http://davespicks.com/writing/programming/mackeys.html

Dave Polaschek compiles a comprehensive list of lots more keyboard shortcuts for use at boot time and later.

172 Change the Startup Disk

The boot volume selection screen and the many different key combinations you can use to control how your Mac boots are useful indeed, but they're only one-time solutions (see **170** **Select the Boot Volume at Boot Time** and **171** **Boot from Different Disks Using Keystrokes**). If you want to switch permanently to a different boot volume instead of selecting it from the selection screen every time you start up the computer, use the **Startup Disk Preferences** window to change your default startup volume.

See Also

→ **170** Select the Boot Volume at Boot Time

→ **171** Boot from Different Disks Using Keystrokes

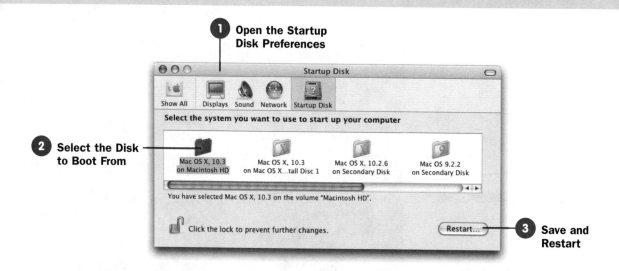

1 Open the Startup Disk Preferences

2 Select the Disk to Boot From

3 Save and Restart

1 Open the Startup Disk Preferences

Open **System Preferences** using the **Apple** menu. Click **Startup Disk** to open the **Startup Disk Preferences** window.

2 Select the System to Boot From

TIP

If you select a Mac OS 9 system as your default boot volume, your computer will boot into Mac OS 9. However, if you want to switch back to Mac OS X, you must use the **Startup Disk Control Panel** in Mac OS 9—it's available from the **Control Panels** submenu of the **Apple** menu, and it works very similarly to Mac OS X's **Startup Disk Preferences** window. Bootable volumes are shown in a hierarchical manner; click the icon of your Mac OS X installation, save, and restart back into Mac OS X.

Wait a few moments for Mac OS X to detect all the available bootable volumes. All the volumes appear in the window, each one (except the **Network Startup** option) represented as a system folder. Each folder is labeled with an operating system version. The icon representing the volume you normally boot from is selected.

Click the icon representing the volume from which you want to boot. This can be a Mac OS X system, a Mac OS 9 system, or another kind of bootable volume.

3 Save and Restart

When you have selected the boot volume you want, click the **Restart** button. On the confirmation sheet that appears, click **Save and Restart**. When you do this, the Mac saves low-level information that tells it to boot from the new volume the next time it starts up.

The Mac will restart and should boot into the system installation that you selected.

18

Rescue Operations

IN THIS CHAPTER:

Not even a Mac is perfect. The truly die-hard Apple fans might not like to admit it, but even the best-designed computer in the world is a machine—and as such, it's subject to the unpleasant realities that all machines face: mechanical failures, misconfigurations, and obsolescence. That shiny new Mac you brought home and took lovingly out of its elegantly packaged carton is virtually guaranteed to be too old for you to use within a few years. Parts break and have to be replaced. New applications demand more memory, faster video cards, and bigger hard disks. And by the time you've installed a couple of dozen applications on your Mac and built up music and photo libraries to enjoy in your leisure time, the newest software on the market will seem as though it's designed to require a computer just a *little* bit faster than the one you've grown so comfortable with.

Living with your Mac, by necessity, means not just having the skills to operate your software and the operating system to get the most out of them. It also means being able to repair your system when something goes wrong, to upgrade it when you need to extend its lifespan, and—when you finally upgrade to a new Mac—to move your life over to it from your old computer so that you don't have to start over from scratch.

173 Back Up Your Information

Before You Begin

✔ **29** Configure Networking Manually

✔ **50** Sign Up for .Mac

See Also

→ **176** Move Your Data to a New Mac

→ **179** Archive and Install a New Mac OS X Version

Apple knows that one of the biggest problems with computers is the fact that they sometimes fail. Hard drives crash, laptops are dropped or stolen, files are accidentally deleted—and for most people, there's no solution but to start over from scratch. Making proper backups is one of those things that everybody knows they *should* do, but very few people have the patience to actually do it. Backup applications can be expensive, as can the media on which the data is stored. It's like insurance: a significant cash outlay designed to buy assurance that in the extremely unlikely chance of catastrophe, the loss of data can be reversed—and nobody likes paying for insurance.

 WEB RESOURCE

Dantz Retrospect is a full-featured backup suite for Mac OS X that gives you more control over your system's data backups than what Apple **Backup** offers.

http://www.dantz.com

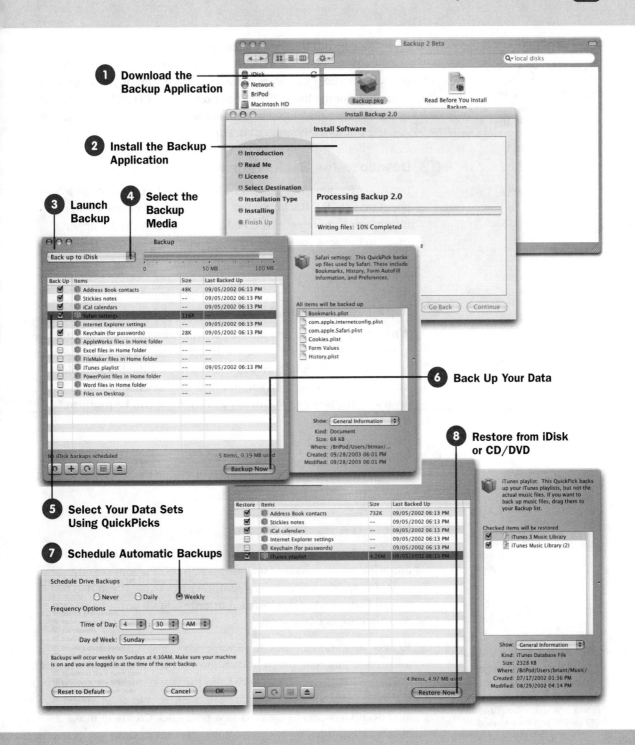

1 Download the Backup Application

2 Install the Backup Application

3 Launch Backup

4 Select the Backup Media

Install Backup 2.0

Install Software

⊖ Introduction
⊖ Read Me
⊖ License
⊖ Select Destination
⊖ Installation Type
⊖ Installing
● Finish Up

Processing Backup 2.0

Writing files: 10% Completed

Backup 2 Beta

iDisk
Network
BriPod
Macintosh HD

Backup.pkg   Read Before You Install Backup

Q▾ local disks

Backup

Back up to iDisk

0   50 MB   100 MB

Back Up	Items	Size	Last Backed Up
☑	Address Book contacts	48K	09/05/2002 06:13 PM
☑	Stickies notes	--	09/05/2002 06:13 PM
☑	iCal calendars	--	09/05/2002 06:13 PM
☑	Safari settings	116K	--
☐	Internet Explorer settings	--	09/05/2002 06:13 PM
☑	Keychain (for passwords)	28K	09/05/2002 06:13 PM
☐	AppleWorks files in Home folder	--	--
☐	Excel files in Home folder	--	--
☐	FileMaker files in Home folder	--	--
☐	iTunes playlist	--	09/05/2002 06:13 PM
☐	PowerPoint files in Home folder	--	--
☐	Word files in Home folder	--	--
☐	Files on Desktop	--	--

No iDisk backups scheduled   5 Items, 0.19 MB used

Backup Now

Safari settings: This QuickPick backs up files used by Safari. These include Bookmarks, History, Form AutoFill Information, and Preferences.

All items will be backed up
Bookmarks.plist
com.apple.internetconfig.plist
com.apple.Safari.plist
Cookies.plist
Form Values
History.plist

Go Back   Continue

Show: General Information
Kind: Document
Size: 68 KB
Where: /BriPod/Users/btman/...
Created: 09/28/2003 06:01 PM
Modified: 09/28/2003 06:01 PM

6 Back Up Your Data

8 Restore from iDisk or CD/DVD

5 Select Your Data Sets Using QuickPicks

7 Schedule Automatic Backups

Schedule Drive Backups

○ Never   ○ Daily   ◉ Weekly

Frequency Options

Time of Day: 4 ⇡ : 30 ⇡ AM ⇡

Day of Week: Sunday ⇡

Backups will occur weekly on Sundays at 4:30AM. Make sure your machine is on and you are logged in at the time of the next backup.

Reset to Default   Cancel   OK

Restore	Items	Size	Last Backed Up
☑	Address Book contacts	732K	09/05/2002 06:13 PM
☑	Stickies notes	--	09/05/2002 06:13 PM
☑	iCal calendars	--	09/05/2002 06:13 PM
☐	Internet Explorer settings	--	09/05/2002 06:13 PM
☐	Keychain (for passwords)	--	09/05/2002 06:13 PM
☑	iTunes playlist	4.26M	09/05/2002 06:13 PM

iTunes playlist: This QuickPick backs up your iTunes playlists, but not the actual music files. If you want to back up music files, drag them to your Backup list.

Checked items will be restored
☑ iTunes 3 Music Library
☑ iTunes Music Library (2)

4 Items, 4.97 MB used

Restore Now

Show: General Information
Kind: iTunes Database File
Size: 2328 KB
Where: /BriPod/Users/briant/Music/
Created: 07/17/2002 01:36 PM
Modified: 08/29/2002 04:14 PM

NOTE

Apple **Backup** is only one of several data backup applications commercially available for the Mac, and you might decide that it isn't full-featured enough to meet your needs.

That's why .Mac includes a data backup program, and a very good one at that. **Backup**, as it's called, can archive all your important data to CD, DVD, an external or network drive, or to your iDisk if you've purchased enough storage there. If you have a writable CD or DVD drive (or an external FireWire drive) and a .Mac account, you don't have much of an excuse for not making regular backups.

❶ Download the Backup Application

Log in to the .Mac Web site and click the **Backup** icon in the left panel to go to the **Backup** page. A large site full of step-by-step tutorials and strategies is online here, as is a link (in the upper right) to the download page for the Backup application. Download the most recent version available, which at the time of this writing is **Backup 2**.

❷ Install the Backup Application

When the disk image has finished downloading, it automatically mounts in the Finder; if it doesn't, locate it (on the Desktop, usually) and double-click it to mount it. Double-click the **Backup.pkg** file to run the installer. When prompted about whether the installer can "run a program to determine if it can be installed," click **Continue**.

❸ Launch Backup

After the **Backup** application is installed, navigate to it in the **Applications** folder and double-click it.

❹ Select the Backup Media

The drop-down list in the upper-left corner of the **Backup** application window lets you choose your backup media. You can only choose a media to which your computer can write; if you don't have a SuperDrive, for instance, but only a CD-R burner, you can back up only to CD or iDisk.

 NOTE

CD- or DVD- burning both require a full .Mac account. If you have a trial account, it will not allow backups to CD or DVD to be created.

To back up to an external or network drive, first make sure that the drive is mounted on your Mac and that you are able to write to it. Then select **Back up to Drive** from the menu and click the **Set** button to open a sheet where you select whether to open an existing backup location or create a new one. Click **Create** to make a new backup target. In the navigator sheet that appears, go to the location on the external or network drive where you want to save your backed-up data. Specify a descriptive name for the backup location (such as **FireWire Drive**) and click the **Create** button. Backup is now set to use that location as its target.

❺ Select Your Data Sets Using QuickPicks

The main window of the application lists QuickPicks, which are prepackaged collections of data associated with certain conceptual areas that aren't easy to find by simply navigating through the system's folders. For instance, Backup will back up your Safari bookmarks and Keychain passwords, even if you don't know where in the system such things are stored. Just enable the check box next to each collection of data that you want to back up.

As you click each QuickPick check box, the usage bar at the top of the window updates to reflect how much space the backup will take if you're backing up to iDisk. The darker orange bar indicates space on your iDisk that is already used; lighter orange is the segment that will be used by the next backup, using the current QuickPicks.

If you back up to CD, DVD, or an external drive, some additional QuickPicks are available—namely, the ones that take up a lot of space, such as your iTunes music and your iPhoto Library. These data collections are likely to be far too large to back up to iDisk, so they're available only for CD or DVD backups.

❻ Back Up Your Data

When your backup configuration is complete, click **Backup Now**. If you're using iDisk, your data will be backed up and transferred to the .Mac servers; if you're using CD or DVD, you will be prompted to insert a blank disc. If your backup data set will span more than one disc, you will be prompted again for another disc at the appropriate time.

❼ Schedule Automatic Backups

You can optionally set up automatic, scheduled backups to iDisk. Click the **Schedule** icon at the bottom-left of the **Backup** window (which looks like a calendar). In the dialog box that opens, choose whether to back up daily or weekly, and select a time range (in the middle of the night is a good bet), and click **OK** to set the schedule.

 TIPS

You can back up different sets of data to different locations. For instance, you can create a small set of critical files to back up daily to your iDisk, and set your huge iTunes **Music Library** to be backed up weekly to an external drive. It's a good idea to set up a more frequent backup scheme for the parts of your system that are changed most frequently.

If you schedule automated backups to an external or network drive, make sure that the drive is mounted and available at the time the backup is supposed to run! If **Backup** can't access the drive, it won't be able to back up your data.

⑧ Restore from iDisk or CD/DVD

If you should need to restore from your backups, because of a cata-strophic hard drive failure or because you accidentally deleted an important file, the restore process is simple. Just select **Restore from iDisk** or **Restore from CD/DVD** from the drop-down list at the top left of the **Backup** window. A list of the files and QuickPicks that were backed up onto the selected media appears. You can navigate to individual files and drag them into the Finder to restore them; or you can click **Restore Now** to restore all backed-up files to their original places on the disk.

174 Create and Encrypt a Disk Image

KEY TERM

Disk image—A file that contains, in effect, the contents of an entire disk. Double-clicking a disk image file mounts its contents as a virtual disk in Mac OS X.

Mac OS X relies heavily on *disk images* for a lot of its archival and data transfer tasks. Disk images allow you to transfer the virtual equivalent of a physical disk, complete with a label, folder hierarchy, file system meta-data, and other features such as user agreements and password protec-tion. A disk image can be readily burned onto a CD or sent as an email attachment. When you work with a disk image, you use the same mech-anisms you do for a regular disk.

To work with disk images, the application to use is **Disk Utility**, located in the **Utilities** folder inside the **Applications** folder.

In addition to disk images, Mac OS X allows you to archive any number of files and folders into a single Zip file, directly from the Finder. Select all the items you want to archive, right-click or **Control**+click one of the items, and select **Create Archive of <*filename*>** (or **Create Archive of # items**, if you've selected multiple items) from the contextual menu. A Zip file is created in the same folder window you're working in, with the same name as the file you selected if you only selected one item, or with the name **Archive.zip** if you selected multiple items. You can then trans-fer this archive file to other computers with email or other file-transfer methods, and the folder structure will remain intact.

Double-click an archive file to expand it into its original contents. If you archived only a single item, the item is re-created in the same folder; if you archived multiple items, they are re-created in a new **Archive** folder.

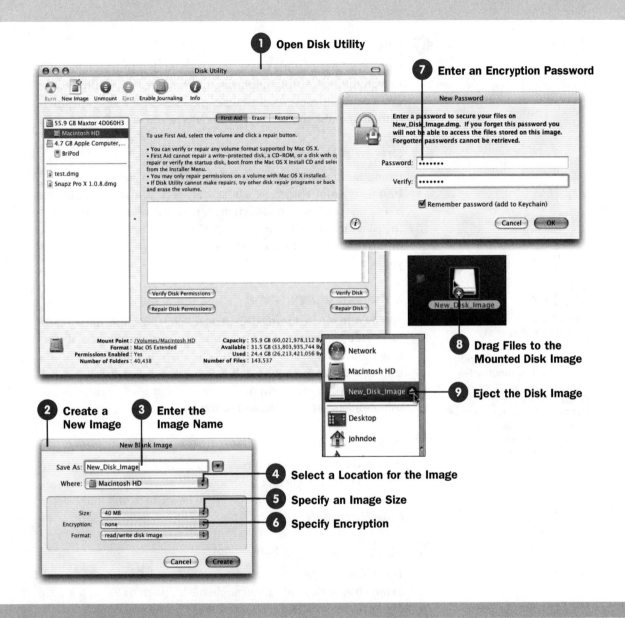

1 Open Disk Utility

7 Enter an Encryption Password

Disk Utility

Burn New Image Unmount Eject Enable Journaling Info

55.9 GB Maxtor 4D060H3
Macintosh HD
4.7 GB Apple Computer,...
BriPod

test.dmg
Snapz Pro X 1.0.8.dmg

First Aid | Erase | Restore

To use First Aid, select the volume and click a repair button.

• You can verify or repair any volume format supported by Mac OS X.
• First Aid cannot repair a write-protected disk, a CD-ROM, or a disk with o
repair or verify the startup disk, boot from the Mac OS X Install CD and sele
from the Installer Menu.
• You may only repair permissions on a volume with Mac OS X installed.
• If Disk Utility cannot make repairs, try other disk repair programs or back
and erase the volume.

New Password

Enter a password to secure your files on
New_Disk_Image.dmg. If you forget this password you
will not be able to access the files stored on this image.
Forgotten passwords cannot be retrieved.

Password: ●●●●●●
Verify: ●●●●●●

☑ Remember password (add to Keychain)

(Cancel) (OK)

Verify Disk Permissions   Verify Disk
Repair Disk Permissions   Repair Disk

Mount Point : /Volumes/Macintosh HD
Format : Mac OS Extended
Permissions Enabled : Yes
Number of Folders : 40,438

Capacity : 55.9 GB (60,021,978,112 By
Available : 31.5 GB (33,803,935,744 By
Used : 24.4 GB (26,213,421,056 By
Number of Files : 143,537

New_Disk_Image

8 Drag Files to the
Mounted Disk Image

Network
Macintosh HD
New_Disk_Image
Desktop
johndoe

9 Eject the Disk Image

2 Create a
New Image

3 Enter the
Image Name

New Blank Image

Save As: New_Disk_Image

Where: 📁 Macintosh HD

Size: 40 MB
Encryption: none
Format: read/write disk image

(Cancel) (Create)

4 Select a Location for the Image

5 Specify an Image Size

6 Specify Encryption

A disk image can contain much more information than a Zip file can.
Disk Utility lets you create, modify, and encrypt disk images of any
important data that you might have, protecting you from data loss and
security intrusions if you keep the resulting disk images in a safe place.

① Open Disk Utility

Open the **Applications** folder, then go into the **Utilities** folder and launch the **Disk Utility** application. When the **Disk Utility** window opens, all your attached disks are listed in the left pane, along with all the disk images that you have created or opened recently.

② Create a New Image

From the **Images** menu, choose **New**, and then choose **Blank Image** (or **from Folder**, which lets you select a folder to make into a disk image). You can also create a new disk image by clicking the **New Image** button in the Disk Utility toolbar. This command brings up the **New Blank Image** dialog box, where you specify your options for the new disk image.

> ### ⚑ TIP
>
> The volume name—the label that will appear under the disk image's (also called a *virtual disk's*) icon when it is mounted—is initially the same as the saved filename of the disk image itself. To change the name of the volume, simply rename it in the Finder as you would any other item.

③ Enter the Image Name

Specify a filename for the disk image. Remember, this file should be interoperable with Windows and Unix systems, and the **.dmg** extension will be added automatically when the file is created. Choose a filename that doesn't have any spaces or special characters in it, just to ease compatibility with other platforms. Consider using underscores (_) instead of spaces.

④ Select a Location for the Image

Choose a folder from the **Where** drop-down list or press the down arrow to reveal the detailed navigator pane. Navigate to the location where you want the image file to be created, and make a new folder if necessary.

⑤ Specify an Image Size

The dialog box provides you with several predefined sizes, designed to match specific kinds of burnable media (such as 93MB for a Zip disk, 610MB or 660MB for a CD, and so on). If you don't have enough hard disk space, some of the larger sizes will be grayed-out. You can also specify a custom size if you desire.

⑥ Specify Encryption

Encryption protects the contents of the disk image with a password. An encrypted disk image can be slower to create and access, but it's a very useful feature if secrecy is important to you. Select **AES-128** encryption (the only encryption scheme available—don't worry, it's a very good one). Then click the **Create** button.

7 Enter an Encryption Password

If you chose encryption, you are prompted to enter a password (and verify the password) after the image is assembled. The password is hidden from you as you type it, so enter it carefully.

8 Drag Files to the Mounted Disk Image

After you click the **Create** button, the disk image mounts and appear in the Finder. (The original **.dmg** file is unaffected and remains wherever you created it.) It now behaves just as though it were another disk, of the size you specified. You can drag documents and folders to it until it's full; each time you change the contents of the virtual disk, the disk image file itself is updated.

9 Eject the Disk Image

When you're done modifying the disk image, drag it to the Trash to eject it, or click the **Eject** icon next to its icon in the Finder. The **.dmg** file, which still exists wherever you created it, can now be burned to a disc or transferred over the Internet, and its contents will be just as you set them.

175 Restore the System to Factory Settings

For every story of a brand-new Mac wowing its owner right out of the box, there's another, quieter story: The one that tells of an old, much-loved Mac that the owner has to sell or give away to a new home. After all, nobody wants to throw away a Macintosh. Besides, a Mac can often remain useful for years after a Windows PC of the same age has been junked.

Before you pass your Mac on to a new owner, you should clean it up, just as you would an apartment that you're moving out of. Cleaning up your Mac means removing all your data from the hard disk so that none of it remains for the new owner to find. Fortunately, with a Mac, it's fairly easy to revert to near-factory condition. You don't have to reformat the hard disk or reinstall the operating system. All you have to do is create a new account, remove your old one, and remove a few extra items before it's ready for a new owner.

Before You Begin

✔ **146** Add a New User
✔ **173** Back Up Your Information

See Also

→ **8** Revert an Application to Factory Settings

→ **176** Move Your Data to a New Mac

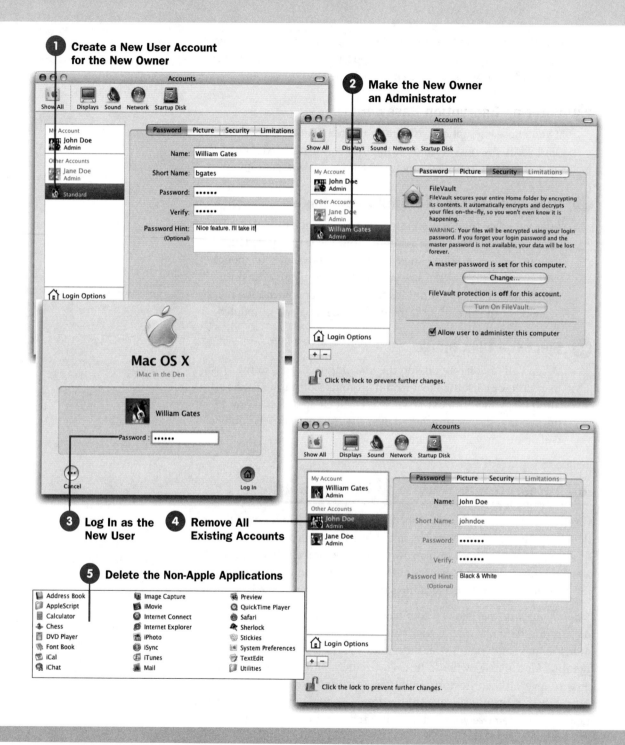

1 Create a New User Account for the New Owner

2 Make the New Owner an Administrator

3 Log In as the New User

4 Remove All Existing Accounts

5 Delete the Non-Apple Applications

1 **Create a New User Account for the New Owner**

Open the **Accounts Preferences** window (click **Accounts** in the **System Preferences**). Create a new user by clicking the + icon at the bottom of the user list; fill in the user's full name, choose a short username, and enter the user's password (twice).

2 **Make the New Owner an Administrator**

Click the **Security** tab and then enable the **Allow user to administer this computer** check box to make the new user an **Admin** user for the computer.

Depending on your (and the new owner's) circumstances, you might want to set the computer to automatically log in to the new owner's account when you start it up. To enable this, click the **Login Options** button at the bottom of the user list and then enable the **Automatically log in as** check box. Select the new owner's account as the one to log into automatically.

3 **Log In as the New User**

Make sure that you have everything you need from your account copied to an external disk or a new computer—you're about to delete your account, so take a last look around. (See **176** **Move Your Data to a New Mac**.) Then select **Log out John Doe** from the **Apple** menu.

At the login menu, select the new owner's user account and log in.

4 **Remove All Existing Accounts**

Open the **Accounts Preferences** window again. Select each user account except for your own (the new owner's account) and click the − button at the bottom of the user list to delete each account. When the confirmation dialog box appears, click **Delete Immediately** if you want to remove each account permanently and right away; if you prefer to keep each account intact as a disk image that you can then copy to another computer (in case you forgot anything), click the **OK** button instead. See **151** **Delete a User** for more information on deleting users.

NOTES

Be sure to use a password that the new owner will be able to enter easily the first time—this isn't intended to be a secure password. It's just meant to be temporary, until the new owner can log into the computer and change the password to something of his own choice. For instance, use a password like **ChangeMe**, if only because the new owner will have to change it to something better—or face the embarrassment of having to type **ChangeMe** every time he wants to log in.

Make sure that no other users are logged in. If there are, get each logged-in user to log in to her active session and then log out of it. Each user's account will be deleted, so make sure that each user has gotten everything important out of her **Home** folder.

NOTE

You can now safely give the computer to the new owner, for all intents and purposes in the same condition as if it had just arrived from the factory.

5 **Delete the Non-Apple Applications**

Now that the user accounts have been returned to the factory-pristine condition as though the new owner were the one who first bought and set up your Mac, the only thing remaining is to remove the applications you installed, if you don't want the new owner to be able to use them. Naturally, if you like, you can skip this step—and the new owner will have access to all the third-party applications you've installed.

If you want to return the Mac to its original state, navigate to the **Applications** folder in the Finder, and drag all applications—except for the ones originally included by Apple—into the Trash. In the screenshots for this task, you can see basic contents of the **Applications** folder, as packaged with a new Mac.

Select **Empty Trash** from the **File** menu in the Finder to permanently erase all the applications you just removed from the system.

176 **Move Your Data to a New Mac**

Before You Begin

✔ **146** Add a New User

✔ **173** Back Up Your Information

See Also

→ **175** Restore the System to Factory Settings

If you buy yourself a new Mac, after the first few hours of elation at how much faster it is, there's always the inevitable crash of realization: You have to somehow get all your data from your old computer to your new one. Preferably, you want to be able to get all your applications, all your music, all your photos, and all your documents onto the new system so that you don't have to reconstruct anything. This can seem like a daunting task, and indeed it can be an involved one. But taken one step at a time, moving your data to a new Mac can be a fairly seamless procedure.

1 **Create a Secondary Admin Account on the New Mac**

On your new Mac, open the **Accounts Preferences** window (click the **Accounts** icon in the **System Preferences** application). Use the + icon at the bottom left to create a new user account; this account will be temporary, so don't worry about what full name and password to use. Just make sure that it's something easy to remember.

Click the **Security** tab and enable the **Allow user to administer this computer** check box. This gives the secondary user the power to manipulate the files and folders in your primary account.

2 Log In as the Secondary User

Log out of your primary account. Then, in the login window, select the secondary user account and log in.

3 Turn On Personal File Sharing on the Old Mac

On your old Mac, open the **Sharing Preferences** window (click the **Sharing** icon in the **System Preferences** application). Under the **Services** tab, enable the **Personal File Sharing** check box to turn on file sharing.

4 Mount Your Old Hard Disk onto the New Mac

Make sure that both Macs can detect each other on the network. To do this, open the Finder on the new Mac and click the **Network** icon; browse into the **Local** folder to locate your old computer by name. Double-click its name (or click the **Connect** button in Column view), and enter your account information to get the list of available *shares*.

In the Finder on the new computer, select the old computer's main hard disk to mount onto the new computer.

5 Copy Your Old Library Folder to the New Mac

Navigate into your **Home** folder on the old computer's mounted hard disk. Click and drag the **Library** folder onto your new computer's Desktop.

6 Launch the Terminal

Navigate into your new computer's **Utilities** folder, inside the **Applications** folder. Double-click the **Terminal** application to open up a new Unix shell window. This is necessary because you're going to be doing some tinkering with user permissions that is actually easier to do at the Unix level than through the Mac's normal interface.

Type **cd Desktop** and press **Return** to move into your **Desktop** folder.

TIP

Both Macs must be connected to the local area network (LAN). You can do this by plugging both computers into a hub, or by using a computer-to-computer AirPort network. If you don't have a network hub, you can use a crossover Ethernet cable to connect the two computers together directly. Make sure that it's a *crossover* cable—if it's a standard Ethernet cable, the two computers won't connect properly.

Library

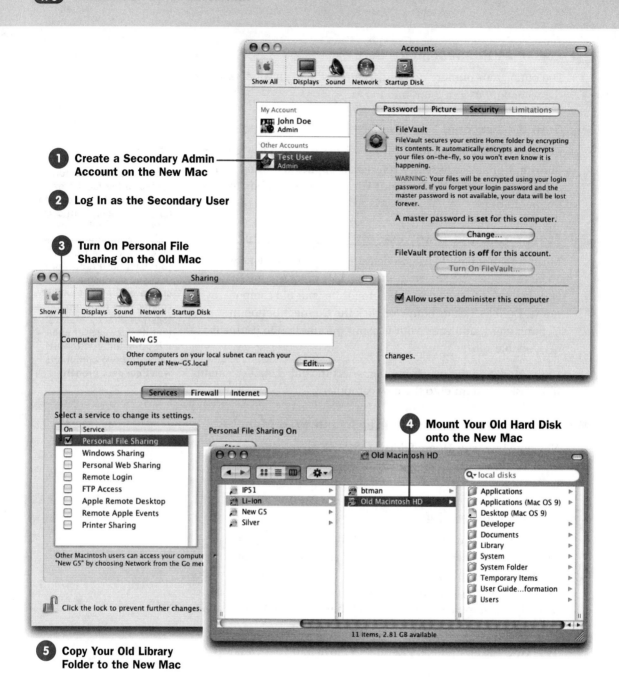

1 **Create a Secondary Admin Account on the New Mac**

2 **Log In as the Secondary User**

3 **Turn On Personal File Sharing on the Old Mac**

4 **Mount Your Old Hard Disk onto the New Mac**

5 **Copy Your Old Library Folder to the New Mac**

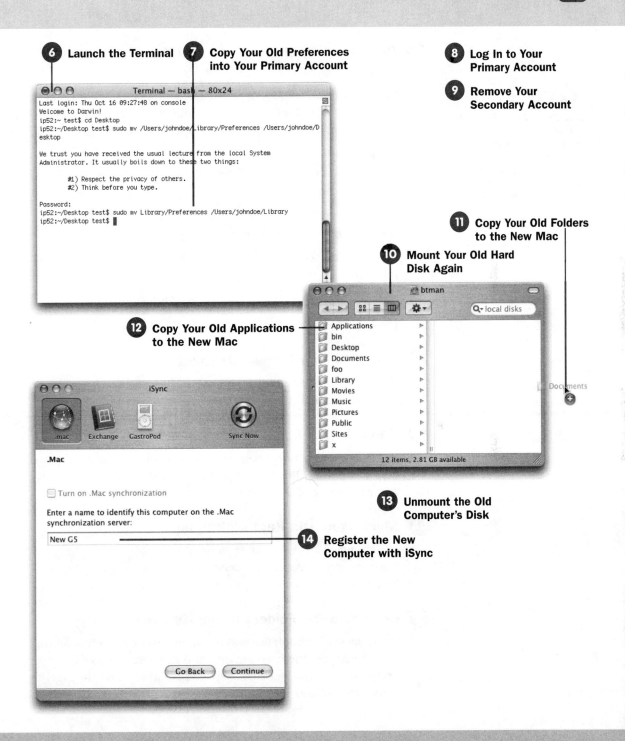

6 Launch the Terminal

7 Copy Your Old Preferences into Your Primary Account

8 Log In to Your Primary Account

9 Remove Your Secondary Account

```
Terminal — bash — 80x24
Last login: Thu Oct 16 09:27:48 on console
Welcome to Darwin!
ip52:~ test$ cd Desktop
ip52:~/Desktop test$ sudo mv /Users/johndoe/Library/Preferences /Users/johndoe/D
esktop

We trust you have received the usual lecture from the local System
Administrator. It usually boils down to these two things:

        #1) Respect the privacy of others.
        #2) Think before you type.

Password:
ip52:~/Desktop test$ sudo mv Library/Preferences /Users/johndoe/Library
ip52:~/Desktop test$
```

11 Copy Your Old Folders to the New Mac

10 Mount Your Old Hard Disk Again

12 Copy Your Old Applications to the New Mac

```
btman
◄ ►   ▦ ☰ ▥   ✱▾            Q▾ local disks
    Applications    ►
    bin             ►
    Desktop         ►
    Documents       ►
    foo             ►
    Library         ►
    Movies          ►
    Music           ►
    Pictures        ►
    Public          ►
    Sites           ►
    x               ►
            12 items, 2.81 GB available
```

Documents

13 Unmount the Old Computer's Disk

```
iSync

.mac    Exchange   GastroPod        Sync Now

.Mac

☐ Turn on .Mac synchronization

Enter a name to identify this computer on the .Mac
synchronization server:

New G5

        Go Back      Continue
```

14 Register the New Computer with iSync

7 Copy Your Old Preferences into Your New Primary Account

NOTE

This step takes all of your old computer's application preferences and copies them into your primary account on the new Mac.

In the **Terminal** window, type the following to move your primary account's current **Preferences** folder into that account's Desktop so that you can browse it later for any items you might need:

cd Desktop

sudo mv /Users/johndoe/Library/Preferences /Users/*johndoe*/ Desktop

Where *johndoe* is the short username of your new Mac's primary account. Enter your account password when prompted for it.

Then type the following to move your old computer's **Preferences** folder into the new computer's primary account:

sudo mv Library/Preferences /Users/*johndoe*/Library

Close the Terminal window.

8 Log In to Your Primary Account

Log out of your secondary account and then log back in to your primary account on the new Mac.

9 Remove Your Secondary Account

In the **Accounts Preferences** window, select the temporary secondary account and click the – button at the bottom of the user list to remove the secondary account.

10 Mount Your Old Hard Disk Again

On you new Mac, navigate to your old Mac again under the **Network** icon in the Finder. Connect to the old computer and mount its main hard disk onto your new Mac.

11 Copy Your Old Folders to the New Mac

Open the shared hard disk and navigate to your old **Home** folder. Drag the **Music**, **Pictures**, **Movies**, and **Documents** folders off it and onto your new Mac's Desktop; you can then move their contents into your existing multimedia folders using the Finder.

12 Copy Your Old Applications to the New Mac

In the mounted disk from your old computer, navigate to the **Applications** folder. Locate any applications you want to copy to your new computer, and that you would rather not (or cannot) simply install cleanly from a freshly downloaded version. Drag these applications to the **Applications** folder on your new Mac to copy them over.

13 Unmount the Old Computer's Disk

When you're done copying applications, drag the old computer's mounted hard disk to the Trash or click the **Eject** button for that disk in the Finder.

14 Register the New Computer with iSync

Open iSync and click the **.Mac** icon in the top toolbar; in the .Mac settings pane, register your new computer with .Mac so that iSync can synchronize all your personal information to your new computer. From the **For first sync** drop-down list, select the **Erase data on computer then sync** option and click the **Sync Now** button to propagate all the existing data that's on .Mac into your new computer's Address Book, iCal, and Safari databases.

After the sync process has completed, your user environment on your new Mac should be (for all intents and purposes) just the same as on your old Mac—except faster!

 TIP

It's best to avoid copying applications from one computer to another if you can install them as fresh copies, or if you have the installation discs you can use in a new clean installation. Copy applications from the old computer only if you have no other way of obtaining them for the new computer.

---

177 Verify and Repair a Disk

Hard disks have a bad habit of deteriorating over time—perhaps more so than any other component in a computer. This is especially problematic in that your hard disk isn't just a component that you can replace; it's the permanent memory for your computer, the place where all your accumulated data and important documents are stored. If you haven't done a backup (and why haven't you?), and your hard disk goes bad, you will likely be willing to do just about anything to get that data back.

Before You Begin

✔ **19** Add a Newly Installed Hard Disk to the System

✔ **173** Back Up Your Information

See Also

→ **174** Create and Encrypt a Disk Image

→ **178** Restore or Duplicate a Disk

---

1 Boot from a Different Disk

2 Open Disk Utility

3 Select the Disk to Verify

4 Verify and Repair the Disk Permissions

5 Verify and Repair the Disk

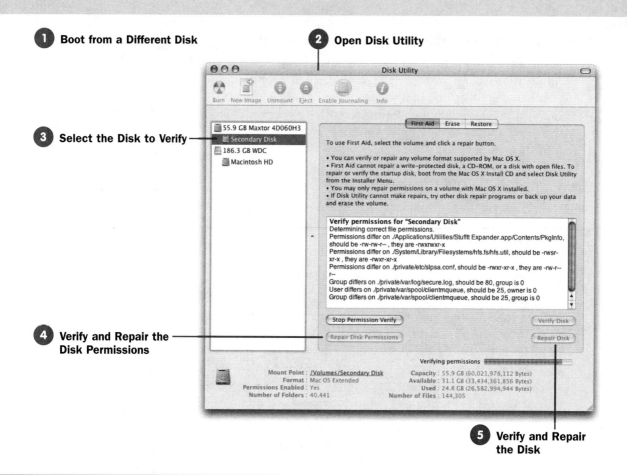

NOTE

You must be logged in as an Admin user to verify or repair a hard disk.

The **Disk Utility** program, located in the **Utilities** folder, provides a handy way to perform quick repair operations on your hard disk—operations that have a surprisingly high success rate in many cases. **Disk Utility** can examine the Unix permissions on your hard disk and detect discrepancies that might cause instabilities in your system; it can also correct those errors for you. What's more, **Disk Utility** can scan your disk for surface defects (the most common cause of data loss from deterioration over time), and even "repair" these errors by recovering the data in the defective regions and copying it to a healthy part of the disk.

① Boot from a Different Disk

Determine whether the disk you want to inspect is your Mac's startup disk. If it is, you won't be able to do repairs on it while the Mac is booted from it. Boot the system from an external backup disk or from the Mac OS X installation CD to do repairs on your main startup disk. See **171** **Boot from Different Disks Using Keystrokes**.

② Open Disk Utility

Navigate into the **Utilities** folder inside the **Applications** folder. Double-click the **Disk Utility** icon to launch the program.

③ Select the Disk to Verify

From the list in the left pane of the **Disk Utility** window, select the disk you want to examine for errors. You can select an entire disk or a single volume within that disk. Click the **First Aid** tab to access the disk repair functions.

④ Verify and Repair the Disk Permissions

Click **Verify Disk Permissions** to begin a scan of the permissions of all the files on the disk. This process will take several minutes; **Disk Utility** reports all its findings in the status window.

⑤ Verify and Repair the Disk

To perform a surface scan of the disk, click **Verify Disk**. This process can take several minutes or up to an hour or more. The results of the process are shown in the status window.

If **Disk Utility** reports correctable errors in the status window, and you want to recover your disk and make it usable again, click **Repair Disk**. **Disk Utility** will again unmount the disk and attempt to repair any surface inconsistencies that it detected during verification.

When **Disk Utility** has finished the repair process, restart your computer using the regular startup disk (if necessary); with any luck at all, your disk will be back in working order.

However, even if you were able to resurrect your disk using **Disk Utility**, be aware that any surface defect that causes you to do a repair is an indication of an aging disk that should be replaced. Consider buying a new hard disk for your computer, and by all means back up your data using the .Mac **Backup** application as described in **173** **Back Up Your Information**. At the least, copy your files to CDs or DVDs!

 TIP

If you notice results in the status window that indicate a possible reason for an instability in the system, repair the permissions by clicking **Repair Disk Permissions**. This process, too, can take some time. When the repair is complete, however, your Mac OS X system and its applications might behave more predictably if you've been seeing a permissions-related problem.

NOTE

To do a surface scan of the disk, **Disk Utility** must be able to unmount it from the system. Make sure that you are not using any applications or documents on that disk, or **Disk Utility** will report an error and fail to perform the verification.

178 Restore or Duplicate a Disk

Before You Begin

✔ **173** Back Up Your Information

✔ **177** Verify and Repair a Disk

See Also

→ **20** Partition a Hard Disk

NOTE

You must be logged in as an Admin user to restore or duplicate a disk.

Using the **Disk Utility** program, you can quickly and easily make duplicates of entire hard disks or volumes, or restore a hard disk to a known reference "image"—a technique commonly used in computer labs and business environments where a network administrator must be able to ensure that multiple computers are all "cloned" from a known software state.

Disk Utility can start with either a disk image file or a physical disk (either a hard disk or a CD); you can even specify the URL of a disk image to fetch from an Internet location. The application takes a new disk, initializes it, and then writes the source disk or disk image onto the new disk.

A typical useful application of this technique is if you buy a new disk to replace an aging or deteriorating hard drive; all you have to do is mount the new disk, launch **Disk Utility**, specify the existing disk as the source and the new disk as the destination, and click **Restore**. Then you can boot your system using the new disk, and your system will be as good as new!

1 Open Disk Utility

First make sure that the disk to which you want to restore is mounted on the Mac. See **19 Add a Newly Installed Hard Disk to the System** for more information on adding additional disks.

Navigate into the **Utilities** folder inside the **Applications** folder. Double-click the **Disk Utility** icon to launch the program. Click the **Restore** tab at the far right of the **Disk Utility** window to access the **Restore** functions.

2 Select a Source Disk or Disk Image

TIP

To use a disk image file, click the **Image** button next to the **Source** field and navigate to where the disk image file is in the navigation pane that appears.

Determine which disk you want to use as the source for the restoration process. You can select any disk in the system, including your startup disk if you want to clone it onto a new disk. Drag the disk or volume from the left pane of the **Disk Utility** window into the **Source** field to select it.

3 Select a Destination Disk

You can specify any mounted disk in the system as the destination disk, with the exception of your startup disk and any disk (such as a CD-ROM) that is not writable. Drag a disk or volume from the left pane of the **Disk Utility** window into the **Destination** field.

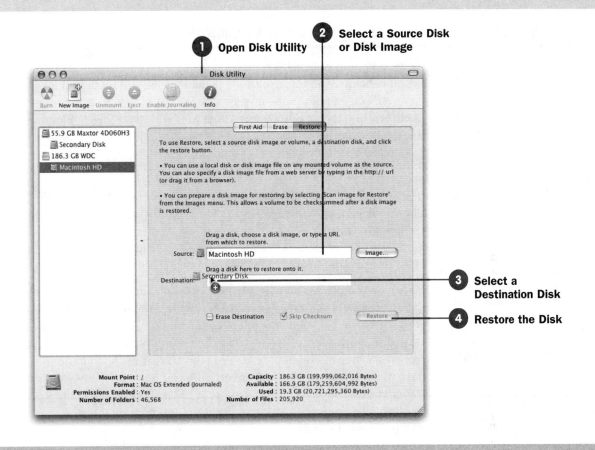

① Open Disk Utility

② Select a Source Disk or Disk Image

③ Select a Destination Disk

④ Restore the Disk

④ Restore the Disk

When you're ready to copy the source disk to the destination disk, click the **Restore** button. **Disk Utility** begins the process of "dubbing" the first disk to the second. The process might take several minutes to an hour or more, depending on the size of the source disk you're using.

When the process is complete, you can browse the destination disk and verify that the duplication process took place correctly. You can then remove the disk and install it in another computer, or remove the old disk from your Mac and use the new one if you're moving your data from an old disk to a new one.

💡 TIP

If you're particularly concerned about data integrity, you can elect to have **Disk Utility** do a *checksum*—a mathematical verification of the data written—after the disk is restored. This can be done only if you're using a disk image file. Select **Scan image for Restore** from the **Images** menu and navigate to the disk image file to prepare the image for restoration with a checksum.

179 Archive and Install a New Mac OS X Version

Before You Begin

✔ **1** Install an Application from Disc or Download

✔ **173** Back Up Your Information

See Also

→ **175** Restore the System to Factory Settings

NOTE

Another installation option is **Erase and Install**, which erases all the contents of your startup disk before installing the new version of Mac OS X on it. This option is helpful for systems that have been repeatedly reinstalled and reconfigured to the point where the new version of the operating system cannot be installed cleanly on top of it.

TIP

If you want to keep your user environment intact (as well as all the files inside your **Home** folder, such as your iTunes music, your digital photos, and your important documents), make sure that the **Preserve Users and Network Settings** check box is enabled. If you don't select this option, you will have to go through the **Setup Assistant** screens to set up your primary user account from scratch again.

The next version of Mac OS X that you install on your computer, in its default behavior, will install on top of your existing installation. If all goes well, you will put in the disc, go through the guided installation procedure, and then continue using your Mac with the same configuration settings you had been using previously. A standard Mac OS X installation adds new features to your existing system, but doesn't give you any further insight into the upgrade procedure.

When troubleshooting an installation of Mac OS X, sometimes it's helpful to be able to examine the files in the previously installed version of the operating system, compare files from one version to another, and revert to earlier versions of the files if necessary. To do this, the Mac OS X **Installer** program provides a helpful option called **Archive and Install**.

When you use the **Archive and Install** option, your old version of the operating system is cleaned from the hard disk—essential in many cases where the old version is full of conflicting files from multiple earlier installations—but it's preserved in a folder on your disk called **Previous Systems**. The new version of Mac OS X is installed cleanly and without conflicts with earlier versions, and it even preserves your user environment; but you can access the old system files (for troubleshooting purposes or to recover important data) by browsing the **Previous Systems** folder.

1 Insert the First Mac OS X Installation Disc

To begin installing the new version of Mac OS X, insert the CD-ROM labeled **Mac OS X Install Disc 1** (or something similar).

2 Start the Installation Procedure

In the CD-ROM Finder window that opens, double-click the **Install Mac OS X** icon. The **Installer program** opens and prompts you to enter your user password (as a security precaution, to make sure that you aren't an intruder who sat down while a legitimate user was logged in). Then you are asked to click the **Restart** button to begin installing Mac OS X.

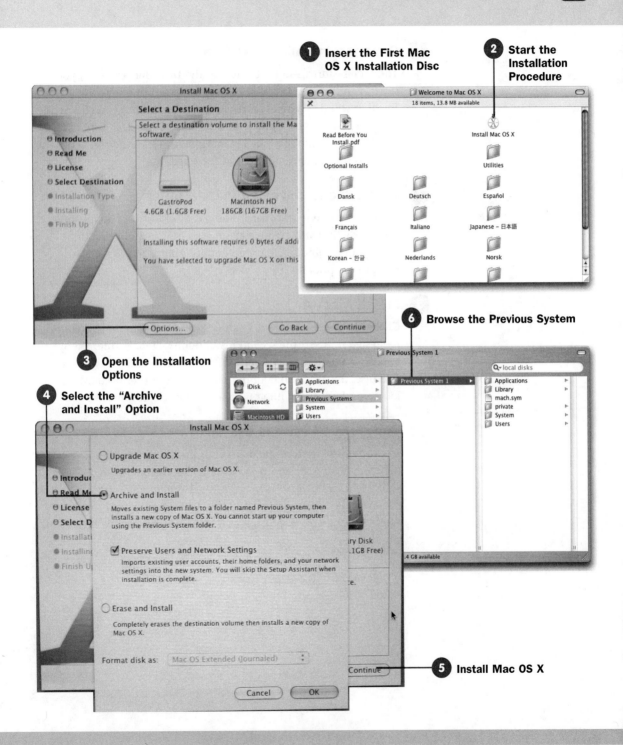

1 **Insert the First Mac OS X Installation Disc**

2 **Start the Installation Procedure**

6 **Browse the Previous System**

3 **Open the Installation Options**

4 **Select the "Archive and Install" Option**

5 **Install Mac OS X**

3 Open the Installation Options

The Mac restarts. After it boots into the **Installer** program, you start to go through the introductory screens that tell you what the Installer will do. When you reach the screen where you choose the disk onto which you want to install Mac OS X, select the appropriate disk (generally the Mac's primary hard disk) and then click the **Options** button at the bottom of the screen.

4 Select the Archive and Install Option

Click the **Archive and Install** radio button to select the installation mode that will create a clean Mac OS X installation but preserve your original system for your later perusal. Click **OK** to accept the options.

5 Install Mac OS X

Click **Continue**. Mac OS X installs itself on your system. You are requested to insert the second installation CD-ROM after the system restarts. After reading and installing the contents of the second disc, the Mac will boot into your primary user account (or the login window, depending on your **Automatic Login** settings).

6 Browse the Previous System

To access the files that make up your previous system, navigate in the Finder to the **Previous Systems** folder. Inside this folder are subfolders for each previously installed system, differentiated with numbers (**Previous System 1**, **Previous System 2**, and so on). Select the one you want and browse its contents for the items you want.

Index

Symbols

Numbers

A

C

D

How can we make this index more useful? Email us at indexes@samspublishing.com

569

Dock
  applications
    adding to, 43-44
    launching, 6-7, 11
    managing, 44-47
    removing, 11
    switching windows, 46
  customizing, 442-444
  dragging, adding to, 44
  Finder, 10-12
  Folders, adding to, 44
  hiding, 443
  items, adding to, 44
  magnification, 443
  minimize effect, 443
  question mark (?), 44
  sizing, 10
  Trash can icon, 10
    burning CDs/DVDs, 11
    disconnecting servers, 11
    ejecting disks, 11-13
    retrieving items, 11
  windows, sending to, 13
Dock Preferences, 11, 442
Dock, Dock Preferences command (Apple menu), 48
documents. *See* files
Documents folder, 13
domain controllers, 133
domains, 111, 133
downloaded files, 38
downloading
  applications, 36-39
  fonts, 296
Draft mailboxes, 215
dragging applications, Dock, 44
drawings
  creating in AppleWorks, 286-288
  saving, 286
drivers
  printers, installing, 305
  tablets, installing, 281
DRM (Digital Rights Management), 323
Duplicate button, 160
Duplicate command (Action menu), 75
Duplicate command (File menu), 75, 367
DV (Digital Video), iMovie
  Camera mode, 373
  clips, arranging, 377-380
  Edit mode, 373
  effects, 380-383
  exporting, 389-392
  importing, 374-376
  limitations, 373
  lossless, 373

movies
  creating, 371, 374-376
  saving, 376
overview, 371-374
soundtracks, 386-388
stills, 384-385
transitions, 380-383
DV (Digital Video) camcorders, connecting, 376
DVD-Rs, burning, 78
DVDs (digital versatile discs), 316
  burning, 11, 77-80, 393
  chapter markers, 393-395
  inserting/ejecting, 78
  playing, QuickTime Player, 321
Dynamic Host Configuration Protocol (DHCP), 109-112

E

Edit button, 399, 480
Edit Configurations command (Configuration menu), 124
Edit Locations command (Location menu), 160
Edit menu commands
  Copy, 72
  Paste, 522
  Show Clipboard, 72
  Special Characters, 509
  Split Video Clip Playhead, 380
  View Options, 23
Edit mode
  iMovie, 373
  iPhoto, 351
Edit Printer List command (Printer menu), 304
Edit Script button, 90
effects
  DV (Digital Video), iMovie, 380-383
  Flash, alerts, 503
  Genie Effect, 47
  Minimize, Dock, 443
  Scale Effect, 48
Effects button, 381
Eject button, 342
ejecting
  disks, 11-13, 22
  iPod, 342
ellipsis (...), entering, 509
eMacs, opening, 149
email
  addresses, adding to contacts (Address Books), 403
  attachments
    finding, 206-210
    reading, 206-210
    saving, 209

F

G

H

I

How can we make this index more useful? Email us at indexes@samspublishing.com

575

M

N

How can we make this index more useful? Email us at indexes@samspublishing.com

581

O

P

How can we make this index more useful? Email us at indexes@samspublishing.com

583

Q

R

S

How can we make this index more useful? Email us at indexes@samspublishing.com

587

How can we make this index more useful? Email us at indexes@samspublishing.com

589

U

V

Virtual Private Network (VPN)
  configuring, 122-124
  status, displaying, 124
Visit Page button, 413
voice recognition
  Apple Speakable Items, 498
  attention signal phrases, 497
  speech commands, 499
  Talking Alerts, 495-597
  text-to-speech recognition, 495-597
voice-overs, movies (iMovie), 388
volume
  alerts, 503
  changing, 317-319
Volume icon, 318
Volume slider (iMovie), 377
volumes
  boot, selecting while booting, 534-536
  naming, 546
  shared files, 127
  startup, 20
VPN (Virtual Private Network)
  configuring, 122-124, 159
  status, displaying, 124

W

waking computers, passwords, 465-466
wallpaper, changing, 431-434
warchalking Web site, 151
warm boot, 20
Watson, channels, 250
WAV file formats, converting, 503
Web browsers
  Defaults, selecting, 228-229
  history, 242
  Safari, 38, 228, 242-244
Web pages (.Mac)
  creating, 172-175
  managing, 175
Web Proxy (HTTP), 116
Web searching, Sherlock, 247, 250-252
  channels, 247, 250-251
  language translation, 251
Web sites
  accessing, 141-142
  Ambrosia Software, 347
  bookmarks, 230-231
    accessing, 232, 235-238
    adding folders, 232
    deleting, 232
    moving, 233
    naming, 232
    synchronizing, 233-235

cookies, removing, 240-242
Dantz Retrospect, 540
Dave Polaschek, 537
Google, 230
iCalShare, 409
Lemke Software, 346
Palm, 418
.Mac, 169, 421
Panic Transmit FTP, 246
SnapBack, 238-240
warchalking, 151
X icons, 434
Web surfing
  Cookies, removing, 240-242
  FTP server connections, 244-247
  overview, 228
  Safari, reporting bugs, 242-244
  Sherlock, 247-252
  SnapBack, 238-240
  Web browsers, selecting defaults, 228-229
  Web sites, bookmarks, 230-233
    accessing, 232, 235-238
    adding folders, 232
    deleting, 232
    moving, 233
    naming, 232
    synchronizing, 233-235
WebDAV servers, 409-411
Webmail (.Mac), 175-179
WebMail Preferences, 178
WEP (Wired Equivalent Privacy), 156
window control buttons, 12-13
Window menu commands
  Buddy List, 260
  Font Book, 297
  Minimize, 47
  Rendezvous, 138
windows
  accessing, 49-52
  applications, switching, 46
  Buddy List, opening, 260
  closing, 12
  columns, 24, 26
  Exposé, 437
  Finder, 10-12
    Action button, 27
    Column view, 25-26
    contents, 21-23
    customizing, 30-34
    disk structure, 20-21
    ejecting disks, 22
    Get Info panel, 29-30
    hiding data sources, 28
    hiding toolbar, 28

How can we make this index more useful? Email us at indexes@samspublishing.com

591

X-Z

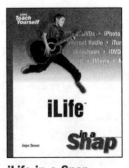

Key Terms

Don't let unfamiliar terms discourage you from learning all you can about Mac OS X. If you don't completely understand what one of these words means, flip to the indicated page, read the full definition there, and find techniques related to that term.

.Mac   *Apple's centralized network service, available for a yearly fee, that allows you to publish the products of your creativity online and make all your Macs operate as one.*   102

1-Click ordering   *A technology that allows you to predefine your credit card information at the server, so that you can later purchase items online with a single click.*   167

Active Screen Corners   *Also known as "Hot Corners," this feature allows you to trigger certain functions by moving the mouse pointer into different corners of the screen.*   437

Admin user   *A type of user who is granted the capabilities to change global settings, install applications, and make other changes to the behavior of the entire system.*   468

AirPort   *Apple's brand of wireless Internet connectivity devices.*   103

Alias   *A pseudo-file that, when opened, instead opens a real file, application, or folder elsewhere in the system.*   69

Antialiasing   *The technical term for "smoothing," as with fonts or diagonal lines.*   430

AOL Instant Messenger (AIM)   *One of the leading instant-messaging applications used by millions of people.*   254

AppleTalk   *Apple's own networking protocol.*   117

AppleWorks   *A suite of productivity tools that includes a word processor, a spreadsheet program, a drawing program, and more.*   285

Application   *Also known as a program, any piece of software you run within Mac OS X.*   14

Archive   *A collection of documents, folders, or applications packed into a single file, which is usually compressed.*   38

Authentication   *To enter a name and password, usually for an Admin user.*   469

Automatic login   *When you start up a Mac with this option enabled, the computer enters a predetermined user's login session automatically.*   455

Bookmark   *A reference to a favorite Web site to which you want to return to in the future.*   230

Channel   *Any of the dozens of specialized service screens available in Sherlock.*   247

Conduit   *A piece of software hiding under the surface of Mac OS X that transfers a certain kind of information to and from a digital device such as a PDA.*   419

Contact sheet   *A group of thumbnail images gathered together onto a single sheet.*   352

Cookie   *A piece of information that some Web sites store on your computer to store your preferences for the site, or your username and password.*   240

Directory server   *A centralized service that provides complete names for all the company's employees and mappings of full names to email addresses.*   222

Disk image   *A file that contains the contents of an entire disk.*   38

DNS servers   *Computers on the network that provide a mapping between numeric IP addresses and textual hostnames; this mapping is the Domain Name Service, or DNS.*   111

Domain   *Centrally managed groups of Windows computers with centralized password management and administration.*   133

Ethernet   *A low-level communication protocol that involves cables that end in RJ-45 jacks, which resemble large phone jacks.*   103

Exposé   *A feature that allows you to shrink all your windows temporarily so that they all fit on the screen and you can select the one you want.*   437

File Transfer Protocol (FTP)   *A method of transferring files from one computer to another.*   245

Firewall   *A piece of software that runs at the very innermost level of the operating system (the kernel) and manages all the Internet communications in and out of your Mac.*   515

Folder action   *A script attached to a folder that, when triggered by certain events, performs some function.*   88

iLife   *The packaged combination of iTunes, iMovie, iPhoto, and iDVD.*   316

Ink   *Apple's handwriting-recognition technology.*   281

Input menu   *A tool that lets you quickly open an input palette or switch to a special input method to enter special characters or non-Latin languages.*   450

IP address   *A unique numeric address that identifies your computer on the Internet.*   110